MW00997255

THE MOOSE THAT ROARED

THE MOOSE

Keith Scott

THAT ROARED

The Story of Jay Ward, Bill Scott, a Flying Squirrel, and a Talking Moose

THOMAS DUNNE BOOKS
ST. MARTIN'S PRESS NEW YORK

Courtesy of Bill Scott

For Bill Scott (1920–1985)

THOMAS DUNNE BOOKS.
An imprint of St. Martin's Press.

www.stmartins.com

Book design by Lovedog Studio

Library of Congress Cataloging-in-Publication Data

Scott, Keith.
The moose that roared : the story of Jay Ward, Bill Scott, a flying squirrel, and a talking moose / Keith Scott.
p. cm.
ISBN 0-312-19922-8
1. Bullwinkle show (Television program) 2. Ward, Jay. 3. Scott, Bill. I. Title.
PN1992.77.B86 S375 2000
791.45'72—dc21

00-025478

First Edition: July 2000

10 9 8 7 6 5 4 3 2 1

CONTENTS

Acknowledgments ix

Foreword by Chris Hayward xiii

Introduction xv

1. **WATCH ME PULL A RABBIT OUTTA MY HAT,** or Here's Lookin' Up Your Ancestors 1

2. **CRUSADER RABBIT: HIS RISE AND FALL,** or You Are Now Entering Frostbite Falls 14

3. **TIME FOR THAT JOLLY JUGGLER, BULLWINKLE,** or Bill Scott, Moose of Letters 31

4. **THE ROCKY ROAD TO TELEVISION,** or That Voice, Where Have I Heard That Voice? 44

5. **SPONSORED SQUIRREL,** or How Green Was My Contract 65

6. **HOW TO CUT CARTOON CORNERS,** or Mexico City Mishmash 74

7. **GRINGOS, HEPATITIS, AND MUCHO LOMA,** or You Can't Make Fun of Pancho Villa 86

8. **SQUIRREL ON THE TUBE,** or Watts Gnu with You? 97

9. **STARRING THAT SUPERSONIC SPEEDSTER,** or Time for That Dancin' Fool, Bullwinkle 105

10. **AND A HOST OF OTHERS,** or Now It's Time for Another Special Feature 117

11. **1960: PONSONBY, PILOTS, AND A SUPER PULLET** 130

12. **AD AGENCY, NETWORK, AND SPONSOR,** or You Think I Want Every Tom, Dick, and Gordon In On the Plot? 143

13. **1961: BULLWINKLE HITS THE BIG TIME,** or Don't Go Getting Swelled Antlers 160

14. **BULLWINKLE MEETS THE PRESS,** or All the Moose That's Fit to Print 181

15. **1962: IT'S MY PARTY AND I'LL LAUGH IF I WANT TO,** or Moosylvania Mania 190

16. **1963: A DAY AT THE NUT HOUSE,** or What Do They Do on a Rainy Night in Coney Island? 211

17. **SILENTS IS GOLDEN,** or The Greatest Waste of TV Time Since *The Bullwinkle Show* (*Fractured Flickers*) 224

18. **BULLWINKLE'S LAST STAND,** or It's a Frog-Eat-Frog World 234

19. **THIS IS WHAT I REALLY CALL A MESSAGE!** or 'Twas on the Good Ship *Guppy* (The Quaker Commercials) 243

20. **TV OR NOT TV,** or Watch Out for That Tree! 256

21. **OUR FEARLESS LEADER,** or What Was Jay Ward Really Like? 277

22. **WELL, BULLWINKLE, IT LOOKS AS IF OUR TIME HAS JUST ABOUT RUN OUT,** or But, Rock, I Need Retirement Like a Moose Needs a Hat Rack 294

Appendix 1. A Who's Who of Jay Ward Productions 315
Appendix 2. Revisiting the Jay Ward Recording Sessions 347

REFERENCE SECTION

Synopses and Voice Credits for the Jay Ward Cartoons 355
Fractured Flickers Episodes and Voice Credits 410
On-screen Credits 415
Miscellaneous Material and Extra Show Animation 418
Pilot Films 420
Miscellaneous TV Commercials 421
Commercials for the Quaker Oats Company 423
Glossary of Animation Terms 426
Bibliography 428

INDEX 433

You Got the Credits, Bullwinkle?

or Here Are a Few of the People Who Made This Impossible! (Acknowledgments)

This book has been an eight-year labor of love. It's also been a difficult one to write simply by dint of geographical distance, and more than most authors I have needed the transoceanic help of others to bring the book to its final stages.

It's obviously somewhat presumptuous to attempt to chronicle twenty-five years in the life of a cartoon studio, particularly when one was not there at the time. Which is why those who *were* there will always do the best books on animation (the lively memoirs of Shamus Culhane, Chuck Jones, and Jack Kinney provide ample proof). The job itself becomes even more of a jigsaw puzzle with the death of several key participants. Until recently, in fact, those brave souls who wrote about any aspect of animation history had very little in the way of reference material or even basic starting points. The task involves much primary research, and, regrettably, various pioneers are now gone to the big storyboard conference on high. Fortunately, I got off to a great start in 1970 when I began my correspondence with the late Daws Butler, Bill Scott, and Paul Frees, and the still highly active June Foray.

The many interviews and meetings with these giants of the cartoon-voice field formed the basis of this book. June Foray has been a wonderful friend for twenty-five years. It was truly one of those magic moments that happen once in a lifetime when I finally worked with her in early 1992, on recording sessions for Universal's "Rocky and Bullwinkle" theme-park shows.

In 1973 I met the supposedly elusive Jay Ward; he was a great help for the next twelve years, especially in fleshing out innumerable details that form the historical chapters within these pages.

Particular mention must be given to Skip Craig, a most loyal friend, who has been unfailingly helpful, meticulous, and patient, and happily blessed with an extraordinary memory. Skip, Jay Ward's chief film editor from 1959 to 1984, is already well known to several entertainment researchers for his incredible help on books concerning Spike Jones and old-time radio; his enthusiasm is unflagging, and he's truly one of the gentlemen of this world.

Above all it was Bill Scott who proved truly invaluable, taking me under his wing—or antlers—by inviting me to Jay Ward recording sessions, writing newsy letters, and supplying research materials. Bill selflessly spent ten years loaning—or simply giving me—copies of his files, correspondence, master tapes, and cels (long before animation art was known to be a hot item); not to mention the many hours I got to spend in his hilarious company. His patience with a decade's worth of often arcane questions knew no bounds, and it is to him that this book is fondly dedicated.

Of tremendous help in verifying facts and fleshing out much needed background were the many other people who were there when Jay Ward Productions was happening. My heartfelt thanks to the following for giving of their time and memories: Alex Anderson, Roman Arambula, George Atkins, Gerard Baldwin, Bruce Burness, Allan Burns, Lucille Bliss, Howard Brandy, Myrtis Butler, Frank Comstock, the late William Conrad, Trilby Conried, Helen Craig, Jim Critchfield, the late Shamus Culhane, Sam Clayberger, Dennis Farnon, Stan Freberg, Mr. and Mrs. David Frees, Fred Frees, Joy Terry Frees, Alan Foshko, Rose Frees Ginsberg, William Hanna, Helen Hanson, Chris Hayward, Linda Hayward, Jim Hiltz, Bill and Mary Hurtz, Chuck Jones, Francy Jones, Chris Jenkyns, the late Lew Keller, Leonard Key, Ted Key, Bob Kurtz, Bill Littlejohn, Bob Mills, Alice Morita, Charlotte Morris, Luther Nichols, Gary Owens, Peter Piech, Don Pitts, Erv Rosenfeld, Dorothy Scott, John Hamilton Scott, Al Shean, Shirley Silvey Berg, George

Singer, Fred Steiner, Darlene Turner, the late Lloyd Turner, and Al Wilson. (If the elusive Bill Oberlin and Chris Allen are still alive, please contact the author!)

For reasons that go beyond this book, I owe enormous thanks to Ramona and Tiffany Ward, who now run Jay Ward Productions in its fortieth year.

Others who helped in generous fashion, beyond the call of duty, include the regular band of dedicated animation enthusiasts: Karl Cohen, Fred Patten (both of whom had already conducted splendid research on the *Crusader Rabbit* era), Charles Ulrich, editor of the newsletter *The Frostbite Falls Far Flung Flyer*, Robert L. Stone, David Mruz, Duane Dimock, Ronnie Wise, Mark Evanier, Jerry Beck, Leonard Maltin, Steve Worth, Peter Greenwood, Raymond Cox, Hames Ware, Graham Webb, Mike Barrier, and the indispensable Mark Kausler. Institutional help came from the Margaret Herrick Library at the Center for Motion Picture Study and the USC Cinema-Television Library's energetic curator, Ned Comstock.

Supplying endless tapes and rare recordings were John and Larry Gassman, Ted Hering, Dick Mullins, Don Aston, and undoubtedly the world's most painstaking recording perfectionist, my funny friend Ken Greenwald. Always there in the nick of time with much needed assistance on additional audio and video material were two of the best in the business—the ineffable Brian Bogle and the gifted voice artist Corey Burton (whose taste and judgment concerning voice work and Jay Ward cartoons are second to none).

Special thanks also to Debbie Cohen, Bart Pierce, Michelle Katz, Nancy Cushing-Jones, and Cindy Chang (Universal City Studios Publishing Rights), Neil Rosini, and especially my literary agent, George Wieser, for hanging in there. My splendid editor, Barry Neville, made a large-scale, judicious decision regarding a total reorganization of the chapters; the result is a much better book. (I would like to thank the copy editor, Adam Goldberger, too, as well as Brian Mulligan for the great design job and Elizabeth McNamara for her help with legal matters.)

A tip of the hat to the following organizations for providing invaluable contacts and permissions: AFTRA, the American Federation of Musicians, Dubs Inc., 5-2-5 Post, the Performing Rights Society (London), the Screen Actors Guild, the Screen Cartoonists Guild, the UCLA Animation Department, the Writers Guild of America, West, 20th Century–Fox (Ashley Simmons), *Newsweek* (Randy Shapiro), the *Los Angeles Times* (Permissions Counsel), Quaker Oats Company (Janet Silverberg), and *Variety* (Gene Byrne).

The generosity of various individuals above extended to their loaning research materials, artwork, and valued photographs; those who agreed to interviews made the project come alive with their memories and gave the book the human touch needed to prevent its becoming a mere catalog of names and dates. The book will gush occasionally; if at times it reads more like a fanzine, I make no apologies.

Finally, to my wife, Sue, whose love and patience helped me through the rough spots, and whose forbearance in teaching me to handle the intricacies of that modern minefield, the PC/word processor (when I still have trouble with leaking ballpoint pens), was worthy of a medal.

Foreword (or Glancing Backward) by Chris Hayward

My writing tends to be economical. Depending on the occasion, bordering on the cusp of terse. Yet when the subject of Jay T. Ward is broached, launching warm reflections of my halcyon years laboring under Jay's nutty auspices, I can get downright verbose. Stay tuned.

Sadly, Jay is no longer with us. Prolific Bill Scott predeceased Jay. Even boon companion Lloyd Turner is trouting on that heavenly lake in the sky. Contemplating these losses, I suddenly realized that at long last, sans emotional restraints, I could now set the record straight—tell the truth about the working environment, the creative restrictions Jay imposed. Aside from monetary considerations (which Uriah Heep would have envied), there were none.

It was an insane but joyous atmosphere.

Al Burns, George Atkins, Chris Jenkyns, Alex Anderson, Jim Critchfield, Jim MacGeorge, Al Shean, Pete Burness—all were freewheeling, outrageously independent talents, each contributing to that madcap era when

---

Chris Hayward is one of the veterans of TV comedy. His impressive résumé includes scripting classics of the genre like *Get Smart* and *Barney Miller,* not to mention *The Smothers Brothers Shows, He & She* (for which he won an Emmy), and, in his own words, "the all-time TV stinker," *My Mother the Car.*

limited animation—in the right hands—could be unlimitedly funny, refreshingly original, and, wonder of wonders: timeless.

Allow me to reflect. Briefly. Back in the early 1960s, Lloyd Turner and I had three things in common (besides writing for Jay Ward Productions): insatiable thirsts, the capacity to make Jay howl with glee, and a bum left arm.

Lloyd's was the bummier. He had lost most of it below the elbow in a woodworking class. "No, sir, that table I'm making doesn't have five legs—one of them belongs to me." As for myself, as an eight-year-old, I chased one of my sisters through a sliding glass door. The door was closed when I reached it, but not after I went through it. I came out of the episode with my left arm atrophied for life, which meant that thirty or so years later, Lloyd Turner and I couldn't row a boat.

But physical limitations didn't prevent us from playing golf. Particularly when Jay would command us to participate in one of his maniacal golf tournaments. On one special occasion we were instructed to be packed and waiting at the curb. Jay would pick us up. However, since he had designated this a "mystery" tournament—destination unknown—what the hell were we supposed to pack? Slickers? Luau shirts? We endeavored to outwit him. Our unworthy opponents—a foursome from San Francisco and lifelong buddies of Jay's—were scheduled to join us at the ultimate playing site.

We got lucky. The first airline we contacted at LAX confirmed that Jay had arranged a transfer for the northern contingent to a smaller aircraft destined for Phoenix. We packed for heat. It was one of the few times we ever got the better of Jay. Oh, we lost to the guys up north.

ADRIFT ON LAKE ARROWHEAD
CHRIS HAYWARD

Introduction

In the entire history of TV cartoons, there has been only one show which could boast dialogue like this:

Rocky: Bullwinkle, you know what A-bomb means!
Bullwinkle: Sure! A bomb is what some people call our program.
Rocky: I don't think that's so funny.
Bullwinkle: Neither do they, apparently.

Puns, satire, irony—the TV shows featuring the earnest young hero Rocky the Flying Squirrel and his slightly dim-witted sidekick Bullwinkle J. Moose are today the most beloved and respected cartoons from the period that has officially been designated the "baby boom era."

The Rocky and Bullwinkle cartoons have attained legendary animation status, helped along at first by film festivals and cult retrospectives dating from the mid-1980s, when those baby boomers' offspring began to come of age. The phenomenon became especially apparent with the release of the Disney–Buena Vista videocassettes in early 1991: their instantaneous leap to the top of the *Billboard* video sales charts was both a joyous vindication for toon cultists, and a sad reminder of television's lack of progress over the last thirty years. Indeed, even when Rocky and Bullwinkle's adventures first aired, from 1959 to 1964, TV was being criticized for its follow-the-leader mentality (everyone remembers FCC chairman Newton Minow's famous remark about "television's vast wasteland").

This abiding popularity is easily explained. The squirrel and moose, thirty-nine years old as this is being written, have hardly dated. Even acknowledged live-action comedy classics from TV's Hall of Fame, though still hilarious and as popular as ever, can be said to be "showing their age." Today's viewers have to adjust their mind-set, in a sense casting themselves back in time à la Mr. Peabody, to enjoy much of old television in context. To appreciate certain vintage shows involves overlooking deficiencies in technical quality and near-alien cultural references. Mostly the effort is well worth it, particularly as a fascinating sociological mirror of the times. Some old masters like Jack Benny, Dick Van Dyke, *The Twilight Zone*, and *The Honeymooners* have proven spectacularly successful, with books devoted to the series, and healthy sales of home video reissue packages.

Of course, the flip side of this equation reveals that, in truth, the list of great old TV shows ripe for revival is not an overly long one. In fact, with various noble exceptions, much early television now seems quaint, or, to be charitable, historically interesting at best. And some shows were, frankly, abysmal: how many people, apart from terminal couch potatoes, would truly sit still in today's high-tech TV climate with its endless viewing choices—satellite, cable, DVD, interactive—through even one episode of *My Little Margie, Tales of Wells Fargo,* or *The Tab Hunter Show*?

Happily, Rocky and Bullwinkle belong to the classic pedigree. The unassuming moose and squirrel—along with their cohorts in cartoon mayhem and glorious hyperbole, like Dudley Do-Right, Peabody and Sherman, Boris and Natasha, and the rest—work just as well now as they did three decades ago. The cartoons dared to be smart and funny. They still come across as smart and funny, reminding us of a time when the sole purpose of cartoons was laughter—not tie-ins with unprepossessing plush toys, or the dictums of network censors concerned with cutting jokes and substituting tedious "new age" relevance.

Today, with the sole exception of *The Simpsons,* the Jay Ward cartoons remain a pillar of comic sophistication in the mainly witless animated pantheon of *Beavis and Butt-head, Biker Mice from Mars,* and environmentally concerned *Cartoon All-Stars to the Rescue*. The adventures of Rocky and Bullwinkle taught an entire generation the art of parody. While most early TV cartoons involved mice belting cats with mallets, or bears stealing pies from a windowsill guarded by a bulldog, the hip young moose and squirrel were concerned with Congress, the cold war, and TV itself. And let's not forget those deliberately dreadful puns—people and places like Doctor Bermuda Schwartz, Maybe Dick the Wailing Whale, Wossamotta U., art critic Sir Rulion Blue, Whynchataka Peak, Sir Hillary Pushemoff, the Guns of Abalone, the village of Daniels on the Rocks, and Upper Whatchacallitstan.

Subversive and irreverent, multilayered and surreal, topical and rapid-fire: these amazing little cartoons consistently burst the balloons of pomposity in all walks of life. In the flurry of articles which appeared following the astonishingly rapid success of the video releases, such notables as Steven Spielberg, Matt Groening (creator of *The Simpsons*), and author Ray Bradbury effusively sang the praises of Rocky and Bullwinkle.

Thanks to our furry heroes, the world of TV animation was given a breath of fresh air, and those who were seduced by the peculiar comedic charms of producers Jay Ward and Bill Scott were changed forever. This book presents the full story behind these witty cartoon shows and their peerless creators.

Before heading into the saga of these animated iconoclasts, I feel that a personal note is in order for those readers about to embark on this journey into the zany land of Jay Ward Productions. What better way to start than by saying that I love Jay Ward cartoons, and have yet to meet a fellow enthusiast who can match my not-quite-sane level of worship. Let me explain this unabashed addiction.

Australia, for various reasons including our much smaller population, was a good eight years behind the U.S. media revolution: we didn't begin receiving television broadcasts until 1956. By 1960, my family had had TV in our house for about twelve months, when suddenly *Rocky and His Friends* arrived down under. I had already fallen in love with American cartoons like *Crusader Rabbit, Huckleberry Hound,* and "Tom Terrific," and by then (although just six years old), I sensed my life was going to be inextricably bound to Hollywood cartoons, for which I was showing an awareness beyond my years. I harbored an especially keen interest in the funny voices heard in these animated baby-sitters.

In fact, I was exhibiting the symptoms of the classic cartoon junkie at this tender age. Compared to my contemporaries, who were "getting a life" by tearing up the football field or discovering go-carts and pogo sticks, I was one of that odd flock who were drawn, like moths to a flame, to comic books (I was a budding cartoonist), comedy, and TV animation. So when Rocky and Bullwinkle entered my life, I felt like I'd reached a nirvana-point of no return. Never again would I find a cartoon series like this: it was truly different. Although aware that many of the jokes were beyond my comprehension, I knew that this singular TV show would become a lifelong study. Of course, when something has that kind of impact on one's formative years, it's very hard to shake. Even then, while a mere schoolkid, I had made up my mind that one day I would enter the field of animation, comedy, and voice impersonations. As to how, I had not the slightest idea.

Over the next ten years, my interest in Rocky and Bullwinkle became more and more scholarly. The bottom line: I was "hooked" beyond help, obsessed with finding out all I could about Jay Ward Productions. I started writing letters. I wrote to TV stations, radio stations. And I found myself desperately wondering about such earthshaking matters as: Where was Jay Ward Productions located? Who or what was P.A.T. (listed in the credits)? What did the voice actors look like? Who, in fact, did each voice? Even more to the point, who was the mysterious Jay Ward? And most intriguingly, who wrote all that funny dialogue?

My ear was especially taken with actors Daws Butler and Paul Frees, and I determined to meet these heroes of mine. They held me enthralled the way football stars and giants of the music world appear to people with possibly saner tastes. I thought of writing to these legendary voice actors. But at that unworldly point in my life I was so in awe of them that the thought of sending letters filled my insides with butterflies.

Then, just as I was entertaining thoughts of giving up this insanity and settling down to be a teacher, a high school friend's father, on a whim for which I'll always be thankful, loaned me the double Capitol record album *The Best of the Stan Freberg Shows*. This contained beautifully written comedy highlights from Freberg's fifteen-week 1957 summer radio show on CBS. I was as entranced by his humor as I was by Jay Ward's. Within the album covers, lo and behold, were pictures of Daws Butler and June Foray. They looked human, even friendly.

That did it—naively I wrote to Daws Butler care of Screen Gems TV, which distributed Hanna-Barbera's *The Huckleberry Hound Show*. And in December 1970 I received a long and warm letter from him. I was dumbfounded: here in my own room was a reply from the voice of Yogi Bear! In it, he enclosed extras I hadn't thought of requesting, like photos and drawings of all his characters. Best of all, he filled me in on who did the various other voices in Jay Ward's cartoons.

Daws mentioned Bill Scott, who of course only appeared on the *Bullwinkle* titles as coproducer, never taking a voice credit. I had no idea he did voices. I wrote to Bill Scott in 1971, and was again amazed to receive a long letter, plus many cels and photos, again unsolicited. I wrote back, and he encouraged me to correspond. A couple of years later I enclosed some amateurish but detailed episode guides to the Jay Ward cartoons which I'd been working on for several months; Bill wrote back, telling me he was now using them as reference in his office. (Years later he told me the reason he'd originally replied to me was because he'd seen in my first epistle exactly the same obsessive enthusiasm he'd had for cartoons as a seventeen-year-old.)

To top all this, he copied my latest letter and sent it to June Foray. Fate stepped in—she had just met someone exactly like me, the poor sap. He was about my age and lived in California. His name was Corey Burton, and he too was obviously as far off the deep end as I, having shared my lifelong fascination with these voice people and Ward cartoons. June Foray was the catalyst for the erudite letters we sent each other beginning in August 1971. Corey has remained one of my close friends for these twenty-eight years. I must admit to being jealous of him in the first year of our acquaintance: he had been taken by June Foray to actually sit in on several Jay Ward recording sessions for Cap'n Crunch and Quisp-Quake commercials.

Meantime, my other vocal hero, Paul Frees, had made contact and sent me a personalized tape from his home studio. It wasn't too long after this that Corey and I began the long process of getting our feet in the door of professional voice-acting work in our respective countries. By then I'd met Bill Hanna and worked at his new Sydney Hanna-Barbera wing for six months; one of his animators—bless him—gave me my first voice-over assignment in late 1972. But the best was yet to come.

After eighteen months of correspondence and much trading of cartoon sound tracks and record albums featuring Jay Ward voice actors, Corey Burton and I met. I'd entered a quiz in the local *TV Times* (one of those "win a trip to Hollywood" contests, in which the questions involved movie trivia). I came home to find a letter from the magazine telling me I had won the trip. I made careful plans and was soon on my way. I spent the most amazing four weeks of my life in Los Angeles, thanks mainly to the unbelievably gracious hospitality of Jay Ward, Bill Scott, Daws Butler, June Foray and her terrific late husband Hobe Donovan, Paul Frees, and Chris "Hoppity Hooper" Allen.

This occurred in April 1973, when all these people were active and highly visible in the industry. I'd assumed they wouldn't have the schedule or the inclination to spend time with some punk kid from seven thousand miles across the Pacific. I was wrong. When these people heard I was in town, they went out of their way for me. Bill Scott took me to lunch at the old Frascatti's restaurant (opposite Jay Ward's studio); I curse the fact that I didn't take a cassette recorder—he talked for three hours on the history of Jay's cartoons, and finally asked me to write this book. Daws Butler invited Corey and me for a whole day at his home recording studio. I met the hilarious Paul Frees at a voice-over job at the late Radio Recorders, then Hollywood's oldest sound studio. June Foray took me to a recording job presided over by animation legend Chuck Jones, still another of my heroes. And I was invited to a session at Hanna-Barbera's studio, where I met Tom Bosley and other cartoon actors. All these voice people loaned us rare tapes from their private collections.

And then there was Jay Ward Productions. Before I won the trip, Corey Burton had told me about the store Jay had opened just a year earlier. Tantalizingly, it was called Dudley Do-Right's Emporium. He mentioned something which had me salivating—the shop sold cassettes of genuine old radio shows featuring Paul Frees, Bill Conrad, and others from Jay's cartoons. Obviously, this would be my first port of call. The day after we arrived, I left my parents scratching their exasperatedly tourism-oriented heads and caught a bus down to Jay Ward's store. Jay's wife, Ramona, who won't remember this incident, was working behind the counter and told me that the catalog of radio shows was put together by one Skip Craig.

Of course, being an avid watcher of the *Bullwinkle* credits, I recognized Skip's name as the film editor. Mrs. Ward informed me that he worked in the building behind the store. I met Skip Craig five minutes later and discovered to my delight that he, too, had been like me as a youngster—his obsession had been with Spike Jones and the City Slickers. I was crazy about Spike Jones, too, so Skip and I quickly ended up friends; he has since proven to be one of the most generous people I've ever met.

Most rewardingly, I met Jay Ward himself and was instantly charmed by his jolly and easygoing nature. He was sharp: he picked up on my fan worship and wasn't threatened by it. Instead, he patiently answered myriad questions with his razor-sharp memory. Looking back now, I believe—as corny as it sounds—that trip was meant to be. I returned home with a sense of professionalism, a seriousness of purpose that seemed to go full circle back to those heady feelings I'd experienced as a six-year-old cartoon buff.

In the years that followed, I became established in Australia as a cartoon and commercial voice actor, and stand-up mimic. During this time I kept corresponding with the Jay Ward folk. Later, I regularly visited Corey Burton in California, and we reverentially kept up our Holy Grail–like visits and interviews with these comic masters until their untimely deaths. In those years I was able to sit in on some of Ward's recording sessions as a pro, not just a gee-whiz fan.

Finally, in 1992, Corey Burton and I received the ultimate reward for our lifelong championing of Ward Productions: we got to work together in some Hollywood recording sessions with our heroine, June "Rocky" Foray. We were the actors chosen to re-create the voices from *The Bullwinkle Show*. It was as if Bill Scott and Paul Frees had yelled from their resting place, "Oh, damn, let these guys have the job or they'll never shut up. They sure as hell didn't when we were there."

By the time Jay Ward died in 1989, I had amassed a vast collection of research material on his studio and professional life. I determined to write this book as a thank-you for the hundreds of hours of pleasure he gave me and thousands of other cartoon buffs, and for the fact that I feel he was largely responsible for my career. This, then, is not a biography of Jay Ward; rather, it's an affectionate appreciation of his legacy and a history of his television career.

My biggest regret is not doing this book years ago, when my idols were still around. Although Bill Scott had asked me to write it during my 1973 visit, I procrastinated, knowing I wasn't really ready. In the two and a half decades since, my enthusiasm has never waned, and in the actual process of putting the book together I have been delighted to meet many more players from the Jay Ward story, particularly his splendid writers and artists. I'm even more delighted to report that they are as fascinating and funny a bunch as I'd suspected.

And of course to this day, I'll drop everything for a tape or TV showing of a Jay Ward cartoon. So, as a certain flying squirrel would have it, "Now here's something we hope you'll really like!"

1

Watch Me Pull a Rabbit Outta My Hat,

or Here's Lookin' Up Your Ancestors

He was a guerrilla fighter armed with humor and art, leading the fight against boredom.

—*Luther Nichols, on his lifelong friend Jay Ward*

For one brief decade, 1959–68, the funniest, all-stops-out zaniest cartoons ever made for television emerged from a tiny building on Sunset Boulevard in Hollywood. This was the home of Jay Ward Productions, undoubtedly the most eccentric animation house in the movie capital. Visitors were greeted by a sign on the door proclaiming, "The only animation studio certified by the Pure Food and Drug Administration." But eccentricity aside, Jay Ward Productions, while never a household name on the Disney scale or even the Hanna-Barbera scale, became a Hollywood success story boasting some of animation's all-time beloved characters. Most satisfyingly, Rocky the Flying Squirrel, Bullwinkle J. Moose, and the other great toon stars from this studio represent the all-too-rare triumph of comic integrity over TV expediency.

When *Rocky and His Friends* burst onto America's home screens at 5:30

P.M., November 19, 1959, it was seemingly just one more in a mushrooming number of TV cartoons. But it soon became apparent that this show, starring the unlikely combination of a moose and squirrel hero-team, had something totally different about it. It was off-center: funny, very sharp, and, in the opinion of several television people, almost "too good"—i.e., too hip, too sophisticated, and certainly too fast-paced for the majority of TV watchers.

They were partly right: hip and fast it was. Yet somehow this wickedly witty animated potpourri proved accessible to all manner of viewers, from toddlers to grandparents. Still, during "Rocky and Bullwinkle" 's first two seasons, the corporate powers—sponsor and network—kept asking, "How is this possible?" They kept interfering too, to no avail.

After all, this was unheard-of. Satire was normally frowned upon as a dicey prospect in the world of mass entertainment; but in a children's cartoon series? Predictably, the "suits" regarded it as axiomatic that a TV show boasting such perception and wit would only appeal to a so-called elite. But the nervous pundits had missed the point. Producers Jay Ward and Bill Scott weren't concerned with being clever. They simply wanted two things: a high-quality show and one that was consistently funny. This was a tall order in the fiercely competitive rat race of network television, yet they did the show they wanted year after year. In 1961 Ward told an interviewer, "We aim at neither adults nor children. Our goal is to achieve the ultimate in comedy, including subtleties which escape the youngsters but which evoke response from adults."

Speak to anyone who worked with Jay Ward and you get the same fact over and over: he simply went about his creative way quietly and determinedly, remaining steadfast in his one abiding conviction—no one would interfere with his artistic control. Essentially, Ward was a gentle maverick with an enormous sense of fun, although he could be tough. His many admirers labeled him a visionary.

Not that talk of grand visions took place at Ward's studio; as writer Allan Burns hastens to explain, "Jay would have punctured that balloon very quickly." Actress June Foray, famous as the voice of Rocky the Flying Squirrel, noted, "Jay was a very perspicacious man who always knew precisely what he wanted." Invariably what Ward wanted was something funny, which is what the viewers got: the shows were funny all right. But beyond this they felt oddly different from any competing cartoons. Each element within the *Rocky* show was informed by a mind-set and comic sensibility then unique to TV. The writers didn't talk "down" to the audience, yet they didn't talk "up" either. Although brilliantly satirical, there was nothing self-conscious or highbrow about the shows. Indeed, a salutary self-deprecation was always lurking in the scripts.

In a nutshell, then, Messrs. Ward and Scott were two producers who cared not a jot for statistics showing what the viewers might accept. Not for them the cold, by-the-numbers findings of market research; rather, they flattered their audiences by presuming that people who watched television actually had brains. The audience, in turn, recognized a truly rare bird among TV shows—one that didn't insult their intelligence.

And so it remains today: *Rocky and His Friends* and *The Bullwinkle Show* are regarded as the most hilarious cartoons from television's golden age. International animation journals still place the moose and squirrel at the top of polls listing the hundred best TV cartoons of all time. While there have been other sharp satirical cartoons (like *Roger Ramjet,* one of Bill Scott's all-time favorites), no one quite brought off animated satire with the aplomb of Ward and Scott, who laced it with subtlety and a quirky charm. George Atkins, a writer of the "Fractured Fairy Tales" segment, opined, "The show was always the very special province of the brighter, more aware young viewer who cherished *Bullwinkle's* irreverence, the range of its satire, the presumption of the viewer's higher intelligence, the urgency and seriousness of subject matter—ever thickly encased in utter ridiculousness, and the always convincing high quality of its voice-work."

The sheer breadth of subject matter in one of Jay Ward's TV offerings was also unique. Consider the format of most half-hour cartoon shows; They're either sitcom oriented, from *The Flintstones* all the way through *The Simpsons,* or they're in the adventure genre, from *Jonny Quest* through *Teenage Mutant Ninja Turtles* (imagine the latter satirized by the Ward crew). And if they were anthologies they featured endless variations on one theme.

What Ward and his hardy band of iconoclasts offered was essentially an animated variety show: the mock adventures of "Rocky and Bullwinkle," in which public and private institutions were lampooned gently but soundly, sat cheek by jowl with fairy tales and fables, history and poetry, melodrama, and even the TV format itself. And all in a breathless thirty minutes. It was enjoyed by older viewers who discussed the show's witty cultural allusions the next day over coffee breaks. Meantime their kids had eagerly lapped up the adventure angle and were recounting the cartoons in the playground. Two audiences in one; it would be thirty years before *The Simpsons* repeated this phenomenon.

As well as being years ahead of their time, it was their ability to appeal to both age groups—albeit on different levels—that truly set the "Rocky and Bullwinkle" shows apart. The vast majority of TV cartoons are too childish for parents to sit through, and the genre has acquired a deservedly low reputation. Of the hundreds of animated series aired since 1959, most have proved unimaginative and predictably repetitious. How many times can a cat outwit a dog, or a bunch of one-dimensional teenagers outrun a ghost? Leonard Maltin, in 1975, aptly described them as "assembly line shorts grudgingly executed by animation veterans who hate what they're doing." "Rocky and Bullwinkle" stood out as a welcome oasis in a mostly mirthless desert.

Without intending to, Jay Ward and company gave comedy fans a cult series boasting the twin stamps of intelligence and plain silliness from the first episode to the last. This is a pretty rare achievement in the advertising-and-ratings-driven world of TV: a show which generates the feeling of a fun-filled secret ("This is ours and nobody else gets it") for aficionados while being thoroughly enjoyed by the mainstream audience.

As Bill Scott saw it, "All smart people loved Bullwinkle. *The Bullwinkle Show* has the most loyal and the most intelligent audience, but it was never number one. It's a special show for special people and it's long-lived and always funny, but never the number one [ratings] grabber."

A few weeks before his death in 1992, Lloyd Turner, one of Ward's top writers, reflected, "You know, when our little gang of misfits were running amok pissing out all that uninhibited, unsupervised, completely unique unsalable piffle (unsalable to anybody but Jay that is), we had no idea we were making thunder. Out of the lack of good sense to know any better we were idea alchemists making magic. It was a time of enchantment. We created Saint Elmo's fire that is burning as brightly today as it did thirty-three years ago."

So just who was the elusive Jay Ward, besides being prime perpetrator of all the animated nuttiness? He was born J Troplong Ward in San Francisco on September 20, 1920. The unusual middle name was French in origin, being his mother's maiden name; the J had no period after it, so that he could choose a name he wanted later (it was originally to be Joseph, his father's name). A gifted student, Ward grew up to become a kind of kooky David O. Selznick of animation, and an enigma to all but his closest associates and friends. Of all the legendary names in the labyrinth of cartoon history, Ward is the least chronicled. He is also the one whom animation buffs most want to know about.

Veteran cartoon director Lew Keller lunched with Jay Ward for years, even after the studio ceased activity. He spoke of Ward's childhood: "Jay's parents separated when he was young. His father was in real estate and he lost a lot of money in the depression; then he moved to New York and became a wine wholesaler. Jay was an only child and was brought up by his mother, Juanita—they were very close. She had a rooming house on College Avenue, and she was a well-known singer-dancer who loved to travel. [Her professional performing name was Juanita Holmes.] It was only years later, after Jay was married, that he finally met up with his father again."

One of Ward's closest friends from the age of six was Luther Nichols. As next-door neighbors, they went from grammar school through high school and on to college at the University of California, at Berkeley. He recalls, "Jay and his mother were not well off. The rest of us were comfortably middle class, but Jay had a mainly improvident childhood. And it affected him. This and the lack of a father figure were really what imbued in him that extreme independence. Jay was very proud, and he had a strong sense of needing to make it on his own, and on his terms alone. The estrangement with his father was a major—*the* major—influence in his life."

During his college years, Jay Ward, in collusion with pals Nichols and Alex Anderson, was a principal founder of a mythical institution called the Meadowbrook Athletic Club. Nichols explains, "Meadowbrook was dedicated to the proposition that inferior athletes could, on a given day, beat superior athletes if they had a certain amount of luck, guile, and Jay on their side. We played baseball and basketball for endless hours at Emerson and other playgrounds in the city, and when we weren't playing we were betting on our favorite big-league teams. Jay had a gambler's instinct even then; in fact I was his prime source of income in those early days." Anderson adds, "The perpetual trophy of the UC gym still bears the Meadowbrook name, attesting to Jay's success." Ward's loyalty to UC Berkeley remained throughout his life. He made regular donations to the Bancroft Library, and was a chairman of the Robert C. Sproul Club and an honorary member of the Cal marching band.

Nichols recalled some early examples of Ward's lifelong fun-oriented nature. "Jay was noted for his prodigious consumption of ice-cream sodas. Never vanilla, that wouldn't be Jay: as you would expect, he went for the offbeat flavors like pistachio and rainbow specials. I remember when Jay got one of his first sports cars; it was a real pretty MG with a right-hand drive. At the time Jay owned this huge Saint Bernard dog named Brandy, and he'd place the dog in the left-hand side of his car. Then he'd slide down the seat as far as he could while he drove, so it looked like the dog was driving! People would see this big dog with its huge tongue hanging out and brown hair flying about. Wherever they went people were startled and Jay would get these double-take reactions that he just loved. This was an early indication that Jay was going to be creatively different—one of the great gag men of our time."

Intriguingly, the story of Jay Ward's outstanding career in animation—via his first star character, the legendary *Crusader Rabbit*—is a classic example of how showbiz immortality can often hinge on the twin intangibles of good timing and fate.

Ward completed his undergraduate work at UC Berkeley, receiving an A.B. in May 1941. Following this, he commenced postgraduate studies in business management at the Harvard Graduate School of Business Administration. These were interrupted when, despite his poor eyesight, he was drafted. During World War II Jay Ward served in the Army Air Corps. In 1943, after two years of service, he married his wife, Ramona (or "Billie," as she had been known since childhood). They had met in Massachusetts while Jay was attending Harvard.

Ramona Ward explains, "After the war, [Jay] took his army shirt off and never put on a uniform again." Returning to Boston, he completed his remaining year at Harvard while earning some income as a floorwalker in a department store. "Even after he returned to Berkeley, he never wanted to work for anyone but himself, despite a lot of good offers. He decided on real estate."*

In 1972, Ward, interviewed for the Southern California newspaper *The Tattler,* explained, "I was going into the real estate business in Berkeley, California. I wasn't too crazy about real estate, but I had to eat." In fact, young Realtor Ward might have continued plying this halfhearted career choice for years, but for a freak accident that was about to change everything in his life.

At the age of twenty-six, Jay Ward, recent recipient of a February 1947 master's degree, went to work. The postwar housing boom was strong, and J. T. Ward Realty and Insurance Company was soon open for business at 3049 Ashby Avenue, Berkeley, near the majestic old Claremont Hotel. He worked from a small green cabin that boasted a bright majenta door—the color magenta was to be Jay's sales gimmick. The rustic building was situated adjacent to a babbling brook.

Ramona Ward recalls, "It was only his first day in the office, and that

*In 1960, Ward was interviewed by the *Berkeley Gazette;* the article revealed that he inherited the real estate business from his father.

afternoon he was stepping out the door for the mail." As Jay stood chatting with the postman, a nearby lumber truck lost brake power, went out of control, and careered crazily down steep Tunnel Avenue. With the lights against him at the Ashby Avenue intersection, the driver suddenly lurched to his right. Ward caught the full force of the truck as it crashed, full-speed, through the front window of his office, crushing him under the vehicle and pinning him against a wall.

Seconds before being hit by the runaway truck, Ward was reading a poem to his mailman. This was part of a letter he had just received from his close friends Milton and Barbara Schwartz. Barbara had composed the verse as a good-luck gesture to Jay on his first day in the new business. Jay's lifelong pal Alex Anderson recalls, "Barbara felt guilty for a long time afterward, along the lines of 'If only I hadn't written that poem.' "

As a *Los Angeles Times* retrospective article reported, "Hauled out of the ensuing carnage, it looked as though Ward would be blinded and crippled for life." As it turned out, the result could have been even worse. Still, the impact broke one of Ward's knees and caused much further damage, not the least of which was psychological: as Ward's animation director Bill Hurtz maintains, "That was the start of Jay's lifelong claustrophobia—it haunted him the rest of his days." Ward sustained terrible muscle injuries and was temporarily blinded by grains of the sand which bordered the nearby brook.

Ramona Ward recalls that horrific day: she was about to walk their first child when she received an ominous telephone call from the police, informing her that Jay had been rushed to nearby Alta Bates Hospital, at Ashby and Regent Street. As the facts became clear (the mailman had been thrown forty feet upon collision), one rather callous female neighbor answered Ramona's anxious question concerning her husband's whereabouts with a dismissive, "Oh, he's dead!"

The convalescence proved long and painful: Ward wore a cast for the next six months, followed by leg braces. Indeed, during the first few days a doctor seriously considered amputating one of Jay's legs. Upon his recovery Ward returned to real estate, this time at a new address, 2 Tunnel Road, Berkeley. But this stint didn't last long. Within a short time Jay would be the manager of a company pioneering cartoons for the embryonic medium of television. This rather amazing career switch teamed Jay Ward with his first partner in the animation field and his friend since childhood, Alex Anderson.

Also born in September of 1920, fifteen days before Jay, Alexander Hume Anderson, Jr., was a native of the Bay Area. He and Ward were friends from the age of nine. As Anderson recalled, "Jay was a unique individual. At school he always gave the impression he knew more than the teachers. Just before they separated, Jay's parents had taken him on a round-the-world trip for about six months; he came back very sophisticated compared with all us other kids. Jay devoted enormous time and energy to his love of sports—tennis, baseball, softball, track and field, basketball, bowling. How he managed to maintain a high grade average and combine this world of sport, I'll never know. He was always very sharp. Later in life he struck me as P. T. Barnum, the ringmaster, with the world as his circus. Jay is the most memorable character I ever knew."

They attended elementary school and high school together, ending up as fraternity brothers at Cal. In their junior and senior high school years in the 1930s they sold wreaths and Christmas trees each December. Anderson quipped, "It was a seasonal business."

Alex Anderson came from an artistic family. Two of his uncles were cartoonists, one of them being the famous Paul Terry, head of the New York–based Terrytoons studio. Terrytoons's three decades of theatrical animation had produced such stars as the popular Mighty Mouse, Heckle and Jeckle, and Gandy Goose. During boyhood summers before enrolling at UC Berkeley, Alex, having displayed early artistic ability, apprenticed at Terry's studio. Here he learned the animation business thoroughly in all departments. "I was sort of the heir apparent. My uncle got me started in the whole idea of making cartoons." Even as a young man, Anderson knew he was more interested in writing than drawing. (Nevertheless, Bill Scott maintained, "Alex was one of the finest and funniest animation artists around, and a wonderful draftsman. His storyboards are just a delight to work from.")

While in his early twenties Anderson saw Walt Disney's newest film, *The Reluctant Dragon* (1941). The movie contained a sequence in which humorist Robert Benchley previewed a cartoon featuring the genius infant Baby Weems. Unlike traditional "full" Disney animation, the Baby Weems episode was presented via storyboard sketches which were bolstered by strong narration. The segment was highly effective and left a big impact on Anderson, who felt that this method could be employed as a viable form of animation: "The sequence was done with stills, production shots, and so on—it resembled a moving comic strip, and had a lot of vitality." He believed he could produce a cartoon series in this simplified visual style "if the story was worth telling."

Little did Anderson realize at the time that his moving-comic-strip idea would finally evolve into what is popularly called "limited animation." The

Disney film, along with Alex's talks with veteran Terrytoons artists (who demonstrated cutout animation and other artistic shortcuts learned in the silent era) proved influential. They instilled in Alex Anderson his eventual idea of producing cartoons for the emerging medium of television. TV was already being regarded as the entertainment big time of the future, and Anderson quickly saw vast potential in employing this simplified method of animation for the home screen. Most importantly, it could be specifically designed for a small budget. In 1946, following college graduation and World War II service in naval intelligence, Alex Anderson commenced another stint at Terrytoons in animation and story editing. This time he broached his idea to his famous relative, Paul Terry.

Uncle Paul, however, wanted no part of this—his cartoons were distributed internationally by 20th Century–Fox, and he told his nephew, "If I have anything to do with television, Fox will dump me just like that." Terry received the lion's share of his funding from the giant movie company. At the time, the film studios looked on TV with a paranoid fear. They regarded the upstart medium as archenemy number one, feeling certain that the death knell of the motion picture industry was about to be rung. Anderson adds, "Uncle Paul was actually very sweet about it; he told me he understood my enthusiasm, because I was the same age as he was when he'd started Terrytoons. He encouraged me to go ahead, even offering me the use of his camera department."

Undaunted, Alex Anderson decided to proceed. With several cartoon concepts brewing in his fertile imagination, he felt determined to give it his best shot. One of these concepts led to *Crusader Rabbit*. It resulted from the talks between Anderson and Terrytoons background artist Arthur Bartsch. Woodshedding new ideas for a cartoon series, they especially liked the feel of a two-character team: "We felt the main character should have a strong personality within a little body. Then we partnered him with a kind of passive, amiable buddy who was encased in a large, threatening body." This was effectively a comedy team in the classic tradition of physical mismatch, such as Laurel and Hardy or, more recently, Basil and Sybil Fawlty. From this point, the characters became animals, and finally, a rabbit and tiger were chosen.

In early 1948 Anderson left Terrytoons and returned to the Bay Area. He said, "I was in New York at the time Jay had the truck crash accident. He was recuperating; he was wearing leg braces and undergoing physical therapy. I visited him when I returned and talked to him about my idea of animation for television, and in fact I didn't even think he'd be interested. But he came out of the water like a trout! He wanted us to try TV. Well,

I was happy, because Jay had recently come back from Harvard and I knew nothing about how to run a business." Alex adds that Ward was into a lot of ideas at the time: "He was an aggressive entrepreneur and he could see what I wanted to do." And so they decided to go into business.

Jay Ward was as much a visionary as Alex Anderson. Although he knew virtually nil about cartoons, he had always possessed a keen eye for spotting talent, and the allure of showbiz appealed strongly to his personality. As Ward recalled, "A lot of our friends said that we were tackling a project that was too big. But we just felt that it could be done. Remember, this was 1948 and TV was in its infancy. At the time, Berkeley didn't even have a TV station." Alex adds, "We believed it would work for us. There was virtually nothing on early TV but wrestling matches."

Like Anderson, it didn't take Ward long to see a healthy future in television, the dynamic new postwar industry. Ramona Ward said, "During his recovery, Jay spent a lot of time reflecting on the future," while Jay added, "Those six months gave me lots of time to think." He saw the gigantic potential of TV as a long-term business opportunity (years earlier in New York, Jay had witnessed a television demonstration which made a lasting impact on him). Ramona relates, "We even had a small set which stood idle for months before TV broadcasting began. Jay would say, 'When it comes, we'll have a show ready.' " She recalls that early in their daunting new venture Anderson suffered occasional pangs of cold feet but Ward would gently spur him on.

In the summer of 1948, they took the plunge. That May, Jay Ward and Alex Anderson formed Television Arts Productions, Inc., Berkeley, California. When interviewed about this period, Ward recalled, "I think my greatest advantage was that I had no advantages. By that, I mean I just didn't know anything! And I was too dumb to know how little I knew. We started, you know, with only $50 and the desire to do it ourselves." On July 26, 1948, they officially began work in a temporary studio at 111 Sutter Street, Berkeley (home of NBC). The rented office was several floors up—no chance of runaway trucks here. Anderson recalls the rent being a bit steep, "but Jay felt that the modern office would add some prestige to our little company."

Their first undertaking was a pilot film, most of which was made by just the two of them. This was a fifteen-minute TV proposal featuring three cartoon items, "Hamhock Jones," "Dudley Doright of the Mounties," and "Crusader Rabbit." The pilot was given the umbrella title *The Comic Strips of Television*.

It was mostly written by Anderson; Ward helped contribute story gags.

Crusader Rabbit, TV's first original cartoon star. *Courtesy of Alex Anderson*

Alex was responsible for the fullest piece of animation: the well-remembered opening scene featuring Crusader Rabbit galloping toward us astride a horse. It quickly became apparent, however, that there was simply no way Anderson could complete all the artwork alone, so the intrepid young TV pioneers began hiring a small staff. Their first employee was Gerry Ray, a former Disney animator. Next came British-born Tom Stanford, who worked their Kodak Cinecamera (bought, says Alex, "from an army surplus store") and performed the editing chores. Years later Stanford won an Oscar for his work on *West Side Story* (1961).

In 1981, Anderson told animation historian Karl Cohen, "Jay Ward was very much a part of the pilot, not just the business manager. Jay worked as a consultant whenever needed, did some writing, gave guidance, and took charge of the sound production. He also acted as script editor." In fact it was Ward who suggested the name of the eventual TV series, seeing their rabbit star as a crusading adventurer à la Don Quixote. Alex recalls, "One of Jay's main functions on the production end was at Sound Recorders studio. That became his main thing—he was good at it. He was always a good editor, and he had the ability to hear if something wasn't right, or if it was a really good take. We did several episodes in a session." The recording studio was where Ward's true creative gifts emerged.

Wayne Stahmer, an owner of Sound Recorders in downtown San Francisco, suggested the actors who are heard on the pilot sound track. Jay Ward's first starring voice was Lucille Bliss, who played the heroic little Crusader Rabbit.

Born in New York on March 31, circa 1927, Bliss grew up (near vocal colleague June Foray) in Springfield, Massachusetts, and eventually settled in San Francisco. Her mother was a famed concert pianist. While still in high school Bliss began working in radio shows originating from San Francisco. Her first series was *Professor Puzzlewit*. In 1948, her mother told her of auditions being held for a cartoon in which the lead was to be either a dog or a rabbit. She met Ward and Anderson: "Alex told me, 'Crusader is a feisty little character who, visually, will walk like my young son.' He then demonstrated the walk for me. So I said, 'Hey Tiger, Tiger! I'm Crusader Rabbit,' and they yelled out, 'That's it. Great! That's just the voice we want!' "

Lucille worked with actor Vern Louden, who played the affable tiger, Rags. Louden was later a producer-director at KGO, ABC's San Francisco outlet. Character specialist Russ Coughlan and narrator Roy Whaley, both seasoned radio artists, were also snapped up by Television Arts. Like the staff, the voice actors did the pilot on spec, as Ward and Anderson had practically no funds. Ward recalled, "When we first started, we were so dumb we even shot the film upside down. That's right. We took it to a friend and had him run it through his projector and it came out upside down. At first we thought he had goofed, but he hadn't."

Upside down or not, the pilot film was finally completed in September 1948. In the first cartoon, "Hamhock Jones," a zany Sherlock Holmes spoof, the title character is introduced as the world's most amazing detective. Dr. Soufflé warns him about the notorious Siamese twins, Otto and Blotto Pretzel. Otto is the good twin and brother Blotto is evil—a visual gag shows Blotto drinking, and Otto suffering the hangover. Scientist Otto develops a gas called Votain, which can turn Democrats into Republicans and vice versa. When Blotto steals his brother's formula, Soufflé seeks the great detective's help. "Hamhock Jones" was the series for which Anderson held the highest hopes, even though he told Karl Cohen, "Jones was not all that personable a character." Gerry Ray felt "Hamhock Jones" was "a great idea."

The second item was "Dudley Doright of the Mounties." Rather different from the cartoons we know today—even Dudley's surname is unhyphenated—this story is set in Deepfreeze Landing. The entire cartoon, "The Ballad of Bashful Bess," unfolds in Robert W. Service rhyme, as Dudley, inspired by Nelson Eddy, gives chase to the hiss-able villain Sidney "the Snake" Snodgrass, who has abducted the fair and lovely heroine, Bess Blushmore. Dudley sports a somewhat effeminate voice, and the episode effectively

Crusader Rabbit and Rags the Tiger seem to be in agreement.
Courtesy of Alex Anderson

parodies old-time Yukon melodrama. One of Alex's obvious influences was Tex Avery, who had directed two fine theatrical cartoons based on Service poems, *Dangerous Dan McFoo* (Warners, 1939) and *The Shooting of Dan McGoo* (MGM, 1945). Bess even resembled Avery's MGM sexpot heroine from *Red Hot Riding Hood* (MGM, 1943).

Completing the reel was "Crusader Rabbit," which proved to be the successful item. Anderson notes that Crusader was modeled after MGM's freckled, bucktoothed 1940s child actor Jackie "Butch" Jenkins. The rabbit's appearance in the pilot is different from his later series look. Here he boasts whiskers and a slightly grungy demeanor, while Gerry Ray softened him for the TV episodes. In fact, the eventual TV show continues on from this episode, in which Crusader ventures to Texas to help his cousins the Jackrabbits, who are being systematically banished from their home state. He persuades a docile circus tiger named Rags to assist him, thus kicking off the fabled careers of television's first original animated stars.

2

CRUSADER RABBIT: HIS RISE AND FALL, or You Are Now Entering Frostbite Falls

In October 1948, Jay Ward and Alex Anderson presented their *Comic Strips* audition film to NBC. Ward flew to New York City and met Russ Johnson, NBC's director of video film shows. Jay learned that the network only wanted a five-minute show. Leonard Key, a close friend of Ward and Anderson since college, recalls, "The NBC guys called Jay and said, 'We like *Crusader*—we're impressed with it, it has potential.' Then they asked him, 'But who are you guys?'—meaning Jay and Al had no track record in the business. They said, 'You're from Berkeley and you have a three-and-a-half-minute pilot; well fine, but we want a responsible person behind it.' So they struck a deal with Jerry Fairbanks." Fairbanks, a seasoned and resourceful filmmaker long associated with Paramount, had signed an exclusive five-year contract with NBC in January 1948, appointing him sole supplier of all film shows for the fledgling TV network. Unlike many of his Hollywood cronies, the savvy Fairbanks recognized television's huge potential early on, much like Ward and Anderson.

Jay's next stop was Hollywood, where he met Fairbanks, who became the nominal supervising producer of the project. Len Key explains, "Jerry Fairbanks, financed by NBC, agreed to guarantee the *Crusader Rabbit* series and get behind it, if he could own the negatives." Anderson told animation scholar Fred Patten, "Actually Fairbanks had been identified to us as an

'NBC film adviser' who would handle prints and distribution. To this day I have no clear idea what his contractual arrangement with the network might have been." In any case, Fairbanks and Television Arts signed an agreement to produce 130 episodes of *Crusader Rabbit*. NBC supplied the money to Fairbanks, who paid for raw film stock and other production costs, advancing a sum each week to TAP for animation and voice-recording fees. Fairbanks would handle the marketing and publicity. Work commenced on the first five *Crusader* episodes in late 1948, and Ward and Anderson began hiring an art department.

The staff at Television Arts quickly swelled in size and talent: early artists included Chuck Fuson and Spaulding White, both of whom had been with Disney; former Terrytoons director Volney White; commercial illustrator Russ Scholl; and two newspaper cartoonists, Ted Martine and Bob Bastian, who was the longtime political cartoonist for the *San Francisco Chronicle*. The first staff members, like Ray and Stanford, stayed on. The camera department soon included Robert Oleson and Jack Williams, later with NASA. Jay Ward prepared the exposure sheets for the cameramen.

Thirty years on, Gerry Ray enjoyed recounting "the feeling of fun and camaraderie" which was ever present in the Berkeley-based enterprise. Several more excellent animators were soon hired, including Jerry Bowen and Bob Bemiller. Some, like Ray and Lee Mishkin, would be back with Ward eleven years later on *Rocky and His Friends*. For a month or so, even the legendary Grim Natwick toiled on *Crusader*—Natwick had created Max Fleischer's Betty Boop and had helped on the Snow White character for Walt Disney. Young first-time animator Bob Mills proved a quick study, starting as an inker, and eventually becoming the show's production manager.

Television Arts soon moved to a permanent location. The new studio complex was crowded, cramped, and hot, being composed of a converted garage with an apartment above it. This facility was located in the backyard behind Anderson's parents' house at 2733 Stuart Street, Berkeley. The kitchen and living room became the art department, while the writers worked from the bedroom. The business office was downstairs in the garage, next to the camera room.

With several scripts ready, the first set of sound tracks was recorded. Lucille Bliss remembers, "We'd record at night from nine o'clock, sometimes until four in the morning. Then I'd have to go straight to college. The studio was on Powell Street, and we'd do one week's worth of episodes."* She adds, "There wasn't much money at times. Jay would always joke and say, 'All right, it's pay time—who needs it the most this week?' " Bliss, who received $5 an episode for the pilot cartoons, saw her earnings soar to $30 a segment following the sale to NBC.

When TAP's artwork was completed, the materials were again shipped to Hollywood, where Jerry Fairbanks supervised postproduction at his Sunset Boulevard studio. He added background themes from a stock music library, then dubbed the tracks and had prints struck. The total cost per cartoon was roughly $2,500. Fairbanks said, "*Crusader Rabbit* was very limited. They often contained fewer than four cels per foot compared to ten times or more the amount for full animation. They would simply plan a story line so we could reuse some of the animation with a different background." Where theatrical animation had cost thousands of dollars per minute of film, Television Arts managed to make each episode cost-efficiently, for what are now unbelievably low prices.

January 1949 saw a flurry of press releases: one notice in *Broadcasting-Telecasting* read, "Animation for *Crusader Rabbit,* as the series will be known, is to be done by Television Arts Productions, Berkeley. The firm was recently organized by J. Troplong Ward, San Francisco radio producer, and Alexander Anderson, former animator and story editor of Terrytoons." At this point Television Arts had five films in the can, and an additional thirteen scripts ready.

But in early February 1949, NBC decided not to go ahead with the original plan. After viewing the first five, they felt that instead of networking the series, it would do better in syndication. *Daily Variety* reported, "As a result of the NBC snub, Fairbanks will peddle the pix himself. [The] Firm will make 130 reels and offer them to video outlets." In fact, *Crusader Rabbit* was not actually syndicated; rather, it was sold by Fairbanks via a method known as spot-marketing—that is, the cartoons were distributed to individual NBC stations with built-in commercials.

Following a promotional party thrown by Fairbanks for the media press and their kids on March 25, 1949, NBC occasionally test-screened the early cartoons. They finally ordered (i.e., paid for) sixty-five more editions of the series in August. Television Arts went back to work, and the sixty-five ep-

*TAP's facilities were limited, so the masters were sent to Hollywood and transferred to optical negative film.

isodes, produced at the rate of five a week, were completed by November 1949. This brought the total to seventy episodes, containing four complete adventure-serial stories (or "Crusades," as Fairbanks's publicity crew nicknamed them). There followed a two-month grace period until January 1950, when NBC ordered the remaining sixty episodes of the advertised package. The sixty new segments amounted to three more "Crusades."

With the additional sixty episodes on order, the Television Arts team was kept busy from New Year through the summer of 1950. Meanwhile Fairbanks spent considerable time selling the show on a city-by-city basis to NBC affiliates. When the Carnation Milk Company came aboard as sponsor in mid-June, the diminutive rabbit was ready to make his TV debut. Fairbanks followed up with some promotional work (our hero was billed as being "Two and a Half Carrots Tall"). *Crusader Rabbit* finally premiered in Los Angeles on August 1, 1950, at 6:00 P.M. on station KNBH. Ultimately, the series ran on more than two hundred stations.

Television Arts' *Crusader Rabbit* series proved that limited animation was indeed a viable TV prospect. The chancy experiment had worked; without realizing the full impact of what they had done at the time, Anderson and Ward had made a not inconsiderable mark upon show-business history. Indeed, *Crusader Rabbit* was the foundation for what is now a multi-million-dollar TV phenomenon. In a very real sense, Anderson's cheap little "moving comic strip" was one of the most influential things to happen in animation for many years.

Watching the old episodes today, Alex Anderson feels, "They're really pretty primitive." While this is no doubt an accurate assessment by today's technical standards, the show's visual quality is secondary to its overall impact on future TV programming. Certainly, *Crusader*'s influence on Hanna-Barbera's 1957 *Ruff and Reddy*—the show that truly kick-started the TV animation bandwagon—is undeniable.

As Jerry Fairbanks told Gary Grossman, author of *Saturday Morning TV,* "At the rock-bottom prices the networks or stations were able to pay for programming then, we had to develop shortcuts." To keep the show within the minuscule budget, the well-made sound tracks carried the momentum; the format reappeared in 1959 with Ward's *Rocky and His Friends,* albeit far more frantically paced. The animation was described by Anderson as "sort of moving storyboards with a walk cycle." In fact, the movement is mainly limited to stationary cutout figures with mouth movements, eye shifts, and various changes of expression created on cel [celluloid sheet] overlays. Bob

Bemiller recalled, "We kind of invented limited animation with the six basic mouth movements. . . . We pioneered slugging the boards and timing the stuff down to the second. We didn't have the budget to edit it later, like they did in theatricals."

Animator John Sparey, who joined the enterprise in mid-1950, added, "They didn't use cel paint on cels, but car lacquer!" Bold black outlines were employed to ensure that the artwork stood out on the tiny TV screens of the era. To compensate for the visual restrictions, audience interest was maintained by much camera movement and those clever sound tracks in which the narrator described most of the action. Gerry Ray told Fred Patten, "They got something like $2,700 or $3,000 an episode. So it worked out to about $3 a foot that stuff was produced for. Three dollars per 35-mm foot, in 1949 when we started this stuff."

From the outset the writing set a high standard. When *Crusader* went to air it not only held the small fry spellbound, it had the same effect as the concurrent puppet show *Time for Beany:* the humorous scripts began attracting an unexpected adult following. Animator Bob Mills observed, "Jay and Alex shared a similar sense of humor—they both laughed at the same things."

Anderson's storyboards were beefed up with extra gags by Hal Goodman and Lloyd Turner; Turner would be one of Jay Ward's top cartoon writers a decade later. "Lloyd came up to the Bay Area for a while and worked on the show," said Alex. Turner recalled, "In 1948, Alex was in Los Angeles. He'd gone to see the Cartoonists Guild, 'cause he was looking for writers. He got my name and I went to see him at a motel in Beverly Hills. I drew a few pictures for him and told him a few jokes and he said I was hired; would I be able to work in Berkeley? I said yes, because my dad lived up there and worked in a bank in Oakland. So I went up and I met Jay, and our personalities clicked, it was like love at first sight.

"Upstairs in this converted garage they had a cubicle-like deal with all the artists, and a tiny area where they put me and another writer named Ralph [*sic*] Goodman. So I wrote gags and turned them in to Alex. That only lasted a few months because they ran out of money for writers, but it was a real interesting time being in on the ground floor as far as early TV cartoons were concerned. I knew Alex for many years and played a lot of golf with him and Jay. Actually Jay and I were the real buddies. I never really got to know Alex that well as a person."

Another staff member was singled out by Anderson as a major contributor to the unique comedy within the cartoons. Joe Curtin, a Canadian artist who had worked at Terrytoons (and hated the place as much as the boss's nephew), was, recalls Anderson, "Very clever. He was a big help in the writing and he had a great sense of humor, of what would or wouldn't work. He was a marvelous influence." Gerry Ray added, "Curtin was a very funny guy from a place called Guelph, Ontario." One of Curtin's tasks involved transcribing the narration into script form from Anderson's storyboards.

Once on air, Crusader and Rags quickly proved popular. The format was timeless: our two heroes lived in an elfin glade called Galahad Glen and would travel anywhere to fight for right. One adventure took the rabbit and tiger to India to prevent Rags's cousins, the Indian tigers, from having their stripes removed to make India ink. Another great tale landed the boys in Merrie Olde England of the tenth century, defending the honor of Sir Chester Chilblain's lovely daughter. And a really wild plot found them journeying to Ireland to dispose of a giant named Finn McCool XIII, who had thoughtlessly driven all the leprechauns from their homeland.

These truly imaginative stories featured great villain characters, like the unctuous Dudley Nightshade, mad scientist Belfry Q. Batts (whose secret fantasy was to be a cowboy star), a two-headed fire-breathing dragon named Arson and Sterno, the Rajah of Rinsewater, Babyface Barracuda, and the menacing Black Bilge the Pirate, whose inevitable parrot was named Garlic. Our two stalwart pals received an occasional assist from Garfield Groundhog. Plucky Crusader, with his memorable husky voice, became an identifiable hero to the younger viewers. His slow-talking sidekick Ragland T. Tiger ("Rags" for short) proved a likable second banana. Like *Time for Beany*, the *Crusader* TV show was a clever departure from Alex's uncle's *Farmer Alfalfa* and similar creaky silent-vintage cartoons, then being sold for the new home screen. A neat combination of comic chapter-play adventure laced with suspense and hip dialogue, *Crusader Rabbit,* like Jay Ward's later shows, immediately appealed to two age levels.

The pun-laden scripts spoofed dramatic conventions, movies, songs—in fact, whatever inspired Anderson and Ward at the time. The show occurred at one of those cyclical times when comedy attitudes change. During World War II the escapist humor had been brash, broad, and loud: Abbott and Costello movies, the wild Warner Brothers cartoons of Bob Clampett, Bob Hope's radio show, etc. By the time *Crusader Rabbit* debuted, a satirical edge had crept in. This would be an era of clever verbal humor, led by *Time for*

Beany, Stan Freberg, and Mort Sahl. The satiric tone was tempered in Alex Anderson by a storytelling ability which was marked by vivid imagination, gentle wit, and a quiet style all his own. It was admired by many skilled artists, who hung on Anderson that most enviable of titles, a "cartoonist's cartoonist."

Bob Ganon, manager of animation house TV Spots, referred to a purity and innocence within Anderson's satire. Bill Scott felt that "Alex was never topped as a writer in this field." Examples of Anderson's influence on Scott's later scripts for *Rocky and His Friends* can be found in trademarks like the narrator saying, "As our story opens today" or "Don't miss our next episode." Indeed, as early as the second episode, Crusader breaks the "fourth wall" and talks back to the narrator.

As Leonard Key put it, "Jay and Alex were a magnificent team. Alex was a terribly funny man, and brilliantly creative. He was shy and self-effacing, even at school, but he had a lot of the actor in him. And Jay was insanely brilliant at promotion and ideas—he was one of the greatest showmen who ever lived, even though he was plagued by his lifelong nervous condition stemming from the accident."

An early review gave the show a terrific rap.

> *Crusader Rabbit* is a loveable, determined doll of a rabbit whose creators [*sic*], Fairbanks Studios, put him through paces and feed him dialog apparently designed for children, but with such tongue-in-cheek that at times the nightly 5 minutes could hold its own with a popular threesome [*Kukla, Fran and Ollie*] no longer seen locally. . . .

One thing *Crusader Rabbit* had over Jay Ward's later cartoons was Fairbanks's professional sound tracks: regrettably, most of Ward's early *Rocky and His Friends* shows were badly dubbed and mixed in Mexico City. In *Crusader Rabbit* the two-reel comedy sound effects were addressed intelligently, and the library music for the backgrounds was well chosen and unobtrusive.

There was a second grace period after the first 130 episodes were completed. This lasted six months, from July 1950 until January 1951. To keep the staff busy while NBC made up its corporate mind to renew, Ward was able to obtain animation work for some early television commercials, including spots for Italian Swiss Colony wine, Kraft cottage cheese, and Carnation's Friskies dog food (sponsor of Crusader). During this period some new cartoon ideas began to emerge from the Berkeley-based animation company.

One was a storyboard for "The Adventures of Duffy Dobbs, Private Eye," while sundry other TAP concepts included "Samson of Swillwater Creek," "Gloria Monday," and "Wormwood Scrubs." Most significant, however, was a presentation storyboard called *The Frosbite Falls Review*. This proposal featured a colorful array of creatures, including the very first appearance of our heroes Rocky the Flying Squirrel and Bullwinkle, billed here as "the French-Canadian Moose."

A year or so before, Anderson had had a dream in which he attended a poker party with a large, goofy moose. "I brought along this stupid moose who was doing card tricks. I woke up feeling embarrassed—I thought, you've been working too hard." Anderson told the *San Francisco Chronicle,* "There's something majestic about a moose. They're macho, but they have a comic aspect, with that schnozzola of theirs. There are few other creatures so begging to be caricatured." At the time in Berkeley there was a car dealer named Clarence Bullwinkel (Anderson recalls, "He ran a Ford agency on College and Claremont Avenues in Oakland"). Jay and Alex agreed that Bullwinkel was a funny name, and after respelling it the moose had his moniker. As for the squirrel, Anderson explained, "I had worked on *Mighty Mouse,* and he flew around. I didn't understand the mechanics of how a mouse flew—or, for that matter, how *Superman* flew. But flying squirrels do fly, and that gave him the mantle of 'superness' without having to stretch the truth." Actually, Rocky was originally to be a plain squirrel with artificial wings!

In *The Frostbite Falls Review,* Rocky and Bullwinkle were just two characters in a large cast—others included Sylvester the Fox, Flora Fauna, Blackstone the Crow, and Oski the Bear. The premise had these animals broadcasting a television show from their own station, located in the North Woods. While the moose and squirrel look familiar, they have none of the touches that Bill Scott gave them eight years later in the *Rocky* pilot (except that Rocky was intended to fly to the aid of others—that stayed). Anderson explained, "It seemed like a good format: to make satirical comment on TV, including ourselves."

Cartoon historian David Mruz interviewed Jay Ward in 1980, and learned the origin of the name Frostbite Falls. "As a kid, Jay was a big fan of the University of Minnesota Golden Gophers. Before Alaska had become an American state, International Falls, Minnesota, was known to millions who

Introducing the all-star cast of the
FROSTBITE FALLS REVIEW
For years these amazing creatures have been hiding their dramatic abilities away out yonder in the great North Woods. Now at last, through the wondrous medium of television, they plan to launch their remarkable talents upon our unsuspecting nation.

The Frostbite Falls Review, a cartoon idea that failed to sell, and which featured the first appearance of Rocky and Bullwinkle. *Courtesy of Alex Anderson*

heard radio reports on the nation's weather as the 'Ice Box of America.' Living in America's ice box was Jay Ward's idol, Bronko Nagurski, who owned and operated a gas station in International Falls. This was a natural for Ward when they needed a setting for a spin-off series for his [eventually] lawsuit-plagued *Crusader Rabbit*." Several scripts were prepared, but the Frostbite Falls proposal failed to sell.

Meantime *Crusader Rabbit* was finally given its third go-ahead. NBC picked up TAP's option in January 1951 for a further set of sixty-five episodes. This time, however, the network requested five episodes a week; for the previous batch, the Berkeley team had been completing only four weekly. Anderson says, "We did 195 episodes, and that consisted of the three sets. Well, on the third batch we decided it was just getting too difficult to maintain a pool of talent in Berkeley, so we discussed shifting to Los Angeles."

Television Arts moved to Hollywood in February 1951. Anderson said, "I finally bit the bullet. We worked from an animation facility—you couldn't really call it a studio—behind a big market in Hollywood. It was a row of bungalows. I was writing up here in Berkeley, and constantly going down to L.A. with the story lines—I rented a motel room—and we completed the third set." Ramona Ward recalls, "Their studio was on Kingsley Drive, off Sunset Boulevard. Jay and I took the family, and for a year or so we lived down by the beach in Santa Monica." Anderson spent most of his time in Berkeley, as the writing and voice-recording remained up north. Several of the staff weren't interested in relocating, so Ward had to recruit about 50 percent new people, some of whom answered an ad that TAP placed in *Variety*.

Bill Littlejohn, who later animated the "Dudley Do-Right" episode opening in 1961, remembers his first association with Jay Ward ten years earlier, when Television Arts moved to Los Angeles. Littlejohn was business agent for the Screen Cartoonists Guild when Ward came to register his Hollywood setup. Bob Mills and Chuck Fuson came down from Berkeley, while Gerry Ray and John Sparey rejoined the TAP team. Ray told Fred Patten, "I did the [story] boards. Alex wrote the stuff and I boarded it. The writing was really excellent. I have nothing but the sincerest admiration for Alex. And Jay also, because Jay always had the feeling for that type of humor. Although Jay was not a writer, he was able to spot it, bring it along, develop it, coddle it, encourage it and laugh it along."

Bill Hurtz recalled meeting his future boss in 1951, when Ward visited famed cartoon studio UPA. The artists there told Ward how they all rushed home to watch *Crusader* every evening. "When he came by we said, 'Hey, he's got this great kid's show on TV. . . . The guy's got great stories.' That's what we were impressed by—because drawing doesn't impress us that much—and we said yeah, this is the way it should be done. So we'd cut out from work and get home by 5:15 or 5:30, whenever it was, to watch *Crusader Rabbit*. When he came down to visit us he was thunderstruck to see that we were just as interested in what he was doing as he was in what we were doing."

But so much for the best-laid plans of rabbits and men: Jay Ward soon discovered there would be no further "Crusades." Six months after moving production to Los Angeles, the sixty-five new episodes were in the can. A long fallow stretch began in July 1951, while they waited for a renewal, this time in vain. Anderson jokes, "The patient was a success but the operation died! NBC didn't renew; we weren't particularly worried, we just regarded it as another hiatus. When you're that young, your ego is pretty indestructible." By the end of summer, Ward began laying people off. Some accepted outside work. Finally, in early 1952, Ward and Mills—resigned to the bad news—packed up all Television Arts' belongings and returned to Berkeley, where the artwork was put into storage.

Anderson recalls, "For the moment there was no income, so I took a job with the ad agency Guild, Bascom and Bonfigli in San Francisco. Jay went back into real estate, along with several other things. As usual he had a lot of irons in the fire, like Ward-Walker coffee—this was gourmet coffee twenty years ahead of its time—and Mr. Dingle soda-fountain drinks, as well as various other business ideas. And he played a lot of tennis and golf. Anyway, the so-called hiatus turned out to be five years in length before *Crusader Rabbit* was revived."

These five years, involving a complicated legal battle, were to prove a dark period for Television Arts. In hindsight, Ward and Anderson would doubtless have preferred hibernating with the rabbit and tiger in Galahad Glen.

Before winding up the Hollywood operation, Fairbanks and Ward had become concerned that NBC wasn't promoting its smaller shows, in particular *Crusader Rabbit*. Instead, the network appeared to be throwing all its resources into their splashy variety spectaculars featuring Dinah Shore and others. Ward, convinced that his rabbit's marketing potential was being squandered, came to an agreement in which Fairbanks would buy the cartoons back from NBC and promote them himself, with profits to be split fifty-fifty between TAP and Fairbanks. And so on February 1, 1952, Fairbanks signed a contract to buy back all his films from the network for $170,000.

Fairbanks planned to market his library, via distributor Consolidated Television Sales, as a "show-starter" package to new TV stations in America and Canada. Unfortunately, as Bob Ganon recalled, "Jerry Fairbanks had been in financial difficulties all his life." Fairbanks couldn't afford to pay NBC the lump sum, so the network mortgaged his films in a scheme whereby he would pay back the sum of $8,000 per month. But even this proved risky; the youthful and bustling TV industry had rapidly outgrown Fairbanks Productions, whose older film shows already looked a little shopworn. Consequently, his income had dropped markedly.

Within several months it became clear to the NBC brass that Fairbanks would default, so in January 1953 they foreclosed. Anderson said, "Fairbanks had put *Crusader* and his other TV series up as collateral—but he couldn't repay, so NBC auctioned the films off. I remember the morning we found out. Jay called me and said he'd seen this announcement in *The Hollywood Reporter* which said NBC has 195 *Crusader Rabbit* films on the block." Ramona Ward recalls, "Jay was very upset. He flew to New York that same day and tried to put a stop to the sale." Sadly, he was unsuccessful. And this was just the start of the protracted troubles that followed.

By June 1953, NBC had sold all Fairbanks's films, including the little rabbit's "Crusades," to Consolidated Television Sales, which had had the distribution contract with Fairbanks. But when this company also went belly-up, in mid-1954, it was bought by wealthy Shull Bonsall, a shrewd and well-heeled Los Angeles businessman who, according to Gerry Ray, "specialized in buying bankrupt companies with worthwhile assets." Thus, Bonsall acquired the negatives to the *Crusader Rabbit* films and continued their distribution.

Meanwhile, Anderson and Ward were far more concerned with their immediate financial well-being. Always under the impression that the original deal with Fairbanks guaranteed them half the profits on the series, they found they were suddenly being stonewalled by everyone now involved with the *Crusader* library, all of whom denied any such rights existed. Alex said, "Jay and I always felt it was a strange coincidence that the NBC executive who brought Fairbanks into the picture [Russ Johnston] subsequently quit the network and joined Jerry Fairbanks Inc. as a vice president. We certainly were not a party to the NBC loan and maintained that our interest in the films could not thus be disregarded."

And so, on October 19, 1953, Television Arts Productions went to trial in Los Angeles against Fairbanks, NBC, and anyone else now connected with the films. The case dragged on for over three years, but ultimately Anderson and Ward lost. Alex said, "There was indeed litigation. . . . We learned to our dismay that with a few legal loopholes . . . our 50 percent equity in the films had disappeared." One of these loopholes found that the contract which supposedly guaranteed Ward and Anderson half the profits was deemed a "personal agreement" with Fairbanks, and this had been voided when Fairbanks lost the films to NBC. To cap this, the judge ruled that there were in fact no profits to be divided: unfortunately, the series hadn't broken even.

But our feisty little rabbit and his placid tiger pal wouldn't sit still for long. During this sobering experience with Fairbanks and NBC, Ward and Anderson kept busy with their real estate and advertising careers. Then in late 1956, Jay Ward and Len Key discussed a revival of *Crusader Rabbit*.

Leonard Key was the same age as Jay and Alex; they'd all attended University High School in Oakland, then UC Berkeley. Key had played football, and sports-nut Ward dubbed him "Big Len" (while Key's nickname for Ward was "Jazef"). He had occasionally dropped in on Anderson and Ward in their garage studio during production of the early *Crusader Rabbit* films in Berkeley. Lucille Bliss recalls Len and his cartoonist brother Ted sitting in and contributing occasional opinions or ideas. Key recalls, "We were all close friends and we all thought this idea of the Laurel and Hardy type of cartoon team was great." He loved the characters, and had long felt proud of Television Arts' achievement.

Key explains, "I'm a workaholic; I'd been in radio and TV for some time and I was forever doing a deal for someone—I was always involved in far too many things at one time." He dearly wanted to see Ward leave the world of real estate and return to animation, feeling, "Jay had a genuine talent for this field, and I knew he was real eager to get back into cartoon production."

Constantly keeping his ears open to all that went on in the industry, Key learned that the present climate strongly favored TV animation. He felt the timing was now perfect to resurrect *Crusader Rabbit* for all new episodes: "The early series was way ahead of its time. And anyway, very few people owned TV sets back in 1949. But now thousands of people had television in the home and the business had caught up: kids loved cartoons, which meant big advertising bucks. So one day I called Jay and told him I had a great idea: let's do another 195 episodes! Jay was willing and eager, but he was busy with the court case and couldn't devote himself full-time. So he decided to look for an acceptable animation outfit to which he would assign rights. I became the manager of the project."

Ward approached the famed *Tom and Jerry* director William Hanna, who expressed interest in the idea. Still with MGM, whose theatrical cartoon division was inexorably winding down due to rising labor costs and the inroads being made by television, Hanna and some associates were keen to enter TV animation. They had been impressed with the original *Crusader Rabbit* and, after studying the series and discussing ways of improving on the artwork, decided to try some episodes on speculation.

Hanna flew to New York to talk with Ward about the business angle. He then met Anderson in San Francisco to discuss the creative aspects of the property. Hanna recalls, "I'd never met Anderson, so he said he'd greet me at the airport, and that I'd recognize him because he'd be wearing this big Russian hat." The upshot of these meetings was that Hanna and the talented animator Mike Lah formed an independent studio called Shield Productions, Inc., with design artists Don Driscoll and Don McNamara as partners. Shield was to make new *Crusader Rabbit* episodes in color. The staff consisted mostly of MGM artists. Lah told Fred Patten that Ward encouraged them to open the studio. The Shield people would fund the *Crusader* series themselves, and be paid when Ward sold the show.

This time around, Alex Anderson wasn't really interested. He says, "By now, I was a vice president and creative director at an ad agency, and I had a family. So I was rather reluctant to go back to a ninety-hour week with the prospect of not much money." Still, he agreed to help with the scripts, part-time, and wrote some material. Key opines, "Frankly, I felt they both had a 'bad taste' in their mouths from the earlier experience. But I knew Jay was very keen to return to TV on a full-time basis."

Len Key began working on packaging the new *Crusader* "strip" (TV terminology for a Monday-to-Friday show, one episode a day). Again, it was planned for a full TV season running thirty-nine weeks, or 195 weekday episodes. The Shield staff recorded some voice tracks and began work on the new *Crusader* cartoons. If nothing else, Key was certainly energetic. He composed a sales program guaranteeing "195 episodes comparable in quality to the older shows," and by hopping planes, city to city, "I built up interest in the show amounting to some $4,500,000 in potential contracts. All the folks in TV programming departments still loved *Crusader Rabbit.*

"Finally some guys at RCA put together a deal. I got a very good reaction. They were originally a radio syndication firm and this was to be one of their kickoff TV series. It would be on a two-year unlimited-run basis. The cartoons were budgeted at $3,000 each. I hired a damned good lawyer and we were in the final stages of negotiation." Key and some acquaintances invested money in the project for a share in the property.

Suddenly new trouble loomed. Shield Productions had been working for three months, with several shows under way, when legal rights to the characters began being questioned. Jay Ward hadn't mentioned his currently pending lawsuit with Fairbanks, feeling confident that his attorney, Ted Chester, would soon win the case. But now Shull Bonsall—who had basically liquidated Fairbanks Productions and thus owned the negatives to the original *Crusader* films—wanted to make his own color *Crusader Rabbit* series through TV Spots, a small commercial animation studio he had bought in 1954.

Bob Ganon, general manager of TV Spots, got Bonsall enthused about producing "entertainment" animation to supplement their regular TV commercial assignments. Bonsall was eager, having seen the healthy ratings for cartoons like *Popeye* and *Bugs Bunny* once the film studios finally released their backlogs to television in 1956. Understandably, he regarded the old *Crusader Rabbit* films he now owned as a viable property. As before, Ward didn't bring this new matter up with the Shield people, assuming that though TV Spots might have their old cartoons, he and Anderson indisputably owned the character rights.

Events began to snowball. Shull Bonsall contacted Len Key, and they met in New York for lunch. Key discovered "just how tough and shrewd Bonsall was—which made sense—he was a bean counter from way back when he made a pile of money out of laundromats." Bonsall offered half the income from the old films and a fifty-fifty deal if he could make the new ones through his TV Spots studio. Key remembers Bonsall saying, " 'I've checked you guys out—you could use the money.' " Key stalled, saying he had to consult Anderson and Ward. He phoned Jay, who responded, " 'Big Len, tell him no—we'll do it ourselves. Besides, Bonsall is one of the people we're suing, and we don't want to deal with him.' " Key informed Bonsall that Ward and Anderson weren't interested, but thanks anyway. "The contracts were all made up, and we were ready to close our deal with RCA."

Bonsall then intimated that Key and Ward were making a big mistake. "And with that veiled threat," remembers Len, "he showed me his financial record, and said, 'I've got a lot more money than you guys.' Soon after, we got a call from Bonsall's lawyer, Donald Dewar, saying they would sue us and claiming that Television Arts didn't have clear title to the property." Then RCA called Len, reporting more trouble: Bonsall's lawyer had also phoned them, claiming "lapse of copyright and unfair competition," his pitch being that the new Shield episodes could not be guaranteed to be of comparable quality.

"In reality," Key explained, "Bonsall was simply making it impossible for us to continue. It was slam-dunk—he told us that our retainer for an attorney would cost us $40,000, and that we were looking at a five-year court case! None of us could afford it, so of course Bonsall won. He got the characters by simply paying Jay and Alex $50,000. Jay was very disappointed in the outcome; and at the same time he was happy the mess was over, because it would free him up to do other things."

By now Bill Hanna and associates had quit. At first Ward had assured Shield Productions that he and Anderson owned the characters and that work should proceed. However, Shield's attorney advised Hanna to dissolve the *Crusader* project: there was no written contract with Ward protecting them from Shull Bonsall's claim, and thus there seemed little chance of selling the Shield episodes to a sponsor during this ongoing mess. Eleven color episodes went down the drain. When Shield offered to sell their work, they couldn't reach an agreement with Bonsall, so the finished cartoons disappeared into the vault forever. The final result was that Bonsall's TV Spots took over Shield's work and position.

To tidy up the matter of character rights, in June 1957, Bonsall bought Ward and Anderson's corporation, Television Arts Productions, for $50,000. Anderson recalls, "Shull Bonsall was pretty slippery. I remember Jay bringing word of Bonsall's offer—not just for the rights to *Crusader* but for TAP itself. He gave us something like three days to take it or leave it. We finally agreed, with the proviso that Jay and I retain some equipment and the rights to all our undeveloped properties."

RCA and its lawyers were understandably angry, having advanced $9,500 and committed themselves, to no avail. Key was certainly embarrassed: "My stockholders were furious." And what of Bill Hanna? Just as MGM closed its theatrical animation division, George Sidney of Columbia/Screen Gems offered Hanna financing for a new animation studio if Screen Gems could have the famous MGM team of Hanna and Joe Barbera. The Shield staff joined the new Hanna-Barbera Productions and commenced work on *Ruff and Reddy*. The rest is TV cartoon history.

Meanwhile Ward and Anderson's older *Crusader Rabbit* films were being distributed by George Bagnall and Associates. As Len Key saw it, "Bagnall was small-time; he had a bunch of crummy films and old shorts—he was lucky to get *Crusader*." TV Spots eventually went on to produce 260 new color episodes of *Crusader Rabbit*. Bob Ganon even approached Anderson to write the scripts. Under the circumstances, however, Alex was hardly interested. A new cartoon writer, one Chris Bob Hayward, got the nod. Anderson said, "To be fair, the new *Crusader* show had some excellent people working on it, and the results were very good." (Chris Hayward later became one of Jay Ward's top writers.) Bob Bemiller and John Sparey, who had worked on the original series, were now with the TV Spots *Crusader* crew, Bemiller becoming the show's director.

The one thing Shull Bonsall didn't get was the rights to Anderson and Ward's other characters, including a certain moose, squirrel, and mounted policeman. Ward had been back in real estate for almost six years, always intending to return to TV when possible.* Now, in mid-1957, Ward felt it was time once and for all to get back. Anderson comments, "Jay Ward Productions eventually rose like a phoenix out of this mess of legal nightmares."

With his beloved animated offspring Crusader Rabbit and Rags the Tiger now in the custody of stepparents at TV Spots, a bruised but wiser Alex Anderson was happy to pursue a full-time career in advertising. Jay Ward, meanwhile, was at a crossroads. As columnist John Stanley observed, "Ward went back to making more money in real estate, but with the decided goal that he would one day return to cartoon producing, fulfilling his dream." Return he did, although for a couple of years Jay's "dream" played more like a fractured Stephen King nightmare.

*Ward kept his real estate business running. It was, as he put it, "something I can return to when they kick me off the air." He finally sold it in 1986.

3

Time for That Jolly Juggler, Bullwinkle, or Bill Scott, Moose of Letters

The years 1957–59 marked the formative period of Jay Ward Productions. During this time Ward teamed with the incredibly gifted Bill Scott, and with the help of promoter Leonard Key, our favorite squirrel and moose finally got to be TV stars. But the machinations of finding a sponsor and a bankroll turned out to be as complex as the longest Rocky and Bullwinkle adventure: the heroes and all the cliffhangers were there, but the script wasn't nearly as funny.

At least Jay felt secure about one thing: although Alex Anderson had departed, his place was filled by a talent that was his equal.

Jay Ward Productions would house many top-line talents, but without Bill Scott there might never have been a *Rocky and His Friends* or *Bullwinkle Show,* at least as we know them. He was the head writer, coproducer, and undisputed creative force behind the cartoons; as well, he provided the voices for most of the star characters, giving witty vocal life to Bullwinkle, Mr. Peabody, Dudley Do-Right, Fillmore Bear, George of the Jungle, Super Chicken, and Tom Slick.

Scott is often described in Rocky and Bullwinkle articles as the "soul" of the shows, and his stamp is dominant in the cartoons. The whole tone of Jay Ward's output is a direct reflection of Scott's unique creative personality.

Not counting his brief appearance in a 1950 storyboard developed by Alex Anderson, "Bullwinkle J. Moose" as we know him was actually born William John Scott on August 2, 1920, in Philadelphia. From the age of five Bill Scott grew up in nearby Trenton, New Jersey. When he was fifteen it was discovered he had contracted tuberculosis, and in early 1936 his father, a machinist, and his mother, a waitress, moved to Denver, Colorado. The climatic change seemed to do the trick, and happily, Scott's bout with TB didn't recur.

An animation buff from the age of four, Scott was hooked for life after seeing a Felix the Cat cartoon. "I can remember the first cartoon I ever saw, and in fact the first gag in the first cartoon I ever saw; it starred Felix, and I was entranced by the fact that this little black thing could run across the movie screen. In those days of course it was all silent film, and in order for a character to show any kind of reaction, he did what they would do in comic strips, which was to have exclamation points or question marks appear over his head. So Felix, being pursued by a dog, stopped, turned, did a take, and a large exclamation point appeared. He grabbed the down-stroke of the exclamation point with one hand, and used it as a bat to hit the period, which acted as well as a ball and knocked the dog out cold! Well, I was dazzled, and I've been dazzled by animation ever since. I realized even then that it was an art with which you could do anything, and I was tickled to death with it. So, as I say, I was an animation nut from the word go: I was probably the only seventeen-year-old in Denver who memorized all the credits on the cartoons."

Attending South High School in Denver, young Bill spent his formative Saturday afternoons keenly studying animated films in Colorado movie houses. He graduated from the University of Denver in 1941 with a B.A., majoring in theater and dramatic arts with a minor in English.

For some time, Scott had been allowing his performing skills to flower. From 1938 to 1942 he was a freelance radio actor on stations KOA, KLZ, and KVOD. When he was eighteen he joined the Denver Children's Theatre, where he met Dorothy Williams, whom he married four years later. Dorothy was a high school senior studying drama when they met. They were soon staging puppet shows in the window of a Denver department store and in theaters. "We gave them 'Cinderella,' 'Rapunzel,' and 'Rumpelstiltskin,' but the kids could hardly wait for us to get off so they could see *The Lone Ranger*."

At the same time Scott kept feeding his obsession with animation. "I was one of the thousands who responded to the Walt Disney nationwide talent search by drawing Goofy and Pluto. I loved to do this, although I really didn't have that much drawing ability." Before long he hooked up with Bill Turnbull, another rabid local cartoon buff.

"Turnbull was the only other guy in town who memorized all the credits on cartoons and short subjects. We knew all the names: animators like Phil Monroe and so on. In fact, I knew who all the people were at Warners, Disney, and MGM—these were my heroes. Bill Turnbull was an animation buff to such a degree that he built his own animation crane out of wood plus spit, string, and wire, from a couple of photographs of Disney's famous Multiplane version, and it was an operable machine! We needed material to demonstrate his camera, so he and I began to 'paper animate' just to see how things moved. And this was my first actual experience with animation."

Scott and Turnbull worked together for one summer, animating to some sixteen-inch sound track discs from the movie *King Kong* (1933), more for fun and self-education than anything else. Later, they got to do some title work for some of the Denver movie theaters that screened local advertisements.

"Careerwise I wanted to be a commercial artist very much; I thought that was a fine thing to do. But it really didn't take me long to realize that I was not a good draftsman, and I knew very little about color: two things which have haunted me ever since. I'm a pretty good draftsman now [1981], but then I had more guts than anything else."

Following graduation, Scott became a high school teacher. He taught English and drama for "one traumatic semester [1941–42]—as scarifying to the students as to me—in fact I was trained to be a schoolteacher. Then, when World War II descended upon us, I enlisted in the army in spring 1942, but—through a friend—I was able to attend aerial photography school. Cameras were another hobby, and besides, the photo school was located near Denver."

Qualifying as a lab technician at photography school, Scott was assigned to Peterson Field Air Force Base in Colorado Springs. Soon after, his unit was ordered to transfer to California. But because Scott was acting in a fund-raising play staged by the camp newspaper (he scored the lead role in *The Man Who Came to Dinner*), Special Services reluctantly put him on detached service for one month. When the play ended its run early, Scott enjoyed a brief furlough, then took the Chief to Los Angeles. After a confusing run-around, during which Bill was listed as AWOL, he discovered that his camera crew was stationed at the First Motion Picture Unit, a division of the Eighteenth Air Force Base Unit. The FMPU—a military organization—

Bill Scott, with the Bullwinkle puppet for which he provided the voice, entertaining a group of children in 1961. *Courtesy of Bill Scott*

housed many of Hollywood's finest filmmakers, who were busy producing training and instructional films for the war effort. It was located at the Hal Roach Studio in Culver City, former home to Bill's comic idols Laurel and Hardy. Upon arrival, he was informed he was too late: his combat camera crew had already shipped out, and young Bill Scott was suddenly a "private without portfolio."

As he told interviewer Paul Etcheverry, "When I walked into the orderly room of the unit itself, just to report for duty, I was sent in to see the personnel officer, who was Ronald Reagan! Quite a jolt for a Denver boy." (Reagan narrated many of the films the unit produced.) Soon after settling in, Bill was amazed and delighted to learn that within the walls of the First Motion Picture Unit there existed a large animation wing, featuring veterans from Disney, Fleischer, and MGM. Without hesitating, Scott hightailed it to the cartoon department. He eagerly explained his background to commanding officer Rudy Ising, who in civilian life was one half of the famed Harman-Ising cartoon team late of Warners and MGM. Ising managed to effect a transfer for Scott, from the film-loading bay to the cartoon unit, and Bill began his famed animation career as a lowly gofer.

"When I was assigned to this animation department I thought I'd died and gone to heaven, because all these people whose names I had memorized from screen credits were sitting near me at the next desks—and doing much better work than I was." The unit was assigned three major tasks, as Scott explained. "Firstly, we turned out general instructional films: we did one called *Camouflage*, for example, and we used a little chameleon character as the lead, with the voice of [actor] Jimmy Gleason. That was the first film I did a voice for, by the way—I did a Texas accent. Secondly, we did specific training films for gunners, teaching them how to use gun sights. We had an animated cartoon character called Trigger Joe, who was our hero in a thing called *Position Firing,* about the K-10 and K-11 gun sights.

"The third thing was that one whole section of the animation unit worked just on doing maps and topographical things for fighter pilots. This later developed into a program that took up a whole soundstage using 3-D models. We had a whole model of the island of Japan, and the animation people were employed every day, painting and repainting the whole 'countryside' as it would appear before and after bombardment. So the pilots who flew over were essentially flying their approaches and so forth before they ever got there: every landmark! This was a strange kind of thing for animation people to be doing, but it was the biggest bunch of artists and painters they could lay their hands on." Virtual reality half a century ago!

Scott was stationed there until his discharge from the air force. "I didn't do animation per se; I started out washing cels (the lowest of the low), then graduated to being a painter, then an inker. But my draftsmanship and patience weren't good enough to even follow a traced line with a pen, so they put me on as an 'in-betweener.' I was a fairly unsuccessful one, but fair enough to become a rather poor assistant animator for Phil Monroe. Phil and I got along very well; we had a similar sense of humor and we liked each other."

It was here that Scott first met Bill Hurtz, who would spend twenty-five years at Jay Ward Productions. Hurtz recalled this period vividly; in 1977 he delivered a witty speech when Scott was honored by ASIFA, the international animated film society, in which he said, "Scott was an outsider. He had never worked in Hollywood. What he lacked in background, he made up in brass. Instead of being in awe of all these animated biggies, he assumed an arrogant stance that soon irritated most of us into taking a second look at him."

While an assistant animator, Scott graduated to the Frank Thomas unit: "I moved to doing assistant layout for John Hubley, then working on story and storyboard for Frank Thomas." These two artists proved a major influence on Scott during his increasing immersion in all areas of cartoons. Thomas was one of Disney's famous "Nine Old Men." "I respected Frank Thomas. He was always a very kindly man, which is what I needed at the time. Apparently, he could see things in me that I and other people couldn't see, and he went to bat for me a number of times. I was one of the few people in that unit who remained there; a lot of them were being drafted into other units, or shipped out for overseas duty in combat camera work. Well, my position was tenuous because I'd had no experience or background in animation. I was the newest of the new boys. Yet Frank helped me, and I respected him for that, and I did the best that I could for him. Not only was he loyal to me, but I was drawn to his splendid, dry wit. A very sharp, intelligent man."

As for the time he spent with John Hubley, his future boss at UPA, Scott reflected, "I loved 'Hub' as a leader. He was the guy way out on the end of the string, pulling animation as a medium after him, as far as its expanse and what it could do. He was one of the first to bring both social and moral passion into animation, and to expand the frontiers beyond what it had been: moving versions of old German fairy-tale illustrations. To where we realized we could learn and utilize the art of Picasso, Matisse, Dufy; anything you could visualize could be animated. That was the genius of Hubley, and it was very exciting to be hooked up to somebody like that. But I could never say he was a mentor because we operated in such different spheres. His was very much in the realm of the visual. Mine was not—I was never a very good artist or painter. Hubley couldn't lead me anywhere because I was on a different road."

Scott's experiences in the FMPU animation wing proved an invaluable crash course for his future career. "I spent all my spare time trying to learn how to draw. People like Bill Hurtz and Phil Monroe were superb draftsmen and great animators, and there I was, trying to scratch their breakdown drawings." As he told Jim Korkis, "They were both very nice, and they'd cover up my mistakes for me. And all the time I was doing layout, we were working on storyboard too. So I had quite a range of jobs in the animation industry while I was still in the service."

Scott credited his native comedic bent as being the true reason he was able to last there. Bill Hurtz explains: "The favorite indoor sport of all animation cartoonists is the drawing of a series of gags, inspired usually by a guy telling of some exploit of the night before. Scott would have forever remained an outsider had he not responded to the challenge of the gag series with some hilarious drawings which easily matched the best of Hubley's or the others.' "

When the war ended in 1945, Bill Scott was still a PFC, so he applied for Officer Candidate School. After six months he rose to the rank of second lieutenant, explaining, "I graduated just in time to be separated from the service, and joined the army reserve. True to form, I remained a lieutenant for the next ten years." Meanwhile, his on-the-job training in each area of cartooning had given Scott the necessary confidence for his next career step. And what a step: the fabled Warner Brothers cartoon studio. After his discharge in 1946, he recalls, "I just kicked around for a while." Finally, seeking work, he went to his former CO, Rudy Ising. Ising asked around, but nothing much happened until Scott got a call from Warner Brothers.

Phil Monroe had gone to bat for Bill by speaking to Chuck Jones; fortunately, Jones was amenable to trying out some new people. Scott said, "Because I'd worked for Phil as an assistant, he recommended me as a story man. A fine fellow named Lloyd Turner and I started out as apprentice story men, as a team." As Turner recalled, "When I became an apprentice writer, I was teamed with Bill Scott. He was so bright: he could draw like mad, and he was a funny guy. He taught me an awful lot. What a great guy; I couldn't think of anyone better to learn the business with than Bill Scott."

Turner and Scott worked as a team for about a year, during which they found themselves in a competitive situation. Scott dubbed it the "fang and claw system." "We didn't know it but we were in competition with each other. The deal was you went three months at one salary, then three months at the next salary, then you became a journeyman—which gave you a big raise in pay. But Warner Brothers wasn't willing to pay two journeymen, so we were pitted against each other: each of us had to do a story, and whoever's story was best was kept on."

But Bill and Lloyd refused to play this game, working on each other's stories, doing joint jokes. Unbeknownst to the Warner brass, they would simply toss a coin to see whose story would be chosen. "Finally," added Scott, "it wasn't mine: Lloyd was kept on and I was bounced."

Scott was with Warner Cartoons from 1946 to 1947, employed in the Arthur Davis unit. Art Davis had been promoted to a directing position when Bob Clampett left Warners. Scott told Paul Etcheverry, "Art was an ace animator with a delightful sense of humor. But Artie was scared shitless; he knew he was trying to cut it amongst some very big talents and he was very nervous.

We had a terrible time selling stories to him. . . . He really wasn't all that sure of our talent, and he certainly wasn't sure about what was funny himself. He was pretty much put in the same spot that Lloyd and I were in: 'You're here on a provisional basis and you'd better shape up or ship out.' "

The time Scott spent at Warners proved highly educational, and he got to work with several of his early heroes. The jam sessions for each cartoon featured the established Warner story men Mike Maltese, Tedd Pierce, and Warren Foster. "You couldn't get any better than that—they were sensational people!" Scott was able to sharpen his own considerable comedy skills, which later blossomed into his distinctive style at Jay Ward's. In the Davis unit, Bill thoroughly enjoyed working on Daffy Duck's character, while he and Turner had a hand in the Goofy Gophers' unique delivery.

"At Warner Brothers I had to use my own technique, which involved a lot of in-jokes, dialogue jokes, and crazy character things. I know we had our Shakespearean dog in there at one time, and we had the two Alphonse and Gaston–type gophers; we had a lot of fun with those. But I have a feeling that my kind of humor was considered too cerebral and literary for my then current boss, Eddie Selzer." Selzer was the somewhat humorless business manager of Warner Brothers Cartoons.

The credits on the Warner films are rather arbitrary, and true authorship is now virtually impossible to determine. For instance, Scott remembered working on *Mexican Joyride* and *Catch As Cats Can,* even though these two films list Dave Monahan as sole writer. And although he and Turner share a writing credit on *Bowery Bugs,* Scott always insisted, "I never got to do a Bugs Bunny film, much to my disappointment."

Bill Scott left Warner Brothers in 1947, grateful for the experience: "I developed a real sense of animation timing, of how long a scene should be to work for an audience. I'm glad I had the opportunity to work there. The people were great and I had fun." Bill Hurtz quipped, "Scott lasted one year. His natural gift for not knowing his place as low man on the totem pole might have contributed to his leaving."

Scott next moved to Paramount via producer Jerry Fairbanks's Apex Films in 1947. "I plummeted downhill to doing *Speaking of Animals,* a live-action series done with animated mouths where animals told funny jokes to each other. They won an Academy Award one time for making a bunch of cows move back and forth while someone sang 'Cow Cow Boogie.' It was not what you would call one of the pinnacles of animation." (The series began in 1941 as novelty one-reelers developed by Tex Avery, who worked on the first three.) It was here that Scott first worked with Stan Freberg and June Foray, who supplied some of the voices.

In his publicity autobiography Scott wrote, "My major chore was inventing clever dialogue for okapis, fruit bats and other curious beasts. A year later I got into an altercation with an aardvark over the way a scene should be played, and left in high dudgeon when I found that the aardvark swung more weight with the front office than I did." In fact, Scott was fired, the victim of a personality clash with producer Lou Lilly, a former writer-artist at Warner Brothers (Lilly wrote Bob Clampett's 1944 *Hare Ribbin',* among others).

In early 1948, Bill Scott decided to get something out of his system: a long-held dream of acting on Broadway. He, Dorothy, and their nine-month-old-son, John, packed off to New York. Dorothy explains, "I had come into some inheritance money when my mother died, so we were able to afford this trip, as long as we eventually got work. But Bill got the feeling it wouldn't be what we thought when some radio and theater people in New York told him that he wouldn't get acting jobs because he was *too* versatile!" Scott directed a couple of plays. Then, dejected, the family returned to the West Coast six months later.

At this time a friend managed to get Bill and Dorothy interested in the idea of running a doughnut shop in the Crenshaw district of Los Angeles. This venture lasted less than a year ("An even more hideous experience than the cartoon business," joked Bill Hurtz). As Scott told Jim Korkis, "By working only twelve hours a day, six days a week, we managed to lose only about $1,000 a month!" Then fate stepped in once more.

In early 1949 Scott received a call from writer Charles Shows. "Charlie and I had worked together on *Speaking of Animals;* by now he was writing on *Time for Beany,* so I went over to this ratty old writer's building on the Paramount lot and joined that crowd. Charlie and I spent somewhere between six months and a year writing that show. And that was writing fifteen minutes a day for live television, which was pretty fascinating. It was Bob Clampett's show, and fortunately for our collective sanity, Clampett never did very much on the actual production. He'd show up about half an hour before and scuttle into the booth, stay throughout the show, and then scuttle right out again. So we didn't see very much of Bob, except when it came to getting a new show up or something like that.

"We were given a lot of leeway; it was pretty much whatever you wanted to do. We had no strictures and we'd carry on one *Beany* adventure for what seemed like months. 'The Search for the Two-Headed Freep' was the one that

I came in on. One reason this story went on so long was that we couldn't find an ending for it! Nobody could figure out what a two-headed freep looked like (except that it was unusual—most freeps have three heads). It was a fine and fertile show—we had a lot of freedom. If we wanted to do a song, we'd just say 'Cecil sings "Ragmop," ' and Stan [Freberg] would start singing it. We never thought about getting approvals or clearance or paying a royalty, or any of that jazz. We'd use the daily news. Whenever we needed a cutaway for a headline we'd just pick up the daily paper and paste a fake headline on top. It was a great show to work on, and it was a very exciting show to be with because it just took off like a rocket.

"And that's one of the things that hurt really, 'cause the show started to make a piss-pot full of money, of which we got absolutely none. I mean Charlie and I were working at that time for $75 a week. I think [actors] Stan and Daws Butler were really up there in the chips, I think they got $150! And these were two stars of a national TV program. At one point, there being no videotape in those days, the thing was shown on kinescopes in like forty markets across the country and it must have been taking in about $150,000 a week. Well, it led to a great deal of tension between us and Clampett, culminating in a decision we gave him on a new show called *Buffalo Billy*. We wanted a raise and the question came up as to who would bell the cat: who would actually present this petition to Clampett? And I like a nut said, 'Sure, I'll do it.'

"So I intercepted Bob on his way home and said we'd like him to hear some of our ideas on the new show. Bob flicked his horn-rimmed glasses up and down and said, 'Sure, Scottie, I'll have a look.' This was a Friday night. Well the following Monday, the cast gathered for breakfast at Armstrong-Schroeders in Beverly Hills.* I was not invited: Clampett's attorney had called me that Saturday and effectively told me that my services were no longer required. When Freberg asked, 'Where's Bill?' Clampett flipped his glasses and said, 'Well, Bill isn't with us anymore.' That shocked the shit out of everybody. It really scared them! So that was the end of my stint with Clampett; but it was an exciting time."

As Bill Hurtz saw it, "*Time for Beany* took Bill Scott out of the apprentice

*Stan Freberg insists that Scott recalled the wrong eatery: "It was actually O'Blath's Café, on the corner outside the Paramount gate, where we learned of Bill's fate."

class and into the pressure cooker. Looking and listening to Freberg and Butler got him into the art of hand puppetry." During his KTLA stint, Scott did occasional bit voices for incidental characters and even played a giant in one story. This experience was used to advantage later when Scott manipulated the Bullwinkle puppet in 1961.

The Emmy-winning *Time for Beany* influenced Jay Ward mightily as well. In later years Ward was desperate to do a comedy puppet show; the *Beany* chapter-adventures resembled not only the style of his *Crusader Rabbit* series, which aired during this period, but also the later "Rocky and Bullwinkle" segments. As well, the witty house style of *Beany* was carried on by Ward: two of his top writers, Chris Hayward and Lloyd Turner, put in time on Clampett's show.

Bill Scott's next move took him to the revolutionary cartoon studio United Productions of America in 1950. He had already moonlighted there during the war, helping out with in-between work on the political cartoon *Hell-bent for Election* (1944) when UPA was Industrial Film and Poster Service.

"Again I was recommended by old cronies: in this case Phil Monroe and Bill Hurtz, whom I'd been with back at the First Motion Picture Unit, put in a good word for me. UPA had just signed with Columbia, and they were looking for new series and new ideas, and once again I was teamed with another writer, Phil Eastman. Our first job was the second Magoo picture. They had already made a picture called *Ragtime Bear* [1949], and Magoo seemed to be a viable character, so Phil and I were given the task of doing the next Magoo picture to see if the character would really work. We did, I think, the next three."

As Hurtz wryly recalls, "When Hubley asked him on board to work on their new Columbia release, Bill accepted with a tiny semblance of humility—he was teamed with Phil Eastman, a quiet man of great talent. It was love at first sight. They collaborated on all the first great shorts about Mr. Magoo. They had to match up to John Hubley's creative standards. This was complicated by John's peculiar genius for not knowing what he wanted until the work was done. Scott and Eastman would recuperate at the Smokehouse, a nearby restaurant [in Toluca Lake], and bandage each other's bloodied psyches."

Of his time at UPA, Bill Scott said, "I was fortunate enough to be with some of the finest talents in the biz. I cowrote the adaptation of *Gerald McBoing-Boing,* and John Hubley and I wrote *Rooty Toot Toot.* And I did the adaptation of *The Tell Tale Heart* for Ted Parmelee." The latter, co-written with Fred Gable, was his personal favorite: "What a thrill. I got to direct James Mason."

By the time Scott joined UPA, the studio had a noticeable attitude, indeed a snobbery, about it. "You never mentioned Warner Brothers, although some of the veterans who had originally been with Warners had in truth thoroughly enjoyed their time there." On the other hand, UPA being what it was, the elitism was justified. The UPA philosophy was honest: an attempt to escape from the rigidity and formulas of what animation was perceived to represent—cute (Disney) or brash (Warners/MGM)—and to expand and experiment with the potentialities of design, motion, and graphics.

Things progressed well for Scott at UPA until studio politics (fueled by the House Un-American Activities Committee), combined with an acrimonious factional split in the animation union, caused a shake-up which affected many jobs. "UPA was pretty left-wing. Phil Eastman was fired, and to keep it from looking political, they fired me too. I left UPA, under somewhat of a cloud, in 1952. After our time there, Phil and I freelanced for a while, then he moved to Connecticut."

Following this, Bill Scott found himself at producer John Sutherland's organization. Sutherland Productions specialized in nontheatrical animation: "This was a dazzling experience, as well as ulcerating. I wrote institutional, educational, and just plain propaganda films for big business like GM, DuPont, AT&T, Union Carbide, and the American Petroleum Institute. I wrote apologies, excuses, and descriptions. We did TV commercials and industrials. These were in essence didactic films: films to persuade, films to impress. A fascinating time—painful but fascinating."

Scott told Jim Korkis, "I had to write animated cartoons on why fishing laws are vital to us, or about DuPont employee benefits." And Bill Hurtz's opinion: "Scott became a writer and vice president for John Sutherland and he hobnobbed with tycoons. This was not his finest hour."

Scott added, "I disliked what I was writing, but I wrote it because the money was good. About once a year, I'd get fed up and march into the office to say I couldn't do it anymore. Every time I'd open my mouth to complain, they'd stuff it with money. I worked with some of the greatest wheelers and dealers and corporate pirates, as yet unhung, that I've ever met.

"Finally I just couldn't take it anymore: I'd lied for four years, and that was enough. I've tried not to do that since. Everything I'd thought or suspected about big business turned out to be absolutely true, and I just couldn't deal with that after a while. That's the only job I ever quit; fortunately, I was fired from everything else! After Sutherland I went back to UPA for a bit, and worked on the late, lamented *McBoing-Boing* TV show."

In 1956 Scott became "assistant producer" on CBS-TV's *Gerald McBoing-Boing Show,* UPA's venture into the world of television cartoons. Used to the luxury of producing eight theatrical shorts annually, UPA was now expected to make a full half hour of animation per week. Bill observed, "They'd got about halfway through this enormous enterprise, and suddenly someone realized that nothing was funny." The producer was Bobe Cannon, a brilliant and sensitive director. Cannon was not a "conventional" animator, in that he actively hated broad humor. However, this was commercial TV calling, so Cannon requested that Scott come on board and "doctor" the show, to make it, as Scott put it, "more roughhouse. You see, everything was very artistic and the graphics were sensational, but there were no jokes! So somebody prevailed upon Bobe Cannon, who had never been a very big fan of mine, to ask me in as his assistant. I had to try to inject some humor, some point of view, or some satire into the stuff.

"Well I tried my best but it never did get off the ground. There were a number of independent and very self-centered (I don't mean that as a pejorative term) people on this TV show, who wanted their own pictures done exactly their own way. They had no training in humor and in fact they really didn't appreciate humor very much. Yet they each had the full responsibility of turning out a short film on a very scant budget. Of course, when someone like me came in to try to inject something else—or make a joke—there was a great deal of resistance. So I don't know how effective I was at all."

The twenty-six shows premiered December 16, 1956. They went way over budget, and enjoyed only low ratings. Scott didn't hang around: "After that I freelanced for a year or so, writing commercials for Storyboard [Hubley's animation company] and Quartet Films, and I did a couple of pictures for Walter Lantz when he was working for the State Department. Also, some freelance work for Sutherland, Four Star, Playhouse Pictures—oh, and some time spent on the Magoo feature film."

In 1957, while Bill Scott was freelancing for various animation houses, he was contacted by old crony Charlie Shows. Shows, who would soon be busy writing Hanna-Barbera's new *Ruff and Reddy* series, recommended Scott as a writer for Shamus Culhane Productions. And it was here that Scott and Jay Ward would first meet.

4

The Rocky Road to Television,

or That Voice, Where Have I Heard That Voice?

By 1957, the highly regarded veteran animator Shamus Culhane had enjoyed a decade of heady success in the TV commercial field. Now he was trying for the burgeoning TV cartoon bandwagon. According to Bill Scott, "Shamus had become very interested in producing a series through his new West Coast studio." Culhane was offered a series of five-minute cartoons (totalling 195 episodes) for Interstate Television. Needing money at the time, he agreed to do the series. Aware of Jay Ward's desire to make a new cartoon show, Culhane offered the Interstate project to Jay, who would produce and develop the property in Hollywood. The title of the proposed show was *Phineas T. Phox, Adventurer*. Scott recalled the series being "really sort of another version of *Crusader Rabbit*. It starred a fox who was a detective, and his assistant, who was a dumb bear called Bonaparte. The whole thing was a takeoff on Sam Spade."

Production was already under way when Scott came on board. Ward had asked Jerry Fairbanks to recommend a good cartoon writer, and Charlie Shows came to mind. Shows, in turn, suggested Bill Scott, as they had both written for Fairbanks's *Speaking of Animals* theatrical shorts and TV's *Time for Beany*. Culhane was impressed by Scott, calling him "a very cogent man. What I liked about Bill was that he had the same ideas concerning animation dialogue as I did, which meant not just having stupid words that talked down to kids."

Unfortunately, Jay Ward and Shamus Culhane quickly had a major falling-out over Ward's production methods. Culhane recalled, "The storyboards were looking just like the old *Crusader Rabbit.* In my opinion these came across like a series of still drawings that were too primitive—it just looked cheap." Characteristically, Ward stuck to his guns. According to designers Bill Hurtz and Al Shean, this was not the way Shamus Culhane liked to be treated: he was the boss.

Hurtz remained a close friend of Culhane (who died in 1996) offering, "Shamus was irascible—in fact almost as irascible as old Art Babbit [a revered animation figure formerly with Disney and UPA]." Al Shean was working at the Culhane Productions head office in New York at the time. Shean, himself a highly independent character, found Culhane to be "impossible and neurotic." An ego clash between Ward and Culhane seemed a foregone conclusion; and in fact Ward and Al Shean were to clash in much the same fashion years later.

What Culhane needed was a producer, not a singular entrepreneur like Jay Ward. Always suspicious of Ward's friendliness with many of the animation staff, Culhane accused him of questionable ethics and staff poaching. *Phineas Phox* proceeded without Jay, who felt deeply insulted. He walked out on Culhane—fittingly, this incident occurred on Friday the thirteenth. Ward had just made plans for a recording session, and was ready to hire the following actors: Paul Frees, Peter Leeds, Larry Dobkin, Hans Conried, Stan Freberg, and Mel Blanc. With this cast and Ward's love of recording work, the *Phineas* sound tracks would undoubtedly have been splendid.

The acrimonious experience with Shamus Culhane was the last straw for Ward, who swore that from this point on he would work only for himself. As for *Phineas,* Bill Scott recalled, "Jay dropped out of the project, then Charlie dropped out, and I wrote a couple more episodes. Shamus kept making noises like a producer, but the scripts were tampered with too much for my liking. Then it kind of just floundered and died sometime in 1958.

"But Jay was enthused. He'd gotten his feet wet with Hollywood animation again, and this time he wanted to do it properly. Anyway, a few days later Jay wrote to me and asked if I'd be interested in working with him on another series. So I met with him, and he pulled out some ideas that he and Alex Anderson hadn't been able to sell—particularly one called *The Frostbite Falls Review,* which concerned a TV show, sort of like *Hee Haw* combined with *The Today Show*. All the characters were animals, in a 'rube' setting; kind of a small-town comedy.

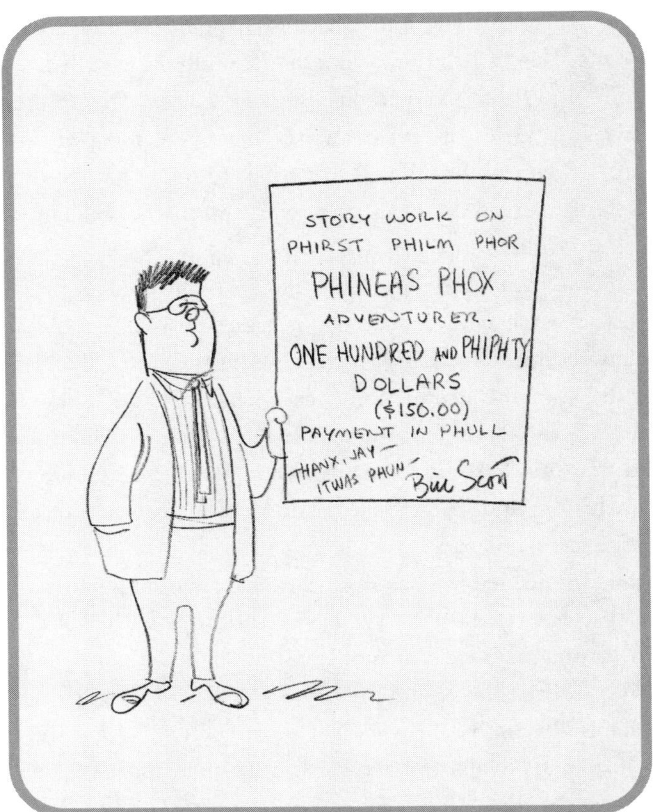

Bill Scott's characteristic humor is evident in this self-drawn invoice. *Courtesy of Bill Scott*

"Jay was very entranced with the same kind of characters he'd had in *Crusader Rabbit,* which was the little guy teamed with the big guy. In this *Frostbite Falls* show there was a flying squirrel named Rocky, and a moose named Bullwinkle. Jay asked if we could do an adventure strip with these two characters, and I said, 'Well, sure. Why not? Anything for money.' So we wrote a script together which became the pilot film."

Scott remembered that Rocky was basically a Crusader Rabbit clone in the original *Frostbite* storyboard; he was redesigned during pilot production. Alex Anderson consulted in the early stages, but he considered Scott a fine writer and soon dropped out of the picture again. It was during this embryonic period that Ward first learned of Scott's amazing vocal talents. As they cowrote the script (Jay was story editor, while Bill honed the actual jokes), Scott would read the dialogue aloud in various voices, "and Jay was just delighted, he'd fall about laughing. Then when we discussed hiring people for the pilot, I asked him, 'Who do we get to play Bullwinkle?' and he said, 'Well, you do it.' So I said, 'Sure, why not. Sensational!' So I read the role of Bullwinkle. . . . I didn't know that I was going to play that part; it had never entered my head."

In late 1957, following the split with Culhane, Ward's old college friend Len Key came aboard again, his recent embarrassing experience with the aborted revival of *Crusader Rabbit* notwithstanding. Key recalls, "It's a small world. I was working at Shamus Culhane's head office in New York. I was vice president of sales for TV commercials, and I had a few things going on the side, outside Culhane's shop. Well, Jay asked me to help him sell his proposed *Rocky* cartoon. I was busy as hell, but I'd just set up a company called Producer's Associates. I knew a guy named Roger Carlin, and I'd been helping him out; he'd been bounced from a job at MCA and he was flat broke. Hell, for a while there I'd kept his mother and sister alive—he had nothing. Anyway, I needed someone to run this sideline company if I put up the money. Carlin was a great one for grand schemes and he certainly had the gift of the gab." (Key's company was later renamed K-C Enterprises before finally becoming P.A.T., of which more later.)

By Christmas 1957, Ward and Scott completed the storyboard for *Rocky the Flying Squirrel*. Having written it together, they quickly established a rapport. Scott received $150; if the pilot film sold, he would receive another payment of the same amount. Ward was eager for the pilot to sell quickly and loved the idea of having the experienced and talented Bill Scott for the series. Meantime, Scott continued freelancing on TV commercials for Storyboard, Playhouse, Four Star, and other production houses. He even wrote some magazine articles.

When it debuted in 1950, the original *Crusader Rabbit* had been ahead of its time: for starters, there simply weren't that many owners of TV sets back then. Its renewal prospects were further hampered by the FCC's five-year "freeze" on new television stations (1949–54). But now, several years and millions more viewers later, the timing for TV animation was just right. Cartoon "strips" (i.e., Monday-to-Friday shows) were needed for the new fall TV season for about forty top markets. "We felt we could do a series of these 'strips' and really murder the TV cartoon market," said Len Key, "and so I agreed to try and sell Jay's *Rocky* pilot, even though I was still at Culhane's."

Never too happy working at Culhane Productions, Key, like Ward, was interested in calling his own shots. Besides, he dearly wanted to work with Jay. He began absorbing any gossip concerning the cartoon business. The then-hot topic of discussion in animation circles was cheap runaway production. "Runaway" simply meant that part of the cartoon-making process was performed outside the United States, under American supervision. The most likely locations were Japan and Mexico, both countries having active animation industries. In his memoirs Disney veteran Jack Kinney points out that the real clincher, apart from cheaper labor costs, was a ten-year tax break for American companies abroad. Key was impressed; he and a partner quickly formed a tie-up with the Tokyo-based Tojo Studios. The first proposed deal involved a budget of $800 per four-minute cartoon, to cover below-the-line costs.

This so-called below-the-line work entailed the actual laborious process of animation—the thousands of individual drawings, and inked and painted cels. (The earlier above-line stages involving storyboards, model sheets, layouts, and sound track were handled Stateside.) Supervision would be handled by a top U.S. cartoon director and one or two animators and layout artists, all of whom would travel to Japan. At this time, Jay was considering having music for *Rocky* composed by Fred Steiner, a brilliant musicologist then living in Mexico City. (Coincidentally, Mexico was where the below-the-line activity finally began eighteen months later.)

By now, Ward's enthusiasm was fully rekindled. He told Key that his New Year's resolution for 1958 was "to become a big producer"—without Alex Anderson, who had a secure job and didn't want to move south. Ward, determined to proceed with his *Rocky* pilot, also had "millions of ideas for shows—some good, some terrible—even live-action." He went to Los Angeles in early February, working part-time out of a small office at 5631 Hollywood Boulevard (home of the Raphael G. Wolff animation studio). He began afresh with the time-honored theory which states, "Hire the best talent available and you can't fail." He started scouting top cartoon writers. Ward always felt the key to a good series was the writing, whether for animation or live-action. His creative showman's flair had resurfaced, this time to stay. As he told Len, "You know me, I'll try anything—send me ideas." Even the death of his mother in mid-January 1958 didn't slow him down for more than a week or so, and he continued developing various TV concepts.

Besides writers, Jay also began a lifelong relationship with his superb voice talents. Besides Bill Scott, already cast as Bullwinkle, the *Rocky* pilot required sharp, incredibly versatile actors to handle the multitude of characters and

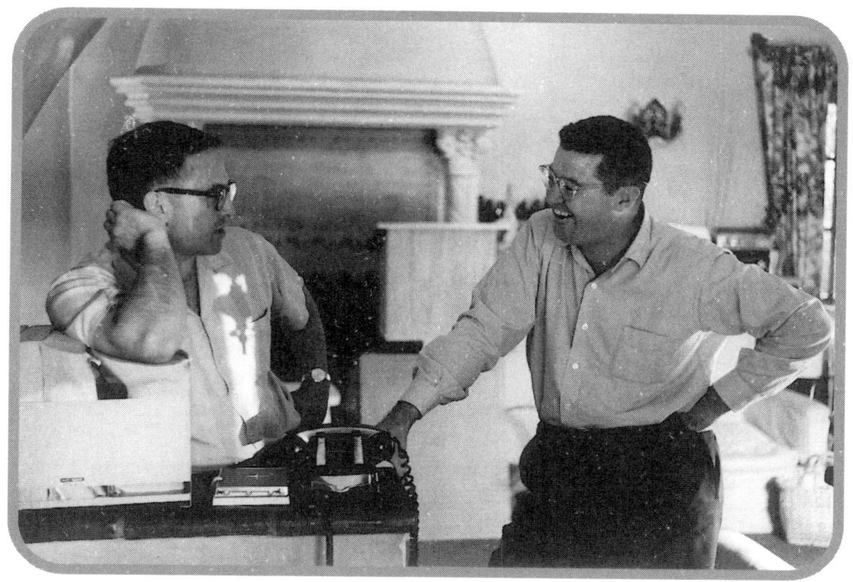

Jay and Bill in animated (ouch!) discussion at Ward's Andalusia Arms apartment. *Photo by Leonora Miller, courtesy of Bill Scott*

clever dialogue. It got them in Paul Frees, June Foray, and narrator Bill Conrad.

Paul Frees was born Solomon Hersh Frees in Chicago, Illinois, on June 22, 1920. He grew up in Albany Park and attended Von Steuben Junior High. Frees displayed several creative talents as a small child, and possessed a pigeon chest that helped him produce, according to his brother Dave, "a beautiful voice." He grew up to be one of the most versatile voice artists in TV history.

After winning several amateur-hour contests, Frees went on the road as a teenager. As the MC for the Hull House troupe of performing youngsters he sang, tap-danced, and did impressions. Later he worked solo, and orchestra leader Benny Meroff suggested he change his name. So Paul Frees became Buddy Green, the "Prince of Impersonators," and worked nightclubs, then did radio work in Chicago, appearing on dramatic shows. Drafted into World War II, he was wounded in the Normandy D day invasion and received the Purple Heart. While recuperating in Los Angeles for eight months, he attended Chouinard Art Institute on the GI Bill, having originally planned an artistic career. But Frees suddenly needed money when his young wife, Annelle, was hospitalized; he returned to radio, and with his vibrant, sonorous voice soon became a highly successful actor on big-time network shows like *Suspense, Escape*, and *Rocky Jordan*.

Tragically, his wife died before her twenty-first birthday, and to hide his grief Frees became busier than ever with radio work. He also intensified his lifelong private interest in police matters, sparked by his wartime experience with Special Services; years later he was living a strange double life as a special assistant to the Narcotics Division of the FBI while doing crazy voice-over work during the day. In 1949 Paul Frees started doing animation voices for Disney and MGM (as Dick Lundy's *Barney Bear*). Earlier, he had cut some great comedy records with Spike Jones and the City Slickers.

His colleague Daws Butler observed, "Paul was like nobody else. His speaking voice was magnificent, he could sing, he did narration, he was a fast study with an impish sense of humor, and his rhythm and timing were just natural. He and Bill Conrad would get going during the sessions and rag each other. Conrad was always doing jokes about Paul, but with great affection. Paul was very verbose, with a million stories; you'd never get a session started with him." Skip Craig recalls, "Paul Frees constantly had a compulsion to be 'on.' I always felt that if he was stuck in a recording session until two in the morning he would still be trying to entertain the one person left in the building." June Foray added, "Paul was a nut!" but she knew there was actually a sad clown under the surface: "He never really grew up. He married six times, but he was like a child, emotionally. He hid a troubled private life with his silly facade."

These observations were accurate: above all else Paul Frees was a show-off, albeit a hugely talented one. He revelled in the Jay Ward recording sessions, speaking fondly of them as "the happiest days of my life. As far as the Jay Ward organization is concerned I would give my eyeteeth to work for them. The things we did were so clever and beautifully written, and done with such a light heart; I would gladly have paid them!" Although Frees wasted an inordinate amount of studio time and tape stock, Jay Ward loved every minute of it.

Frees's characters seemed endless, and Ward's cartoons would prove to be his greatest showcase. Bill Scott called him "the single greatest voice artist I've ever heard; his voice was like a cathedral pipe organ." In the opinion of Chris Hayward, "Paul Frees was the best sight reader of all time."

As a youth, Frees had been blessed with a supersensitive mimic's ear. Like a human sponge, he absorbed every character he heard in radio and movies, often joking, "I make my living from dead people." After his own distinctive touch was added, they emerged as the gigantic cast he became for so many of Jay Ward's toons: 325 Rockys, 91 Peabodys, 100 Hoppity Hoopers, 39 Dudleys, and hundreds of commercials, often cast as blustery colonels, corporate heads, mayors, naive southern youngsters, cowboys, gangsters, and spies, and in an unending array of colorful burlesque dialects. And let us not forget his most famous Jay Ward role, that truly funny character and crumb of all crumbs, Boris Badenow.

While Frees and others, like Warner Brothers voice expert Mel Blanc, were exceptional talents within a relatively tiny circle of voice actors, June Foray is truly unique. Over a half century of performing, she is still the preeminent female voice artist. And what an artist: her characters have yet to be topped for flavor and humor. Her range is awesome, from babies through little-boy characters (such as our stalwart hero Rocky) to the raucous tones of her excellent Marjorie Main imitation, and even a great barnyard rooster takeoff. Her wicked witches have been without equal, and her shrewish wives (Aesop's "The Wolf in Sheep's Clothing"), snooty society types (the customer in the "Fractured Fairy Tale" "Little Red Riding Hood"), and famous "Brooklyn Princess," not to mention her other Jay Ward starring roles—Nell, Natasha, Ursula—display an ear perfectly attuned to vocal subtleties and comic dialect.

Foray was born on September 18 in Springfield, Massachusetts. Her musical mother tried to interest her in dance, but June preferred acting, starting at age twelve in straw-hat theaters and local radio. The family moved to California in the early 1940s, and after both acting and writing *Lady Make Believe* for station KECA, teenage June Foray graduated to motion-picture dubbing and network radio, doing drama (*The Lux Radio Theatre, Red Ryder, Sherlock Holmes, The Count of Monte Cristo*) and comedy, stooging for Danny Thomas, Steve Allen, Jimmy Durante, Bob Hope, and Phil Harris. Later she did TV, appearing on *Carson's Cellar,* in which she performed on-camera sketches with Paul Frees. She began doing animation voices for Universal (Walter Lantz's *Eggcracker Suite*) and Paramount (*Speaking of Animals*), where she first met Stan Freberg. In the 1950s she worked for Disney (*Cinderella, Peter Pan, Trick or Treat,* and playing Mrs. Goofy), MGM (*Tom and Jerry* and Tex Avery cartoons), Walter Lantz (as Knothead and Splinter), UPA (*The Lady in Black*), and over forty of the sublime Warner Brothers cartoons.

When Capitol Records began their spoken-word division, A and R man Alan Livingstone astutely contracted Foray, Daws Butler, Stan Freberg, Mel

Blanc, and the veteran dean of voice men, Pinto "Goofy" Colvig. Between them, these artists did over one hundred children's records, including many adaptations of Disney cartoons (*Ferdinand the Bull, Pinocchio*). "Then Disney's people started asking, 'Who's this girl doing all the voices? We'd better use her!' " says June, explaining how she came to work almost exclusively in animation.

June Foray also worked with Freberg and Butler on Capitol's "adult" comedy records like *St. George and the Dragonet* and *Little Blue Riding Hood.* In 1954, Foray continued her association with Freberg on the offbeat CBS radio comedy *That's Rich;* and in 1957 she was a regular in his legendary series *The Stan Freberg Show*. June did some of her greatest work here, calling on many of the characters she would soon play for Jay Ward.

She described her initial meeting with Ward to animation historian Milton Gray. "In 1957, my agent called and said, 'There's a man named Jay Ward. I don't know him, he's never worked for Disney or Warners or MGM, and he would like you to do a series. They would like to make a demo film, and try to sell it. Would you be interested?' I said, 'Of course, I'm always interested in something like that.' I met Jay at the Tail of the Cock, on La Cienega, and he was sitting at the bar. He bought me a couple of martinis before lunch, and I wasn't used to drinking before lunch. I was feeling very high in my martini glass by the time we had lunch, and I said, "I'll do it, I'll do it, for free even! I'll be happy to do the demo for you!' We recorded the first demo in 1958 at Capitol Records, in one of their tiny little recording studios. Paul Frees, Bill Scott, and myself. This was just *Rocky,* it had nothing to do with 'Fractured Fairy Tales' or 'Dudley Do-Right.' "

Discussing the work procedure with Jay Ward, June recalled, "We'd read around the table, tell jokes, laugh at the funny dialogue—because it was brilliantly written—then we'd do it on mike for time, and then record. We did five segments in an hour, then just sat around and laughed and told jokes. [It] remained a beautiful family.

"Jay was always astute. I'd say, 'What kind of voice do you want the princess to be?' He'd say, 'Brooklyn.' I'd say, 'Gee, I was Brooklyn in the last one, don't you want something different?' He'd say, 'No, give us the Brooklyn.' And he was right. He was very precise in what he wanted, and he was correct."

In 1960, an ABC-TV publicity release stated, "June thoroughly enjoys creating and developing new voices. Having decided to concentrate on this talent, she's always listening for new voices, then she tapes and files them in her personal library."

Bill Scott had suggested Frees and Foray long before he knew he'd be their costar. When Gary Owens interviewed Paul Frees on radio late in 1970, he mistakenly asked his guest how he happened to land the role of George of the Jungle. Frees immediately corrected him, saying, "No, George is actually Bill Scott, who is Jay Ward's partner and the best dog-gone voice man in the whole TV cartoon business." Ten years later, Frees told this author, "If Bill Scott hadn't been a writer, he would have been right up there at the top of the tree along with me and a few others, doing voice-overs."

Daws Butler, in the TV documentary, *Daws Butler: Voice Magician*, elaborated on Scott. "To me, Bill Scott was one of the most talented actors in town. His dialects, his characters, the top of his voice—the bottom of his voice, and such inventive ideas: he had a sense of humor all his own and was an actor all his own. I had tremendous respect for him as an actor, and we loved to work together. I'd like to give him credit as a person, as well as being a terrific actor, comedian and writer—he had it all."

In sheer volume of cartoons, Bill Scott performed the largest amount of voice work for Jay Ward; he was in almost everything, missing just one recording session in twenty-five years when he had a cold (in five "Fractured Fairy Tales," Paul Frees substituted). Scott did comic vocal sound effects, rewrote scripts during the sessions, and directed the other actors. He was far and away the wittiest of the entire bunch, and possessed a consummate writer's flair for understanding jokes: one take, and Scott had it.

The pragmatic Bill Scott was a stickler for "doing it": at the sessions, he would go along with the nonsense, even, publicist Howard Brandy recalls, "instigating some of it, saying, 'Let's see how soon we can get Bill Conrad to break up!' But only to a point. Then he'd take over, saying, 'All right—let's do it, then we can get outta here!' " This was understandable in light of Scott's coproducer title: fun was fun, but only as much as the budget would allow!

Scott was able to match Frees and Foray character for character, earning their complete respect; he'd been known to them mainly as a writer in the period before Jay Ward Productions. "I was a very quick study, and I'd blatantly steal my bit voices from Paul," admitted Scott. "One thing I was able to do was make my voices 'clean.' " By "clean," Scott meant they weren't foggy or gravelly.

While Scott lacked the rich vocal timbre of Frees and Conrad (he would never be a narrator in their class, and never cared to be), he was regarded by the other actors as the most brilliant player on the team. They were in awe of his writing ability—as Jay's former secretary Linda Hayward recalls, "Bill was an absolute speed demon with his scripts." And his penchant for comic dialects proved a perfect partnership with Paul Frees. For example, in one "Peabody" episode Frees played Wilbur Wright with a booming southern tone, while Scott essayed his brother Orville in a high-pitched Carolina whine.

Scott's Gestapo-esque Fearless Leader was a terrific voice and provided a neat contrast to Boris's Slavic groveling. Scott even did a few crazy imitations (Edward G. Robinson, Chico Marx, Wallace Wimple, a superb Bob Newhart, Eddie Lawrence) as well as helping June Foray out on occasion: he played a great witch, as his voice was able to be pitched just right for a slightly dizzy female character.

By contrast, with his gruff "pomegranate" voice, William Conrad was, like Paul Frees, one of the most familiar narrator-announcers in the United States. By the time Conrad and Frees began working for Jay Ward, their distinctive deep, rolling voices were being heard on countless commercials and movie trailers, following long stints in radio.

In 1991, referring to his sessions with the *Bullwinkle* gang, the self-effacing Conrad said, "I never really felt like I was part of that team." When it was suggested he was being too harsh on himself, he elaborated, "Well, I mean I couldn't compete. I loved working on the show; they were a hell of a lot of fun, but those other people could do all that crazy stuff and all those great voices. That wasn't my thing at all."

Millions of *Bullwinkle* fans disagree with the late Mr. Conrad. "Bill Conrad's narration set the pace for us," said Bill Scott. "When you get that big voice going all-out frantic saying, 'Little realizing that right behind them was a sinister shadow'—boy, you've got to energize yourself and be ready to follow his voice immediately."

Conrad was born in Louisville, Kentucky, on September 27, 1920. The family moved to California, where he began in radio as a junior announcer in his teens. After serving in World War II as a fighter pilot, he returned to radio, and also played various movie parts. Conrad was regarded by his peers as one of the finest audio actors of all time; in his long-running role of Marshall Matt Dillon on CBS's *Gunsmoke* (1952–61) he set new standards of subtlety in air drama. By then he had done thousands of transcontinental

Radio Days

When quizzed on his background as a superb cartoon voice, Bill Scott explained, "In my college days, I was a radio actor in Denver. I didn't make much money at it but I was always available, and I did a couple of national broadcasts from Denver playing various cowboys. I did a whole series of air force programs out of Lowery Field, doing the standard bottom-of-the-rung stuff. But always doing more than one voice; in those dear dead, rotten days you only got paid for the session, and if you could hire an actor who could play four characters, well that was great because you only had to pay him once! So of course the people who could do multiple voices were much in demand.

"At one time, for a period of six months or so, a girl named Lenore Geller and I did a comic soap opera together, doing all the characters. [Bill's wife Dorothy remembers, "Bill helped write this show: it was called *The Tweetles.*] We had like twenty-one characters that we were playing. So I had that kind of background. Great training—lousy pay!

"I didn't do much with it until later. I did one voice in the air force and I think that's all I did. Then at UPA I did a few fill-in voices here and there, and I did a song on the *McBoing-Boing Show,* but not full-time until my association with Jay."

In fact, Scott performed quite a few voices for Sutherland and UPA. Among others there were theatrical cartoons like the *Magoo* and *Pete Hothead* series, and *McBoing-Boing Show* TV entries including *The Sleuth*, a "prehistoric" cartoon with Bill and Dorothy providing the vocals, and *Mr. Tingley's Tangle*, which Bill narrated in rhyme. Earlier, Bill and Dot could be heard in *Man Alive*, a 1952 instructional short sponsored by the American Cancer Society, directed by Bill Hurtz. And as dialogue director on the 1959 *Magoo* feature *1001 Arabian Nights*, Scott can be heard in a couple of bit parts.

The Jay Ward studio ceased production in mid-1984. Scott had seen it coming, so in January that year he recorded a demo tape to promote himself for freelance voice work. Almost immediately he was hired by Disney and worked on their new TV cartoons, playing Moosel on *The Wuzzles* and Gruffi Gummi, Sir Tuxford, and Toady on *Gummi Bears* until his death.

broadcasts. He and Paul Frees had been acting side by side since 1945 and had long ago established their off-mike personas: Conrad was a man's man who would brook no nonsense, coming across as slightly intimidating with that gruff voice and confident air; Frees was the perennial "nut"—the court jester who invariably reduced the macho Conrad to shrieks of laughter. Bill Conrad was one of those actors who really got the giggles, and was therefore an immediate favorite target of the ever-mischievous Frees. By the time they worked together on *Bullwinkle,* they knew each other's styles the way twins know each other's moods.

Early in his association with Jay Ward (in August 1959), Conrad suggested that he could "double." Bill Scott remembered this incident: "He came into one session, and he was telling Jay, in his colorful language, that he could do more than just be the narrator. You know, like 'I can double, Jay. I can do voices and accents as good as these bastards.' Well, that day there was a character in one of the scripts, the last one we did that night. He was called Sam. Sam was a little native on Bloney Island. So Conrad tried it, and he retried it! Jay kept saying, 'You sound just like Bill Conrad," so we finally gave the part to Paul Frees. Well, Frees was just relentless—he ragged Conrad about this for years. He'd say, 'Bill Conrad is the man of a thousand voice! And he can hardly manage that one!' I think Conrad got bored occasionally, so I'd write some bit in for him from time to time."

What Scott had forgotten was that two years later, almost to the day, Conrad finally did play a native called Sam in "Rocky" episode 220. In fact, in the recording session held a week earlier he had played both a native and one of Santa's elves.

This was actually a gag reward for the previous two years of ribbing, which culminated with the May 12, 1961, issue of *The Hollywood Reporter,* which solemnly announced, "Jay Ward Productions will go a third cartoon series try with a 'Sam the Native' pilot. Bill Conrad's been firmed for the voice of Sam, the friendly cannibal." Ward and Scott had sneakily planted the item.

In truth, Conrad could double. On radio he played many fine, believable characters in dramatic shows, but they weren't cartoony enough for Ward's style. Then too, Conrad shared a common trait with Hans Conried: whenever they did double, their own voices were so distinctive that they had a difficult time disguising their vocal timbre. Expert multivoice people like Frees and Foray could "hear" their tones as they were portraying characters, and knew how to mask their own voiceprint.

Conrad's performances in the "Rocky and Bullwinkle" episodes were

Rocky the Flying Squirrel. *Courtesy of Universal Studios Publishing Rights, a Division of Universal Studios Licensing, Inc.*

highly enjoyable, especially in the later seasons, when the narrator was included in the plots. In one episode a cop removes the gag which Boris has tied around the narrator's mouth, but in doing so he rips off the poor fellow's mustache; Conrad gave hilarious, if painful, voice to the now whiskerless storyteller.

For fifteen years, Bill Conrad was a rock-solid part of the Jay Ward sound. In a TV interview in 1980, he said, "I think I learned more about pace and comedy working with these people than in any other enterprise I've ever been involved in." The last of the original Jay Ward male voices, Conrad died of heart failure on February 12, 1994.

Following a test taping at Capitol Records, the recording session for *Rocky* was held at Universal Recorders on February 11, 1958, with Conrad, Frees, Foray, and Bill Scott performing their classic roles for the first magic time. Four takes and it was done: Rocky, Bullwinkle, Boris, Natasha, and the narrator spoke their first hilarious lines. Scott earned an extra $100, and Ward was ecstatic. He wrote to Scott, saying, "I loved your work on the recording." In March, Ward Productions was legally incorporated.

Eager to assist Jay on the *Rocky* pilot film, Len Key put in a word for Al Shean, later one of Ward Productions' most valued employees. Shean was a gifted character designer and storyboard artist. Key said, "Shean was John Hubley's number one guy on the creative end at UPA, a good story man, almost as good as Al Anderson on his character drawings, and an excellent layout man; and like me, he wanted out of Shamus's studio." Shean was interested in both Ward's *Rocky* concept and the prospect of working in Japan. So was Fred Charrow, another top artist then at Culhane's New York shop and formerly with TV Spots.

But as things turned out, Key's recommendations were too late: Ward had already begun the animation on *Rocky*. Two Hollywood artists, Sam Clayberger and Roy Morita, handled all the artwork for Jay's film. Bill Scott had spoken to the two UPA designers, who agreed to work on the *Rocky* pilot in their spare time. So did editor Skip Craig, also at UPA. Craig eventually dubbed the finished film at TV Recorders.

At this point, Len Key was already gearing up to send materials to Japan. Although he felt confident about a national sale for *Rocky,* Key believed that the financing would have to be reasonably low-budget because the characters weren't established yet. He was looking in the area of $1,500 per episode (had their show featured *Peanuts, Pogo*, or any other famous entity, they could have asked $4,000 per segment).

Key was a diligent worker. Before long he had several sponsors interested in the plucky flying squirrel and his slightly moronic moose buddy. A top contender was the lucrative Canada Dry ginger ale company. Key knew that the TV animation market was out there and that their timing was very good. During 1958, in fact, any cartoon that was well made (à la *Crusader Rabbit*) and cost around $1,500 per episode was considered to be automatically in the TV stakes, with or without a national sponsor.

Meanwhile, Jay was being given a crash course in the current West Coast animation scene by Bill Scott, who had innumerable contacts. Although Shull Bonsall had beaten him to the punch with the color *Crusader Rabbit* series, Ward was now confident he could do better.* Besides *Rocky,* he commenced work on a puppet show, similar in tone to *Time for Beany,* and was nego-

*Len Key had learned that Bonsall wasn't working the new Crusader deal with RCA or the original series' distributor, George Bagnall; rather, he had set up Regis Films, his own distribution wing.

tiating to have the marionettes built in mid-March. This project, planned as a fifteen-minute daily serial, was named "Carrots and the King."

The lead characters were Carrots, a redheaded eight-year-old boy, and Mr. Waldo Wadsworth, who proclaims himself a king after finding a lost mine deed. The Waldo character, an unemployed Shakespearean ham actor, was obviously the template for Waldo Wigglesworth in Jay's later *Hoppity Hooper* cartoons. (King Waldo was still being considered for a full-length animated feature three years later; Jay commissioned Chris Jenkyns to develop the project, but nothing came of it). Several character names in Bill Scott's *Carrots* script reappeared later in the "Rocky and Bullwinkle" stories, including General Broadbeam and Baby Face Braunschweiger.

By now it was clear that Jay Ward was not simply competing with Shull Bonsall. He was already displaying the ahead-of-his-time creative showmanship for which he later became legendary. Ward, lining up staff and talent, wanted to expand into all the fields he liked: comedy, satire, jazz, sports—he even had an idea for an audience-participation TV show where viewers would send in predictions of football scores. In early March animation on the *Rocky* pilot was nearing completion, and Ward, still residing in Berkeley, returned to Hollywood to supervise the camera work. He sent a copy of the storyboard to Len Key, who showed it to Al Shean. A splendid artist with high creative standards, Shean completely flipped over it. Then it was sent to Canada Dry for perusal.

By the end of March 1958 the pilot film, now officially called *Rocky the Flying Squirrel,* was ready. Key began toying with the idea of buying Academy Productions, an East Coast animation firm.* He wanted a facility for producing commercial spots, industrials, and TV cartoons. But Jay much preferred the idea of basing his own studio in Hollywood, and expressed disdain for commercials because of his aversion to creative interference. Right now he wanted to stick exclusively with entertainment films, especially as Bonsall's new version of *Crusader Rabbit* was selling like hotcakes.

A print of the completed *Rocky* pilot was sent to Key. He thought it was superb and immediately began hawking it around. The response was excellent. Read Wight of Mathes Advertising showed it to his client, Canada Dry. The account executive for Cocoa Marsh, a chocolate marshmallow drink,

*Academy, formerly Tempo Films, was formed by UPA's original founders, Dave Hilberman and Zachary Schwartz.

also loved the film, while one distributor who screened it offered $3,500 per episode for an outright sale of sixty-five episodes. Although excited about the latter reaction, Ward felt that percentage ownership was preferable.

So did Len Key, who was aware that many ad agencies were into the payola game (involving questionable kickbacks) at the time; he warned Jay to make sure they had a good up-front profit before signing with a distributor. Industry practice meant that Jay would have to relinquish full equity in *Rocky*. The usual deal was 50 percent for the financing company. TV financing involved the cost of film prints, advertising, promotion, and legal fees. Hanna-Barbera, for instance, funded their early cartoon series with Screen Gems on a loan basis with interest.

One reaction to the *Rocky* film was already prophetic: "Good, but too sophisticated." Interestingly, all the parties who screened the pilot felt that the title should have been "The Adventures of Bullwinkle the Moose" (prescient, considering Bullwinkle actually inherited the show in 1961). While Ward was certainly amenable to suggestions, he couldn't see what was wrong with *Rocky the Flying Squirrel* as a title. Key's follow-up task involved working on a comprehensive merchandising and promotional campaign to help speed the sale.

By July 1958 things were looking to the big time. Canada Dry was almost at a firm deal, involving 195 episodes of *Rocky* at $5,000 each. Also in the pipeline was a possible production deal with Nabisco and King Features in which Ward and Key would subcontract animation for a series of new *Popeye* TV cartoons. Topping this off, Cocoa Marsh had ordered a tentative contract drawn up for *Rocky*. And now Jay had a second pilot film ready for Len to sell. This was *Jam Session*.

An enthusiastic jazz buff, Jay had conceived a TV series which would showcase the great jazz artists of the day. By the end of March he decided on the title *Jam Session* after rejecting "Jazz World, U.S.A." Following initial preparations, including hiring Monte Kay to line up top talents like Dave Brubeck, Ward filmed the first sequence on June 2 at the Red Onion nightclub in the Bay Area. The shoot was hampered by temperamental musicians, distractions from a gaggle of bohemian characters who "hung out" all day, and a number of technical problems.

Ward was disappointed with the quality of the rushes (the audio was poor), but after seeing the final cut he felt pleased. Skip Craig said, "Jay showed me the film one time, and it was pretty good. But it was basically cool jazz. Mort Sahl was in it doing a stand-up routine." Earlier, Ward had considered humorist S. J. Perelman and TV critic John Crosby as hosts before deciding on the controversial new comic Sahl, who later became an ardent fan of Jay's satirical cartoon shows. The film was directed by Bob Henry, who was associated with much big-time TV variety, including *The Dinah Shore Chevy Show* and *The Nat King Cole Show*. In late June, Jay headed for New York with a print.

Then, just as Leonard Key was working like a veritable Mr. Peabody, the very worst thing happened. In July, Key recalled, "Jay came back east and he stayed less than a week. He was very nervous; he said he wasn't feeling well, and could I finish selling the films without him." Ward flew back from this meeting and became seriously ill with a chronic nervous attack. The flight was further hampered by terrible weather conditions, and Jay began hyperventilating. According to Skip Craig, "Somebody did the worst possible thing and gave him oxygen. It nearly killed him." The net effect of this incident was that Ward's synapses were destroyed, and his health would never be the same. Jay thought he was dying on the plane and recalled seeing his life pass before his eyes three times while being restrained by several members of the cabin crew.

The aircraft had to make an emergency landing in Salt Lake City, and Ramona Ward drove all the way from Berkeley to bring him home. He was hospitalized for a month. The immediate effects of his illness took a long time to wear off; indeed, it took Ward many years to recuperate. He became agoraphobic. Ramona Ward recalls, "There was a long period following that plane flight where his food would have to be brought to the apartment. Jay would open the door and take the meal inside. Eventually, he was able to cure himself by degrees. He wanted to conquer his fear, so he started by walking out of the apartment to get his mail at nighttime." However, she adds, "Jay never fully regained his health, and he had many relapses to the end of his life."

While shocked and concerned for his old college chum, Len Key kept working for a sale on *Rocky*. His older brother, nationally famous cartoonist Ted Key, expressed an interest in helping on storyboards while Jay recovered. As Len was keen to have other cartoon ideas to fall back on, Ward kept himself busy while bedridden by devising a second cartoon series, to be set in the Old West. This was tentatively called "The B Boys"—the characters being a beaver, a burro, and a buffalo. For this project Ward considered hiring Bill Scott for scripts and Alex Anderson for model sheets. Sadly, it never saw the light of an animation desk.

Jay was informed that his recovery would take months. To make matters worse, the previously rosy picture regarding *Rocky* looked a lot different by late August. The Canada Dry people were playing a waiting game while they considered changing ad agencies. As a result, they became shy about investing money in new TV shows. Len Key, feeling the deal slipping away, tied up his second choice, Cocoa Marsh.

Key insisted that the Tojo team in Japan would handle all below-the-line work on *Rocky,* although the Edwards animation studio in Montreal was also considered.* Meanwhile, the waiting game went on. At one point Canada Dry came back to the negotiating table, then stalled again. When Cocoa Marsh began hedging, Maypo and Carnation (the original sponsor of *Crusader Rabbit*) expressed interest in *Rocky*. Even the agency for Bosco made inquiries; but none of this interest looked likely to culminate in a firm deal.

Ward's already serious nervous condition was inflamed by all this indecision. Bob Mills, a veteran of the early *Crusader Rabbit* shows, now ran his own animation studio. He recalls, "Jay came to visit me while he was still sick. He brought the *Rocky* pilot film to show me, but when we sat down to watch it we found he'd forgotten the sound track. This was completely out of character for Jay, and I suddenly realized just how ill he was—he was kind of disoriented."

Meanwhile, in early October 1958, Len Key closed a financing deal on *Rocky* with Peter Piech. A former journalist who ended up in TV film sales, Piech had a reputation as a crackerjack seller; he was interested in the distribution and merchandising of TV properties. Unemployed at the time, he had been brought into the project by Roger Carlin. "After several meetings," Key explains, "we decided to work together as Producer's Associates of Television [P.A.T.]. Actually, Carlin was going to run the company, and we had his lawyer, Charles Haydon, to do the contracts. Peter would handle the distribution for a 5 percent piece of the action, and my job was sales and sales promotion."

Piech and Key agreed to finance the *Rocky* series. As president of P.A.T., Piech's duties would be administrative, such as advancing the moneys for production. Key added, "Jay's responsibility was that of any executive producer or packager—to line up good people to do the work."

Rocky looked set to go, and Key felt sure that one of the potential sponsors

*Edwards employed the Norman McLaren team and had an excellent animation track record. Because of the Canadian ties to the British Commonwealth, the films would qualify as quota, which meant an instant guaranteed sale in Canada, England, and Australia.

was about to commit. On October 11, P.A.T. drew up a firm plan of action for 195 episodes with a $1 million guarantee of sales within two years. Key heard through the grapevine that considerable enthusiasm was brewing for *Rocky* back east: "It was felt that the pilot story was as good as the old *Crusader Rabbit,* while the production values were much better."

P.A.T. was soon set up at 500 Fifth Avenue, and eager to get started. Ward would supervise scripts and storyboards, while subcontracting any domestic animation to a mutually acceptable company. Key suggested temporarily appointing Bill Scott in the producer's role (Scott was already slated for the writer-director position). Ward consented, adding that he would reclaim the production reins once he felt better. By now it was confirmed that he had suffered a total nervous breakdown.

In fact, Ward's illness had prevented him from meeting with Bill and Dorothy Scott when they visited San Francisco. This incident embarrassed Jay; he was incredibly frustrated, convinced that his physical condition was holding up the sale on *Rocky,* not to mention the filming of his puppet show. But he was still coming up with ideas for cartoon series. Bill Scott remained highly enthused after hearing Ward's clever town-that-time-forgot premise for "The B Boys" show proposal.

By August, Scott had left UPA for the third time, following a stint as dialogue director on the Mr. Magoo feature film *1001 Arabian Nights.** He was freelancing for Shamus Culhane (whose *Phineas Phox* series was floundering after ten storyboards) and Quartet Films, who kept providing him with TV commercial assignments. During this job-to-job period, Scott noticed a lot of new TV cartoon pilots around town. He became more and more interested in seeing *Rocky* take off. Ward wrote to Len Key, emphasizing, "Bill would be wonderful for the series. He's the best man that I know of—and he knows all the good writers in Hollywood."

Then at long last Jay Ward's run of bad luck seemed set to change. In the final week of October, Charles Hotchkiss from the Dancer-Fitzgerald-Sample (D-F-S) advertising agency spoke to Jay in San Francisco. Hotchkiss was put in touch with P.A.T., who arranged a screening of the *Rocky* pilot. It was favorably received, as Key explains: "Charlie Hotchkiss showed it to D-F-S. They liked it and they showed it to General Mills, their top client." It appeared that *Rocky the Flying Squirrel* was about to get the long-awaited go-ahead.

With D-F-S suddenly expressing keen interest, Ward was urged by Peter

*Jack Kinney (ex-Disney) the film's director, took Scott's place.

Piech to start thinking of ideas for new *Rocky* episodes, with the series expected to air in the fall of 1959. But Ward's seesawing ill health worsened just as P.A.T. commenced preproduction. Key points out, "Jay's condition was being compounded with extra nervousness about selling the show." So a revised contract was drawn up giving Ward $2,500 for the first *Rocky* episode and a royalty of $125 for each new one, at the same time assigning Bill Scott 25 percent ownership of each cartoon he produced until Ward recovered.

Bill Scott wrote to Key, saying, "As you know, *Rocky* was Jay's original idea and he and I wrote the pilot together. I'm glad he feels that he can go on with it because I have a lot of respect for Jay and we work well together." Scott waited for the impending go-ahead, expecting a lot of fun on this project along with a nice bundle of money to boot.

Unfortunately for Jay Ward, his jazz-show pilot didn't sell, although it came close: a European friend of Len Key almost secured a British deal for twenty-six episodes to be financed by Harry Saltzman (later the coproducer of the James Bond films); and a Canadian network deal for thirty-nine shows had been discussed. Neither one, however, eventuated.

Late in the year, with P.A.T. set up and closing in on the *Rocky* deal, there was talk of financing thirty-nine segments of *Jam Session* for the fall of 1959. They went as far as planning a possible coproduction between the United States and France, where American jazz was, and is, positively revered. But by Christmas, 1958, Ward faced the music (don't pardon the pun—an occasional one seems mandatory in a book on Jay Ward): there was just no market for his show.

In December, P.A.T. signed contracts with Ward and Scott. Financing was planned for between 195 and 250 five-minute episodes, and there were discussions about possible commercials employing Rocky and Bullwinkle. Now things began to move. Aside from the *Rocky* project, P.A.T. was approached by Albert Kanter, the head of *Classics Illustrated Junior,* for a series of animated fairy tales. Key asked Scott to write and storyboard the first episode for $300; it was to be based on *Classics'* comic-book version of "Goldilocks and the Three Bears." The brief instructed, "Be funny but still charming—updated but not sophisticated." Scott began toying with this in his spare time. Key and Carlin booked a flight to Japan to check on the animation studio's progress. Christmas and New Year celebrations passed, and Jay Ward looked forward to a less traumatic year ahead. Unfortunately, he wouldn't get this wish.

5

Sponsored Squirrel, or How Green Was My Contract

At the start of 1959 Jay Ward's health bounced back a little, at least to the point where he felt more confident. He was, however, still delicate, and P.A.T. temporarily put Alex Anderson on alert. For *Rocky the Flying Squirrel* now had a sponsor.

A deal was cut with the breakfast-cereal division of General Mills. The giant food group, founded in the 1920s and based in Minneapolis, was anxious for a children's cartoon show which could work for it the way *Huckleberry Hound* was working for its rival, Kellogg's. General Mills was ad agency D-F-S's biggest account, and a powerful TV player. One of its longest-running sponsored shows was the *The Lone Ranger*.

At the time General Mills' top dogs were Lowry H. Crites, the marketing manager, and Cy W. Plattes, advertising manager, and later vice president, along with Jerry Souers, program and media director. Plattes was the real fan; a showbiz buff, he was in awe of Jay Ward and Bill Scott. Peter Piech recalls, "Lowry was a staid old man but a really great guy, and Cy was a lot of fun because he absolutely relished the aura and excitement of being around show business and show folk."

In January, with Ward's health still fluctuating, Leonard Key discussed the situation with Bill Scott. It transpired that *Rocky* had been sold on a promise of superlow cost, based on Japanese runaway animation. But behind the scenes things hadn't gone as smoothly as hoped. Key and Roger Carlin returned from a disastrous pre-Christmas trip to Tokyo: "We'd gone to Japan, where we found that there was no deal—it had blown up in our faces! The so-called animation studio didn't exist. There were just chalk marks on a vacant lot. They'd intended to finance the building with our show contract. It had been a total waste of time; they tried to ply us by getting us drunk and supplying geisha girls."

Hurriedly, Mexico City became the new talking point. Key explained, "When we did the *Rocky* deal, we had mentioned the feasibility and low price of animation in either Japan or Mexico to Charlie Hotchkiss, our contact at Mills' ad agency. Of course he got very enthused. Then when Japan bombed out on us, Roger Carlin said that Piech knew someone in Mexico—this rich general contractor named Gustavo Valdez. Valdez really wanted to get into the animation business, so we both flew down to meet him. Valdez was a multimillionaire, and I can remember having lunch at his magnificent home. We discussed our pickup with General Mills, and he agreed to join the project. He would build a brand-new cartoon studio, from scratch!"

Thus, the sponsoring division of General Mills discovered runaway animation. Highly enthused, Hotchkiss informed his client that it could save almost $500,000 a year by having the drawings done outside the United States. Valdez's new animation studio, Val-Mar Productions, was hastily assembled. Key recalled, "It was Hotchkiss's idea to visit down there, and his reports painted a glow all over Madison Avenue. Between his optimism and the BS of Roger Carlin, I don't think [account exec] Gordon Johnson or the client knew what the hell was happening."

Bill Scott, interviewed in 1981, remembered the Mexican experience this way: "Val-Mar was a kind of rich man's toy. This fellow Gustavo Valdez was a very wealthy man from a number of other enterprises. He just wanted to get into [animation], and was able to work out a sort of under-the-counter operation with the then advertising agency people, and some people from General Mills, who all had a little piece of the action. It was put together in a fairly sleazy fashion. The promoters [P.A.T.'s salesmen] of this thing presented it to the Mills people as a way of doing it. I assume they'd asked Jay if he thought it could be done in Mexico, and Jay had said, 'Why not? We've got the animators; there's no reason it can't work, animation's the same anywhere, etc.' But I don't think he was fully aware of how primitive the Mexican animation [staff] was at this time.*

"But it wasn't Jay's decision or the Mills decision to go down there. It was the decision of the people who were putting the show together for a price, and we very quickly learned that the enterprise was going to need a great deal of supervision up close."

Artistically, the Mexican situation would prove highly frustrating to Ward, as Scott explained. "Jay has great respect for animators: for American animators, and particularly for animators who 'animate.' In other words, he's really not terribly interested in people who just make things move. He loves actors and performance. Some Jay Ward favorites were Bill Littlejohn, Ben Washam, Phil Duncan: really fine animators who truly understand that animation is much more than just movement. It's acting, it's observing, it's seeing and reporting, and character, and satire—in motion as well as word. Which is why our stuff, even when limited, always had strong posing and 'acting.' Especially when the budget allowed it, like our Quaker spots and *George of the Jungle*.

"So I think that Jay was considerably stung by the product that came from Mexico, and he was determined forever after to make real animation."

As director Bill Hurtz clarified, "In an effort to cut costs, the advertising agency that had the General Mills account invested in this cartoon studio in Mexico. Then they made a contract with Jay which agreed that we'd write the stories, direct them, design them, and assemble them, but that the animation and backgrounds and the ink would be done in Mexico. Now that's where the most number of people come into the process. This was nothing that Jay was particularly fond of."

The fine details of the Mexican tie-up remain somewhat cloudy to this day, and depending on surviving participants' memories proves both selective and hazardous. But perhaps the most succinct summation was provided by Bill Scott, who for years bemoaned the fact that when Jay Ward took ill, some "high-rolling deal makers with friends in the ad agency" took over selling the show. Scott informed Jim Korkis, "So nobody could claim it was a direct conflict of interest, the people involved would have 'hidden stock' in this company called P.A.T., which had controlling stock in the Mexican company."

*In fact, Ward was strongly opposed to the Mexican farm-out from the start.

The original 1959 model sheet for Rocky and Bullwinkle. *Courtesy of Universal Studios Publishing Rights, a Division of Universal Studios Licensing, Inc.*

With Key and Carlin setting the deal, P.A.T. became partners in the south-of-the-border studio. They clinched the *Rocky* deal by convincing General Mills that investing money and equipment in the animation house would mean a magnificent tax break and an attractive production-cost factor. Val-Mar could also be a facility for cheaply made animated commercials, even if *Rocky* should prove unsuccessful. The show contracts were finally signed in March 1959.

In fact, General Mills bought the series *Rocky and His Friends* when P.A.T. sold it to them as a kids' show for a kids' time period. It was intended by General Mills to reach a specific children's audience for fifty-two weeks, at the lowest possible cost. Unfortunately, P.A.T., via Len Key and Roger Carlin, sold the show at a frankly ridiculous price. The sales campaign was based on the pitch that *Rocky* would be the most original TV show of its kind, which was reasonable enough. The trouble stemmed from basing the show on the quality of the pilot film, which Jay Ward and Bill Scott had made with minimal funds, naturally assuming that if the series sold, the visual quality would be far superior to the primitive cutout animation of the pilot.

But in a truly rash move, P.A.T.'s sales team assured General Mills there would be "no extra animation involved" if the series was made in Mexico at Val-Mar. They promised a lower price than Hanna-Barbera, whom Mills had also considered. Ward Productions was employed by P.A.T. as an independent contractor, although Jay Ward had cannily insisted on a contractual clause allowing him and Bill Scott the final say on quality control. A second premature promise stated the show would air twice weekly starting September 29, 1959; in fact, air-time had already been purchased from ABC.

The crux of the problem was that Key and Carlin had impetuously convinced both themselves and General Mills that the Mexican animation facility could produce at a very low cost. Neither party entertained the possibility that there was in fact a distinct lack of talent down in Mexico. Rather, in their haste to cut a deal, they blithely assumed that the product would roll out without a hitch and onto the airwaves.

The ad agency sent various American artists to Val-Mar, competent journeymen animators like Bob Schleh and Harvey Siegel. They also sent Bud Gourley, a production manager with live-television experience. But it was immediately apparent that these people weren't the A-class talent needed to whip the fledgling Mexican operation into shape.

Above all else, however, the *Rocky and His Friends* show contract proved the major stumbling block. Incredibly, in the agreement signed in March 1959, the original price per half-hour show was $8,520. This paid for two runs, with no union fee payments. And this at a time when, as Bill Scott wrote in a contemporary article for *Broadcast* magazine, "an average good one minute TV commercial costs between eight and nine thousand dollars." Skip Craig recalled, "The budget was impossible. It was just too low, and the show couldn't be produced at that price."

Aside from the lack of renewal increases and the unfair position on rerun payments, the contract meant General Mills could purchase the U.S. television rights to all the *Rocky* shows outright after a mere two runs. Finally, P.A.T.'s biggest tactical blunder was executing the General Mills contract without fully consulting Jay Ward and Bill Scott, who didn't see the agreement until four months later. Understandably, this fomented several weeks of time-consuming resentment.

And it was now that Ward and Scott suddenly discovered to their mounting trepidation that the show for which they were contracted was to be a half-hour series. In fact, fifty-two half hours, to air twice a week on ABC starting September 29!

Up to this point, Jay and Bill had assumed they were to make a five-minute daily cartoon. But as we have seen, General Mills wanted a longer kids' show to compete with Hanna-Barbera's Kellogg's-sponsored cartoons, while ABC-TV was looking for a show to fill the 5:30 P.M. daily time slot, a scheduling hole created by the recently canceled *Mickey Mouse Club*. This was the first of several disquieting signs that Ward and Scott, out of sight in sunny California, could easily be steamrollered by upcoming events.

With time running out, Jay and Bill had to formulate a thirty-minute TV show for their next meeting. Somewhat desperate, Ward submitted the synopsis of his fifteen-minute show "Carrots and the King," for which the puppets had already been constructed. But while Ward believed "Carrots" could make up part of the half hour, Piech informed him that the puppet market was too elusive.

At this point Len asked his brother Ted Key to come up with possible ideas for the *Rocky* show. A weekend meeting was set up in April 1959 in Los Angeles to discuss the show format with the ad agency. At the Hollywood Roosevelt Hotel, Jay and Bill met with Len and his cartoonist brother Ted, who introduced his witty concept, called "Danny Daydream," which would soon evolve into the "Peabody's Improbable History" segment. Also present were Roger Carlin (he and Len representing P.A.T.) and Gordon Johnson. Johnson wielded considerable clout, being the top decision maker at Dancer-Fitzgerald-Sample, where he was senior vice president and account executive for General Mills.

There was a disturbing dynamic to the meeting. Len recalls, "First Johnson was late—he was bragging how he wouldn't take a cab from the airport and had demanded a limo." And in a 1985 radio interview Bill Scott disclosed, "I didn't know about Mexico [being confirmed] at this point. As I was walking across the parking lot to the meeting with sponsor and network and whomever, the two gentlemen who put the show deal together bracketed me like two rogue elephants around a tame elephant and said, 'If anyone asks about Mexico, say we can do it!' Sure enough, almost the first question I was asked was, 'Do you think the show can be made in Mexico?' " Scott had to fake his enthusiasm, while Jay Ward, never comfortable about runaway animation, felt extremely wary.

It was now disclosed that P.A.T. had sold the show to General Mills for a very low price, contingent on the artwork being farmed down to Mexico.* As if this wasn't bad enough, Jay and Bill learned why they hadn't known sooner about the change from a five-minute show to a half hour: the contract between Mills and P.A.T. had been signed a month before, without Jay and Bill being consulted (in fact, Jay Ward wouldn't see that contract until July). He and Scott were thunderstruck at what they sensed was a lemon in the making.

Years later Bill Scott told Jim Korkis, "It was the most cockamamie, warped . . . deal," then added, "I can't help but think that's how most television shows get put together and financed. I was naive about these things even though I had been in the business for a while. After about two years in business with Jay, we learned that when somebody uses the phrase 'We're not looking at this from just a current viewpoint; we're talking about a long-term commitment,' that a 'long-term commitment' meant they wanted a piece of the action."

Fortunately, the meeting proved a success in the creative aspects of the show. First, a title was decided on. The series would be called *Rocky and His Friends* (a takeoff of *Arthur Godfrey and His Friends*). Then the format

*Ward and Scott were informed they had to coproduce the entire series with no additional moneys—save percentages of the show elements—while deferring their salaries until show delivery.

was set: for each half hour, there would be two "Rocky" chapters, a "Fractured Fairy Tale," a "Peabody," and a short segment called "Bullwinkle's Corner."

On the Monday following the meeting, Jay and Bill began working in earnest on the scripts. Scott quickly brought writers Chris Jenkyns and George Atkins into the fold, and soon after, Chris Hayward joined this elite literary circle. Ward now worked all week in Los Angeles. At first he commuted to Berkeley on weekends; later that year he took a combination office–Spanish hacienda apartment on Havenhurst Drive, just off Sunset Boulevard on the cusp of West Hollywood. It was soon crammed to the rafters with Jay's miscellaneous collectibles, including old puppets, carved tiki gods, and funny hats.

Skip Craig said, "By the time I joined the outfit late that year Jay had his small studio just up the road from the apartment." This was actually an old house once lived in by actor Fess Parker. A trade item mentioned, "Film editing was performed over the range in the kitchen, animators were in the living room, and there was a projection screen over an old bed in a back room." The building, west of the late Schwab's Drug Store, is still the Ward Productions office today. Jay told the interviewer, "Instead of expanding our facilities, we're the only studio in town trying to contract. We'd be condemned if there was enough to condemn."*

The month of May 1959 proved frantic. Several scripts were completed, and the first two recording sessions were held. The Mexican operation was revving up, and the voice actors were put under contract. Stone Associates was tied in as the merchandising agent by P.A.T., again without consulting Jay Ward, who told Piech that he wasn't happy with this arrangement.

Scott and Ward collaborated on the scripts for the first two "Peabody" cartoons. Scott wrote all the "Rocky" episodes, while he and Chris Jenkyns did the first four "Fractured Fairy Tales." Supplies were bought, Moviola equipment was rented, Bill's wife, Dorothy, filled in as temporary secretary, and the first layouts were done by freelancers David Hanan and Bernie

*Skip Craig adds, "Next to the house-studio, on the corner of Sunset, was a shack, where the Dudley Do-Right Emporium now stands. For a few years this site became a famous hot dog stand called the Plush Pup. Later, 8218 Sunset was for sale, so Jay bought that property and that became his large studio, and for a while we even used the building in between during the busiest years. By 1971 the Plush Pup was gone and by the end of that year the Dudley store was ready."

Gruver. Alex Anderson even contributed two "Fractured Fairy Tale" scripts ("Puss in Boots" and "Hansel and Gretel"). Ward and Scott cowrote the commercial and sponsor intros, and Scott scripted several "Bullwinkle's Corner" segments.

Also in May, the gifted UPA animation director Ted Parmelee signed a contract with P.A.T. as a freelance director. Bill Scott, a close friend, had recommended him. Parmelee was employed for twelve months at $300 weekly. Jay Ward continued to scout for staff, and soon the invaluable Al Shean, who had been on the fringes of the project for some time, joined the outfit.

Feeling the need for one more writer, Scott approached his ex-UPA collaborator Phil Eastman. Eastman wrote to Bill, stating, "You and Jay have a great deal more to offer than Hanna-Barbera." Scott offered Eastman $300 for each "Fractured Fairy Tale" script. But Eastman had been burned by CBS and Terrytoons. He had written two episodes of "Tom Terrific" and was paid so little it was almost on-spec money. When the cartoons were repeated four times he received nothing. Thus, Eastman demanded the reasonable price of $500 per "Fairy Tale" script, including storyboards, at the rate of one per fortnight. Alas, the P.A.T. budget was simply too low. Fortunately, Chris Hayward proved a fast and facile writer. Later in the year Hayward put in a word for the very funny Lloyd Turner, who completed Ward's scripting team.

The Mexican studio began preparing for the work to come. Then, just as it looked like the worst was over, the real trouble began. So much trouble, in fact, that Rocky and Bullwinkle almost never made it to TV.

6

HOW TO CUT CARTOON CORNERS,

or Mexico City Mishmash

The moose and squirrel's Mexican adventure began with a phone call in the first week of June 1959. Jay Ward and Bill Scott were busy with preliminary work on early scripts and the day-to-day setting up of Ward Productions when Carlos Manriquez telephoned from Mexico to announce that his team was ready to begin preproduction on *Rocky and His Friends*. Ward and Scott relayed their best wishes to Ernie Terrazas, who, according to Bill Hurtz, "was a great source for animators."

Terrazas had been busy scouting animation talent, especially bilingual artists fluent in both Spanish and English. He'd approached people like Bill Melendez, a highly dependable ex-UPA/Warners man; the talented veteran Rudy Zamora, whose credits went back to the 1930s with Disney and Max Fleischer; and others, like Xavier Atencio, Bill Perez, Emery Hawkins, Howard Baldwin, Bud Partch, Carl Urbano, and Tom McDonald (indeed, the last five had already worked in Mexico). He was also on the lookout for young artists who could be trained on the job.

Jay Ward mailed storyboards, scripts, track readings, and raw magnetic film for the first cartoons to be made at Val-Mar. These were two "Fractured Fairy Tales" ("Goldilocks" and "Jack and the Beanstalk"). He also sent the all-important character model sheets and mentioned that Al Shean, his excellent model artist, would be visiting Mexico to help demonstrate the desired layout and design style. As Bill Hurtz explains, "Al drew perfectly for Jay

Ward cartoons." Terrazas was instructed that each "Fairy Tale" would run five minutes (or 450 feet). The *Rocky* show's opening titles were awaiting approval, but Ward was lobbying to do these in Hollywood. Meanwhile he suggested that the Mexican editing team begin by compiling a sound effects library.

Next Ward contacted Laboratorios Mexica, informing them he was producing fifty-two half-hour 35-mm color films. He priced the cost of developing negatives, dailies, and composite and release prints in Mexico. Meanwhile Frank Comstock's catchy theme music for *Rocky and His Friends* was recorded in mid-June, in a Mexican sound studio. Back in Hollywood, Ward Productions' freelance team commenced animating the show titles and Jay invoiced the first bills back east.

Alarmingly, two sets of payments were delayed by P.A.T. Because of this Ted Parmelee refused to go to Mexico, and a spooked Jay Ward feared that within a mere month of setting up his studio, word of late payments would spread, and his name as an animation employer would be "box-office poison." In addition, the creative writing was affected; it's well-nigh impossible to write comedy when the mood is upset, especially by the prospect of no food on the table. So Scott phoned Piech, telling him, "All work has been stopped." A recording session was canceled and no more writing or storyboards went ahead. Before long, outstanding payments were four weeks late. Ward and Scott were fighting mad and threatened breach of contract. Musician Frank Comstock was also awaiting his payment.

The ad agency was quickly made aware of what had transpired. Ward began demanding certified checks. The mess would be resolved within a month, but not before some amazing revelations. Basically it was learned that P.A.T., the company which was to finance *Rocky and His Friends,* had no money!

P.A.T. had planned to borrow on the General Mills contract in order to obtain enough money to produce the show. But according to Len Key, P.A.T.'s bank, Manufacturers Hanover, would not lend because of the Mexican production tie-up.

As Key explains, "To start the enterprise rolling I'd signed a performance bond with American Surety, a huge Triple-A insurance carrier in New York—this guaranteed completion and delivery of the films. Then I took that and the General Mills pickup to Citicorp in Mexico and got an appointment with the manager, who was an American. I wanted Citicorp to finance the production. He looked at the bond and the Mills pickup, then he looked at me and said that he couldn't do it. We were Americans in Mexico City, so he said, 'We don't deal with gringos—gringos don't win in Mexican courts!' This meant we couldn't collect if the Mexico City studio defaulted. I vividly remember that day because it shocked the hell out of me." With the surety bond deemed worthless, Key's bank was understandably loath to release funds.

Panic set in. General Mills still loved the pilot and sorely wanted to compete with Kellogg's *Huckleberry Hound.* So at this point, in order to save the show, Gordon Johnson persuaded the ad agency to guarantee a loan of $125,000 from the Chemical Corn Exchange Bank. He then purchased stock in P.A.T., along with his close friend Robert Travis (already extremely wealthy from his family's Ohio-based glass business), and between them they suddenly owned 60 percent of the company.

In fact, the entire stock of P.A.T. was pledged to the ad agency pending repayment of the loan. Of course, this meant that P.A.T. was now controlled by D-F-S, meaning the creative cartoon makers in Hollywood could be big-brothered by the agency heavyweights who were now effectively executive producers. As Alex Anderson observed, "It seemed to be a classic case of conflict of interest."

At least Jay Ward felt relieved over one point—to date he had signed no legal agreement on character merchandising, and he made sure those rights were not released at this time. On July 10, D-F-S paid all the outstanding bills. Production on *Rocky* could now resume.

Peter Piech said, "The Chemical Corn Bank was the first bank to ever invest in television—this was years before. They loaned money for TV production through the Bank of America. I took pride in the fact that once we'd ironed out these early problems, the *Rocky* enterprise was able to liquidate this loan six weeks early."

We can only wonder whether this mess might have been avoided had Jay Ward's illness not occurred. If nothing else, Ward was astute—he had an MBA from Harvard and was meticulous with his records. From the outset, Bill Scott felt that P.A.T.'s sales team was to blame for hasty decisions. He said, "The way the show had been put together always seemed a little shady to me." This hardly augured well for a harmonious business relationship. Adding to the mess, Ward and Scott held fast to their standards of creative excellence. The amateurish Mexican situation would remain a sore point over the next two years.

Al Levy, a friend of Len Key, was working at Talent Associates, and there was some early talk of TA paying off P.A.T.'s creditors and financing *Rocky* as a Hollywood-based operation. But it came too late. Gordon Johnson was in at P.A.T., with financial backing from Bob Travis, and the Mexico City tie-up proceeded. Key remembers warning Jay Ward, " 'You're dealing with a very tough . . . bunch.' [These people] were gambling on Jay and Bill playing ball so that Ward Productions could repay writers, voices, and so on."

Happily for all, General Mills loved the show. Key said, "The bosses at Mills thought the sun rose and set on Jay and Bill as far as cartoons were concerned." The client, in particular cereal top-dog Lowry Crites, was insistent upon them. This was the godsend: it meant that Ward and Scott's position was strong; considering P.A.T.'s recent financial hiccup, General Mills could just as easily have gone courting another outfit like Hanna-Barbera.

With work on *Rocky* now under way, Key took a few weeks off in Europe on a separate business venture. He and a friend bought into a diet soft drink project (called No-Cal) for the armed forces. It didn't make the big time; as Len reflected, "How stupid that idea was, trying to sell soda pop to nations of wine drinkers. Anyway, while I was gone, P.A.T. aced me out of the company that I'd basically set up. I got screwed out of the deal. I got back to find they'd changed the locks on the doors! To this day I believe it was because Johnson wanted to run the show, and I think he felt I knew the cartoon field better than he. And of course I was close to Jay."

Although Peter Piech was P.A.T.'s nominal president, it seemed to Len Key that Gordon Johnson was really steering the ship. Piech's relationship with Jay Ward improved after the initial financing debacle was rectified, and he settled into his main role of administration and salary payments. A year later he and Ward became business associates in merchandising. As Piech puts it, "Jay and I were a team—P.A.T./Ward—for the next thirty years."

Meanwhile, Key was depressed and shaken. He admits to part of the blame concerning the original contract and budget: "I was naive about the animation game in the area of timing. Looking back, I realize they couldn't have produced the shows as quickly as the contract stipulated. But I'd always acted with good intentions; I got the impression that Carlin . . . cooked this up so all the blame for contract troubles would look like my fault, and that I had done damage to Jay and Bill."

Characteristically, Ward remained loyal to his friends. He stuck by Len, who offered to work exclusively for Ward Productions, acting as Jay's East Coast representative. For the third time—following their earlier experiences with Jerry Fairbanks and Shull Bonsall—Ward and Key agreed that the television business was more than simply fickle; in fact it often resembled a minefield.

Feeling none too certain about *Rocky*'s long-term prospects, Ward began pushing for a second TV series. He revived his thoughts on a comedy puppet show, still feeling it couldn't miss. Meantime, Key went to work as head of sales for Ward Productions and soon had various major accounts like Tootsie Roll and Sealtest expressing interest.

In mid-1959 Key heard that the *Alvin* property was up for grabs and that animation firms were being scouted. But Ward wasn't interested in subcontracting on other people's characters. The only exception would be for a prestigious theatrical release. Rather than *Alvin,* which ended up being produced by Format Films, Jay investigated the idea of a feature-length cartoon starring Winnie the Pooh.

Key learned that Ward would have to get the consent of both the A. A. Milne Estate and NBC, which had a seven-year option on Pooh from 1957 to 1964. NBC suggested Ward undertake a Winnie the Pooh pilot. If they liked it they would commission a series of thirty-nine episodes, or possibly a TV special with full animation.

When the *Rocky* deal was finalized in June, Jay Ward was given the official go-ahead to commence production. The first finished animation by Ward's freelance Hollywood team consisted of several items. They produced the first *Rocky and His Friends* "show opening," rarely seen nowadays. This featured the General Mills logo, and a scene in which Rocky and Bullwinkle light fireworks. It ends with the boys being chased over hill and dale by a gigantic Catherine wheel which runs amok.

Next came the "Rocky Episode opening," with the plucky squirrel demonstrating some flashy flying while Bullwinkle paints a sign—the luckless moose ends up being caught in some laundry hanging on a tenement washing line. General Mills suggested making an alternate ending to this, so as to have a different gag lead-in to the second episode (there were always two "Rocky" episodes per half hour). Then came the surreal "Rocky episode closing" featuring the boys popping up in a daisy patch; the "Fairy Tale opening" with the giant and the dwarf; the "Fairy Tale closing," in which a piece of chalk writes "the end"; the "Peabody opening," featuring the march with Cleopatra and the grouchy little street sweeper; the "Peabody closing"; and two show bridges ("Time for that dancing fool, Bullwinkle!" and the moose as a klutzy magician pulling a bear out of his hat). They also

Notes on the Val-Mar Studio Staff

Gustavo Valdez (*Studio owner*). Of Aztec Indian descent, Valdez had already made his fortune in paving and as the waterworks tender for Mexico City. "He was the chief money behind Val-Mar," according to Bill Hurtz. "His father was the governor of Sonora, and his mother took the children to Texas, then on to Los Angeles. He attended UCLA on an athletics scholarship, became a baseball pro, then graduated as an engineer. And he was a really neat guy." P.A.T.'s Peter Piech, who had controlling stock in Val-Mar, said, "Valdez, being a contractor, had the animation studio built to specifications: a hacienda with six levels, the bottom one containing the camera department. The studio was in his wife's name, and his family were in on the payroll. Jesus Martinez was his brother-in-law." In fact Bill Hurtz recalls Val-Mar "being set up, in effect, for Martinez" and being "a new, contemporary building." Writer George Atkins visited the facility after it had been operating for one year, and remembers, "They'd had an earthquake, which effectively split the building in two. I went up to the top floor to see ink and paint, and there was just a rickety plank to walk across, with certain death below if you lost your balance!"

Piech believed that "Valdez, this fantastically wealthy road-builder, wanted to get into animation because of a latent artistic frustration." In early 1959, P.A.T. and ad agency Dancer-Fitzgerald-Sample signed a contract with Val-Mar, specifically to produce *Rocky and His Friends*. Bill Hurtz told cartoon scholar Charles Ulrich that account executive Gordon Johnson "engineered setting up the studio in Mexico City, and I think privately put in cameras and things. He was a participant in the making of the show." Val-Mar, a contraction of Valdez and Martinez, was the studio's original name. A year later it was changed to Gamma Productions (Gamma rhymed with llama).

Jesus Martinez was appointed administrative head of the studio. As manager, he wanted to take over the scheduling and quality control departments when Bill Hurtz's three-month tenure was up. Martinez (known to all as "Chuy") had been trained as an architect. While he was good at gathering and charting information, he didn't analyze well. According to production manager Bud Gourley, Chuy was the type who needed things clarified over and over.

Ernest Terrazas was a veteran animator. Bill Hurtz recalls, "He was good at command but never followed through on promises. And he lacked conviction. Actually, at first Ernie was drunk. . . ." Fortunately, Terrazas was creatively gifted in story and taught most of the young artists, who looked to him as a leader. Hurtz adds, "Ernie buckled down somewhat after I left. He drew well, and he'd been well trained at Disney on storyboard."

Carlos Manriquez was a thirty-year veteran: he'd worked at Disney as a background artist, with stints at CBS and on Warner Brothers cartoons, in the Chuck Jones unit. At Val-Mar he was named the first supervisor, in charge of three areas: checking, ink and paint, and camera. In the early days he spent most of his time vying with Martinez and Terrazas for the top position. Although this politicking meant time was lost on his cartoon duties, Hurtz felt that Manriquez showed far more aptitude than the other two as a candidate for executive material.

Several Americans traveled south as the studio was being set up. Bill Hurtz recalls that **Edwin A. Gourley** (nicknamed Bud) was hired as "the expediter—he dealt with the Mexican authorities, including a guy named Vasquez in customs. There were no [legal] work permits, so Bud was always 'mysteriously' tipped off to any Labor Department inspections. The story can be told now that Bud smuggled highly expensive polished Belgian shotguns into Mexico for rich clients. Bud was basically what you'd call an 'operator.' "

Of the American artists, Hurtz noted that **Bob Schleh** was "a nice, quiet chap from New York. He was an odd duck; he never hung out with the rest of the guys. I think he committed suicide—at least I know he died a very early death. And **Harvey Siegel**, a commercial artist, was also sent down by the New York people. He was a good layout man and he'd been with Shamus Culhane." **George Singer**, who joined the team several months later, was, says Hurtz, "a good journeyman artist. Earlier, he couldn't get into UPA's circle [he was at UPA, but after Hurtz had left], but he certainly worked for Hanna-Barbera for years afterward." These were the main early players; including assistant animators, in-betweeners, ink and paint personnel, and others, Val-Mar boasted a sizable staff.

Meanwhile, back in Los Angeles, Jay Ward's early staff consisted of layout artists Sam Clayberger, Bernie Gruver, and Sam Weiss; storyboard artists Shirley Silvey, Roy Morita, Chris Jenkyns, Al Shean, Al Wilson, Art Diamond, and Adrienne Diamond (the two Diamonds weren't related); directors Gerry Ray, Ted Parmelee, and Pete Burness; and film editor Skip Craig (and occasionally Roger Donley). For cartoon titles and other below-the-line work originating from Hollywood, Ward employed Barbara Baldwin, Bob McIntosh, Mary

Cain, Hedy Munk, and Connie Pinard Matthews (ink and paint), Bob Maxfield, Frank Braxton, Edward DeMattia, C. L. Hartman, Lloyd Rees, Tom McDonald, Ben Shenkman, Ben Washam, Phil Monroe, Fred Madison, and Spencer Peel (animators), Max Morgan (camera), Sam Clayberger and Dean Spille (backgrounds), and various other freelance artists.

A note about terminology: Ward's team in Hollywood "predirected" the material sent to Mexico. This meant that storyboards and exposure sheets were fashioned for the Mexicans, who would be under U.S. supervision at Val-Mar. The layouts, timing, and camera action were already prepared. The work in Mexico City was "below-the-line," that is, the labor-intensive end of the operation. The glossary at the end of this book will help those readers unfamiliar with animation terms.

made two commercial intros: one had Bullwinkle as an artist ("I just paint what I see"), while the other showed him getting tangled up in some film which breaks loose from a recalcitrant movie projector. Finally, the Hollywood outfit was asked to animate "Rocky" episodes 7 and 8.

Meanwhile, the main animation for *Rocky* was due to commence in Mexico City. After speaking at length with his old *Crusader Rabbit* animator Gerry Ray, recently working in Mexico at the Thompkins Studio, Ward became highly doubtful about the Mexican team's ability, and he realized they would need considerable supervision.

When ad man Charlie Hotchkiss visited Mexico City in mid-July he reported that the studio was okay and the job could be done. Key, however, remained skeptical: he knew that all Hotchkiss had actually seen was a six-story building, one animation stand, and a few desks and tables. Still, Jay Ward was willing to bend a little on Mexico, since he and Hotchkiss hit it off well on a personal level.

Finally, just before August, the Mexican unit announced they were ready to start. Protesting Hotchkiss's choice for animation supervisor, Ward and Scott got their way: the award-winning UPA designer-director Bill Hurtz was sent to Mexico City for quality control. A top artist, Hurtz's credentials were impeccable. To Jay and Bill, this was the first really positive thing to happen since the deal had been cut.

Hurtz recalls, "My job was to put the men to work, and essentially to see to it that they did it with a degree of acceptability, that is, as well as possible, because Jay did not control the Mexican operation."

Thus Bill Hurtz would be judging the product on a daily basis, keeping in mind the Mexican team's budget and time factor. Indeed, this was the crux of Jay Ward's problem with D-F-S in 1959: he wanted to help the Mexicans reach their goals, but he refused to sacrifice quality. And when Jay refused, he meant it. Aware that both the show budget and the delivery dates were unrealistic, he gave Hurtz the authority to reject any artwork not up to scratch, even though the ad agency was already pushing for speed: *Rocky and His Friends* was still expected to air twice weekly from September 29.

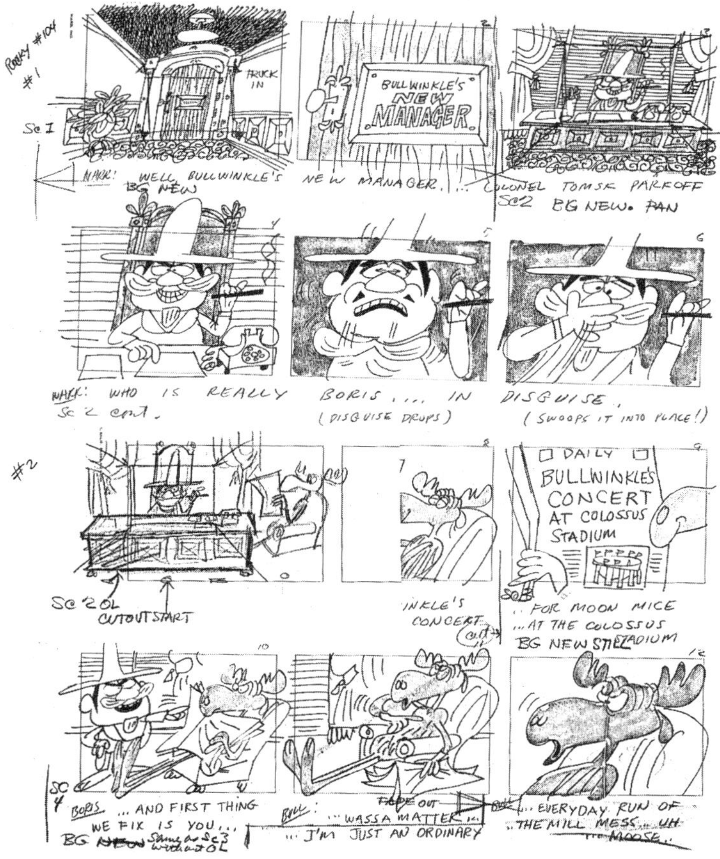

An example of a storyboard for a Rocky and Bullwinkle adventure. ***Courtesy of Universal Studios Publishing Rights, a Division of Universal Studios Licensing, Inc.***

Ward issued a set of guidelines to be followed for his style of cartoon: "Layouts—must be uncluttered, easy to 'read,' with a liberal use of close-ups and many different angles for staging; Animation—should be drawn as humorously as possible; Backgrounds—good coloring is needed, but be careful to emphasize how it looks on black and white TV; Ink and Paint—heavy outline required on figures; Editing—the sound effects are very important; Dubbing—ensure that voices are very clear, and the sound effects are loud."

Hurtz was instructed to make sure each artist worked on just one series (for instance, only on "Peabody" cartoons). He'd already determined that a single cartoon would take between five and six weeks, from layout through final cut.* With Jay's guidelines in place, Bill Hurtz arrived in Mexico City on July 20, 1959, to find that things weren't quite ready. And that's putting it mildly.

In fact, Hurtz probably felt like escaping to the island of Moosylvania—anywhere but this studio! For starters, Val-Mar was still without a telephone and an English-speaking stenographer. To make matters worse, importing magnetic film from Los Angeles to Mexico meant lengthy customs holdups. Hurtz was relieved to learn that Ward's Hollywood team would handle the sound effects and dubbing in this early stage. Although confident in some of the animators, Hurtz found the layout department to be woefully inadequate. In fact, layout, the very blueprint of a cartoon, was this studio's major pitfall. Jim Hiltz and Gerard Baldwin, who flew down with Hurtz on short-term P.A.T. contracts, found themselves doing double duty: redrawing layouts as well as directing the cartoons.

The work practices were certainly different. Hurtz recalls, "At first, the Mexican people—animators, inkers, and painters—would be sitting in this big room, like a union hall. They would wait their turn, and when a cel was ready, each person would come and get a single cel at a time. It was cheap labor—I think in those days they were paid something like ten cents a cel."

Artistic matters aside, Val-Mar was also shaping up as a corporate nightmare. Basic organization within the studio was virtually nonexistent, although Hurtz felt somewhat reassured when he met the financial backer, Gustavo Valdez. He found Valdez to be "a truly remarkable man: straightforward, realistic, and forceful. He was a fine fellow. He would take us out every weekend and show us a grand time." At this point Valdez appeared to be the project's greatest asset (assuming his patience held out).

Hurtz, however, couldn't perform miracles. Even if the Mexican studio had been capable of Disney quality, P.A.T.'s budget was utterly unworkable. Ward pointed out that Hanna-Barbera was making its shows for a production cost of $21,000 per half hour, or two and a half times more than the *Rocky* show budget. In fact, Jay reckoned his cartoons should have been

*All "Rocky" episodes would run three and a half minutes (315 feet), each "Peabody" was four and a half minutes (405 feet), and the "Bullwinkle's Corner" segments ran one minute (90 feet).

budgeted higher than H-B's, explaining, "Our stories have much more dialogue, movement, changes of scene, more voice actors, and so on."

From the start, Ward and Scott had misgivings about the shabby way contract decisions were reached without their being involved. Ward, who had graduated from the Harvard Business School, informed Gordon Johnson that it took time to develop and train staff, especially a staff of about one hundred who couldn't speak English!

Certainly Jay found the early days of the *Rocky* operation confusing; once Mexico began gearing up, he had to get used to the geographical situation for his virtually daily correspondence to Mexico City, Minneapolis, and New York in this era before fax and E-mail. Thus, while General Mills and ABC had contractual approval on the scripts, voice recordings were often completed before the client saw those scripts. Promised delivery dates were already being broken by Val-Mar in August, and Ward knew they'd never get to air by September 29, the contracted date. Further, he warned Johnson that twice-weekly broadcasts were an impossibility for at least six months. The folks in New York finally started listening to him, and many differences were ironed out over the next year.

While Ward was delighted with the "Fractured Fairy Tales," D-F-S and the sponsor griped about this show element more than any other. They felt that several stories were too similar in content, and that their cost was too high. As early as April, Ward and Scott had warned Johnson that the "Fairy Tales" would require more work: the characters were new in each story, which meant more animation and extra model sheets. And the scripts were more intricate, being five minutes in length. Overall, Jay was completely opposed to the agency viewpoint. He felt the "Fairy Tales" were so fresh and funny that they could have been shown theatrically and held their own with the contemporary Warner Brothers and UPA releases.

Ward was highly versed in the technical aspects of animation, but for the first couple of months he got the impression that his suggestions were being systematically ignored by the ad agency, which appeared to be trying to call all the shots. Eventually Jay won his argument—indeed, the budget was increased to a far more workable figure, as will be revealed. But for most of 1959 Jay Ward, leery of the whole *Rocky* enterprise, was eager to put his energies into other projects which he felt could be managed far more realistically.

7

Gringos, Hepatitis, and Mucho Loma, or You Can't Make Fun of Pancho Villa

In early August, when the Mexican animation commenced, Bill Hurtz quickly faced a discomfiting reality: the first two shows contained far more animation than D-F-S had deemed acceptable. This was blamed on hasty planning, but was no doubt unavoidable in such a new setup. Still, the tiny budget was blowing out, and inevitably, the unrealistic request came thundering from New York: Hurtz had to "make the next films simpler." Additional animators were being hired when Gordon Johnson (whom Hurtz called "the man with the muscle") arrived in Mexico. Hurtz, Gerard Baldwin, and Jim Hiltz called a meeting in Johnson's hotel room.

Hurtz told fanzine publisher Charles Ulrich how he got Johnson to bend a bit: "I made a pitch there. I said, 'Gordon, these stories are glorious!' We were getting about a third of what Hanna and Barbera were getting. . . . I said, 'For God's sake, this is the best stuff in town. Why can't we get at least as much as Hanna-Barbera?' And he says, 'Well, we're not buying Hanna-Barbera.' And he says, 'Furthermore, you could photograph the storyboard on this show and it would still play.' And he was oddly right, you know, in a way."

Hurtz, aware that his goal was the delivery of ten finished items for two half-hour shows by September 7, pleaded with Johnson to allow Ward's team to handle the layout work. Grudgingly, Johnson agreed. Hurtz told Ulrich: "So the layouts were done up in Hollywood and then shipped down with the exposure sheets. So the 'look' of the show was on it, and the timing was ours; it's just what made them move was done in Mexico."

Gerard Baldwin and Jim Hiltz decided not to stay in Mexico City after their three-month contracts were up, although both men remained with Ward Productions in Los Angeles. Meantime, Bill Hurtz tore into the work in late August and early September and really left Val-Mar bloodied. He praised the ink and paint department ("They were really fast: they were the people who pulled the show out of the bottomless abyss"), but found the constant checking and supervision to be personally tiring. With the first films due back from the lab, Hurtz began seeking a competent background artist: "The local painters had absolutely no sense of color scheme."

Veteran animator Dun Roman was set to arrive in late September to take over Jim Hiltz's position.* Aside from Roman, Ward wanted a second supervisor in Mexico to succeed Bill Hurtz, also due to return Stateside. The brilliant *Mr. Magoo* director Pete Burness was working for Jay in Los Angeles, but he wasn't interested in relocating (a pity, since Burness spoke fluent Spanish).

Hurtz recommended that Val-Mar employ a full-time Spanish-speaking animation supervisor to stabilize the staff, increase the output, and be responsible to Dun Roman on quality control. The ad agency came to the rescue by hiring Rudy Zamora, a highly skilled animator. Zamora was a full-blooded Mexican with vast experience at Disney and many other studios. Shamus Culhane noted, "Zamora's mother actually nursed Pancho Villa." Happily, Zamora spoke perfect Spanish. He was also a witty man whose irreverence meshed well with Ward's. He was to prove invaluable.

On September 14, Bill Hurtz shipped the first batch of completed films to Jay Ward. Hurtz knew they were "pretty poor—in fact, some of the work was frankly embarrassing." But he was confident the next ones would be better: apart from hiring a Texan artist named Frank Hursh for backgrounds, Hurtz felt that the Mexicans' grasp of continuity was slowly improving. Besides which, regular art classes were being held for the animators.

Unfortunately, more serious setbacks arose. Ward informed Gordon John-

*Earlier, Roman and Hurtz had both worked at Shamus Culhane's Hollywood studio.

son that by Hollywood standards, the Mexican lab was simply too slow. This was the first hint of the delivery problems to come. Delivery dates were the major bugbear as far as D-F-S and ABC were concerned.

When Jay Ward screened the first finished films—consisting of the first four "Rocky" episodes and the earliest samples of "Bullwinkle's Corner," "Fractured Fairy Tales," and "Peabody"—he was very disappointed. In fact, mortified would be more accurate. The pictures were riddled with technical errors: cel spots, camera shakes, poor poses, bad lip-synch, and often terrible color. Ward immediately ordered a slew of retakes.

Upon his return to Hollywood, Gerard Baldwin informed Ward that Val-Mar's work was improving a little each day, and that he had felt some satisfaction in seeing the studio taking shape. But overall, he warned Jay, there was still a hell of a way to go. It was fortunate indeed that the experienced Dun Roman agreed to take over. Bill Scott and Al Shean flew down with Roman, carrying a pile of Ward's instructions for the retakes. Just as they arrived in Mexico City, Bill Hurtz contracted severe hepatitis and arrived back in Los Angeles very ill.

Hurtz recalls, "I was somewhat conservatively inclined, so I decided to get some injections to be on the safe side for health reasons. Well, my doctor's father recommended a health clinic in Mexico to continue the shots once I got there. Within a few weeks I contracted a pretty severe bout of hepatitis—I spent a week in bed, then found I was still very ill, with a high fever. I was almost due to return to L.A. anyway. So Dun Roman effectively took my place, and he got me on a plane back to Los Angeles. It turns out I was pretty much bedridden for six months, and although limited in my activity I was able to do some work from bed with exposure sheets, storyboards, and timing until my health returned."

He was still well enough, however, to give Jay Ward a disturbingly detailed report:

1. Val-Mar Productions desperately needed a qualified office manager. "Chuy" Martinez was incapable of anticipating troubles ahead of time, repeatedly ending up in hot water when purchasing materials (running out of cels was a regular problem).

2. There was no one controlling the studio's schedule. Information about delivery dates and the number of shows actually in production was vague at best. Carlos Manriquez had kept some output

records, but was burdened with too many other duties, such as checking.

3. As for the directors, while Terrazas and a good animator named Lopez were okay on rough layout work, Hurtz felt that the particular U.S./Jay Ward style of humor was definitely not their strong point. More layout artists were needed to back up Harvey Siegel and Bob Schleh.

4. Before the arrival of background artist Frank Hursh, Val-Mar had hired a hopeless group of poorly prepared artists on a piecework basis. Apart from having no taste in color, they were paid so poorly that morale problems were hurting the show's prospects. Hursh badly needed a background assistant, while Bill Hurtz recommended that the color system be standardized to Hollywood methods.

5. The checking on the first seven pictures was irresponsible: someone rushed the films into ink and paint before the drawings were checked following animation. Ward ordered many retakes, and to the white-lipped horror of D-F-S, the first two shows went way over budget.

6. Hurtz recommended that the ink and paint department use the sturdier .005-sized cels, and that new paints be ordered from Hollywood. The lighting in the ink and paint room was atrocious—people were coloring and cleaning cels in near darkness. Something called dustproofing was also to be introduced!

7. Finally, the camera department was faulty: there were no air hoses to clean the cels, and this area, too, was extremely dusty. Air-conditioning should have been mandatory. Camera number two was improperly lined up, while camera number one had no electric platen. They had to use a hand platen, "which went out with the Civil War" according to Hurtz, and shadows on the cels were the result of uneven hand pressure. Even basic storage facilities were lacking. It appeared to Hurtz that Gordon Johnson had been well and truly "stabbed" by the camera suppliers.

8. Ernie Terrazas often didn't show up at work, and too often Valdez was unavailable to consult.

If this was a frightening report, Dun Roman was to fare even worse. From the moment he arrived at Val-Mar, he observed an endless string of production meetings eating up valuable studio time. And he fully agreed with Hurtz: there was a crying need to continue with the Hollywood-executed layouts. Strangely enough, he and fellow veteran Rudy Zamora clashed at first on the question of "quality" in the animation. (One glaringly atrocious example was a Natasha "walk" scene in the second "Rocky" episode, which frankly resembled the work of a kindergarten class.) Roman decided that Al Shean would handle all "Fractured Fairy Tales" storyboards (Shean's stuff was extremely inspiring to the Mexicans). Roman, meanwhile, would personally handle the "Peabody" storyboards.

Roman hated the place at first. It seemed to him that interoffice communication was nonexistent, and he felt that the work was being sabotaged by people childishly bucking each other at every turn. Then there were the logistical problems: Bud Gourley was late with scheduling details, Charlie Hotchkiss from the ad agency was being ineffectually picky (forever gauchely asking, "Why is quality so important?"), paint supplies ran low and were not reordered in time, the lab screwed up a second delivery to Jay Ward, and several animators didn't stick to their roster. In fact, the whole Mexican experience was playing like a bad cartoon with Captain "Wrongway" Peachfuzz in charge.

Overall, the main battles in 1959 concerned budget versus quality. One month into production, the agency naively ordered the amount of animation cut down so as to conform with the *Rocky* pilot, which Bill Hurtz had deemed "pretty crude, visually." Next, Johnson accused Ward of using more drawings than Hanna-Barbera. Jay stuck to his guns, patiently explaining that his cartoons had much more substance than H-B's: more scene changes, a much faster pace, more voice actors, and so on. Again, these were facts he had mentioned four months earlier. While initially frustrated, once the Mexican team was under way Ward had continuous ammunition to prove his points.

He also informed D-F-S that editing and film-development costs had been underbudgeted. As a temporary measure he suggested that the Mexicans work only on the "Rocky" episodes; the rest of the half hour could consist of filmed puppet songs and a redubbed foreign cartoon. Once the Mexican team was trained properly, the other cartoons could be reintroduced. Although his idea was not approved, a brain wave of Scott's was. This involved having Rocky and Bullwinkle introducing the show segments in "bridges" running fifteen seconds, including the first example of Bullwinkle's inept magic ("Watch me pull a rabbit outta my hat").

By September, the agency finally realized that Jay hadn't been kidding. The Mexican facility displayed none of the professionalism P.A.T. had promised. Indeed, the staff's glaring inexperience had already cost the project oodles. Gordon Johnson and the D-F-S executive committee set out to hire a permanent production supervisor. D-F-S had expected ten cartoons a week from Val-Mar, but veteran animator Bill Hurtz, who had been sent to Mexico to oversee, told Johnson that the most anyone could expect at this point was five segments weekly. They'd have to build from there.

A nervous Gordon Johnson, rapidly going over budget, decreed that *Rocky and His Friends* be edited and dubbed at Charlie Kimball's Mexican studio rather than in Hollywood. Ward's film editor, Skip Craig, explained, "Jay didn't want to do this. But we were running behind, and we couldn't get the retakes done in time. When the first show went to air we had to stick a title card in one "Peabody" scene which said, 'Sorry, we couldn't make it!' Also there were customs delays; they had to pay duty on 35-mm film stock, so I had to send 17.5-mm sync tape down there." While the tape didn't incur customs, it was an extra problem in cost and time.

It was also glaringly obvious that P.A.T. hadn't figured on the contingencies and expense of long-distance phone calls, equipment breakdowns, shipping costs, and so on. The airdate was postponed two weeks, to October 13, but Ward maintained there was still no way they'd be on air that quickly: the Mexican sound studio had no music tracks and sound effects beyond the first two half hours, and the first three shows required animation retakes galore.

By now Gordon Johnson was probably wishing to be deported to Pottsylvania. It wasn't the first time he had to go back to ABC and the cosponsor (Sweets Company of America, makers of Tootsie Roll) to request yet another delay. Jay Ward's timing was on the button: he accurately predicted the airdate would be November 19, 1959.

At a mid-October meeting with General Mills, D-F-S agreed that to save much-needed time, Ward and his team could edit and dub the completed third and fourth shows. They insisted, however, that all subsequent post-production be handled in Mexico.

The opening titles, animated in Los Angeles, pleased D-F-S. So to help speed up the Mexican output, Jay was given the nod to produce two "Fractured Fairy Tales" in Hollywood ("Beauty and the Beast" and "Rumpelstiltskin").

At this point, the ad agency made a snap decision which utterly infuriated Jay Ward. For what turned out to be three weeks, he and Bill Scott were ordered to put a hold on new script writing, effectively freezing all Hollywood activity, until Mexico "proved itself." If satisfied, the agency would then look to amend the basic agreement and increase the budget. Ward, who disliked being pushed around in this manner, was nobody's fool: to keep his Hollywood team busy during the layoff, he cannily requested permission to complete storyboards, sound recording, and editing of material already paid for. This consisted of eleven "Rocky" episodes, two "Fairy Tales," and fourteen "Peabodys." Meanwhile Jay had to content himself by experimenting with a laugh track for *Rocky and His Friends* (mercifully abandoned after the first four shows).

The wasteful freeze lasted over three weeks, occurring just as the Hollywood crew finished the animated show titles, including billboards for Tootsie Roll and General Mills. This work cost almost $25,000—over budget by $7,000, but still totaling only half the cost of equivalent animated commercials. The work was done on a job basis by Ted Parmelee, who produced and directed. It proved time-consuming, for Parmelee needed traveling time and extra artists. The "Peabody" opening, featuring the Cleopatra parade, proved particularly intricate and cost a lot in color work (ink and paint, and checking). But he did a great job.

Meanwhile, ABC started panicking about the scripts. Jay took an especially stubborn stand when it came to his writers. And in this area the D-F-S creatives were on Ward's side—they loved receiving the scripts each week. As for General Mills, they were fair, albeit conservative. They were mostly concerned with "too much inside showbiz stuff" and any mocking of the defense forces. ABC, regarded as the most lenient of the networks, was basically policy-conscious: they were worried about mentioning brand names and by voice impersonations of real people.

Back in Mexico, Roman grew ever more peeved at the combined Val-Mar/D-F-S modus operandi. He felt threatened if he ordered retakes, even though his position was supposedly paramount. And it should have been; as Hurtz emphasizes, "Dun Roman was excellent. His work went back to Disney's *Mother Goose Goes Hollywood* [1937], and he was a very funny man, besides being a good story man." Ostensibly, no work could proceed to ink and paint, finished background, or camera without Roman's okay, yet he had an inescapable feeling of being powerless. Too often the ad agency thrust a half-baked definition of "limited animation" at him, and he believed that he was being manipulated into accepting below-par quality. In essence, Roman had to "recheck" the checkers.

Adding to his troubles, the Mexican executives were constantly jockeying for position; these ego-tripping office politics slowed down the output even further. Roman requested more experienced people in Los Angeles to help with layout, suggesting artists he knew were up to the job, like Paul Julian (ex-UPA and Looney Tunes), Chuck McElmurray, Bernie Gruver, and Sam Clayberger. Further, he informed Ward that simply getting to see the rushes was difficult: the lab was miles away and Val-Mar had no moviola (an early editing-viewing machine), with the incredible consequence that the animators didn't get to see their own work. Roman longed for the professionalism of Hollywood. After a month in Mexico he was steaming when he learned that the lab still hadn't been given a shake-up regarding late delivery.

Roman was enough of a realist to see that a degree of racial tension was at work. From day one the locals had perceived the Americans to be resentful of Mexico, and, consciously or not, had expected a patronizing attitude from these expatriate artists. This paranoia, coupled with their annoyance at Ward's insistence on the retakes, hardly augured well for a smooth operation. On the plus side, Roman was pleased to observe a gradual softening of this hostile "gringo" mind-set.

Meanwhile the aggravatingly dumb mistakes made by the Mexican management team continued into 1960. Cels and paint, even drawing paper, kept running out; and, incredibly, when Bill Scott visited the studio in Roman's first week, a strike occurred when an executive questioned the cost of a new roll of toilet paper. To cap it all, Roman and Zamora not only had no desks, they had to share one chair.

These far from mild annoyances were coupled with even larger concerns. Minor earth tremors periodically knocked the cameras out of alignment, while disease proved a very real problem in the city. Usually one key man was absent each week because a family member was ill. Roman believed this was the intangible factor behind the late deliveries. To be brutal, the city was rife with disease at the time, a fact he sensed was concealed by both the local and American press.

By October, the third full show was ready for viewing. These episodes would be the last where Bullwinkle talked through his snout, Ward insisting he be given a proper mouth. Although the animation had improved slightly, Roman told Jay, "Some of it is still vile, only saved by Bill's scripts and the sound tracks." Overall, Dun Roman believed that most of the animators and in-betweeners were afraid to seek help from either himself, Rudy Zamora, or Ernie Terrazas because they would "lose face." Hurtz had already sensed this. Fortunately, this barrier slowly crumbled as the Americans made an extra effort to be gentle and friendly.

Despite all his woes, Roman cared enough about the show to make creative changes, even to model sheets from Hollywood. For instance, in the "Peabody" episode "Lucrezia Borgia," Lucrezia was changed from a beastly hag to a knockout, if chubby, lady. Bill Scott agreed with the alteration, characteristically adding, "The way women are drawn in our business today, one would assume all the artists are fags." With the broad accent that voice actress Dorothy Scott gave Lucrezia, Roman felt it would be better to make her a Gina Lollobrigida type. Meanwhile, he begged for a moviola and the on-air date was shifted back yet again.

After viewing more finished material, including the fifth "Rocky" episode, Jay Ward agreed that the work was improving. Unhappily, however, of the layout people to whom he spoke—topflight artists like Sam Weiss, Tony Rivera, Bob Dranko, Ted Parmelee, and Sam Clayberger—none wanted to go to Mexico. And Ward was still fuming about the three-week freeze on writing imposed by D-F-S. He told Johnson it was "a stupid decision." In fact, had it continued, Jay would have gladly quit the *Rocky* project in early November, just a fortnight away from the show's premiere.

Actually Jay could have been even pickier on retakes, but he only ordered them when a gag or story point could be better presented, or a technical fault was truly bad. Had he wanted, he could have demanded a hundred more: the third show had scratched cels, cel movement when characters walked, foreground movement, flares from the lights, shadows, unusually high amounts of paint changes, and terrible character models. Ward kept insisting on—and Val-Mar finally got—their long-awaited moviola.

Happily, news reached Ward that General Mills' reaction to show 1 was ecstatic. Now feeling more confident, he backed Dun Roman all the way. The show contract plainly stipulated that Ward and Scott had final say on quality control. Agency bigwigs Hotchkiss and Johnson fought this tooth and nail, but Jay Ward was tough. Artistically speaking, both his TV show and his reputation were at stake. He couldn't stand the amateurish-looking character poses, so in a blunt note to D-F-S he and Al Shean defined limited

Style guide from *Rocky and His Friends* for early merchandising use. *Courtesy of Universal Studios Publishing Rights, a Division of Universal Studios Licensing, Inc.*

animation as "cycle animation that was to be *well drafted*." Ward and Scott also requested many extra head and body movements in future cartoons, Bill Scott despising "the constant sight of two heads conversing, otherwise known as Hanna-Barbera palsy." As Jay explained, "If limited animation is well made it will 'read' funny instantly to the audience."

At this time Jim Hiltz, Gerry Ray, and Pete Burness were handling the

Hollywood predirection. The ad agency managed to get more American artists to relocate, sending Joe Montell for layout assistance. Montell had worked on backgrounds for MGM theatrical cartoons with the legendary Tex Avery.

General Mills' response to show 2 was even more enthusiastic. And finally, after six agonizing months, a compromise was reached: the budget would be substantially increased. As a trade-off, Ward had to grudgingly bow to ad agency "financial" pressure by allowing all shows from the fifth one to be edited and dubbed in Mexico. The sound quality would nose-dive from Skip Craig's excellent standard to a year of muddy distortion on the Mexican elements, with truly ludicrous sound effects tossed in willy-nilly. Meanwhile, on November 11, Gordon Johnson had lifted the Hollywood production freeze. The final on-air date was set: *Rocky and His Friends* would debut on November 19, 1959.

8

Squirrel on the Tube, or Watts Gnu with You?

Despite the imminent premiere of *Rocky,* Jay Ward found the deal with General Mills to be pretty sad, particularly when additional intelligence indicated Hanna-Barbera was profiting handsomely. Kellogg's paid about $50,000 for each *Huckleberry Hound* and *Quickdraw McGraw* show over two years, with a firm guarantee of four showings. Being in color, the syndication repeats were cream, along with merchandising and foreign sales. Jay's plans were competitive with Hanna-Barbera's, but while H-B churned forth series after series, Ward's many ideas seemed to go nowhere. In fairness it should be noted that H-B had the clout of Columbia Pictures behind them, while Ward remained a tiny independent.

Still, his rival's early success spurred Jay to attempt expansion. Len Key began work on a prospectus for their new corporation, Jay Ward Films. Ward geared up for a new puppet show and various other projects. He planned 52 episodes each for a second half-hour cartoon show, a half-hour satirical puppet series called *The Watts Gnu Show* (for which a pilot was filmed), the juvenile puppet show *Carrots and the King,* and a half-hour series showcasing international animation which Ward's team would redub in English. Also on the drawing board was a daily five-minute strip cartoon of 260 episodes, and a feature-length cartoon film, *The World of Winnie the Pooh.* By Christmas 1959, there was even talk of a movie-length adaptation of *Mad* magazine for Paramount. The profit potential was calculated to be around $30 million with further ideas down the track. Indeed, one of them, *The Watts Gnu Show,* almost sold.

A comedy revue with puppets, *Watts Gnu* was the show Jay Ward tried in vain to sell for three years. The lead character was a gnu, and his voice was a light, happy one very close to Bill Scott's natural sound. Every time Watts came to a word that began with the letter *n* he added a hard *g* sound at the beginning—such as his closing song, "G-never, G-never Be G-nasty to a Gnu." Skip Craig noted, "The puppets were almost life-size, and boy, they were ugly! Really gruesome. Except for the lead character, Watts. He was kind of cute."

But Ward's bad timing struck again. Had he waited, say, fifteen years, the market would have been just right for puppets: certainly Jim Henson's *Muppet Show* proved a gigantic success. In 1959, however, puppets were simply considered out. Jay's pilot film had several close calls at being sold, but it was just not meant to be.

With production on *Rocky and His Friends* under way, Ward was keen to pursue his comedy puppet show, and he began developing it in mid-1959. The production-cost factor was considerably lower than in animation: the staff would consist of about fifteen people (where animation staff levels were one hundred or so), and the financing was tiny by comparison—cartoons took five months from inception to delivery, while puppets would take just two months at one-sixth the budget. The then-prevailing industry wisdom was that puppets were unsalable, which to Ward was pure balderdash. As long as the show was funny, he believed, it would sell. He and Bill Scott conceived the series as a comedy-variety show with songs and sketches. In Jay's words, "It soon became a kind of *Steve Allen Show* with puppets, with bits of old newsreel footage for blackout gags. Bill dubbed the show 'Hellzapuppets'!"

By August 1959 the songs were ready, a script was written, sets were being designed, and the puppets were constructed. Ward asked Leonard Key to start selling the show, convincing him it would be great. It was filmed in early October. When Key saw the finished product he absolutely loved it, feeling the term "puppet show" was a misnomer; it was, he felt, comedy pure and simple, and he began enthusiastically pushing it to the ad folk. The N. W. Ayer agency flipped over it, and D-F-S told Bob Baldwin (Ward's West Coast salesman) that it was "great, but we don't want to invest beyond *Rocky* right now."

Unfortunately, Ward and Key struck out. It was generally felt that the show was too sophisticated, new and different, and in fact it received mostly adverse comments like "Neither fish nor fowl" and "How can you sustain this type of material week after week?"

As for the show itself, Chris Hayward and George Atkins wrote a script jam-packed with skits. Indeed, for a half hour it now comes across as too "busy." Unfortunately, it lacked the charm of *Time for Beany*, which had featured highly likable characters. Watts Gnu was a friendly enough personality, but was more of an MC who joined in some of the sketches rather than being someone that kids could relate to.

Compounding this, the show played a little too satirical. *Beany* had tempered its adult barbs with a fun story line and atmosphere. The *Watts Gnu* jabs seemed to be an excuse to simply parody television, which would work nicely today when everyone is media-savvy and saturated with the medium. Back then, however, it was too soon; people were still happily entranced by the novelty of TV sets in their living rooms. Finally, a gnu may simply have been too oddball a species for a lead character.

Within the *Watts Gnu* pilot, however, there were some entertaining items on display. The songs and special material by Leon Pober and Forman Brown were excellent. Bill Scott and Paul Frees did a Peter Lorre–Boris Karloff duet, lamenting the newer wave of late-fifties horror film, like *The Blob*. Frees also played a Colonel Blimp type who, while cooking in a cannibal stew pot, sang "Never Raise Your Boy to Be an Explorer." There was a cowboy takeoff called "Half Shot at Sunrise," a *What's My Line?* parody, and a slushy romantic ballad featuring a Jeanette MacDonald–Nelson Eddy couple. Their operatic love duet was punctuated with funny muttered asides about how they couldn't stand each other.

Chris Hayward recalls, "*Watts Gnu* was shot on a big sound stage over three days with really great sets—very expensive, but it just lacked that little something." It was directed by Alan Lee for Consul Films. The pilot was shot in color, and described in the sales brochure as "containing original music and live-action camera techniques, enhancing comedy which is at once satire, slapstick and ridiculous."

Jay Ward didn't want to share ownership of the show, so the only firm offer, from ABC-TV and Dan Melnick (a future executive on *Get Smart*), fell through at the eleventh hour. With *Rocky* soon to air and new cartoon ideas in the pipeline, Ward put *The Watts Gnu Show* on hold for what he thought would be one season, but it was never to achieve series status. Alas, Jay didn't get to do his long-cherished puppet show.

How TV Cartoons Were Sold in the Late 1950s

By 1958–59, the demand for cartoon product on TV was inexhaustible: most of the major movie studios weren't producing theatrical cartoons anymore, and their backlogs—long since sold to television—were almost depleted. Agencies and sponsors now turned to independent producers for their animation needs; the profit potential in cartoons had proven spectacular in a medium barely a decade old.

Shows like *The Mighty Mouse Playhouse, The Gumby Show, Tom Terrific,* and of course *Crusader Rabbit* (both the new color ones by Shull Bonsall, and Jay and Alex's older ones, which were still in distribution) bore out these money-spinning statistics. Hanna-Barbera's instant success with *Ruff and Reddy* and *Huckleberry Hound* had solidified the credibility of made-for-TV cartoons.

It hadn't taken long to see that while the life expectancy of a live-action series was generally five to seven years, the average cartoon could foreseeably be earning money from each succeeding generation: their audience was constant, replenishing itself with a brand-new group of young viewers every two to three years. Bugs Bunny, after all, had entertained this generation of sponsors when they were in knee pants; the sassy rabbit, indomitable as ever, was now entertaining their children and grandchildren. By the late 1950s some animated TV shows had made financial history with the salivating accounts people, who saw the demand for new cartoons getting stronger with each season. TV had proved to be truly insatiable!

As for actually getting a show on the tube, here's how the scene worked when Jay Ward was pitching his *Rocky* concept. After completion of a pilot film, the company's sales staff went to work via advertising, notices in trade journals, and contact with network and agency people. The successful result of all this legwork meant a national sponsor and a network showing of the proposed series (the early radio tradition of sponsorship was adopted by TV from the start—it began fading out in the late sixties).

At this time there were several types of arrangements made in the sale and financing of films for TV. A network could buy a property from a producer and then seek a sponsor. More often (and the way that *Rocky* was sold), a sponsor who had previously contracted for network airtime would buy a property upon advice from its advertising agency. Still another method was syndication, in which the network wasn't involved; instead, the property was sold for distribution in various market areas through independent TV stations.

The next step was obtaining the working capital needed to kick-start production of the show. Arrangements were often made with the purchaser to advance funds. Also, banks or other private sources could advance these funds by discounting of the sales contract—or a share in the profits from the show. Those people and institutions who financed television shows soon discovered that TV film properties had one very attractive feature: they enjoyed a long period of earning power simply by being shown over and over (and with cartoons, research showed that children liked to watch reruns time and again).

Thus, cartoons were considered a safe bet. They had a life span of generations, and it was expected that production costs would be recovered after one run, while profit margins on the reruns would be high. To add cream on top, revenues from foreign sales and licensing rights to the characters were there for the taking.

Character licensing, in particular, interested Jay Ward and Peter Piech. They knew the spectacular revenues to be gained from the subsidiary rights to cartoons and puppet shows. Previous success stories in the arena of licensing and merchandising TV properties included *Howdy Doody, The Mickey Mouse Club,* and *Popeye.* If just one character from *Rocky and His Friends* connected well, the earnings could conceivably be in seven figures.

• • •

Rocky was due to premiere when Len Key, by now Ward's full-time East Coast contact, called Gordon Johnson. They kissed and made up over Key's ousting from P.A.T. Len's brother Ted always felt that Johnson "loved playing top dog, and threw his weight around a bit too much." Len wasn't too shocked to learn that Roger Carlin had been bounced from P.A.T. In fact Carlin had been paid out. He had continually alienated Ward and Scott, made false promises in Mexico, and in recent weeks had been making deals all over town, misusing P.A.T.'s name. Soon after being given the heave-ho, the hapless Carlin suffered a fatal heart attack. (His last credit was as executive producer of *The Mighty Hercules* cartoons for Oriolo Productions.)

Rocky and Bullwinkle's most famous shtick—pulling the rabbit outta the hat. *Courtesy of Universal Studios Publishing Rights, a Division of Universal Studios Licensing, Inc.*

Peter Piech said, "Carlin had a kind of sad life. He certainly made some errors but I liked that boy, and I'll always be grateful to him for introducing me to *Rocky the Flying Squirrel*."

Ward viewed the fifth complete show, the first to be dubbed in Mexico. As he'd feared, the sound quality was poor; there was much distortion and no equalization, and the voices were muffled. Most noticeable were badly judged sound effects which often drowned out the dialogue, a problem that continued for three years. To add to his misery, there were ongoing visual problems with embarrassing character poses, thousands of spots and scratches on the cels, shoddy camera work, and increasing evidence that the language barrier at Val-Mar resulted in poor mouth-sync and a lack of understanding of the jokes.

But technical problems notwithstanding, at long last on Thursday, November 19, 1959, *Rocky and His Friends* premiered, in a late-afternoon lineup which included reruns of *Rin Tin Tin* and *My Friend Flicka*. *Rocky* even benefited from a strong lead-in show, *American Bandstand*, which was highly popular. The audience who tuned in that first broadcast saw something entirely different in TV cartoons.

It began at the Slick Observatory: "An international group of scientists, eggheads, and double-domes" peered through a giant new telescope and were shocked to see a moose and squirrel returning from the moon. Before the next three minutes were up we'd learned that these two Minnesota residents had tried to bake a quick-rising cake, the ingredients of which blew them and their stove to this lunar outpost. During this incredibly frantic cartoon; politicians were ridiculed, the media were lampooned, and cold war spies were glimpsed.

Thus from the earliest broadcast it was apparent that *Rocky*'s story lines were densely packed, especially when compared with the simplistic plots seen in other cartoons shows of the era. The opening story is the most remembered, and the most repeated. At forty episodes it's also the longest. This epic tale, concerning the hunt for Mooseberry rocket-fuel formula, is an adventure steeped in satire and themed around the then-topical U.S.-Soviet space race. The many atmospheric set pieces include the moon sighting, Rocky and Bullwinkle working for the government, Rocky's encounter with the air force, Boris loose in the Minnesota woods, the moon men onstage in Las Vegas, a crazy canoe trip down the Potomac ("Stroke!" "Bail!"), a surreal ocean liner voyage, a stopover on tiny Bloney Island, the scary dictatorship of Pottsylvania, scaling the Grimalaya Mountains, encountering the "Abominomibububble Snowman," the return to Washington, and the moon mens' failed attempt to become U.S. citizens.

The serialized story set the tone for the rest of the long-running series, introducing that master of disguise Boris Badenov, his equally evil cohorts Natasha Fatale and Fearless Leader, their menacing boss Mr. Big, mild-mannered moon men Cloyd and Gidney, and dizzy Captain Peter "Wrongway" Peachfuzz. If at times it seemed like the story was being chopped and changed as it went along, well, it was! Bill Scott remembered pinning to his desk a note which read, "Don't forget the plot!"

And the reaction? Industry bible *Variety* critiqued *Rocky and His Friends*, and by the high standards of that famous showbiz journal, the following can be considered a rave review:

> Rocky and His Friends *are the kind of cartoon characters that should win a place in the heart of the moppet audience and a sigh of relief from parents. The approach to kid humor is intelligent; maybe not as subtle as*

Huckleberry Hound, *but a thankful departure from the violent slapstick that makes up the bulk of tele cartoon fare.*

Jay Ward and Gordon Johnson looked set for a long relationship and soon got used to each other's peccadilloes. Bill Hurtz described Johnson as "a typical harried Madison Avenue type, very punctual and businesslike," while Key observed that Johnson and Ward, although they liked and respected each other, marched to totally different drums. "There were constant year-in-year-out gripes from Gordon. It was always, 'Well sure, the work is good, but what's the point unless it comes within budget,' or 'All this artistic control is a waste of time; hell, General Mills is happy—that should be enough!' " Hardly a meeting of the minds.

9

Starring That Supersonic Speedster, or Time for That Dancin' Fool, Bullwinkle

"Rocky and Bullwinkle" was the Jay Ward super cartoon. As Ward himself acknowledged, "It's by far our biggest hit and our longest-running on television." The most famous characters in the Ward Productions canon, Rocky and Bullwinkle are, today, animation legends occupying, along with Bugs Bunny, Donald Duck, and Popeye, places on the top rung of cartoon superstars. It took our heroes longer than the others because for many years it was hard to find the moose and squirrel, apart from night-owl or early-to-rise syndication spots. But thanks to the proliferation of cable and satellite TV services and the video revolution, our boys—like a fine wine aging with time—are now respected and loved by an ever-growing legion of cartoon buffs worldwide. And well they should be: their adventures are the most brilliantly written TV cartoons of them all. There is a timeless quality to their gag-filled serials, transcending those very elements within the cartoons which are, in fact, dated by recent history—including events like the moon landing, the end of the cold war, the effective dismantling of Communism, and the decreased role of old-style espionage agents (to the abiding chagrin of one Boris Badenov).

One of the most intriguing aspects of the "Rocky and Bullwinkle" cartoons is that much of the satire remains relevant to the present generation, who are weaned on an irreverence that their parents didn't experience. The media-literate kids of today, with so much television available, are exposed to constant cynicism and, after Watergate, a diminished respect for public institutions. Hence the rise of modern cartoon stars like Bart Simpson and Beavis and Butt-head.

But let this audience watch a few of the old "Rocky and Bullwinkle" cartoons and it soon becomes obvious that nothing is new under the sun: the moose and squirrel were just as "in your face" as today's TV rebels. The military and the government, two pet targets of the "Rocky and Bullwinkle" scripts, were far less likely to be lampooned when these cartoons first went to air, before JFK and Vietnam. Rewatching the shows now, in a vastly changed world, they appear light-years ahead of their time.

In fact, bright kids about to enter the twenty-first century may well find *Bullwinkle* sociologically fascinating, akin to old issues of *Mad* magazine. Of course today's problems—mass unemployment, homelessness, urban poverty, overpopulation—don't get a satirical look-in on *The Bullwinkle Show*. Forty years ago there were different priorities: the big concerns back then were paranoia about Communism, the ever-present threat of nuclear attack, and UFOs, all of which are addressed wittily in the Jay Ward cartoons.

But far more than the comedy content, it's the tone of "Rocky and Bullwinkle" which today's fans embrace. An aura of skeptical uncertainty, endemic in a world economy burdened with trillion-dollar debt and downsizing, hangs over the new millennium, a feeling similar to the general malaise felt during the Great Depression. It's often been noted that in tough times, those in need of an escape turn to the release offered by comedy for a welcome wry laugh at shared misfortune. In particular, comedy with an edge, containing jokes that don't just play safe but tell a few home truths. The moose and squirrel strike that chord with today's audience: despite dated references to Eastern Bloc dictatorships and mainframe computers, the cartoons overflow with great jokes and puncturing satire. It was the first show in the history of TV animation to blatantly—healthily—thumb its nose at the establishment. In today's parlance, it had "attitude."

Then too, besides being charming and tightly written, the stories featured truly memorable characters blessed with that intangible quality which guarantees immortality: we liked them. Rocky was the likable hero, Bullwinkle the likable smart goof, and the friendship they shared was comfortable and believable. We even cared about them, something that can't be said for many other TV cartoon characters. Boris and Natasha, their perennial foes, were

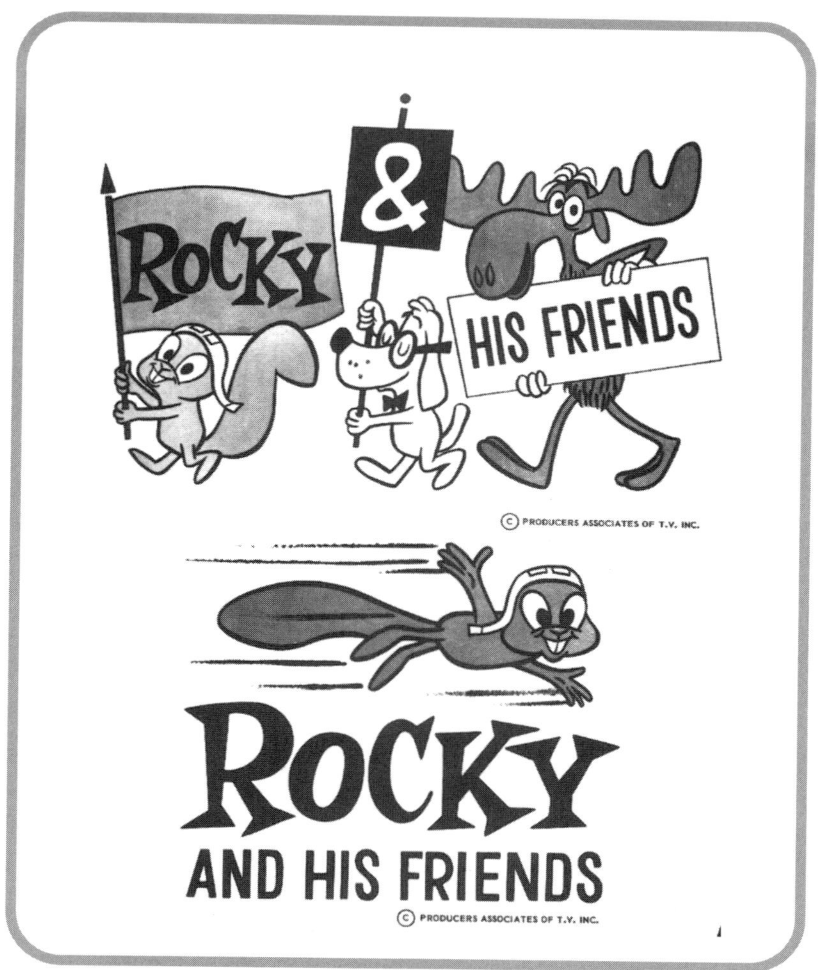

Publicity art for *Rocky and His Friends*. *Courtesy of Universal Studios Publishing Rights, a Division of Universal Studios Licensing, Inc.*

more simply out-and-out villains—funny, stock baddies—yet they still held our interest. The semiregulars, like Captain Peachfuzz and moon men Cloyd and Gidney, and even the recurring bit players Chauncey and Edgar, were good comedy characters. Some were more well-rounded than others, but what made them all come to hilarious life was the writing talent of chief scribe and coproducer Bill Scott.

Scott's classy cartoon scripts were tempered by his innate taste. While some comedy writers are occasionally guilty of overstepping into cruelty or cheap shots, Bill Scott made his satiric points with great subtlety, coupling this talent with a keen understanding of dynamics: change of scene, change of tempo, funny incidental characters, occasional slapstick and reliable old low comedy. And always with that uncanny knack of writing a show which pleased all age groups.

As with *Crusader Rabbit*, Jay Ward's landmark cartoon series (from which, Scott maintained, he learned all his writing tricks), the "Rocky and Bullwinkle" stories were presented as chapter-plays, like the blood-and-thunder movie serials of yore. They would often ramble on through all manner of side stops and convoluted plot twists to the eventual righting of wrong by the two befuddled heroes. The cliffhanger episodes always ended with punned alternate titles. Scott was a master at these, admitting, "I love puns, wordplay—the worse the better. If people groan, that's sensational." In one segment, for instance, as a giant snowball hurtles downhill toward our heroes, narrator Bill Conrad somberly intones, "Don't miss our next episode, 'Avalanche Is Better Than None,' or 'Snow's Your Old Man.' "

Thirty-five years on, the series still works its magic. Like the zanily complex story lines, the lead characters have stood the test of time: Rocky the Flying Squirrel and his pal Bullwinkle J. Moose are now cartoon immortals. Not bad for critters from a modest little shack in Frostbite Falls, Minnesota. Although the action in most of their stories began in this town, the moose and squirrel were seasoned globetrotters, constantly off on one adventure after another. In fact, in one episode Bullwinkle brings up this very point, asking, "Say, Rock—does anybody ever wonder where we get all the money to gallivant around the world like we do?"

Rocky was a simple, likable hero. Although equipped with all the typical Boy Scout virtues, he was never cloying or sweet. Hokey smoke, no! Rocky was clever, optimistic, and often slightly naive ("That voice—where have I heard that voice before?"). Adorned in his aviator's helmet, which was removed in only a couple of episodes, Rocky was the epitome of a resourceful hero, using his flying prowess to advantage in various chapters and always highly protective of the mighty moose. For the youngest viewers, of course, Rocket J. Squirrel was the one they could relate to. And because the show was self-reflexive, Rocky was always completely aware of his role: "Have you forgotten, Bullwinkle—we're TV heroes!" Writer George Atkins points out that the squirrel was the most generous star in TV history, graciously letting the moose become the headliner when they changed networks, and never batting a competitive eyelid.

Bullwinkle J. Moose is today regarded as the greatest TV animation star of them all. The "smart goof," as Bill Scott called him, was, quite simply, a very funny character: the sidekick to the nominal hero who finally became the real star of the proceedings. The upright moose often displayed his mighty muscle-power, but just as often proved how much he really needed Rocky ("I can't swim!"). Bullwinkle even occasionally got the air of the playboy about him: when Boris was disguised as a female moose, our hero flirted outrageously ("Well, howde-do-do-do!"). And he was the plot pivot time after time—baking a fudge cake from his grandma Moose's recipe, inheriting Uncle Dewlap's mine, stepping on the Rue Britannia inscription, receiving a college football scholarship, going to Hollywood to be a star, taking a shirt to a Shanghai laundry, offering to go fishing for a whale, and attending a Missouri convention where, thanks to a certain piece of head wear, he (temporarily) became the smartest moose in the world.

And Bullwinkle was always the source of the most hilarious wordplay. He'd constantly wisecrack in the face of danger, a trait which Bob Hope exhibited in his classic old films (Bill Scott acknowledged these as one of his own early comic influences). For instance, when the feared Mister Big points a gun at our heroes and threatens, "Gentlemen—I'm afraid your hour has come!" Bullwinkle pointlessly asks, "Is that standard time or daylight saving?" And the moose's personal logic seemed to come straight out of Gracie Allen. When the boys are locked in a car being driven by a remote-controlled mannequin, Rocky suddenly realizes: "He's a dummy!" To which Bullwinkle admonishes, "Please, Rocky—you're speaking of our host." The squirrel doesn't give up: "No, Bullwinkle, he really *is* a dummy! You know what that means?" Finally grasping the situation, the moose answers profoundly, "Yeah—he must have cheated on his driver's test!"

Then of course there were our favorite double-dyed villains. That master of disguise Boris Badenov and his slinky Slavic "girl-fiend" Natasha Fatale were prime candidates for top place in the baddies hall of shame. Bill Scott even based their looks on the husband and wife in the *Addams Family* magazine cartoons. Boris was completely devoted to his vocation of villainy, and was the world's most avid fan of all that's downright rotten. Yet he would prove to be the champion underachiever within his chosen profession. His totally inept ways kept him from ever winning, as the moose and squirrel lucked out again and again. But Boris was nothing if not persistent. A graduate of USC (the Ukrainian Safeceracking College), Boris would diligently

Boris Badenov—a true master of disguise. *Courtesy of Universal Studios Publishing Rights, a Division of Universal Studios Licensing, Inc.*

consult his *Uncle Vanya's Fireside Crookbook* to no avail. When foiled, Boris would shout "Raskolnikov!" in tribute to the murderer-cum-hero of Dostoyevsky's novel *Crime and Punishment*.

This was the type of joke revered by Bullwinkle's more intellectual viewers, who had already chuckled over the name Boris Badenov, a punning variation on the protagonist of Mussorgsky's opera *Boris Godenov*. His Pottsylvanian dialect was supplied by Paul Frees; it was based on Balkan character actor Akim Tamiroff with a dash of Yiddish inspired by the Mad Russian, a comic character heard years before on Eddie Cantor's radio show. Dressed in black, with dead-white skin to offset his somber fashion sense, Boris was a great cartoon character—the perennial loser, related by fate to the hapless Wile E. Coyote of Chuck Jones's *Road Runner* series.

His partner in crime was the lovely Natasha, a slender Mata Hari type who towered over Boris. Sharing his white complexion, she at least wore eye shadow and a purple skirt (red in the final season). She also shared Boris's ability at aliases and disguises. Her pet name for Boris and others was the Tallulah Bankhead-esque appellation "dollink." Sometimes it seemed as though Natasha could have been a saint, had the criminal lifestyle not seduced her. For Boris was hardly a gallant companion: when they shared a canoe she did all the rowing ("Stroke! Stroke! Stroke!"), and she was continually being yelled at—"Sharrup your mouth"—by the chauvinistic schnook. June Foray supplied Ms. Fatale with a delightful Mittel European tone, making her sound like the Greta Garbo of cartoon land.

Boris and Natasha appeared as the boys' archnemeses in all but four of the twenty-eight adventures. Boris himself was in one of those other four stories ("Buried Treasure"), uncharacteristically labeling himself Baby Face Braunschweiger and leading a group of three tough hoods called "the Light Fingered Five Minus Two." Apparently Boris and Natasha must have agreed to some sort of trial separation. Although, come to think of it, it was never mentioned that they were married!

The three stories which didn't feature the Pottsylvanian no-goodniks were written by Chris Hayward and Lloyd Turner: these were "The Three Mooseketeers," "Mucho Loma," and "The Ruby Yacht," adventures which took Rocky and Bullwinkle to France, Mexico, and Pakistan, respectively. Bill Scott observed, "Chris Hayward loved exotic foreign locales—cloak-and-dagger stuff." But Boris and Natasha certainly appeared in some of Hayward and Turner's work: it was one of their stories which took our heroes to Shanghai, where the rotten spies were holed up.

Ward and Scott always went to great lengths to ensure that Boris and Natasha were perceived as Pottsylvanian spies, not Russian. Peter Piech half-jokingly said, "We perpetuated the cold war! When the show went on in Japan, two or three weeks later the Soviet cultural attaché put it in a really bitter way to the Japanese Foreign Office that this TV show was 'persona non grata,' and it was taken off the air by the Japanese network. It didn't return for about six months; so yes, it did irritate the Russians a bit."

Bill Scott loved recounting the time ex-UPA artist Meyer Schaefer vacationed in Russia: "Meyer was a very nice guy who worked for us, and later went into the animation-supply business. Anyway, he goes to Russia and he gets interviewed at one point by a customs official who asks him what kind of profession he's in. 'I'm an artist,' says Meyer. 'I work in animation.' 'Oh,' says the Russian, 'for Walt Disney?' 'No,' says Meyer, 'I work for Jay Ward.' 'Jay Ward?' 'Yes, Jay Ward does *The Bullwinkle Show*.' Long pause, then the Russian says, 'This is TV show that has Russian spy?' And poor Meyer was left sputtering and perspiring as this man walked off with his passport and didn't come back for quite a while. Meyer was thinking, 'This is it! I'm going to end up on the Gulag!' But he finally got his passport back."

Two of Scott's most well-remembered characters made it into just three adventures. These were the moon men, Gidney and Gloyd. Scott explained,

"Jay and I figured that the names we would most hate to have been born with were Sidney and Floyd, and so the spelling was changed and we had names for our moon men." They appeared in the first story and were integral to it, then returned in the fourth story, "The Monstrous Mechanical Moon-Mice." Scott recalled, "I only reintroduced them for this story, because I was interested in whether I could revive what were, after all, pretty one-dimensional characters; the same thing with Mr. Big. None of them could have been milked time and time again." The Scrooch-Gun-toting lunar-tics made one final bid for cartoon stardom in the last five chapters of the "Kirward Derby" plot, mainly because the sponsor and ad agency remembered them, and requested their revival on NBC prime time to see if they had merchandising potential.

The Peter Lorre-ish Mr. Big was too minuscule to really frighten us. Bill Scott recalled, "I'd done all I wanted with Mr. Big: in the end, he didn't really work and he bored me." A threatened presence in the first story, he was seen only in "Upsidaisium" and "Moon-Mice." Scott's second master villain, however, was Fearless Leader, top dog in Pottsylvania's pecking order and a superb bad guy. This hawk-faced nasty with the unsightly Teutonic dueling scar appeared in only seven stories. Originally meant to be named Central Control, Fearless Leader was a memorable heavy, evoking quakes of terror in his two bumbling underlings.

The likable, totally befuddled Captain Peter "Wrongway" Peachfuzz appeared in only 8 of the plots. Even Chauncey and Edgar, Scott's incredibly taciturn townsfolk, only appear by name in 22 single episodes out of 326. But every cultist and fan remembers, "Now there's somethin' you don't see every day . . . ," and it seems like they made many more appearances than is the case. (Actually they did reappear, six times on *Hoppity Hooper* and once in a "Super Chicken.") These colorful sideline characters are etched into the minds of Bullwinkle fans, who, collectively, tend to think that the moon men, Peachfuzz, and others were in almost every episode.

Modestly analyzing his comedy, Scott said, "The sophistication of the humor, if such it be, is that Jay and I do things that we think are funny." Like other comedy writers who leaned to the satirical (such as Stan Freberg and Tom Lehrer), Scott despised the misuse of positions of power. His "Rocky and Bullwinkle" stories are rich in bumbling or corrupt generals, mayors, bank presidents, politicians, governors, network executives, totalitarian power brokers, and individuals like Pericles Parnassus, a takeoff on the megarich Aristotle Onassis. With the four years he'd spent at John Sutherland Productions fresh in Scott's memory, many "Rocky and Bullwinkle" stories feature boardroom meetings similar to the yes-men style of Stan Freberg's wickedly biting Capitol recording *Green Chritma*. From Scott we learned about power plays in the corporate corridors of the World Economic Council, the Frostbite Falls Foistboinder Company, and the World Shipping Office, at the University of Wossamotta, and in party meetings in Pottsylvania such as the one which launched a car called "The Assassin–8."

Scott's love of puns, and his sheer mastery of when to let one fly, is evident in place names like the mountain called Whyntchataka Peak, and Boris's many aliases, such as the removalist Van N. Storridge. Wordplay was always lurking, often noticeable in the byplay between the offstage narrator and the on-camera characters. Scott recalled, "That stuff used to crack me up when I was younger—in the Bob Hope and Bing Crosby *Road* pictures, where they'd talk to the camera, and make gags about being in a movie." Typical examples occur in the cliffhanger climaxes; take episode 92, in which the narrator breathlessly asks, "Will Bullwinkle be able to extricate himself?" and the moose yells back, "I will as soon as I get loose!"

Scott's grasp of political satire seemed ahead of its time, especially for a TV cartoon. When Rocky is stuck on a speeding missile, a general yells, "That squirrel is headed straight for Washington!" Suddenly concerned, Bullwinkle replies, "Do you really think he can carry the farm vote?" And the following example is a great illustration of the oft-repeated statement that these cartoons could be appreciated on different levels each time a fan returned to them, slightly older with each viewing. It's an exposé of Pottsylvanian life from the thirtieth "Rocky and Bullwinkle" episode:

Narrator: Pottsylvania was a country composed entirely of spies. Even as schoolchildren, Pottsylvanians were taught only the ABC's—assassination, bomb throwing, and conspiracy—with an occasional course in advanced sneaking and prowling.
Schoolmaster: Congratulations, Feodor. You graduated magna cum louse!
Narrator: And every conversation had at least two meanings.
Gottwold: Hello, Vanya.
Narrator: Translation: We're going to blow up city hall tonight.
Vanya: Hello, Gottwold—how's the boy?
Narrator: Translation: Sounds like fun—who'll be inside?

Gottwold: Just fine thanks.
Narrator: Translation: Who cares?
Vanya: Well, see you later, Gottwold.
Narrator: Translation: The party starts at seven, bring your own bomb.
Gottwold: Bye-bye, Vanya.
Narrator: Translation: Bye-bye, Vanya.
(we see Vanya blown sky-high.)

The cartoon catchphrases created by Bill Scott are now part of the vocabulary of an entire generation and their offspring: expressions like "Hokey smoke" (Rocky's catchall exclamation); "Mighty moose muscle"; "That voice, where have I heard that voice before?"; "Say the name"; "Sharrup your mouth!"; and "You serrit, kiddo!" Like all comedy writers, Scott frequently used whatever came into his head or was close at hand; the young audience had no idea that the moniker Captain Peter Peachfuzz was actually based on the name of the show's executive producer, Peter Piech, or that the good captain's ship, the SS *Andalusia,* was named for the Havenhust Drive apartment block where Jay Ward lived, the Andalusia Arms. These, however, weren't intended as smug in-jokes, simply convenient devices.

As well, Scott had a singular quirk of creating oddball W. C. Fieldsian expressions for the moose to use as expletives: "Aw, crabapples," "Oh, butter balls," "Shuckin's and cobs." And he displayed a wonderful ability to parody melodramatic conventions in vaudevillian style—one character would discover something momentous and ask, "You mean . . . ?" and another character would immediately jump in on this gravid moment with, "Yes!" Sometimes the narrator floridly announced Boris as "That crumb of crumbs," or "That schlemiel's schlemiel," or even "That snake in the grass—that perfidious scoundrel," to any of which Boris would musically yell, "Say the name!"

In one of the later episodes (255), the show's comedy style, indeed the show itself, is well and truly razzed, as this self-referential exchange demonstrates:

Rocky: You know, what we need is a good hiccups doctor.
Natasha: Boris, you heard?
Boris: I heard.
Natasha: Dollink, that's your cue! You're supposed to show up disguised as hiccups doctor.

Boris: Natasha, I can't do it!

Natrasha: Boris, why not?

Boris: This time they're sure to recognize me!

Natasha: They never have.

Boris: Seventy-nine disguises I used on those two—not one did they ever see through.

Natasha: So?

Boris: The law of averages is turning against me.

Natasha: It wouldn't dare! Boris—you're forgetting article six of *The Villain's Handbook*.

Boris: Article six?

Natasha: Yes—look here.

Boris: "There is nobody so stupid as the hero of a TV cartoon show." Well, maybe you're right—come on.

Rocky: As I was saying, what we need—

Boris: (*interrupting*) Allow me to introducing myself.

Rocky: Who are you?

Boris: I'm the ship's medical officer.

Bullwinkle: Ship's doc?

Boris: (*cringing at the pun*) Of course they do!

Rocky: That voice, where have I heard that voice?

Natasha: See, dollink?

Boris: I see it but I don't believe it!

The structure of the "Rocky and Bullwinkle" episodes was based on Alex Anderson's modus operandi for the first *Crusader Rabbit* cartoons a decade earlier. It consisted of a narrator imparting an urgent sense of adventure fraught with peril, counterpointed with puns and gags. Bill Scott always acknowledged, "Alex was the best. My God, he was a great writer. He was the master animation writer; I learned everything about cartoon serials from his work."

Scott further clarified the "Rocky and Bullwinkle" house style in a 1971 letter: "The basic format—a continued story told in many episodes, with strong emphasis on dialogue and plot rather than on sight gags and animation—was originally used by Alex and Jay on *Crusader Rabbit*. Rather than starting, as Disney did, with the concept of animation as a kind of surrogate live action, we started with the concept of animation as a comic strip, and moved the characters only when it was essential to. Of course, in

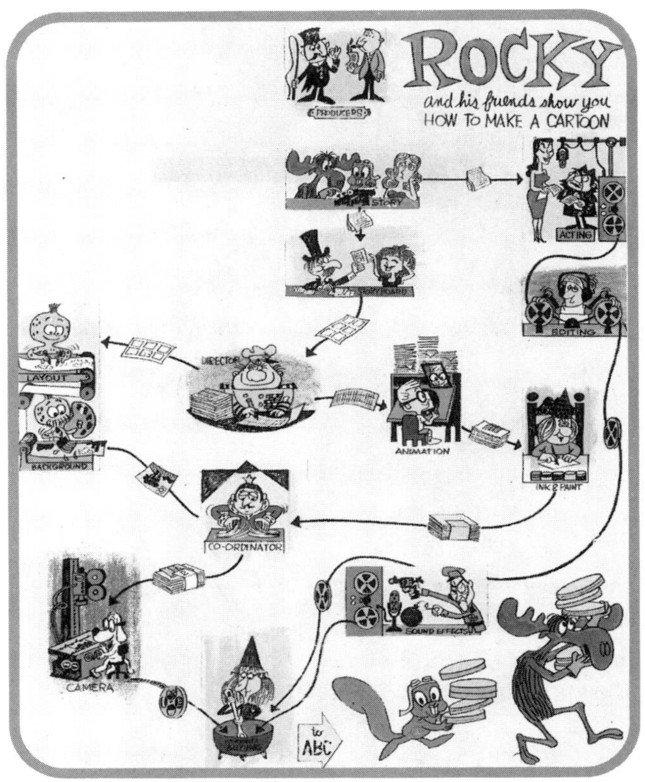

How to make a cartoon, the Jay Ward Productions way. *Courtesy of Universal Studios Publishing Rights, a Division of Universal Studios Licensing, Inc.*

order to do that, the camera angles had to be numerous and the plot lines and dialogue had to carry the weight."

It obviously worked: as time goes on, the "Rocky and Bullwinkle" cartoons gather more and more avid followers. Little did Jay Ward and Bill Scott realize, while honing their pilot script in late 1957, that the mostly modest moose and the feisty young squirrel from the unassuming little burg of Frostbite Falls, Minnesota, would become the animation superstars they are today.

10

And a Host of Others, or Now It's Time for Another Special Feature

The cliffhanger adventures of the moose and squirrel were just one of several zany attractions in Jay's new cartoon show. The supporting features are just as revered today, in particular the first element, "Fractured Fairy Tales." This was one of Jay Ward's favorites (beaten later by "Dudley Do-Right of the Mounties," which seemed to be top choice of all at Ward Productions).

Bill Scott called the "Fairy Tales" "superb—we had such great writers on the show and telling them to make up their own fairy tales was like giving whiskey to the Indians. 'Eight Princesses and an Owl' [sic] sounds like it was written by the Brothers Grimm. But it was George Atkins. Parody, lampoon, and satire. They had it all. They were the most imaginative part of the show."

Early in the production of the *Rocky* show, Ward was sorely concerned about the quality of the Mexican animation, so it was decided to pull a few of his favorite "Fairy Tale" scripts back to the Hollywood studio. Later, several were subcontracted to TV Spots. This is why sharp-eyed viewers will note better animation, striking layouts, and unusual graphics in the UPA style. Several employ a distinctive method of blending all-white characters against full-color splash-type backgrounds. This different look was the first of many characteristics unique to "Fractured Fairy Tales."

Not since the classic theatrical cartoons from Warner Brothers a generation earlier—like Tex Avery's *The Bear's Tale,* Friz Freleng's *Little Red*

Riding Rabbit, and Chuck Jones's fabulous Three Bears series—had anyone so mocked the sacred area of children's bedtime stories. A special overall whimsy permeated the "Fractured Fairy Tales," and, as usual, the Jay Ward trademark was well in evidence: strong, well-paced writing—laced with puns—and excellent voice acting by *Rocky* regulars June Foray and Bill Scott, and the legendary voice artist Daws Butler.

Then too, Scott's choice of actor Edward Everett Horton as narrator was one of the all-time great casting decisions. "He was hired," said Scott, "to lend a certain air of reverence to otherwise irreverent stories." Horton had previously worked for Scott in 1957 on *The Gerald McBoing-Boing Show,* narrating a fairy-tale cartoon called "The Unenchanted Princess," which could be considered a rehearsal for Ward's series. Horton's restrained and wry delivery of these sly little tales was a delight. He was also clever enough to send up his own screen image of the dithering, nervous characters he had played in the 1930s and 1940s. His patented giggle was often heard echoing the audience's groans at the outrageous pun endings of these tales: "The bee stings in life are free" was just one painful example.

A major influence on "Fractured Fairy Tales" was Stan Freberg. Six years earlier, Freberg and Daws Butler cowrote a spoof of *Dragnet* entitled "St. George and the Dragonet" which was a huge success for Capitol Records. The revisionist fairy-tale settings of this and its flip side, "Little Blue Riding Hood," were employed to great effect, particularly the use of period icons—dragons, knaves—mouthing hilarious anachronisms and TV-cop colloquialisms. Also, the voices on Freberg's recording were performed by Foray and Butler. Foray played a Brooklyn princess, a grandmother, and Little Blue Riding Hood, while Butler essayed a Jerry Lewis–like knave and the fire-breathing dragon. These voices would turn up repeatedly in "Fractured Fairy Tales."

Furthermore, Jay Ward had long been highly impressed by *Time for Beany,* the TV puppet show featuring Freberg and Butler. It, too, had appealed to both kids and grown-ups, and was very much on the wavelength of Ward's work. Bill Scott had written *Time for Beany* in 1949–50, and after a year of five-day-a-week contact with the actors, he knew their talents inside out. Thus the Freberg connection can't be overstressed.

Certain characters voiced by these players became particular favorites of Jay Ward, and he requested their presence again and again. June Foray did a great Marjorie Main battle-ax voice; it was heard as either an old hag or a fairy godmother. She had also played a "regulation" Margaret Hamilton-

Daws Butler

In the insecure, often bitchy field of acting, Daws Butler was universally known as the nicest man in the business. A gentle, kindly person, he elicited warm praise and respect from practitioners of a notoriously jealous profession. Bill Scott said, "Daws was a great guy. He never made an enemy, and he never stopped working on new accents and characters."

Born Charles Dawson Butler in Ohio on November 16, 1916 (in one "Aesop" episode a Butler character delivered the in-joke "My mother's living in Toledo"), Butler was a chronically shy youth. He forced himself to perform in Chicago and Midwest nightclubs, describing it as "a kind of self-inflicted therapy." Following naval intelligence service in World War II he moved to California, ending up on network radio shows like *Al Pearce and His Gang, The Whistler,* and *Suspense.* In 1948 he began making animation inroads with legendary cartoon director Tex Avery at MGM. His big break came with TV's hit puppet show *Time for Beany* in 1949. Once established, Butler worked for Capitol Records (along with his *Beany* cohort Stan Freberg), doing albums for both children and adults. He was soon established in TV commercials, and theatrical cartoons for Walter Lantz, UPA, Warner Brothers, and the MGM team of Hanna-Barbera.

Daws Butler was to the formative years of TV animation what Mel Blanc was to theatrical cartoons: the king of the hill. He first worked for Jay on the aborted 1956 revival of *Crusader Rabbit,* recording some episodes as Rags the Tiger's new voice. In the *Rocky* series, Ward astutely cast him in the "Aesop" fables and "Fractured Fairy Tales," which proved the perfect showcase for Butler's truly oddball flock of voices. In the mid-sixties he was the star player in the Cap'n Crunch commercials, and also performed in Jay's later cartoons and unsold pilots. In *George of the Jungle* he played almost all the sundry mad villains out to get George and Super Chicken, while in "Tom Slick" he was the wretched mechanic Clutcher.

In his early days with Jay, Butler was something of an outsider compared to the rest of the team, his main work deriving from the Hanna-Barbera dynasty; indeed, in one "Fractured Fairy Tale" ("The Teeth of Baghdad"), a Bill Scott–voiced citizen of Iraq asks Butler's character—a rug seller—"What are you, a spy from Hanna-Barbera?"

Butler didn't receive, and in fact didn't request, screen credit following the first season of *Rocky*. By then he was entrenched at H-B, whose shows were sponsored by Kellogg's; it would have been problematic to be credited on Jay's cartoons, which hawked cereal competitor General Mills' product. "Jay would jokingly refer to Daws as a traitor—a defector to Hanna-Barbera," jokes Howard Brandy.

Butler was a splendid comic actor, with the emphasis on "actor." His delivery displayed great sensitivity. A writer, and later an experienced dramatic teacher who loved language, Butler despised what he called "cosmetic readings." More than most, he took the cartoon business seriously, insisting that animation voices weren't meant to be simply "funny voices," but flesh-and-blood "characters."

There were several of these "characters" which Ward insisted Butler reprise time and again. The one affectionately dubbed "the fag prince" was heard in countless "Fairy Tales" and was reemployed later in "Tom Slick," "Super Chicken" (swishier than ever as Prince Blackhole of Calcutta in "The Elephant Spreader" episode), and the title role for an unsold pilot, "Captain Cutlas." Then there was the Jerry Lewis–like voice which Butler used for Quaker Oats spokes-character Quisp. This was also heard in "Fairy Tales" like "The Little Tinker" and in a "Super Chicken" as the twisted villain Salvador Rag Dolly. Ward loved Butler's Phil Silvers con-man voice, often used for villains (like the Oyster in yet another "Super Chicken" segment).

Of course Daws Butler's most famous character for Jay was the addled Cap'n Crunch, who enjoyed a twenty-one-year run via Butler's talented tonsils.

Although he began as an impressionist, Butler's own vocal resonance was so strong that it inhibited total accuracy. He cashed in by exaggerating famous people, using their speech inflections for crazy character creations, as witness his great Snagglepuss/Bert Lahr voice for Hanna-Barbera. Among the celebrities he mimicked on Ward's shows were George Jessel, Bela Lugosi, Peter Lorre, Richard Haydn, John Wayne, Gary Cooper, W. C. Fields, and Joe E. Brown.

This wide vocal range was even more amazing considering the fact that Butler was already starring as almost twenty voices over at Hanna-Barbera: he had to be careful not to make any character too similar for the Jay Ward cartoons. In fact, the only real crossovers were variations on his *Time for Beany* title voice, a realistic characterization of a young boy (similar to Elroy in H-B's *The Jetsons*), and his Brando-like imitation, used to great comic effect for Hanna-Barbera's laconic house cat Mr. Jinks. This Freberg-influenced character voice was often employed by Ward in "Aesop and Son," and for the husband role in the early "Fractured Fairy Tale" "Rapunzel."

Daws Butler's fruitful association with Jay lasted all the way to Ward Productions' close in the fall of 1984. Following six years of recurring health problems, including a disabling stroke, Daws Butler died on May 18, 1988. Skip Craig recalled, "I was at his funeral. Boy, his memorial service was packed; Stan Freberg was one of the pallbearers."

ish wicked witch voice for both Disney and Chuck Jones: Witch Hazel in Disney's *Trick or Treat,* and in Jones's great Warner cartoon *Broomstick Bunny*. This voice was gainfully employed in the many "Fairy Tales" involving witches in the plot lines. Daws Butler did two characters that Jay adored: a fey, slightly swishy nobleman who was immediately dubbed "the fag prince voice," and an absentminded old gent heard as various kings. The latter was actually a vocal impression of the befuddled 1930s character actor Charlie Butterworth; eventually it broadened slightly to become Cap'n Crunch in Ward's Quaker cereal commercials. Scott was most often heard playing kings, fathers of ugly stepdaughters, and stupid trolls.

Many of the "Fairy Tales" were written by George Atkins. Chris Jenkyns and Lloyd Turner also wrote several apiece, and Bill Scott polished off the final drafts on all of them. The earliest ones, by Jenkyns, fractured real fairy tales by the Brothers Grimm and Hans Christian Anderson. Later, original fairy-story plots were composed. Turner and Atkins wrote quite a few of these. They were so distinctive an element of *Rocky and His Friends* that they remain the strongest memory of the series for many viewers.

They featured a world of dukes, princesses, goblins, magic mirrors, spinning wheels, wicked witches, incompetent witches, gnomes, fairy godmothers, ugly old hags, ogres, trolls, evil queens, enchanted frogs, and bedraggled taxpayers. The economy in these never-never lands consisted not of dollars and cents but kazoos, pazuzas, finsters, kinockers, rinkels, and gold grickels.

An early story was the familiar "King Midas." The Jay Ward house style was immediately apparent in this episode: the fracturing consisted of a take-off on medieval marketing consultants and ad agencies, and the cartoon subtly warned younger viewers about the dangers of greed. Image-conscious King Midas calls a crisis meeting of his advisers—pronounced *ad*visers—Bauble, Bangle, Bead and Benson (suspiciously reminiscent of a top agency of the time, BBD & O).

In "Cinderella Returns," Cinderella is overly concerned with social position; she knows she is "only an—ugh—commoner," but her fairy godmother is owner of Good Fairy Rentals and offers her a deluxe anniversary makeover. The twist ending reveals that the Prince is really a collection agent married to the fairy godmother. In "Riding Hoods Anonymous" by Lloyd Turner, an earnest wolf has decided to swear off eating Red Riding Hood and her ilk by joining the self-help group of the title ("I pledge, I pledge I will not eat; one Riding Hood can still defeat!"). By the end of this tale we are on the poor wolf's side anyway, because Red and her grandmother are a couple of mean-spirited swindlers.

The most famous "Fractured Fairy Tale" was "Sleeping Beauty." The twentieth script in the series, it was written by the witty George Atkins. In this one a Walt Disney look-alike prince refuses to kiss the dozing girl because he suddenly sees a buck in her; he opens an amusement park themed around her dormant form and calls it Sleeping Beautyland. An in-joke featured a character named Yolanda the wicked fairy. In real life Yolanda was the secretary who mailed the weekly checks to Jay Ward from Producers Associates of Television in New York. It is fortunate, too, that this funny segment was one that Jay produced in Hollywood; Bill Hurtz directed it at a cracking pace.

In 1960 Jay Ward, commenting on the latest industry trends, said, "It seems that what you have to do is animated versions of an established TV show. . . . Well, we want to prove we're funny by doing something fresh, not because someone else already has been funny." Trade journals of the era agreed that the "Fairy Tales" were fresh all right: they were singled out in many contemporary articles about television cartoons.

Overall, "Fractured Fairy Tales" ranks as one of the most disarming and timeless cartoon series to emerge from Jay Ward Productions. Thanks to subtle and clever writing they remain fresh and undated over thirty years later. In fact, the scripts easily outclass much of today's animated comedy, and it's hard to imagine their like again.

An "extra added attraction" within the *Rocky* show, "Bullwinkle's Corner" consisted of thirty-nine short segments in which the erudite moose recited poetry containing a goofy twist. Later, the poetry corner was reformatted and became "Mr. Know-It-All." This, too, proved highly popular ("For all you men of letters, here's Mr. Know-It-All." "Hello, Mailmen!"). When *The Bullwinkle Show* was due to premiere in September 1961 the sponsor requested more "Know-It-All" segments, rather than reviving the poems. They also asked for clever ideas to help promote the character merchandise boom resulting from our antlered hero's exposure in his new evening time slot. So a third format, "The Rocky and Bullwinkle Fan Club," appeared.

There were ninety-nine segments that Bill Scott generically dubbed "Bullwinkle's Corner"; they consisted of the thirty-nine in which the antlered star read fractured verse, fifty in which he delivered his professorial "Know-It-All" lectures, and ten of the "Fan Club" meetings.

Bullwinkle was a charismatic presence in these short pieces, and they went a long way toward spinning the moose off into his own series, even if that series was pretty much identical to *Rocky and His Friends*. Some of the poetry readings were memorable—they'd start out straight, then go terribly wrong for our hero. Scott's imagination ran wild for these bits; he often said, "I loved writing these segments; they really were a lot of fun." In "Little Jack Horner," for instance, the pie crust is so hard that Bullwinkle can't stick in his thumb and pull out a plum, while in "Wee Willie Winkie" he is arrested for behaving like a flasher ("Hello, R and I. You got a make on a mug named Winkie?"). In "Simple Simon" the moose and Boris end up doing an Abbott and Costello–style routine over the line "Let me taste your ware" ("My what?" "Not what—ware!"). "Tom, Tom the Piper's Son" plays like a scene from *Dragnet,* while "Tommy Tucker" headlines Bullwinkle as a singing waiter, performing snappy patter songs for the bemused diners.

The "Bullwinkle's Corner" poetry bits remain a delight to revisit. Several of the recitations feature nursery rhymes, while others are adapted from classics (Poe's "The Raven" gets the full treatment with parody verses). Some are lesser-known but evocative pieces like "A Wet Sheet and a Flowing Sea," "Taffy," and "Where Go the Boats?" Bullwinkle interprets them all most entertainingly, living up to his early General Mills publicity as "the intellectual moose." In "Rocky-Bye Baby" he even pays tribute to his employer: he is censored by G. J., who consults with his boss, C. P. These initials referred to Gordon Johnson from the ad agency and Cy Plattes, the boss at General Mills.

The seventh poem, "Taffy," introduces the concept of Boris Badenov making various gate-crash appearances during Bullwinkle's moment of glory. The Pottsylvanian louse appears in several, again demonstrating his penchant for disguise: in "Barbara Frietchie," for example, he plays Stonewall Boris. The no-goodnik also appears in the "Mr. Know-It-All" pieces, constantly thwarting the moose's attempts to demonstrate such subjects as how to hitchhike, how to get into the movies without buying a ticket (naturally Boris is the theater manager), and how to interview a scientist (in this piece, Boris rather pointlessly switches Bullwinkle's brain with that of a chicken). In one "Know-It-All," Bullwinkle even reads poetry again: a satirical dig called "How to Be a Beatnik" makes short shrift of the late-1950s coffeehouse pseudo-set.

Bill Scott wrote the poetry pieces and a few early "Know-It-Alls." Chris Hayward and Lloyd Turner scripted many of the latter; George Atkins and Allan Burns contributed several. Hayward remembers, "Lloyd and I did one that got us a complaint from the consulate of India. Bullwinkle was demonstrating how to do magic, and he put a large cow inside a box, then stuck swords through the sides. They objected to Bullwinkle's closing line: when he looked inside the box, he said, very slowly, 'Holy cow.' "

The "Fan Club" segments were neatly played. Rocky, Bullwinkle, and Captain Peachfuzz form an uneasy alliance with Boris and Natasha until, in one segment, the superspy can stand the goody-goodiness no longer. He creates, instead, Boris's Fan Club, for lovers of skullduggery ("Double your pleasure, double your fun, join Boris's Fan Club and learn hit-and-run!"). The funniest of the "Fan Club" pieces is the episode in which the cast performs a creakingly bad melodrama entitled "She Can't Pay the Rent": even Dudley Do-Right treats us to a cameo appearance in this one.

The mellifluous moose acquitted himself with distinction in "Bullwinkle's Corner," demonstrating his stunning versatility in each segment. It's no wonder he got his own show!

Actually Bullwinkle's poetry career was revived after the 1961 *Bullwinkle Show* premiere on NBC. The ad agency came up with two ideas for Cheerios commercials, and Bill Scott wrote a third one. These spots were animated in Hollywood. Bullwinkle plugged the Cheerios catch phrase "Big G—Little O" with the following rhymes: "Thanksgiving," "Old Mother Hubbard," and "It's Not That I Don't Trust You, William Tell." The spots were pleasingly executed, with Boris making a costarring appearance in the first, and Dudley Do-Right guesting in the second.

• • •

"Sherman—set the WABAC Machine for 1959."

Finally there was "Peabody's Improbable History," one of the best-remembered of Jay Ward's cartoons. Mr. Peabody, the genius dog who lives in a penthouse apartment, and Sherman, the young boy he adopts, travel through time in the WABAC (pronounced Way-Back) Machine, which was the canine's own invention. This cartoon segment was a sort of updated version of H. G. Wells's *The Time Machine.* But while Wells's characters merely observed the passage of history, Peabody participated, and was in fact the direct cause of each event ending up safely in the history books. As Ward put it, "The comedy came from the fact that all these famous historical figures were complete boobs."

It was true: if Peabody and Sherman hadn't traveled back in time, Zebulon Pike would never have discovered Pikes Peak—he suffered from an embarrassing fear of heights; Leonardo Da Vinci wouldn't have painted the Mona Lisa, as Mona had a toothache and couldn't produce her inscrutable smile; Richard the Lionhearted would forever have remained chicken-hearted; and Alexander Graham Bell, who gauchely asks Peabody, "What's a telephone?" would merely have invented an Alexander Graham cracker. In each story, Peabody has his paws full: John Sutter doesn't recognize "little yellow rocks" as gold; the first man to cross the English Channel can't swim; and Whistler paints his mother's chair—minus his mother.

Cartoonist Ted Key created the original "Peabody" concept for the *Rocky* show in his East Coast studio; at first it simply involved the funny gag of a dog who had a pet boy. The idea was presented at the initial *Rocky* think-tank meeting in Los Angeles; Key's dog-boy idea was tentatively called "Danny Day-Dream" and, in the development stage, involved the idea of time travel, possibly via a time machine.

In 1992 Key spoke to animation scholar Karl Cohen, who revealed that Key's idea for Peabody and Sherman "came from watching animals. Ted Key notes, 'We all take orders from our cats,' and from that observation he thought up the perverse angle of switching roles so a smart dog owns a boy."

The idea was enthusiastically received, and by the end of May, Ward and Scott had modified the format, using character models drawn by Al Shean. The dog, originally called Beware, was now a superior genius type à la Clifton Webb: Ward had suggested a voice based on Webb playing his Mr. Belvedere role. Renamed Peabody, after Bill Scott's own real-life dog, the genius beagle invents his own time machine. The series title became "Peabody's Improbable History," and the boy was now called Sherman, named by Scott for Sherman Glas, a technical director at UPA.

Ted Key was happy to give his approval to this handling of "Peabody," and he felt that Ward couldn't have found a better working partner than Bill Scott. "Bill's talents were exceptional. And I felt that Horton as narrator for the 'Fairy Tales' was just perfect. He had just the right Alice-in-Wonderland quality, the suggestion of unreality needed for counterpoint." Key made up a list of ninety-three possible subjects for "Danny Day-Dream," from Robert Fulton to Stanley and Livingstone in Africa. Most of these ended up as "Peabody" episodes.

Ninety-one wild plots were scripted. In each episode, Mr. Peabody had to come up with the last-minute solution to help these figures of history achieve that for which they were destined; indeed, without the little white hound the course of human events might have gone terribly wrong.

Mr. Peabody possessed supreme self-confidence, and had no qualms reminding us that, thanks to his superior intellect and perception, the final historical outcome was his. And why shouldn't he brag? Don't forget, it's our Peabody who draws up the blueprints for the Great Pyramids.

The character of Peabody was the most improbable thing of all. An upright dog, complete with red bow tie and thick spectacles, the brilliant and rather pragmatically egotistical beagle had one endearing eccentricity: a compulsion for spouting the worst puns in the history of wordplay. The cartoons invariably end with one of these. Writer Chris Hayward, who composed the bulk of the "Peabody"s himself, admits, "Sometimes the puns came first, then I'd work backward."

As the series went on, the plots got wilder and the pace picked up; both "Peabody" and "Rocky and Bullwinkle" grew ever more frenetic with each season. In an early episode showcasing Stanley and Livingstone, Peabody easily deciphers the African natives' gibberish, explaining, "I invented that gibberish." But in the later segments, the scripts were almost Monty Pythonish in their escalating nonsense. "They were totally written to please ourselves," says Hayward, who recalls the story concerning Mata Hari being chock-full of his most outrageous puns. Not only is an optometrist named Dr. Focals, but Mata Hari is discovered standing "by Focals." Next, Peabody unlocks a safe in England—this time we're informed he didn't invent the combination; it's simply the same as the phone number of his aunt in Peoria. Finally, when Mata flies to safety in a giant blimp, Peabody ends the episode with his all-time most excruciating pun: "One nation indirigible" . . . ouch!

Walter Tetley

Sherman was played by Walter Tetley, who throughout his life specialized in child-voice roles. Tetley possessed a fine sense of wise-guy comedy.

Born Walter Campbell Tetzlaff in New York City on June 5, 1921 (although some sources indicate 1915), Tetley was a child performer of Scots ancestry, on his mother's side. His made his debut at age seven, dressed in a kilt, performing Sir Harry Lauder imitations. He was considered a precociously gifted artist, and received a ton of work while still a very young boy.

Tetley made thousands of radio appearances from 1930 through 1958. During the 1930s he worked with the biggest stars of the medium, including Fred Allen, Jack Benny, and W. C. Fields, all of whom were impressed by the lad's flair for comedy. In 1938 he moved to Hollywood for a West Coast broadcast by Allen, and stayed to act in MGM films. While doing the rounds of radio-show auditions, Tetley met comedian Hal Peary, who later employed the young actor as his nephew Leroy on *The Great Gildersleeve*, which ran on NBC for seventeen years. In the late 1940s Tetley played his most hilarious role: the sarcastic delivery boy Julius Abruzzio, who made life miserable for fall-guy Phil Harris on *The Phil Harris–Alice Faye Show*. His first animation work came via Walter Lantz (Tom Thumb, Jr.), and Tex Avery, in the 1941 Warner Brothers Looney Tune *The Haunted Mouse,* after which Lantz cast him as Andy Panda in theatrical shorts 1945 to 1949.

Like Dick (the voice of "Speedy Alka-Seltzer") Beals, Tetley was an actor who, due to a hormonal condition in which he never grew facial hair, always sounded young. In effect, his voice never broke. In the 1940s, at the urging of his parents, Tetley was treated by a urologist and actually grew several inches.

Bill Scott cast Tetley in the role of Sherman. Scott had been familiar with his work in radio and animated commercials. In fact, they had worked on *The Gerald McBoing-Boing Show* a few years earlier, in the "Dusty of the Circus" series. Scott nicknamed Tetley "the Squire of Malibu," and thoroughly enjoyed working with him on the "Peabody" episodes, noting, "Walt was a total professional."

Tetley created a likable child in Sherman, who occasionally made mistakes and got on the genius hound's nerves, but was ever loyal to Peabody and a pretty fair student. Sherman would groan as loudly as we did at "his master's" puns. Chris Hayward loved Tetley's voice. "I would write this stuff, and like all writers you hope that you get these tracks back that approximated what you'd written, and I'd always hear these great, great line readings by Walter—his voice was just marvelous for that Sherman character. It was such a sensational sound."

Tetley was highly active in charity work for the handicapped. The victim of a serious motorcycle accident in the late 1960s, Walter Tetley suffered several bouts of poor health in his last years, and died on September 4, 1975.

Bill Scott wrote the first episode, while the second—featuring Napoleon—was a collaboration between Scott and Jay Ward. Then Hayward came on board, "and I ended up writing most of the 'Peabody's myself. I did a few with Lloyd [Turner]; we'd just look at a list of historical figures and pick one." Scott remembered that performing the voice of Peabody was difficult. "It was that very precise, supercilious Clifton Webb imitation. I'd speak very rapidly and softly, but to achieve the sound I had to tighten my lips, and this impeded me somewhat. I'd have to redo a lot of Peabody's lines because I'd just start stumbling over the words, with my mouth stretched so taut."

The range of famous characters covered in the "Peabody" cartoons makes them one of Ward's most fascinating creations. There is an erudite quality to Scott's Peabody voice that still plays well; Leonard Maltin even ventured the plausible opinion that many a school-age youngster learned some nuggets of history by watching these zany little forays through time. While the canny canine's cartoons lack the atmospheric charm of the fairy tales, which are based on beloved literary favorites, the "Peabody" format is a comedy classic based on one of the most effective devices—the simple reversal: in this case, dog has pet boy.

For old movie buffs, a fun part of the "Peabody" cartoons is identifying the voices Paul Frees impersonates. Frees played the bulk of the historical identities, several of whom were based on impressions of vintage movie actors. It was vastly amusing hearing Alexander Graham Bell talk like Jack Benny, or having the Sheriff of Nottingham look and sound like Charles Laughton at his hammiest. And the "Peabody"s gave Frees more scope for his exotic, flavorful foreign accents than any of Ward's other shows; Daws Butler called Frees "a great dialectician."

The one disappointing aspect of "Peabody's Improbable History" is that, visually, the cartoons were some of Ward's crudest, being animated in Mexico (except for the Pancho Villa episode, made in Hollywood to avoid Mexican censorship problems). The first forty segments were unprepossessing, and the audio was muddy. Slowly the Mexican studio improved, and the final"Peabody"s weren't as bad. But no matter—the scripts and voice work were always a treat.

Finally it should be noted that, during the first twelve months of *Rocky and His Friends,* the "Peabody" cartoons resulted in several headaches for Jay Ward. The ad agency and sponsor blue-penciled the scripts, regarding various historical names as sacrosanct. A sidebar on page 154 discusses some of these panic ploys, but in fact the only official complaint was a letter from some humorless descendants of Jim Bowie, who were angered by the segment in which Peabody helps the frontiersman discover his famous Bowie knife.

11

1960: Ponsonby, Pilots, and a Super Pullet

Soon after *Rocky* went to air, Len Key learned that Jay Ward and Bill Scott were gaining a reputation for artistic difficulty. He suspected Johnson was responsible, calling him "a Machiavelli in my book. Albeit a charming one." He added, "Frankly, Gordon Johnson talked too much. He partially damaged the Ward-Scott reputation with idle blather about artistic temperaments and late scheduling." In fact, Len felt that Johnson may even have been subtly queering deals to keep Ward and Scott exclusively with *Rocky* and D-F-S.

If anything, it was the fear of late deliveries which temporarily hurt Ward Productions. Charles Ulrich interviewed Bill Hurtz, who clarified this issue: "I was taught at Shamus Culhane that if you missed a deadline, you never worked in TV again, because the airtime had been contracted for. If they could have taken you out and shot you, they would have. But next to that, you were permanently barred from employment by missing a deadline."

Actually, our fearless producers had sensed this brewing in the first few months. But aside from the agency carping, the sponsor and Jay Ward enjoyed a good relationship from the start. In mid-November, Key was informed by Peter Piech that General Mills was so enthused about the *Rocky* show—even before its first airing—that they were discussing slotting it into a 7:30 P.M. Sunday spot on NBC. Further, General Mills assured Len Key that Ward Productions would definitely do any "Rocky and Bullwinkle" commercials, from script through finished product, at the full going rate.

Then came the best news of all after such a torturous year: the *Rocky and His Friends* budget was more than tripled, to $26,000 per show, and was given a revised and much fairer seven-year contract. There would be proper union fee payments, and increases of 15 percent with each renewal. Announced in December, it felt like a Christmas present. Even so, this substantial hike came only after Jay Ward spent several months educating the agency and sponsor about the hard realities of this venture, and after General Mills had seen some of the finished work. The result, while far from perfect (Ward and Scott had to agree to relinquish some quality control), was at last financially workable. The one unhappy clause for Jay: General Mills would eventually own U.S. television rights to all the half-hour shows in perpetuity.

Johnson and his accountants, who had lived with vain hope for six months, initially resisted the budget increase but finally agreed with Ward about the Mexican situation, which to any remotely interested observer was a mess, both financially and creatively. In fairness, the Mexican setup could have been an excellent proposition after eighteen months of staff training, had the material meanwhile been produced in Hollywood—a fact which Ward had predicted months earlier.

But while the worst period for Jay Ward and *Rocky and His Friends* was over, there were still many niggling problems to come.

Trying to make the best of the situation, Ward set himself and Val-Mar a new target for 1960 whereby all predirected cartoon material was to reach Mexico at set times: six to eight weeks ahead of the delivery date for "Rocky" and "Bullwinkle's Corner" segments, and five to six weeks ahead for "Fairy Tales" and "Peabody" episodes. The year 1959 came to a close, and the worst was finally over, the improvements due in no small part to the Herculean efforts of Bill Hurtz, Dun Roman, and Rudy Zamora in Mexico.

When Dun Roman's contract was up he left early in the new year. As 1960 rolled around, Ward informed Zamora that a competent animator named George Singer would be arriving. Singer recalls, "Gordon Johnson hired me in New York. I'd just returned from England and for a month before going to Mexico I worked in Pete Burness's room at Jay's Sunset Boulevard studio, so that I could absorb the characters." Johnson also hired Americans Dave Fern and Dan Jurovich.

For the next few months Ward was constantly annoyed by the abidingly poor quality of the sound effects. And with good cause: there were either no effects where there should have been, or they were totally inappropriate. Worse, they were often distorted to the point where dialogue was drowned out. The one saving grace for Jay was that the animation continued to improve.

With George Singer taking Roman's place, Ward felt confident that Rudy Zamora could handle both the directorial chores and overall studio supervision. He was most happy with Zamora and believed that one supervisor was now sufficient. Zamora maintained regular requests for Hollywood materials, especially layouts—by March the Mexican animators were actually ahead of the Los Angeles–based layout artists!

Indeed, by the start of 1960, production on *Rocky and His Friends* was progressing smoothly. This year the adult nature of the *Rocky* show became the prime issue. In January 1960, Jay Ward was advised that General Mills wouldn't approve the "Peabody" script about Francis Scott Key, in which Peabody helps compose "The Star-Spangled Banner," warning of potential trouble with patriotic groups and educators. And ABC began expressing concern over some of the voices that Paul Frees and Bill Scott were doing—it was felt that the burlesque dialects might offend certain ethnic groups. Cited were the "Peabody" stories on Confucius, Vasco Balboa, and Lord Francis Douglas, the latter of which featured a broad Italian character.

Compounding this, General Mills instructed Ward that in the future, the "Peabody" episodes must steer clear of American historical figures. The Wright brothers episode was blamed: General Mills was panicking about possible adverse reactions from teachers and aeronautical groups. Soon afterward the scripts featuring Paul Revere, Stephen Decatur, and others had the sponsor nervously believing they'd be accused of "encouraging children to laugh at American history"; this, of course, was what Jay and Bill wanted kids to do! Ward was polite about most of this, but, as was his wont, he stuck to his opinions. In particular, he felt that the Wright brothers story was fine, and he didn't budge. Six months later, he got his way, and the episode was approved. (The situation was identical three decades later: Nickelodeon fought similar battles in 1991–92 over *The Ren & Stimpy Show*.)

Meanwhile, in January 1960, Jay Ward announced two new projects. The first was "The Piper's Show." This was planned as a half-hour series featuring the best cartoons and puppet films from all over the world. A well-known host would introduce each film, and an animated piper with appropriate musical accompaniment was to provide a backdrop for the host between items. Ward's team would supply the translation script, narration, and music. The demo film was a twelve-minute award-winning Czechoslovakian stop-motion puppet short entitled *The Lost Sentry*. Ward made arrangements with New York distributor Rembrandt Films, whose manager, Bernhardt Hurwood, was a former film editor who had once worked for Jay in that capacity. Ward redubbed the sound track of *The Lost Sentry* in November 1959, employing the distinguished European character actor Walter Slezak as narrator. The English language script was by Chris Hayward, with new music by Frank Comstock.

Originally the piper character was to have a name, and the series was to be called "Pongo Presents." Ward then decided it needed a more rarefied feel, so the title was changed to "Monsieur Pipeaux." He was talked out of this, and it became simply "The Piper's Show." Jay Ward and Len Key both felt that the redubbed version of *The Lost Sentry* was so good it could have been released theatrically.

The second item was "Cosgrove the Magician," planned as a series of five-minute cartoons for a five-day-a-week TV format, possibly for the six and eleven o'clock news periods.

But strapped by P.A.T.'s original, barely workable budget, Ward had no spare money to make up presentations for new cartoon shows. Once *Rocky* was on the air he urged Len Key to raise the funds to finance his new projects. Another new cartoon idea was already under way by early 1960. Chris Jenkyns had storyboarded a "Fractured Fairy Tale" about a small jumping frog, and Bill Scott felt that the character could be a series lead. The frog, first called Hippety Hopper, was renamed the Green Hopper and finally Hoppity Hooper. By month's end a storyboard was ready, and the voice track was recorded on February 2. "Hooper Productions" shares were sold to Jay's employees in order to finance this pilot. Skip Craig says they contributed "$500 each, and this bought a quarter of one percent of the show to each of us."

The series was originally intended to be made up of a half hour consisting of three episodes of "Hoppity Hooper," supported by "Clobbered Classics" ("in which we [would] poke fun at such classic stories as *The Three Musketeers* and *A Tale of Two Cities*," said Jay). Chris Hayward's *Musketeers* pastiche had been written in 1959.

In addition, Jay was thinking of revising the 1948 Television Arts property "Dudley Doright of the Mounties," although it would be another year and a half before that intrepid Canadian bungler became a TV star. Ward described this in the *Hoppity Hooper* prospectus as "a mounted policeman of the far north, in a satirical hair-raising series of adventures in the style of old melodramatic theatre." In the same prospectus Ward described the character of Waldo as "A wolf in wolf's clothing," although in the *Hoppity* series he was actually a fox.

A third project was a series concept called "The Super Chicken Show," from an idea by Chris Hayward and Lloyd Turner. This show would be designed for regional and syndicated sale. A pilot film was prepped.

Chris Hayward recalls, "It didn't really work—we wanted to try some 'name' voices, so General Mills wouldn't feel they were too similar to *Rocky*'s cast." The actors suggested ranged from Carl Reiner to Dennis Day, with Don Knotts finally landing the title role. Comedian Louis Nye played faithful Fred. Both these players were popular members of Steve Allen's TV stock company. Considered for the narrator were Herschel Bernardi (the voice of Charlie Tuna), Westbrook Van Voorhis (famed *March of Time* narrator), and Don Wilson, Jack Benny's longtime announcer. The part finally went to radio veteran Marvin Miller, who had worked with Paul Frees for several seasons on TV's *The Millionaire* and narrated Bill Scott's *Gerald McBoing-Boing* cartoon at UPA. All these performers were proficient, but somehow their voices didn't work for such a crazy cartoon. Two weeks later several supporting characters were redone by Bill Scott and Mel Blanc.

This would be the only time the brilliant Warner Brothers' voice artist would work for Ward. In fact, as hilarious as Blanc's voices were, he didn't seem to fit into the slightly nutty family feel of a Jay Ward session. Blanc was always supremely professional but came across as a little cold to Ward, while Scott said, "I never much cared for the experience of working with Mel." (Daws Butler and June Foray echoed the opinion that Blanc was a bit aloof, though strangely enough Paul Frees would always emphatically state, "Mel is the undisputed king of the cartoon voice world; nobody comes close to Mel Blanc!")

Although the storyboard and sound track were completed, in which the formidable chicken battled the notorious brothers Henry and Edsel Fraud, the board was never shot.

Tentative support segments for this show included "Farcical Fables," which surfaced again in 1960 as "Aesop and Son," "The Piccadilly Squares," and "Colonel Swagger of the O.O.E." (short for, what else, Office of Odds and Ends). If nothing else, the timing for these ideas was good.

It was now confirmed that three animated series had been sold for nighttime viewing: *The Bugs Bunny Show, The Flagstones* (soon retitled *The Flintstones*), and *Mr. Magoo*. A cycle was starting with evening cartoon shows, and Ward wanted to ride in on it; he and Scott were confident that they were the best of the current crop.

But it was simply a case of expecting too much too soon, and fund-raising proved impossible. Discouragingly for Jay, the only solid results were renewals of *Rocky*. In fact, Ward's next series, *Fractured Flickers,* was still four years away, to be followed by *Hoppity Hooper*. Slowly, Ward faced the reality: he was already being labeled "ahead of his time." Roughly translated, this meant Ward and Scott were considered a bit too "clever" (read "subversive"). And, once it began airing, so was their cheeky little cold war cartoon show, which many TV executives thought too daring in the conservative Eisenhower-era climate of 1959–60. Bill Scott recalled an executive once shaking his head and muttering, "You're too funny—we can't have that."*

In March 1960 it was announced that *Rocky* would expand to twice-weekly showings after summer. There were some who felt that this move was the ABC network's attempt at sabotaging *Rocky,* hastening its cancellation by playing two seasons' worth of material over just one year. But with the release of January's ratings figures, the previously pessimistic at D-F-S, and those within the hallowed halls of ABC, were surprised and delighted to see *Rocky and His Friends* come in at the number one show position, way ahead of firmly established *Rin Tin Tin* and *My Friend Flicka*. The next survey saw a 13.9 rating, which was the number one position for all daytime shows. Needless to say, General Mills was very happy.

D-F-S, meanwhile, was acting antsy about the second "Rocky" story line. The "Box Tops Robbery" caper is a lighthearted dig at the show's real-life breakfast cereal sponsor, General Mills. The hook to this story is that the health of the world's economy relies on cereal box tops and their accompa-

*One small example of their outré humor serves as an illustration. In October 1959, Jay Ward and Bill Scott came up with the name "Ponsonby Britt, Limited," as the new title for their corporation. Finally deemed too facetious, the name Ponsonby Britt, O.B.E., was retained in the cartoon credits as a long-running in-joke. The fictional Mr. Britt was listed on-screen as the mysterious executive producer of all Ward's shows. Scott said, "We had no executive producer, so we felt we should make one up." The exotic Ponsonby was even given an official biography for a press release. It was exactly this sort of frivolous japery which led to the perception that Ward Productions was a little too self-indulgent for its own good.

nying giveaway premiums. Rocky and Bullwinkle continue their battle with Boris and Natasha, becoming entangled with police, economists, and the banking system. In one scene, a frantic teller rushes into a bank president's office, yelling "Mr. Friendly," as we see a sweet little old lady groveling on the floor. Mr. Friendly irritably turns to his underling, hissing, "Arbogast, please! Can't you see I'm foreclosing a mortgage!" The story line, watched gingerly yet good-naturedly by the sponsor, concerns the dastardly Boris Badenov counterfeiting cereal box tops ("the real basis of the world's monetary system") so he can monopolize the redeemable goodies market.

General Mills affably agreed to go along with the story as long as they weren't embarrassed. But the agency, fearing the worst, insisted Ward and Scott cut it to twelve episodes. Bill Scott—who had planned this "as the story where the heroes capture Mr. Big, and embarrass Boris by temporarily shifting the world economy to box bottoms!"—had to leave Mr. Big until the next story. (The legend persists that General Mills demanded that this story quickly grind to a halt. The less romantic truth is that it was actually convenient to cut off at twelve chapters: the first twenty-six half-hour shows contained two "Rocky" episodes each—namely, these twelve and the forty Mooseberry Bush chapters—making a clean "repeat" block for twice-weekly summer reruns.)

With a renewal looming, the Mexicans had to give the "Rocky" episodes top priority. With Val-Mar still not up to speed, it was deemed necessary to pull the "Fractured Fairy Tales" back to the States. This delighted Jay Ward, who got the nod to do some at his studio. At this juncture, Bob Ganon of TV Spots, which was experiencing a seasonal dry spell, agreed to a subcontract arrangement. General Mills would pay TV Spots for thirteen "Fractured Fairy Tales" at a cost of $3,750 per episode. Their first assignment was "Pinocchio."

TV Spots was given the third "Fairy Tale," "Rapunzel," to study as the benchmark. Ward Productions supplied TV Spots with above-the-line materials—writing, sound track, storyboards, and model sheets. Ganon's team did the rest. Jay Ward felt a twinge of poetic justice, now that Shull Bonsall's studio was working for his show.

Animator Gerry Ray told cartoon historian Fred Patten, "I had a great compliment! I came back from Mexico and directed a couple of 'Fairy Tales' for Jay when they were just starting out, and animated them—animated one and directed a couple—and then they ran out of money. I went and got a job somewhere else, and then they gave me something like thirty-nine [*sic*]

'Fairy Tales' which I directed and produced at TV Spots for Jay. They were such fun to do!"

In April 1960 Jay approved a new model sheet which modified the appearance of Rocky the Flying Squirrel, who was to be drawn "cuter" and with better-looking goggles. At this time, the Mexican censor rejected the "Peabody" script "Pancho Villa." Following a month of stalemates, Ward decided to make this episode in Hollywood—it would be the only "Peabody" segment not produced in Mexico. Meanwhile, the ad agency, though anxious that all the show elements remain on schedule, gave temporary top priority to a grab bag of new General Mills billboards and *Rocky* show opening titles. These were important because *Rocky and His Friends* had been renewed for twenty-six weeks.

April proved even busier with extracurricular work when Johnson decreed that new episode openings for "Peabody" and "Fractured Fairy Tales," and four show "bridges" would be added to Val-Mar's schedule. Ward had no reason to panic—Rudy Zamora and Bob Schleh were extremely proficient. By now the Mexican team was well motivated, and before the month was over the following items had been realized: "Rocky" opening 3 (featuring Rocky's high dive into the tub of water), "Rocky" opening 4 (with Bullwinkle as a mountain climber), "Peabody" opening 2 (in which Peabody and Sherman use various means of transportation to travel through history), "Peabody" opening 3 (in this one Sherman inspects a series of museum paintings), "Fairy Tale" opening 2 (with Bullwinkle as a clumsy ballerina), and "Fairy Tale" opening 3 (featuring the witch and her magic wand).

Topping off the increased workload, a new one-and-a-half-minute *Rocky* show opening was commissioned in early May. Director Pete Burness laid out the poses (this is the well-remembered opening that begins, "A Thunder of Jets in an Open Sky . . ."). By the end of the month the "Box Tops Robbery" adventure had been completed. The Mexican studio, at last, looked reliably efficient.

In May 1960 Jay and Bill finally got around to recording some songs and sample dialogue for "The World of Winnie the Pooh," which they planned as a feature-length cartoon. They secured the services of the fine British comedy actor Reginald Gardiner to narrate the storyboard; Scott and Gardiner performed a delightful song called "Three Cheers for Pooh." Alas, this project went nowhere, and the "Pooh" characters finally ended up in Walt Disney's stable.

Also in May, a newspaper feature, "Letting Adults In on Laughs," by *San*

Diego Union TV-radio columnist Donald Freeman, boasted interviews with Ward and Scott publicizing *Rocky*'s expansion to two showings a week. This was the first time the larger public was made aware of the level of humor in the cartoons, even though many adults wouldn't see the show for another fifteen months, when Bullwinkle moved to prime time.

It began,

> Who are Jay Ward and Bill Scott? To begin with, both are on the plump side and each, confiding to you, expresses the solemn view that the other looks like a bespectacled fire hydrant. Both Ward and Scott breathe creative gifts in abundance.
>
> "We work well together," said Mr. Ward, who takes delight in the fact that he drives a 1948 Packard, "because I am nearsighted and Scott is farsighted. We discard our glasses and we see things quite differently. However, we agree on food—our favorite combination is pizza and popcorn. Brain food, you know."

Freeman mentioned they were also at work on "Super Chicken": "This one," Ward explained, soberly, "is about a chicken who thinks he's Superman, but he's really chicken."

Finally, the supporting features of the *Rocky* show were enthused over by our erstwhile producers.

> Scott said, "First shot out of the box, we have Peabody the genius dog who invents a time machine and this starts us off on a whole series of improbable histories. There's one about Napoleon suddenly finding himself hopeless in battle, someone having stolen his suspenders. Napoleon therefore is unable to salute, to draw his sword or to order his troops forward."

Ward's principal complaint to Gordon Johnson concerned Mexico's consistently poor sound effects and dubbing work. Jay believed that even if an audio expert from Hollywood went to Mexico, as D-F-S suggested, it wouldn't help: rather than being a technical matter, the basic problem was the comedy judgment of the Mexican editors. In turn, the Val-Mar team complained about their tight schedule. One half-hour 35-mm print had to leave Mexico City by plane each Saturday night, clear New York customs by Tuesday, and arrive at ABC on Thursday, for the following Thursday's telecast. This was a lot to expect from a facility which had been utterly out of its depth only six months earlier.

With the show to air twice weekly, D-F-S had requested additional lead-in materials for commercial intros, and these were written and voiced in March. This new material would provide greater variety on these "seen-every-day" show elements, and Johnson budgeted $2,000 per minute. The lead-ins, in order of scripting, were commercial intro 3 ("Eenie Meanie"); "Fairy Tale" bridge 3 ("Jolly Juggler"); commercial intros 4 ("Fan Mail from Some Flounder"), 5 ("Bullwinkle Is a Dope"), and 6 ("Private Bullwinkle"); "Fairy Tale" bridge 4 ("Baritone Solo"); "Peabody" bridges 2 ("Get Another Hat"), 3 ("I Take a Seven and a Half"), 4 ("Don't Know My Own Strength"), and 5 ("This Time for Sure"); and show close 2 ("You Got the Credits?"). These elements were animated in Mexico.

Concurrently, six commercials were approved by General Mills. Ward was asked to produce these in Hollywood. They plugged three cereals: Trix (featuring Bullwinkle as a troubadour and at his breakfast table), Cocoa Puffs (with Bullwinkle as a singer and a TV announcer), and Jets cereal (with Bullwinkle in a bicycle race and as a boxer). The moose and squirrel also appeared for the new cosponsors in commercials for Peter-Paul candy and Dentyne.

With the contracted fifty-two "Fairy Tale" scripts completed, General Mills gave Jay the go-ahead to animate more of them in Hollywood to speed their completion. During renewal discussions, Mills requested a change in "Fractured Fairy Tales" for the upcoming season. Ward's team came up with the Aesop's fables idea, and a storyboard was made up for a pilot episode, "The Lion and the Mouse." The sponsor was enthusiastic about the new concept.

Finally agreeing with Ward that the audio work emanating from Mexico was terrible, especially in the "Peabody" cartoons, D-F-S promised to rectify the problem. At this point—summer of 1960—the "Rocky" episodes were officially given top priority: writing, voice recording, and all below-the-line work was intensified because the somewhat shell-shocked Bill Scott would be taking a well-earned one-month vacation at the end of June.

Each Friday Ward mailed predirected materials to Mexico for at least three "Rocky" episodes, and any completed storyboards for "Bullwinkle's Corner" and "Peabody." By June, Val-Mar productions commenced work on the first episodes in the "Rocky" story "Upsidaisium," as well as two new cosponsor billboards: one each for Peter-Paul candy and American Chicle Company, makers of Dentyne.

Because the Val-Mar team was tightly committed to turning out the many "Rocky" episodes, George Singer and Dave Fern received overtime for their work on the new billboards. So did Bob Schleh and Rudy Zamora, who handled the new show titles. The work involved fuller animation because it was to be seen daily and had to look slick.

At this point several changes occurred. James G. Stewart from Glen Glenn Sound visited Mexico to analyze the audio problems. Glen Glenn was the Hollywood studio at which Ward's voice sessions were recorded, and Stewart was head engineer on most of them. His credentials were distinguished to say the least: he had been the sound man on Orson Welles's 1941 masterpiece *Citizen Kane*.

Rudy Zamora, meanwhile, had had quite enough of Gordon Johnson's blaming him for Val-Mar's scheduling problems. Johnson had consistently pushed him, so the free-spirited Zamora left at the end of the half-year mark. He had certainly been a great help, and in fact seven years later would be back with Jay Ward working on *George of the Jungle*.

Bob Schleh, always a competent artist and organizer, took over Zamora's position as studio production manager. A Mexican animator named Sandoval became the new—and apparently quite strict—animation supervisor. It was decided that Harvey Siegel would personally supervise all future layouts, which had become too diverse in style from cartoon to cartoon. Ward still urged the Val-Mar team to conform to the style of Al Shean. This was a wise ploy, since the Mexicans had long considered Shean Jay's most talented designer and openly admired his work. Frank Hursh, now the full-time color consultant on *Rocky and His Friends,* began experimenting with a more sparkling "contrasty" effect on the background art for the benefit of black-and-white TV reception (still in the majority of households at that time). As for animation, Schleh felt that the "Peabody" story "Guglielmo Marconi" showed tremendous improvement. One other good omen: the cel handlers were at last wearing gloves!

In August 1960 Sal Faillace, an excellent animator fresh from Lars Calonius Productions, arrived at Val-Mar to assist the Mexican animators with character poses. And Jim Stewart's trip had proven beneficial—at St. Angel Studios, where the audio dubbing was performed, a new German sound system was installed, replacing the tired and unversatile equipment they had been using. At last the sound tracks became crisper and brighter.

This period in Val-Mar's history marked the first anniversary of operations, a year of turmoil, confusion, and plain hard work. But the improvements were undeniable. Jay Ward made it clear to Gordon Johnson that if the ad agency hadn't been so panicky, the Mexicans wouldn't have reciprocated. Ward had always insisted on having a quality show but had found it difficult producing by long distance to Mexico City while the agency called the shots from New York. And he made it a point to periodically reemphasize that all the scenes should be kept simple and easily read.

The first birthday of the Val-Mar studio brought it a new name, Producciónes Animadas Gamma SA (translation: Gamma Productions). As Peter Piech says, "When the enterprise became Gamma Productions it was a vastly more professional operation, and all the early problems were solved." Bob Schleh was confident of smooth sailing for the upcoming production schedule. Schleh believed that each individual cartoon would take five weeks, from receiving storyboard to final camera, and that five or six cartoons could be produced concurrently.

After several fruitless months trying to raise moneys for Ward Films, Len Key and Jay Ward decided to part company. Key felt that Ward was too unbending on money matters for his own good: he had almost sold Jay's "Watts Gnu Show" pilot to ABC-TV ("It was a deal for $30,000 per show"), but Ward had insisted on full ownership, and the network brass had told them to take a hike. Besides, Key wanted to pursue other interests, including a return to his main love, the Broadway theater; he was soon a shareholder in *The Night They Raided Minsky's*.

On June 28, 1960, Jay Ward received good news. General Mills was picking up the option for twenty-six new Rocky shows, providing all "Peabody" and "Bullwinkle's Corner" segments were predirected in Mexico from this point. The Mexican schedule would be intensified as the remaining "Rocky," "Peabody," and "Bullwinkle's Corner" episodes had to be ready by October 6, the start of the fall season.

Ward, now busy with the two renewals totaling fifty-two shows, had relaxed somewhat; in 1959 he hadn't been sure if *Rocky* would prove to be a mere one-season wonder, and he had been scrambling for other ideas. Now, with the financially healthy budget and renewal, he could afford to put some of these projects on hold. The parting was amicable, and the ex-Berkeley schoolmates stayed in touch.

In June 1960, Jay Ward Productions signed a three-year deal with Neufeld, Rosen, Bash & Associates for network representation in the sale of all properties. NRB had entrée to many network honchos. They immediately commenced discussions with NBC to clinch a deal which would see Bullwinkle Moose starring in his own prime-time show a year later. Unfortunately, Jay's new packaging firm didn't appear to do much with the rest of his portfolio: "Watts Gnu," "Super Chicken," "Hoppity Hooper," and a special called *The Magic of Christmas*. While Jay was in a hurry, NRB was willing to wait.

12

AD AGENCY, NETWORK, AND SPONSOR, or You Think I Want Every Tom, Dick, and Gordon In on the Plot?

Like any TV show, *Rocky and His Friends* was a hectic, full-time commitment for many people, fraught with the myriad day-to-day hiccups endemic to television production. Keeping the enterprise on an even keel involved much correspondence, compromise, and to-and-fro between Jay Ward and Dancer-Fitzgerald-Sample, advertising agency of record for General Mills, the main sponsor of *Rocky*. The countless details on each and every aspect of the show were finalized between Ward in Hollywood and the influential Gordon H. Johnson in New York (D-F-S's immediate contact with Ward on the West Coast was the efficient and popular Betty O'Hara).

During renewal discussions, General Mills requested a few more changes. It was officially decided that "Aesop and Son" would replace the "Fairy Tales." Mills and the agency were still battling the scripts, insisting they were aiming only for kids, and Jay was ordered to monitor the writing much more closely "in the areas of adult sophistication and foreign accents." Ward stood firm, telling Johnson that the scripts were *not* that far over the heads of kids.

Meanwhile, the second *Rocky* season kicked off with the moose and squirrel's second-longest adventure yarn, running thirty-six episodes. This was one of Rocky and Bullwinkle's greatest stories. The magnificent moose inherits a mine deed to Mount Flatten, a "floating mountain." Our boys discover that it contains an amazing antigravity metal called "upsidaisium." Naturally, Boris and Natasha want this precious metal for their nasty little country, in order to solve its chronic parking problem. In this story we finally meet the feared Pottsylvanian evil-meister, Mr. Big. Once again the meandering plot features swipes at Communism, while Bill Scott gives the U.S. military bureaucracy special satiric attention, with klutzy characters like the flustered and incompetent General Broadbeam in the hilarious scenes in Fort Knick Knack. He also takes an amusing jibe at the parochial inhabitants of small towns, including one tiny village called Buzzard's Craw, and another lazy little hamlet whose blank-faced denizens impassively observe the huge mountain flying by overhead ("You know, Lem, it sounds so all-fire good, I plumb wish I was facin' the other way").

The "Monstrous Mechanical Moon Mice" story returned to some of the early devices: the moon men return, and Mr. Big continues his life after disappearing into the heavens while holding a chunk of upsidaisium. Two more institutions are razzed: teenage singing idols (with Boris disguised as a send-up of Elvis Presley's manager, here called Colonel Tomsk Parkoff) and the public's insatiable love affair with television. When all the TV antennas in town are mysteriously broken, people sit doggedly in front of their sets refusing to budge; one pathetic man decides to watch his washing machine ("Love these sea stories!"). In the two episodes where Bullwinkle and Boris engage in a dueling-singers match, there is a charming feel to the songs Bill Scott sings as Bullwinkle. This was a true signpost of Scott's unique humor. As he explained, "The veteran Disney animator Frank Thomas taught me these old English music-hall numbers when I worked with him at Fort Roach during the war."

The tale of the fabled Oogle Bird (pronounced "Boid" in authentic Flatbush dialect) is set on the island of New Greenpernt, ruled by King Bushwick "the Thoity-thoid." This nifty story is set off by Bullwinkle's weather-forecasting bunion. Boris Badenov tries to woo the famous fortune-telling Oogle Bird in yet another disguise, as the romantic Charles Boyoogle. Interestingly, Boris imitates a voice for the only time in his career—in all his other disguises he employs only visual alter egos. Besides the great Charles Boyer imitation, actor Paul Frees supplied another uncanny vocal copy for King Bushwick, who sounds eerily like Ed Gardner's Archie character from the old radio comedy *Duffy's Tavern*. Receiving Bill Scott's barbs this time are Washington bureaucracy, the U.S. Air Force, and TV weather people. A great Scott throwaway gag features the out-to-lunch Captain Peachfuzz, now making a living as the nation's chief weather forecaster. He achieves his nightly prognoses blindfolded, by hurling darts at a map; when one dart lands in the exact middle between sunshine and cloud, he says to "tell 'em it'll be unsettled!"

The "Rue Britannia" story was the first "Rocky and Bullwinkle" script not written by Bill Scott. Chris Hayward and Lloyd Turner wrote a fast-moving plot set in England. It involves an inscription—reading "Rue Britannia"—found on the sole of the moose's hoof, which will net Bullwinkle an inheritance of £1 million if he can survive a week in Abominable Manor; as the moose admits, "Shucks, I've been livin' in an abominable manner all my life!" The two new writers grasped the characters to perfection, and the puns are very Hayward and Turner-esque: the Earl of Crankcase, the law firm of Lamb, Curry, and Rice, and an outrageous cliffhanger title, "Mourning Becomes Electra-cuted." This tale also benefits from Chris Hayward's penchant for classical-style mystery and intrigue.

Next came the "Picayune Pot" story, an enjoyable cops-and-robbers saga from Bill Scott, who seemed to be experimenting with the dastardly Boris—this time minus Natasha—by placing him in the role of a Chicago-style gangster rather than a master spy. This tale involves a hunt to find buried treasure in publisher Colonel McCornpone's newspaper contest. More and more, from this story on, the omnipresent narrator was engaging in byplay with the on-screen characters (Boris: "Hey, wise guy—quiet!" Narrator: "Well I whispered, didn't I?"), and in fact Bill Conrad played a couple of larger incidental roles in this story. The banking system received another dart from Scott's poison pen, with the local Frostbite Falls branch manager again dubbed Mr. Friendly. And again he runs the Farmers and Swineherds National Bank.

"The Last Angry Moose" was Rocky and Bullwinkle's first ministory. Running a mere four episodes, this is a delicious parody of Hollywood mores, moviemaking, and 1950s method acting. Bullwinkle decides to go to Hollywood and become a movie star, but learns that he must take Brando-like courses in slouching and mumbling. He is also given a new name, Crag Antler! June Foray did a great imitation of the vicious Tinseltown gossip Louella Parsons, while ever-versatile Boris disguised himself as Alfred Hitchhike, D. W. Grifter, and Gregory Rat (the originals—Hitchcock, Griffith, and Ratoff—have yet to file suit).

The final story, before NBC inherited the cast for the revamped *Bullwinkle Show,* was a fine adventure concerning "Maybe Dick," the legendary Wailing Whale. In this tale, the leviathan of the deep has been swallowing whole ocean liners and throwing the World Shipping Council into panicsville. A neat Bill Scott pun has Bullwinkle chastising the great shipping tycoon Pericles Parnassus: "Boy, for a powerful magnate, you sure don't pick things up very fast." Paul Frees supplied the voice of Parnassus: it was an imitation of comic actor Harry Einstein (in real life, the father of comedian Albert Brooks). Einstein created a Greek dialect character called "Parkyakarkus," heard on radio shows with Eddie Cantor and Al Jolson in the 1930s. Our old nemesis Boris is disguised as Captain Horatio Hornswaggle, and he and Natasha have somehow acquired a pet gorilla named Rollo. This funny script closed the second and last series of *Rocky and His Friends.*

Jay received a new directive: the "Rocky" episodes had to be delivered earlier. Ward happily agreed, requesting he be allowed to handle more of the workload in Hollywood. "Rocky" production was being stepped up because it was now decided that from January 1, 1961, *Rocky and His Friends* would be telecast three times a week (Sunday, Tuesday, and Thursday). More writing was commissioned to complete "Rocky" scripts up to episode 104. The General Mills commercials had taken time to do properly, and more were being prepared. By mid-1960, Jay Ward's Los Angeles team had completed various commercials, three "Fractured Fairy Tales," the "Aesop" pilot, and one "Peabody" episode. Ward requested an additional seven "Fairy Tales" for his own studio, and he was given the go-ahead.

Actually, Jay inherited more work than he had expected. Two new commercials for General Mills' "hot" cereal Wheathearts were added to the Ward Productions timetable, via the Knox-Reeves ad agency. These featured Peabody and Sherman.

When Jay saw the first annual accounting from P.A.T. in July, he was shocked by the high cost of the Mexican operation. On the basis of just one "Fractured Fairy Tale," he calculated that he could produce each cartoon $4,000 cheaper, and with far greater quality. Before he cooled off, Ward had even begun looking into the feasibility of sending Bill Hurtz to Japan for below-the-line work.

Yet D-F-S kept trying to exert control over Jay's studio. For example, they asked Ward to send far more detailed script summaries to the sponsor, claiming that General Mills had been very upset by the "Box Top Robbery" plot. Jay fought this point and won—he knew Mills had been reasonable, and suspected Gordon Johnson was playing power politics. As for the detailed script outlines, Ward cagily asked for a $200 fee for each one, telling Johnson, "When we write stories, we obtain the barest thread of a plot and then write as we go." The request for script outlines was never heard again, but Ward didn't let it rest there, adding, "We have always tried to write as funny as we know how." He considered Johnson's theory—that the show was "geared for children who don't understand this type of humor"—to be "hogwash."

Twenty-six "Aesop and Son" scripts were commissioned in mid-July, just as *Daily Variety* officially announced, "*Rocky and His Friends* has been renewed for 26 weeks by General Mills. Program shifts to Thursday and Sunday at 5:30 on ABC-TV, replacing *Lone Ranger* in the Sunday slot. Show had the highest Nielsen rating last season of the daytime shows." Feeling more confident, Jay Ward began openly defying Johnson's orders.

It was pointed out by Jay that although they had the number one daytime show, they could rate even higher if there were fewer repeats on the show, and some publicity. He reminded Johnson that in the seven-odd months the show had been on the air, there had been absolutely nothing of any promotional nature in the newspapers. Quizzing Johnson on this, Ward pointed out that publicity equaled sales of General Mills products, high show ratings, and a skyrocketing profile.

In fact, in 1961 TV reporter Dwight Newton revealed, "This week, I had the grim pleasure of introducing Jay to Ell Henry, ABC's West Coast publicity chief. They had never met!" The article explained that "ABC wanted *Rocky* like a hole in the head but General Mills, taking a mad gamble, had forced the issue. ABC scheduled it apparently hoping nobody would see it, and never promoted it."

Pressing on, Ward mentioned that the elimination of the "Fairy Tales" was "a dumb idea" caused by D-F-S worrying about similar story lines, such as the four variations on "Sleeping Beauty." In reality, many letters sent to P.A.T. proved that the audience had loved the "Fractured Fairy Tales."

"Finally," Bill Scott recalled, "Jay became unflinchingly tough." Pointedly, Ward asked Johnson, "Why do D-F-S and Mills think they know more about producing a cartoon show than we do?" He added that D-F-S could have a true TV winner if they would stop fighting the production of a good show. And as proof, he reminded them that his five predictions had come true:

1. Not getting on air by September 1959;
2. Not getting on air twice weekly by November 1959;
3. Not being able to stay on twice weekly with new material;
4. The need for a higher budget from General Mills; and
5. The higher cost of the Mexican operation, which was supposed to be far cheaper.

Deflated, Gordon Johnson agreed with Ward, admitting that ABC had been shy on publicity due to the uncertain delivery dates. ABC now promised Jay some promotion in the fall, adding that the 5:30 P.M. Sunday period was an excellent position for the show—in fact, it rated the highest of all children's weekend time slots.

It was agreed by all concerned that the Mexican operation had finally picked up the pace under head animator Bob Schleh, with production output now ahead of schedule: in the month of July alone they shipped ninety-three and a half minutes of completed animation. This was an incredible improvement over their one year of operations. TV Spots raised their price after the first thirteen "Fairy Tales," due to industrywide wage hikes, and Bob Ganon contracted for nine more, agreeing to ship the "Androcles" and "Beauty and Her Beast" stories, predirected, to Mexico.

Meanwhile, the "Bullwinkle's Corner" segments were ordered to be changed from one minute to one and a half minutes, as there was less advertising time on Sundays (for the weekday broadcasts the show's end titles were trimmed by thirty seconds). In September "Bullwinkle's Corner" was modified. Instead of being the Bard of Minnesota, the moose now became Mr. Know-It-All, giving ludicrous lectures and pointers on various subjects. D-F-S ordered five more of the old one-minute poetry format, for a total of thirty-nine, and commissioned the longer "Know-It-All" format to follow.

Several merchandise items featuring the show characters came on the market in August 1960. Ward and P.A.T. had entered into a fifty-fifty licensing agreement six months earlier; there was now a potential weekly audience of 50 million. Meanwhile, the agency informed Jay that General

Mills would be requesting a replacement for the "Peabody" episodes. Ward and Scott mooted an idea called "Oliver's Twists"—Oliver was to be a W. C. Fields type who enjoyed telling tall tales. They also tried to sell *Hoppity Hooper* and a new cartoon concept called "Simpson and Delaney" to D-F-S, but as separate shows distinct from *Rocky and His Friends*.

"Simpson and Delaney," with a sample episode written by Bill Scott, was shown some initial interest. The show was to be a series of continuing episodes à la *Hoppity Hooper*. It centers around a lovable rogue named Delaney who runs a cheap and tacky circus (Delaney's Greater Combined Shows) with his girlfriend, Daphne. They have very few customers, mainly because Delaney and Daphne are also the only performers, donning various tacky guises like the Barfolas or Benzino the Fire Eater and His Flame.

One day a dull-witted customer named Simpson shows up, telling Delaney he wants to be an actor. He has no talent, but Delaney sees a buck in him because the large lad is obviously a perfect strongman act. Simpson is transformed into a masked wrestler, until he is pitted against a rival circus owner's gorilla. Ward and Scott were enthused about this idea.

The month of October saw Pete Burness make a brief journey down Mexico way to adjust and guide several model sheets for character consistency, especially on Rocky and Boris. Schleh still felt it was essential to get all the Hollywood assistance possible, and requested a more comprehensive supply of model sheets for nonregular characters, such as the historical figures in the "Peabody" episodes (Pizarro, Shakespeare, Daniel Boone, Jesse James, and Louis XVI), and the "Monstrous Mechanical Metal-Munching Moon Mice" for the latest "Rocky" story in progress. By this point the "Aesop and Son" segments were also in production, replacing "Fractured Fairy Tales."

Schleh informed Ward that the seventy-first episode of "Rocky" marked a turning point in quality at the Mexican setup. Twenty episodes later he announced, "Our artwork is finally respectable!" Certainly, compared to the work being turned out twelve months earlier, everyone could now feel justifiably proud. In retrospect, the schedule that the New York connection had imposed on Val-Mar—a green outfit burdened by a major language barrier—seems positively staggering, and their relatively rapid improvement was remarkable.

Also in October 1960, Jay Ward chatted with San Francisco–based journalist Jim Scott. Scott, familiar to Jay from his Berkeley Tennis Club days, wrote an interesting article for the *Berkeley Gazette*. It revealed that *Rocky* was by then TV's highest-rated daytime show (and had been on the air less than a year), and that the *Rocky* pilot film had cost only $5,000. The author noted, "General Mills paid him for 78 shows. Coming up are *Hoppity Hooper, Watts Gnu* and *Super Chicken.*" The article offered a valuable account of what it was like at Ward Productions back then. "I toured Jay's three buildings on Sunset Boulevard—his office is in an apartment in a Spanish courtyard. There he and his co-producer, Bill Scott, run the show, which includes 25 (temperamental) artists. In addition, Jay maintains a unit in Mexico City, where more than 100 cartoonists ink out the bulk of his work. In his Sunset studio the artists come and go as they please. Some work from their homes. The most industrious seemed to be a little guy who was turning out merchandising ideas for Jay's weird creatures. Actors, directors, animators, musicians and designers also are involved."

Employee Marcelle Philpott was interviewed; she felt that Ward was successful because he and he alone handled all these artists. "They respect him," she said, "because he does only quality work, and is such an understanding and warm person. He's fair with everyone. They wouldn't work with anyone else."

Ward was described as a brilliant organizer who worked a seven-day week, still operated his Domingo Avenue realty business, and was still a member of the Berkeley Tennis Club. The report also revealed that *Rocky* had been sold to Australia (the first foreign sale). Jay Ward finished with, "This work is fun, Jim—actually, I'd be doing it if I didn't make a darned cent."

In November 1960, Sal Faillace was appointed the new animation coordinator for *Rocky and His Friends,* replacing Ernie Terrazas, who was promoted to a full-time director position. Faillace decided to conduct weekly animation classes to further improve the level of draftsmanship. Bob Schleh wrote to Jay Ward, mentioning that the eighth "Aesop" cartoon showed tremendous improvement, being the best work they had produced yet. Ward was finally confident enough to allow four and a half minutes of material to be directed on-site in Mexico each week, providing continuity of work for Gamma. In early 1961, Bill Scott revisited the Mexican operation. This time he departed feeling much happier.

Meanwhile the new package of twenty-six *Rocky* shows was a month away from completion by late November 1960. Suddenly General Mills decided to renew again, this time for a full fifty-two shows instead of the usual twenty-six. This was great news for Jay Ward. The price was 15 percent higher than the first series, and all reuse fees would be paid properly. In fact, this new show order, timed for the fall 1961 season, exceeded $1.5 million. Best of all, the renewal meant continuity of work, starting with 104 new "Rocky" episodes to be scripted.

Following this heady news, a fresh set of show titles was ordered, as more variety would be needed with the increased exposure. These titles would be produced in Mexico. Discussions began in November for a daily version of *Rocky,* in a fifteen-minute format, to take advantage of the burgeoning merchandise. All "Rocky" episodes ordered from Mexico were now given A1 priority; the already large backlog of "Fairy Tales" and "Peabody" would be used for reruns.

By now audiences were seeing Jay's newest cartoon, "Aesop and Son." As charming as these cartoons are, the plain truth is that "Aesop's Fables" was the poor cousin of "Fractured Fairy Tales," created because the ad agency insisted that "Fairy Tales" was the weakest element in the whole *Rocky* show. (In fact, they were so wrong about this that "Fractured Fairy Tales" was reinstated after "Aesop" 's thirty-nine segments were broadcast.) The idea of fables came to Jay Ward and Bill Scott as a viable alternative: they were still thematically linked to fairy stories, and Aesop's Fables were as popular with young children as the Grimms' and Hans Christian Andersen's output.

During the writing of the pilot episode, "The Lion and the Mouse" (the first "Aesop" cartoon to be aired), the series title was decided on. Originally Aesop was going to narrate the stories "straight"—there was no Junior. The show was called "Fractured Fables." This was replaced by the working title "Addled Aesop," until the format of father and son was decided on. The highly amusing Charlie Ruggles was the favored choice for Aesop's voice, since it had been decided to continue the tradition of having this show element narrated by a revered and venerable character actor from the movies.

Many of the fables were written by Chris Hayward and Lloyd Turner, which explains these cartoons' similarity to the punned closing between Peabody and Sherman. Aesop would relate the fable, capping it with a moral. Junior, in turn, would bounce his own word-playing moral back on Dad. And as with most of Jay Ward's cartoons, puns are a real big deal. Aesop Junior is as ready as Mr. Peabody to end each segment with a wisecrack, but thanks to the sensitive playing of Ruggles and Butler, the boy never seems smart-alecky. The puns are more of a warmhearted father-son tease than anything else.

Show Notes for 1959–60

The original order was fifty-two shows. With 2 "Rocky" episodes per show, the total reached 104 episodes. From November 1959 to May 1960 the first twenty-six half hours aired. These consisted of episodes 1–40 (the Mooseberry rocket-fuel story) and 41–52 ("Box Tops Robbery").

The next twenty-six half hours were ready following the summer break, and the show aired twice weekly, Thursday and Sunday. It was discovered that the Sunday and Thursday station programming lineups were different in ten market areas, so it was necessary to run a separate series of "Rocky" stories for the different days, as follows: Sundays (September 25, 1960, to January 22, 1961): Rocky episodes 53–88 ("Upsidaisium"); Thursdays (September 29 to November 17): Rocky episodes 89–104 ("Metal-Munching Moon Mice"). General Mills didn't want to air reruns from Thursday November 24, so D-F-S, confident of a renewal for twenty-six more half hours, asked Bill Scott to hastily write a new story that would finish in six weeks (i.e., 12 episodes). The result was episodes 105–116 ("Greenpernt Oogle"), which aired from November 24 to December 29. The renewal was signed in November.

Then from January 1961 the show was aired three times weekly—on Sundays, and twice during the week (Tuesdays and Thursdays starting January 3 and 5). For the weekday telecasts, reruns began from episode 1, while the Sunday shows featured all-new episodes.

Following the "Upsidaisium" story, which ended January 22, there were twenty weeks left of the renewed twenty-six (the first six weeks employing "Greenpernt Oogle," mentioned above), so D-F-S offered Jay the choice of either a long 40-episode story or several shorter adventures. Ward chose the latter; from January 29 the following stories were aired: episodes 117–124 ("Rue Britannia"), 125–138 ("Buried Treasure"), 139–142 ("The Last Angry Moose"), and 143–156 ("Maybe Dick"). To lighten the task of Bill Scott, Ward commissioned Chris Hayward and Lloyd Turner to write one "Rocky" story when this schedule was being thrashed out in July 1960. They wrote the "Rue Britannia" story.

When the renewal was signed, two extra decisions were reached in order to keep the writing staff busy. "Aesop and Son" had comprised 26 episodes in the earlier renewal of twenty-six weeks. The next renewal was for fifty-two weeks. General Mills wanted a new cartoon element, so an additional 13 "Aesops" were commissioned, with the remaining thirty-nine weeks reserved for the new segment. Sponsor and ad agency had to eat humble Cheerios, for viewer mail was so strong that Ward's beloved "Fractured Fairy Tales" returned.

Secondly, following the first 52 "Peabody" episodes (and the follow-up batch of 26 totaling 78 "Peabody"s in all), an extra 13 were ordered for the upcoming fifty-two week renewal. As before, General Mills requested a new element for the remaining thirty-nine weeks of the contract. Thus the intrepid Dudley Do-Right of the Mounties joined the cast.

Nonetheless, the lad is quite sharp: to "The Wolf in Sheep's Clothing" Aesop appends the moral "Appearances are often deceiving," but Junior comes back with a beauty: "Always be alert, whether awake or a sheep." In another sheepdog scenario ("The Hound and the Wolf"), the poor dog's set of false teeth are stolen by a crafty wolf. Aesop's point is "Barking dogs seldom bite." But Junior can't resist the retort "Nothing dentured, nothing gained." The stories themselves are guilty, too; in one episode a female frog is called Ann Phibian.

Hayward remembers writing the two fables featuring a bandit called "The masked Clock." Chris Jenkyns's more whimsical style is recognizable in "The Sick Lion" and in an episode that NBC's Standards and Practices tried to reject. Jenkyns explained, "I'd written an 'Aesop' about a cat and a hen who fall in love; NBC had script approval, I guess, and someone there told us this was tantamount to doing a story about interracial marriage. Anyway, Jay told them they were being ridiculous and that my script was funny. It went to air."

While the animation is often pretty awful, the "Aesop and Son" cartoons are a delight to the ear. Charlie Ruggles's narration is just right. For the younger audience he has a perfect old-storyteller voice; strangely, Ruggles did not receive screen credit. The rapport between Aesop and Junior is natural, and their father-son relationship is believable due to the fine playing of Ruggles and Daws Butler. Butler, as Aesop Junior, demonstrated his awesome range and acting talent; Junior is a credible twelve-year-old kid voice, not a vocal distortion. Daws was forty-four when he portrayed this role. And

Rocky and Bullwinkle vs. the Censors

In 1961, TV columnist Dwight Newton wrote, "The TV nets are appalled by Jay Ward's cartoon endeavors because he is a nonconformist, a great dissenter, a stinging satirist, a sort of modern day Mark Twain in an industry that forever trembles at the thought of possibly offending a viewer or an advertiser." In its first twelve months Rocky and His Friends was the subject of much to-and-fro when it came to script approval by General Mills and ABC-TV. Although approval was standard industry practice, the unique nature of Jay Ward's cartoons caused much panicking and compromise. The first problem was the "Fractured Fairy Tale" called "Beauty and the Beast." The ad agency felt this contained subject matter that was far too adult: an ugly and promiscuous beast strikes out with every woman he woos in his efforts to get kissed, which will change him into a handsome prince. The episode's payoff was the problem. The beast proves to be a fake—he's not really a handsome prince. As he tells the narrator, "Look, Bud—you get kissed your way and I'll get kissed my way!" Ward was finally allowed to do this as written.

Several minor script objections, laughably puritanical by today's standards, included "Fairy Tale" 30 ("Aladdin's Lamp"), which contained the word "darn": General Mills felt this would lead kids on the road to swearing. And episode 20 ("Sleeping Beauty") featured a bubble gum reference which upset the co-sponsor Sweets Company of America, who'd turned sour on any candy mentions after a saltwater taffy gag in "Peabody" 8 ("Sir Walter Raleigh").

In an early Rocky episode ending the narrator announced the double title "Canoe's Who," or "Look Before You Leak." The agency requested that the second title be changed, and an alternate line was recorded at the next voice session ("The Vulgar Boatman"). But Jay wasn't happy—he won his point by embarrassing the agency people about their dirty minds, especially considering that viewers could plainly see a leaky canoe when the title was being announced. "Look Before You Leak" was back in, but a compromise was reached by having the audio fade out as the line was heard.

But the biggest problem for Ward occurred in "Rocky" episode 32. Natasha is disguised as an Indian princess in a scene where she, Rocky, Bullwinkle, and Boris, all joined by a rope, are climbing a snowy mountain. When they realize they're lost, Natasha says, "Great Spirit say go this way." They fall, and the vexed Boris declares, "Great Spirit goofed!" That line caused the agency and sponsor to hit the roof; the boss at General Mills was very religious and superpatriotic, and there was much argument about the Great Spirit line mocking "the Indians' highest deity." Jay lost this one, with the upshot being that the ad agency began watching future scripts far more intently.

If the agency liked a script (as in the case of "Peabody" 22 ["Robin Hood"] or "Fairy Tale" 17 ["King Midas"]) they would say, "All OK and very funny." But if there were problems their memos went into amusing detail—at least by today's *South Park* standards. For example, "Peabody" 21 ("Louis Pasteur"): "Episodes like this one and Alfred Nobel scare the living hell out of us. Over the years these guys have been built up as prestige figures and national heroes. We can hear the phone ringing right now from the French Embassy complaining about our making a comic strip figure of their boy Pasteur." "Peabody" 24 ("Ponce de León"); "This is a hilarious episode, but we do bear down a little hard on the diaper talk. Can the flag on page 1 be a bib instead of a diaper, and can we also avoid the tie-in with the Spanish flag?" "Fairy Tale" 19 ("Little Red Riding Hood"). "We wonder whether the gag about the Freeway will be understood nationally. Here in the East, for instance, highways are not called Freeways. And the line 'Here's the latest thing from Africa . . . number one boy.' We don't want the NAACP breathing down our necks." "Peabody" 14 ("Confucius"). "In this one ABC objects to the Chinese pidgin English which contributes to a stereotype of the Chinese race offensive to people of Oriental origin."

If it wasn't the ad agency, it was the network, as in these remarks from Bernardine McKenna of ABC Continuity Acceptance. "Rocky" 29: "The satire on hair oil TV commercials is rather unfair." (Regarding the hair-oil spot, D-F-S actually disagreed with the network—and they were ad people!) "Peabody" 12 ("George Armstrong Custer"): "There are an awful lot of arrows protruding fore and aft from an awful lot of soldiers in this episode. Though the bit is intended for laughs, don't forget how many parents feel about unnecessary violence in children's shows." "Fairy Tale" 12 ("Tom Thumb"): "I find the whole tenor of this episode objectionable. Juvenile delinquency is not something to be treated flippantly. Please have Tom become something other than a mixed-up JD with a souped up butterfly, leading a juvenile gang on 'candy heists.' THIS EPISODE IS REJECTED." (It went to air.)

But most of the comments came from the ad agency. Regarding the Peabody cartoons, they pleaded with Jay to stay away from names like Nobel and Pasteur who were "associated with prestige and public service in the public's mind." Mills suggested the ending of the Pasteur episode with the Shrimp Louis pun would be lost on most adults and all children, adding, "Think we are getting a little sophisticated." For the Robinson Crusoe episode (#23), they urged the deletion of a "fish on Friday" tag joke, fearing trouble from Catholic viewers, and the elimination of the expletive "darn right." For #25, "Leonardo da Vinci," the concerns were with the Italian accent used for da Vinci which "appears dangerously close to caricature." (It was!)

The Fairy Tales fared no better. "Sir Galahad" (#16) elicited a query on "whether the writers aren't getting a little too preoccupied with show biz," while #19, "Red Riding Hood," again caused concerns about broad dialects: "Red's Greek accent . . . might offend people of Greek nationality." PC Police forty years ago!

And the famous "Sleeping Beauty" episode caused nervous tremors about the references to Sleeping Beauty Land (by inference Disneyland) resembling a low budget circus "or Coney Island sideshow." There were fears Disney might bring defamation proceedings because of the coupon book bits, and the "avaricious counting of money in three scenes."

By 1960 the complaints appeared less frequently; as the show caught on and ratings climbed, many of the earlier concerns dwindled. There were still a few though: the "Snow White" segment was called "definitely a poor story for kids," who wouldn't get the stock-market storyline. And, "no more Americans in the Peabody scripts." They allowed "Sitting Bull but not George Washington" (i.e., no Native Americans, but real ones were OK—times were sure different!). They added, "Couldn't you build histories around Cheops building the pyramids or the Trojan Horse," and suggested the Vikings, Marie Antoinette, and Catherine of Russia as possible subjects (indeed some were used).

But by far the most interesting reaction came from D-F-S concerning the "Rocky and Bullwinkle" story about counterfeit box tops. Although General Mills was a little concerned about a satire on their very lifeblood, the "Great Spirit goofed" line was infinitely more bothersome to them than this story. It was the agency people who were far more panicky. Their main worry concerned the takeoffs of cereal premiums, with so much of their work for Mills involving these items. The premiums in Bill Scott's original story draft were ordered changed before recording commenced. Originally, Boris was offering "a combination atomic whistle and poison ring." D-F-S suggested changing this to atomic roller skates. They also suggested one that Jay Ward liked so much he used it in the revised script verbatim: "An English yo-yo that whistles 'On the Road to Mandalay.' "

within the cartoons, he did some of the kookiest character voices he ever played, matched beautifully by Bill Scott, who costarred in all the fables. Most of them, in fact, are really dialogues between Butler and Scott, who together played what amounted to an entomologist's and zoologist's life study—an incredible range of animals. They portrayed frogs, sheepdogs, wolves, foxes, bears, lions, eagles, beetles, earthworms, canaries, mules, jack-rabbits, mice, cats, and owls. And all the owls seem to talk like Cap'n Crunch! Indeed, there are very few human characters in these stories.

June Foray appeared in only eight of the episodes, so perhaps Aesop was a trifle misogynistic. At least in "The Rooster and Five Hens" she made up for it, playing all five Leghorn sisters. "The Hare and the Tortoise," Aesop's most famous morality play, was tackled by Ward's team, who even offered up a sequel. Perhaps the funniest episode was "The Centipede and the Snail": these two losers are not only superdumb, with voices to match, but are the most eccentrically designed cartoon animals to be seen in a long time.

The pilot film, the opening title (with Junior using a jackhammer to add his name to the credits), and a few episodes were animated in Hollywood by the Ward outfit, but the bulk of the "Aesop"s were executed in Mexico. They do look slightly better than the early "Fairy Tales" made by the Gamma Productions team, mainly because "Aesop and Son" began production after the Mexican unit had been in operation more than a year. By this stage Gamma was a little more together.

One extra twist to the tale: the ad agency was eager for an animated Cheerios commercial to feature their newest stars, Aesop and Son. Two spots were produced at Ward Productions, but the voices of both characters were done by Daws Butler. Butler recalled, "Charlie was a great personality and we hit it off real well. But I ended up doing Aesop in the TV commercial because he was out of town or something. I loved the music of his voice—

"I never could do Edward Everett Horton, but with Charlie Ruggles I seemed to fall into being able to do that."

In early November 1960, Ward was contacted by New York–based record producer Arthur Shimkin of Hudson Productions, then the audio wing of Simon and Schuster. Shimkin was assigned to produce a Golden LP (containing five tracks per side) for the children's market. This was the quickest project Jay Ward ever undertook: a month from receiving the phone call, the record *Rocky and His Friends* was being pressed (it was released in March 1961). The budget was $4,300. Dennis Farnon, who had impressed Ward and Scott on the *Winnie the Pooh* session, composed and arranged eleven musical items. The dialogue was written by Paul Parnes, who quickly deduced that Ward's cartoon sound tracks didn't require visuals. Two "Peabody" episodes, two "Bullwinkle's Corner" segments, and a "Fractured Fairy Tale" were dubbed from studio masters, then linked with the new material, which was themed to appeal to an individual child playing the album. (For another "Fairy Tale," Jack and the Beanstalk, Bill Scott revoiced Daws Butler's lines, as Butler was then under contract with Colpix Records, which released LP versions of Hanna-Barbera shows; however, this "Fairy Tale" was eventually discarded from the album.)

The music was put down in three hours on November 18 by Dennis Farnon and an orchestra. On November 23, voice tracks and song overdubs for the Golden Record were taped with the characters of Rocky, Bullwinkle, Peabody, Sherman, Natasha, Boris, Cloyd, and Gidney. Bill Scott's twelve-year-old son John got in on the act, joining his famous costars for some handclapping sound effects. Arthur Shimkin was delighted with the results.

On November 29 that same busy week, Hans Conried along with Frees, Scott, and Foray spent a long evening recording all the loop lines for the pilot film of *Fractured Flickers*. They did two segments, "Tarfoot of the Apes" and "The Giddyap Kid," and two days later Conried filmed his host segments. Then on December 5 and 7 the music cues were recorded, again by the versatile Farnon. (They included his great Jazz Age title music for the animated *Fractured Flickers* opening.)

The year 1960 was also noteworthy for a short-lived but noble project called the "Jay Ward Productions Workshop," which commenced in November. The idea was to sponsor a sixteen-week class in the techniques of movement and design for the increasing trend toward adult TV cartoons so that "a sense of satire and parody in design would be imparted to younger artists." The class was held one night a week. Promising students were selected by Ward Productions, which supplied classrooms, materials, and teachers. (These were Bill Hurtz and Bobe Cannon [1911–64], the brilliant UPA director of classics like *Gerald McBoing-Boing*.) There were no fees charged. Hurtz recalls, "We ended up only doing about six weeks' worth of lessons." Bill Scott was one of several lecturers in a similar course at the University of Southern California starting in 1961, and he was part of a founding movement to install animation courses at West Coast universities.

The workshop idea was suggested following the rapid success of *The Flintstones* and *The Bugs Bunny Show* in evening prime time. By now Jay Ward and Bill Scott were well aware that General Mills and the NBC network were expressing considerable interest in the *Rocky* show characters for a nighttime slot.

13

1961: Bullwinkle Hits the Big Time, or Don't Go Getting Swelled Antlers

Happily for Jay Ward, the year 1961 began with a big announcement: NBC would air the next "Rocky and Bullwinkle" series in evening prime time for the new fall season, kicking off September 24, 1961. This switch to the most prestigious network and an adult time period was the result of months of negotiations between general Mills, Ward's sales agents Neufeld, Rosen, Bash, and the National Broadcasting Company. The network was eager for a prime-time cartoon show; the success of ABC's *The Flintstones* meant there was a large market for nighttime animation which appealed to both adults and children. NBC bit the Bullwinkle bullet, and publicity would soon be vital.

A sound track for Jay's "Simpson and Delaney" project was recorded in January 1961. Dennis Farnon composed the title music, and Scott sang two songs for the pilot track, which was to be presented with an accompanying storyboard. Ward budgeted the series at $75,000, but it didn't sell. Maybe it's just as well, because Simpson was mighty like Fillmore Bear and the opportunistic Delaney was a ringer for Professor Waldo, both from the later *Hoppity Hooper* series.

Following a year and a half of diligent work in Mexico, Bob Schleh left the *Rocky* show on February 3, 1961, transferring to a directing position on Peter Piech's *King Leonardo* series for Total Television, also being made at Gamma (though the first few Total cartoons were animated at TV Spots in

Hollywood). Sal Faillace took over as production supervisor on the Jay Ward cartoons, and work continued steadily on "Aesop and Son," "Bullwinkle's Corner," and "Peabody" segments south of the border.

March 1961 saw the release of the Golden children's record album *Rocky and His Friends*. Later that month D-F-S met with the U.S. Treasury Department to discuss a tie-in for a schools-targeted public-service project, "The Rocky-Bullwinkle Savings Stamps Club and Peace Patrol." This was the first truly big publicity break for the characters. A short film featuring the moose and squirrel, timed to coincide with the fall premiere, would eventually reach about 10 million children in schools nationwide.

By now the media were informed of Rocky and Bullwinkle's network switch to prime time, resulting in a flurry of press items.

The story "Ward-Scott on Animation Spree" from *Variety* (February 22) reported, "Ward and Scott have sketched out plans for the production of *Green Hopper,* a 30 minute show revolving around a frog, wolf and bear; *Simpson and Delaney*—a Laurel and Hardy animated duo, and *Super Chicken*. Hopper was being shopped around the ad agencies. Previously completed and in the offing is *Fractured Flickers,* a show comprised of footage from silent pix which is re-edited to bring about unusual and funny situations. Each show will cost in the neighborhood of $50,000."

The article revealed that Ward was building up a large library of background music themes. Also discussed were the imminent release of the Golden Record album and "plans for a 90 minute animated spectacular for TV, aimed at children (and those oldsters too that dig the cartoon bit), during Christmas season. The special will be peppered with carols, hymns and Christmas stories."

Far and away the most interesting print coverage was the extensive interviews with Jay Ward, either solo or with Bill Scott. In stark contrast with Jay's later reputation as a constantly giggling eccentric who wouldn't talk to the press [his variable health was the main reason he appeared reclusive], a review of this contemporary reportage proves otherwise. It shows Ward to be a sharp interviewee who definitely knew the value of publicity.

From the aforementioned *Variety* article: "Both Ward and Scott are of the opinion that animated cartoons are misjudged by ad agencies as shows only for youngsters. 'That's not so,' they chorus, 'all ages of the TV public respond to animation. Look at the reaction of cartoons in use as commercials.' "

Jay expanded on this subject when speaking to (Los Angeles) *Herald-Tribune* columnist Joe Hyams in April, explaining: "Cartoons are the only

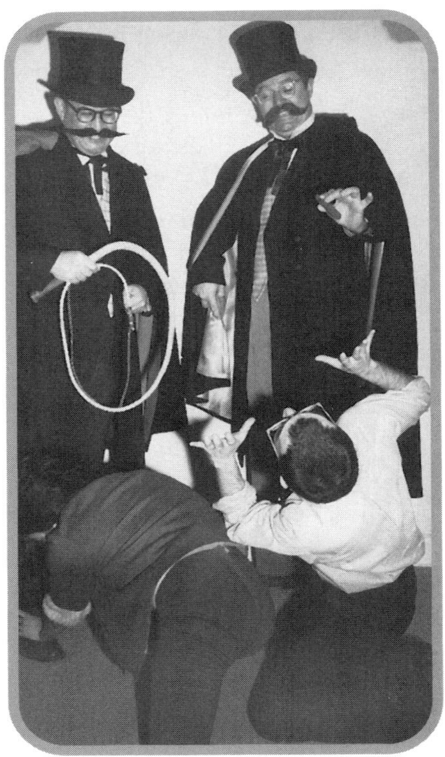

Bill and Jay in melodrama mode. *Courtesy of Bill Scott*

medium people love as a medium—even when lousy. We're a writing studio—we write our shows as funny, sharp and sophisticated as we can make them. Even though animated shows have a large audience of kids, you have to remember it's the same kids who watch *The Untouchables, Twilight Zone* and Bob Hope. Kids today are exposed to an adult world and they're sharp. Our stuff is sharper and more sophisticated than many of the dramatic shows. Everything we do is a satire and whimsy—that makes the fun."

Scott: "We're the only two animation people in the world who haven't worked for Walt Disney. Our shows differ from Donald Duck and Pluto in two important areas. Disney worked twenty years to get animation to appear as real as possible, and the nearer he got to reality, the duller the shows got. We believe animation should involve a push beyond reality. If you've got a picture that can be done with live characters, you might as well use live characters. We use animation to sell a story, Disney uses the story to sell animation."

Ward: "If you turned off the sound and watched one of our shows, the appeal would be mostly for children. With the vision off and just the sound on, the appeal would be for adults. The whole show appeals to every one. And if you listen, we say things that are mighty sharp."

In July 1961, a piece by Charles Witbeck revealed that Ward and Scott hadn't been able to sell their other TV shows. Scott: "We know we're funny. The problem has been to get air time when someone can see us. We take the blame—we didn't make a major sales effort. We didn't go around banging doors and pushing. We were too busy making shows. Suddenly we learned there is a tremendous difference between sales acceptance and public acceptance."

Columnist Charles Denton's report: " 'We've been overlooked,' said Jay Ward. "We try to make fun of things people know about because they're the funniest. But at the same time, we refuse to draw parodies on existing shows. We took *Watts Gnu* and *Fractured Flickers* to one agency guy and he looked them over and said we didn't have the right idea about TV cartoons. "What you have to do," he told us, "is to animate an established show and give it a little twist." Well, we want to prove we're funny by doing something fresh, not because someone else already has been funny. MCA is planning an animated cartoon of *Fibber McGee and Molly*. We were asked to animate it, but turned it down. That's just the sort of thing we don't want to get into.'

"Bill Scott added, 'The one thing that gave us heart was *The Flintstones*. It's so mediocre we became convinced that anything acceptable would really go over."

Jay: "We aim at neither adults nor children. Our goal is to achieve the ultimate in comedy, including subtleties which escape the youngsters, but which evoke response from adults."

Scott: "No one resents a cartoon character, so instead of someone getting sore when an animated figure satirizes in a biting way, he'll smile and say, 'Isn't he cute?', but let a 'live' character utter the same thoughts and there are cries of anguish from here to the most remote ratings-survey outpost!"

Martin Williams wrote a perceptive piece about limited animation shows for Evergreen Review. In "A Purple Dog, a Flying Squirrel and the Art of Television," he praised "unpretentious little programs with artistic energy and fine comedy, supposedly designed for children, and, at their best, unique comic experiences." He correctly surmised that the sound tracks were all-important: "The creative core of these shows lies in the writing, then with the highly resourceful people who do the voices—not to mention the sound effects." After giving a nice rap to Hanna-Barbera's "Quickdraw McGraw,"

"Augie Doggie," and "Snagglepuss," he added, "*Rocky and His Friends* is in some ways a more sophisticated affair, and it never risks the occasional calculated cuteness of the *Huckleberry* shows. It abounds in lampoon, burlesque and wild puns. The fall will bring Ward and Scott's color *Bullwinkle Show*—superior comic entertainment."

Strangely enough, Williams, who praised Hanna-Barbera for their earlier shows, went on to describe the nighttime *Flintstones* as "humorless, derivative and noisy." (Several items came down hard on the family from Bedrock; ironically, *The Flintstones* would prove the biggest success story of any cartoon show from this era.)

Around the same time, columnist Dave Stringer wrote a similar article; again, Hanna-Barbera's earlier shows were praised. Then Stringer added, "The newest and in many ways the most promising entrants in the TV cartoon field are Jay Ward and Bill Scott (a graduate of 'Mr. Magoo') and their *Rocky and His Friends* series. They proceed in a barrage of puns the kiddies may or may not catch. By all odds the best things the *Rocky* show does are its 'Fractured Fairy Tales.' Narrated by Edward Everett Horton, they are perhaps as funny as any animated works you've ever seen."

And on April 27, 1961, *The Village Voice* published an unsigned testimonial called "The Perils of *Rocky*": "*Rocky* abounds in wildly energetic, punning, burlesquing low comedy, but it frequently achieves some fine lampoon as well—like the hilariously discomforting reactions of the citizens of Frostbite Falls when they all lost TV reception. The writers and the talented quartet who do the voices carry a heavy burden, but the stylized drawing is beautifully complementary, and that wonderful surrealist moment at the end of each Rocky episode when a blank-faced Rocky and Bullwinkle sprout out of the ground in the middle of a daisy patch is about as close to a visual masterpiece as TV has to offer."

To maintain their audience share, ABC decided to rerun the older *Rocky and His Friends* in a daily fifteen-minute format. All the element openings were eliminated, including the twenty-two-second "Rocky" opening, and the credits were shortened. This "new" *Rocky* show would be an individual station operation, and to the delight of Ward and Johnson, market after market immediately offered excellent time slots.

Jay now had the opportunity to establish Ward Productions in the "Class A" nighttime category. His new NBC series was named *The Bullwinkle Show,* and D-F-S commissioned all-new "Mr. Know-It-All" segments to pro-

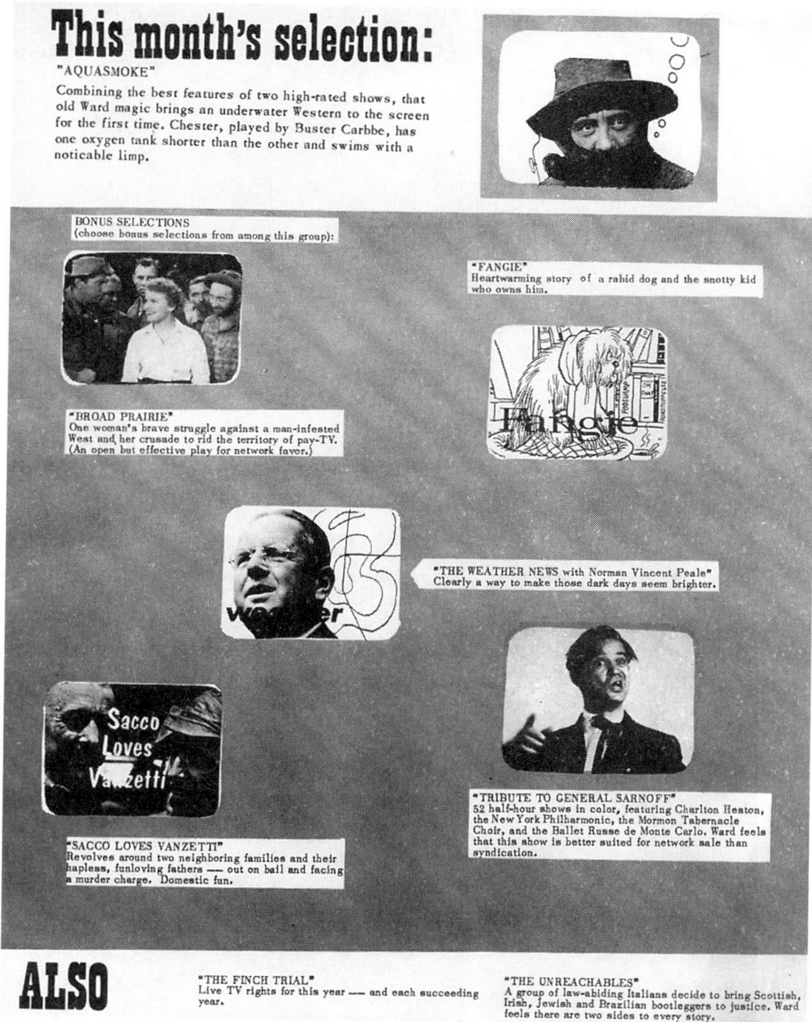

An example of the crazy mailers for "Operation Loudmouth."
Artwork copyright © 1961 by Ward Productions, Inc., courtesy of Skip Craig

mote the mighty moose's title stature. For the first time in two years of operations, Ward was actually asked to write "sharp, adult subjects." Gordon Johnson requested new opening title animation from Ward's Hollywood studio for Bullwinkle's starring vehicle, while "Dudley Do-Right of the Mounties" was approved as a new element, each episode to run four and a half minutes.

Once the NBC *Bullwinkle Show* deal was firmed, Ward decided to devote more time to the publicity arena. The Mexican studio was handling the bulk of physical cartoon production, and, as Bill Scott said, "Jay kind of buried himself in promotion early in the game." Then too, Cy Plattes, Ward's pal at General Mills, was keen to publicize the new *Bullwinkle Show's* airing in prime time on the then top network. In the first week of April 1961, Jay sent out the first of his zany publicity mailers. To promote the evening show, he and his new PR man Howard Brandy concocted a gigantic media barrage.

The promotional blitz was named "Operation Loudmouth" and officially kicked off in August 1961. Four months earlier a teaser series of zany mailers—produced in-house at Ward Productions and written by George Atkins and Allan Burns—began appearing once a week for thirty-nine straight weeks, reaching over 1,200 ad agencies, columnists, and disc jockeys throughout the country. The mailing list eventually swelled to over 3,000.

Part of this intense publicity drive was Jay and Bill's own decision. As *TV Guide* reported, "To put it bluntly, Ward and Scott and Bullwinkle were not selling. 'We had to do something about it,' explains Ward, a round, bespectacled man who describes himself as a chuckly butcher. 'We had to let people know that we were funny and creative. So we invented what we call "Operation Loudmouth," to influence the opinion makers.' These, in Ward's opinion, were some 400 people, the heads of agencies, certain columnists and disc jockeys. 'Then we found everybody wanted in,' Ward says."

The mailers consisted of visually arresting one-sheets containing ludicrous and attention-grabbing headlines, most of which satirized contemporary politics and TV. One of them urged its readers to "Earn Big Money or Fabulous Prizes for helping promote *The Bullwinkle Show*," explaining this could be done by "hitting Mao Tse Tung with a bowl of tomato chow yuk while yelling 'Bullwinkle!' " Or readers should "Soak Fidel Castro's beard with gasoline, using your official Bullwinkle water pistol, while yelling 'Bullwinkle, si—tractors, no!' " Soon after their kickoff the mailers featured hilarious cartoon drawings and gags by young Allan Burns, a recent recruit to Jay's writing staff (had Burns lived on the East Coast he would surely have been one of *Mad* magazine's top contributors).

George Atkins recalls, "My greater pride was in the creation of Jay's 'mailer' idea and the writing of the material for these weekly mailings—after a couple of months writing these while in L.A., Jay allowed me to run off to Mexico City and Acapulco for several months and to mail my material from there. I thought the very talented Al Burns was only doing the layout and artwork for these efforts, but when I made my first trip home I discovered that he was adding material to many of them—and the truly galling part for me was that everything he added was excellent. I also discovered that the mailers had caused quite a sensation in the networks and agencies and that my absence had allowed me to be the forgotten man in the whole procedure."

The irresistibly silly mailers featured themed spoofs like the "Film Series of the Month Club" whereby one could purchase six Jay Ward TV series at the list price of $2 million each and get a seventh absolutely free; or "Jay Ward's Pyramid Club," where you bought one Ward TV show and sent it off to the ad agency at the top of the list of other buyers; when your name hit the top you'd get 2,458 series for the price of one. Then there was the Jay Ward Peace Corps (to "underdeveloped ad agencies and sponsors"), or Camp Oona-Oki-Chobee, a retreat for harried TV personnel, where top sports events included Indian wrestling with network vice presidents.

There was even a special suicide campaign in which top dollar was offered to anyone who went over Niagara Falls dressed in a Bullwinkle suit, or who "splattered into Lenin's Tomb in a 1938 Hudson Terraplane called 'The Bullwinkle Special.' "

Character merchandise from *Rocky and His Friends* had sold well for several months, Ward's commission enabling him to fund this self-promotion. As early as April the trades announced the impending nonsense. From the *Hollywood Reporter:* "Jay Ward and Bill Scott are spending a lot of loot to bring laughs to some 800 press, network and ad agency execs with their weekly 'Operation Blabbermouth' [*sic*] circulars. Very funny *Mad* Magazine–type stuff. They'll also shell out coin for blimp advertising and sky-writing stunts for their *Rocky and His Friends.*"

As part of the publicity Ward's three other properties were announced as available for syndication: *Hoppity Hooper* (budgeted at $22,000 per show), *Fractured Flickers* ($15,000 per show), and *The Watts Gnu Show* ($25,000 per show). None, however, sold at this time.

Happily, the decision had been made to broadcast *The Bullwinkle Show* in color. At the time, the biggest noise in the TV industry concerned "color-casting." There were about 1 million color sets in use by mid-1961, and the figure was growing rapidly. Jay was pleased: he knew that cartoon shows were twice as effective on TV when seen in color.

By July, D-F-S's Charlie Hotchkiss informed Ward that thanks to the great advance publicity, some sixty major ABC stations had ordered the shorter *Rocky* series, while NBC was already getting fabulous acceptance for the upcoming *Bullwinkle Show*.

The animated titles for both shows were completed quickly. *The Bullwinkle Show* opening utilized a snazzy Broadway premiere theme with flashing signs and neons, with our antlered megastar adorned in top hat and tails, while the *Rocky and His Friends* titles employed a circus-style theme. The *Rocky* set was completed first, as prints had to be struck for many individual stations, a complicated and time-consuming procedure back then before film shows were stored on videotape.

In Mexico, midway through 1961, Sal Faillace requested extra design assistance for the new NBC segment "Dudley Do-Right of the Mounties." Model sheets and color cels of the main characters were sent to Mexico. Ward Productions was making the first "Dudley" episode in Los Angeles, and Jay was highly enthused about his new character. He told one columnist, "I personally feel that the 'Dudley' episodes will be the big hit of the show, and I am using our best directors to help it off on the right foot." The first "Do-Right" cartoon was ready by early August.

George Singer departed after eighteen months at Gamma, returning to Hollywood. Upon completion of the "Aesop and Son" episodes, it was decided that the Mexican team would handle the new series of thirty-nine "Fractured Fairy Tales." By the end of 1961, over half the "Dudley" cartoons were completed, and Sal Faillace took a Christmas break; Jaime Torres Vasquez assumed the production reins.

One of Jay's most legendary cartoons, "Dudley Do-Right of the Mounties" would debut on the first NBC telecast. Reviving Alex Anderson's 1948 concept, then overhauling it, Ward assigned Chris Hayward and Lloyd Turner to write the first thirteen scripts. Hayward, a vintage movie fan, came up with the signatures which set "Dudley Do-Right" apart, putting it in the cult area of something really special.

There is indeed a brilliant comic quality to the "Dudley" cartoons. When screened today to an audience of seen-it-all industryites, they still elicit tears-in-the-eye belly laughs. The combination of razor-sharp wit and the feeling of tribute evoked by gently poking fun at a time when *The Perils of Pauline* was taken seriously is as fresh today as when these animated gems premiered in September 1961.

Chris Hayward recalled that the only brief he and Turner were given by Ward was, " 'It's about a stupid Mountie.' So we said, 'Anything else we need to know?' and Jay said, 'No . . . just have fun!' " Hayward's special

Dudley, Nell, and Horse. *Courtesy of Universal Studios Publishing Rights, a Division of Universal Studios Licensing, Inc.*

touches involved affectionate put-downs of the filmmaking conventions of a bygone time. They include the old-fashioned visual of an iris-in/iris-out accompanying scene changes, and silent movie titles appearing on screen. Blending in well with the puns and incredible energy of the Ward house style was the ambience of turn-of-the-century melodrama, especially helped by Hans Conried as the voice of the hissable archvillain Snidely Whiplash. In fact, Conried maintained, "I never thought of Snidely as a characterization—I thought the role was designed for me!"

The other voices of "Dudley Do-Right" were just as funny. More than any of Ward's other series, the "Dudley" cartoons were perfect for a stentorian narrator. Paul Frees reveled in the mock-serious *March of Time* vocal style, which was counterpointed by the sheer stupidity being enacted on screen; Bill Conrad performed this chore for the final nineteen scripts, giving hilarious solemnity to opening lines like "Niagara Falls! And sometimes it doesn't," or "The Iron Horse! Nickname of the first transcontinental train, and real name of an animal that ran dead last at Hialeah!"

As for the title character, Bill Scott's strangulated voice characterization had two sources. One thought that naturally sprang to mind was the operatic voice of Nelson Eddy, who had played a true-blue Mountie in the famous MGM musical *Rose Marie* in 1936. Besides Eddy's, Chris Hayward had always found the voice of Johnny Weissmuller funny. The Olympic star and muscular Tarzan of the screen spoke in a high-pitched whine, especially noticeable in the Jungle Jim series. By combining these two vocal sounds and imbuing the character with a self-righteous goody-goody attitude, Scott and Hayward set Dudley's voice and character for all time. He was unquestionably the squarest dolt in the annals of cartoon history.

Indeed, his moral rectitude was apparent from the start. In one early episode a man declares, "This is about the squarest Mountie I've ever seen." This prompts Dudley's commanding officer, Inspector Fenwick, to ask our hero, "Dudley, how do you feel about Lawrence Welk?" The true-blue one replies, "Only terrific, Inspector—that's real toe-tapping music!"

Inspector Fenwick, Dudley's often flustered superior, was a Paul Frees specialty: an excellent imitation of British actor Eric Blore, the eternal valet in the Fred Astaire–Ginger Rogers musicals like *Top Hat* (1935). Fenwick's blustery pronouncements, in that plummy and slightly effeminate voice, were all the funnier considering he was in command. His daughter Nell was played by June Foray in a voice she remembered using as a child, "a voice reeking with terribly proper, overenunciated sweetness." Funnier still was the fact that Nell, the light of Dudley's life, was not only a thirty-seven-and-a-half-year-old spinster, but madly in love with the hero's horse to boot. Whether trapped in a sawmill (à la silent heroine Pearl White), becoming a lawyer and getting the villainous Snidely off the hook, or knitting a suit made out of marigolds, sweet Nell was many times the pivot for the plot of an episode.

Snidely Whiplash was simply one of the most dastardly villains of all time. Perennially foreclosing mortgages and slithering under doors, he was above all the classic black-caped, mustache-twirling rogue we loved to hate, helped by the great voice of Conried at his most John Barrymore–like. Snidely's main henchman was Homer. Rollo was another sidekick in two episodes, and once, when Whiplash "created a Finster," his assistant in the eerie laboratory was named Tor, a reference to Ed Wood's Z-grade horror film star Tor Johnson. This role was played by Paul Frees in an obsequious Boris Karloff imitation.

Chris Jenkyns wrote various "Dudley" segments, and the final set sprang

Hans Conried

Of all Jay Ward's voice actors, Hans Conried enjoyed the highest public profile. He was a most popular TV performer, known for portraying the zany character of the Lebanese national Uncle Tonoose on *The Danny Thomas Show.* He also made many panel appearances on *The Jack Paar Show* and the charades-based programs *Pantomime Quiz* and *Stump the Stars.*

An erudite man, Conried was a true "personality"—a tall, angular actor who was a real-life Shakespeare expert, and the possessor of a devastating dry wit. As Bill Scott said, "Hans would not suffer fools gladly; he could be withering." Scott directed the recording sessions for the *Gerald McBoing-Boing* TV show in 1956, which had featured Conried narrating the "Favorite Painters" series. Jay Ward had always been entranced by Conried's voice and flamboyant aura (which Hans admitted was based somewhat on his idol, John Barrymore). Conried had worked with Ward's actors on many radio shows since the 1940s. Whenever possible Ward would employ Hans Conried, who was one of the most strikingly individual actors in Hollywood, and a genuine original.

Born in Baltimore, Maryland, on April 15, 1917, of Austrian parentage, Hansel Conried graduated from Columbia University and did a year in summer stock. He became a Hollywood radio actor in 1935. To the end of his life he championed radio as his favorite work, stating, "It truly was the most civilized medium." He became a mainstay in drama (*Suspense, Lux Radio Theatre, The Orson Welles Almanac*), later specializing in comedy programs, often stealing the show from such stars as Eddie Cantor and Burns and Allen. Conried essayed funny dialect roles as a regular on *My Friend Irma* and *Life with Luigi,* and appeared in over seventy films and countless TV guest shots.

Conried married Margaret Grant, then an assistant in NBC's West Coast Special Events Department, in 1941. They had four children (Trilby, Hans III, Alexander, and Edith); as he remarked, "I collect Shakespeareana, books, stamps, Japanese swords, Oriental art objects—and children."

Perfect casting for the world-weary host of *Fractured Flickers*, Hans Conried was also con man supremo Waldo Wigglesworth in the *Hoppity Hooper* series. From the late 1960s Conried toured extensively in summer stock and lectured on the Bard in schools and colleges, thus being unavailable for Ward's last series, *George of the Jungle* (although he did narrate the "George" pilot). He returned for a few Quisp & Quake commercials playing the villainous Simon LeGreedy, a ringer for Snidely Whiplash.

Discussing Ward's shows in a 1970 radio interview, Conried said, "They were ostensibly tailored for children, but we had an awfully good time making them. It's a very adult humor. Bill Scott, who wrote them, is a brilliant man. And we had more fun than we should have in those recording sessions."

Following World War II service as director of Radio Tokyo, Conried became an authority on Japanese culture. In later years, Conried and Ward shared an interest in Oriental art, particularly Japanese.

After suffering a stroke in 1974, Hans Conried slowed down slightly, but he worked steadily until his death on January 5, 1982. Conried will always be remembered as an integral member of Jay Ward's team. One of his finest moments came at the opening of a *Fractured Flickers* episode, when he looked straight into the camera and pompously proclaimed, "Tonight's program is proudly brought to you by the makers of—*mistakes!*"

again from the fertile minds of Hayward and Turner. There would be many quotable lines from these thirty-nine films, particularly in the narration; one episode opens with Conrad booming, "Dawn: the time of day when Pearl White got up and ate her serial."

Memorable, too, is the music heard in the "Dudley" cartoons. Fred Steiner and his father, George, composed a slew of piano tracks that, when sped on tape, authentically re-created the sound of rinky-dink silent-film accompaniment. This gave the "Dudley" episodes a true touch of class. Jay Ward certainly felt the "Do-Right" cartoons were classy; taking no half measures, he appointed Oscar-winning UPA director Pete Burness to take charge of the series.

The "Dudley" scripts were classified by a numbering system. The "official" titles listed in this book's episode guide were used by Jay Ward Productions but were constructed by ad agency Dancer-Fitzgerald-Sample for archival purposes. The episodes by Hayward and Turner can be recognized by the silent-film-style titles on-screen, which included parodies of vintage movie credits: in seventeen episodes, Snidely Whiplash and others are introduced by the "actor" portraying them, such as "Dudley Do-Right played by

Dewar Diddy, Nell Fenwick played by Sweetness N. Light, Snidely Whiplash played by Madison A. Swill." Hayward said, "I remember writing in one that Horace Heights played a mountain" (this was a pun on the name of 1940s orchestra leader Horace Heidt).

One of the funniest "Dudley"s was shown just once before being pulled from the P.A.T. vault forever. It was the third episode, "Stokey the Bear," which aired October 13, 1961. Director Lew Keller said, "Jay always went to the office real early, like seven A.M. or seven-thirty, so this is like a couple of mornings after 'Stokey' goes to air. He and Skip Craig are the only ones at work so far and suddenly there's a loud knock at the door." Skip Craig, laughing in hindsight, picks up the story. "Yeah, Stokey the Bear—this pyromaniac bear with a Mountie hat who looked exactly like Smokey the Bear, and he ended up burning down Chicago. So it plays on-air and boy, it really hits the fan. . . . They heard from the Forest Service and I think it even shook Jay up, because they were threatening jail: 'Smoky the Bear is protected by Congress, you people can go to jail!' So this little guy shows up from the Forest Service, and he's got the green coat and the hat like Dudley Do-Right, the squarest little twerp, and he had this lady secretary with him. And we have to show him this segment on the Moviola, and he gets up close with this grim face, and he's watching intensely, and really telling Jay 'What's going to happen to you people!' He never cracks a smile through the whole thing, but his secretary's standing behind him desperately trying to stifle laughter. I don't know if they made [Jay] destroy the negatives. Anyway, now there are only thirty-eight 'Dudley's. I was proud of those; they were the only ones we did full postproduction on, so I love the 'Dudley's, too."

An unsigned newspaper story from 1964, "Bullwinkle Creator Welcomes Lawsuits," featured an interview with Jay Ward; one section reports: "The only case Ward ever lost ('we settled out of court') involved an animated animal called Stokey the Bear, who went around setting forest fires. 'The Forest Service nearly had apoplexy over the show,' Ward recalls. 'I didn't know it at the time, but there is something called Smokey the Bear, and it's protected by the government. I understand it is used to promote fire prevention. Sounds incredible but that's what I've been told.'

"The Forest Service threatened Ward with a fine and jail sentence. But only after the sponsor in Minneapolis ordered films of the Stokey episode destroyed did Ward give in."

Ironically, in 1967 Ward produced a set of public-service TV commercials for fire prevention. They feature the "Bullwinkle's Corner" format, with

Bullwinkle reading poems extolling the genuine Smokey the Bear ("To see that fire never catches, Smokey's friends don't play with matches"). All had been forgiven!

Jay Ward was never happy with the budgetary restriction allowing Charles Kimball's postproduction team in Mexico City to dub the cartoons. He insisted the "Dudley" episodes be dubbed in Hollywood. Happily, D-F-S gave him the okay on this, which is why these films don't suffer from distorted sound effects and muddy voices. And considering the delightful background music in each "Dudley" segment, it is a great relief the series wasn't assembled south of the border. More than any other, the "Dudley" cartoons demonstrate exactly what Ward meant when he said the Mexican outfit never truly mastered the feel and comedy timing of the sound tracks in which he took such pride. Skip Craig was relieved: "The stuff from Mexico was horrendous. I was always worried seeing my name on the credits, and panicking that people would think the bad sound was my fault."

It's a safe bet that "Dudley Do-Right of the Mounties" is the one Jay Ward cartoon series which holds up after thirty years without losing any impact. By today's rapid-pace standards it's possible they are more popular now than in 1961: they move quickly, they are uproariously funny, and they work after repeated viewings much the same as *Get Smart* still does (significantly both Chris Hayward and Lloyd Turner wrote for that revered series). While there were the occasional weak episodes of "Peabody," "Fairy Tales," and "Aesop," there is never a "Dudley Do-Right" that disappoints. No wonder it was Ward's favorite of all the cartoons in his canon. Happily, too, he was allowed to animate a handful of them in his own studio.

In the first week of August, Gordon Johnson began scouting for a *Bullwinkle Show* cosponsor; he tied up with Ideal Toy Company. The material for the shows was already being formatted. This didn't take long: of the seventy-two new "Rocky and Bullwinkle" episodes required for thirty-six weeks, 90 percent were already written and recorded.

At the end of August, General Mills bigwig Cy Plattes previewed the first prime-time show. He was highly enthused and noted, "extremely high caliber . . . great titles . . . loved 'Mr. Know-It-All' . . . 'Aesop,' was excellent." He congratulated Jay and Bill on "a great opening show." Strangely enough, though, he criticized the "Dudley Do-Right" episode. To him, it seemed too hurried in parts. He suggested the following (this note is amusing today, as if Plattes missed the satire completely):

> Firstly, he requested the announcer read the line beneath each cast member—i.e., "Dudley Do-Right as played by Sid Gould."
>
> Next he asked that the silent movie–style title cards ("Please remove hat") be deleted, and begged Jay and Bill to stress the fact "that this is an old-fashioned opera type of thriller" (surely blatantly obvious already!).
>
> Finally he felt that the cartoon would be "stronger" if the old-fashioned melodrama context was eliminated entirely, then nervously added, "the melodrama reference is okay, provided we beef up the links so that the audience gets the idea."

This type of directive, although intended to help, made Jay Ward cringe. Ward and Scott always presumed the audience *was* intelligent enough to "get the idea." More likely, Plattes was simply unfamiliar with the "Dudley" cartoons at this point. His note seems confused and self-contradictory. Indeed, a couple of months earlier he had seen the raw dialogue script and loved it.

By now General Mills had opened its coffers to help the publicity push, and Jay, happily subsidized, decided to go to town. He and Howard Brandy began dreaming up lunatic ways to really send *The Bullwinkle Show* off with a bang. In short order, Brandy made arrangements for several live events back east, via his New York associate Alan Foshko.

Meantime, the first big media stunt would be the Bullwinkle statue dedication and unveiling in Los Angeles. This idea had fantastic possibilities, and Ward was excited, telling reporters, "We'll be giving a street dance and block party as part of the whole show, to set the stage for a wonderful week to start our TV show."

To prepare everyone for the statue ceremony, a special West Coast *Bullwinkle Show* premiere was held in late August. Members of the press and their children were invited. This resembled a typical gala Hollywood premiere, with the Jay Ward twist added. Ward and Scott hired the works: mammoth searchlights, huge balloons, a red carpet, and the plush Screen Directors Auditorium theater on Sunset Boulevard. The fun began when the famous stars who attended were deliberately ignored in stony silence while members of the press were greeted effusively with wild cheering supplied by an offstage sound track. Jay and Bill carried on this charade dressed in white ties, tails, and toppers, along with white Bermuda shorts and black sneakers. The invitees got pairs of tickets to widely separated seats, to accommodate Hollywood couples who weren't on speaking terms. Ward explained, "This proved no problem; there were no ushers." Bill Scott served as MC and announced all arrivals at the microphone.

This "premiere to end them all" was proudly announced as running "a full 28 minutes!" The first episode of *The Bullwinkle Show* was screened, but during the slots for commercial breaks the audience was treated to special live performances of advertising spoofs featuring onstage appearances by June Foray, Bill Conrad, Hans Conried, and Bill Scott. Ward's staff dressed incongruously, sporting Bullwinkle beanies with antlers, while refreshments were served in the lobby by famed Hollywood caterer Dave Chasen. *Variety* reported some jealous sniping from Universal-International, who were staging the premiere of their current release *Come September* the same evening. But even this early, NBC was apparently nervous about their new TV show. The *San Francisco Examiner*'s Dwight Newton wrote, "450 swells and belles attended, but NBC's only representatives were two press agents who came late and left early. They didn't even send a cameraman." Many big TV names attended, including, said Newton, "an ardent Bullwinkle fan named James Garner."

Howard Brandy then accompanied Bill Scott on a six-city follow-up promotional tour in which local press heavyweights were invited to lunch and a screening of the show. The first stop was New York City, where Scott participated in a Madison Avenue revivalist march with "Salvation Army" costumed girls waving signs urging, "Repent, Sinners—Watch *The Bullwinkle Show*." Similar media previews followed in Philadelphia, Boston, Detroit, and Chicago, winding up in Minneapolis, home base of General Mills.

On September 17, one week before *Bullwinkle* went to air, Elizabeth Sullivan's article "Moose on the Loose" described a preview lunch hosted that day by Bill Scott. It mentioned show highlights like "Aesop and Son" and "Watts Gnu" (it seems that for a short time "Watts Gnu" was to be an occasional show segment), and touched on Jay Ward's background, Gamma Productions, the voice actors, and the upcoming block party. "Jay Ward Productions' staff of employees have, in their collective careers before joining Jay, won a total of 72 major awards; have won nine Oscars with honors at film festivals in Nice, Cannes and Edinburgh. Ward and Scott are both brilliant at satire."

Following the press previews, Scott flew back to Los Angeles, where, with barely time to wash behind his antlers, he participated in the big Bullwinkle block party and statue unveiling.

Howard Brandy had suggested the statue idea in April, when he first hooked up with Ward. The moose monument was constructed by Bill Oberlin, former art director on *Time for Beany*. Oberlin, who landed a gofer job at Ward's via Chris Hayward, had a reputation around town as a clever jack-of-all-trades. After he fashioned the fourteen-foot-high Bullwinkle statue it was put into place in the first week of September and covered with canvas until the big night. Skip Craig explains, "The statue was made by Oberlin out of layers of gauze and cement. Opposite us then was this famous statue of a Vegas cowgirl who was dressed in a bikini and holding her hat, so we had the moose statue looking just the same." Bullwinkle turned on precisely the same cycle as its "sister" statue, the Las Vegas Sahara Girl, rotating atop a billboard directly across the road.

Special handouts were issued to press editors, and then five hundred additional invitations went out. To commemorate the occasion, attending celebrities and press reps would place their elbow prints and signatures in blocks of cement at the entrance to Jay's main office. "Elbow prints mean they won't spill their martinis," explained Ward. There were all kinds of extra gimmicks under wraps, and Ward expected about three thousand people for the huge street dance he had planned. An area on busy Sunset Boulevard was roped off between Crescent Heights and Harper for the unveiling of the Bullwinkle statue, and on September 20, the party kicked off.

Skip Craig recalls, "It was a real big production that night; there were tables spread out all over, a tattoo booth, and I think there was even a kissing booth. On the corner by the savings and loan was where Jay had the bandstand set up with full orchestra, playing these big fanfares. Bill Scott was dressed in his Teddy Roosevelt costume—he went around blowing a bugle. Later on all these extra people started turning up. It was wild, like real mob scenes."

The eighteen-piece orchestra, dubbed "the Bullwinkle Philharmonic," was led by composer Dennis Farnon, who commenced proceedings with some distinctly tongue-in-cheek music, including little-known melodies like "The Bullwinkle Suite," "Hippos I Have Known," and "Side View of a Western." Bill Scott, cast again in the MC role, delivered a comical opening speech, after which Farnon treated the crowd to more of his arcane music. Next, Scott roasted the surprised bandleader, who was due to leave for England. Then the orchestra offered "Bullwinkle Meets the Count." (Much of this oddball music was similar to the backgrounds heard two years later in *Fractured Flickers*. "They were all themes from our tracking library," explains Skip Craig.)

Later in the evening some classy straight dance music got everyone hopping, with numbers like "Why Don't You Do Right," "Three Little Words," and "Isle of Capri" blaring across the Strip. When the dance bracket ended, Jay Ward delivered a comical address parodying the Emma Lazarus poem that adorns the pedestal of the Statue of Liberty (". . . your huddled mooses yearning to breathe free"); then finally the Bullwinkle statue was unveiled by guests Jayne Mansfield and Los Angeles County sheriff Peter Pitchess. This was followed by thank-you speeches from Gordon Johnson and Cy Plattes of General Mills, after which a fanfare led into the ceremonial "Moosylvania March."

As Jayne Mansfield kept busy signing autograph books, the combined efforts of the city, county, and state police were needed to keep at least one lane of the famous Sunset Strip open; Sheriff Pitchess had arranged the necessary permits for the event. Skip recalls, "Jay had a sign put up for the passing motorists: 'Don't complain or we'll block this lane, too.' The orchestra was kept busy all night; there was nonstop dancing in the street."

As *TV Guide* reported, "5,000 milling, screaming, caterwauling celebrants showed up—and this was a completely booze-less do, something almost unheard of in Hollywood. However, some 10,000 cups of coffee were consumed, 1,000 cartons of popcorn distributed, and 3,000 Teddy Roosevelt 'Rough Rider' hats given away." Countless straw hats with moose antlers attached were also handed out. The festive occasion included free food, with hot dogs courtesy of the Plush Pup [where Dudley Do-Right's Emporium would stand a decade later], a stilt walker, and an organ grinder with accompanying monkey. There was coverage by *Life, Look, Newsweek, Time,* United Press International, Associated Press, and the NEA, and newsreel films by 20th Century–Fox and NBC.

Jay Ward told the media, "It had all the elements of a riot." Traffic was tied up for hours, but Ward had no qualms. He proclaimed the statue "my cultural contribution to the city of Hollywood." And the sponsor saluted Jay and Bill "for a tremendous promotional job on *The Bullwinkle Show*." The statue itself was truly Bill Oberlin's masterwork. Chris Hayward says, "Nobody knew how it worked but Oberlin. We finally discovered that he could start and stop its rotation with just a simple little matchstick."

Before 1961 was over there was further promotion. As Skip Craig said, "These were definitely the wild years of Jay Ward Productions." A Bullwinkle and Rocky float formed part of the Rose Bowl parade, while General Mills' publicity team—the Kalmus Company—did a magnificent job in the

Bill Scott, Los Angeles County sheriff Peter Pitchess, and Jay Ward unveil the moose monument. *NBC photo, courtesy of Bill Scott*

Macy's Thanksgiving Day parade with a truly gigantic Bullwinkle helium balloon, costing a cool $20,000. Jay Ward took part in a Thanksgiving parade at San Francisco's Union Square, and Bill Scott participated in the Hollywood Santa Claus parade.

Jay, dressed in a Napoleon costume, led a "Sing Along with Moose" ceremony. Teenage models joined passing Christmas shoppers to sing parody songs from "The Bullwinkle Songbook," accompanied by the Guckenheimer Sauerkraut Band. Local disc jockey Al Collins, who weighed two hundred pounds, strolled around in a vast pair of army fatigues lettered "This Space for Rent." Various satirical songs were heartily sung, extolling subjects like foreign aid to Mars or payola at NBC, while one ditty, a spoof of "Love and Marriage," had something to do with *Gunsmoke* regulars Matt and Chester sharing Miss Kitty. Invited reporters were awarded zany commendations like "The Boris Badenov Medal of Dishonor for Valor in the War Against Clean Living," or medals "For Arousing Public Apathy to *The Bullwinkle*

Repent Sinners: Bill Scott leads a parade down Madison Avenue to publicize *The Bullwinkle Show.*
NBC photo, courtesy of Bill Scott

Show." At all these events, Ward and Scott were amazed at the tremendous crowd response to Bullwinkle. Ward told the General Mills brass, "I'll bet no other show has such loyal fans—when they like us, they go all out, saying, 'Best show on television.' Modestly, we agree."

14

Bullwinkle Meets the Press, or All the Moose That's Fit to Print

The new nighttime *Bullwinkle Show* featured story lines even faster-paced than before, and Jay Ward produced some truly hilarious shows. The character design was better, even if the animation was still aesthetically lacking. Gone forever was the slightly tentative feel of those early segments in the Mooseberry Bush story. The sound tracks were louder as well; Bill Conrad's narration is so changed from his subdued style of two years before that it seems as though he's two entirely different actors.

The longest story on the NBC run was telecast first. This was the saga of the fabulous "Kirward Derby." The organizers of the annual Missouri Meese Convention invite Bullwinkle to attend. He and Rocky set off, only to run into a 150-year-old feud between two warring clans, the Hatfuls and the Floys. After the first twelve episodes the story gets around to its real point. Fearless Leader and his eternally sniveling minions, Boris and Natasha, are seeking a derby hat which has the ability to impart great intelligence to its wearer. As legend has it, the hat, housed somewhere in Missouri, can only be found by the stupidest bubble head in the world: enter one Bullwinkle J. Moose. The hat is named "the Kirward Derby." This little joke was the first of several which landed Jay Ward in hot water after only six weeks on the new network.

It just so happened there was a real-life announcer known as Durward Kirby. The TV sidekick of comedian Garry Moore, Kirby was then cohosting *Candid Camera*. In early November 1961, *Bullwinkle's* executive producer, Peter Piech, received a letter from Kirby's lawyer stating that the use of Kirby's name, or a simulation thereof, "has resulted and will continue to result in substantial damage to him including damages which may not be ascertainable in dollars."

Demand was made upon *Bullwinkle Show* distributor P.A.T., sponsor General Mills, ad agency D-F-S, and the NBC network that each immediately "cease and desist," with a possible lawsuit implied. As editor Skip Craig recalls, "Kirby was a stuffed shirt. That was just ridiculous. Jay's lawyer was instructed to reply by saying, "Tell Mr. Kirby that he has our permission to name any one of his hats after any character in our show.' " In fact, Ward actually sent Kirby a hat. Then he replied to Kirby's lawyer: "The only other names for the Derby—Kentucky and Brown—were already taken. We had toyed with the idea of calling it the Bullwinkle Bowler, but discarded this as being too chauvinistic. Please sue us, we love publicity." As he told the press a year later, "Whenever anybody says they are going to sue us, we always tell them we will send our lawyer right over to help them draw up the papers. Nobody has ever accepted the offer."

NBC was nervous about any misunderstandings, and elected to call the hat "the magical derby" in program listings. Columnist Dwight Houser, a big fan of Jay Ward's, slyly observed, "Ward Productions is ignoring the cease and desist order. Myself, I don't think Kirby has a legal leg to stand on and, if anything, the Derby nonsense will just make his name a little better known. Did that ever hurt any TV personality?" The issue was soon dropped.

Actually, this was the second time a showbiz personality had complained. Skip Craig said, "Earlier, during the *Rocky* show, Red Skelton's attorney made a phone call to us and said that Bullwinkle sounded too much like Skelton's character Clem Kadiddlehopper. Jay said, 'Great! Can we send you the tapes? We want the publicity!' " Soon after, Jay promised the Skelton people that in an upcoming show, he would have Bullwinkle make a complete denial of the charges—by giving an impression of Kadiddlehopper to show the vocal difference. The complaint was never heard again. (Presumably, it had never occurred to Skelton that Clem sounded a little like Edgar Bergen's dummy character Mortimer Snerd, or even a bit like Walt Disney's Goofy.)

But back to *The Bullwinkle Show:* it remains to say that the story of the "Kirward Derby" is one of the all-time greats in the series. It reintroduces the moon men, and its atmosphere is reminiscent of the moose and squirrel's earliest adventures, even mentioning the long-lost Mr. Big. Bill Scott takes potshots at Washington, the cold war, Elvis Presley, Albert Einstein, and any number of other targets. At twenty-six chapters it's the third longest story.

The next plot was also lengthy. It ran eighteen episodes and contained some great moments. The boys buy the Lazy Jay Ranch in Squaw's Ankle, Wyoming; one thousand acres for $28. They soon discover it's a most unusual ranch. They won't be raising cows, steers, or sheep. No, this is in fact a worm ranch ("Gittalong there, worms!"). The worms are to be raised for bait in the nearby fishing resort of Angel's Cramp. Boris is after some valuable rocks on the ranch, and disguises himself as Black Angus, a Scots cowboy. This story marked the beginning of the wilder humor to come: at one point in the story, Boris tears up the script, and the narrator doesn't know what's happening. Along the way, we are introduced to Finkelberries (different from Mooseberries) and a monster called "the Wutzat."

With their next story it almost seemed like Rocky and Bullwinkle had wandered into a "Fractured Fairy Tale" by mistake. One of the original Three Musketeers, Athos (now almost ninety years old), mistakes the boys for his two long-lost companions-at-arms. So Rocky becomes Porthos, and Bullwinkle is, what else, Aramoose! By the end of this somewhat unusual chapter in the lives of our heroes, good king Once-a-Louse is restored to his throne, while the nasty François Villain is reduced to pruning Limburger lilies, the natural flower of Applesauce-Lorraine, the province in which this crazy story takes place.

The following saga—"Topsy Turvy World"—saw the addled Captain Peachfuzz make his NBC debut. Reensconced as the bumbling head of G-2, Peachfuzz commissions the lads to solve the problem of the world turning sideways, and the consequent change in international weather patterns. Frostbite Falls is now on the equator and windy Chicago is where Honolulu used to be. Of course, Boris is behind this; disguised as Colonel Oglethorpe Peachtree, his plan is to take over the new North Pole and become the next Santa Claus, thus carrying presents *up* chimneys instead of *down*. The action centers on the island of Riki Tiki, with Bill Conrad gaining his moment of immortality as Sam the Native.

This was the story which really embroiled Jay Ward with network censors. According to *TV Guide,* "NBC objected to an episode in which Bullwinkle and his pal Rocky parachute into a cannibal pot (a routine almost as old as slapstick itself) on the grounds that 'the need of peoples everywhere to be represented with dignity precludes the out-of-context use of cannibalism.' This struck Ward as too outlandish to take seriously. He ordered the figures redrawn as pale-faced replicas of his partner, Bill Scott, and himself, complete with spectacles. Later he was to grumble: 'Cannibalism? To eat a moose and a squirrel?' " The continually humorless intractability of NBC was to become a sore point with Ward.

When *The Bullwinkle Show* went on air, immediately preceding the debut of Disney's much-touted *Wonderful World of Color* on ABC, critical reaction was overwhelmingly favorable.

> In the Bill Scott–Jay Ward creation, we watched Bullwinkle J. Moose, Rocket Squirrel, Boris Badenov and Natasha Fatale acquit themselves with distinction once more. (Fred Danzig, UPI)
>
> I am not very often the enchanted type, but I think I'm going to be, Bullwinkle-timewise. (Henry Mitchell, *Memphis Commercial Appeal*, September 25, 1961)
>
> Bullwinkle, a moose with a twinkle, should delight adults as well as kids. (Larry Wolters, *Chicago Sun*, September 25, 1961)
>
> Bullwinkle is a show that has an adult script to go with the cartoons. (Frank Judge, *Detroit News & Times,* September 25, 1961)
>
> It may be a race between parents and the kids as to who will get to the TV set first for *The Bullwinkle Show.* Not only were the lines clever in the opener of the series, but the situations were offbeat and sophisticated. (Eleanor Roberts, *Boston Traveler,* September 25, 1961)
>
> *Bullwinkle* surely can't miss . . . *Bullwinkle* is a great big hit. (Tom Mackin, *Newark News,* September 25, 1961)
>
> The half-hour is loaded with satire and wit—much more than *The Flintstones* for example. There was a delightful "Fractured Fairy Tale," and "Dudley Do-right." Cheers for *Bullwinkle*. (Richard Shull, *Indianapolis Times*, September 25, 1961)
>
> *Bullwinkle,* the befuddled moose, premiered breezily. The animated color was not as brilliant as perfectionist Disney's, but the fun substance

> was richer in both broad humor and subtle satire. (Dwight Newton, *San Francisco Examiner,* September 26, 1961)

After deciding that Disney's hour lacked laughs, Judy Williams went on to write,

> Now *Bullwinkle* is another matter. He's kind of an Ernie Kovacs in animation. I'm prejudiced, I admit. I saw the premiere of his show, and met his producer Jay Ward. I was impressed. (*Indiana News,* September 25, 1961)

One highly complimentary review came from Canada:

> Bullwinkle is a wall-eyed amusing moose who last year was one of the friends in ABC's *Rocky and His Friends.* He proved so popular with the sandbox set that NBC offered him a starring role in prime-time.
>
> Level of humor in all this is for some reason far higher than in the later situation comedies, including *The Flintstones.*
>
> Funnier and less sloppily sentimental than most of Disney's creatures, Bullwinkle Moose, Rocket Squirrel, Boris Badenov and a host of smaller sketches handled themselves with zany distinction last night.
>
> (Jon Ruddy, *Toronto Telegram,* September 25, 1961

Finally, to go full circle, Donald Freeman, author of the first major Rocky and Bullwinkle article in early 1960, penned a most favorable critique in the *San Diego Union:*

> **HAIL TO BULLWINKLE**
>
> *The Bullwinkle Show,* a new animated cartoon epic gracing NBC, I will sum up in one extravagant phrase—it's wild and wacky and wonderfully funny. In short, I'm hooked.

The Bullwinkle Show premiered with a new twist, a live puppet of Bullwinkle J. Moose hosting the show and introducing the cartoons. Ward was the instigator of the puppet, the idea being to introduce the show to the wider audience and set up the zany style with Bullwinkle's offbeat remarks.

Show Notes for 1961

The Bullwinkle Show was commissioned for the full network season of thirty-nine weeks, including three definite dates where the show would be preempted. Thus, thirty-six weeks containing seventy-two new Rocky episodes were written. These were 157–164 ("The Three Moosketeers"), 165–182 ("Lazy Jay Ranch"), 183–208 ("Missouri Mish Mash" featuring the infamous Kirward Derby), 209–222 ("Topsy Turvy World"), and 223–228 ("Painting Theft"). There were three extra dates when the show didn't air, so the final three half hours (containing the six episodes of "Painting Theft") were tentatively slotted for either the 1962 summer break, to be followed by a rerun of the Kirward Derby saga, or to open the 1962–63 season in September. The latter scenario occurred.

The on-air schedule was different from the writing sequence. On Ward's recommendation, the Kirward Derby story aired first, from September through December. The "Lazy Jay Ranch" story ran from December 1961 through February 1962, followed by "Three Moosketeers" in March and "Topsy Turvy World," which ran from April to June. The latter story was the final script, the agency specifically requesting it run just fourteen episodes in order to fit the season.

Bill Scott wrote most of these; the two shorter stories ("Painting Theft" and "Three Moosketeers") were written by Chris Hayward and Lloyd Turner. These two gag men were certainly busy in 1961, penning the final 13 "Peabody"s, the first 13 "Dudley"s, and several "Aesop"s and "Mr. Know-It-All"s. Chris Jenkyns wrote the middle set of "Dudley"s.

On February 15, 1961, Fred Steiner conducted a recording of several new music themes composed for the network change. More music was taped in June, when an extra session saw Bill Scott, Paul Frees, and June Foray recording promos for the NBC premiere. These were much more adult ("Watch it on NBC—the National Bullcasting Company!").

Skip Craig said, "I was tickled by the puppet. The jokes were good-natured. I remember once [the puppet] told the kids to go look in Daddy's pants pockets for those green pieces of paper with people's faces on them, and send them in to Bullwinkle." These bits, written by Bill Scott who handled and voiced the puppet, were pithy and irreverent. And NBC absolutely hated them!

In Ward's opinion, good or bad press meant little in the long run: rather, *The Bullwinkle Show* would simply follow the path of his previous work, including *Crusader Rabbit,* a path which started slowly, then gathered steam after a few months. Analyzing this further, Jay pointed out that his cartoons were "different in both angle of humor and fast pacing"; as he saw it, this took a while for viewers to get used to, but they were gradually won over.

Noting they were up against tough competition with perennial family favorite *Lassie* on CBS, Ward expressed concern about Bullwinkle's second-rate lead-in show. This was *1-2-3—Go!,* a mediocre careers-oriented educational show, whereas CBS's lead-in was the strong performer *Mister Ed.* Ward requested more on-air promotion from NBC, and decided to really go all out to boost the show himself. Apart from the "Savings Stamps Club," there would be floats in two huge events, Macy's Thanksgiving Day parade and the New Year's Tournament of Roses parade. An enormous merchandising campaign was planned for 1962, involving over forty companies and more than two hundred items, including soap, books, and a ton of toys. And Jay, meanwhile, was going to build on his madcap "Operation Loudmouth" publicity drive with more baroque attention-getting stunts. In just six months, his mailer campaign had resulted in over four hundred newspaper mentions.

In late October 1961 Ward Productions made up storyboards for three new Cheerios commercials, two of which were based on fine ideas from D-F-S's creative department. These showcased the "Bullwinkle's Corner" format, which meant the audience enjoyed the return of Bullwinkle the soulful poet ("It's not that I don't trust you, William Tell, it's just that I have Cheerios to sell").

Newsweek (December 4, 1961) noted that after just two months on NBC, Ward's famous censorship and legal problems were already legend. Thirty-five years on, these anecdotes are still the ones remembered as headline material in the Ward Productions saga.

For the sake of accuracy, here's the *Newsweek* report, which appeared after only eight editions of *The Bullwinkle Show* had aired:

> It is a pertinent comment on the status of the American parent that *Bullwinkle* is getting shellacked by CBS's *Lassie* in all the ratings, and it is a crying shame, too. For *Bullwinkle* is not only the funniest—to

adults, anyway—of the plethora of new cartoon programs, but it is the most courageous program on the air. In two months' time Bullwinkle J. Moose has antagonized its network (NBC) and its sponsor (General Mills), as well as comedian Red Skelton, announcer Durward Kirby, and the whole U.S. Forest Service. No other moose can make that statement.

Created with loving care by a pair of uninhibited, 41-year-old producers, Jay Ward and Bill Scott, whose proudest boast is that they never worked for Walt Disney, the show is a blurred pastiche of puns and one-liners, larded into mock adventure stories, fractured fairy tales, and mutilated Aesop. It doesn't sound that controversial, but the truth of the matter is that Bullwinkle's troubles began the moment he opened his mouth. Friends of Red Skelton took to remarking to the comedian that Bullwinkle's voice sounds exactly like that of a Skelton character called Clem Kadiddlehopper. Skelton's lawyers kicked up such a fuss that Bullwinkle was forced to make a formal denial on the air (in a voice that sounds exactly like Clem Kadiddlehopper's). Durward Kirby, for his part, has shown displeasure over a new hat Bullwinkle is wearing—a bowler called the Kirward Derby.

A mainstay of the Bullwinkle show is Dudley Do-Right, a Canadian Mountie of shuddering impeccability. In one adventure, Dudley's arch-enemy, Snidely Whiplash, got hold of a forest-fire-minded bear named Stokey and hypnotized him into setting fires instead of preventing them. This brought the U.S. Forest Service around to Ward and Scott's door, and produced angry smoke signals as far away as Minneapolis, land of the free and home of the sponsor.

Bullwinkle's most portentous battle is still being fought. Animator Ward (whose latest song, "Santa Is a Dirty Old Man," may or may not be released in time for the Christmas rush) dutifully submitted to NBC a story line in which Bullwinkle Moose and Rocky Squirrel plunge out of an airplane and fall straight toward a waiting group of cannibals and their steaming cauldron. NBC nixed this immediately, on the ground that cannibalism is impermissible. Whereupon Ward and Scott raised the delicate moral issue of whether it is cannibalism to eat a moose and a squirrel.

NBC is still pondering.

The Bullwinkle Show had been on the air just a few weeks when Ward was informed that a strong, loyal group of viewers was building. Unfortunately, the healthy trend soon went into reverse. This was big-time stakes now: NBC expected a 33 percent share of the audience or they would simply find a replacement show for the 7:00 time slot. Nighttime TV was, after all, simple bottom-line economics: if Bullwinkle delivered the desired share he would stay where he was. General Mills had gone all out and obtained an incredible 172 out of 185 NBC markets. The network informed Johnson that the share was possible with this coverage if the show could attract more children; industry research showed that every youngster brought along at least one adult for that time slot.

NBC's own in-house research had certainly proved one point: kids also hated the Bullwinkle puppet. Perhaps they sensed it spoke adult-style humor, although they seemed to love "Fractured Fairy Tales" most of all, and those scripts weren't exactly juvenile fare. Overall, though, General Mills and Ward were optimistic, feeling that *The Bullwinkle Show* would build momentum, especially over the winter. Jay was determined to stay for a second NBC season, not wanting to appear, as Johnson so sensitively put it to him, "like a first-year failure."

The network got its wish, and the puppet host quickly vanished. Bullwinkle's barbed jokes made NBC extremely nervous, as will be revealed. Ironically, after just two months on the air the Bullwinkle puppet experiment was deemed so disastrous that D-F-S queasily instructed Jay Ward and Bill Scott to "stay away from inside or showbiz-type humor." And with that thunderous order ringing in their ears, our fearless leaders continued to make the funniest cartoon show on TV.

15

1962: It's My Party and I'll Laugh If I Want To,

or Moosylvania Mania

Looking back in 1971, Bill Scott recalled, "As the show continued, our sponsor insisted on shorter and shorter stories so that they'd be more flexible in syndicating it. Though oddly enough, the Mooseberry Bush is the one story that's repeated over and over." Scott and Ward were busy in the closing months of *Bullwinkle* production with their new *Fractured Flickers* series, along with fine-tuning a Cap'n Crunch pitch for Quaker Oats and pushing *Hoppity Hooper* for a sale. Jay was also steeped in his various wacky promotional gimmicks. Writers Chris Hayward and Lloyd Turner inherited the bulk of the remaining "Bullwinkle" episodes, keeping them busy through 1962; Scott wrote the circus story and the moose's last two adventures.

In January 1962 an excellent story by Roger Beck appeared in *TV-Radio Mirror*. Here Jay Ward, ostensibly the great recluse, spoke perceptively and at length about the show, touching on his theories of animation and comedy.

> We're also asked if we pattern our characters after real people. Of course we do. They're all takeoffs on real people. Look around you. It's been said that Bullwinkle comes across like Clem Kadiddlehopper, but we didn't intentionally pattern him after that Red Skelton bit. Bullwinkle's a 'smart sort of a dope,' like Clem or Mortimer Snerd or

> a character out of Artemus Ward. He's a very simple guy who comes up with smart cracks.
>
> Our main characters are basically characterizations of people in general, and of types more than just anybody specifically. For example, Boris Badenov is our villain and he's ALL bad. Rocky, our other hero, plays it straight and is all good. It's all a takeoff and satire on melodrama.
>
> We once even had a crooked guy named Murgatroyd Cornelius Applefinger, who opened a talent agency under his initials of MCA. Everybody knew that was a jab at Music Corporation of America, the biggest agency of them all. [*Ward was referring to the "Aesop and Son" entry "The Fox and the Hounds."*]
>
> We've not only offended people—without meaning to, of course—but we've also had trouble with countries. The story of Pancho Villa almost got us into a jam in Mexico and I think our new character, "Dudley Do-Right of the Mounties," may be the hit of the show. But I won't be surprised if we're at war with Canada over him within the year.

A month later, Harold Bender interviewed our intrepid coproducers, and the report, "Building a Better Moose Trap," appeared on February 25, 1962. Again, Ward gave voice to a slather of fascinating comments following Bender's comment that "the tongue in cheek, offbeat stories, like 'Fractured Fairy Tales,' are giving the cartoon series a 'way-out' distinction and a gradually growing audience."

> Ward: "If we paid attention to the lists of Do's and Don't's supplied by network, sponsor and agency, all we could say would be hello and goodbye. And we'd even have to shorten that a little. In one of our *Rocky and His Friends* programs we had a sergeant gently poking fun at an army general. Our sponsor General Mills let us know they did not think this funny. It was okay to spoof a private but not a general, particularly as they had a retired general on the board of directors. We've ignored the list of taboos ever since we were told we couldn't make fun of *The Lone Ranger*—or his horse," chuckles Ward. "The reason was that the sponsor had sponsored the Lone Ranger for many years before taking us on. But the horse taboo was the final straw."

The zany promotional parties intensified in 1962. Peter Piech expressed reservations: "I always wondered why Jay let Howard Brandy talk him into spending all that money on those publicity stunts; it simply wasn't necessary to promote *The Bullwinkle Show,* because as far as publicity was concerned General Mills had more clout than a visitor from another planet." In hindsight, none of it actually made much difference to the show ratings. But, boy, did they have fun there for a while. Particularly at a notorious bash known as "the Picnic at the Plaza."

This New York–based stunt was set up by Howard Brandy to entertain the press and potential *Bullwinkle* sponsors for the upcoming fall TV season, the moose's second on NBC. The staid and very proper Plaza Hotel in New York City was the site of this Ward bash: a picnic-style dinner party, held not in nearby Central Park, but in the Plaza's own Grand Ballroom. Because it was a "picnic," Ward naturally wanted to import ants ("elegant ants used to caviar and shad roe"). At first the already nervous hotel management gave him a resounding no.

Sure enough, a real old-fashioned picnic took place. Ward had sod and grass trucked in to cover the floor of the swank Persian Room. Guests consumed caviar out of lunch boxes on red-checked tablecloths while two dance bands played. A barbecue was held, and along with the endless champagne, there were fortune-tellers, pickpockets, and a photographer who snapped pictures of guests sticking their heads through holes in wooden panels with silly paintings on one side. The big finale to the dinner was a flambé dessert. It was ceremoniously brought in by marching waiters as the lights were dimmed in the ballroom. So many people turned up that the picnic baskets ran out, which caused a minor commotion.

In the spirit of authenticity, Jay Ward brought in his picnic ants. But, "possibly fearful of the wrath of Plaza management, or worse, a monstrous exterminator bill," he kept them safely enclosed in glass. Bill Scott recalled, "They were like these really big ant farms." Howard Brandy was responsible for the ants concept. "I thought it would be funny to invite 10,500 guests, 10,000 of whom were ants. To be truthful, Jay didn't care for them!"

Ted Key vividly remembers, "Jay had a giant stuffed animal in his room at the Plaza; it was a present for Bette Davis, who was a guest at the picnic, and it was well known that she loved stuffed toys." A laughing Peter Piech recalls the normally reserved General Mills people really letting their hair down: "Old Cy Plattes was swinging from a tree." June Foray remembers

Gordon Johnson, Bill Scott, Cy Plattes, Jay Ward, and Peter Piech.
NBC photo, courtesy of Bill Scott

the function as "a wonderful night. Jay had the press there, and they were in abundance. I still have a picture from that night with myself and the staff from *Mad* magazine. My husband and I had a great night there. And Bill Scott was sitting with us, too."

Nineteen sixty-two saw the final fourteen "Mr. Know-It-All" segments completed. Rocky and Bullwinkle also appeared in commercials for Garden of Toys, Presto sparkle paints, and Soaky bath products. In July, two new animated promos appeared for *The Bullwinkle Show*.

Bullwinkle J. Moose also made his newspaper debut this year. In July, the syndicated *Bullwinkle* comic strip began its three-year run. Jay asked P.A.T. to negotiate the deal. Peter Piech said, "I had a lot of newspaper contacts with my journalistic background. A friend of mine who got the strip under way was John Ossininkle, who had been at the *New York Times*. It started with the McClure-Bell syndicate, then John took it to the *New York Times* syndicate. We later had an offer from Simon and Schuster to put the comic strip into book form, on one condition: we had to eliminate Boris Badenov. They were worried that if Boris was in the book, it could affect the nation's chance for détente! So we turned the book down."

The comic strip, though never widely distributed, was beautifully drawn by the late Al Kilgore, who had previously written some "Rocky and Bullwinkle" comic books, published since July 1960 by Dell (and later Gold Key). Kilgore was much liked among the cartooning fraternity. He was regarded as something of a human dynamo, having written and drawn books, distributed movies and been a founding member of the international Laurel and Hardy fan club, "the Sons of the Desert." Kilgore got on famously with Jay Ward and worked for him over a five-year period, even storyboarding some Quaker cereal commercials. He also worked for Piech on the *Underdog* series, for which he did storyboards and predirection. Kilgore said, "Jay Ward gave me total freedom. I find him to be a lovable kook, as well as a brilliant businessman."

By mid-1962, Ward's Quaker oats commercials deal had been signed, while the loony promotional stunt called "Moosylvania" was under way.

To really promote *The Bullwinkle Show* and its famous dim-witted star, Ward, Brandy, and the creative staff came up with the idea of petitioning for statehood for the moose's birthplace. This was inspired by a Bullwinkle adventure concerning "the dreadful little place called Moosylvania," which had just been scripted. Linda Hayward, Ward's secretary at the time remembers the "Moosylvania" campaign only too well. For months she had to take care of a ton of enthusiastic fan mail.

In the middle of 1962 Skip Craig was approached by Ward and told, " 'You're gonna buy an island!' 'Okay, Jay, whatever you say.' I'm from Minnesota, so Jay sends me back there to buy him an island in the Lake of the Woods. Jay already has these fight songs composed for this wild idea for Moosylvania statehood that he and Howard cooked up.

"So, off to Minnesota I go. He gives me a blank signed check, and he's laughing his head off saying to me, 'Ha ha ha—you'll be up by Canada, so if you try to fill this check in, it won't cash anyway, ha ha ha. . . .' So I go back home and I get in touch with my uncle, who's a surveyor and knows all about this stuff. We go to some county seat up there and into the courthouse, and we start looking up maps for owners of islands. Jay wanted it on the American side; there's hundreds of islands on the Canadian side and maybe only seven on the American. Anyway we track down a few people, and we're told, 'Nobody's gonna sell you an island.' But we finally found a dentist

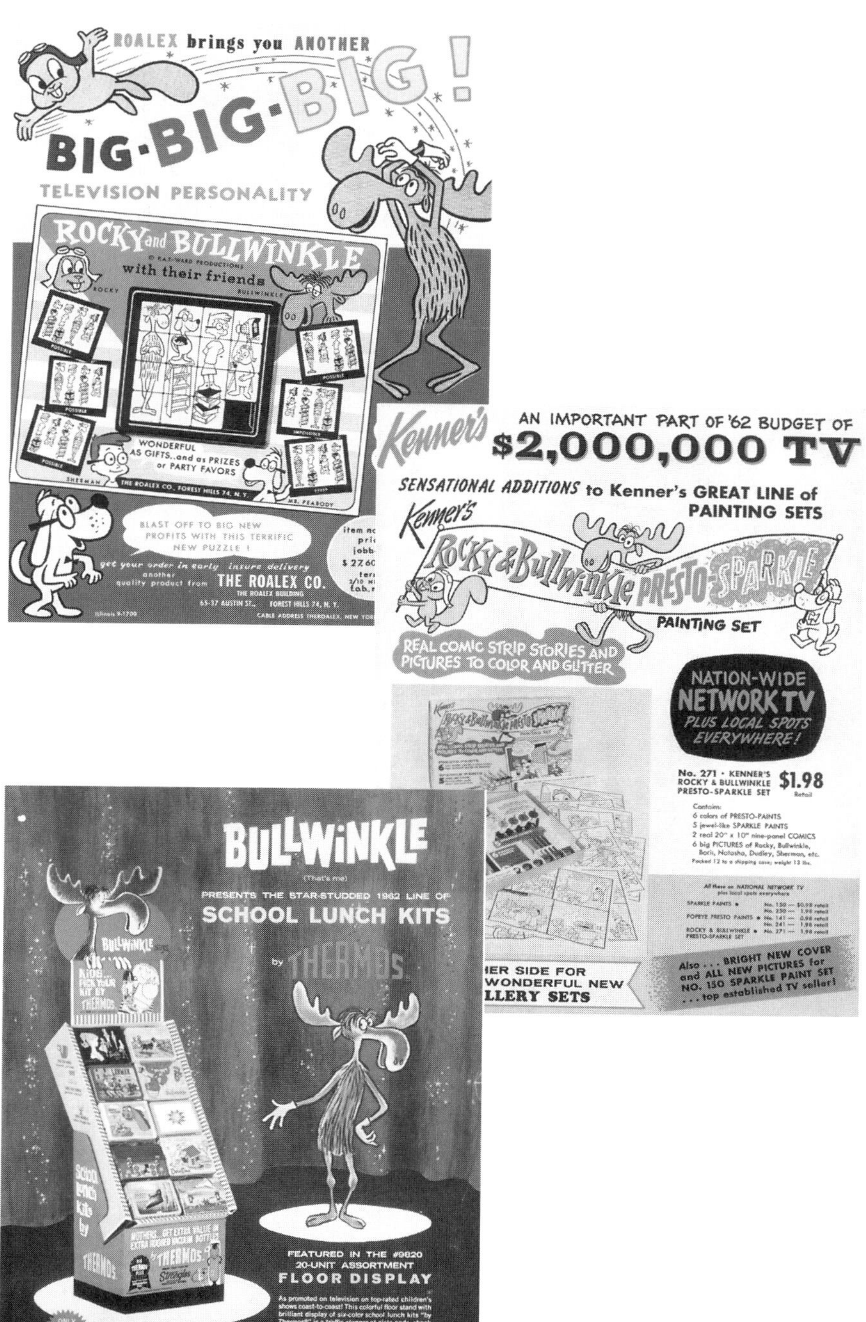

Artwork copyright © 1962 by Ward Productions, Inc. Characters courtesy of Universal Studios Publishing Rights, a Division of Universal Studios Licensing, Inc. All rights reserved. Photos courtesy of Bill Scott

who's got this dinky little island, and he thought this was hilarious. 'Gee that's funny!' he said. But he still wouldn't sell it. So I called Jay and told him, and Jay said, 'Okay, lease it.' So we drew up this agreement, and this guy leases the island to Jay for three years for publicity purposes only, and he's going to use Jay's money (about $1,500) to build a fishing shack; he's already got this pile of lumber out there. So he was delighted.

"Then my uncle and I hired this single-engine seaplane and this guy's going to fly us out to take some pictures of our island. On the way out there, he buzzed the shore and said, 'I'm gonna find you a moose.' And he did! He's yelling out, 'There's a moose—hey, Bullwinkle!' So we fly out there and take pictures. There's a swampy area, and a hilly area—really a pretty little place. Then the pilot says, 'Gee, I hope it doesn't blow up a storm—we could be stuck here for three days!' Lake of the Woods is huge: you get out there and it's like ocean, you can't see the shore.

"So I brought back the color slides and this little lease on the 'Moosylvania' island, and Jay goes from there. He gets these petitions drawn up and this political bandwagon is made up from this panel truck; they do it up with plastic braid, and he has a band organ installed with a big PA system. Jay is decked out in this Napoleon-type costume with a cocked hat and a sword, and Howard has this Dudley Do-Right uniform. They get all these leaflets about 'Moosylvania' printed up and they hit all these towns and have these wild parties with this band organ playing. In several towns they nearly got arrested, just for being noise nuisances."

In early September Alan Foshko became involved. Brandy arranged for Foshko to be their East Coast connection for this and all follow-up events. Foshko planned a special "Moose's Day Parade" for November 16, 1962 (a week before the annual Macy's Thanksgiving Day Parade), as the grand finale to the "Moosylvania" statehood push. Brandy and Foshko maintained an itinerary which was carefully followed.

And so the final week of October 1962 saw Jay Ward embarking from California on the tightly planned, and totally crazy, cross-country promotional tour. His mission: to gather votes for a petition to incorporate Bullwinkle's homeland of "Moosylvania" as the fifty-second state in the Union (Ward told the press he believed Mississippi would probably end up being the fifty-first). He and Howard Brandy set out in their gaily decorated Ford sound truck and calliope combination, complete with a loudspeaker blaring "Moosylvania" songs which had been recorded in Hollywood on October 2 by the Randy Van Horn Singers. Ward was outfitted in a multicolored,

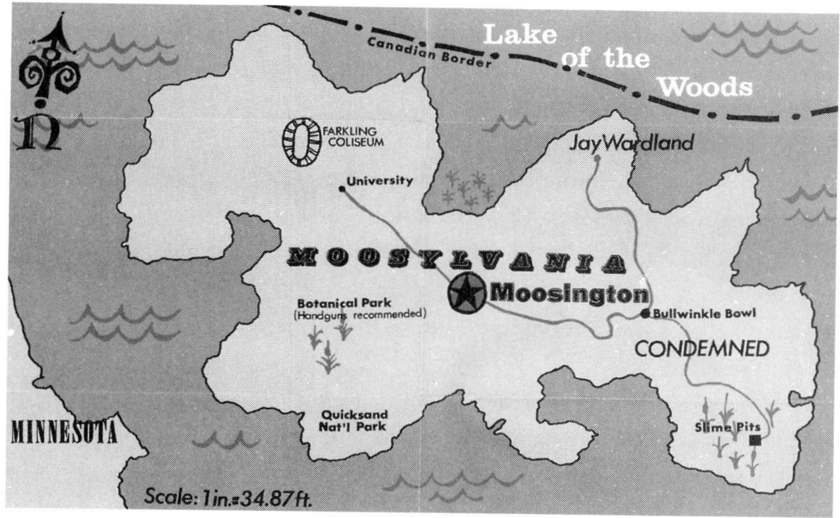

Copyright © 1962 by Ward Productions, Inc., courtesy of Ramona Ward

plumed commander's hat of questionable ancestry and his Napoleon costume, while Brandy was dressed in a Dudley Do-Right suit. They equipped themselves with flyers, leaflets, songbooks, and thousands of balloons, which were filled with helium and released at each stop-off point. Brandy recalls, "I blew up more balloons than Disneyland does in a year."

Triumphantly, they paraded through twenty-two cities. In each town, Ward merrily drove through the main intersection, stopping traffic and pausing only for television and press coverage, preplanned by Brandy. Parades were staged along the main stems of Denver, Chicago, Dayton, Cincinnati, and Cleveland. Chris Hayward recalls, "Jay often drove like a speed demon. His legs would bother him so much that he'd be pounding them with his fists, and he'd break the speed laws." (The pain was a legacy of his traumatic 1947 accident in Berkeley.)

In Pittsburgh Jay Ward appeared on the local host segments of an episode of *The Mickey Mouse Club,* and actually got everyone to sing Mickey's song by spelling out "M-i-c-k-e-y M-O-O-S-E."

Bizarre press conferences were held in each town, all following a set format. After the truly silly "Moosylvania" songs were played, Wilkie buttons and drinks were distributed. Then it was time for Jay Ward to face the reporters. He invariably elicited an opening laugh being dressed like a booby-hatch Napoleon, and the meet-the-press sessions were played as mock-serious affairs. Much of his comedy material was written by Al Burns.

Jay Ward was introduced as Moosylvania's "ambassador pauci-potentiary." Once at the lectern, he commenced proceedings by expressing an intense concern for his territory's future political situation. A planted reporter asked, "Are you in favor of reapportionment for Moosylvania?" To which Ward answered, "Yes!" "Reapportionment on the basis of population, or area?" Again he answered, "Yes!" After the laughs died down he added, "In either case, it wouldn't matter. Moosylvania has no people and it's composed entirely of quicksand. We have an a-cameral legislature and an absentee governor who lives in a summer state house in Minnesota, and a winter palace in Palm Springs."

Next he described Moosylvania's highway department committee, which sat in absentia. "The last six surveyors we sent out to find hard spots in the quicksand have never been seen again." Also mentioned were Moosylvania's state flower (what else—the Venus flytrap), the state bird (a gnat), and the fact that you could reach Canada via a fourteen-mile footbridge owned by Toora-Loora Goldberg ("the toll is $12.83 each way, since there are few immigrants who survive to make the round-trip"). As the island's ambassador, Ward claimed diplomatic immunity, and he was adamant that as soon as statehood was granted, Mooslyvania could qualify as a disaster area. "It would make a good retreat in case of thermonuclear war. Enemy bombers would take one look at it and figure it had already been hit." Finally, Ward announced that Moosylvania had petitioned to join the United Nations: "We're a natural for the Insecurity Council."

Following dinner Ward handed out badges bearing inscriptions like "Fink of the Month" and letter sweaters worn by the "Moosylvania University Farkling Squad." After mentioning that they now had thousands of signatures on the statehood petition, he admitted, "Three of them are real. The others came from Chicago voter registration lists."

Invariably quizzed on the sport of farkling, Jay Ward had some convenient answers up his sleeve. "Farkling is Moosylvania's state sport. The teams line up, and the match starts only when the referee cries, 'Foul!' Each time a player is caught playing fair, the captain of the other team gets three blows below the belt or a free pistol shot at the opponents' cheering section." Inevitably asked how farkling got its name, Ward replied, "It was invented by Abner Baseball."

Drinks and dessert were consumed, and the final gag was a beauty. Ward and Brandy stole silently away and drove to their next destination, leaving the bewildered press people to divvy up the $250 check!

The next stop-off was not so amusing. While en route to their final eastward destination of New York City, Ward and Brandy stopped off in Washington. After driving around the city, they decided to take their wildly decorated truck right up onto the White House driveway. Jay hoped they could get an endorsement from President Kennedy, who was well known for having a sense of humor. In they drove, with banners waving and the calliope blaring loudly, only to be turned away by a grim-faced security agent who didn't think this campaign warranted the president's immediate attention; in fact, at one point he began to reach for his gun. Jay Ward told one reporter, "Before I knew it, sixteen guards were upon us. The sergeant asked, 'Waddaya tink yer doin'?' I told him I was asking for statehood. He gave us thirty seconds to get off the driveway, but I claimed diplomatic immunity."

Brandy recalls his feelings of genuine terror that fine autumn day. "We had a network photographer, and the NBC publicist was Pat Humphrey, Hubert Humphrey's daughter-in-law. We've got the petition of signatures rolled up like a big roll of toilet paper, and Jay showed it to the uniformed guard. Jay says, 'We want to see President Kennedy.' The guard says, 'You can't!' Jay tells him, 'You don't understand, we've got a petition for statehood.' The guard looks at us like it's get-out-the-butterfly-net time. Jay pressed on, convinced the guard didn't appreciate the idea. He says, 'If President Kennedy knew what we were doing, he'd want to see us. He has a sense of humor!' I keep saying to Jay, 'Let's get out of here.' But Jay says, 'No—the guard could at least be civil to us.' I see the publicist turning white, like she's going to die of embarrassment.

"While all this is going on the loudspeakers are blaring out the Moosyl-

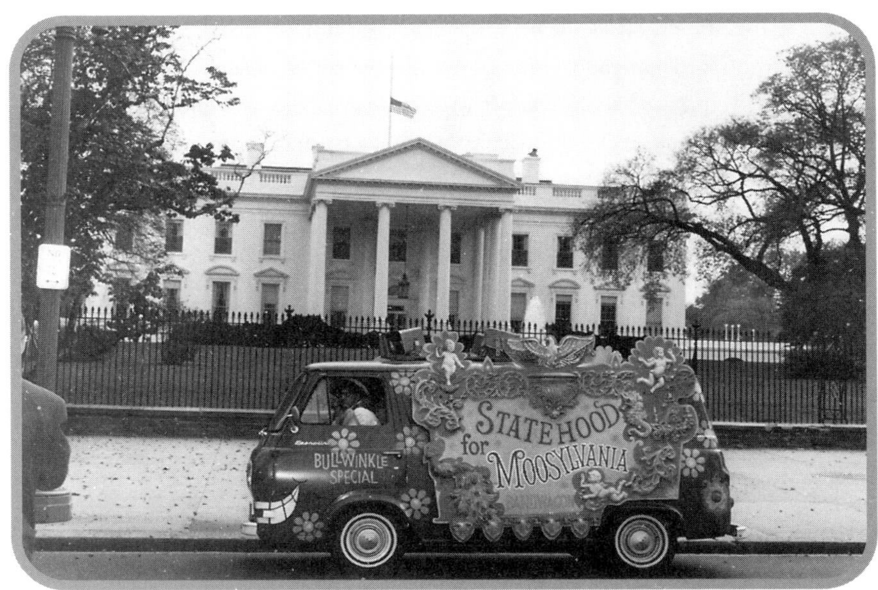

Jay and the sound truck outside the White House. *Courtesy of Bill Scott*

vania songs. They can hear it on the other side of the Potomac. Finally, the guard says to get out of here immediately, and he unsnaps the strap over his gun."

Reluctantly, but hastily, they left. Later that day Brandy, still dressed in his Dudley Do-Right costume, took photos of this incident to the Associated Press. "I tell the AP guy, 'I've got some great pictures for you.' He says, 'Are you jokin', kid? Come over here.' He shows me the photos coming off the wire. You could see Russian trawlers and warheads off the coast of Florida. We'd landed right in the middle of the Cuban missile crisis! Jay called me 'Fink Brandy' for months after that."

According to the November 14 *Radio-TV Daily,* "The entourage was turned away because the request must come by U.S. Mail, and, they were told, be accompanied by some 200,000 signatures. Presently, the 'Moosylvania' movement has upwards of 30,000 endorsements and the number is skyrocketing as a result of tie-in promos." In truth, Ward's little stunt was considered irritatingly frivolous in this tension-packed week: the world was holding its breath as the missile crisis unfolded. Bill Hurtz adds, "What got Jay into trouble was their sound truck screaming out the Moosylvania fight song. Sound trucks aren't allowed inside the nation's capital. When the red-faced cops ordered him out, Jay drove around to the other gate. The story hit the

Show Notes for 1962

Rocky episodes to number 228 were due to conclude in June, and Gordon Johnson had already convinced General Mills to renew for the fall season (the new cosponsor was Emenee Industries, makers of musical and electronic toys). The twenty-six-episode Kirward Derby story reran in the 1962 summer break. Ward knew that continued exposure on the network meant big bucks from merchandising revenue and a gradual audience increase, so in late 1961 he and Johnson planned enough material to air for a further two years. In fact, 1962 saw ninety-eight new "Rocky and Bullwinkle" chapters rushed through.

During the Christmas break in 1961, the writers sharpened their pencils and wits again. Between January and May, thirty-two new episodes were written and recorded. Once animated, this meant sixteen new half hours would air from September 1962 through February 1963, to be followed by reruns. The thirty-two new episodes were 229–232 ("The Guns of Abalone"), 233–240 ("Treasure of Monte Zoom"), and the very funny Bill Scott scripts "Goof Gas Attack" (241–248) and "Banana Formula" (249–260), the latter cowritten with Lloyd Turner.

Johnson also commissioned Scott to begin writing a new story in time for the next renewal discussions. This was a smart ploy, indicating, even before the green light, D-F-S's confidence in the show. It was also important because there were new personnel at General Mills. This time Johnson got the sponsor to approve a further sixty-six episodes, clinching it by convincing them it was their last chance to take advantage of the current price for Mexican production. This meant a rush job on scripts and recording. Writing commenced in the summer recess, and by December 1962 the episodes were recorded and ready for animation. Johnson had requested sixty-six because his plan involved using twenty-six (or thirteen half hours) for the upcoming 1962–63 season, instead of the earlier planned reruns. Then for the 1963–64 season he would have forty episodes left for twenty half hours (September 1963 to early 1964). The reruns would follow from there.

At this point a discrepancy should be noted. Although the final show for 1962–63 ends with "Rocky" episode 260, the next series begins with episode 301. This break was Peter Piech's idea: the writing and voice recording of episodes 241–260 had been rushed and out of sequence, resulting in some scripts for "Banana Formula" being misnumbered. The resulting confusion temporarily sent the New York accountants up the wall! To avoid further mix-ups, a clean round number was approved when production resumed in July 1962. Readers will note that the final "Rocky" episode is 366, but because this forty-figure gap was created, there are really only 326 chapters in all (for 163 half hours).

The rush writing job resulted in the following stories: 301–310 ("Bumbling Brothers Circus"), 311–316 ("Mucho Loma"), 317–322 ("Pottsylvania Creeper"), and 323–326 ("Moosylvania"). This batch gave Johnson and Ward the first thirteen half hours in their plan; then the final twenty shows consisted of "Rocky and Bullwinkle's" last forty episodes: 327–332 ("The Ruby Yacht"), 333–338 ("Bullwinkle's Testimonial Dinner"), 339–344 ("The Weather Lady"), 345–350 ("The Louse on 92nd Street"), 351–362 (the famous football story "Wossamotta U"), and 363–366 ("Moosylvania Saved"). Alas, this last tale marked our fur-clad heroes' swan song.

wires and the press called it the greatest stunt since J. P. Morgan had a midget sit on his knee in Congress."

On November 20 Ward told a press conference, "A lot of people, a lot of critics and NBC people, say aren't we in bad taste doing this whole Moosylvania statehood bit with Berlin and Cuba and all that—and we've come up with what I think is a fine answer to this criticism. It's 'Yes.' It's been an exhilarating trip. We've found that when we get into a town the mayors have been so courteous and friendly when they've ordered us off the streets. Very nice!"

It seemed mighty unusual for a painfully shy man like Jay Ward to be dressed in a Napoleon suit, doing all this attention-getting shtick. But as Bill Hurtz explained, "The costume was his way of hiding behind a character, and in fact many actors admit that they, too, are uncomfortable as themselves."

As planned, the Moosylvania stunt climaxed in the Big Apple on Friday, November 16, with "the Moose's Day Parade," Alan Foshko's trump card. This event was two months in the making; it involved a motorcade down Forty-fourth Street, starting at Eleventh Avenue, with 250 show business personalities and press taking part. They ended up at Sardi's restaurant for lunch. On hand was the Sardi's bus transporting a six-piece band, Jack Douglas and the chorus line from *How to Succeed in Business Without Really Trying,* and other performers from *Night Life, Mr. President,* and *Take Her, She's Mine* (all then-current Broadway successes); several of the famous participants were Foshko's clients. Foshko provided bunting, banners, Moosylvania balloons, posters, a Bullwinkle suited actor, a Mountie suited actor, ice-cream vendors, policemen, and a flatbed truck for the marching band.

Fourteen gaudy vehicles tied up traffic in busy midtown streets for almost an hour. Alan Foshko recalls, "I went to the police department and asked for a permit to stage the parade. At first the police were saying no. So I said to the police chief, 'You obviously don't believe in Santa Claus,' and that broke the ice. I got the permission we were after. It was a beautiful sunny day, and we had a tremendous parade. I went to the Metropolitan Museum of Natural History to get a stuffed moose, and we had actress Sylvia Miles elected as Miss Moosylvania. Elizabeth Ashley was voted 'most wanted' by the Moosylvania Mounties, and we had all the comics from the Friars Club, and top disc jockeys. We also found a fabulous sign painter who did some fantastic work. Oh, and there were a hundred white-gloved policemen!"

As usual, Ward had sweatshirts and hats for giveaways, the hats being derbies with antlers. During the parade, picketers carried signs featuring then-topical jokes, like "How come Jackie [Kennedy] never visits 'Moosylvania'?"

The most effective gag came when the three hundred guests finally got to their seats in Sardi's posh second-floor dining room. The swank luncheon everyone envisioned turned out to be hot dogs, sauerkraut, chestnuts, and pretzels served by four hot dog vendors with pushcarts. The total cost that day was close to $4,500, a tidy sum back then. Foshko recalls, "Those scavenger press people literally drank the bartenders under the table!" Eighty bottles of scotch were consumed. One anonymous journalist got so zonked he was found later during dinner hour and fished out of a laundry hamper.

Ward was highly impressed with this effort. Foshko said, "Jay had no idea. He really thought it was only going to be a tiny little parade. It cemented his respect for me and we quickly became very close friends. Jay never expected this, especially the hot dog vendors. Sardi's restaurant begged us not to do that, they wanted to lay on a big Sardi's special luncheon. But the pushcarts turned out to be such a big success that they were used later in John Lindsay's political campaign." Ward's wife, Ramona, who flew back east for the street parade, recalls, "The highlight of the lunch at Sardi's was the appearance of Juanita Hall from *South Pacific,* who sang all her famous numbers in her beautiful voice. Everyone in the audience was reluctant to let her go."

En route back to California, Ward and Brandy hit more towns, including Tulsa, Dallas, and Las Vegas. They finally arrived home in early December. Ward made it in time for the final "Rocky and Bullwinkle" recording session and some fine-tuning of the new Cap'n Crunch pitch, not to mention a well-earned Christmas break.

The final "Rocky and Bullwinkle" record date was held on December 11, 1962, and the Mexican team had plenty of material to keep them busy through the next year. Immediately following the recording, the cast hastened to Jay Ward's studio for an "elbow bending" party with family and friends—in fact, their elbow prints are still in the cement outside Ward's former building at 8218 Sunset Boulevard. Hans Conried and his wife joined the talented revelers.

A footnote to the Moosylvania campaign was the fate of the cross-country truck: it wound up on a Hollywood used-car lot owned by actor Ben Alexander (Jack Webb's longtime sidekick on *Dragnet*). He finally sold the vehicle, but only after denuding it of its antlers and the steam-making apparatus attendant upon the calliope.

In 1962 the "Rocky" and "Fractured Fairy Tales" segments rolled off the Mexican assembly line without a hitch. The Gamma team had certainly come a long way since the stumbling days of 1959. After three years, day-to-day operations were efficient and trouble-free. By early May, the final "Dudley Do-Right" and "Fairy Tales" segments were shipped to P.A.T. All that remained were the "Rocky" episodes and a few episodes of "Bullwinkle's Corner."* At year's end, "Rocky" episodes were the only *Bullwinkle Show* element awaiting completion, production on them continuing well into 1963.

With two years at Gamma under his belt, Sal Faillace resigned on August 31, 1962, citing personal reasons (he would, however, return to work on Piech's *Underdog* series). Harvey Siegel took over as studio production manager, with Joe Montell replacing Siegel as head of layout.

*Ostensibly for a bit of show variety, but in fact to subliminally remind viewers of the many merchandise items now on the market, ten "Bullwinkle's Corner" segments were transformed into the "Rocky and Bullwinkle Fan Club."

• • •

A brilliant second season of *The Bullwinkle Show* commenced in September 1962, with a very funny story by Chris Hayward and Lloyd Turner. In "Painting Theft," Bullwinkle whitewashes his chicken coop so the hens might lay more eggs in the brighter surroundings. But he unknowingly whitewashes over ten old masters stolen from a Paris art museum by Boris, who has stashed them in Frostbite Falls. Philistine Boris must now buy them back. The script gets in some neat digs at the pretensions rampant in the art world, particularly critics (one of whom is called Price McVincent). They proclaim the moose's sloppy whitewashes—like "Vanilla Ice Cream Spilled on a White Sheet #2" or "White Cow Eating Marshmallers in a Snowstorm"—masterpieces.

The plots and gags now moved at a blistering pace. Next on the moose's agenda was another short story of four episodes entitled "The Guns of Abalone." This was the only time a contemporary movie, in this case the 1961 blockbuster *The Guns of Navarone,* was employed as a plot device. Forced down on the Rock of Gibraltar, Rocky and Bullwinkle once more tangle with Boris and Natasha. Boris plans to use the guns to take over the world, but, fortunately for all of us, he aims the five cannons at each other. At one point our heroes face a firing squad; given a last request, they naturally ask "Not to be shot!" This reasonable request must, of course, be granted.

The following tale unfolds with Boris and Natasha in Minnesota. The perpetual no-goods are seeking the Lost Treasure of Monte Zoom. This turns out to be a fourteen-karat-gold-plated car known as an Apperson Jackrabbit. In this rapid-fire script, we discover that Bullwinkle is an avid bird-watcher and that Boris has a day job he can always go back to ("Throwing rocks at the UN Building"). This story's funniest moment: the boys, trapped in the town water system, interrupt the off-key singing of a Frostbite Falls tenant, who is blissfully warbling "My Sweet Virginny Pride" in his bathtub when they unexpectedly emerge from his shower nozzle.

The next adventure in the hectic lives of our stars was one of their wildest. In "Goof Gas Attack" some of the top scientific minds in America begin acting like morons and addlepates. It transpires that Boris and Natasha possess a Goof Gas gun. The sinister gas is responsible for the personality disorders. Boris plans to take over when the nation is riddled with simpletons. Again, Captain Peachfuzz employs the boys to help—after all, how could

Goof Gas harm the moose, the biggest goof of all? This hilarious story is one of the strongest, with many bit characters becoming dunderheads, and another terrific Bill Scott joke: in Washington, a politician gets up and rambles, "I propose we set up a $20 million inquiry to look into government spending!" To which the boys reply that Washington couldn't possibly be harmed by Boris, because what the congressmen speak is already Goof Gas.

This great story was followed by another classic, chock-full of belly laughs, concerning a secret formula called "Hush-a-Boom." This recipe—for a silent explosive—is hidden inside a banana eaten by Bullwinkle, who amazingly remembers the details of every meal he ever ate. The formula (H_2O NH_3 C_2H_5 PDQ U_{235} and a pinch of salt) is, naturally, craved by Boris, Natasha, and Fearless Leader. Our heroes, along with the intrepid but muddleheaded Captain Peachfuzz (in his swan song), survive a weekend at Boris's mysterious Kitchy Itchy Lodge. Boris even makes a tape recording of Bullwinkle blabbing the formula, but all to no avail: he and Natasha are ignominiously arrested for being mere litterbugs! A wild scene features two *Dragnet*-like army police who tie and gag the moose and squirrel. They also gag the narrator; in the next episode, when one of the army cops rips the tape off our storyteller, his mustache is painfully removed too. Lloyd Turner wrote this terrific tale, with revisions, as always, by Bill Scott.

This season had seen *The Bullwinkle Show* shifted by NBC to 5:30 on Sundays. It was at this point that a less rosy picture of the network and its politicking with Ward's show emerged.

NBC was highly sensitive about jokes at their expense. The most conservative of the networks, they were frankly horrified by the *Bullwinkle Show* puppet host in 1961. From the start the puppet had sent up the sacred medium responsible for its exposure, dishing out snappy jabs at the pompous way in which "color-casting" had been publicized.

Early in the series the antlered puppet proclaimed, "Attention, black-and-white TV viewers! Would you like to see *The Bullwinkle Show* in color tonight? Just follow these easy instructions. Think of Mr. Khrushchev's latest speech. Have you got it? Think of your next year's income tax. Now think of the mean things Mr. Disney said about your black-and-white set. Makes you see red, doesn't it? I thought so. So now in glorious red color, here's *The Bullwinkle Show*."

Adding salt to the wound, in one of their zany promotional mailers called "Sing Along with Bullwinkle" Ward's team included a parody song which cuttingly satirized NBC's recent low ratings. Then there was the zinger in which the puppet introduced a "Fractured Fairy Tale" as "an empty piece of fatuous prose . . . you know, like TV's Code of Ethics."

In fact the sassy glove-puppet had well and truly blown it back on his very first nighttime show. At the end of that episode, our mooster of ceremonies declared:

> Well, the old clock on the wall says it's time to go—actually, it's a new clock and all it says is "ticktock." But that's television, and we gotta go anyway. But first a message to all you KIDS who are watching. Did you know that the knobs on your television set will come off if you pull on them? Right now, why not pull off the knob that changes the channels? It's loads of fun, and that way you'll be sure to be with us next week—and the week after that, and the week after that, and the week after.

Now it was NBC's turn to see red. First a young girl in Des Moines and then several other moose-minded kids complied with Bullwinkle, to the horror of their aghast parents. The network was furious, telling the press that twenty thousand or so kids had wrecked their family TV sets. Jay Ward told General Mills that he didn't for one minute believe this spurious, inflated figure, but to mollify NBC, the Bullwinkle puppet apologized thusly:

> Well, good-night time is here again. How time flies when you're having fun, and not getting paid. But before we go, a word with you kids who are watching. A couple weeks ago I told you to take the knob off the TV set so you'd be sure to stay tuned to *The Bullwinkle Show*? Well you can put it back now—if you can find it. A little glue will hold it in place. On the other hand, a lot of glue will keep it stuck on this channel. So use your own judgment, and a lot of glue. Bye.

As before, NBC brass weren't impressed; now they feared the FCC would have them on the carpet. To top it off, Jay released this press statement: "We've asked the network to give us a commendation for keeping an audience until the repairman gets there."

That did it. NBC angrily requested the puppet be removed. As *TV Guide* reported, "Everyone from the Press Department to Continuity Acceptance was nervous. NBC press representatives somehow mysteriously failed to

Moose of distinction.
Artwork copyright © 1961 by Ward Productions, Inc.; photo courtesy of Bill Scott

show at certain Bullwinkle functions, like the *Bullwinkle Show* premiere, for instance, and had to be reminded—by the ad agency handling the General Mills account, as it turned out—to show up at future ones."

Even before *Bullwinkle*'s on-air debut, NBC had been miffed by the publicity stunt in which Bill Scott picketed Madison Avenue with beautiful mission girls dressed in Salvation Army costumes left over from *Guys and Dolls*. They carried signs reading, "Repent Sinners—Watch *The Bullwinkle Show*" and jokingly paraded in front of the headquarters of rival network CBS, whose irate brass phoned NBC and threatened to call the police. NBC reportedly told CBS, "It's not our band—pinch 'em." Ward was upset: "We asked the network to send a photographer down to take pictures. But they said, 'NBC will not participate in such a loathsome event.' "

Jay Ward, who always viewed a lack of humor with deep suspicion, refused to admit an NBC press agent to his Picnic at the Plaza Hotel bash six months later, even giving the man who did the barring an engraved medal. Jay had learned that some top NBC brass were unhappy about the entire show deal. Weeks before going to air, Jay's nutty publicity machine suggested the network change its name to "the National Bullwinkle Company." Rather than seeing the joke, NBC was too stunned to answer.

Closer to the first broadcast, Ward Productions made several twenty-second promotional films in cartoon form. In one, a husband and wife were talking about TV and wound up in an argument about a moose being called Bullwinkle. Hubby's final words were, "How would you like a belt in the mouth?" It was funny to all but NBC, "because it smacks of violence." The network phoned Ward, advising him that the twenty-second plug for the show would not be aired, then asking him to kill a funny takeoff on NBC's "Living Color" peacock logo (the Bullwinkle puppet had oven-roasted the bird, a joke that again had the big wheels in a state of shock). Bill Scott dubbed NBC "Nothing But Chaos."

But as a *TV Guide* article from August 1962 revealed, the reality was that D-F-S and General Mills had been "mad at NBC all year." Originally the ad agency had contracted for the 6:30 P.M. time slot on Sundays, but NBC had pushed the show back to 7:00, where it faced tougher competition. At renewal time, Mills insisted they didn't want the show scheduled at 7:00 again. The network was deliberately slow to respond, so General Mills shopped around. When archrival CBS offered 6:30, NBC finally came back offering 5:30, which was actually a good time.

But during all this corporate role-playing, the press somehow got word that *The Bullwinkle Show* had been canceled. Although this was untrue, NBC appeared to have led the trades on a wild moose chase for a time by arrogantly delaying the announcement of *Bullwinkle*'s new time slot. Rumors of *Bullwinkle*'s demise led one newspaper to quote "network sources" stating, "*Bullwinkle* definitely will not return next fall." Of course, when NBC finally announced the moose's new time, Ward's crew had the last word again. In their next mailer they announced, "It is with great ennui and profound personal apathy that the National Broadcasting Company announces the renewal of *The Bullwinkle Show* for the 1962–63 TV season. It will air at 5:30 P.M. on Sundays, a time slot once occupied by *Omnibus*. Oh well, it's in color."

Jay Ward, for once only half joking, told a reporter, "General Mills keeps sending us threatening notes. NBC doesn't like us. They don't speak to us. They bar us from their parties. Everybody in power hates us; but [at least] the people like us."

And in a rare serious moment, Jay revealed, "If we can stir up people, for or against us, we'll be satisfied. We think TV should create controversy and not be bland." He concluded with something he seemed to believe: "NBC tries to pretend we're on another network!"

Eventually NBC would relent, making allowances for Ward's eccentric ways, and a better relationship was finally cemented. Jay allowed, "Really, any network that would carry *Bullwinkle* can't be all bad." But it must be noted that once *The Bullwinkle Show* and NBC parted company, Ward and the Sarnoff network were never to speak again.

16

1963: A DAY AT THE NUT HOUSE, or What Do They Do on a Rainy Night in Coney Island?

Production on the remaining "Rocky and Bullwinkle" episodes continued in Mexico, while the daily fifteen-minute *Rocky* show expanded from fifty to ninety markets. Jay's *Watts Gnu* pilot film was revised: the hilarious "Fairy Tale" "Sleeping Beauty" and a "Fractured Flicker" were added to it, replacing some of the weaker sketches. It was screened for General Mills, who received it most enthusiastically. But it would never sell. This was a real blow for Jay Ward, who had wanted a puppet show for years.

Ward's history of bad timing continued to dog him. The *Fractured Flickers* pilot was shown to Frito-Lay, who loved it, although they requested "better quality" once it aired. But at the eleventh hour it was found to be too late: the company had committed $1 million that very week to sponsoring the high school drama series *Mr. Novak*.

Early in the spring of 1963, *The Bullwinkle Coloring Book* (designed by Al Kilgore) was released. It was heavily promoted on TV, via Cheerios and Gold Medal flour, thus reaching two audience age groups. The book sold well. During this period an interest was expressed in making the *Bullwinkle* cartoons available for the 8-mm home-movie market. Peter Piech looked into it, but nothing came of this.

Meanwhile the madcap publicity stunts continued into 1963, kicking off with "Jay Ward's New Year's Eve Party," held in the month of March!

For Jay's PR man, Alan Foshko, this stunt was a personal favorite. On March 19, 1963, Jay Ward and friends took over Budd Friedman's Cafe Improvisation, then a relatively new coffeehouse in New York's West Side theater district. Foshko remembers that "the Improv" hadn't yet officially opened. Those brave souls who participated in the "Moose's Day Parade" were now invited to enjoy a gala New Year's Eve party—celebrated nearly three months late. Ward explained, "I couldn't spend New Year's with my New York friends last year, so I decided to do it in March."

Six-foot-long hero sandwiches and spaghetti were served, and the guests celebrated the arrival of the New Year four times, at 11:08, 12:47, 1:15, and 3:30 in the morning. Appropriately, New York was blanketed by a freak snowstorm that evening. When the assembled guests looked out to see a white street, one woman yelled, "Betcha Jay arranged that, too!" In typical Ward style, a sign on the wall read: "Please try not to eat and drink too much. This party is only deductible up to $200.00." Hundreds of guests attended, and dancing went on into the wee hours. Many famous Broadway names were present, including Michele Lee, Hermione Gingold, and Lee Grant, along with the obligatory TV and press representatives.

A greeting was hung on the restaurant's front door to give arriving celebrants a hint to the tone of the evening ahead. The notice solemnly asked, "How come you never invite Jay Ward to any of your parties?" It was followed by one next to the coatroom proclaiming, "Anyone who wants to reciprocate, Jay is free next Monday." Throughout the night the guests spotted many other signs of a similar bent, including one contemporary piece of satire hanging from the chandelier. This one stated, "Anyone who wants to help invade Cuba after the party, please see Jay Ward." Ward even got in a plug for his animated offspring with one printed announcement proudly boasting, "Another big first for Bullwinkle—winter reruns!"

In a publicity release, Ward said, "The world is a pretty serious place. I feel that people are entitled to a laugh to break the monotony. The parties? I think everybody gets a kick out of an offbeat party, that's why I like to give them." To which Foshko added, "Yeah, but the guy who really has the most fun of all is Jay himself!"

For April, Ward planned to hold the first formal in the Hilton ballroom—the first because the Hilton Hotel was not completed yet. He envisioned providing his guests with plastic helmets and boots in case of falling cement, but this concept was turned down by the Hilton's justifiably nervous promotional office. Foshko remembered another idea that almost happened: "Jay and I wanted to hold a big party in an apartment building, with the ploy being that each apartment you went into was holding a different theme party—in one room there would be a birthday, another would be celebrating a wedding, a third would be a sweet sixteen, and so on." Instead, the next stunt became "Jay Ward's Homecoming Party."

In late April, Jay threw his "Coming Home Party" on the campus of Columbia University. Asked why, he replied, "Because I'm leaving for California in the morning." But had Ward really attended Columbia? "No, the only college I attended was Moose U. in 'Moosylvania.'" Actually it was Harvard, but they had declined to cooperate. "In truth," Alan Foshko admits, "Columbia University was my old alma mater. They agreed to do this in exchange for a donation."

This event was billed as "A Homecoming Week party especially for those who never had a home to come home to." The normally hallowed halls were comprehensively signposted, ensuring that the revelers knew this wasn't to be an academic evening. For instance, a sign on one wall read, "Have you ever noticed how much Jay looks like Ben Casey?" (TV's Dr. Casey was played by actor Vince Edwards, who was the Brad Pitt of 1963.)

The heretofore staid campus was decorated with streamers and banners. Partygoers arriving by car observed scores of students dressed in striped jackets and straw hats; stationed at strategic points along the way, each one held up a sign announcing "Jay Ward's Homecoming, Class Reunion and Big Game Night Party," and directing the guests to John Jay Hall, where the wingding would take place. Once inside, the invitees were greeted by the entire marching band from Manhattan College, who cheerfully donated their services to the cause. Attractive Columbia coeds handed out registration cards and ID tags. College dink hats, pom-poms, pennants, and huge corsages were presented to all revelers prior to their entering the candlelit and gaily festooned "rathskeller" (as a publicity release described the room).

From then on Dixieland jazz, raccoon coats, booze, and hamburgers were the order of the evening. A popular attraction was team mascot Barbara Henning, a pretty blonde of unique proportions, who was safely ensconced in a six-foot cage. In all, more than five hundred guests showed up.

Counting balloons, helium, flowers, costumes by Brooks Van Horn, megaphones, "Hello" tags, signs, and publicity, the party expenses cost Jay Ward around $700, with food and drinks on top. He donated $500 to Columbia University.

Thanks to all these nonsensical stunts, *The Bullwinkle Show* and Jay Ward Productions had received plenty of publicity. Bullwinkle even appeared in the first installment of NBC's summer musical series *The Lively Ones*; animated in Hollywood, with the moose rotoscoped (animation traced from live-action reference) to the choreographer's steps, Bullwinkle danced the bossa nova (with star Vic Damone) and heckled musical director Jerry Fielding. And some excellent Bullwinkle publicity occurred on April Fool's Day, 1963, with *TV Guide* publishing a droll supplement section put together by the resident zanies of Jay Ward Productions.

Meantime, Jay Ward's biggest project in 1963 was an outgrowth of his plans to expand beyond animation: *The Nut House,* a one-hour live-action comedy pilot.

The Nut House was Jay Ward and Bill Scott's only excursion into live-action television. As Scott recalled, "CBS approached our studio. They wanted a fast and zany show. So that's what they got."

In late May 1963, CBS and Jay Ward signed a contract for the development of a weekly one-hour comedy-variety series to go out live during the 1964–65 season. The network, unsure if Jackie Gleason would be back (they had given in to letting the Great One do his show from Miami), decided to give Ward's studio a crack at comedy after being impressed by the "Operation Loudmouth" PR campaign and Jay's growing comic reputation.

George Atkins recalls, "CBS had allocated a $20,000 writing budget at the time for a comedy pilot. So all these writers were hired, as well as us at Jay Ward's. But guess whose stuff ended up being used on the show? Ours did! Of course, by the time all the outsiders had been paid, even though their stuff was junked, we only received our usual low salary. But the sketches we did were terrific. Chris and Lloyd came up with that beautiful big finale piece called 'Alvin.' " The show's concept did not allow for name stars; rather, this would be a showcase for "second bananas," along the lines of the legendary Olsen and Johnson Broadway show *Hellzapoppin!*

Bill Scott enthused, "The show was very funny. We had every writer working on it, and some are now big, big names in TV and motion pictures. One of the contributors was Paul Mazursky, and of course we had our own crew. And all the cast were young up-and-coming comics who were brilliant actors: people like Jane Connell, Andrew Duncan, and others from the Second City Troupe.

"The sight gags cost a lot of money, sometimes just for one gag. The joke that really stunned CBS was a scene at a bachelor party in which a cake jumped out of a girl. [This skit didn't make it to the final show.] Our final sequence started out as a small joke—the 'Alvin' number. This army guy goes into one of those 'make a record' booths, and he starts to do this recording for his mother. And it goes into a bit where he ends up being 'produced' like a big-time star. That was about all there was to the joke. Well, Jay spotted that fact, so he said, 'Let's expand that—let's see what happens after that.' So it ends up as a huge production number, with all these gags; two guys are behind the booth writing a Broadway-type score, a girl is painting the album cover, and so on. Very funny piece.

"Anyway, they looked at the budget for this whole show, and it was just outrageous. Nobody would ever have gone for that at the time. And as I maintain, the idea was used, nay, ripped off, later by George Schlatter. It became *Laugh-In* and made them all a fortune!"

Skip Craig remembers the show as "just a hodgepodge, but some very funny stuff, and some good young comics. But it lacked the thing that made *Laugh-In* successful, which was the linking device of a front star, like the team of Rowan and Martin." Lloyd Turner was a big supporter of this pilot: "It had a beautiful cast and fine production. It was too far ahead of its time for CBS, but our *Nut House* was swiped by Schlatter for NBC later. We should have had that show, we wuz robbed."

By early November 1963, the show was ready to go. The casting was completed, and Johnny Mann was signed for choral direction. With his usual offbeat generosity, Ward surprised all his *Nut House* actors with extra money to tide them over through rehearsals. The cast began rehearsing three weeks before the shooting date.

Jay Ward jokingly reported budgeting the show at $200,000, telling the press, "It's thirty thousand for production costs and the rest for fun, promotion, and press parties!"

Originally some of the sketch ideas were to be employed in a second comedy pilot Ward and Scott had in mind. This was called "Inside at the Outside," which was to have been hosted by a different comic each week, including Shelley Berman, Bill Dana, and Bob Newhart. Instead, the material was combined with *The Nut House* skits. Jim Stanley (associate producer of *Sing Along with Mitch*) became coproducer, with Emmy award–winner Charles S. Dubin hired as producer-director. Jerry Fielding (who had last conducted the Bullwinkle bossa nova) was slated as musical director. Herb Ross came aboard as choreographer, while special musical material was composed by Marty Charnin, Mary Rogers, and Jim Rusk.

Ward and Scott decided to borrow from the techniques of rapid cutting and swift action normally seen in cartoons. Jay told the press, "It's a potpourri of music, gags, dances, and sketches in live action with a smattering of animation—no use in getting Bullwinkle mad at us. He holds a grudge a long time. It's a little bit of a different idea in variety shows. It has no big star, no serious moments, no schmaltz, no name guests—in fact, for a while, we thought of calling it 'Dr. No.' "

The versatile performing troupe consisted of Ceil Cabot, Jane Connell, Fay DeWitt, Andy Duncan, Don Francks, Tony Holland, Adam Keefe, Muriel Landers, Marilynn Lovell, Mara Lynn, Len Maxwell, jazz trumpeter–comic Jack Sheldon, and Alan Sues (later a *Laugh-In* regular). Several of these performers had worked with such stars as Sid Caesar and Danny Kaye. Hostess Kathy Kersh, a former beauty queen as Miss Rheingold, played "the Nut House Squirrel Girl," a takeoff on the Playboy Bunny.

Meanwhile, behind the scenes things weren't so rosy. As with his earlier experiences at two other networks, Jay Ward soon discovered CBS was panic-stricken over his approach to comedy. The CBS brass were bothered by the show's lack of cohesion, and grumbled about the absence of a guest host. Several scripts were nixed by the CBS Program Practices division during preproduction. "They have been slashing away at my sketches," lamented Ward, "and at this point I am not sure what will end up on the cutting-room floor." Later he added, "The twenty-seven different show segments range from a five-second blackout to an eight-minute finale which is probably the biggest cadenza since The 1812 Overture."

Of the actual shooting, Skip Craig ruefully recalls "Jay's typically good timing. The day we taped the show at CBS was the day of [John F.] Kennedy's funeral. That whole weekend of the assassination and funeral, we were finishing it. And Allan Burns had written this really nice program to be given out to the studio audience . . . and there were Kennedy gags in it! He had a football lineup with Bobby Kennedy as Right Brother and so on. I remember screaming, 'Al!' He had to madly change the thing and rush it to the printers." Al Burns remembers the large fold-out program he designed as "cumbersome."

Once the special was edited, the real showdown took place between Jay and Ward and CBS. Out went a brief act in which a pitchwoman stepped onstage and declared, "I'd like to show you my Maidenform bra" as she shucked her blouse. Then out went all the scenes involving a gorilla who walked through the set with the CBS eye-logo attached to its derriere. Out, too, went a skit in which an unlucky commuter was trampled flat by the far-out regulars of a subway coffee shop. Finally, out went any hopes of a weekly series, although an indignant CBS got salvage money by airing a tamed-down version of Ward's pilot at 10 P.M. one hot summer evening, when few would be watching.

Yet for a short time before it finally aired (September 1, 1964, as a replacement special), Jay Ward and a couple of CBS sympathizers, thinking optimistically, were looking into the possibility of doing a Broadway show from the sketches. Due to a programming shakeup, CBS reran the doomed pilot on New Year's Eve 1964, while the option to go to a series ran until February 1965. But it wasn't to be: the network's top brass simply found Ward and his show too way-out.

Unfortunately for Jay, *The Nut House* tested poorly, too. George Atkins remembers (through rose-colored glasses), "Critical reaction was excellent." But in truth, most critics deplored the sketches as stale and embarrassingly broad, although each felt the concept was laudable and a relief from the various bland Donna Reed–type sitcoms then in abundance. By today's standards, the show comes across as tame and a little disappointing. The technical achievements of the 1990s, such as digital effects and computer graphics, weren't in existence then, and the black-and-white program looks primitive now. Still, for 1963, it must have seemed revolutionary: *That Was the Week That Was* had yet to be telecast, it was four years before *Laugh-In* debuted, and twelve years ahead of both NBC's *Saturday Night Live* and the first U.S. appearance of *Monty Python's Flying Circus.*

But by being so different *The Nut House* alienated over 80 percent of the audience, who found the show either too silly to enjoy, or overcrowded with material and disconnected. "Much of the program's broad humor, satire, spoofs or burlesque went over the heads of most people in the audience," said a CBS program research report, which admitted that a small minority "enjoyed *The Nut House,* calling it clever, witty and different."

The bits that worked best were the short cartoons, which must have told Jay and Bill something. Pete Burness directed these pieces. The opening animation, featuring a squirrel cracking open a large nut, is similar to the opening cartoon titles on *Fractured Flickers*. A catchy musical theme was composed by the prolific Fred Steiner.

The opening sketch, in which a milk bottle is left near a manhole cover and a hand (resembling Thing from *The Addams Family*) grabs it and leaves change, was called "the best part of the show" by many, who felt the remainder quickly nose-dived into frantic and objectionable material. A skit in which death row prisoners sang barbershop-quartet-style songs was funny but went on too long (of course, many sketch shows are guilty of that crime to this day), while the showpiece, "Hello, Mom! This is your son Alvin," elicited a fifty-fifty response from "enjoyable" to "exaggerated and ridiculous."

The cast was considered highly talented, and the singing and dancing were complimented, but overall *The Nut House* didn't stand a chance. It was, in the classic Jay Ward Productions pattern, simply ahead of its time. The most intriguing footnote to *The Nut House* saga was the list of possible choices for cast members. Ward and his team had considered hiring such future stars as Woody Allen, Mike Nichols, Peter Falk, Tommy Smothers, Mel Brooks, Sandy Dennis, and Jo Ann Worley.

By August 1963, Desilu, the sales agent for *Fractured Flickers,* had a hundred-odd syndication markets signed up for the first thirteen shows (ten of which were already in the can). A New York press screening for *Fractured Flickers* had already been held at the intimate Johnny Victor Theatre in the RCA Building on June 1, 1963. This function, naturally, was given a true silent-movie-era treatment. There was free liquor (billed as "vintage—early bathtub"), and the bash was lavishly catered. A rinky-dink piano player was employed, and the knockout Barbara Henning made her second appearance at one of Ward's happenings: here she was dressed as the function's "1920's girl." Gordon Novelties supplied long cigarette holders, headache bands, Roaring Twenties armbands, and other period icons.

Alan Foshko was pleased with the turnout: representatives from fifteen magazines, as well as *Variety* and the other trade papers, showed up. Unfortunately, the Decoration Day holiday took its toll in absentees, and the function was jinxed by a terrible rainstorm—an uncanny omen for Jay's next event.

The press screening, in fact, was merely a warm-up for the biggest bash Foshko ever threw, and what was effectively Jay Ward's last publicity hurrah: the "Coney Island Film Festival." For this event the inimitable Alan Foshko pulled out all the stops.

As early as April 1963, Foshko had been formulating his idea for "Jay

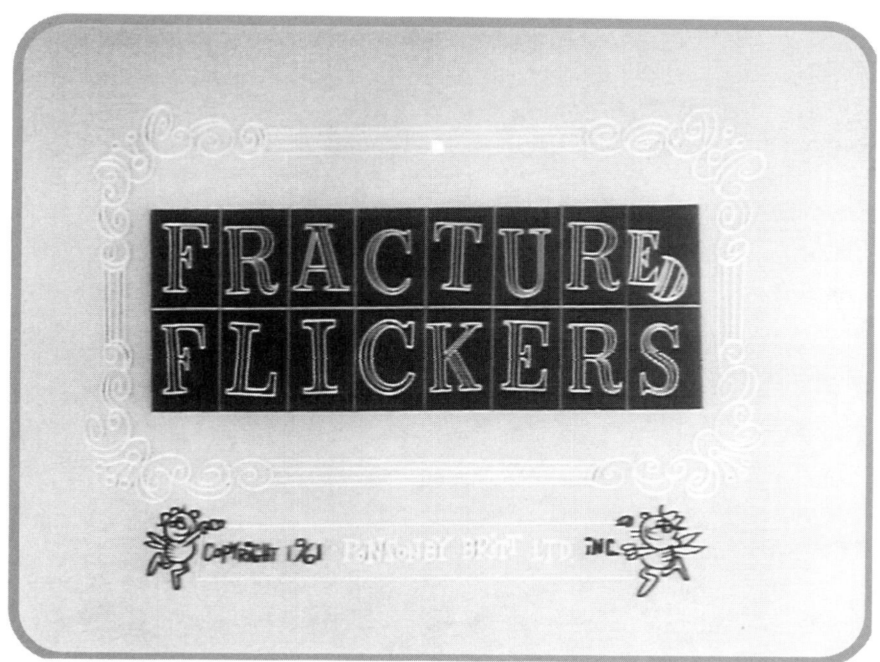

The *Fractured Flickers* opening logo. *Courtesy of Ramona Ward and Tiffany Ward and Jay Ward Productions, Inc.*

Ward's Coney Island Film Festival." He recalls, "This was the best thing we ever did, and it turned out to be a truly gigantic evening." By June, preparations were under way. Timed to coincide with the prestigious New York Film Festival, which would open two nights earlier, Ward's own cockeyed shindig publicized the New York television debut of *Fractured Flickers,* in itself something of an "antifilm" TV show.

Ward's stunt was comically promoted as the next logical film festival after those of Venice, Cannes, and San Francisco. Coney Island, the famed seaside resort often referred to as New York's "Hot Dog Beach" or "Pizza-Knish Shores," was the location chosen to provide a fun backdrop to an out-of-left-field film festival in which, naturally, only Jay Ward telefilms would be shown.

With heavy advance press blitzes on both coasts provided by Howard Brandy and Alan Foshko, the media were soon aware that this would be the most lavish promotional affair since Mike Todd's 1957 bash at Madison Square Garden for the premiere of his movie blockbuster *Around the World in 80 Days.*

The groundwork for the stunt required exhaustive preparation. In July, Foshko secured the services of Hebrew National Kosher Foods, which would cater for three thousand guests, supplying endless frankfurters, salami, mustard, cold cuts, rolls, rye bread, pickles, and relish. The Jantzen Swimwear company happily confirmed a tie-in by donating six genuine old-fashioned bathing suits for the festival, and a grand prize of two swimsuits to each of the eight winners of a "Miss 1919" contest. Meanwhile, Maysles Films agreed to record the highlights of the night for posterity.

To promote the Coney Island stunt, Jay appeared on the then one-year-old *Tonight Show Starring Johnny Carson*. Billed as "Rhinestone Jay Ward," he sported a genuine rhinestone monocle and a huge salami, but the appearance wasn't too successful. Skip Craig said, "It was embarrassing—Jay froze and started laughing; he and Carson didn't know what to say to each other, and the interview was over real quick." Chris Hayward recalled, "Carson couldn't believe he'd come out with that bologna, but that was Jay's way of hiding; he didn't really want to do it. He was out of the TV studio and on the elevator before the next commercial break was over."

The big night finally arrived on Thursday, September 12, 1963. Approximately two thousand people had been invited from the press and TV fields, with Jay Ward paying all expenses. What this meant was that Jay paid for everyone's transport to Coney Island by subway! At 7:00 P.M. three vintage ten-car BMT subway trains made the first of several round-trip express routes to Coney Island. It would be the only time in history that dining cars were added; indeed, the first time a subway was rented for an entire evening.

The New York City Transit Authority okayed the train rides. Foshko recalls, "Looking back now, I don't know how I managed to get those permits." The contract cost $1,200. This paid for six round-trips from Manhattan to Coney Island, including insurance, security, power for lighting, and cleanup costs. The waiting guests were greeted by a new look to the normally drab subway platform. Authentic 1880s gas lamps were imported from Baltimore, and brightly colored fountains exuded the fragrance of Revlon perfume. The delighted invitees journeyed on vintage 1920s subway cars that had been brightly decorated for the evening. Live Dixieland jazz was played in the aisles. Gifts and tote bags, courtesy of East House, were supplied. These were filled with period items: for the women, there were rope necklaces, drop earrings, Prohibition-era makeup, headache bands, false eyelashes, and cigarette holders, while the men received straw hats, cigars, canes, bow ties, and vests. A buffet of cold cuts and Pepsi was provided by Hebrew Kosher for each car, while the scent of Revlon perfume was piped through the ceiling fans.

When the train arrived at the Stillwell Avenue terminus, a delegation of Brooklynites wearing Dodger uniforms greeted the passengers. This was followed by a spectacular fireworks display over the Atlantic Ocean. "We even had Gene Krupa playing on the subway platform," Foshko recalls. The trains made trips at 7:30 and 8:30, with an extra midnight celebrity express for theater folk. Return trips were booked at 1:00, 2:00, and 3:00 A.M., with Ward adding, "There will also be special buses, followed by ambulances."

Once off the train, the guests adjourned to the magnificent new $3 million Astroland Amusement Park. The varied entertainment included a Mack Sennett–style bathing-beauty contest, two fashion shows, jazz bands, endless free rides, and, of course, continuous screenings of eight *Fractured Flickers* in the "Palais de Festival" area. Genuine Bathtub Gin Punch was to be served from authentic 1920s giant bathtubs, along with Ballantine beer and Taylor champagne (the New York State champagne). Liquid refreshment flowed all night long from the 1920s "Speak Easy" bar, which stretched half a city block in length.

Throughout the evening, silent-movie-era nostalgia was laid on thick: there were flagpole sitters, marathon dancers, and "Dimpled Dollies" on display, along with costumed actors dressed like Rudolph Valentino, Theda Bara, and other early silver-screen notables. Jay Ward himself played a Diamond Jim Brady role—he carried a bag filled with rhinestone rings for all the women present.

The "festival" part of the evening was played totally tongue-in-cheek, as only Ward could do it. Foshko succeeded in getting the statuesque Jeri Archer (measurements 42-25-36), from the current Broadway play *Little Me,* as MC. All the big movie companies received genuine invitations to enter. "For instance," said Ward, "20th Century–Fox received a formal, written invitation to enter *Cleopatra* in the silent picture category, but we never heard from them." Of course, everyone present was in on the gag: *Fractured Flickers* would obviously make a clean sweep of the prizes.

Capping the already satirical tone, an actual awards show was staged; sure enough, every category was mysteriously dominated by *Fractured Flickers*. Nominations included "Sickest Film"; "Best Film Made Without a Camera"; "Most Serious Comedy"; "Best Foreign Film with an All-Male Cast, Except for Six Leading Ladies and Other Women"; and "Nicest and Most Talented Producer (Jay Ward)." Needless to say, Ward was the sole judge—and winner—in the festival competition.

A magnificent time was had, but true to form, Jay Ward's parade was rained on. Actually, the rain came in buckets, proving a record New York downpour. Foshko said, "I was willing to take out rain insurance with Lloyd's of London. It would have cost $500. But Jay was so hyped up and excited that he said no. He believed that it wouldn't rain. One of the guests was TV weather girl Gloria Okon, and Jay said, 'Gloria won't let it rain.' But there were four damned inches that night!" Foshko's memory might have been hazy; according to Charlotte Morris, a close friend of Jay and Alex Anderson since college, Jay *did* pay for rain insurance. She attended the Coney Island party, and remembers huddling with scores of other people under a pavilion when the deluge came. "Jay told me that night that he was insured with Lloyd's for rain." That didn't help the thousands of invitees and gate-crashers who were reduced to squeezing into sheltered pavilions with no access to the scattered refreshment stands and rides. But the ankle-deep water didn't seem to dampen any spirits, as the guests continued dancing on indoor tables. (Actually, the real bummer was that the storm prevented the truck delivery of the advertised Bathtub Gin Punch.)

"The Coney Island Film Festival," precipitation and all, cost Jay Ward around $50,000. He estimated that three quarters of that fee went down the drain with the rain. As June Foray recalls, "It was a fantastic evening, but it pelted down soon after we got off the train. I had a fur coat on and I looked like some bedraggled animal. Nobody could go on any of the rides after a while. But we had a marvelous time on the train. Bill Scott and myself were the only voice actors there, I think.* I still have the earrings they gave us that night."

Looking back on this period with nostalgic fondness, Alan Foshko points out, "These stunts were done with sweetness and a certain innocence, and I don't believe that they would be possible today. There was a sense of enthusiasm. We were all so young, and nothing seemed impossible. And the Coney Island party was a truly fabulous night. It felt like you were part of a movie. Everyone was walking around so mystified and so happy. Four thousand people finally turned up that evening.

"And my relationship with Jay was the best part of the deal. In those days Jay loved an event, he loved 'capers' and being a part of something that no one expected. He really felt like he was alive. Jay was truly my pal; in fact, there was quite a chemistry there from the start. We'd do special things together, like our progressive dinners. We'd start with egg rolls in a Chinese

*Hans Conried, the star of *Fractured Flickers,* was previously engaged and couldn't attend.

restaurant, then soup in an Italian restaurant, then a steak at some other place, dessert at a French restaurant, then coffee and drinks somewhere else. We both shared a bit of a childlike quality in our natures—we were sort of like Huck Finn and Tom Sawyer.

"Jay and I laughed all the time. One time we had the giggles, and we went to the theater together, along with Jay's secretary, Linda. We saw *The Riot Act,* and we ended up laughing so violently that we got hysterical and had to leave. Poor Sylvia Miles was onstage at the time. Jay loved absurdity and he was a sweet man. He was the most unique client I ever had, and everyone on my staff adored him. The Coney Island bash was the last one we did. But I held a final farewell party in my apartment, where everyone had to bring a present that cost under a dollar."

Indeed, Coney Island would be the last big Jay Ward publicity party. It occurred less than two months before the assassination of John F. Kennedy. Foshko, along with several others, believes that fate had a hand in the timing. "In my view, the world changed from that day [Kennedy's death]—Jay and I changed, the industry changed, and the city of New York changed. But overall the mood of the times changed forever. As they say, that was the day America lost its innocence.

"The change in Jay was obvious. Within a couple of years he felt betrayed by some people, and a little disappointed in life. He didn't want to produce TV shows anymore. Physically he was not that well. Also it should be pointed out that anyone who has had such a fabulous taste of the high life reaches a point where there simply has to be a swing to the other side." Howard Brandy agrees with Foshko, adding, "Jay never really wanted to be a public figure, and by this time he felt he'd done it all." For the next few years the publicity reverted to the mailers, with the highlight being the studio's annual Christmas cards. For the 1964 card, Jay had an enormous reproduction of Bullwinkle, dressed as Santa Claus, holding a tiny card simply marked "Joy."

Following the Coney Island function, there was a unique PR bash on the West coast. The Exotique Dancers' League of North America held their sixth annual convention at the swank Bel Air Hotel on November 12, 1963. Buxom president Jennie Lee named Bullwinkle J. Moose their "Male Personality of the Year." (Previous winners had included Mike Connors, Tony Curtis, and Walter Winchell.) Ward and Bullwinkle were honored, with the girls performing a bump-and-grind fashion show. Apparently this wingding got a little out of hand—Skip Craig said, "Yeah, out of hand is an understatement: they were thrown out of the place!"

17

Silents Is Golden, or The Greatest Waste of TV Time Since *The Bullwinkle Show* (*Fractured Flickers*)

"It drove us to drink!" exclaimed writer Chris Hayward, referring to the blood, sweat, and tears behind the making of *Fractured Flickers;* his wife, Linda, added, "And it practically ruined Chris's eyesight." Hayward came up with the concept for the silent-film spoof, undoubtedly the quirkiest show to emerge from Jay Ward Productions, and physically the most difficult to make. Debuting in October 1963 and running for twenty-six half hours, *Flickers* was first dreamed up four years earlier. Hayward cowrote the pilot film for Jay Ward's unsuccessful puppet series concept *The Watts Gnu Show* with George Atkins, and, being an ardent silent-movie buff, he included a couple of blackouts containing old film footage. Afterward Hayward broached the idea of an entire comedy show based on silent films. He recalls, "I said to Jay, 'Instead of "Fractured Fairy Tales," how about "Fractured Flickers"?' Well he seemed to like this idea, so I went to work on it." Bill Scott remembered, "Jay asked me if we could use this [film] material and joke it up and I said, 'Sure.' "

The concept was beautiful in its simplicity. Vintage films would be re-edited into crazy new stories, with the writers creating wildly incongruous material to be read in funny voices over the mute images. This had been done before, on *The Ernie Kovacs Show* for example, but no series ever used the concept as slickly as *Fractured Flickers*. The show managed to perfectly evoke that long-ago era when movie directors wore leather thigh boots and shouted through megaphones.

Reverence, however, was hardly this show's byword: Lon Chaney in *The Hunchback of Notre Dame* (1923) no longer haunted the cathedral, but became instead a sappy cheerleader named Dinky Dunstan. This skit, written by George Atkins, is one of the all-time favorites, often included in compilations of Ward's output. John Barrymore in 1920s *Dr. Jekyll and Mr. Hyde* remains a scientist, but is now a valiant chemist in search of the perfect chocolate seltzer drink. In *Blood and Sand* (1922), Rudolph Valentino plays an insurance salesman, not a matador. And a once grim William S. Hart cowboy saga suddenly concerns the tribulations of a used-horse salesman.

A year after "Watts Gnu" was completed, the pilot film for *Fractured Flickers* was prepared. On December 1, 1960, actor Hans Conried was filmed on a small soundstage hosting the show and introducing two flickers. During the same week, versatile composer Dennis Farnon recorded the theme music and various background pieces. Then the films "Tarfoot of the Apes" and "The Giddyap Kid" (or to give them their original titles, *Tarzan of the Apes* [1918], and the William S. Hart western *On the Night Stage* [1915]), having been matched to the script via the painstaking process of slaving over a hot Moviola, were "looped." Looping is an industry term: the voice actors recorded the dialogue while watching short loops of edited film so that they could approximate, as much as possible, a semblance of lip sync.

The half-hour pilot script was written by Chris Hayward and Lloyd Turner. Once the films were reassembled, voices were provided by Hans Conried, who narrated, Paul Frees, Bill Scott, and June Foray. Next, editors Norman Schwartz (who only worked on the pilot) and Skip Craig added the hilariously silly sound effects, and the "fracturing" was done. The pilot was finished off with some fine title animation completed in early 1961. This featured caricatures of various pioneering movie types: a Theda Bara vamp, a swashbuckler, a cowboy, the Keystone Kops, and a dastardly villain who turned up several months later as Snidely Whiplash in the thematically similar "Dudley Do-Right" cartoons. The storyboard and design were by Bill Hurtz, and Jim Hiltz directed the animation.

In this audition film, Conried played a host who was different from the straighter presenter that he became in the series. To start with, he wasn't called Hans Conried; rather, he played a flamboyant thespian named H. Carleton Fothergill. It was a role which suited the arch Conried perfectly:

this cheap little series was way beneath Fothergill's dignity, and so he sneered his way through the show with magnificent disdain. The only reason he actually had the gig in the first place was because his agent had lost him in a canasta game. At the end of the show he is chained to a table to prevent his escaping. This humorous linking material was written by Bill Scott.

Although a much tamer host in the twenty-six episodes produced between 1963 and early 1964, Conried masterfully conveyed the Jay Ward philosophy: a sly undertone ran through all his on-camera pieces, indicating that nothing should be taken seriously. And while many of Hollywood's sacred cows were mocked, nothing was mocked more consistently than producer Ward and the show itself. Chris Hayward recalls, "Allan Burns wrote all those live pieces for Hans—all the guest interviews, all the payoff stuff, 'Good evening,' etc. Just marvelous stuff." (Bill Scott also claimed credit for much of this material.) There were many gags about the low budget and tacky quality of *Fractured Flickers,* and the ever-present possibility of lawsuits from beleaguered silent stars. Indeed, the real-life Lon Chaney, Jr., threatened to sue following the "Dinky Dunstan" sketch, which mangled his famous father's hunchback role—he labeled the skit "a shameful, irresponsible act against an indefensible screen immortal"—and Joan Crawford described the series as "a horrible idea."

Skip Craig recalls the low budget and severe time constraints of putting together each episode. "We were on a tight schedule, and Jay's idea of a cutting department was two guys, once a week! *Flickers* was impossible. Every Monday morning we had to make loops of all the pictures so they could record the dialogue that night; then that stuff would come back in to us each Tuesday morning. And at the same time we also had to dub the previous week's show. I had to synch all the dialogue, and cut the music so it would time out, and Roger Donley threw in the sound effects. And we managed to get out a show a week with two guys—boy, it was a bear! I remember at one point on *Flickers,* Jay hit financial difficulties and Glen Glenn [the recording studio] wouldn't go on till they got paid. The lab did the same thing. So we did two shows at Ryder Sound and another lab."

The source of the film material was the late, and controversial, Raymond Rohauer. Rohauer ran the Coronet Theatre revival cinema on La Cienega Boulevard in Los Angeles, and was regarded as the most energetic film collector of his day. He was responsible for unearthing and saving all the Buster Keaton material. In fact, he befriended Keaton, and managed to resurrect the fabulous comic's career.

In 1954, while managing the Society of Cinema Arts in Los Angeles,

Rohauer was contacted by actor James Mason, who had bought Buster Keaton's house. Mason had discovered a gold mine of valuable film stored in the basement. This was Keaton's personal collection. Rohauer, an ardent Keaton admirer, helped the down-on-his-luck comedian restore his decomposing nitrate films; then he formed a corporation through which Keaton could regain control of these films, which until then were tied up with the Joseph Schenck family. Over the next decade Rohauer arranged enormously successful in-person screenings of Keaton's masterpieces in Europe. Significantly, clips of Buster turn up in virtually every episode of *Fractured Flickers*.

When Rohauer tied up with Jay Ward and *Fractured Flickers,* he was curator and program director for prestigious film archives like the Gallery of Modern Art in New York. He was paid a flat fee for each *Flickers* episode. Writer-artist Chris Jenkyns recalled, "Rohauer was a man totally immersed in silent film. It was his whole life. He must have spent all his time in a vault, because in real life he looked sallow—white! It seemed as if he came out from under a rock." Linda Hayward, then Jay's secretary, says "Rohauer was a strange kind of guy. I used to tease Jay about him because the man was miserable. I'd say, 'Jay, he hates everyone: men, women, children, dogs, cats!' Rohauer was an angry man."

Bill Scott, who also loved silent films with a passion, worked closely with Rohauer in the selection of clips. But there was a personality clash: Howard Brandy remembered, "There was really only one person I ever heard Bill Scott say he couldn't stand, and that was Ray Rohauer." As Scott put it, "Some people will tell you [Rohauer] is one of the greatest conservators of American film and other people would say he's the biggest bandit and should be hung. I guess there's a little bit of both in him . . . but he had available to him just huge numbers of old films for which he had the television rights for a number of years." Skip Craig points out, "Rohauer was absolutely legit on the Keaton films—he'd been on probation earlier for violating Chaplin copyrights."

Jay Ward and Bill Scott aborted a distribution agreement with British-based Independent Television Corporation (ITC), run by Lew Grade. The New York branch of ITC liked the pilot film. In early 1962 they struck a deal with Ward Productions whereby they would finance half the cost of producing thirteen initial shows. The remaining thirteen would be made exclusively in the United Kingdom, and broadcast there prior to the U.S. airing.

ITC had been involved in various American coproductions since the mid-1950s. Indeed, some of the films to be used on *Flickers* were old British product in order to satisfy a quota regulation. In February 1962, Bill Scott traveled for three weeks to England, where he screened ninety-six films sourced by Rohauer; most of them were British prints of American movies. Chris Hayward recalls, "Rohauer was well known in England." Scott ordered what was usable shipped to Hollywood. But once the first couple of episodes were shown to ITC, their management team began dictating rules on quality control. The British deal soured and Desilu Productions took over in October 1962, paying Ward $10,000 per episode to cover production costs. *Fractured Flickers* was distributed by Desilu Sales on a first-run syndication basis to various stations, beginning in September 1963.

By mid-1963, Desilu had lined up a hundred-odd markets, and the public was soon made aware of the impending shenanigans thanks to the enormous press coverage for Jay Ward's most ambitious promotional gimmick, the "Coney Island Film Festival," at which *Flickers* was previewed to the press. There were ten episodes ready by then; the final sixteen were finished through 1964. On his one-year-old *Tonight Show*, comedy connoisseur Johnny Carson urged viewers to tune in to *Fractured Flickers,* calling it "substantially funnier than anything else in prime time."

When *Fractured Flickers* premiered, it received mixed notices:

> The dialogue was bright and the sequences nicely covered, and it made for an altogether delightful few moments. *(L.A. Outlook,* October 18, 1963)

> A good, intelligently trivial way to start an evening of serious viewing, like watching a frisky old Pete Smith movie short before the big picture. It's pure and obvious celluloid patchwork with lots of its comedy strained; but it's funny enough. (Jack O'Brien, *New York Journal-American,* October 1963)

> As is true of *Bullwinkle,* it is impossible to write down lines from *Fractured Flickers* and make anything hilarious of them. You have to hear them to laugh. So tune in. (Joan Waller, *CUE,* October 1963)

But *Variety* (October 2, 1963) was somewhat more subdued, sniffing:

> *Fractured Flickers* lacks the satiric subtlety and restraint to entice the sharper, more selective viewer, but it could become a big favorite with

audiences whose taste runs to hot foots, itching powder, dribble glasses and baby pictures with captions. That, of course, is a sizeable and responsive audience, but it's too bad that the Jay Ward scribblers weren't more inspired because the concept of embellishing silent pix with a new dialogue certainly seems to lend itself to richer, more provocative comedy than the rather obvious, pedestrian gaggery for which the writers have settled. . . .

Among the flickers unspooled on the premiere were a bullfight sequence re-edited to get the matador gored, and a 1918 *Tarzan* segment (re-dubbed "Tarfoot of the Apes") starring Elmo Lincoln. Host Hans Conried, an excellent choice for the assignment, also conducted what amounted to a fractured interview with guest Rose Marie.

A regular *Flickers* feature was the weekly chat between Hans Conried and a famous guest star. There was even a special treat for Jay Ward buffs: in one episode Conried conducted a witty tête-à-tête with the venerable Edward Everett Horton, our fondly remembered narrator from the "Fractured Fairy Tales" cartoons.

The "fractured" interviews were scripted in the same ironic tone as the flickers themselves. The guests often "complained" about the low payment they were getting on this travesty of a show, or that they were there under false pretenses. Mostly, they acquitted themselves neatly with the urbane "Hansel" (as Bill Scott referred to Conried). Teen pop idol Fabian, a client of Howard Brandy, was surprisingly good, and some truly unexpected talents—Paul Lynde, Allan Sherman, Gypsy Rose Lee, and even the Bullwinkle puppet—entered right into the spirit of the show. In fact, the only guests who seemed a little uncomfortable were Cesar Romero and Zsa Zsa Gabor. (Johnny Weissmuller filmed an interview, but it wasn't used in the series.)

Skip Craig recalled, "Those interview bits were tough. The low budget meant we only used one camera to film all that stuff, so continuity was real difficult to match. They'd do the interview with this one camera three times—a two shot, and two close-ups consisting of Hans, then the guest." Chris Hayward remembers, "The little commercial soundstage we used was pretty shabby." (This was Glen Glenn's facility at the Desilu-Gower studio in Hollywood.)

Scott revealed that two episodes were filmed per session, one in the morning and one in the afternoon, adding that Ward Productions was dealing with a celebrity agency who would often provide a guest whose schedule suited *Fractured Flickers*. "Sometimes we'd find out about [the guest] the day before. So I would then sit down and write an interview—as soon as I wrote it we'd send it out for TelePrompTer, and the star would get there at two-thirty or so and go ahead and do it. Got to meet a lot of famous people and write for them because as soon as you knew who the person was you could write an interview about what that kind of person would do."

The *Fractured Flickers* shows themselves ranged from hilarious to downright bizarre. Skip said, "It was only the first six or seven shows that worked really well. The later ones were just all over the place, with characters not matching, and no attempt at lip synch." While George Atkins agrees with this summation, Chris Hayward offers, "That was because we had no time. The last shows were made when we were on air, so we literally had only a week. On the earlier ones we had lots more time because we didn't have a firm air date scheduled." Certainly the flickers that work best tend to be the longer productions like "Tarfoot of the Apes," "Do Me a Flavor," "The Death of a Traveling Salesman," "The Giddyap Kid," "Dinky Dunstan—Boy Cheerleader," "The Prince and the Poppa," and "The Barber of Stanwick."

George Atkins recalls, "The titles of these works mercifully elude me; I can only remember wisps of content such as Walter Cronkite (Cronker Waltite in our case) involving himself with a guy who piles off the Eiffel Tower to an abrupt stop in the grass below, things like that." Atkins certainly has vivid memories of a topical skit completed in October 1963: he worked on a 1928 British film called *A South Sea Bubble* starring Ivor Novello. Atkins renamed one character Elmo, the lost Kennedy brother. "I did one about a foppy Kennedy brother the family kept under wraps. He was in a terribly big swish about having to stay in hiding and wanted '. . . something like that Senate thing Teddy has.' This thing aired in one market (it was a syndicated show) about one night after JFK's assassination and the station was set upon by a virtual mob of violence-prone avengers. This segment was quickly expunged from all prints and remains forgotten to history."

In 1964, columnist Harold Heffernan wrote, "In spite of Hollywood criticisms, nasty letters and telephone calls, and open demands that the Screen Actors Guide 'do something about it,' *Fractured Flickers* continues to jazz up old celluloid and cause 1964 audiences to wonder how their parents ever swooned over such characters as now pop out at them.

"At Jay Ward Productions, hundreds of films are viewed before one is picked for 'fracturing,' half a dozen projectors are spinning on a full-time basis, as twice that many experts sit there trying to figure out which bits can best be used to break up a TV audience. The old movies plough through at a terrific speed. Oddly, only one of the judging group was wearing specs."

Scripting the shows, said Hayward, "was madness—absolute chaos. Every Monday morning at ten o'clock, Jay and Bill would come in and we'd 'do' the whole show for them. Lloyd Turner would make all the sound effects vocally! To write it we would go through all this wonderful footage, then pick out scenes and write the frame numbers down, and hang that bit on the Moviola rack. Then the next bit and so on; then we'd piece it all together. We had to edit it to write it, with all these crazy, short bits. All the stuff I worked on was mostly mad little eight-second or eight-frame bits. We did all the 'Minute Mysteries.' " And all this some twenty years before the era of digital video editing.

George Atkins adds, "*Fractured Flickers* had to be written on the site of Jay's stacks of ancient film, all of which was like dynamite and was the cause of some catastrophic studio fires in the thirties and forties before nitrate film was copied onto the fireproof stuff. A couple of inches of nitrate film when lit looked like gasoline had been ignited. When I think of working for many months amid this stuff, while smoking visitors toured our converted two-bedroom house, I get visions of Vietnamese Buddhists going up in curls of orange-and-white fire. The process—sitting there squinting into a Moviola and spinning the film onto a superfast moving spool and thereby deep-cutting fingers on a daily basis, wading through miles of nonproductive footage while searching for a comedic idea which might work with a few frames, marking the film we wished to have printed so that Skip Craig, Jay's film editor, could order it reprinted—all of it was the most frustrating and difficult writing job I've ever attempted to perform.

"Jay's budget was way too low. There were five writers and only three Moviolas. This meant your Moviola would be swiped if you had to go to the bathroom, and that meant you'd have to wait and do your stuff later, like, say, from midnight until four in the morning. For a while we had a guy named Art Keene writing and he was really guilty of this practice—he was the type who'd steal your machine if you just stepped out for a hot dog. He wasn't that funny, and personally he was about as popular as ground glass in a bathtub."

On the other hand, Lloyd Turner remembered the entire process being "a joy: it was not a difficult show to do, in my opinion. Chris and I looked at all this funny, funny footage all day long, beautiful stuff with Stan Laurel and so on. I found it very easy. Of course I was lucky that old Chris was such a whiz at the editing. I only have one arm, so I wasn't able to cut the film. Chris was a delight to work with."

Linda Hayward vividly recalls the drinking sessions, mainly because her husband's alcohol intake ranked somewhat below Turner's capacity. "These guys would get mentally wiped out, and they'd go and drink at the Radar Room." Hayward explains, "It was the only way we could get enough false energy to make that ten o'clock Monday morning read-through. Most days we'd get there real early and start on all this film. Some mornings I'd get there at four o'clock—I remember seeing rats scampering across the street—and we'd work until about noon. Then we'd go and get hammered, collapse and go home, sleep it off, then start over again."

George Atkins notes, "It was [writer] Jimmy Critchfield who was really clever. None of us could figure out how to make a funny flicker from the comedy footage. It was easy with the heavy melodramatic stuff. But Critch figured a way to use the comedy films, and these were the flickers where Bill Scott did that Bob Newhart voice as a movie director who says things like, 'Okay, roll the camera now, Morey.' " Hayward and Turner wrote various recurring sketches: the "Minute Mysteries" featuring detective Sherman Oaks (culled from Stan Laurel's 1925 comedy spoof *Dr. Pyckle and Mr. Pride*), and the "odes," which were poems read by Bill Scott in a fine imitation of comedian Eddie Lawrence's character, the Old Philosopher ("What's the matter, Bunky?"). There were regular salutes to famous cities ("That wonderful, wonderful town!"), and a sports series called "Saturday Night," narrated by Paul Frees in the nasal race-commentator voice he later employed for Ward's "Tom Slick" cartoons.

Frees soon ended up the main voice of *Fractured Flickers*. Hans Conried narrated the earlier feature-length *Flickers,* but the recording schedule eventually settled into the regular Monday night looping sessions. Conried, who lectured extensively on Shakespeare, was often unavailable for these. The supremely silly voices heard on *Flickers* were some of the zaniest characters ever played by Foray, Frees, and Scott.

The music for the show was perfect. Canadian-born Dennis Farnon had a great talent for composing themes which sounded so authentic it seemed as if they were originally supplied on discs accompanying the silent films. Much of Farnon's music for the show was recorded between June and September of 1962 in England, where he lived for many years. "Farnon did a tracking library which we used in the series, although for the pilot he scored the music to bar sheets," said Skip Craig. Some shows also feature the familiar piano tracks written by the father-son team of George and Fred Steiner for the "Dudley Do-Right" cartoons.

If seen in reasonably sane doses, *Fractured Flickers* proves a fascinating show which always produces a few hearty chuckles. But it was basically a noble experiment; while there was much funny material contained in the thirteen hours produced, it was a little too off the beaten track (and to be truthful, inconsistent) to be a big-time hit. As Peter Piech puts it, "The show was not strong enough to sustain—you can only milk a cow so long before the teat runs dry. And it was simply unsalable to a network."

The pieces that work the best today are the wonderfully snide Hans Conried links.* Some of the *Fractured Flickers* celebrity interviews have, unfortunately, dated; apart from Rod Serling, Zsa Zsa Gabor, and a few others, younger audiences who catch the show on occasional cable screenings won't know several of the guests. Incidentally, in the tenth show a delivery boy walks into shot asking Hans if he ordered a sandwich: that's Bill Scott making a rare on-camera appearance; in another show he plays a stuntman.

Writer Jim Critchfield, who joined Ward's staff during production of *The Nut House* pilot, worked on the final thirteen *Flickers* shows. He would revive the idea in 1966, when *The Garry Moore Show* commissioned several comedy blackouts from the Ward studio.

*Following *Flickers* there was talk of Ward Productions making another TV vehicle to star the saturnine Conried—as host of a comedy-game show, originally heard on radio, called *So You Want to Be an Actor?*

18

Bullwinkle's Last Stand, or It's a Frog-Eat-Frog World

By late 1963, with the end of *The Bullwinkle Show* in sight, D-F-S finally gave Ward the go-ahead on a new cartoon series. After almost four years in the waiting room, the feisty frog Hoppity Hooper was finally given a shot at stardom. *Hoppity* would be cosponsored by General Mills and D-F-S's new toy account, De-Luxe Reading. The four episodes were ready in time to be previewed in March 1964 at the annual toy fair, where they went over very well. A series was scheduled for the fall season on ABC at 12:30 P.M. Saturdays, with *The Bugs Bunny Show* as a strong lead-in. Fifty-two episodes, each running four and a half minutes, were ordered (two per show for twenty-six half hours).

General Mills laid down some new conditions for the tiny green star. The stories had to be written strictly for a juvenile audience, and the sound tracks were to be a little slower and clearer for this age group. The September 1964 debut of *Hoppity Hooper* coincided with Bullwinkle's return to ABC for Sunday reruns at 11:00 A.M. Although Hoppity Hooper effectively replaced Bullwinkle as Jay Ward's new "star," it was like Tammy Bakker replacing Mother Teresa: the pint-sized frog didn't enjoy one iota of the moose's popularity or classic status.

Hoppity Hooper is something of a forgotten Jay Ward Production. The *Hoppity* cartoons concerned the close-shave adventures of a frog, a fox, and a bear who traveled from town to town in the fox's patent-medicine van. These days it can be hard to find *The Adventures of Hoppity Hooper* on television.

Animated in Mexico (and as such, the last series Gamma Productions worked on for Jay Ward), the show was deliberately slanted more to kids than the "Rocky and Bullwinkle" series. That's not to say the humor was childish, but the stories were less concerned with *Bullwinkle*'s adult-style subjects—intrigue, spies, and history. The comedy centered mainly on the character of Waldo fleecing various victims and getting his comeuppance in the end.

Opinion is divided: Bill Hurtz didn't particularly care for this series ("I didn't really do that many"), while writer Jim Critchfield called it "three characters in search of a premise." Chris and Linda Hayward felt the show was a real letdown compared to Jay Ward's earlier cartoons. On the other hand, Skip Craig enjoyed it very much, while Ward and Lloyd Turner absolutely loved it.

The series had a comfortable small-town ambience about it. Hoppity, Waldo, and Fillmore the Bear seemed to exist in a rather indefinable cartoony "time," a distant relation to "Fractured Fairy Tales" in mood, whereas the "Rocky" and "Peabody" stories were closer to reality, or based on actual historical figures. This atmospheric feel to *Hoppity Hooper* is due in no small measure to writers Chris Jenkyns and Bill Scott, who had both worked on early "Fairy Tales."

The sound tracks, as usual, were paramount. Hans Conried played the rapscallion fox named Professor Waldo Wigglesworth, a snake-oil salesman of the old school. Scott played the simple-minded Fillmore Bear, and Chris Allen, returning four years after recording the pilot, portrayed the title part of the heroic little frog. Bill Scott told Jim Korkis, "I especially enjoyed working with Hans Conried and a cute gal named Chris Allen—Chris was a writer, not a voice person; all she could do was this little-kid voice."

The stories were narrated by Paul Frees, using a slower storyteller-type voice. The first two episodes, recorded in 1960, feature radio actor Alan Reed as Fillmore. By the time production began, Reed was firmly contracted to Hanna-Barbera, playing Fred Flinstone. Scott's replacement voice for Fillmore—which on General Mills instructions had to sound totally different from any character in "Rocky and Bullwinkle"—was a friendly "dumb" voice, much like the wolf's in the "Fairy Tale" "Riding Hoods Anonymous."

Pete Burness directed the *Hoppity* pilot, for which Bill Hurtz designed

Four publicity poses from *Hoppity*. *Courtesy of Ramona Ward and Tiffany Ward and Jay Ward Productions, Inc.*

the opening show titles. These were classy silhouette graphics, animated by Gerard Baldwin, who recalls being a bit miffed that "we had all put money into the series to fund the pilot, but the rights were given up when it got on air. Jay paid us back our money so we weren't able to share." Dennis Farnon composed the title music back in 1960, and the closing theme was a later piece he had written in England entitled "Olga Moletoad's Ride."

General Mills bought the series in late 1963, just as the final "Rocky" episodes were coming off the animation assembly line. Production commenced in mid-January 1964. The *Hoppity Hooper* cartoons were predirected in Hollywood by Bill Hurtz and Pete Burness. Almost a hundred were animated in Mexico City; episode 2, the pilot film, was made in Los Angeles back in 1960, and Ward's team animated one "Hoppity" adventure in 1964.

Only the "Hoppity" episodes were new. It had been decided they would be "wraparound" segments for repeated elements from the earlier "Rocky and Bullwinkle" shows (i.e., "Fairy Tales," "Aesop," and "Dudley Do-Right"); a happy decision, because Ward's team was now frantically busy animating commercials for the Quaker Oats Company. As Bill Scott saw it, the show packagers "primarily wanted a longer [continuing] main segment" which would give them a better shot at selling a show in syndication rather than to a network.

The *Hoppity Hooper* characters were well-rounded. Vocally, Hoppity sounded genuinely childlike and winsome; the juvenile audience related well. Fillmore, the bugle-blowing bear, was a simple soul and another of Bill Scott's great "dumb" voices, a lot more naive than Bullwinkle. The youngsters would feel for Fillmore too. These virtuous characters were ever loyal to the mendacious rogue Professor Waldo; strangely, the latter would also come across sympathetically, being avuncular and protective of his two meal-ticket companions.

With Waldo, however, one's sympathy went only so far. He was a money-hungry scoundrel all too aware of his own shortcomings. Conried and the writers gave him the personality of a pompous, W. C. Fields–like braggart who was something of a failed actor and it was a great characterization. His florid speech was punctuated with expressions like "Hour of mischief!" and "My sainted Aunt Agnes." He never called Fillmore by his correct name—instead, the poor bear was designated Fensdorf, Athelstane, and countless other demeaning appellations. Waldo would also regularly go into spasms of physical jump-and-jive, shrieking, "I've got it!!!" as he hatched his fraudulent plans.

The stories often concerned new schemes and scams dreamed up by Waldo, such as his detective agency or his idea to market Wottabango Indian Corn Elixir. In other scrapes the characters found themselves trapped in fairy-tale settings (the Mole community in "Diamond Mine") or fantasy lands ("The Traffic Zone"—Paul Frees narrated these four episodes in a hammed-up Rod Serling voice). The boys lived in the prosaic little town of Foggy Bog, Wisconsin, just as Ward's other heroes resided in small towns like Galahad Glen and Frostbite Falls. In fact, thanks to Waldo, the boys were often about to be tarred and feathered by sundry creditors in their hometown at the start of a new adventure.

Lloyd Turner recalled the "Hoppity" cartoons as having no boundaries and thus being inspiring to write. "The characters and adventures were what I call probable/impossible. I wrote a lot of those, and I loved them. It was a delight to work on. And Bill Scott would always add something to any script. He'd punch them up, but that never bothered me."

Turner wrote an affectionate ribbing letter to Jay Ward years after leaving the studio; it was published in a writers' journal. At one point he reminded his former employer,

> Your instincts were usually right on—if you thought a script was good, it usually was. But on a few occasions your judgment shorted out (maybe too much ice cream). Especially when we'd wire brush you on some idiosyncrasy. Remember "Defier"—the first horse in your "Bullwinkle" stable of race horses? It had good blood, but it was a textbook loser. You'd grab me and say, "No workin' today—we're going to the track." Defier was running. (Sometimes the writers would grumble: How come we'd get laid off or denied a raise, and you'd pay $15,000 for a horse?) One of your celebrity friends said, "No way I'm betting on that beetle." But I did. Defier lost. That's loyalty. So I wrote a "Hoppity Hooper" where Hoppity and Uncle Waldo meet a con man and buy a horse called Big Dud. It can't run, steps in his bucket (like the real Defier) and goes to sleep within 40 feet of the finish line. I did a lot of horse jokes—it was truly inspired. You hated it. "If I was in the bum business, I'd want ten more just like you," you said. It went into production because nothing else was ready and everybody else loved it. "Funny stuff," you decided later and would quote my jokes back to me.

Several in-jokes were employed for the adventures of the amiable amphibian: racetrack star Leadfoot Lew Keller was a character name based on animation director Lew Keller. In a golf story an announcer calls out the scores of golfers named Ward, Hayward, and Turner; and there were even crossover appearances by Bullwinkle, Dudley Do-Right, Boris Badenov, and, showcasing the influence of writer Bill Scott, our old cameo stars Chauncey and Edgar.

Following their initial airing, the twenty-six half-hour shows were repackaged by P.A.T. with different components and began syndicated life as *Uncle Waldo's Cartoon Show.* The final twenty-six shows joined this canned version when the network run finished on September 2, 1967. *Hoppity Hooper* was the last Jay Ward TV series made under the P.A.T. coproduction banner. When Ward's next cartoon series went to air, animation fans would notice a distinct improvement: *George of the Jungle* was made entirely in Hollywood.

• • •

Meantime *The Bullwinkle Show* had moved to Saturday morning for its third and final NBC run in 1963–64. It featured ten stories. These were enjoyable if somewhat inconsistent, but a definite disappointment after the quicksilver comedy of the previous season. Unlike the earlier material, the new scripts often seem deliberately truncated, with an occasional comic misfire along the way. The first story was, however, a beauty. The Bumbling Brothers, Hugo and Igo, run a circus in which Boris is employed as a lion tamer named Claude Badley—a wince-inducing pun based on the name of real-life animal trainer Clyde Beatty. The story reveals that Bullwinkle has yet more untapped musical talent—he's a Hum-a-Comb virtuoso. In one scene Ward and Scott get in a little zinger aimed at NBC's censorship division. Rocky, tied to a stake, is about to be cooked by a giant Indian. The plucky squirrel whips out his contract, defiantly telling the huge Apache, "The network says, quote—'No cannibalism on TV!' " Fortunately, Bullwinkle's insipid music causes the tribe to do a rain dance, destroying the fire. At the end of one episode the narrator bursts into helpless laughter at one of Scott's awful puns, and our indignant heroes have to take over his announcing chores.

After this, our vacation-bound boys travel to Mexico and meet "a pail-banging, cymbal-crashing, cap-shooting desperado." That's how Guadalupe Rodriguez is described; he keeps the villagers of Mucho Loma (English translation: Much Mud) awake at night and is a badly wanted man. Perennial innocents Rocky and Bullwinkle drive into the town, are hauled before a judge and given either ninety-nine years in jail or the option of capturing Zero (Guadalupe's nom de crime). An unusual story, this seems more like a serial for Crusader Rabbit and Rags the Tiger, and was in fact written by Chris Hayward, who had scripted the color *Crusader* yarns. There is no sign of Boris and Natasha, and while the moose and squirrel acquit themselves dandily, it seems like this is slumming time (as in Hayward's earlier "The Three Mooseketeers"). The outrageous and self-reflexive wordplay abounds: Bullwinkle yells, "That Zero feller got away Bill Scott–free," and corrects the word *jaywalking* to "Jaywarding." The next storyline was plainly inspired by Roger Corman's recent schlock epic *The Little Shop of Horrors* (1960). Boris gives Bullwinkle a plant to enter in the annual Frostbite Falls Flower Fair, but it is a Pottsylvania Creeper, a carnivorous plant which proceeds to devour several hapless citizens. This funny story revealed the depths of Fearless Leader's depravity as he and Boris observe the Creeper about to swallow Rocky. Fearless Leader orders Boris to turn his back, explaining, "There's only one thing better than looking at something wonderful." Boris timidly asks, "And that is?" To which his sadistic superior gleefully answers, "Keeping somebody else from seeing it!!"

In "Moosylvania," a rather self-indulgent minidrama running four chapters, Boris discovers that the quickest way to acquire a lifetime supply of fiendish tricks is to hold an evil contest ("I like evil because . . . in twenty-five words or less"). Bullwinkle attempts to file statehood for his birthplace of Moosylvania, and Boris disguises Butte, Montana, to look like Washington, D.C. As we have seen, Jay Ward and staff adapted the plot's statehood gimmick far more interestingly, to real life, actually leasing an island, which they dubbed "Moosylvania."

The next four stories each unfolded in six-episodes increments. The "Ruby Yacht" saga was built on a truly wicked pun. In the eleventh century, poet Omar Khayyám wrote the famous *Rubaiyat*, a eulogy to wine, women, and God. In the twentieth century, Bullwinkle, down by the shores of Veronica Lake, discovers a jewel-encrusted dhow which is—well, obviously—the Ruby Yacht of Omar Khayyám! With this plot device painfully in place the moose and squirrel are kidnapped by a vizier working for the pasha of lower north Pakistan, who desires the fabled yacht for his bathtub. Rocky and Bullwinkle are taken, via the SS *Plankton,* to the remote city, where they endure the threat of being thrown into a snake pit and a palace trial. During one of the recording sessions for this story, Bill Scott, then everyone else, got the giggles when he and Paul Frees again played two *Dragnet*-inspired customs men. The line that tickled Scott's fancy occurs when one of these deadpan officials matter-of-factly tells a sailor, "You have scurvy, sir—get off the boat and eat some oranges!"

Next, the boys take a trip to Ed Foo Yung's Chinese Laundry—in Shanghai, China. This occurs when Bullwinkle's only shirt needs to be washed; he urgently requires the garment for an upcoming testimonial dinner to be held in his honor. Coincidentally, of course, Boris and Natasha happen to be in Shanghai. Boris is trying to smuggle an atom-bomb watch into the United States inside a laundry package. When Bullwinkle is mistaken for the agent One-Ton Lee, he is given the package. Boris tortures Bullwinkle by sadistically forcing the moose to watch while Natasha devours a delicious chocolate-marshmallow-strawberry hot-fudge sundae.

The story of Ruth Booth, the weather-predicting fortune machine, is a fanciful tale; hardly one of the boys' strongest stories, but at least they get to go to Watchowee Falls. The silliest moment, however, is a true animation non sequitur, as Boris Badenov is placed in a duel. He is set up with seconds and an umpire; but the narrator informs us that "it was such a beautiful day, everyone decided to have a picnic." Thus Boris and his opponent just keep walking and nobody remembers to yell "fire" after ten paces. Finally, we are informed, "the whole thing simply blew over," and the plot returns to where it left off. Even *Ren & Stimpy* creator John Kricfalusi never pulled off an audacious gag like this.

Boris Badenov displays a rare moment of humanity in the next story. He reveals that he actually has a hero: Boris's role-model in perfidy is the kingpin of gangland crime, Fingers Scarnose ("The Louse on 92nd Street"). No one has been brave enough to testify against the notorious and feared Scarnose—that is, until Bullwinkle. But Rocky must protect his pal until trial day, so they hide out at a mink farm, where the moose must pretend he's a mink; Rocky advises him, "Try and look expensive!" Boris even gets to disguise himself as a witch and gives Bullwinkle a poisoned apple—naturally, there's a bomb inside.

The penultimate "Rocky and Bullwinkle" story, at twelve segments, is one of the most repeated in syndication, along with the early Mooseberry Bush adventure. This crazy tale finds Bullwinkle being put on a football scholarship at Wossamotta U. The college (school colors: Ocher and Alice Blue) is desperate for a new football lineup because they haven't had a win in twenty-two years. But Boris and Natasha enter the stakes, and Bullwinkle is quickly tempted to throw the game. This story actually came about as a gentle in-house jab at Jay Ward's lifelong love of college football.

As a boy in the 1930s Ward had listened, enraptured, to radio broadcasts of football games starring his hero Bronko Nagurski, who played for the University of Minnesota Golden Gophers. Nagurski, who also played professionally for the Chicago Bears and became a pro wrestler, lived in International Falls, and indeed Frostbite Falls was Ward's and Alex Anderson's tribute to that chilly locale. The fine "Wossamotta U" script, by Bill Scott, contains swipes at university boards, gambling syndicates, the sport itself, and a notorious secessionist patriot named Colonel Jefferson Beauregard Lee, who oozes naught but mindless southern jingoism. Boris forms a team of thugs and goons called the Mud City Manglers. Supersadist Fearless Leader is their coach, dressing these brutes, rather incongruously, in women's clothing.

The rather anticlimactic finale for our dynamic cartoon duo—just before they put their feet up to enjoy the benefits of syndication heaven—featured a return to "the dreadful little spot called Moosylvania," where Rocky and Bullwinkle happen to be on vacation. Fearless Leader and Boris turn Moosylvania Island into a disaster area by spreading the rumor that our boys are marooned. Thus, emergency rations galore begin arriving; the villains plan to steal these in order to prop up the faltering Pottsylvanian economy. This short tale was the last of the twenty-eight loony adventures featuring our furry fighters for truth and justice.

Bill Hurtz told Charles Ulrich, "One of the theories behind General Mills and Dancer not going on with the show was that they had enough [episodes]. They said that there'd be another batch of kids coming along. And they'd just simply reissue them."

So ABC picked up the reruns, and the mighty moose played constantly on his old network on Sunday mornings from 1964 through 1973 (the series even enjoyed a brief NBC network revival in 1981–82). A decade later, in July 1992, the old cartoons, now in restored prints, received a new lease on life when they began screening on Nickelodeon's "Nick at Nite" cable service under the title *Moose-a-Rama*. And in mid-1996, General Mills struck a deal with Ted Turner's Cartoon Network, ensuring that the old "Rocky and Bullwinkle" adventures will be delighting new generations of cartoon buffs for years to come. (Internationally, the "Rocky and Bullwinkle" library has been let loose in over twenty countries since 1960.)

In fact, the Jay Ward cartoons have never really been off the tube. The syndicated version of *The Bullwinkle Show* has been seen in various markets since the 1960s, even playing alongside a different version in 1969–70. This was *Dudley Do-Right and His Friends,* another of Peter Piech's Filmtel repackaging jobs: two "Dudley" cartoons bookended various rerun elements from both Ward Productions and Total TV (of which more later). Thus began the confusing spate of shows featuring "Aesop and Son" next to "The King and Odie," or "Fractured Fairy Tales" followed by "Commander McBragg." This situation led various TV historians to believe that Jay was responsible for a batch of rather unfunny cartoons.

19

THIS IS WHAT I REALLY CALL A MESSAGE!

or 'Twas on the Good Ship *Guppy* (The Quaker Commercials)

"Ahoy there, shipmates!" The Quaker Oats Company began its twenty-two-year association with Jay Ward Productions one weekend late in June 1962. What was undoubtedly Ward's best business deal had almost accidental beginnings. Twenty years later, Bill Scott recalled, "The studio was pretty much closed up; we were in summer vacation mode. One day [during this break] the advertising people for Quaker phoned, and our secretary [Linda Simmons] enthusiastically told them Jay would be delighted to submit a proposal on a character they had in mind: a character called Captain Crunch. 'Why certainly,' she told them, 'Jay would be glad to.' Of course, Jay hated commercials! He never wanted to do them."

Chris Hayward agrees: "A friend of mine was Harry Koplin. I'd worked with him on some TV game shows and now he was in advertising. He asked me to set up a lunch date with Jay because he felt that Rocky and Bullwinkle were just perfect for commercials. But after their meeting Harry came back to me and said it was hopeless. Jay absolutely hated everything about commercials and wasn't interested." The truth of the matter is that Ward was always amenable to advertising work; it was agency interference he loathed. He would only produce commercials if granted total creative freedom, and cited Stan Freberg and John Hubley as role models.

All this was about to change. As Scott recalled, "This Captain Crunch project was actually a brilliant notion; a clever fellow from Compton Advertising [Bruce Baker] came up with a wonderful concept for selling a kid's cereal. It had never been done before: that was, to research and find out the thing that kids most liked in a cereal, then to make that the name of the cereal and the name of the eventual character. That is, tie the whole thing together and then totally aim it to animated TV commercials.*

"Well, the research proved that what children liked the most was a cereal with 'crunch.' So the character—and the food—was called Captain Crunch. They shopped around a number of other studios. Then when Allan Burns impressed them with his character ideas, we had quite a job trying to enthuse Jay to even submitting for it at first.

"Allan was a very creative fellow. It was he who really came up with the format. The crew of children on the boat, you know—A,B,C, and D, which was Alfie, Brunhilde, Carlyle, and Dave, plus Seadog. And Cap'n Crunch himself was a splendid character: the bumbling little old man five hundred years old who sailed the seven seas all his life with his crew of bright young kids. This whole little family was all Allan's invention. He did the preliminary designs, then later a fellow named Charlie McElmurray did some additional design work on the captain, but it was pretty much Al Burns's fertile imagination. The scripts were then turned over to me. I inherited that and I've now [1982] written about three hundred of them!"

By the time Cap'n Crunch cast off, children ruled breakfast time. Since the mid-1950s, cereal commercials had formed a huge corner of the ad business. And their animated spokes-characters had assumed at least as much importance as the breakfast foods themselves. Many hit campaigns featured cartoon stars. These were either originals like Kellogg's "Snap, Crackle and Pop" or General Mills's "Trix Rabbit," or licensed spokestoons from sponsored TV shows, such as Yogi Bear for OK's, and one Bullwinkle J. Moose for Cheerios. Importantly for all concerned, a character who clicked could generate massive sales, not only of breakfast cereal but of scores of tie-in-spin-offs ranging from mugs to money boxes.

*Scott's recall is slightly inaccurate: it was Ken Mason, at the time a Quaker vice president, who conducted the original research; Mason then left it to Baker and Compton's creative team for the eventual ad campaign.

Courtesy of Quaker Oats Company

• • •

Following two and a half years of product development, dating from early 1960, the Quaker Oats Company was finally ready to enter the "presweetened" breakfast cereal field. And animated commercials would soon be a prime requirement. William Ayers and Bruce Baker of Compton Advertising approached various Hollywood animation houses. Bill Hurtz said, "They saw Hanna-Barbera, Disney, and a couple of others." Baker had been aware of the Ward team since 1959, when his animator friend Dun Roman had put in a word for Jay. In any event, Ward Productions was an obvious frontrunner through their association with competitor General Mills. By this time they had notched a solid three years' experience in the kids' cereal advertising arena via Rocky and Bullwinkle.

In the last week of June 1962, Linda Simmons answered Compton's fateful phone call. She said, "I remember the following weekend [on June 28] when they got together with Allan, because I was making coffee all day for everyone." Al Burns recalled, "Jay had decided there'd be a vacation for all, starting July first. He'd already left; he was driving to a fishing vacation on an island near Vancouver. Suddenly these guys from Compton Advertising turn up at the studio. I was there alone, and the Captain Crunch idea came up during our conversation.

"Roy Morita was in town, so we both went up to Jay's apartment, and we ended up with all these drawings and paper all over the floor. We started coming up with the series—the kids, Seadog, and even the pirate Jean La Foote. Then they left, and I wrote and storyboarded the stuff in two days."

Less than a week later, Burns's ideas and characters received an extremely positive reaction back in Chicago. Harry Johnson of Compton contacted Jay Ward, asking for an outline and costs. Realizing this project would be both financially rewarding and independent of P.A.T.—thus no Mexican animation!—Ward rethought his position on commercials. Bill Scott recalled, "When the cereal company came to Jay about doing this stuff he said no. I was the one who said, 'Look, we can have some fun with a sea captain and a gang of kids. He could go around the world and be a real bumbler.' Jay relented and said, 'Okay. But we'll only do it as long as it's fun."

Ward connected with Doug Jamieson of Chicago-based Quaker Oats Company, requesting an advance of $2,000 for writing and storyboarding two short intros and two one-minute test commercials, along with some preliminary character voice suggestions. Jay soon learned that Quaker's top man, Ken Mason, was a huge fan of *Bullwinkle* and enthusiastic about the Ward's studio's involvement.

In short order, with Quaker's promise of no artistic meddling, Ward became highly enthused about developing the Captain Crunch character (renamed "Cap'n" in one of the earliest recording, sessions, when June Foray mispronounced "Captain") and producing commercials at the full Hollywood rate. He discussed profit sharing of the character, and merchandising rights.

The Quaker account people at Compton were most impressed by the humor and zany creativity at Ward Productions. They sent the storyboards back to Jay's team for fine-tuning in early August. The completed boards were then filmed. These were very well received—Bill Scott had even come up with extra scripts. In September, Ward and Scott were asked to attend a meeting in Chicago. Jay, however, was busy formulating the big Moosylvania statehood publicity campaign and overseeing work on the forty remaining "Rocky" episodes and his new *Fractured Flickers* series.

Instead, Bill Scott attended the meeting with Allan Burns (who, of course, was already familiar with the project). Both men made a huge impression on Bruce Baker. As a result, they were asked to supply storyboards for six ten-second spots, three sixty-second spots (including one of the first commercials completed, "The Wild Man of Borneo"), one sixty-second jingle (for the early commercial "Singalong with Cap'n Crunch"), and the development of the Jean La Foote pirate character, as well as tapes of the final Cap'n Crunch voice. This meant a ton of work in just a short time. But it was vital to get it finished, for Compton's plans included a one-year test market run during 1963–64.

Work began in earnest. First the character needed a distinctive sound. Daws Butler said, "I fully expected the ad people would audition about fifty actors for the role." He and Jay Ward sat around for a few hours trying different approaches, until Ward suggested, "Why don't you do that absent-minded-king voice you used in the 'Fractured Fairy Tales.' " This voice was energized slightly, and the good Cap'n was suddenly brought to life. Long one of Butler's personal favorites in his large flock of characters, he described Cap'n Crunch as "a loyal old man who loved his crew; he was a combination of great sincerity and stupidity. He started out old and stayed old."

On November 2, 1962, the first recording session was held; though Bill Conrad was the first announcer, Paul Frees soon took over the role. Following this, the test animation was directed by Pete Burness. Compton viewed the finished work early in January 1963 and loved it. In fact, the Ward team's commercials were the hit of Compton's big marketing presentation to Quaker management.

With the upcoming test-market time frame set for fall 1963, Jay Ward was asked to help design Cap'n Crunch comic books, package backs, character premiums, and store displays. He also produced a five-minute film short, "Cap'n Crunch Sails Again," for the sales team. Ward negotiated a healthy creative retainer, and the Cap'n Crunch years were under way. Captain Horatio Magellan Crunch would become the second-longest running cereal character of all time, after Kellogg's Tony the Tiger.

Final recording sessions were held in April and July of 1963. The classy-looking animation was soon ready, resulting in the first commercials for the twelve-month test period that kicked off in September, covering six cities. This campaign proved a major success. Exactly one year later, the good Cap'n set sail for homes all over the United States with his familiar cry of "It's got corn for crunch, oats for punch, and it stays crunchy even in milk."

They had a hit. The campaign proved so strong, in fact, that Quaker immediately ran into a supply-and-demand crisis. Plant production lagged and stores quickly ran out. A special plant was built for Quaker to handle the product shortfall. In very short order Cap'n Crunch was outselling fifty-five competitors, whose combined sales represented half a billion dollars a year. The national children's audience had gone wild, relating especially well to the crew of animated kids on board the good ship *Guppy*.

Bill Hurtz remembered, "Jay had a very lucrative contract with Quaker and he received the red carpet treatment for twenty years. The commercials had very high budgets, and we must have done twelve to fifteen every year. Really a good deal." As Skip Craig put it, "The Quaker thing pretty much kept the studio going for many years. It kept us all employed." For a 1988 *Los Angeles Time* article, Al Burns quipped, "We didn't care, but it turned out to be a big account. It got Jay two racehorses." Skip Craig adds, "Not only racehorses. [Jay] was able to build two beach houses. And then there were the fancy cars, and all the art that he bought!"

Ward's studio received a budget of $100,000 for the first year. For a time in the late 1960s Cap'n Crunch market research proved he was the most popular animated character on TV. Jay Ward truly enjoyed making these commercials, and referred to the Quaker Oats Company as "Gentlemen—with a sense of humor." In fact, Jay and Ken Mason became such good friends that Jay and Ramona vacationed on Mason's island in Wisconsin and at his house in Maine. Mason attended the 1969 wedding of Jay's daughter Tiffany.

In late 1964, the Cap'n Crunch commercials began airing nationally. As Bill Scott explained, "We made our commercials as much like entertainment cartoons as possible, with the sales message limited to one line." The spots proved enormously popular, and were linked to a clever use of premiums such as treasure chests and rings included in the cereal packages. The Quaker Oats Company was delighted, and eager for Ward Productions to help on the creative development of its next line of cereals.

March 1965 saw the first recording session for Quisp and Quake, another long-running Ward commercial series. These memorable characters were created by Bill Scott, in association with ad agency Papert-Lois-Koenig. The cartoon spots were variously directed by Hurtz, Pete Burness, and Lew Keller. Their frantic sound tracks featured Daws Butler as Quisp, a propeller-headed extraterrestrial. Quisp sounded like the manic Jerry Lewis–style voice Butler had supplied in "Fractured Fairy Tales" like "The Little Tinker." Quisp, who hailed from the Planet Q, looked rather like the moon men Cloyd and Gidney from *Rocky and His Friends*. Bill Conrad supplied the booming voice of Quisp's archrival, the powerful Quake, a he-man. (But Quake still called his mother "Mama." She was voiced by the ubiquitous

QUAKE: WAIT!
PULLING CANOES OFF THE ROCKS TAKES STRENGTH,
LIKE I GET FROM QUAKE,
QUAKE
QUISP
MY Q-SHAPED CEREAL WITH THE POWER OF AN EARTHQUAKE.
(He lifts
an enormous rock

Quisp and Quake commercial storyboard. *Courtesy of Quaker Oats Company*

June Foray.) Paul Frees was the tag announcer and often doubled as a villainous character, like the notorious Barbary pirate known as "the Caliph of Fornia."

Quisp constantly touted his "quazy energy cereal" and feuded with Quake, who in turn plugged his "earthquake-powered cereal from the center of the earth." This on-camera rivalry ingeniously inspired factions of loyalty among kiddie consumers for one or the other brand ("Quisp or Quake—which would you choose?" asked the early commercials). In late 1968, the somewhat gruff Quake character, who was researching negatively, was streamlined. He transformed from his burly miner guise into a superhero costumed Australian-hatted cowboy and began hawking his "new and improved cereal." (Quake was finally eased off the supermarket shelves with the appearance of the new orange-flavored Quangaroos.)

Originally budgeted at $40,000 annually, the Quisp-Quake spots translated into further income and regular work for Jay Ward's animation team. By early 1966, Ward was enthusiastically overseeing the many recording sessions required for these commercials, and was proud of the fine animation emerging from his studio. As Leonard Maltin wrote in 1975, the Quaker commercials "are better in every way than most of the shows they interrupt."

(Crushes it with his bare hand)
QUISP: IT'S TOO LATE FOR THAT!
QUISP
WHAT WE NEED IS SPEED, LIKE I GET FROM QUISP,
QUISP
THOSE SUGARY LITTLE FLYING SAUCERS OF QUAZY ENERGY.
QUISP
(Quisp holds out his cereal package,

Quisp and Quake commercial storyboard. *Courtesy of Quaker Oats Company*

Bill Hurtz recalled, "This was full animation with all the stops out. We had the money to do fine work, and we used the best people around: Bill Littlejohn, Frank Smith, and Ben Washam, who was Chuck Jones's number one guy—I kept taking Benny away from Chuck! And one of Jay's favorites, the late Phil Duncan, loved to do Cap'n Crunches, so we'd mail the storyboards to him, up in the Sierras."

Maltin observed, "Quaker [gave] Ward amazing freedom . . . and enough money for him to turn out a finished product much handsomer than any of his shows ever were! The studio [was] able to do pencil-test dry runs—a luxury it could not afford under network budgets and time restrictions." Animator Bill Littlejohn qualified this, adding, "Even though the work was much better than the Mexican stuff, the system wasn't geared to fine animation. The challenge was to get as much motion out of as few drawings as there were. And this motion and pace was what Jay loved."

The cast of crazy animated characters grew larger over the years, as Ward added excellent commercials for Quaker's Burry Cookies division and Aunt Jemima frozen waffles. Besides Cap'n Crunch and the *Guppy* crew, there were many other memorable creatures, like C. B. "the Crunchberry Beast" (for Cap'n Crunch with Crunchberries), Smedley the Elephant (Cap'n Crunch's peanut butter cereal), Simon the Quangaroo (orange-flavored Quangaroos), Captain Vitamin, the later King Vitaman and his nervous lackey Sir Cravenleigh, Professor Goody and Wallace the Waffle Whiffer (Aunt Jemima's frozen waffles), Harold the Giant (Scooter Pies, from the Cap'n Crunch cookies division), Harry S. Hippo (fruit-flavored Punch Crunch), Koko the Seal (Koko Crunch), and Officers Hi and Lo (low-sugar Hi-Lo's). A fine short-lived series featured Quincy Quaker, "Son of Quaker Oats," for Frosted Oat Flakes. Quincy was played by Dick Beals, who doubled as dialogue coach for the various child actors heard on the sound tracks of these spots.

Even the onetime supporting characters were as zany and humorously designed as those in Jay Ward's earlier cartoon shows. Cap'n Crunch faced innumerable foes like Mopey Dick, the amorous Magnolia Bulkhead, and the vicious Captain Blah. Over two decades he also encountered old friends like Wilma the White Whale (for Vanilly Crunch), Ponce De Leon, and Robinson Crusoe. There were spin-off product commercials for Cap'n Crunch cookies, Cap'n Crunch's instant hot cereal, and even a short-lived instant cereal drink—Cap'n Crunch's Ship Shake ("Any way you make it/ If you stir it or you shake it/It's Ship Shake")—which, unfortunately, proved a flop.

The voices were set from the start and never changed. Often an established TV or theatrical cartoon character would vary slightly until settling into its famous sound: for instance, Bugs Bunny and even Bullwinkle changed subtly over the first year or so of their screen lives. But Cap'n Crunch and his loyal crew, and Quisp and Quake were identical from the first recording to the last. This reflected the different approach to sound tracks in the advertising field, where a character's voice was refined and tested for weeks before approval.

Most of the support characters were performed by the virtual one-man theater Bill Scott, who also wrote the bulk of the many scripts (though Lloyd Turner contributed a few). Scott portrayed the faithful Seadog, Jean La Foote "the barefoot pirate," La Foote Junior, the Crunchberry Beast, Smedley the Elephant, Sir Cravenleigh, Captain Vitaman and his wonder dog Lester, the Waffle Whiffer, Harry S. Hippo (who sounded like Filmore Bear from *Hoppity Hooper*), Simon the Quangaroo, Jester from the Land of Half, Koko the Seal, the Hi-Lo Munchster, and Chockle the Blob (whose muttered

"Yeah, yeah, yeah" sounded like a precursor to Dustin Hoffman's *Rain Man* character). Scott's longest-running Quaker role was young, gap-toothed Dave, one of the kids from the Cap'n's exuberant crew.

June Foray portrayed the ponytailed crew member Brunhilde, along with Tugboat Granny and Mother Lode, Quake's ever-concerned mom. As busy as he was portraying the dithering Cap'n Crunch, Daws Butler also found time to play Alfie, the bespectacled crew member of the good ship *Guppy*. In the Aunt Jemima spots, Butler was Professor Goody, and he essayed the Burry cookie spokes-character whose giggle was borrowed from 1930s character actor Hugh Herbert. Paul Frees became Harold the Scooter Pie Giant, Mister E ("the Mysterial Cereal," a ringer for Orson Welles's radio character the Shadow), and Count Awfullot in the later Halfsies spots.

The short-lived Captain Vitaman character was originally given a celebrity voice: he was played by Peter Graves, then riding the crest of popularity on *Mission: Impossible*. When a couple of follow-up versions of the Vitaman character failed to click, he was revamped to a medieval setting and became King Vitaman. His Majesty's voice was provided by actor Joe Flynn, familiar as the dyspeptic Captain Binghamton from *McHale's Navy*. The first King Vitaman spots were subcontracted to Michael Lah's animation outfit, Quartet Films, before the Ward studio took over. As Bill Hurtz informed cereal-box expert Scott Bruce, the original Vitaman "was a funny cereal because when it first came on the market, the vitamins used in it spoiled on the shelf. The taste of the thing would fizzle out in a few weeks. That just about ruled out the success of the product." Quaker's head chef had to hastily adjust the palatability of this line. The animated series was short-lived, soon making way for a live-action king.

King Vitaman was the last original "star" commercial character from the Ward Productions stable. The final decade from 1974 to 1984 was dominated almost exclusively by Cap'n Crunch and his sundry Crunch cereal spin-offs. Each year saw a number of commercials for Cap'n Crunch cereal, Cap'n Crunch with Crunchberries, and Cap'n Crunch's Peanut Butter cereal. These three lines became the mainstays of production for Jay Ward, although Harry the dancing pink hippopotamus hawked fruit-flavored Punch Crunch in 1975, and Jean La Foote even ended up with his own cereal, Cinnamon Crunch, for a time (these short-lived extra product "lines" were known in the cereal game as "flavor flankers"). In 1982, Cap'n Crunch introduced his final family member, Cap'n Crunch's Choco Crunch cereal. By now, captain and crew were being seen in some elaborate and lush-looking commercials set on Crunch Island.

In each Cap'n Crunch commercial, the befuddled captain had to retrieve his purloined cereal by listening for its telltale sound. He would then remind the embarrassed culprit (usually pirate Jean La Foote), "You can't get away with the Crunch, 'cause the crunch always gives you away!" The only other cereal projects that Ward worked on in this late period were Quaker's new low-sugar Halfsies and Hi-Lo's; these commercials, riddled with months of revisions, were very tame when compared with the oomph of the first Quisp-Quake melodramas, which had moved with the energy of the old "Dudley Do-Right" cartoons.

From 1977 the spots lost much of their comic sound and fury and, though still charming, were more closely targeted to a juvenile audience. A major reason was the advent of Action for Children's Television (ACT). This Boston-based organization was spurred on to success by growing community disgust with violence on television—a reaction in 1968 to the assassinations of Martin Luther King, Jr., and Senator Robert Kennedy—and it quickly grew to national prominence and membership. While their motives were pure, ACT's inroads meant that animation would suffer its mightiest blow: the nervous reaction by the networks stifled creativity with a plethora of new and often silly no-no's. By 1977, the Children's Advertising Review Unit was established by the Council of Better Business Bureaus to set guidelines for sponsors, thus effectively lobotomizing an already spayed animal.

Bill Scott informed author Gary Grossman, "We've had to remove the Captain's sword. He can't even brandish it anymore. And we're forced to use boxing gloves on the ends of sticks for comics fights." Scott was disgusted with the most ludicrous rule, which called for the removal of "jeopardy," telling Grossman, "Captain Crunch is a sea captain, an adventurer who encounters strange beasts, animals, wild-looking natives, pirates, and typhoons. Each cartoon gets us right up to the brink of the abyss as far as the program-practices people—the censors—are concerned, because it envisages peril, violence, jeopardy, and all those wonderful things with a dreadful name which make cartoons. There's no stomping or running. We can't show the flexibility that animated characters are known for. Once we lock ourselves like that, we might as well be doing live-action programs."

By the early 1980s the Ward-Quaker relationship began winding down. Aside from ACT, there were various other factors at play, not the least of which was the advancing age of some of the principals. Daws Butler—Ward's vocal linchpin—suffered a heart attack, followed by a debilitating stroke in early 1982, and his Cap'n Crunch line readings were seriously affected. Bill Scott ended up having to coach him by reading each line aloud; Butler would then repeat Scott's delivery and record line by line. (The stroke affected the right periphery of Butler's brain, making it impossible to see small words like *a* and *the*.) Paul Frees, by this time residing permanently in Tiburon, Marin County, phoned in his lines from his home studio after 1980.

During this period, much creativity in TV advertising continued to be bombarded by ever more committees, rules, and regulations which further stifled the freewheeling feel of the funny spots made a decade before. Although Bill Scott still wrote the scripts, change was in the air. Commenting on the overall state of animation and commercials in the mid-1980s, Daws Butler remarked, "The writing has gotten to a pedestrian level. I don't blame the writers. I blame the networks; they simply beat the scripts to death. They rewrite and rewrite, then they rewrite it again." Jay Ward became increasingly disenchanted, and toward the end was content to simply go through the motions.

Hurtz told Scott Bruce, "Jay didn't want to be told what to do. He got along famously with Ken Mason, Quaker's CEO, but when Ken retired, things started to go downhill. We went through three or four sets of Quaker executives. Every year the contract was renewed. Then in the early eighties, Quaker created its own in-house advertising agency [Adcom]. The agency started submitting scripts to Jay. Jay wanted nothing to do with them; he wouldn't even look at them. Finally it got so bad, it took four or five of Bill Scott's scripts to get Quaker's approval. Jay finally rebelled and said, "Hey, I don't need this anymore.' "

Neither did Bill Scott. In 1981 he said, "Way back when we started, Jay stipulated to Quaker that we'd do these things as long as it's fun. Well, it stopped being fun a long time ago." Aware of the new generation of young turks—those art directors and writers now flexing their creative muscles—Scott told Ward that he wouldn't take the changed circumstances any longer. He certainly didn't need the work; at sixty-three, Scott was getting lucrative offers from the celebrity-speaker circuit and cashing in on the many residuals the Quaker spots had paid him over twenty-one years. Besides it simply wasn't enjoyable anymore. Hurtz said, "Jay knew that the end was in sight." Skip Craig recalls, "One day I heard Bill Scott ask Jay, 'You want to do any more of this crap?' and Jay said, 'Nope!'" Nobody was surprised when Quaker canceled the contract and took its business to another animation studio. As June Foray recalls, "The last session was in the spring of 1984. Jay said, 'That's a wrap!' and it was the end of an era."

Thanks to the VCR, Jay Ward's cereal kingdom lives on today. Bootleg video compilations of these commercials reveal that during his association with the Quaker Oats Company, Ward produced some of the funniest, fastest, and best-looking animated TV spots of all time. Bill Scott maintained that the major reason for Ward's Quaker Oats deal was simply "Jay's way of supplying employment to his friends and keeping the studio open." Still, for someone who supposedly didn't care for advertising in the first place, these miniclassics remain one of Jay Ward's finest cartoon legacies.

20

TV or Not TV, or Watch Out for That Tree!

Although heavily into the Quaker Oats commercial assignments, Jay Ward was still eager to expand beyond the cartoon field. In June 1964, various program ideas for the upcoming 1965–66 TV season were being developed. Jay Ward Productions submitted a neat concept called "That Was the Town." A proposal for a live-action comedy series, this concerned a township cut off from the rest of the world for fifty years that suddenly has to adjust to modern life. Alas, there were no offers.

Just before Christmas, 1964, General Mills ordered a further twenty-six half hours of *Hoppity Hooper*. Throughout 1965, the writing and recording continued on this series, with the final episodes animated through early 1967.

By now Gamma Productions was busy with Peter Piech's other enterprise, the aforementioned Total Television; in 1961 Piech entered into a partnership with "Buck" Biggers, formerly at D-F-S, scriptwriter Chet Stover, and sound recordist Treadwell D. Covington (unlike Ponsonby Britt, this strange name apparently belonged to a real person). The cartoons produced by Total Television were written and voiced by an East Coast team. They were animated at Gamma, hence the confusion in certain TV reference books, which mistakenly lumped the Total Television output under the Ward Productions banner. These shows—*King Leonardo and His Short Subjects, Underdog, Go-Go Gophers, Tennessee Tuxedo and His Tales*—were pleasant diversions, but definitely not up to Jay Ward's cartoon caliber. Some, like the short filler "Commander McBragg," simply didn't work well, quickly proving repetitious and screamingly unfunny.

In 1964 Harvey Siegel became co-owner of the Mexican studio, with Jaime Torres Vasquez, the firm's longtime traveling troubleshooter. Siegel, a former commercial artist, was head of Gamma Productions until it closed in 1970. Today he remains a top figure in Mexican animation circles.

A 1964 news feature on the Gamma studio explained the daily work procedure for Stateside readers. "Siegel's routine involves receiving a phonograph record of the soundtrack, and a long worksheet with scene-by-scene direction and rough character drawings. 'Then I do some sketch ideas plus a Spanish translation of the story line.' Layout and design chief Joe Montell adds his contribution, then the package moves to the drawing board of Sam Kai, a native of San Francisco. Kai points out, 'For this sort of show, you have to go overboard on the movements and gestures.' " Siegel recounted an amusing anecdote from the awkward days in 1959 when "special paints were unavailable. Importing them proved a huge drain on the budget, so we discovered we could get by using ordinary flat house paint!" Returning to the present, he added, "We are now able to produce 14 minutes of animation a week which translates to roughly 2,500 drawings or 150 scenes, with a daily average of a thousand cels."

But as much as the Mexican team had improved, it was obvious to even casual viewers that the sloppy mistakes continued right up to the last: Boris's mustache disappearing and reappearing, cels wobbling, Sherman with no hair, Bullwinkle with no nostrils or no ears. And of course once Jay Ward experienced the exhilaration of working full-time on the Quaker cereal spots in late 1962, there was no question but that he would only animate in Hollywood from then on.

Certainly there's no escaping the evidence: everything from Ward's Sunset Boulevard outfit looks superb by comparison: countless Quaker Oats commercials, *George of the Jungle,* and special animation for *Fractured Flickers* and *The Nut House*. Bill Scott recalled, "More and more we would try to pull some of the work back to Hollywood." And Jay Ward vowed that he would never again be involved with runaway animation.

So was it all worth it in the end? The 1964 news item neatly summarized the catch-22 concerning runaway animation. "It was found that while production costs are somewhat lower than in the U.S. customs duties and the time-consuming red tape involved in doing business south of the border virtually wipe out these advantages, or any tax gain that might accrue from a venture in a foreign country."

Peter Piech states that the Mexican cartoon outfit existed from 1959 to 1970; the final assignments for Gamma were the later shows for Total Television, such as *Go-Go Gopers* and *Klondike Kat*. Piech comments, "There were over one hundred people on the payroll by then, and most were veterans of *Rocky and His Friends*. This artist community had stayed very solid over the years. It was an artistic reservoir of established middle-class people who moved on into the advertising and film industries." Piech recalls that when Gamma Productions ceased operations, "seven and a half cameras, and some other equipment, purchased originally for Val-Mar from as far away as New York and Japan, were donated to the Cartoonists Guild."

There is an ironic footnote: today there is unanimous feeling that the blunder-filled Mexican animation is actually one of the abiding charms of the "Rocky and Bullwinkle" shows. Indeed, many Jay Ward buffs feel that if the moose and squirrel had enjoyed slick and smooth artwork, it would have detracted from the series' unique verbal humor. In any event, a fun aspect of watching the Mexican-made cartoons is spotting the nondeliberate mistakes!

Meanwhile, Ward produced his funny pilot film of *Super Chicken.* In late 1964, with *Hoppity Hooper* pleasing General Mills, Ward was asked to submit a pilot film of his 1960 concept "Super Chicken," but with some changes. A new script was written by Lloyd Turner, and the characters (though still the same visually) were overhauled once more. Unlike the 1960 version of the superfowl, Ward didn't bother with outside voices; Bill Scott played Super Chicken, and Paul Frees was his valet, Fred. William Conrad (soon to begin his second Jay Ward stint as the voice of Quake in the upcoming Quisp and Quake cereal commercials) came in a couple of weeks earlier, on February 22, 1965, to record the *Super Chicken* pilot, playing his great omniscient narrator. In fact, it's a pity this was the only time Conrad was involved with *Super Chicken*—his narration here was vibrant and funny. (Frees narrated the TV shows, but he had too much to do and his commentary voice sounded a bit flat at times.)

In the film, directed by Bill Hurtz, Eggs Benedict, owner of the world's largest chicken ranch, goes crazy, becoming a mad criminal intent on getting rid of Super Chicken. But our hero beats him at every turn, and Eggs is imprisoned time and again.

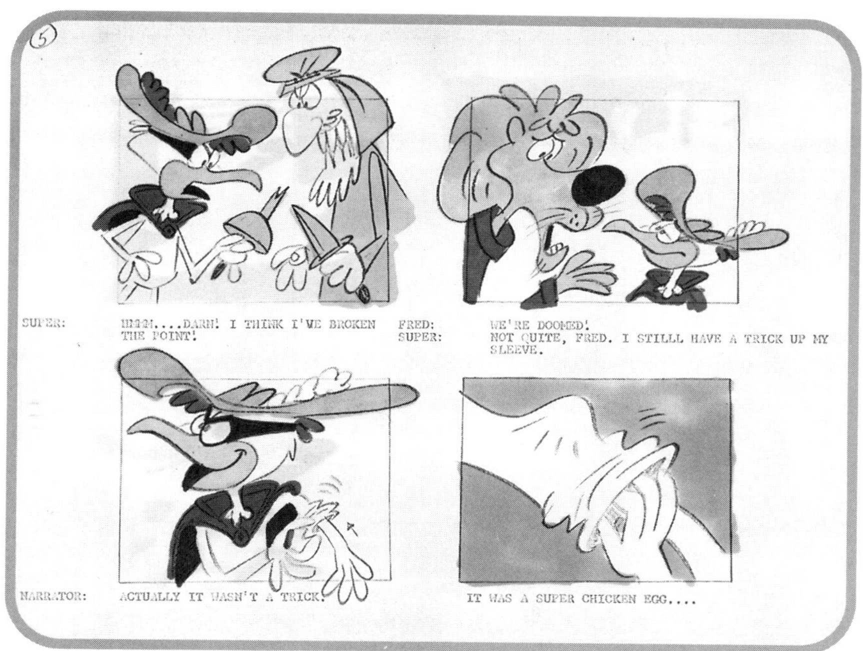

A storyboard from the unfinished 1960 *Super Chicken* pilot. *Courtesy of Ramona Ward and Tiffany Ward and Jay Ward Productions, Inc.*

Super Chicken's secret identity now changed. In the 1960 script he was Nelson G. Cluckerfeller, but in this pilot he became "wealthy play-chicken Hunt Strongbird, Jr." This little joke annoyed certain CBS executives: in the early sixties, James T. Aubrey was the reigning president of CBS Television, and Hunt Stromberg, Jr., was his West Coast programming executive. The ultra-conservative Aubrey hadn't cared for Jay Ward's 1963 live-action pilot *The Nut House,* considering Ward a troublemaker. Of course, this was grist for a satirist's mill, and the Hunt Strongbird name was the resultant jab. But it cost Jay—CBS wouldn't consider any of his animated shows.

Still another cartoon idea was actually green-lighted for production—called "Sir Melvin," this one disappeared to pilot heaven. But a few months after the *Super Chicken* film, another pilot was being prepped, featuring a doltish Tarzan clone who was to become Jay's last big TV success. This was *George of the Jungle*.

Skip Craig says, "George was created by Allan Burns. But originally it wasn't the funny, muscular Tarzan type we know, it was a wimpy little guy in a leopard skin with a tie, who rode around the jungle on his motor scooter.

His rich parents in England couldn't stand him and dumped him in the jungle." As Bill Hurtz notes, "It was lucky that it became the George we ended up with." To this day George Atkins is convinced that Burns named the title character for him. "If my name had been Seymour Atkins it would have been Seymour of the Jungle!"

Directed by Gerard Baldwin, this was the funniest pilot film Jay Ward ever made. A masterful little cartoon, it features great caricatures of Bogart's and Hepburn's *African Queen* characters. Charlie and Rose are villains who decide to steal George's pet elephant, Shep, because the pachyderm trumpets in E-flat, not F-sharp like the others. George is a klutz who swings through the jungle, slamming into every tree. The animation is a delight, and the script by Bill Scott, from an idea by Jim Critchfield, is belly-laugh material. Both this and the *Super Chicken* film were commissioned by General Mills, who ended up passing on them.

Meanwhile, in September 1965 the *Bullwinkle* comic strip was canceled in an action agreed to by all parties. *Broadcasting* magazine noted, "The actual reason is not quite clear. McClure-Bell Syndicate hinted at an editor's opposition to the exclusive property rights held by others. But P.A.T. and the owner attribute the strip's end to a lack of sales effort and push from the syndicator."

The final material for General Mills consisted of several commercials. For Cheerios there was a long-running campaign featuring Bullwinkle, who attempted to execute various funny athletic feats, including a series in which he teamed with the Cheerios Kid. The familiar tag line was "Go! With Cheerios," to which the abidingly accident-prone moose shakily added, "But watch where you're going." These spots were produced by Ward's Hollywood team through 1968, with Bullwinkle appearing in many General Mills print ads as well. There were also animated spots in 1966 for Lucky Charms featuring Boris and Natasha with the Charms leprechaun, and in the early 1970s spokes-Mountie Dudley Do-Right, along with his sweetheart Nell, plugged Frosty O's.

By the time postproduction ended on *Hoppity Hooper,* Ward was having a ball making *George of the Jungle* entirely in Hollywood, and answering to no one.

In 1966, ABC was bidding furiously with the other networks for the then one-year-old Saturday-morning cartoon market, which had proved hugely profitable. Thanks to programming whiz Fred Silverman, cartoon shows were again a hot item. Suddenly Jay Ward found that his timing was, for once, propitious. Late in 1966, Ward's sales team screened his pilot films of

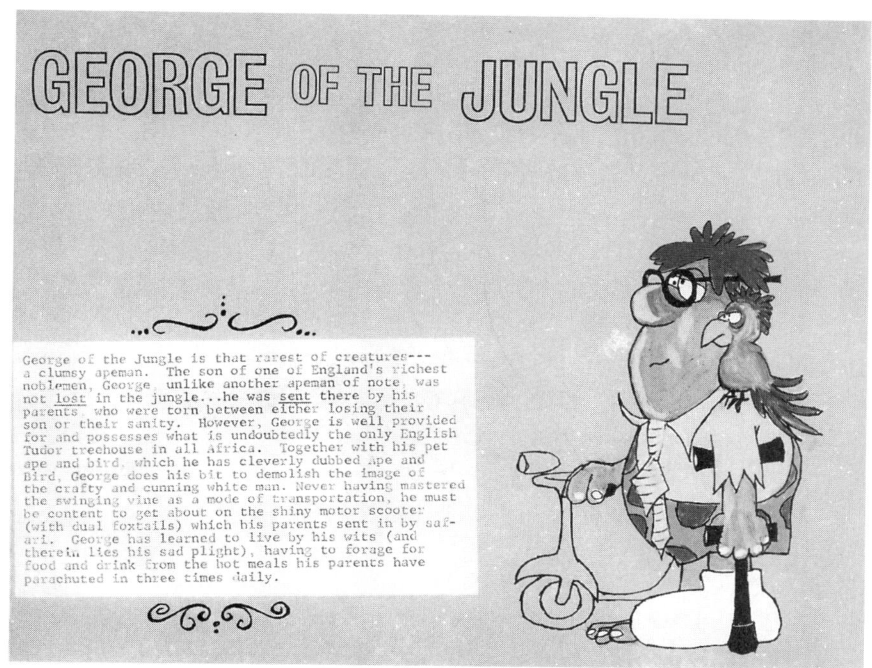

GEORGE OF THE JUNGLE
George of the Jungle is that rarest of creatures---
a clumsy apeman. The son of one of England's richest
noblemen, George, unlike another apeman of note, was
not lost in the jungle...he was sent there by his
parents, who were torn between either losing their
son or their sanity. However, George is well provided
for and possesses what is undoubtedly the only English
Tudor treehouse in all Africa. Together with his pet
ape and bird, which he has cleverly dubbed Ape and
Bird, George does his bit to demolish the image of
the crafty and cunning white man. Never having mastered
the swinging vine as a mode of transportation, he must
be content to get about on the shiny motor scooter
(with dual foxtails) which his parents sent in by saf-
ari. George has learned to live by his wits (and
therein lies his sad plight), having to forage for
food and drink from the hot meals his parents have
parachuted in three times daily.

The original proposal for ***George of the Jungle.*** *Copyright © 1964 Ward Productions, Inc. Courtesy of Bill Scott*

George of the Jungle and *Super Chicken* to Richard Zimbert and Ed Vane of ABC-TV. It impressed them. So did Ward's solid three-year relationship with the Quaker Oats Company, and in early 1967 a letter of agreement was finalized, giving *George of the Jungle* the green light. April saw the first recording sessions, and production commenced. Like Hanna-Barbera and the rest of the TV-toon fraternity. Ward worked to a tight schedule: the show was to start on the air that September for six runs. Thirteen half hours were ordered. Bill Scott recalled, "We made a great pitch to produce some more. They decided on four more—that would make it seventeen [shows]. . . . That's all there was."

Ward received $38,500 per show (the overall budget was $654,500). The cartoons were to be assembled fully in Los Angeles, and Ward was named executive producer. ABC got first crack at "any other Jay Ward television ideas." Production kicked off with an advance of $50,000. ABC retained syndication rights through ABC Films, while the merchandise and syndication profits would be split fifty-fifty.

ABC also had script approval. Their first ruling ordered that Jane, the female character in the *George* pilot, be renamed to avoid a possible lawsuit from the Edgar Rice Burroughs estate. Ward and Scott suggested "Jean," but two days before the first voice session a directive was issued—it had to be a name totally unlike Jane. Bill Hurtz suggested Ursula: his daughter had a friend by that name, and the way Hurtz's little girl pronounced it was similar to George's untutored speech pattern. Ward thought this was funny and also topical: in 1967 one of the most popular screen sirens was Ursula Andress, a onetime guest on Jay's *Fractured Flickers*.

Animation director Bill Hurtz recalled, "We all felt that the *George of the Jungle* series was the best work we ever did. We put much more into it than we could ever get back out of it. Jay lost a fortune on this show. We went up to $150,000 over the budget. But the shows looked beautiful. Jay kept urging us to put more and more animation in this show, and spoke to us of doing it for the glory of the medium. But, boy, it cost us money."

George was the first of a trio of heroes within the half hour, the others being "Super Chicken" and "Tom Slick." The entire show was the classiest Ward ever produced. Lush with color and sight gags, the series was the best-looking example of "limited" animation until the Disney and Warner/Amblin shows appeared some twenty years later. And it's still one of the best written. With an even faster version of the pun-filled mocking style of Ward's earlier shows, the series has become a cultist's classic. Jay Ward's creative team on *George of the Jungle* was one of the most eclectically talented in Hollywood.

The cartoon adventures took place in Africa's fertile Mbwebwe Valley. George of the Jungle was a superguy in the Burroughs *Tarzan* mold. Big, brawny—an Adonis with all the musculature of Sylvester Stallone, and the athletic grace of Jerry Lewis; there wasn't an episode where George didn't swing through the jungle without smashing full force into a solid tree. He was a big, well-meaning klutz, and through all his adventures he was assisted on the path to the eventual routing of wrongdoers by his loyal companions, Ursula, Ape, and elephant Shep.

Ursula, George's live-in girlfriend, was the source of much amusement. George was an unknowing buffoon who obviously hadn't much in the libido department. He occasionally forgot his attractive mate's name; in one cartoon, when Ape referred to Ursula, George replied, "You mean that longhaired fella who never shaves?" The "ape named Ape" was an important player. A large gorilla, he spoke beautiful English in an excellent imitation of Ronald Colman, supplied by Paul Frees. He was erudite and pompous.

Shep was George's faithful elephant. George named him Shep because he

The Tooki Tooki Bird. *Courtesy of Ramona Ward and Tiffany Ward and Jay Ward Productions, Inc.*

believed the huge creature was a puppy: "big, gray, peanut-loving puppy." Shep was Bill Scott's nod to that affectionate musical ode to dog owners, *Old Shep* (in fact, he had named a dog Shep in his 1947 Warner Brothers cartoon *Bone Sweet Bone*). Scott voiced both the monosyllabic George and the distinctive pachyderm trumpetings of Shep. Finally there was the jungle's ineffectual District Commissioner, for whom Paul Frees reprised his unctuous Inspector Fenwick voice, based on British character actor Eric Blore.

George battled a truly odd assortment of characters in his seventeen misadventures. A recurring team called Tiger and Weevil were two nasty hunters who trapped animals for profits; there was Jerry Mander the cutthroat "property developer, sub-divider and general contractor"; Seymour Nudnik, the powerful tycoon (George, of course, thought he was a "typhoon") who wanted to be the new king of the jungle and who wasn't above bribing the Commissioner and animals to vote for him; Dr. Chicago, a garden-variety mad scientist; and the Duke of Ellington, an eccentric big-game hunter who urgently required George's head for his trophy room.

George's famous jungle cry, heard throughout each episode and in the opening theme song, heralded the start of his botched but finally successful adventures. It must be pointed out, however, that without Shep, Ape, and the loyal and ever present Tooki Tooki Bird (the Mbwebwe Valley's answer to AT&T), George would have encountered much more difficulty.

An ape named Ape. *Copyright © 1967 Ward Productions, Inc. Courtesy of Bill Scott*

Bill Scott said, "I wrote all the *George* episodes from their inception." He really went all out in the puns department. Some of them, in fact, were so excruciating that it seemed as though Scott was challenging the viewer to dare him to be awful, or at least to go hoarse from groaning.

The sound tracks were, as usual, a source of hilarity. The villains all sounded mighty familiar: Weevil was Paul Frees's uncanny imitation of Robert Newton's overripe Long John Silver characterization. Bill Scott played a pygmy native called Little Scissor, "the tip-top tailor of Tanganyika," as a funny Edward G. Robinson takeoff.

Daws Butler gave the other nasties his crazy impressions of George Jessel (Dr. Chicago), Phil Silvers (Jerry Mander), and Clarence Hartzell. Hartzell was an actor in the old *Vic and Sade* radio series, on which he played Uncle Fletcher. This voice was used for Seymour Nudnik in the final episode (Ward and Butler reprising him for Professor Goody in the Aunt Jemima waffles commercials). Butler also did a great Richard Haydn voice for Sir Alfred Canine and the Duke of Ellington. Haydn, a unique British actor, was famous for his character of Edwin Carp the fish expert and the caterpillar in Disney's *Alice in Wonderland* (1951); this distinctive voice was also

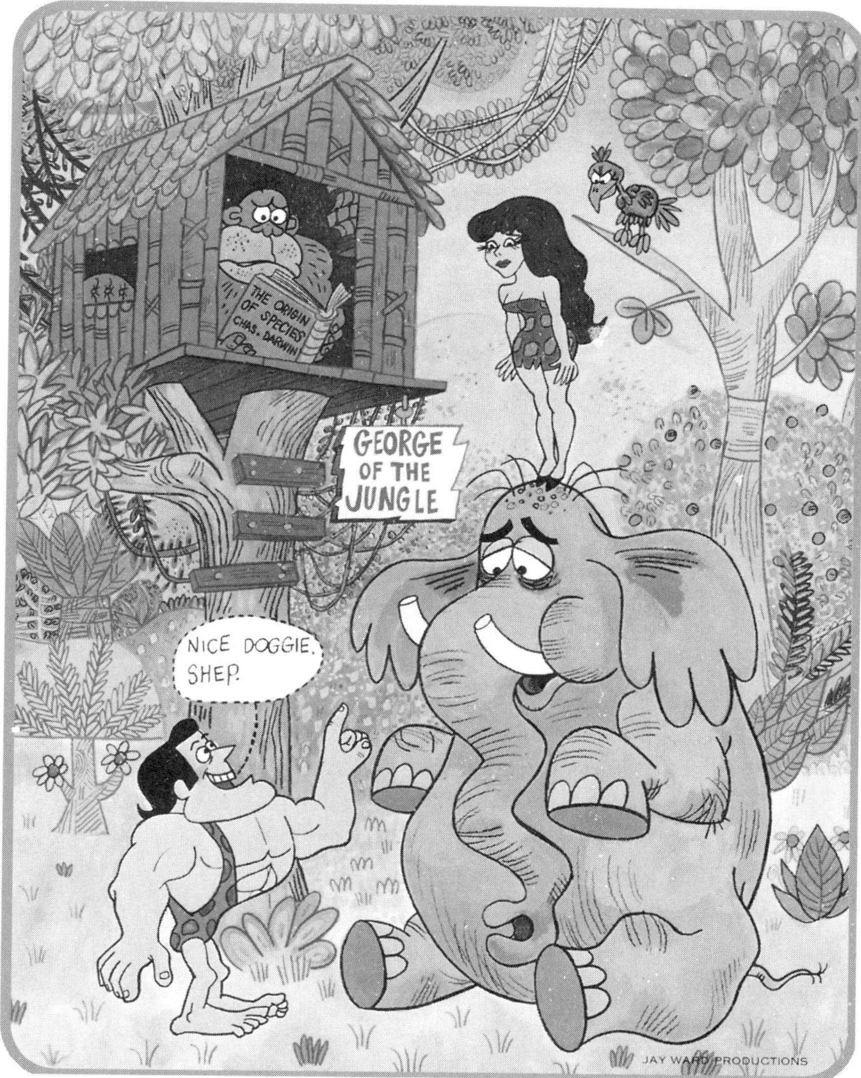

George of the Jungle with his costars Shep, Ursula, and Ape. *Courtesy of Ramona Ward and Tiffany Ward and Jay Ward Productions, Inc.*

borrowed by actor Shep Menken for Clyde Crashcup in the 1961 *Alvin and the Chipmunks* series. As with the "Super Chicken" segments, Paul Frees narrated George's goofy tales in a somber, overly dramatic tone.

A great package of cartoons, the *George* series is remembered instantly by anyone who heard the theme song (invariably, they will happily chant, "George—George—George of the Jungle!"). The fine and flashy animated titles accompanying this music were designed by Paul Harvey. Two gorgeous women accompany George in the opening ("as Fella and Ursula stay in step"), but only one of them appears in the series—after the titles were completed, a ménage à trois was considered unacceptable, and in George's case probably downright impossible.

The well-remembered music for *George of the Jungle* was a departure. Jay Ward's secretary Linda Simmons, who later married writer Chris Hayward, recommended that her boss try Stan Worth as a composer. She had seen Worth performing at Frascatti's restaurant across the road from Ward's studio. Worth and actor-lyricist Sheldon Allman composed various songs for Ward in one long session, including new Bullwinkle and Dudley themes for a projected revival of those characters (the Dudley song contains some funny double-talk nonsense by Gary Owens). Their music for "George of the Jungle" and "Super Chicken" is instantly catchy: the "cartoony" songs mesh perfectly with the trademark Ward Productions nuttiness. They completed the music in August 1967 at the Annex Studio, on Sycamore Avenue. (A tragic footnote to *George of the Jungle* occurred on September 1, 1980, when Stan Worth was killed in a plane crash; the aircraft was an old model he had just finished refurbishing.)

Skip Craig recalls the show getting way behind schedule, causing some major headaches. "The *George* show was tight, the last one especially. I think we got the dailies three days before the airdate, and we had to cut it, dub it, and get our prints to the lab. We were going crazy; it was horrendous that last week trying to get the show done."

The seventeen half hours, containing fifty-one cartoons, were repeated over and over. Bill Hurtz said, "You might say our own successes have been our own undoing." He explained to Charles Ulrich, "Where the costs came, and you couldn't evade them, was in ink and paint. You know, those girls were on salary; they didn't work per cel. They just cost more, 'cause there was more stuff to ink and paint. That's where it whopped [Jay]. But I'm glad he did it. Because it was the best work ever done for Saturday TV, I think."

George Woolery in his book *Children's Television* put it well when he wrote, "Filled with insider gags to please the funny-bone of the producers, *George of the Jungle* overcame its limited animation handicaps through imaginative characters and clever, genuinely witty dialogue, simple enough for children and perceptive enough for adults."

An article in the *Chicago Sun-Times* from 1968 gave the show a rave.

After the reviewer blasted the proliferation of awful superhero-type cartoons, he wrote,

> It would seem the nadir of fatuity to expect a bit of comic fluff like *George of the Jungle* to redeem this cosmic cretinism, but the writers and animators bring it off. The script sparkles with quick wit, both verbal and in the form of sight-gags, and the animation is so superb that every movement occurs naturally and with a telling effect. (I noticed a dozen animators listed in the credits. Evidently the success of *George of the Jungle* owes something to sheer manpower.) George of the Jungle, mighty, leopard-pelted lord of the forest, grabs a vine and swings, his enormous chest vibrating with the familiar Tarzan call. Halfway through his swing—you guessed it—he flattens his skull and all appurtenances and attachments thereto against a tree and slides ignominiously to earth.

Supporting George, Jay's long-awaited "Super Chicken" finally went to air. Of all Jay Ward's animated characters, none had undergone a longer gestation period than "Super Chicken." As we have seen, the idea was first mooted in late 1959 by Chris Hayward and Lloyd Turner.

In Turner's amusing published letter to Jay Ward, he reminded his boss, "Your funny meter was turned off when another writer and I did a takeoff on *Superman* as a chicken, with a dumb lion named Fred as a best friend; they flew around in a chicken coop and fought Dick Tracy–like villains (instead of 'Pruneface' we had a guy called 'The Oyster'). You passed on Super Chicken. Then fate took a hand. The big guns came out from the East and asked, 'What are you doing at the studio now?' You didn't want to say 'nothing'; in desperation you told them about Super Chicken. . . . They bought it and you came back quoting Super Chicken jokes to us."

So which came first, the chicken or the yegg? The original 1960 pilot script was called "Super Chicken vs. Yeggs Benedict." Yeggs was a typical master criminal, and his henchman was named Denver Omelet. Super Chicken's secret identity was J. Pullet Wealthy (a takeoff on billionaire J. Paul Getty), and his sidekick was Lawrence Lion. In this embryonic script the heroes had to overcome the evil depredations of Yeggs and Denver.

With the Yeggs script written, Ward planned a half-hour show to star the mighty fowl. In March 1960, a follow-up script by Hayward and Turner was fashioned into a storyboard, and recorded as two episodes. Several more scripts were written in advance when, temporarily, it looked like Ward might sell the series. Four more years passed before the 1965 pilot film was made.

Because the Hunt Strongbird name gag was still a sore point from the pilot, it was decided to make "Super Chicken" an element of the half-hour *George of the Jungle* show instead of vice versa, although Stan Worth and Sheldon Allman did compose a longer symphonic version of the fabulous fowl's theme song for a possible future series as headliner.

The on-air character was set but for one more change: Super Chicken's ultimate secret identity was, finally, Henry Cabot Henhaus the Third (a takeoff on then ambassador Henry Cabot Lodge). The seventeen episodes went to air and instantly became a cult favorite as popular as the "Dudley Do-Right" cartoons. A couple of the story lines had been written seven years earlier ("Super Chicken vs. the Oyster," "Super Chicken vs. the Zipper") and all that had to be changed in the scripts was Super Chicken's real name, from Nelson G. Cluckefeller to Henry Cabot Henhaus.

"Super Chicken" was a wild, incredibly fast-moving cartoon series that pitted the feeble fowl against a gallery of kooky nasties: the Laundry Man, Dr. Gizmo, the Fat Man (with Paul Frees doing a great Sydney Greenstreet impression), Rotten Hood "and his band of merry man, Fried Tucker," and the Muscle. The chicken and lion lived in downtown Pittsburgh, Bill Scott's birthplace, and Henry's zip code was the same as that of Tujunga, California, where Scott lived most of his adult life. They traveled in an egg-shaped aircraft called the *Super Coop*. Super Chicken obtained all his powers after imbibing super sauce, although he never looked any more muscular. His "cry in the sky" was the old cavalry charge done with chicken clucks which invariably left him coughing and wheezing; Don Knotts had done this in the 1960 version. Fred, the hapless lion, was constantly getting pummeled but remained ever faithful to the plucky bird, who sagely counseled him, "You knew the job was dangerous when you took it, Fred!"

The "Super Chicken" episodes were neatly animated, and the funny scripts were written by Lloyd Turner and Jim MacGeorge, who had performed voice work for Bob Clampett's *Beany and Cecil* cartoons, was well known for his Stan Laurel imitation and was often teamed with Chuck McCann, playing Oliver Hardy. The voice of Fred, Super Chicken's long-suffering valet, was a modified Ed Wynn imitation courtesy of Paul Frees. This gave the lion the necessary nerdlike sound for his subservient role.

Super Chicken and Fred. *Courtesy of Ramona Ward and Tiffany Ward and Jay Ward Productions, Inc.*

Bill Scott played Super Chicken. In the pilot film Scott portrayed him with the Hubert Updike voice Jim Backus had made famous on radio and, later, *Gilligan's Island*, where it became that of rich snob Thurston Howell III. Scott had borrowed this upper-crust voice earlier for *Fractured Flickers,* and reemployed it for Hunt Strongbird, Jr., "wealthy play-chicken." For the series, however, Scott adapted the style used by Don Knotts in the unfinished 1960 pilot.

Within weeks of *George of the Jungle* going to air Ward Productions received a landslide of letters begging for more episodes, especially "Super Chicken." The chicken's irreverent adventures appealed hugely to the hip youngsters who were changing the face of 1960s society. In a TV season of feebleminded sitcoms like *The Flying Nun,* "George of the Jungle" and "Super Chicken" stood alone as the only healthy put-downs. Henry Cabot Henhaus became as cultishly popular as Bullwinkle J. Moose. Today "Super Chicken" remains hilarious, and is a fitting finale to Jay Ward's TV shows. There was, however, one more cartoon on the *George* series, "Tom Slick."

Tom, Marigold, and Gertie. *Courtesy of Ramona Ward and Tiffany Ward and Jay Ward Productions, Inc.*

The opening song pretty much summed him up: "Tom Slick, Tom Slick / Let me tell you why / He's the best of all good guys. . . ." In fact, Tom was so goody-goody he made Dudley Do-Right look like one of the Manson family.

This series had been on the drawing board for a short time. "Tom Slick" was originally to be called "Stretch Marks." This was a race-driving pun courtesy of Lloyd Turner, borrowed from a "Fractured Flicker" he'd written for an auto-race skit. The character was soon renamed "Tom Swift" after the hero of Edward Stratemeyer's boys adventure stories. Finally the appellation "Tom Slick" was chosen, a slick being the name for a trackless racing tire. Tom's timing was just right: the movies *The Great Race* (1965) and *Grand Prix* (1966) had recently been huge box-office hits, and the world's teenagers were then enjoying the slot-car-racing craze.

Approximating Dudley Do-Right in morality and voice (Skip Craig says, "I always wondered why Bill didn't come up with a different sound for Tom; he just did Dudley"), Tom Slick was nevertheless a pretty dull character, freckles and nobility notwithstanding. The difference was that Royal Canadian Mountie Dudley Do-Right was funny. While the racetrack star was also true-blue and pure of heart, he displayed none of Dudley's stupidity and klutziness. Even George of the Jungle was pretty dim; good looks aligned with dumbness made for big laughs. Racing daredevil Tom ended up one-dimensional, as did his saccharine girlfriend, Marigold. Besides, with Dudley and Nell there was that horse to supply the necessary intense, even kinky, dramatic triangle. But Marigold and Tom were always a bit much in the sweetness department. In any of Jay's earlier shows this would have been the subject of barbed ridicule, but not here. The "Tom Slick" cartoons were probably the most disappointing of Ward's oeuvre. Skip Craig says, "They always seemed like they were there to fill up the half hour."

Still, they had their moments. Apart from the great Hollywood animation, the roster of wild incidental characters who appeared one-off in each segment was colorful. And the dialogue was drenched in the usual quota of Ward Productions wordplay. (Tom: "Oh, Gertie. They've got to get up pretty early to catch you." Gertie: "I don't know, it's been so long since anybody tried.") Bill Hurtz said, "They were fairly good, and certainly Hanna-Barbera ripped off the idea for *Wacky Races*—they were watching."

Tom Slick raced anytime, anyplace, and all over the world. And he raced in any medium—in the air, on land, underwater (this was a plot device lifted straight from Blake Edwards's epic *The Great Race*). In each cartoon our hero inevitably lucked out and won. His perfect manners and rulebook mentality were too much for the evil Baron Otto Matic, a double-dyed Germanic villain, "all-around bum sport of bum sports, twisted evil genius and fussy eater." The Baron was voiced by Paul Frees in manic storm trooper style. He was aided in his nefarious schemes by his mechanic, Clutcher, a disheveled toady who was almost a literal grease monkey. Portrayed by Daws Butler using one of his goofiest voices, Clutcher was a hapless soul who was continually being belted on the head with a wrench by the sadistic Baron.* The Teutonic villain was featured in nine of the seventeen stories; aside from him, Tom Slick, like Super Chicken, faced a rogues' gallery of nasty cheats unequaled since Chester Gould's mug file in *Dick Tracy*.

Tom Slick was eternally spouting sanctimonious aphorisms like "There's no such word as 'quit' in auto racing." Gertie Growler, who owned the garage housing Tom's racer, the *Thunderbolt Grease Slapper*, was a sharp-tongued, no-nonsense old dear voiced by Bill Scott as an imitation of Jonathan Winter's Maude Frickert character; frankly, it was Scott's most annoying cartoon voice. Fortunately, Gertie was on the side of the viewer in her queasy reactions to Tom's virtuosity. So was Baron Otto Matic: "I think I'm going to be sick," moans the Baron when Tom meets a clone in good-sport Fledge Sparrow, with whom he exchanges holier-than-thou pleasantries.

The sound tracks for these cartoons were complex. Skip Craig said, "It

*As Ward buff Charles Ulrich astutely pointed out, this type of cartoon violence was totally alien to Ward's usual style.

was the same story as *Fractured Flickers:* two people trying to do a show a week. Roger [Donley] and I didn't have the time, so we got them farmed out to a good cutter named Rich Harrison." In addition to the comic sound effects, there was an extra layer of audio which accurately evoked the ambience of the racetrack. Harrison did eleven of the seventeen episodes, and three each for "Super Chicken" and "George of the Jungle."

The stories were narrated by a ubiquitous Race Commentator, in the nasal voice that Paul Frees had first used for various "Saturday Night Sport" sketches on *Fractured Flickers*. He set the scene with openers like "Welcome to the glamorous, glittering Muncie, Indiana, freight yards!"

The ever present crowd "Yea!"—rendered with weary indifference in each episode—was another Ward-Scott trademark and is a familiar signature from this series, along with George's jungle yell and Super Chicken's "cry in the sky." Most of the "Tom Slick" scripts were written by John Marshall. Skip Craig said, "Marshall was one of the three guys who started Pantomime Pictures. Fred Crippen, Jack Heiter, and Marshall all left UPA. Marshall was eventually with us for a while." Jim Hiltz recalled that John Marshall designed the "Tom Slick" series as well.

The "George," "Super Chicken," and "Tom Slick" cartoons were released by CBS–Fox Home Video in attractive packages, beginning in April 1992, while *George of the Jungle* enjoyed a brief run on the Fox network. In the summer of 1997, the jungle king hit the big time: a successful live-action movie version of *George of the Jungle,* with Brendan Fraser in the title role, was released by the Walt Disney Company, and netted over $170 million worldwide. This book's author was delighted to be booked as narrator of this film.

Aside from his famous cartoon stars, what of Jay Ward's other activities in the 1960s? While the long-running Quaker Oats deal kept the studio busy and financially afloat, the remainder of the decade saw Jay try and fail with TV show after TV show. Following *The Nut House* pilot Ward still had contract time to supply comedy for the CBS network. One series on the drawing board in mid-1965 was called "Officer, You Dropped Your Purse," concerning the misadventures of a policewoman; Jay intended Shirley Jones for the lead. Other CBS proposals included "Uncle Lefty," to star Howard Morris, and "Prince Fred," a vehicle for Sid Caesar as a midwestern dentist who inherits a European kingdom.

Meanwhile, in May 1965, comedian Garry Moore was planning a comeback comedy-variety series for CBS. He began huddling with Jay, trying to work out a deal for a regular weekly feature within the show, either animated or live. Jay's abortive *Nut House* pilot notwithstanding, it was clear that Bullwinkle, with college fan clubs all over the country, was drawing a selective cross section of comedy buffs, including professors, doctors, and government officers. Moore said, "I intend to knock myself out to come up with a different show. One weekly segment will involve the delightful kook Jay Ward, and will be a funny animated comment on various things. Jay is a highly creative talent." Soon thereafter Ward was named Moore's TV producer.

By mid-1966, however, the picture had changed. Jay told reporters, "I was supposed to be the executive producer of Garry Moore's new show, but CBS got nervous about it, and they made Pat Weaver producer and named me contributing producer. Nobody ever heard of a contributing producer—I don't know what it is." Punctuating his words with his familiar snort and laugh, Jay added, "I suppose they'll let me know what I'm supposed to do this summer."

For Moore's CBS show, Jay's team went back to their silent film library. They assembled ten "Flicker Songs"—these were short "flickers" neatly matched to hit tunes of that year. For instance, Nancy Sinatra's "These Boots Are Made for Walking" featured various clips of people with extremely silly footwear, and provided funny visuals to the lyrics. The idea was dreamed up by Jay's new writer, Jim Critchfield. His first one—"I Get a Kick out of You"—had already been made for the 1963 *Nut House* show, but wasn't reused. When Critchfield experienced some personal problems, the"Flicker Songs" were finished off by Lloyd Turner and Jim MacGeorge.

Turner recalled, "I did a few by myself. By this time Chris Hayward had teamed up with Al Burns and they'd left Jay's employ, so Skip Craig would come in and work the Moviola for me. The 'Fractured Songs' [*sic*] were great to work on and they turned out real funny." Skip adds that Bill Scott did a couple, "but Bill chose ballads and they didn't work; the tempo was too slow for the visual gags, whereas Critch and Lloyd used up-tempo songs and the images were cut fast to the beat. The people back in New York didn't really like the stuff we came up with; and besides, Moore's TV show didn't last that long anyway." Once Ward Productions completed the "Flicker Songs," Jay parted company with the CBS network for all time.

Garry Moore did, however, narrate another Jay Ward project which was a direct outgrowth of *Fractured Flickers* and "Flicker Songs." In a deal completed in June 1964, Jay acquired the motion picture rights to the Hal Roach comedy film library, along with Roach's personal services as producer. In two ironic coincidences, the deal was signed on Roach's fiftieth anniversary in show business, while Ward's legal representative in these negotiations was none other than W. C. Fields, Jr. Ward and Scott quickly decided on a feature-length compilation film, *The Crazy World of Laurel and Hardy*. Raymond Rohauer, who had introduced Ward and Scott to Hal Roach, got associate producer billing. The film had the official imprimatur of comedy veteran Roach, who had made these brilliant comedies with Stan and Ollie nearly four decades earlier.

Ward and Scott took executive producer credits. The film was originally called "The Wonderful World of Laurel and Hardy." Along the way the working title changed to "Laurel and Hardy, the Laff-Makers." Bill Scott wrote a warm yet unobtrusive script; Stan and Ollie were two of his all-time comedy heroes. As he put it, "We treated Laurel and Hardy as lovingly as possible. They were comic geniuses, and we try to show them at their very best." He added, "We think it is the definitive Laurel and Hardy picture. We had sixty pictures available to us from Hal Roach, and picked the best stuff from their talkies."

Scott's approach consisted of revealing how the peerless comedy team almost always relied on three major props in every film: doors, hats, and automobiles. As he explained, "We strung together a number of hat jokes one after another, the same with doors and cars. The result is hilarious. We also spliced the 'Hardy clobber.' These are scenes where poor old Ollie gets his lumps but good in about twenty blackouts." With the exception of a clip from the silent *Bacon Grabbers* (1927), the entire *Crazy World* is culled from Laurel and Hardy's sound shorts and features.

Skip Craig: "Everything Bill touched was marked by his genius. He would take a theme and develop it, like the hats or doors, and he'd switch the [sound] track against the picture, or sometimes play gags offstage for an effect. Jay's old Berkeley staffer Tom Stanford did the cutting on *Laurel and Hardy*. He'd been dealing with blowups from 16 mm. When it was finished, I went back to match it and I had the full 35-mm print, which made it easier. I had to be quite meticulous, and go frame by frame, filling in the torn pieces. Jay brought in legit musicians for this project." The score was composed by Jerry Fielding, who had worked with Ward on *The Nut House*. Adds Skip, "The Laurel and Hardy feature played quite a bit; Jay put it on a double bill with *Jay Ward's Intergalactic Film Festival*, which was a compile of a lot of his cartoons and *Flickers*. God, I put together countless prints—I can remember sitting over at DeLuxe for ages and ages doing this."

The Crazy World of Laurel and Hardy had commenced production in 1964. It took almost eighteen months to complete, and was premiered at the Berlin Film Festival. Jay said, "About a year after we started, somebody else [Robert Youngson] did it [a Laurel and Hardy tribute], too, and had it on the market first. For some reason, we're having trouble selling ours. So we sit around and look at it a lot." Originally, Jay intended to hire Stan Laurel as narrator, but the comedian was seventy-four years old and in failing health (he died in 1965). Peter Sellers, too, was considered for the narration chores. But by the time the film was ready, Garry Moore, then working with Jay on the CBS show, got the nod as the film's commentator.

The finished feature, running eighty-three minutes, had its official premiere at New York's Kips Bay Theatre on December 21, 1967. Hal Roach was present, in New York for talks with network brass about a new TV comedy he planned to produce with Jay Ward. This new show, which didn't get off the ground, was to feature brief, diverse sketches. Shades of *The Nut House!*

When work began on the Laurel and Hardy feature, a contemporary news report mentioned, "Jay Ward is looking for all the W. C. Fields comedies in order to do a matching film." Following several delays, this project finally happened, and the Fields compilation, along with various others, was finished seven years later, in 1974.

Meanwhile, during production on *George of the Jungle,* Jay launched a subsidiary recording label, the Mother's Records and Snarf Company. Leah Cohen, sister of Mamas and Papas singer Cass Elliott, was to run the operation, and Jay would supply promotion and wacky album artwork. Singer Teri Thornton recorded several songs, but the Snarf label was another Jay Ward venture that quickly bit the dust.

Various TV ideas kept coming, but by late 1967, after nearly a decade of trying, Ward finally reached the conclusion that the networks were trying to tell him something. Yes, they recognized his unpredictability and genuine funniness. But they knew he was never content to cash in on someone else's cliché—and frankly, he unnerved them. Ward's ideas had nothing to do with the safe formulas of frothy little laugh-track comedies like *I Dream of Jeannie*.

In a rare serious moment, Jay reflected, "The real trouble with TV is that everyone is trying to please someone else. We've stopped going to the networks. They're friendly and nice, but we never get an affirmative answer. I really can't blame the network men. I go in to see them with some far-out thing and they have so many nice, slick shows from Universal or MGM. They go the safe route. Any idea you take to a network has to go through fifteen guys.

Fourteen of them may like it, but if the fifteenth says no, they all want to hedge and take a second look. If it's something wild, they back off."

Ward strongly believed that if an original comedy failed, then that killed it for others. In his view, "I think maybe the kids are the most intelligent audience for TV anyhow. We go our happy way with our cartoons." He concluded, "But we're undaunted. Like true Dudley Do-Rights, we keep trying, ignoring the obvious."

21

Our Fearless Leader, or What Was Jay Ward Really Like?

> We tried to do as many funny things as we could think of that would amuse ourselves. We felt the animation and action would entertain children and we could do our own satire and humor based on our own adult feelings. Our main interest was funny humor.
>
> —*Jay Ward, 1987*

In October 1978 Jay Ward was honored by ASIFA, the International Animated Film Society. For this prestigious occasion, Bill Scott wrote an opening testimonial in which he attempted to analyze his partner of twenty years.

> For a number of years in the animated cartoon industry, one of the most nagging questions that has plagued us all has been: "Is there *really* a Jay Ward?"
>
> People who have seen the "Executive Producer" credit on Jay Ward Productions' cartoons know for sure that there is really a Ponsonby Britt, O.B.E.—but they're not all certain about Jay Ward. I'm here tonight to assure you—and you can check it for yourself—that there really *is* a Jay Ward. Not only is there *a* Jay Ward, there are several *Jay Wards*.

There is Jay Ward the bon vivant and considerate host, who, when throwing a real old-fashioned picnic for a few hundred fans at the Plaza Hotel in New York, wasn't satisfied with serving real old-fashioned hot dogs, potato salad and pickles. He insisted that the caterer supply several thousand real old-fashioned ants.

There is Jay Ward the racing tycoon, owner of the Bullwinkle Stables—so soft-hearted that he bets a bundle on even the slowest of his entries just so the horse won't feel bad after the race.

There is Jay Ward the eternal child, with a sweet tooth approximately the size of a mastodon tusk, who, when expanding his studio, made the first order of business, even before the desks were moved in, the installation of a complete soda fountain. Ours is the only studio certified by the Pure Food and Drug Administration.

There is Jay Ward the TV pioneer who, with his partner Alex Anderson, made the world's first TV cartoon series, *Crusader Rabbit,* when everybody knew it couldn't be done, and were right. He went on to produce, among other projects, *Rocky and His Friends, The Bullwinkle Show, Fractured Flickers,* and *George of the Jungle.*

There is Jay Ward the Berkeley Real Estate magnate, whose first customer on his first day of business was a runaway automobile that came through his front window and carried him right into the hospital.

There is Jay Ward the family man, whose easy going ways and willingness to compromise have led his adoring wife and three children to refer to him by that most endearing of all pet names—"The Chairman of the Board."

There is Jay Ward the art collector, whose magpie mania encompasses everything from merry-go-round horses to wooden Indians, and who has had to move out of two offices because finally there wasn't enough room for them and him.

There is Jay Ward the loyal friend and noted soft touch, who has stuck gamely with and supported some of the most improbable people through some of the most outrageous situations imaginable, and whose ultimate epithet even for people who have done him obvious wrong is "He's a dirty guy." (I've known Jay for 20 years, and I've never heard him say even "damn." Limited vocabulary.)

There is Jay Ward the old Berkeley Grad, who is such a Cal booster that he was selected by the prestigious Robert Gordon Sproul Associates as their Man of the Year. You have to look hard to find Jay's

M.B.A. from Harvard Business School, but his office sports a whole collection of UC drum major's hats.

There is Jay Ward the patron of the arts, whose *first* Man of the Year award came from the American Ecdysiasts Society, a professional association of striptease dancers. Jay hosted a Dansant for these ladies at the staid and stuffy Bel Air Hotel. It got a little out of hand and Jay is now 86'd permanently from the entire Stone Canyon area. But then what are we to say of a man who single-handedly not only made Coney Island a motion picture Mecca, but raised Muncie, Indiana, to its position as sports capital of the universe?

There is Jay Ward the studio boss, who grants to those who work for him complete artistic and creative freedom, as long as what they do is good, funny, and finished yesterday.

There is Jay Ward the fashion plate, who blazed new trails in men's toggery not only by appearing at his son's wedding in top hat, morning coat, and sneakers, but also appeared on the *Johnny Carson Show* wearing a rhinestone monocle and carrying a six-foot salami. Is that class?

All of these Jay Wards sound like men who are constantly on the go, always in the forefront of things, glad-handers, backslappers, and Merry Andrews all. Not so. Jay Ward is, oddly enough, an intensely private person who, given his druthers, shies away from public appearances and interviews, and for whom occasions like this, when he is a center of interest, are difficult and almost painful. And so it is that with all the fanfare and publicity and promotional gimmickry, he still remains something of an enigma to all of us—but an enigma that we who have known him over the years regard with admiration, respect, and affection. He was a unanimous first ballot choice of ASIFA's nominating committee to receive the 'Annie' award tonight.

So will the *real* Jay Ward please stand up?

(In fact, Scott didn't get to deliver this speech—he was caught in a traffic jam and arrived too late. He had to be content to simply present the original copy to Jay.)

A spate of "Rocky and Bullwinkle" retro articles in 1991 took pains to point out that producer Jay Ward was infamous for being reclusive, shy, and mostly unapproachable. Indeed, the *Los Angeles Times* comedy columnist Lawrence Christon found that Ward's reticence had "put a strain on [his] attempt to re-create the era." Time and again Ward was portrayed as a frustratingly elusive showman. Of course, anyone who can put such a personal stamp on a studio and its output is obviously a highly interesting case study. But all we ever get is the recluse: so the question remains, Is that all there was to Jay Ward?

Herewith an attempt to paint a more accurate portrait of Ward, bearing in mind that he valued his privacy above all else. As his wife, Ramona, often said, "Jay never wanted a book written; he was only interested in looking ahead, not back."

Much of Jay Ward's behavior reflected two dominant features in his makeup: a fiercely independent desire for quality, and a lifelong pursuit of fun. These factors, combined with his inherently retiring nature and the poor health he suffered throughout his working life, add up to a fascinating character. Alex Anderson emphasizes that the newspaper reports on Ward were invariably shallow, noting, "Jay was a very complex human being." As we shall see, the "constantly chuckling eccentric" category into which Ward was pigeonholed was just the tip of the iceberg.

Comedy writer Lloyd Turner was one of Jay Ward's close circle of friends. Describing Ward's unique quality as an employer, Turner said, "Jay was childlike, not childlish; there's a difference between the two. But the key to Jay was that everything had to be fun. And the studio reflected that. There were fun-house mirrors in every room, antique barber chairs, and expensive genuine cigar-store Indians; it was like a forest in there. He had a big circus hurdy-gurdy and at the drop of a hat he'd plug it in and play it, and I mean loudly!" When reporters asked Ward about the wooden carousel horses and penny arcade nickelodoens, Jay's invariable reply was, "Life is fun and worth living."

Turner recalled, "We had a popcorn machine, an ice-cream machine with tubs of every flavor plus two types of cone, and a Sno-Kone machine with strawberry and cola flavors. There were boxes of candy, hundreds of flavors of jelly beans, Kit Kats, Snickers bars, and cases of real soft drink—not the diet stuff. We'd all be drinking coffee at eight in the morning while Jay would have a breakfast of Coca-Cola and popcorn, or doughnuts. God, his sweet tooth was legendary!

"He gave us all special nicknames. I was called 'the Old Lloyd-boy.' And I'd say, 'You know, Jay, you have arrested development. You're like an eight-year-old kid.' And he'd love this. He'd laugh and say, 'You know, I think you're right.' Basically Jay hated to be serious and he hated being logical. Everything had to be fun. So it was like working in a fun house, and Jay was our Fearless Leader who led us down the road of total freedom."

A further insight on the subject of Ward as a boss is provided by Bill Hurtz: "I think of all the producers I've ever known, Jay was the best because he innately knew what the role of a producer was: to bring talent together, give them the milieu to work in, then get the best out of them and support them. An example of this concerns people's productivity level at the studio. I was fairly fast on things, Pete Burness was not. Pete took a long time to polish things and work them out very carefully. But Jay said to me once, 'Well, that's his way, and that's valuable. He doesn't have to be as fast as other people.' So Jay made allowances for people's distinct personalities."

Luther Nichols believed that "Jay was a team man. He was, in business, a brilliant recognizor of talent." Writer George Atkins concurred, adding, "While the humor in the cartoons was really a reflection of the total personality of Bill Scott, Jay was the entrepreneurial genius, and that was reflected in the studio itself."

Gerard Baldwin, an animation director who worked four different stints at Ward Productions from 1959 to 1969, described Ward as "a nice man, but very nervous and introverted. There were some demons in him that I could never fathom. See, Jay was a paternal kind of boss. My own nature was such that I didn't join in some of the more frivolous fun-and-games things that went on at the studio. For instance, one day Jay decreed that everybody on the staff would grow a beard, and the person with the best one would be rewarded with an all-expenses-paid trip to Paris. Well, I thought it was all pretty silly and I shaved my whiskers off pretty quickly. So Jay presented me with a Greyhound bus pass to Bakersfield, California."

George Atkins was one of the more eccentric personalities at Ward's. Although he and Jay weren't as close as some at the studio, there was always a mutual respect: "I liked him. Because Jay had a genuine appreciation of what was funny." Ward's inner turmoil, noted by Gerard Baldwin, was attributed by Atkins to "an emotionally delicate condition directly resulting from 1947, when that truck nearly killed him. When I first met him, he was suffering from agoraphobia (a morbid dislike of public places), because of the terrible experience he had been through on a nasty plane flight in 1958, which had amplified his problems of ten years earlier."

As we have seen, in late 1958 and early 1959, Ward was at the worst stage of complications following the nervous breakdown he sustained on the traumatic flight from New York to California. Atkins observed, "In 1959 Jay was in rough shape. He wouldn't come out of his apartment. His shoulder was actually twitching then." Bill Hurtz, recommended by Bill Scott, remembered Jay contacting him by phone. "He said, 'I'm sorry, but I don't go out to meet people. Would you mind coming to see me'—this was a Sunday—'at my apartment?' That was the Andalusia, around the corner from the studio." Hurtz also felt that Ward suffered from a terror of being confined: the truck accident caused "a claustrophobic condition that haunted Jay all his life." Al Shean, who first met Ward back in 1951 at UPA, recalled, "Even in those early days he exhibited some nervous mannerisms." And Skip Craig said, "Until I met Jay, I'd never known someone who laughed nervously at the end of every sentence."

Skip Craig recalled, "Jay was not well for a long time, and he always had the Coca-Cola: he'd be walking around every day with a can of soft drink in his hand." Ramona Ward explained, "He became a cola addict. His nervous system had been destroyed in the airplane and he needed the carbonated liquid to swallow, to keep his breathing passage open."

Of course it's tempting to assume that the ill health which plagued Jay Ward for years, coupled with his native independence, was largely responsible for his studio never making the commercial big time, as Hanna-Barbera's did. Most of his friends and staff, however, feel that Ward was perfectly content with the level of success he attained. And in any event, his product was always far too offbeat for the factory method of much of his competition.

Ward's schoolmate and first salesman, Leonard Key, felt that "Jay had a big ego, but he was nervously shy. The laughter was a facade that masked the recurring bad health. I don't think he ever got over his nervous breakdown. In fact, I saw signs that the breakdown was going to happen: during the period we were trying to revive *Crusader Rabbit* [1956–57] he was in litigation, and he was very nervous. Jay was the greatest showman who ever lived, but I'd observe these extremes—highs and lows. Lavish parties that cost a fortune, by a man who was basically afraid to see people." Howard Brandy and Ramona Ward disagree, however, maintaining that Jay was essentially a "people person"; as Ramona explained, "Jay enjoyed parties as long as he was in a position to get away from the crowd if he felt threatened by his nerves."

Ward's former secretary Linda Hayward recalled, "If Jay overheard something which upset him he wouldn't get into long conversations—he'd be embarrassed. The Napoleon outfit in the Moosylvania campaign: that was a way for him to hide; so was his [later] walrus mustache. And I know for a fact that he didn't really feel comfortable doing that tour in the Napoleon suit. He truly didn't want to do it deep down. Of course having Howard [Brandy] along with him made it a lot easier."

Allan Burns voiced a perceptive comment about his former boss in the 1991 PBS-TV special *Of Moose and Men*. "Jay was unusual. He was very shy; but he thrived on other people's eccentricities, and he wanted to have himself thought of as eccentric. Which is a little difficult when you're shy." Bill Hurtz noted, "Jay's shyness became apparent when, time after time, some newspaper guy would call and want to do a story or interview. Jay would say to me, 'You do it.' And at first I'd say, 'Well look, they want to talk to you—what'll I say?' and he thought for a moment and said, 'Tell 'em there is no Jay Ward!' Of course, he could get dressed up as Napoleon and tour the country for publicity, but like a lot of actors and shy people, in costume he assumed another self."

Skip Craig was a loyal employee from 1959 to 1984. He firmly believes that Ward never made a good business deal in his life: "If Jay was pressured by other interested parties, he would simply give in because he couldn't stand conflict. He actively avoided confrontation of any kind. It was funny really, because in the early days Jay had these big plans each year. We'd sit together in the alcove at his apartment and he'd say, 'We're going to build a dynasty, we're going to have TV series after TV series, and we're all going to retire wealthy with big pensions,' and he had all these big profit-sharing plans that never happened. Jay basically just wanted to have fun, and to laugh his way through life, and go to the Lakers games."

Linda Hayward agrees with Craig that Ward was too soft in his business dealings. "He'd do a lot of stuff verbally; he'd just say 'Okay!' and do a handshake. And those people simply took advantage of that. I mean even though we weren't involved directly, it seemed to us as if Jay gave things away."

In hindsight, Ward's "ostrich" approach can be seen as a defense mechanism—his method of coping with a not inconsiderable arsenal of hard knocks over previous years. Consider his horrific experience with the lumber truck and the lingering aftereffects, followed by the later nervous breakdown and its accompanying phobias. These long-term health problems were further inflamed by messy chapters in his professional life: the vexatious and ultimately futile three-year court battle regarding compensation for the *Crusader Rabbit* series, followed by Shull Bonsall's takeover resulting in Ward's and Anderson's loss of rights to their *Crusader Rabbit* characters. Then too, the first twelve months on *Rocky and His Friends* were fraught with tension: botched financing, an impossibly low budget, and amateurish Mexican animation. It's no wonder Jay Ward "just wanted to have fun" and "avoided confrontation." Indeed, as Ramona Ward suggests, without his expansive humor and childlike enthusiasms, Jay might very well have died several years earlier.

Franky Jones worked as Jay's secretary and production assistant from 1972 to 1982. She described Jay as "completely unique. The nicest boss I ever had, and a pushover. He was somewhat childishly trusting of a couple of people who shall remain nameless, but they took him for a lot of money, and Jay ultimately felt betrayed. He became more and more reclusive, partly because he was very often in pain. You know, he really had difficulty walking, yet he would never complain or tell anyone of his discomfort."

Writer Jim Critchfield, however, disagrees with the theory that Ward never made a good business deal. "No, that's not true. Jay wasn't railroaded by anyone, not for a minute. Normally, if you're with an aggressive person, then, obviously, you'd better take an aggressive stance yourself. But Jay wasn't interested enough to argue. He knew that the P.A.T. [*Rocky* TV show] deal wasn't that great, but there simply wasn't enough money in it for him to be that aggressive."

Bill Hurtz observed both sides of Jay Ward the businessman: "Jay was a very good salesman. The Quaker Oats deal kept the studio going; but, overall, he wasn't an infighter on contracts. On the other hand, he wouldn't be pushed around. From the very beginning with General Mills and their agency, D-F-S, and so on to the last sponsor, Quaker, Jay would not take dictation from networks or agencies. He either did what he wanted to do, or he wouldn't do it, and that meant it had to be fun. [If not,] he'd laugh his nervous laugh and say, 'It's not our kind of thing.' And he was offered [TV] shows time and again that used other characters. But he'd say, 'No, it didn't come from us.' So there were actually many opportunities for Jay to become a kind of corporate monopoly of animation, but he turned them down if it wasn't going to be fun. And this kind of independence did not endear him to the networks."

Critchfield added, "Jay passed up a lot of commercials and shows. He had a lot of very good offers but he'd sit there and he'd chuckle and say, 'Well, I don't think so.' Because if the people involved on a certain project weren't the type of people he felt he could spend time with, well he just didn't do it. He was the type of person who didn't want to cloud up his day if he didn't have to." Lew Keller said, "He was very gutsy that way. If he couldn't do it his way, that was the end of it. Jay didn't care about offending advertisers, he just went for the jokes." Luther Nichols analyzed, "If Jay had a fault, it was stubbornness. He would make up his mind and dig his heels in. And nothing or nobody could turn him around. This occasionally proved hazardous to Jay."

"Jay's Quaker Oats deal," said Bill Hurtz, "was very, very respectable, and he got along real well with one of Quaker's bigwigs [Ken Mason]. The deal was so nice in fact, there was no incentive for Jay to do another series." By the end of the 1960s, the networks were dictating far more policy on creative matters than had been the case a decade earlier, and Ward simply lost much of his enthusiasm for new TV shows. Besides, the Quaker account was lucrative. According to Skip, "He started breeding racehorses, and became very interested in that and other outside activities. Man, he sure went in big for the horses. At one time he owned twenty-seven. He'd get an occasional win but never any big-stakes thing. Jay's racing silks were yellow and orange and the poor jockeys had to wear these crazy clothes with Bullwinkle's likeness on the back." The Thoroughbred horses themselves boasted typical Jay Ward-esque names: Professor McGargle (after a W. C. Fields character), E. Eddie Edwards (often used as a character name on *Fractured Flickers*), Chief Duffy, Chief Dudley, Lucky Coloullah, and Chief Hawk Ear (inspiration for a future cartoon pilot).

Over the years, Ward developed a finely tuned appreciation of art. Lew Keller said, "Jay loved the business and he loved creative people. He thought comedy was the best thing there is. But Jay was also very sensitive to drawing and painting." Bill Hurtz explained, "Jay didn't draw, but he had a great eye for art. And he was the best critic of animation I've ever met. We'd show him a pencil test on the Moviola, and he would go right to the heart of the matter." Alex Anderson confirmed this: "Jay was remarkably quick in the way he absorbed and understood the whole process of animation. Again, he was very bright; during the *Crusader Rabbit* period he had learned the business thoroughly."

At Ward's memorial, Hurtz revealed, "Jay was impulsive: he'd get these sudden 'loves' and everything stopped, and you'd suddenly join him on some journey. Lew Keller and I were taken in noon hours, for a period of three weeks, to acquire an instant art collection. Up and down La Cienega Boulevard, which was then the place to go; he would take about five minutes to see something, then he'd go 'Yep!' and boom, off we'd go to the next place."

Skip Craig added, "In his last years Jay would still get these enthusiasms. I remember when he went crazy for movie posters. He and Howard Brandy would hunt around for valuable originals—Jay paid something like $10,000 for this huge genuine *Frankenstein* [1931] poster!"

During the last twenty years of Jay's life, Jim Critchfield probably knew him better than any other staff member. In analyzing his boss's character he makes some fascinating observations. Critchfield reflected, "Jay didn't like typical. He only wanted to do things he liked, and if you look at the material on his shows, most of it is not mediocre. It compliments the audience far more than the average cartoon show. Of course, Bill Scott is actually the one whose stamp is there in everything. But Jay made it all possible. He brought these talents to a perfect environment. In fact, Jay's ability to select people to work with him—with the exception of myself—was phenomenal. No other studio ever had such a collection of high-quality talent. And they all knew how to react so that they'd please Jay.

"Jay was a witty man, but he was reclusive. Now this was not snobbishness, but you have to understand the key to Jay was that he didn't like mediocrity. Mediocrity is something that's rather common in this business, and, to be blunt, in this world. For instance, if someone had a comment about something in that day's newspaper then Jay was not really that interested. He wanted cleverness. So, if you were a 'character,' if you were honestly different, he'd pick that. Rather than sitting around trying to come up with a contrived sort of a joke, if someone said something that was genuinely witty, then that was a person Jay would like. Lew Keller is an example. Lew [was] a legitimate character. Jay would go with that all the way; he had an incredible brain. He grasped people's characters straightaway.

"Jay was also a little puritanical. He was very strict with himself, and I guess you'd say he was pretty straight. Well, Jay felt that dirty language betrayed a lack of intelligence. If someone came on as crude, it wasn't that Jay would dislike that person; but he thought the crudity itself was just a waste of time." Skip Craig recalls Ward's singular way of categorizing people: "Jay had three classes of people to watch out for: bum, dirty guy, and bad guy; if you were a bum it meant you had to try harder next time, and if you were a dirty guy you were pretty far down the scale of acceptability. But if Jay referred to someone as a bad guy, then forget it! That person didn't measure up to his moral standards and would never be in with Jay."

Was Jay Ward, then, a benevolent despot who expected too high a standard? Critchfield: "Jay was not that easy to be around at times. He could be very demanding, but these moods wouldn't last long. And I knew that if he was really down, he'd be all right if you just left him alone for a while. He would do his downtime, then he'd be cheerful again, but sure, he had a temper." Skip Craig observed the dark side of Ward's personality and felt that it was Jay's perfectionist streak which caused him to act with occasional intolerance. "If you didn't immediately adjust your mind to whatever Jay was talking about when he was in one of these moods, he could really make you feel like you were an idiot." Bill Hurtz agreed, adding, "But of course Bill Scott could be just as temperamental too."

Before Critchfield took over as Ward's sounding board and boon companion, that role was played by Lloyd Turner. Turner recalled, "I really did exert a great influence on Jay. I 'owned' Jay; he just loved my sense of humor and he'd come to me for opinions or to discuss ideas. It was not just a typical employer-employee relationship, because we were like brothers. We socialized, I watched his kids grow up, I was very close to his wife Billie; Jay and I played a lot of golf together and just spent time with each other. It was fun and games all the way, and as a writer there was always that total freedom. I would sum up Jay by saying that he was a super guy, very moral, and supremely intelligent with a highly developed sense of humor. And he was innately a nice man, who remained a dear friend."

Jim Critchfield noted, "Although he was shy by nature, Jay was socially at ease. He wasn't a name-dropper by any means, but he turned down more invitations than most people get in a lifetime." Skip Craig's wife, Helen, was always impressed by Ward's thoughtfulness. Although she only saw Jay infrequently, "he would always take the time to ask about kids and work." Critchfield added, "He was generous, diplomatic, and he had such a brilliant brain—he could read upside down, and he was a speed reader. And he had his nicknames for the staff: Bill Hurtz was 'Master Hurtz,' Lew Keller was 'Sugar Lew,' George Atkins was 'Big George,' and so on. And we all called Jay by his initials, J. T."

If one character trait stood out in Jay Ward's makeup, it was loyalty. Critchfield pointed out that "Jay always believed that loyalty was one of the most valuable human qualities, so he tended to surround himself with great talents who were like-minded. And he was definitely loyal; he was very generous with me. If I needed money, I could always count on Jay for an assignment." Linda Hayward added, "His loyalty was pretty amazing. He would never have let me go. I had to leave if I wanted to move on in the business. He was like a father to me and I felt he really cared. I started there when I was just nineteen and at the time I was such a mixed-up girl. I was very disorganized, and Jay knew I couldn't take dictation: he'd laugh so hard at the mistake-filled letters I'd do for him, then he'd go ahead and send them anyway." Lew Keller sums up: "Jay was a kindly person, and inclined to be paternalistic."

The generous side of Ward's nature made him something of a soft touch, as Linda recalled: "Soft! Jay was the softest touch of all. For ages, there were these panhandlers he'd help out every week, and they each got into a routine of regular handout days. One would be there on Monday, one on Tuesday, and so on. Jay absolutely couldn't say no, and they knew it. He was feeding the homeless years before it was an issue. One time I accompanied him to New York. It was my first trip, and Jay and Alan Foshko took me to a play starring Bea Arthur. And if a panhandler came up to us Jay would just hand out money. It was incredible." Lew Keller added, "Oh yes, Jay was definitely an easy mark for a soft touch."

Equally notable was Jay Ward's attraction to unique characters. For a period in the 1960s Ward became involved with salesman Hal Styles. In 1964 Styles came to Jay with the idea of producing syndicated commercials. Skip Craig recalled that Styles had the gift of the gab: "He was like a sideshow carnival barker. He had a deal going with some Chevrolet car dealers, and the commercial featured a little character which Paul Frees did the voice for; they were just going to use the same footage over and over, and replace each dealership name with a different card on-screen. Styles was the guy who bought all the fancy furniture for the studio, the big desk and so on; he really outfitted the place." Linda Hayward said, "Hal Styles became our salesman for a while—and he sure looked like a real used-car salesman. He never looked like he fitted in at the studio—he'd be the only one there who wore a suit and tie." Ward and Styles produced several commercials for such clients as the Southern California Gas Company.

Several years earlier, Chris Hayward brought another "character" to the Jay Ward studio. The eccentrically talented Bill Oberlin was looking for work at the time. Hayward recalled, "He wanted to do storyboards; I'd helped him get a job doing boards on *Crusader Rabbit* for Shull Bonsall. But Jay put him to work as a runner, doing odd jobs. He actually supported Oberlin there for a while. Oberlin had been the art director on Bob Clampett's *Time for Beany* and at Jay's he built the huge Bullwinkle statue; he also made these little desktop statues of the characters—Dudley Do-Right, Simpson and Delaney, and Cap'n Crunch. And he made one of Jay as a little naked jaybird. We had these tiny

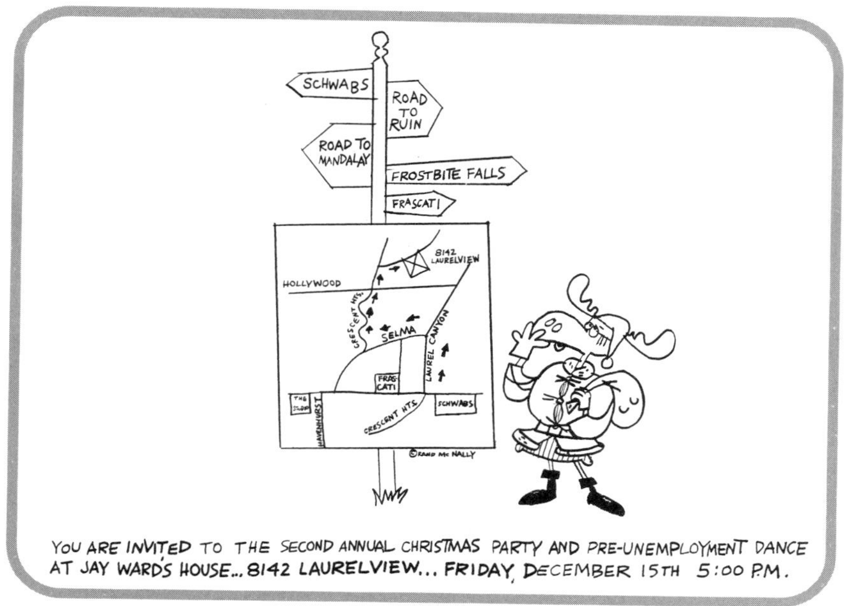

Invitation to a Christmas party at Jay's house. *Original gag drawing courtesy of Bill Scott*

statues down in the basement and when Oberlin would get pissed at Jay over something, he'd turn all these little models so that they'd face the wall, with the jaybird's rear end showing! Later Linda rigged up a can device so that when Jay would come in, she'd rattle the can, and Bill would quickly turn the statues the right way around."

Linda added, "Oberlin was a real character, an absolute original. Jay had a running account at Sears and he'd often send Oberlin out to buy whatever was needed, like nails or whatever it was. Well, one day Jay got his account statement and he suddenly saw that Oberlin had also bought himself a brand-new suit. At Jay's expense!" Skip Craig said, "Oberlin made quite a few motorized miniature versions of the Bullwinkle statue. He was also a brilliant impersonator of W. C. Fields, and when he'd get a performing gig, he'd come in and bum a pair of white editing gloves from me and snip the fingers off them to do Fields. Later Chris and Al tried to write a TV show for Oberlin called 'The Best in the Business,' about a bunch of crazy reporters. But it was never made."

According to the writers, the only negative aspect of working for Ward Productions was payroll. Mentioned in several newspaper accounts are the writers' collective feelings on poor payment. Chris Hayward said, "We all felt we got short shift, although I must say Jay made up for it in other ways." Even at Ward's memorial service Al Burns couldn't resist adding, "Whatever he neglected to pay us in actual living wages, Jay made up for with lavish lunches, golf weekends, parties, trips to the track, ball games. Incredible trips to New York—we flew first-class while Jay, of course, drove. He put us up in the best hotels, fed us royally in the most lavish restaurants, took us to all the hit plays that nobody else could get tickets for, and laughed the whole time."

Skip Craig noted, "There was a somewhat selfish streak in Jay in the later years—he was very generous with funny things, but not on payroll. At first he'd take people back east and they'd go to all the shows. But from the mid-1960s, once he started with the racehorses and breeding them, and filling his house with fabulous art, and turning up in Aston Martins and Jaguars and Porsche Turbos, it seemed like all the toys were for him. It hadn't been that way earlier. Still, everybody loved Jay and wanted to stay there—everyone was loyal to him despite this."

Financial matters aside, the Ward studio held an abiding and peculiar allure for creative people. Lloyd Turner wrote a (published) letter to Ward in which he mentioned, "In spite of sharing working space with rats in the basement and below-the-poverty-level paychecks, you gave us the magic formula for writing: set yourself in motion, open your mind like a floodgate and don't hold anything back. Shed the bonds of convention and restriction and forget the 'can't do's.' The good stuff is in there waiting to surprise you. Throw out what you don't like later."

George Atkins was quick to point out, "All my bad feelings about the way the studio was run financially were counterbalanced by the way Jay made you take great pride in the work. And I *would* feel proud!" It was Atkins who voiced the strongest feelings of ambivalence. "His lack of consideration for our futures, for our financial well-being during our employ with him, was vastly outweighed by the greatest gift a producer can bestow on a writer: the opportunity to do something memorable, something for which the writer could have some pride. He was outrageous, wildly frustrating, infuriating, selfish. Yet he was magnificent in his uniqueness. And so I think of him with affection and gratitude."

Al Burns told the *Los Angeles Times,* "You had wonderful times but no money. I don't think he ever got rich. Or if he did, he didn't show it." And in the same article Chris Hayward stated, "The pay was low and the insecurity great. Jay felt that the writers should pay him! His theory was 'Never show a profit or else you'll have to pay people.' "

Jim Critchfield, however, demurred: "Jay created a fairly big empire and he made the decisions. There's no rule that says you have to share your empire, and by the late 1960s he decided that he wanted to start enjoying his money. Hence the art collection—I was with him when he bought most of the stuff. In fact, there was an undercurrent of competitiveness for some Japanese beads between Jay (who bought them for his wife) and Hans Conried, who was a major enthusiast for Japanese culture."

The most memorable times for Jay's staff members involved the freewheeling fun which was ever present alongside the hard work. Chris Hayward recalled, "There were the famous mystery golf tournaments. You had to be outside your house at six in the morning. He wouldn't tell you where you were going. One trip turned out to be to Phoenix. Actually in Carefree, Arizona, and it was a golf course full of sand traps! Then one time the Ringling Brothers circus was in town, so Jay closed up the studio for the day and took us all there." Billie Ward added, "The Ringling circus visits were an annual event for several years."

Hayward remembered Ward's distinctive handlebar mustache being the result of one of their regular golf matches. "Jay was an excellent golfer. One time we were driving back from Pebble Beach, where we held our annual North-South tournament, and Jay asked us what we'd do for the theme of the next one. I suggested a 'Hirsute' match for which we all had to grow a beard or mustache. Jay grew one that he liked so much, it stayed. The golf excursions were always terrific fun. Another time we all had to 'give a useless gift to someone of your choice.' Alex Anderson gave Jay the wings from a gag United Jewish Airlines frequent-flier prize for one hundred thousand miles. Of course, Jay never flew. I gave Lloyd Turner a small box—he opened it up to find a stainless-steel stroke counter. Jay said, 'I thought it was supposed to be a useless gift.' I said, 'Well how the hell's Lloyd gonna use it, he only has one arm!' Turner had lost his arm in a wood-shop accident.

Lloyd Turner recalled, "Jay was the only boss in the world who would help an employee go AWOL. He'd come in and say, 'There's a race at Hollywood Park or Santa Anita or wherever, and so and so is running,' or he had a horse in the fifth race, 'So let's go! But we can't let anyone see us or they'll all go home for the day, so I'll meet you in my car,' and he'd park his car up on the corner and I'd sneak out! Then we'd spend the whole day there, and most of the time we'd lose money. And as for golf, well when you consider that I only have one arm, I certainly wasn't the best player around; but I was fair, I could break 90. And Jay would just be in one of his fun moods and he'd say, 'Lloyd-boy, you're gonna play real good today and I'm going to drive your score.' Jay had an Aston Martin or whatever the latest car was (he just loved cars and he was hooked on fast sports cars). So I'd get a bit uptight and I'd play badly, I'd shoot up to 110 or 120. And sure enough, Jay would drive us home and he'd get that car up to 120 miles per hour, and he'd just laugh like he was possessed. Old J. T., I loved him!"

One of the all-time famous anecdotes concerning Jay Ward occurred in 1969 at his daughter's wedding, held at the Riviera Country Club. Linda Hayward remembered, "It was a great wedding. And topping it, believe it or not, Jay had rigged up a life-size mannequin, put a Jay Ward handlebar mustache on it and a tape recorder inside its chest. So when the guests went down the reception line they discovered Jay's wife and this mannequin—in place of Jay! The tape inside played Jay's voice as the mannequin greeted all the guests. This was just incredible, and when Chris and I heard our own names mentioned we just couldn't believe it. Poor Billie had to stand there for ages as the guests came down the line again and again to hear the tape."

Bill Hurtz recalled, "The dummy was dressed in a tweed coat, a sweater, knickers, and tennis shoes." Ward and Jim Critchfield had written a raft of one-liners, with Ward recording all his greetings. He satirized his own distinctive laugh, and spouted jokes like "Hi, I'm Jay Ward—anybody want to buy a half-hour TV show? Move down the line, please," or "Hi, I'm Jay Ward—this wedding is costing me a fortune. Watch for me in Bullocks' basement! Keep the line moving please."

At Ward's memorial service Alex Anderson eulogized, "When Jay returned to animation in 1959 it was not so much a studio this time, but rather an amusement park for creative cartoonists, copywriters, and special voices, complete with popcorn machine, soda fountain, calliope, and late hours. Jay the number one sports fan was also Jay the number one merry-go-round, circus, and carnival fan. He was blessed with a great appreciation of talent, and he was able to gather a superb team of writers and artists into his theme park. They would unanimously agree they were given great creative freedom. But with one ever present question: Is this idea/this gag/this script going to be 'J-rated'? A 'J-rating'—Jay's stamp of approval—was a nebulous thing. At times it was Victorian enough to make the Hays Office seem like Sodom and Gomorrah. And yet it could [also] appear antiestablishment, iconoclastic,

Publicity drawing representing Jay Ward's immortal cartoon legacy. *Copyright © 1961 by Ward Productions, Inc. Courtesy of Universal Studios Publishing Rights, a Division of Universal Studios Licensing, Inc. All rights reserved.*

and well beyond the fringe. I doubt that Jay could have written down his code; I suspect his judgments were intuitive and spontaneous.

"I do know he had trouble adjusting to the situation of the ethics currently prevalent in business. He had the silly notion that you should be able to take a man at his word. He couldn't understand sacrificing quality for expediency. Wouldn't it be sweeter if the rest of the world was 'J-rated'?"

Hopefully these random impressions go a little way to fleshing out the unique person that was Jay T. Ward, promotional wizard and magnanimous game warden of the singular theme park in which his hilarious shows were brought to life. Ward was evasive and enigmatic, quiet and diffident. At the same time he was one of the most original characters in Hollywood, as colorful as any of his creations. So how best to sum up this chapter? Perhaps one final Jay Ward joke will suffice: Al Burns reminded the congregation gathered for Ward's memorial, "Jay's stunts were great. In the big ticker tape parade for the then returning astronaut John Glenn, Jay had placed a huge sign with Bullwinkle's face on it, and the words 'Welcome Back, Lucky Lindy!' "

22

Well, Bullwinkle, It Looks As If Our Time Has Just About Run Out,

or But, Rock, I Need Retirement Like a Moose Needs a Hat Rack

Recounting the gradual winding down of activity at Jay Ward Productions, Skip Craig noted, "When *Fractured Flickers* ended, the writers started peeling off sometime around 1964. Al Burns had teamed up with Chris Hayward, and while they were still there they were off the payroll sitting around in our little front room, dreaming up live-action shows for Jay. They came up with *The Munsters* (I think they even offered it to Jay first). Another idea was 'Hark the Harold Angel,' which was written with George Gobel in mind. Lloyd Turner stayed on the longest, and left after *George of the Jungle* with his writing partner, Whitey Mitchell.

"We went way over budget on *George*. Jay was in hock for years, but the Quaker commercials helped pay for it. Jay was certainly having fun personally, and his health seemed to be okay for a long time from the middle 1960s. He was enjoying himself, breeding racehorses, and building houses.

"When his son Ron graduated from Harvard Business School, he took an office in Jay's bigger building on Sunset Boulevard. He was in charge of acquisitions; Jay was going to diversify into other businesses, like soda pop bottling and all kinds of things. But nothing much ever happened.

"The later years just kind of petered out. Jay had finally got his merchandising rights back and the Dudley Do-Right Emporium opened in late 1971. We kept doing the [Cap'n] Crunch commercials, but later on the Quaker stuff tapered off—there were less and less. I think it was probably very difficult for Jay to keep the place open and keep the payroll going. I didn't gripe by then, because I wasn't working that much, and I was moonlighting doing freelance track reading for other companies in my spare time, like Farmhouse Productions.

"But there were always folders full of ideas and plans for new shows at the studio. Jay had really wanted to build a dynasty like Hanna-Barbera in the early days. But things sure didn't work out that way."

Later, when Ward lost money on *George of the Jungle*, his interest waned. Bill Hurtz explained, "With the solid contract Jay had with Quaker, there was really no incentive for him to do another series—the broadcasting rules were much tighter in the late sixties and it sounded like a lot more network interference. In the 1970s Jay did some more pilot films, but he was rapidly losing interest in TV shows. He gave the pilots to Lew Keller to direct, and they cost a bundle—but they looked great! Lew took a long time on them, and Jay never kept too tight a rein over him."

Jay produced two new cartoon pilots. These contained some of the finest animation ever to come out of Ward Productions, and were light-years ahead of the competition at the time. They featured funny sight gags which, for once, equaled the verbal humor. Jim Critchfield said, "These films were kind of a group effort; quite a few people had a finger in them."

The first pilot film was called *Hawkear, Frontier Scout,* directed by Lew Keller in 1969. This funny cartoon could have been a series. Hawkear is a scout in the North Woods of the early nineteenth century. Possessed of incredible super-hearing, he is assigned to track down Mrs. Kinkaid's long-lost baby. Fort commander Colonel Busby asks the distraught woman how long her infant has been missing. She answers, "Forty years." The Colonel incredulously retorts, "Forty years? Why didn't you report this before?" She blithely replies, "I thought I'd just mislaid it somewhere." Hawkear is a Dudley Do-Right type who talks in a funny Gary Cooper monotone, courtesy of Daws Butler. In trying to find the baby, Hawkear causes the first Indian uprising in thirty years. Lloyd Turner wrote a hilarious script, although the final draft was by Bill Scott.

Hawkear and his trusted companion, Pierced Arrow.
Courtesy of Ramona Ward and Tiffany Ward and Jay Ward Productions, Inc.

Scott told Jim Korkis, "I wish [*Hawkear* had sold] because it was an era that nobody had yet gotten into doing, which was early America. It was the Davy Crockett period. I didn't like the animation on that segment nor the character design. . . . I really wanted a slow, dull-looking hero. That slightly stupid voice would have just been hilarious, particularly since his faithful Indian companion was the smart one. We played the Indian (Pierced Arrow) like George of the Jungle with that halting talk, but I really wanted to sharpen the Indian up and make him much more a little wise guy who was way out of his time. It did end up being funny because it was a good story. It was the Wappahoe Indians who couldn't use any violence because we were already in that time period where that was becoming unacceptable. As a matter of fact, the Indians couldn't look like Indians but had to look very much like a bunch of extras playing Indians."

Jay followed up with a second cartoon, *Fang, the Wonder (?) Dog,* in 1971. Lloyd Turner struck again with this satire of *Lassie*. The Appleknocker family owns the world's dumbest hound, Fang (certainly the total opposite of Mr. Peabody). The klutzy canine attempts to rescue Grampa Appleknocker and grandson Freddy from an old abandoned mine shaft. The hapless hound wrecks a shop and causes the police and fire brigade to drive their vehicles into the mine pit. Grampa is rescued but ends up in traction in the local hospital. Why? Because Fang used dynamite to get them out of the shaft. The idea for *Fang* was a decade old; in Jay's zany publicity mailers concerning the fictional "Film Series of the Month," George Atkins had proposed a TV series called " 'Fangie,' the heartwarming story of a family and their rabid dog."

Another cartoon which almost got to the production stage was "Captain Cutlass." Skip Craig said, "This was a funny script. The hero was drawn as a kind of Errol Flynn swashbuckler. They shot a storyboard for this, but Jay just kind of forgot about it and it disappeared. The [voice] track was recorded the same day they did *Hawkear*." In the 1970s Lloyd Turner wrote several other scripts which Ward halfheartedly intended to produce. One was "The Lone Masked Man." Turner said, "This was to be *The Lone Ranger* forty years on, and he's now old and fat. He's got the gout and a shrewish wife, and his companion is Toronto the Canadian Indian." Another script he recalled was "Ragnar the Chicken": "This one concerned a cowardly Viking who is so feeble he can't lift the singing sword his blacksmith fashioned for him. He had to fight a villain whose name was Hanna the Barbarian! Jay loved that."

Regrettably, though, Ward's 1970s cartoon pilots never made it to series status. Back in 1959, when *Rocky and His Friends* first aired, animated TV shows were still considered a relatively oddball area, best left to those "eccentric" artists. A decade later, however, the networks knew exactly what they wanted, and Saturday morning cartoons were destined forevermore to be "trendy," or even worse, deliberately trend-setting: chosen by accountants with little love or feeling for the medium, and whose primary concern was demographics (a word Jay Ward would have hated). By then, there were also much tighter rules governing "children's entertainment," especially with the advent of ACT (Action for Children's Television, the watchdog movement formed in late 1968). This aura of New Age seriousness and rulebook production which kowtowed to special interest pressure groups was anathema to Jay Ward, who could never compromise his own standards. As Bill Hurtz told *Mediascene,* "It's terribly difficult to make a Saturday morning show with a limited budget, and it's not something that Jay's particularly interested in doing unless the means are comfortable enough for him to do what he wants to do. So he hasn't gone out and clawed and sacrificed in order to get another show."

Characteristically, Bill Scott's feelings were more bluntly expressed: "For a while animation was on as family material. But then it was squeezed and squeezed into being considered a kiddie medium. So out went satire because no kids were going to get it. Parody went out, and allusion to anything, and puns. They never thought kids would get puns. The networks were only thinking about how much money the shows were going to make in the children's ghetto they were assigning everything to. And Jay was a very thorny person when it came to dealing with the networks as far as quality control. Our new cartoon pilots fell on deaf ears and stony hearts."

But the slowdown in animation activity didn't herald a stanstill of creativity at the Ward studio. Far from it, in fact. Apart from the fine animated pilots and the ongoing Quaker commercial assignments, there were several intermittent bursts of new production. In 1971, Dudley Do-Right and Nell appeared in two funny commercials for United Bank; two years later the redoubtable Mountie did some cute radio spots, with Bullwinkle as co-spokesmoose, for his own shop, Dudley Do-Right's Emporium. This now-famous memorabilia shop was suggested by Ron Ward. Jim Critchfield worked with Jay on the concept, and the design of the building was handled by old faithfuls Sam Clayberger and Chris Jenkyns. Twenty-nine years on the store is still open and going strong.

During the 1970s Jay Ward produced commercials for several new clients, including a series of funny spots for Shakey's Pizza. Skip Craig says, "Jay and Critch dreamed up these oddball projects. The Shakey spots were done on TV and radio using some incredibly authentic Spike Jones City Slickers–type music. I hadn't even known they were planning this. Joe Siracusa did the arrangements with the other guys and he put the music together. He used George Probert from the Firehouse Five Plus Two, as well as Spike's original musicians George Rock, Phil Gray, and Joe himself. The TV spot featured Joe E. Ross from *Car 54, Where Are You*? He was dressed up in a pink tutu with a fairy wand as the Shakey Fairy. The radio spots were terrific, and the music is very Spike Jones-ish; I loved it!

"They did some other Shakey commercials featuring big sports names like Wilt Chamberlain and Jerry West from the Lakers. They did a kind of blue-screen [special-effects techinque] thing showing the pizza going through

Wilt's body. Jerry West was in one of them but he didn't enjoy the experience at all—in fact, he was really standoffish, as though this stupid thing was completely beneath his dignity." Famed jockey Willie Shoemaker, who rode for Jay's Bullwinkle Stables, appeared in another Shakey's spot.

The best TV commercial Jay Ward produced never made it to air. This was a fine-looking spot for Bubble-Up. Lloyd Turner recalled, "One day Jay came to me and said he wanted me to write it and direct it, and even do all the casting. So I wrote a Western-type thing and we employed Andy Devine and Doodles Weaver, and we filmed them as two really incompetent cavalry guys up in the fort, with arrows sticking through their hats—they were being attacked by Indians." Skip Craig remembered this as "Funny stuff! During the Indian attack we cut in *Fractured Flickers*–type shots. We shot the commercial in a small studio on Pico Boulevard, and Critch and Lloyd were down there for the filming.

"At the end of the spot they spent a whole day shooting these beauty pack-shots of a Bubble-Up bottle with glamorous backlighting—really a stunning-looking shot. But Jay picked out the one shot he loved: an old beat-up can of Bubble-Up with an arrow through it pouring into a glass which overflowed. The drink was spilling all over, and he said, 'That's the shot we're going to use! Well, the client was horrified—they wanted the glamour shot to accompany this mellifluous voice-over. But Jay said, 'No way, I want to put the funny overflow shot in the commercial!' The client said no, so Jay said he wouldn't finish them. And that's what happened; they'd got to the work-print stage, but they were never finished. Len Key was the contact on that, I believe." (True enough: Jay's old crony Leonard Key was an executive with Bubble-Up at the time.)

Bill Scott produced a couple of commercials for various causes like the Mental Health foundation, using Ward Productions facilities. Then in 1974, he began work on several new compilation live-action films for release by Ward Productions. These were along the lines of the earlier *Crazy World of Laurel and Hardy*. Taking advantage of his passion for classic motion-picture comedy, Bill wrote, narrated, and assembled some fascinating retrospectives on comedians Buster Keaton (*The Golden Age of Buster Keaton*), W. C. Fields (*The Vintage W. C. Fields*), and Robert Benchley (*Those Marvelous Benchley Shorts*). All featured lengthy and representative film clips, along with nice cartoon links animated by some of Ward's favorite artists, like Phil Duncan and Ben Washam. The Keaton films, deposited years earlier in Ward's vault by Raymond Rohauer, were simply too good to leave gathering dust, while the rights to further comedy films had slowly been acquired by Ward. As Bill Hurtz explained, "Jay had purchased the old films as an investment."

These compilation features were lovingly completed by Scott and Skip Craig over several years. Skip remembered, "Bill and I didn't have a real system, it was pretty loose. He'd come in most days and run the films on a Moviola, and smoke up the place with those cigars of his, which I hated. He'd just mark a roll of film and yell for me, and I'd do whatever he requested: sometimes he'd switch the sound track for an effect, and he'd theme the pieces of film. The first one was the W. C. Fields movie. There was a sequence in there that no one had seen for thirty years from *Tales of Manhattan*.* We finished it, but our Fields film never played; we'd done some little animated bridges in which Bill imitated Field's voice. But the Fields estate wouldn't allow it to be released; of course, Jay refused to take the bridges out, so that was that.

"With the Keaton material we did *The Golden Age,* which was split into two features. They played a lot in England. The second one, called *Three Shorts,* consisted of *The Paleface* [1922], *The High Sign* [1921], and *One Week* [1920]—it was pretty much just the three stuck together, and linked by Bill's narration. Joe Siracusa did the music, and again he used some Spike Jones people like George Rock; he got these authentic 1912-era pit band scores from Milt Larsen [proprietor of the Magic Castle and Variety Arts Library] and these were real silent-movie scores. They were recorded and interspersed with original piano tracks composed by Johnny Guarnieri.

"Then we did the best of our live-action films—Keaton's feature *The General* [1927]. This time we got the full-aperture fine-grain print from MGM, and it was beautiful quality. Rich Harrison put in the sound effects, and Joe did the music again. We recorded some narration, but we hardly had to touch the film—except we took out most of the dialogue cards, and stuck in some maps and explanatory things. It was a gorgeous picture, and I actually got to fix a tiny cut that Keaton had goofed on—he used to cut all his own pictures. It played recently on HBO.

"The last one we did was the Benchley feature, but that didn't sell. It wasn't really that interesting, and Jay didn't like it as much as the others.

*Fields's portion in this 1942 Fox film had been deleted from the original feature, and was presumed lost to the ages. But in 1996 the complete feature was finally released on video.

We shortened some things, tightened up the films, and added a little animation. This one was fairly easy because they were sound films so they already had their own music; I just think nobody wanted it. Of course, all during the making of these films we still had a pretty heavy schedule of Cap'n Crunch commercials."

In 1974, another project was begun which didn't see a sale. A one-minute animated pilot for a proposed show called "The Lighter Side of American History" was narrated by Jay Ward himself. This was intended to be a series of short animated spots, in the style of a nutty *Bicentennial Minutes*. Skip Craig: "Jay was planning to do fifty-two of these for the Bicentennial TV season [1975–76]; they used cutout pictures from history books." Bill Scott played Abe Lincoln for this pilot, quoting some of that president's bons mots.

In 1977, Scott compiled a series of humorous scenes from great MGM films for a project called "That's Comedy." This film, too, was never completed; the premise involved employing several modern-day comedy names to introduce clips of the older funsters (for example, Mel Brooks on the Marx Brothers, Marty Feldman on Laurel and Hardy, and Chevy Chase on the great supporting comic actors). Skip: "We had the film in work-print form, and for a long time all the different clips of film sat in our front room. But MGM wouldn't like it, so we'd take it back and recut the thing, then they'd complain again. So it never was finished. Tom Stanford, who'd worked on *Crusader Rabbit* years before, came back to cut that one.

"In 1978 Ron Ward went into business with a Harvard classmate in Washington, selling a commodity-trading program. Gradually most of the people still at the studio got into this, to varying degrees. Jay and I were into it the heaviest and I think we spent more time watching Channel 22's financial reports than we did on the Cap'n Crunch commercials. We were dealing in some serious money there for a while!"

Meantime, various portmanteau films featuring the output of Jay Ward Productions were assembled. One of these, put together by Bill Scott, was called *The Nuthouse*. Not to be confused with their 1963 TV comedy pilot of the same name, this featured older clips like a "Fractured Fairy Tale," a piece from *Watts Gnu*, some "Flicker Songs," and some hilarious animated blackouts directed by Bill Hurtz and Jim Hiltz. (Originally made by Ward as a demo reel, the blackouts were picked up for CBS's *The Garry Moore Show*.) Scott used *The Nuthouse* excerpt reel at the various nationwide and Canadian college lectures at which he spoke.

Other compilations included *Jay Ward's Intergalactic Film Festival* (this was the earliest one, made as a supporting feature for road-show engagements of the Laurel and Hardy movie), *Jay Ward Movie Madness, The Jay Ward Total Catharsis, Retrospective and Revue* (intended as a TV special) and *Jay Ward's Film Festival*. The latter was a ninety-minute show packaged by Clem Williams Films for the college circuit, and contained the complete "Wossamotta U" *Bullwinkle Show* adventure interspersed with many other P.A.T.-Ward cartoons.

Ward's classic characters from the General Mills heyday were put into occasional storyboards which, sadly, never sold. One of the first was a fine script by Bill Scott called "Elementary, My Dear Rocky." This was a combination entertainment-educational story about nutrition. Written in 1976, it was intended to be a half-hour cartoon special featuring Rocky and Bullwinkle. The moose and squirrel meet a worm named Woodrow who takes them on an adventure through the human body, as in the 1966 movie *Fantastic Voyage*. Mr. Peabody shows up to assist our heroes, and the requisite intense dramatic conflict is supplied by our old nemeses Boris and Natasha. Scott even composed some Tom Lehrer–like patter songs for this project.

Animation historian Charles Solomon noted that Bullwinkle's ongoing popularity in reruns led ABC to discuss a possible revival of the characters for a special. Ward and Scott considered some ideas based on unconventional holidays. Scott said, "Every so often someone in the lower echelons of TV would become tumescent about the thought of reviving Rocky and Bullwinkle. Our sales force asked us to do holiday specials like those of Rankin-Bass, so that they could be repeated every year. We thought of maybe inventing our own holiday, like Millard Fillmore's birthday, or an April IRS show. Then there were a couple of other ideas thrown around, like a Bullwinkle Valentine's Day special. Finally we thought we'd spoof the event that's the biggest event of them all, the Super Bowl."

This idea became *The Stupor Bowl,* written by Scott and developed with Alex Anderson (who did the storyboard) in 1980. It was to be a one-hour animated special in the spirit of the famous "Wossamotta U" football saga. Rocky and Bullwinkle of the Frostbite Falls Fumblers were pitted against Boris and Natasha's Pottsylvanian team, and even the intrepid Dudley Do-Right was called on to assist our pals.

Scott recalled, "This was a pretty funny show, a good pilot, and we shot straight storyboards. It was very well received. We got a lot of support at ABC, until somebody made the mistake of checking with the NFL. And they didn't like it, particularly as we had personified the owners as stupid

Coda

The fact that Jay Ward's TV series are still popular at the start of a new millenium is cause to celebrate: with reading skills in sharp decline, younger audiences badly need a few more TV shows which not only entertain but also exercise the gray matter a little. It is also highly encouraging to see sharply written cartoon shows like *The Simpsons, Animaniacs*, and even the gross-out excesses of *The Ren & Stimpy Show* and *Southpark* emerging from the bottomless quagmire of mindless action-adventure series which ran rampant throughout the 1970s and 1980s. TV animation has begun looking better, and is gaining a newfound respect, for the first time in years. Most happily, it seems that wit has finally made a comeback.

Research indicates that the present generation of children has been inundated with so much rapid cutting and video-clip-style television that they are endangering their ability to concentrate for extended periods. The sad truth is that the world is much more blasé today than in 1961. Computerization, MTV, unceasing high-tech bombardment: there's far less concentration time in these hectic days, far more junk-filled TV channels available, and way too many demographically targeted cartoons that are often toys before they're TV shows (e.g., *Transformers, GI Joe,* "and all that other repressed, disturbing crap," in the characteristically colorful words of design artist Al Shean). Part of this equation is sheer technological progress. Unfortunately, the flip side has often boiled down to a profit-motivated disregard for viewers' sensibilities: the famous lowest common denominator keeps sinking lower.

As a result, youngsters of Y2K—an era marked by today's disposal of yesterday's hot fad—got bored rather quickly with the more stately tempo of many older TV shows and movies, depriving them of a sense of tradition, let alone of even recent history. Fortunately, this is not the case with "Rocky and Bullwinkle," whose breathlessly fast cartoons are perfectly suited to today's "now you see it, now you don't" pace. The quality dialogue in Jay Ward's shows, at one time considered subversive, engenders a healthy sense of parody in younger viewers who are exposed so much to a medium once rightly dubbed "chewing gum for the eyes." In this sense Rocky and Bullwinkle, already ancient compared to the similarly satirical *The Simpsons* and *South Park*, have indeed proved that they were way ahead of their time.

Put another way. What other TV cartoon show gave us a fairy tale about a naive wolf who is talked into bumping off his own grandmother by an amoral young woman named Red, who sells riding hoods and furs in a Rodeo Drive boutique. With the implied moral: Young wolves must watch out for Hollywood girls. Outrageous, groaningly funny, and pure Jay Ward.

and venal: they were caricatured in our version as a Hugh Herbert giggler, a sexy Mae West type, the Godfather, and Red Skelton's Mean Widdle Kid. These team owners were ready to do anything to win, so Boris is hired to fix the game. Boris disguises himself as Knute Knock-Knee, and Natasha was the world's only Israeli football coach, Oy Vay Simpson!" The NFL threatened that if the show went into production they would take legal action against the eventual sponsor. As Scott told Solomon, "After that it just died. We didn't even get a no." Animation scholar Karl Cohen put it in a nutshell when he wrote, "Ward's specials were just too offbeat for the conservative television industry, and none were made."

One final cartoon pilot salvaged Jay's beloved college-football formula. This was *Rah Rah Woozy,* directed by Lew Keller. Set at ivy-covered Woozy State College, this film stars two lab animals, Morey Mouse and Hamilton Hamster. The brilliant mouse feels sorry for football coach Weepy Mudbank, who has lost every game for thirty years. Morey invents a radio-controlled football, so that the outcome of the big game between Woozy and Wrecker Tech is assured. This last cartoon made by Jay Ward Productions is a fitting close. The limited animation works beautifully, and the pace is excellent, with many rapid-fire gags. As usual, the writing and voice work are flawless. Bill Scott recalled, "Alex Anderson wrote that one and I rewrote it heavily."

The year 1980 also saw an attempt to revive Bullwinkle for a new weekly TV series. As Bill Scott noted, "Now ABC has the hots to do a new Bullwinkle show." The concept involved a mix of the best of the old cartoons with Jay Ward's newer characters from his unsold pilots. Bullwinkle narrated a presentation film, *The New Bullwinkle Show*. It proposed a one-hour TV series to feature, as before, two "Rocky" episodes, along with "Fractured Fairy Tales," "Dudley Do-Right," "Fang, the Wonder Dog," "Super Chicken," "George of the Jungle" (introduced by the moose as "The pride

Dudley Do-Right's Emporium

In 1969 a full-page ad appeared in *Life* magazine announcing the availability of Bullwinkle and Dudley Do-Right wristwatches. Reaction was sensational: almost overnight every last one of the timepieces sold out. It was enough to convince Ron and Jay Ward to open a specialty character shop. What was once the Plush Pup hot-dog stand had declined into seediness. Ramona Ward recalled, "The site had been a very successful indoor-outdoor restaurant until motorcycle gangs overran it. Jay bought out the lease just to help out the neighborhood, and to do something that wouldn't draw such a crowd."

The ultimate mecca for Ward's legion of fans opened its door, cheek by jowl with a fun-house mirror, in late 1971. Dudley Do-Right's Emporium, a souvenir shop—but in essence a Bullwinkle museum—located at 8200 Sunset Boulevard, was ready for business. It boasted a catalog perfectly in sync with the nuttiness of Ward's old cartoons. Jay wanted "high-quality character-oriented merchandise not available in stores" and proclaimed that his little shop was "the rich man's Nieman-Marcus!" It was housed in a small Caribbean-style building, with giant pink "goony birds" on the roof. Why Caribbean? Ward explained, "We didn't want to hurt George of the Jungle's feelings, even though Dudley got his name on the building."

It had been three years since *George of the Jungle* ceased production, and by 1971, Ward, with a still-busy schedule of Quaker cereal commercials, decided to stick mainly to merchandising souvenirs and products based on his family of kooky characters rather than embarking on any new series (as we have seen, he made a few cartoon pilots but, aware that TV was now riddled with regulations, didn't push them hard). The Dudley store was always low-profile—Ward never advertised, and to this day it's open only three days a week.

Dudley Do-right's Emporium sells copies of some original "Rocky and Bullwinkle" scripts, storyboards, and publicity biographies for the main characters. A big seller is the hand-painted scene cels, which can cost as much as $600; collectible cels are big business today, but it's amusing to look back at the catalogs from two decades ago: in those days some of the same cels cost a mere $9.95. How times have changed.

There are colorful character decals, T-shirts, games, music cassettes, pins, bendable dolls, buttons, notepaper, cards, magnets, and badges, as well as the sturdily reliable Hamilton watches, with Bullwinkle and company adorning the watch faces. Originally there were T-shirts featuring Buster Keaton and W. C. Fields, along with Wilt Chamberlain. Ward explained, "*Fractured Flickers* used Keaton and W. C. Fields. So we have an affinity for them. Wilt used to come in here, so we thought it would be kind of fun to sell tank tops emblazoned with his face, too." Ward was constantly paying tribute to his beloved Los Angeles Lakers basketball team.

Over the years the emporium offered some truly wacky items, especially in the early days. The 1974 catalog featured a Super Chicken airplane kit ($2,600), a week of golf lessons with Arnold Palmer at Pebble Beach ($999), a correspondence animation course ($400) and Bullwinkle valet bags, sheets, and pajamas. Under "Erotica," buyers could obtain Natasha's "Evening in Pasadena" spray perfume or Dudley's "Old Saddle Leather" shave and spray deodorant sets ("for men who want to smell like the Old West"). There were arcane books, recordings of the Moosylvania songs, Dudley Do-Right Stetsons, a genuine Swiss army knife, a "Watergate" paper shredder, bird cages, postcards, and cassettes of genuine old-time radio shows. And for twenty-five bucks you could get Jay and his staff to plan your next party for you. Strangest item: orange crates with roller skates attached.

Probably the most reliable items are the T-shirts with iron-on gags in the spirit of the cartoons. There are shirts plugging "Wossamotta U" and "Mr. Peabody's Private School for the Extremely Clever," and iron-ons with Snidely Whiplash declaring, "It's hard to think straight when you have a crooked mind," Natasha's "Kiss me, Dahlink," and Super Chicken's old adage, "You knew the job was dangerous when you took it!"

Twenty nine years on, the merchandise remains excellent, attractive, and guaranteed to create word-of-mouth. New high-quality merchandise of Bullwinkle and company is now on sale at Universal's theme parks in Hollywood and Orlando, Florida, but, of course, all items remain available at our favorite Mountie's faithful old trading post, Dudley Do-Right's Emporium.

of Tarzana and points east"), and "Rah Rah Woozy" ("contains more school spirit than the dean's hip flask!"). Two years earlier Scott had written new single episodes featuring Rocky, Peabody, Dudley, and a "Fractured Fairy Tale" for just such a revival.

Around this time it was announced that the great Warner Brothers ani-

mator Friz Freleng would produce the new *Bullwinkle* series using the facilities of DePatie-Freleng Productions. Scott told interviewer Jim Korkis, "Jay had said he might be interested in having Friz produce the cartoons if we could write the stuff and keep the creative control. But that's as far as it went. It never got to rights. It never got to any commitment." Alas, *The New Bullwinkle Show* didn't get off the ground.

After 1981, things slowed considerably at Jay Ward Productions. The Quaker commercial assignments shrank in volume, while actors Daws Butler and Paul Frees suffered bad reverses in their health. Ward concentrated more and more on the merchandising of his bevy of characters (he could often be found behind the counter at Dudley Do-Right's Emporium). During the previous several years he had sold character licensing rights to various manufacturers of watches, T-shirts, and so on. Newspaper reports in the mid-1980s described Ward spending his time reading, having lunch with a couple of his cronies, doing a little business, and "eating jelly beans ordered from far-flung beaneries around the world." Most of which was true, according to Skip Craig, "except the last part: the jelly beans really came all the way from Burbank, where there was a shop that carried every flavor under the sun."

But Ward continued planning new films to the end of his life. As Craig noted, "Jay was still hopeful that the live-action films were going to make big money, but they never did. Right at the end he was in negotiations to extend his rights to Laurel and Hardy, which he still considered a viable property. And earlier he was planning to do something with the Douglas Fairbanks movie *The Black Pirate* [1926] and a Salvador Dali movie which Roger [Donley] did some work on. He also had the Fred Allen film *It's in the Bag!* [1945], and the one with [W. C.] Fields and Jane Powell called *Song of the Open Road* [1944], but these projects never got started."

The year 1983 saw the opening of a chain of electrified-entertainment pizza parlors called Bullwinkle's Family Food 'n' Fun Restaurants. Alex Anderson remembered, "This was originally Paul Frees's idea. He approached Jay and said he wanted to open a restaurant to be themed around Bullwinkle and the others. I went to discuss it with Paul at his home in Tiburon." Ward and Peter Piech licensed the characters for these diners, which originally featured audio-animatronic versions of Rocky, Bullwinkle, Boris, Natasha, Dudley, and Snidely, as well as Piech's Total TV characters like Tooter Turtle, Tennessee Tuxedo and Chumley, and Underdog. As the customers ate their food, which included dishes like "Bullwinkle's Famoose Pizza" or "Dudley Do-Right's Done-Right Pizza," they watched the characters performing new scripts and songs written by the ever-prolific Bill Scott. The establishments also featured gift shops carrying a range of rare character merchandise, and there were large games rooms. The first restaurant opened in San Jose.

Corey Burton, one of the best of the new generation of Hollywood's cartoon voice specialists, got to work with his childhood idols re-creating some voices for this project. He recalled, "The voice tracks were recorded on May 21, 1982, at Jennifudy Studios. Bill Scott and June Foray did their characters and stripped away twenty years in an instant as they began reading. Serendipity and déjà vu: Rocky and Bullwinkle lived again!" He got to meet the designer-builders of the animatronics. These were Jim Wells and his team at the Only Animated Design and Display Company in North Hollywood, who disclosed they were all dropouts from Walt Disney who had grown tired of restrictions. While they still worked for Disney, either individually or from this outfit, they now got to call all the shots. "The quality of construction and animation they did surpassed even current Disney art of 1982," said Burton. "We were spellbound by these gentle, creative artisans."

Regrettably, several of the restaurants flopped. But not for want of trying, as Peter Piech remembered: "Jay and I both admitted this idea went nowhere, but we were very enthused at first. Jay kept saying, 'Come on, let's go on this.' " Skip Craig, however, saw it differently: "That's not true. Jay was never really that keen about this sort of thing even though he always went along with it. But the deal was lousy—a thirty-year deal which netted Jay peanuts; he really wanted to get out of it." By the late 1990s only a handful of the diners remained.

Meanwhile Jay Ward Productions had also closed. Skip Craig recalled, "We quit production in the fall of '84. The Dudley store did some business, and there was a fair bit of mail order. After we stopped doing the commercials Jay, very generously, said I could use my cutting room as long as I wanted to—in fact he gave it to me, equipment and all. He knew that I had lots of offers to do freelance track reading, and I think he liked to have a little company—someone to talk to. I also brought him his beloved Jelly Bellies from Burbank. So from late '84 till he died, about five years, it was just the two of us, although Bill Hurtz, Lew, and Critch would pop in for lunch at Greenblatts Deli, as in days gone by. I'm still at it in 1999, doing all the TV series, for Disney TV animation, Pooh specials, and the features, both big screen and direct to video. Ironically on the first series, *The Gummi Bears,* June and Bill were reunited doing Grammi and Gruffi Gummi, and Bill was Toady as well. When he died, Corey Burton took over his voices—perfectly! I remember calling Jay in to my editing room to listen to Corey doing Scott's voices. Jay was actually shaken," and finally said, 'That's eerie—it's Bill.' "

In 1985 Rocky and Bullwinkle finally reappeared on TV in a slickly made commercial for Hershey's kisses, in which they revived their old "rabbit out of a hat" shtick. Sadly, it was to be the last time Bill Scott spoke for Bullwinkle. The spot, directed by Sam Cornell and beautifully animated by Chris Rush, made one wish that the old P.A.T. TV episodes had sported this visual quality.

When Bill Scott died on the Thanksgiving weekend of 1985, it was the end of a brilliant twenty-seven-year partnership. Bill Hurtz wrote, "Scott came into his own [at Ward Productions], writing wildly funny stuff with no censorship and no other egos to contend with. With Jay's complete respect, he was his own man. . . . There were other writers, very good ones on the shows, but all their scripts went through Bill for skillful editing and polishing."

An assiduous worker, Scott remained above all else an animation enthusiast. His work was abidingly enjoyable to him: a year before he died he said, "I have the best job in the world. James Thurber once said that even the most pleasurable of occupations would cloy in time. Well, it hasn't for me. Animation can do anything; it can be anything. It is an art form whose potential has barely been tapped. In spite of the fact that I've been in it for forty years, I have a feeling that the medium still needs to be explored and widened, and people still need to know much more about it."

Writing was his other love. Bill Scott asserted that words, whether for reading or writing, had always been an important influence in his life. "I am passionately fond of the English language. I'm a voracious reader. I'm always looking for the felicitous phrase or the perfect pun. I love puns." A quick glance at the first two hundred or so *Bullwinkle* chapter titles listed in this book's episode guide will demonstrate the quality of the groaners he could produce.

His thoughts on writing for animation were expressed eloquently in his many college lectures. Scott had been doing these talks since 1959, when he screened a "Fractured Fairy Tale" at UCLA for a group of students and professionals (including Chuck Jones) and received a tumultuous response. He continued on the college circuit until his untimely death of heart failure on November 29, 1985—just when he and Dorothy were planning a round-the-world trip.

As Lloyd Turner recalled, "It seems like I knew Bill from the 1940s and was in touch until the day he died. Jay called me and said, 'Master Scott has gone.' It was like being hit on the head with a baseball bat. He never got sick and always seemed such a healthy guy. I had nothing but the greatest respect for Bill. He was a highly intelligent guy and he breathed more life into Jay's cartoons than anyone else."

Within the animation field, Bill Scott was regarded by these others as a creative wizard. Lew Keller said, "Bill was immensely prolific. I would put him in the genius range—his IQ was brilliant. And his puns were masterful." Al Burns told the *Los Angeles Times,* "The animation business is strange, but Jay's imprimatur was even stranger. Bill Scott, too, was an incredibly free spirit, and an intelligent man that everyone adored." In evaluating his body of work it's not unsafe to use the word "brilliant," in an industry used to hearing that devalued term on a daily basis.

Scott spent over thirty years writing and acting in community-theater works. At the ASIFA testimonial Bill Hurtz noted, "The most fun he has may be directing and acting together with Dorothy in a theatrical company known as the Church of the Ascension Players. He has done a number of good works for people down on their luck. He would kill me for mentioning them. It would spoil his image." He was also a member of the Board of Governors of the Motion Picture Academy; president of the Hollywood wing of ASIFA; a member of the TV Academy and the NAACP; a soloist with the Canada Savoy, Ltd., Gilbert and Sullivan Troupe (he sang beautifully—it's noticeable in the cartoon); and a retired major in the U.S. Air Force Reserve. A civil rights and antiwar activist (his son John called him "a screaming lefty"), Scott wrote a regular newspaper column for his local Tujunga, California, paper.

As that other Bill put it, one man in his time plays many parts. But perhaps it's enough to quote writer-artist Chris Jenkyns: "Bill was a prince, and surely the nicest guy in the animation business."

Jay Ward lost any remaining interest in creative production without Scott around. Paul Frees died less than a year later on the morning of November 2, 1986, following a few years of health problems. To Jay the fun of cartoon making was gone forever: Scott was now yelling "Shut up, Paul!" in that big recording booth in the sky.

Ironically, Bill Scott passed away just as a major revival of interest in the characters began stirring. He had seen it coming, however: in August 1980, a Jay Ward tribute was held at the Motion Picture Academy with Scott and Hans Conried as speakers. In just a few years these tributes had proliferated. A series of film festivals was held around the country featuring tributes to the Ward studio, including the first of several put together, with Jay's official blessing, by Jeffrey Fuerst at New York's Museum of Broadcasting (now the Museum of Television and Radio) in 1986. This tribute ran all summer. In March 1987, Bill Hurtz and June Foray appeared at the Los Angeles County Museum for a question-answer session at "Rocky and Bullwinkle and Friends: A Tribute to Jay Ward." And in 1987, Jay granted permission for the Seattle Children's Theatre to stage a hit *Rocky and Bullwinkle* musical, faithfully adapted from the cartoons.

Late 1986 also saw the first issue of an unofficial Jay Ward fanzine-newsletter called *The Frostbite Falls Far-Flung Flyer* (borrowed from the name of a newspaper in the Bullwinkle "Ruby Yacht" story). On the tiniest of budgets, editor-founder Charles Ulrich produced a scholarly and erudite journal which overflowed with Ward minutiae and fun Bullwinkle trivia. Over its twelve-year run it became a reliable reference source as well. Ulrich maintains a "Frostbite Falls" page on the Internet.

In 1988 the Walt Disney Company—itself the butt of several good-humored jibes from Ward Productions over the years—purchased home video rights to the complete library of P.A.T.-Ward "Rocky and Bullwinkle" half-hour TV shows. Following several delays, twelve volumes were released by Buena Vista Home Video beginning in February 1991. Sales were instantly phenomenal; in fact, downright record-breaking would be more accurate. The shows chosen were painstakingly restored, with the happy result that the old TV shows had never looked better.*

Besides the video releases and Nick at Nite and Cartoon Network screenings, our Frostbite Falls stalwarts have been in a few new animated commercials for such clients as Target, Taco Bell, and Eveready batteries, featuring fine-looking animation from Kurtz and Friends. This Burbank-based company had great credentials: founder Bob Kurtz began as a young designer for Jay Ward thirty years earlier, when he worked on *George of the Jungle.*

Jay Ward's health began failing in late 1987. Skip Craig explained, "In his last couple of years Jay had started to feel consistently poorly. I knew he wasn't feeling that good because he'd always loved sports, and his biggest enjoyment was going to the Lakers games, and the Dodgers. Now he stopped going. I was his sports friend and it surprised me when he even gave me his beloved Dodgers tickets. He found that he'd contracted cancer that had started in his kidney.

"All those months leading up to his operation he had begun feeling lousy. We used to sit around and say we both hoped we went like Bill Scott: have a quick heart attack and go fast like that, not slowly with cancer. So it was a real shame that Jay lingered."

Ward died in his Los Angeles home on October 12, 1989. Happily, he had lived to see the revival of interest in his most famous duo, Rocky and Bullwinkle. Following his death, his daughter Tiffany revealed, "He felt very good about the shows he created, and that even thirty years later people were watching them. There have been a lot of film festivals in the last four or

*Not too successful, unfortunately, was the 1992 release of the long-awaited film *Boris and Natasha,* starring David Thomas and Sally Kellerman in the title roles. Five years, countless script drafts, and budget problems plagued this movie, which was produced by Kellerman's husband, Jonathan Krane. The result simply wasn't that funny, lacking the intangible Ward magic, even though the subject matter was ripe for a potential comedy classic. It would have been a perfect project for the *Naked Gun* team, who know how to do parody. But to most true buffs, the absence of Rocky and Bullwinkle seemed conceptually askew. As a review in *The Frostbite Falls Far-Flung Flier* summed up, it was akin to making a movie about Wile E. Coyote and excluding the Road Runner. (The same conceptual problems affected the disappointing *Dudley Do-Right* movie in 1999.)

five years." Jay had chosen the material for these; Tiffany Ward observed, "He knew exactly what pieces he wanted. He had an unbelievably sharp brain, and a fabulous memory."

Fearless Leader Ward was gone. One of the most singular figures in the history of animation, his legacy (including over eight hundred individual cartoons) is a monument to good taste and sheer hilarity, and represents the pinnacle of television cartoon comedy. As the saying goes, we shall never see anything quite like them again.

An original drawing for this book by Alex Anderson, creator of Rocky and Bullwinkle, and Dudley Do-Right

BUT WAIT! MOOSE AND SQUIRREL ENTER NEW MILLENNIUM

In June 1991 Jay Ward Productions signed with MCA, then parent company of Universal, granting merchandising, theme-park, and publishing rights to the entertainment giant. After tidying up various legal affairs and establishing a bevy of licensees, Ward Productions, with Jay's daughter Tiffany as manager, is now back in business. One of her first big coups was licensing the klutzy king of the jungle, George.

In July 1997, the Walt Disney Company released their hit feature film *George of the Jungle*. Happily, it retained much of the flavor of Jay's old cartoon series, and was genuinely funny.

Meantime, Ward Productions and Universal Studios have exciting long-range plans for the great Jay Ward stable of cartoon stars.

In 1998 Universal green-lighted two feature films, *Dudley Do-Right of the Mounties* (starring *George's* Brendan Fraser) and *The Rocky and Bullwinkle Movie*. The latter is a big-budget (almost $90 million) feature containing state-of-the-art visual effects by Industrial Light and Magic. In this film, Boris, Natasha, and Fearless Leader are transformed from animated into human form, represented by Jason Alexander, Rene Russo, and Robert De Niro. (Indeed, it is De Niro's production company, Tribeca, that coproduced the film with Universal.) Naturally, Rocky and Bullwinkle are brought out of retirement by the FBI to defeat their old nemeses once more. The truly zany script contains many references to the old cartoons, and this author was both honored and delighted to be cast as the voices of both Bullwinkle and the William Conrad narrator.

In addition, new animated shorts (such as a "Fractured Fairy Tale," from an unproduced Bill Scott script) will accompany these movies. There is also a wide range of new character merchandise and a growing list of international licensees. Plans are now afoot for animated holiday specials and a possible revival of the moose and squirrel in TV series form.

Also in the television arena, Ward Productions spent three years (1995–1998) restoring all the original film elements. Every one of the classic cartoons now looks brand-new, and all the old audio problems have finally been digitally corrected. Universal TV has signed distribution deals with some twenty countries to air this sparkling new set of 160 half-hour shows, ensuring that *Rocky and Bullwinkle & Friends* (the package's title) will be known to new generations worldwide.

At Universal Studios, Florida, the splendid new cartoon character attraction Islands of Adventure features "Dudley Do-Right's Ripsaw Falls" flume ride; again, your humble author, having worked on the ride's sound track, can attest to its accuracy in capturing the melodramatic feel of the old "Dudley" cartoons.

The classic Jay Ward characters have even appeared in commercials on the Internet, winning the creators, Gadfly Communications, an award from Internet World. With still more plans ahead, it appears that Jay Ward Productions intends for our favorite moose and squirrel to enter the twenty-first century with a bang, sassy and satirical as ever.

APPENDIX 1

A WHO'S WHO OF JAY WARD PRODUCTIONS

Through the various interviews conducted for this book there was virtually unanimous opinion on the topic of being an employee at Jay Ward Productions. Although thirty-five years have passed since the busiest period (1959–65), the writers who left for bigger projects—not to mention far bigger salaries—still speak glowingly of their days at Sunset and Havenhurst. So do the artists: director-designer Bill Hurtz summed his boss up for *Mediascene:* "Jay's real genius was as a producer. He has a marvelous instinct for show business and he loves funny stuff. And he's completely dedicated to that."

It was noted in more than one "Bullwinkle" newspaper piece that though the pay was never top dollar and staff were packed into a cramped working space, the casual and lighthearted atmosphere at Jay Ward's seemed to keep everyone happy and content. As Bill Scott told *ADvertising Age,* "We have no taboos here. Everything goes." In 1981 he said, "The joy of working with Jay was freedom. You see, he trusted writers, and he trusted me very much. So that whatever I did, he thought it was funny. And of course that was the catchword. If it was funny, we'd do it. And if we ran into trouble or arguments or any resistance from the networks or the sponsor, or whomever, Jay would immediately go to bat for you, and I mean he'd really lay it on the line. He supported his creative people all the way through."

THE WRITERS

It goes without saying that the verbal humor in Jay Ward's cartoons is their chief attraction. Jay invariably told reporters, "We're a writing studio." Describing his writers for a 1961 radio interview, he quipped, "We keep a couple of peasants bound in the basement. Every once in a while we bring them up and beat them. They come up with some very funny material!" Bill Scott, the head writer and essentially Ward's coproducer, gets a full chapter to himself. But a superb team of resident supporting scribes was responsible for much of the hilarity, and they now get to speak for and about themselves.

Allan Burns An Emmy award–winning comedy writer, and latterly the coproducer of such TV megahits as *The Mary Tyler Moore Show, Rhoda,* and *Lou Grant,* Al Burns spoke fondly of his years with Jay Ward. Born in 1936, Burns began as an NBC page. He wrote comedy as a sideline, including material for Jonathan Winters in 1957. Burns recalled, "Having failed to make the slightest dent in the world of situation comedy, I spent three years designing and drawing greeting cards for the Kardko and Gibson companies. Meantime I'd visit all the animation houses seeking writing jobs—UPA, Disney, Filmfair, Pantomime. But I was never successful at a full-time job. Most days I'd work on the greeting cards, then mope around wondering whether I should have finished architecture school. Then I'd watch TV.

"One day I happened to catch a show called *Rocky and His Friends,* and after seeing the credits and the name Ward Productions, I grabbed my screwed-up portfolio full of my stuff and went there unannounced. I was having a bit of trouble with the receptionist, when a roundish balding man walked in and, hearing of my dilemma, started chuckling. I didn't know who he was. He asked to see some of my work. Then this nice man proceeded to laugh at every one of my drawings. I felt my spirits rising, then he chuckled again and asked what I wanted. When I told him I was after a writing job, he said, 'Okay,' and just like that I was hired. And that was my first meeting with Jay Ward!"

Ward teamed Allan Burns with George Atkins, and they were put to work creating publicity mailers ("Weekly ones, the wilder the better; this was a six-month blitz before *The Bullwinkle Show* started"). Later, Burns wrote and drew two volumes of *The Bullwinkle Sing Along Book* and scripted material for *Fractured Flickers.* Al Burns came up with the format and design for Cap'n Crunch and the good ship *Guppy* crew, and he originated the character of George of the Jungle. In 1963, Burns and Chris Hayward joined forces and created a TV pilot called *Meet the Munsters*. After leaving Jay Ward Productions in 1964, they worked on, among others, *Get Smart*.

Al Burns found it "a revelation working for Jay. It was the first time I realized you could write to please yourself and not somebody else. Not only was it unusual for a producer to trust your judgment and your sense of humor implicitly, but when you'd write something and have absolutely nothing edited, well this was unheard-of. Jay's conviction—that the audience is smarter than the decision makers reckon—was the most valuable thing I've ever learned.

"And to work with this bunch of old-timers when you were just a kid of twenty-five was remarkable. I mean some of these guys from UPA were twice my age. They probably felt like they were on the downside of their careers, but they were great. Men like Pete Burness, who was so gentle, and always dressed in a Brooks Brothers suit and tie to draw cartoons—and all the time he was terribly ulcer-ridden! Bill Hurtz, Lew Keller, and the others: it was like they were either middle-aged or over, or just out of college. There was no in-between age. A real good talented group, and of course Jay and Bill nurtured them, and they protected and sheltered us. They were like these two mother hens of a very odd gaggle of geese.

"The experience was the seminal one of my life," added Burns. "Even after going out solo, or teamed with Chris Hayward (he and I shared a similar sense of humor), all the way through the MTM and Grant Tinker days, I never forgot Jay's unique way of producing a show . . . he let you trust yourself and he made you trust your audience."

As for Jay's own creative touch, Burns described Ward as a "unique appreciator of talent—strange and arcane talents that Chris Hayward said were 'probably unemployable anywhere else in the free world.' You'd shoot some stuff around for Jay; maybe over lunch you had an idea for a 'Mr. Know-It-All' or an 'Aesop' segment, and if he liked the idea and you got a giggle out of him, Jay just let you run with it. One thing I found amusing was that Jay was a little prudish, and was uncomfortable with rough language. And when it came to the voice-recording sessions, Jay kept them separate from the writers. I was curious to see one or two of those but Jay was almost jealous of that. I think that Jay loved the recording studio work more than anything else—that was his main creative thing."

Chris Hayward Master cartoon scripter and another Emmy Award winner, Christopher Robert Hayward was born in Bayonne, New Jersey, on

June 19, 1925. He attended school in Brooklyn: "While there I developed a negative attitude to the New York Giants, education, and police."

In a "biog" for Ward Productions studio publicity, Hayward wrote, "At the age of seventeen I became widely unknown as the New York State champion impersonator of Frank Sinatra, and subsequently I migrated to Hollywood to find success in the music field. I starred on *California Melodies* and Exclusive Records, and toured night clubs throughout Fresno and Denver. I was on my way."

Eventually Hayward ended up at CBS, where he wrote a disc-jockey show for Paul Frees called *My Own Place*. Later he worked on TV game shows. Establishing himself as a freelance writer in the mid-1950s, Hayward branched into animation. He wrote a *Mr. Magoo* demo script on spec and sent it to various cartoon studios. He was soon working on *Time for Beany, Tom and Jerry, Mr. Magoo,* and *Huckleberry Hound*.

When Jay Ward's proposed revival of *Crusader Rabbit* fell through, Hayward ended up writing most of the 1957–58 episodes of *Crusader* for Shull Bonsall's TV Spots. He recalled, "In 1959, I sent a copy of my *Magoo* sample script to Jay and Bill. They read it, and invited me to a screening of the *Rocky* pilot. I found it excellent: frenzied and funny. So I accepted a job with them.

"For the first year or so all the writers wrote at home. But later we wrote under the roof at 8218 Sunset, in fact in what was called the Writers' Basement. Jay would label his writers various funny names, and he'd always refer to us by saying, 'Here are a couple of my aces.' My nickname was 'the Gray Rat' [Hayward was prematurely gray] and Lloyd Turner was always 'the Old Lloyd Boy.'

"The writers took potshots at everything: we were encouraged to by Jay. It didn't matter the target—politics, social status, television, or even ourselves. We were simply given assignments, although I wrote most of the 'Peabody' cartoons alone. I found that working for Jay Ward was free-form, unfettered, clean, and marvelous. In fact, I was spoiled, because in my later career, if anything I wrote was questioned I'd say to the producer, 'How dare you?' Jay was a producer all to himself, despite Bill Scott's nominal coproducer credit.

"I remember Lloyd Turner was the most popular writer to be around in those days. He'd sit with Jay and make him laugh all day long. Lloyd put in the most time there; everyone found him a great source of amusement. Lloyd and I were often teamed. We came up with *Fractured Flickers,* and we revised the 'Dudley Do-Right' concept. I actually brought Lloyd in. I'd met him doing *Time for Beany,* and then I replaced him. After I'd finished Bonsall's *Crusader Rabbit* series, I tried to sell TV Spots a half-hour cartoon idea called 'Sir Loin and the Dragon.' I asked Lloyd to help me on it. Then when I was doing the 'Peabody's I eventually got Lloyd into Jay's place. Lloyd did some 'Aesop's; then we became partners in crime. He just had a marvelous outlook on life." Of their partnership, Turner said, "Chris Hayward was a joy to work with. We were very close for a long time and we did a lot of things together—golf, the track, and a lot of drinking! He's a neat guy and very clever."

As Hayward told *Los Angeles Times* feature writer Lawrence Christon in 1988, "The pay was low and the insecurity great. One Christmas, we went over to Jay's house and he had maps on his door designating nearby unemployment offices." In 1991 he added, "There really wasn't much money, to tell the truth—but there were plenty of extra perks like the golf and the long lunches. Jay was an avuncular producer. He knew exactly what he was after, and he was a fine sounding board. He simply left the writers alone. Not a comma was changed. Yeah, he was creative all right, not in the sense that we or the artists were, yet very creative. And if you could make him laugh, you were in!"

Hayward's wife, Linda, was Jay Ward's secretary from 1961 to 1966. Then known as Linda Simmons, she was just short of her nineteenth birthday when she began with Jay. Following a year in college she was working at a stockbrokerage, when another girl mentioned a friend named Allan Burns. He managed to get Linda a position at Ward Productions, where, as she puts it, "I was a secretary but I didn't even know how to take dictation!" Involved in all the early *Bullwinkle Show* activity, she handled the fan mail and filing, as well as accompanying Ward back east for the big publicity jaunts with Alan Foshko in 1962–63. Linda finally left the Ward studio to join Chuck Barris as production assistant on *The Dating Game*.

Lloyd Turner Skip Craig recalled, "One of Jay's personal quirks was a compulsion to have somebody to talk to, and Lloyd Turner would spend hours most days just laughing and talking with Jay. In the later years when Lloyd had gone out on his own, this role went to Jim Critchfield."

Critchfield (nicknamed "Critch") observed, "Lloyd was extremely funny. The Old Lloyd Boy—Lloyd's gags were terrific, his jokes were classically good. In fact, Lloyd couldn't think up a bad joke. He was the main writer for a long while on *Time for Beany,* and that's one of the funniest shows of all time, just sensational. That's a classically funny show!"

Lloyd Turner enjoyed a highly successful TV career with credits on *The Doris Day Show, All in the Family, Maude, Mork and Mindy,* and *The Jeffersons* among others, but his memories of the Jay Ward era remained his fondest. Turner was born in Winnemucca, Nevada, on August 14, 1924, and attended Fremont High in Oakland. Later he studied at the California College of Arts and Crafts in Berkeley. As Turner saw it, "I always had a funny bone. Comedy just came to me naturally and I was always thinking 'funny.' Originally I was going to be a cartoonist, and I was actually a pretty good one. My ambition had been to work for Walt Disney. Well I met someone who got me into Warner Brothers animation and that was where I met Bill Scott."

Turner was an apprentice and then a full-time, writer at Warner Brothers Cartoons from 1944 to 1947 and even supplied a couple of incidental voices for the Looney Tunes.

In 1950 Turner worked with another young man, one Jay T. Ward, on the *Crusader Rabbit* series, after which he wrote and directed the revered *Time for Beany* from 1950 almost to its demise. He also put in time at UPA before freelancing for Whitman Publishing from 1956 to 1959, where he "wrote comic books until they were coming out of my ears. Comic books featuring all the cartoon characters: from Warners, Disney, MGM."

When Turner joined Jay Ward's in November 1959, he was asked to write a "Fractured Fairy Tale." "Jay explained the fairy-tale idea to me and told me to do anything I wanted. So I wrote a satire of 'Pinocchio.' I gave it to Jay and Bill; Bill read it and said, 'Jay, this is great, I love it!' So I was in, and eventually Chris and I decided we'd collaborate." They went on to write "Dudley Do-Right," *Fractured Flickers,* "Aesop and Son," "Mr. Know-It-All," and even the little commercial bridges like "Fan mail from some flounder" and "Eenie Meanie, Chili Beanie, the spirits are about to speak."

Echoing the sentiments of Allan Burns and Chris Hayward, Turner—guesting on *Good Morning America* in 1986—had this to say about working for Jay Ward: "The creative process when working on these shows was simply a pure delight. And Jay himself was such an easy guy to work for. He just made the experience the epitome of my career. See, he insisted that we write for ourselves. In other words, Jay was one of those one-in-a-million producers who never demanded that you reflect his taste. You were able to try things that you wanted to do. By the way, Jay was able to read upside down, that was the funniest thing of all. If you were sitting across the table from him, he'd look down at your pile of pages and he'd start giggling. I'd say, 'What are you laughing at?' and he'd point to the script which was facing me, and he'd say, 'That joke's pretty funny!' You know, we were once likened to the Algonquin Round Table—this group of like-minded people, all trying to make Jay laugh. A literate circle, except that instead of Hemingway we had a moose!"

In 1988 Lloyd Turner told the *Los Angeles Times*'s Lawrence Christon, "Once, I was facing legal problems. I didn't know who to borrow from—it was either that or jump off the Santa Monica Pier. I told Jay and he whipped out a check for the entire amount. I said, 'Don't you want a note?' He said, 'If you got hit by a truck, I'd feel so bad I wouldn't care about the money.' For a while he deducted payments from my salary to make me feel noble, and then he had the bookkeeper write it off."

Christon's article contained a colorful incident in which Turner recounted the bizarre working conditions at Ward Productions. Christon reported: "There was the office secretary, a sullen virago named Natalie, who spent a great deal of her working hours knitting. One day she marched down to the ratty Dickensian cellar that passed as a writers' workshop—where Turner and Chris Hayward were bent in their labors—to unscrew the solitary bulb that hung over their communal desk, plunging them into darkness. It was strictly an act of malice; but Turner and Hayward thought it was a Ward prank, and set up a water-filled balloon over the door to reward him for his enterprise and curiosity.

"He never showed up. When they realized it wasn't a joke, they stormed up to Natalie, who was intent on her knitting, and said, 'We're top writers here! We're going to the top with this complaint!' Which they did.

"Much to their consternation, they asked Jay—once they'd told their story—'Will you fire her?' Says Turner, 'He laughed so hard at the story that he said, no. In fact, I'm giving her a raise! '"*

In summing up his time in the Bullwinkle bullpen, Turner said, "It was the best time of my entire life and the halcyon of my writing career." When Chris Hayward left Jay's employ, Lloyd stayed to write many "Hoppity

*This anecdote actually concerned Natalie Bernhet, who was "a stunningly lovely lady to look at, a real beauty—but a pretty tough person," according to Linda Hayward. Bill Hurtz recalls, "When Al Burns was starting with us he had quite a crush on Natalie."

Hooper" segments. He left in 1968, after contributing "Super Chicken" stories for the *George of the Jungle* show. A great help to this author, Lloyd Turner passed away following a valiant three-year bout with esophageal cancer on November 30, 1992.

Chris Jenkyns Following stints at Disney, Storyboard, and Playhouse Pictures, Chris Jenkyns began working for Jay Ward writing "Fractured Fairy Tales," his first one being the "Rapunzel" episode. Later he wrote several "Aesop," "Dudley Do-Right," and "Hoppity Hooper" segments. What is unusual about Jenkyns is that he is a fine artist who happens to also write comedy. Linda Hayward recalled, "He was really good, with his little drawings. I used to wait to see his work when it would come into the studio. I'd think, boy that's great stuff." Chris Hayward spoke highly of Jenkyns's work: "His scripts were whimsical, and he'd always supply a great storyboard along with the dialogue."

Chris Jenkyns's portfolio is impressive. Besides his many cartoon scripts, he illustrated eight books, was a professor of animation in Paris, made over a thousand TV commercials, directed PBS live-action specials, worked on over two hundred promos for ABC (including designing their "new look graphics"), specialized in title design (*Grease, The Carol Burnett Show, Hunter, The Duck Factory*), wrote animation shows for thirty years (*Bravestar,* Doctor Seuss specials), and produced titles for news, sports, and election coverages.

Born in North Hollywood on July 3, 1924, Jenkyns served in World War II, then studied at the Art Center School and Chouinard Art Institute in Los Angeles, the Art Students League in New York, and the Academie Julian in Paris. Pat Diska's *Andy Says Bonjour!,* which Jenkyns drew, was judged one of the ten best illustrated children's books of 1954 by the *New York Times.* In 1955 he wrote and designed the film *Petroushka,* the first animated special made for TV. It was shown at the Brussels world's fair.

For many years Chris Jenkyns was an art director and advertising designer. From 1956 to 1959 he received the Art Director's Club Medal for best animated television commercial produced in the United States. He wrote the famous "Ford Dog" commercial, among others.

As Jenkyns remembers, "Bill Scott had put in a word for me. I'd met Bill when I did a storyboard about oxygen at Sutherland Productions. He called me right at the start of Ward Productions. Unlike a lot of other people, I was very happy with the salary I received from Jay, although I was never on staff. I was always a freelance. I'd get an assignment and write at home on weekends."

While freelancing for Jay Ward, Jenkyns set up his own studio (Jenkyns, Shean and Elliott, later Jenkyns and Associates). He recalls basing his scripts for "Fractured Fairy Tales" on Andrew Lang's fairy-tale books, and attempting to find a way to change each classic story for comic effect. Unlike the other Ward cartoon writers, he didn't do puns. Jenkyns remembers seeing an early "Fractured Fairy Tale" several years later on a rerun. This was "The Elves and the Shoemaker" (in which a frustrated artisan desperately wants to fashion a pair of singing shoes). "Watching it, I had only a vague memory of the story, until I heard a character in it give the shoemaker his address, which was 2311 South Budlong. Suddenly I remembered writing this episode, because that was my home address in 1959!"

Jim Critchfield Born in Oklahoma on September 15, 1923, Jim Critchfield gained early experience in radio on the writing staffs of CBS and NBC, later moving into television. With disarming honesty, Critchfield offered, "All during my career I was fighting a battle with booze." "Critch" became one of Jay Ward's closest friends.

Although he'd met Ward in 1959, Critchfield didn't work at the studio until 1963. His first assignment was *The Nut House* pilot. He also wrote for much of *Fractured Flickers* and helped out on the cartoon pilots of the late 1960s and early 1970s. He recalled that Bill Scott would do the final draft of nearly everything submitted: "Bill always plussed it up, and it was better." Critch was also responsible for various offbeat ideas for TV shows and merchandise that, regrettably, never saw the light of day. One concept involved a set of talking clocks which Ward was going to market—they would feature recorded messages with humorous wake-up calls done by the top voices (Bill Scott, June Foray, and Paul Frees). Critchfield said, "Alex Anderson did some artwork on them, and around that same time Jay and I came up with ideas for the shop which was to become Dudley Do-Right's Emporium. In fact, the actual concept for the memorabilia store was supplied by Jay's son Ron."

Writer George Atkins, a close friend of Critchfield, recalled, "Jimmy was an extraordinarily bright and interesting fellow, very talented. But the bottle would get in his way whenever he was offered a big job. He ended up being paid by Jay to do bits and pieces, but in effect he was Jay's office court jester after Lloyd. It's a fortunate thing that Jim finally kicked the alcohol habit."

Lloyd Turner added, "Critch was one of the cleverest people Jay ever employed." A modest and frank person, Jim Critchfield was a pleasure to meet during the research stage of this book.

George Atkins Described by Al Burns as "the largest, wildest comedy writer I ever met and worked with, a perennial bachelor and a very funny man," George Atkins was a true character. Chris Hayward said, "George was a brilliant guy. I thought he was strange because it seemed like whenever he made money, he'd head off to Acapulco. He wrote great gags, yet he couldn't spell the word *cat.*" Bill Hurtz recalled that although Atkins wrote strong jokes and gags, his scripts often had no windup, and Bill Scott would invariably have to round them off with a comic tag.

George Edward Atkins was born in Sacramento, California, in 1931. He began as a writer for Jonathan Winters on *The NBC Comedy Hour* in 1956, then moved to Winters's own show out of New York. Returning to California, he wrote a couple of *Magoo* cartoons for UPA. In the spring of 1959, Atkins was back east again ("writing some god-awful stuff for Terrytoons") when he received a phone call from Bill Scott, whom he had met at UPA. Scott asked him to view the *Rocky* pilot at the P.A.T. office. When Atkins told Scott he'd seen it and loved it, he was offered a job, specifically writing the "Fractured Fairy Tales." ("I hesitated for maybe eleven seconds, then headed back to Hollywood.")

While writing for the cartoons, Atkins created the famous Jay Ward mailers, and later contributed some "Mr. Know-It-All" segments. Atkins soon moved to Tijuana, and Ward allowed him to mail his material from south of the border (Atkins enjoyed a lifelong love affair with Mexico and still lives there today). In 1963 he returned to Hollywood as a writer on *Fractured Flickers.* After writing for *The Nut House* pilot, Atkins was working on the development of *George of the Jungle* in the spring of 1964 when he got an offer to write for a Carol Burnett special. He left Jay Ward's in June, and from that point on wrote sitcoms ("*a Mary Tyler Moore,* thanks to Allan Burns"), variety shows for Tim Conway, westerns, and much more until 1983. Then he reentered the cartoon field: "I wrote more Saturday morning cartoons than anyone—virtually all of it garbage."

"The Ward writing staff," according to Atkins, "all complained about money; while we watched our contemporaries grabbing the big bucks in sitcoms we seethed with jealousy and resentment, regarding things like *Father Knows Best* as the big time and our efforts as little more than a career waiting room. But the one single thing Jay's writers shared was that we wrote to please ourselves—not network ninnies, not toy company yo-yos, not syndication cretins. Just us and, perhaps incidentally, Jay and Bill. And Jay made this possible. He insisted on sole control of the material. And even when he wasn't enthusiastic he generally deferred to the writer's judgment."

Various other writers did short stints at Jay Ward's, including Gary Owens, Bob Arbogast, Art Keene, Jim MacGeorge, and Jack Mendlesohn.

THE ARTISTS

Jay Ward was certainly in the right place at the right time when it came to his art department. As Skip Craig recalled, "Around the time that Jay was starting up, Stephen Bosustow sold UPA to promoter Henry Saperstein, and Herb Klynn took a lot of the people with him to start Format Films [animation studio]. Various others went freelance, then ended up with Jay, mostly due to Bill Scott's efforts, and they were some really great talents." Indeed, the team at Ward Productions was one of the most powerhouse collections in all cartoondom.

Bill Hurtz Born April 7, 1919, in Chicago, animation director and film designer William T. Hurtz received his early professional training at age ten at Chicago's Art Institute. Moving to Los Angeles, he continued his studies at Chouinard Art Institute. While there, he was invited to join the Disney studio in 1938 by their head of art training, Don Graham. After three years there he was drafted, and spent the war at the First Motion Picture Unit. Upon his release from service, Hurtz became one of the first film designers at UPA, working on the Oscar-winning *Gerald McBoing-Boing*. Graduating to the position of director, Hurtz scored a personal best with a fine adaptation of James Thurber's *The Unicorn in the Garden* (1953). A year earlier, he received an Oscar nomination for *Man Alive!* produced for the American Cancer Society.

Hurtz was later an executive at Shamus Culhane Productions, directing animation for Frank Capra's "Science" series, sponsored by the Bell Telephone Company. Next he freelanced as a director of TV commercials, winning several Art Directors' Club awards, until he was asked to join Jay Ward Productions in July 1959, specifically to organize and supervise production of the early episodes of *Rocky and His Friends* being animated in Mexico.

Regarding the show on which he was involved, Hurtz was in no doubt from the very first: "We knew even then that we were doing the best stuff around. I mean, working for Jay on this *Rocky* show was so exciting and so great. We knew we had something that was more than the sum of its parts."

He worked for Ward until the studio closed in the fall of 1984. Still active, Bill Hurtz has for several years been a gracious source of information on the Jay Ward years.

Pete Burness Wilson D. "Pete" Burness was born June 16, 1910, in Los Angeles. He attended the University of Southern California and Chouinard Art Institute, entering the cartoon business in 1931. Burness spent twelve years at MGM's cartoon division followed by a stint at Warner Brothers, animating for Friz Freleng, then nine years at UPA.

As producer-director of UPA's Magoo shorts, Burness won five Academy Award nominations, winning the coveted statuette twice, in 1954 and 1956, for his productions of *When Magoo Flew* and *Mister Magoo's Puddle Jumper.*

Joining Jay Ward Productions in 1959, Burness worked at first on a freelance basis. At one point he left for a position at Playhouse Pictures, before returning to Jay's employ. Bill Hurtz said, "Pete was our truly senior director of animation in terms of age and experience." Burness was one of the most popular people at Ward Productions. Linda Hayward called him "a very sweet man," while Hurtz added, "Pete was a wonderful craftsman, and a very good animator. A very elegant, sweet fellow, but oh boy, what a temper he had. We all nicknamed him 'the Terrible-Tempered Mr. Bang.' "

Burness's tantrums were indeed legendary, as Hurtz explained: "On one of the earliest Cap'n Crunch spots Pete had a spirited disagreement with Jay about the lack of animation in one scene in which the good sea captain was tied up with rope. Jay came in and saw the pencil test, giggled his nervous laugh, and said, 'There's no movement.' Pete said, 'But he's tied up—he can't move!'—and Jay giggled and said, 'Well, I want to see some movement.' Then Jay walked out of the room. Well this got Pete so mad, he kicked a really huge hole in the wall, and that hole remained there for years. Incidentally, later on Pete added some movement just to get back at Jay—the Captain was still tied up, but we animated one of his fingers wiggling." Disney veteran Jack Kinney, who replaced Burness as director of the 1959 Magoo feature film *1001 Arabian Nights,* recalled that while many animators blew their creative stacks on occasion, Pete Burness's stack blowings were in a class of their own.

Bill Scott, discussing the visual orientation of most UPA directors, commented, "Pete was much more in the vein of the Warner Brothers/MGM king of thing. He loved fast movement, impact. He appreciated verbal jokes as well as visual jokes. He had a fine sense of humor himself. He was a delight to write for."

In the mid-1960s, Burness wrote a letter to the British Film Institute in which he stated, "From 1961, I directed for Jay Ward Productions, who are responsible for *The Bullwinkle Show, Fractured Flickers,* and various special films, all for television entertainment. Great credit is due to Jay Ward and his coproducer, Bill Scott. In recent years the limitations of time and money have resulted in too many badly written and poorly produced animated television shows. Jay has been a refreshingly rare bird in effectively insisting on being permitted to develop new concepts and put them together cleverly. The stories are saucy and irreverent and have been great fun to work on. The critics have almost unanimously expressed their approval and encouragement. Jay Ward deserves every bit of it."

When Pete Burness contracted cancer and was too ill to work, Ward graciously kept him on the payroll. He died in October 1969.

Lew Keller "Sugar Lew," as Jay Ward dubbed him, was born in Sacramento, California, in 1912. Keller began in the animation business as a designer; he and Bill Hurtz worked together at Disney during the production of *Bambi* (1942). Later Lew Keller worked as a live-action sketch artist, and ended up at UPA in character design. He graduated to animation director, working on the studio's last theatrical series, *Ham and Hattie*. After another stint at Disney, Keller joined Ward's studio in 1961. Bill Hurtz recalled Keller being nicknamed "the Motor Mouth," and Skip Craig added, "Keller was a good cartoon director, if you could ever get him to stop talking."

Lew Keller was still "doing lunch" with Ward in the last years, long after the studio had closed. He worked on Jay's unsold cartoon pilots, along with Bullwinkle Cheerios commercials and episodes of *George of the Jungle*. Keller observed, "Jay and Bill Scott were never that close socially, but they had the highest respect for each other's abilities. We all felt very good about the work we were doing. This is because Jay wanted to do material that was very original; he simply loved comedy." Keller died in 1996.

Ted Parmelee Theodore "Ted" Parmelee was born in New Brunswick, New Jersey, and at an early age moved to Urbana, Illinois. He attended

University High School, graduating from the University of Illinois in 1935. A freelance illustrator for children's books in New York City, Parmelee later worked in Chicago and finally ended up in Los Angeles. For several years, he toiled for Disney, Warner Brothers, Graphic Films, UPA, Quartet, and Storyboard, later forming his own company, Parmelee-Patin Productions, with Ray Patin.

Parmelee was a close friend of Bill Scott's, working with him on *The Telltale Heart* (1953), a magnificent UPA cartoon, and the later *Gerald McBoing-Boing* TV series. Scott told historian Paul Etcheverry, "Parmelee was very much like Pete Burness. The two of them worked together for quite a while. . . . Their kinds of humor and things they thought were funny were pretty much the same. Ted came much more from a design background. He was a layout man; his pictures always showed a very, very strong personal design influence."

Bill Hurtz recalled, "Ted had several freelance accounts; he didn't want to be with Jay exclusively. His death was a big shock; he and his wife, Miriam, were on his boat with Bill and Dot Scott, when Ted suffered a heart attack. This was in the mid-1960s. Despite Bill's attempt at mouth-to-mouth, Ted died on the way to the hospital."

Gerry Ray Described by Bill Scott as "one of America's finest animators and directors for nearly four decades," Ray got his early training at UCLA, Chouinard, and Disney, and made a pilgrimage to Washington to study with Don Graham, the doyen of Disney draftsmanship. He was Jay Ward's first employee, as animator and director on *Crusader Rabbit*. He was also an animator and director at UPA before rejoining Ward for the kickoff of *Rocky and His Friends,* then directing several "Fractured Fairy Tales" at TV Spots. Later he formed a commercial studio in Mexico City, where he lived and worked for several years, before founding a studio in Hollywood with Disney veteran Norm Gottfredson.

Scott called him "an intelligent, wise, witty, and compassionate man. At the time of his death [early 1984], he was supervising director of Tom Carter's ill-fated *Huck's Landing* feature project."

Gerard Baldwin Born in 1929 in New York City, Gerard H. Baldwin was a fine arts major at Chouinard Art Institute in Los Angeles, and also did a brief stint of study in Mexico. As Baldwin himself quipped, "I gave up art to join UPA in 1950." Apart from time out for service in Korea, he spent the decade working in most of the West Coast cartoon studios (including UPA and Playhouse) before joining Jay Ward Productions in 1959. "That was my first job as a director. Bill Hurtz chose me, and he was a great mentor for me. The first three months in Mexico, with Hurtz and Jim Hiltz, was the only time in my life I felt like a rich man."

A fine animator with a nimble wit, Baldwin once wrote, "Having brainwashed myself into believing that the animated cartoon is a potential high art form, I have had little success in proving this thesis to date." He is surprised but happy that the *Bullwinkle* characters have had a resurgence in popularity. "It was just a job back then. Like any other job, with all the ambition, infighting, and good times you find in any profession. In Jay's cartoons of course, the scripts are everything." Baldwin was still highly active in the animation boom of the 1990s. His older brother Howard was also an animator who often worked for Ward, as did Howard's wife, Barbara, who was a color specialist.

Dunbar "Dun" Roman Veteran animator Dun Roman replaced Jim Hiltz in Mexico City when Hiltz's contract was up, and did much to improve the fledgling Mexican studio's wasteful work practices. Born in New York City on December 24, 1914, Roman attended Townsend Harris Hall prep school, graduating from the College of the City of New York in 1934. Transplanting to the West-Coast in 1936, he worked for Walt Disney, Screen Gems, UPA, and other animation studios (interrupted by a wartime stint with the U.S. Marine Corps and a fling at magazine illustration). Roman also wrote several plays, and had one produced at the La Jolla Theater in 1955. He worked on story for the *Gerald McBoing-Boing Show,* and later at Culhane Productions with Bill Hurtz, who noted, "Dun was a very funny man, and very talented. He died in the mid-1980s."

Jim Hiltz The amiable Jim Hiltz was born in Phoenix, Arizona, on November 7, 1927. Raised in Salt Lake City, he moved to California in 1936, settling in San Diego and graduating from Point Loma High School in 1946. Following army service, Hiltz returned to San Diego as a commercial artist, then spent four years in New York City working on CBS's Terrytoons, and as head animator for Pintoff Productions. From September 1958 he freelanced for many Hollywood animation firms, including Jay Ward Productions. Hiltz was one of the initial supervisors in Mexico when *Rocky* production began in mid-1959—along with Bill Hurtz and Gerard Baldwin.

"My friend Chris Jenkyns had recommended me to Jay. The Mexican studio was pretty shoddy for a while; I used to laugh when Bill Hurtz told me about the Mexican cameraman—he didn't want to be blamed for sloppy-looking work, so he'd cut mistakes right out of the negative!" Hiltz worked at Ward Productions upon his return to Hollywood. "I mainly did the 'Fairy Tales.' Jay had his own style, and he wouldn't delegate; he'd look your storyboard over, and he might say, 'Now—you animate it!' And he wouldn't let you choose your own animators. I remember animating one of Jay's favorites, called 'Cinderella Returns'; Ted Parmelee directed that one. I got to direct my first "Fairy Tale," called 'Rumpelstiltskin'—that was one Chris Jenkyns wrote; he even included that funny little song, 'Scoo scooby doo, Oo bob shebam, I am the Rumpelstiltskin man.'

"The two people I enjoyed working for more than any others were Jay Ward and Ernie Pintoff, for whom I did the Oscar nominee *The Violinist* [1959]—Hubley beat us that year with *Moonbird*. At Jay's there was all the freedom you'd ever need. After I left I worked in Holland for five years, then rejoined Ward's in 1967 for *George of the Jungle*. I specialized on the 'Super Chicken' episodes, and I used to love sitting in Jay's front room with Lloyd Turner and Jim MacGeorge as they wrote them. Old Rudy Zamora came back on board too as an animator. Rudy was so funny: one day we were arguing over a storyboard and he suddenly asked me, 'Tell me, Jim, when were you born?' So I told him, then he asked, 'And in what month?' Then he asked what day of the month. Finally he yells, 'Well, do you realize I was animating in this goddamned business before you were even born?' "

When *George of the Jungle* finished in 1968, Hiltz went to England to work on *The Yellow Submarine*. In 1972 he traveled to Canada; he liked it so much he has lived and worked in Montreal ever since.

Al Shean Design artist Al Shean was born in New York City on September 27, 1930. A descendant of the Al Shean from the famous vaudeville act Gallagher and Shean and a cousin of Maxine Marx (Chico's daughter), Shean won a scholarship to Chouinard Art Institute in California, where he had lived since he was six. Shean worked in the animation industry from 1944, for such companies as Disney, UPA, and Storyboard, with time out for a stint in the Korean War. In the tradition of his distant relative Groucho, Shean possesses an extremely quick and somewhat cynical wit.

A fine artist, Al Shean retains crystal-clear memories of his time with Jay Ward Productions. After working in New York for Shamus Culhane, who was married to Shean's cousin Maxine, he was doing freelance illustration when old acquaintance Bill Scott contacted him early in 1959 (about one year after Len Key had recommended Shean to Ward while selling the *Rocky* pilot film). Shean had first worked with Scott at Sutherland Productions on an industrial animated short about hydra-matic transmission. Scott offered him the prospect of working in Mexico for $1,000 a week, tax-free, with a big house and servants thrown in. Enthused about the offer, Shean made up model drawings for the main characters from Scott's roughs.

Soon after, Shean went to see Peter Peich at P.A.T., bankrollers on the *Rocky* show. "First of all I found it funny just to meet a guy named Piech, and secondly it was funny seeing these lavish offices—when I got there, there were these furniture guys with all this expensive imported Danish teak; I couldn't figure out whether it was being moved in or being removed." Shean learned that Ward and Scott liked his model sheets so much they wanted him to remain in Hollywood. Rather than traveling to Mexico, Shean was kept in California for months. He became Ward's first true employee, and for a short time he did everything in the early part of 1959: model sheets, storyboards, and writing ("This didn't endear me to the Screen Cartoonists' Guild"). In December 1959, Shean left to live in Europe for over a year. While in Florence, he continued working for Ward Productions on "Peabody" and "Fractured Fairy Tales," and the first *Super Chicken* pilot. Shean and Ward had several battles because of late payments ("Al near starved to death there for a couple of weeks," said Bill Hurtz).

In some ways Al Shean did not enjoy the animation business, feeling that the pressure destroyed a lot of creative people psychologically, and too early in their lives. He loved working for Ward and Scott, but personally felt that Jay's cartoons were "not so much 'ahead of their time'—it's just that the TV industry was so far behind!" He found Ward "a very perceptive producer" and felt that "Bill Scott was (and in my opinion remains to this day) the finest animation writer of all time, as well as being one of the most even-tempered people in the business." The independent Shean found studio work ultimately too restrictive. When he finally told Ward and Scott he was leaving, it did not sit well at all.

Sam Clayberger Born in Kulpmont, Pennsylvania, Sam Clayberger was raised and educated in Reading, Pennsylvania. After a brief stint in the air force, he attended Chouinard Art Institute. Clayberger spent years in the animation industry, mainly at UPA and Graphic Films, before joining Ward

Productions. A renowned painter, he has exhibited in many shows and museums.

"Roy Morita and I did the pilot for *Rocky*. There were no animators. Roy was the layout artist and I was a color specialist. The pilot was very rough. The backgrounds were Xeroxes of Roy's layout on cels and then backed with cutout color aid and construction paper plus some painted surfaces (like cel painting). We had stuff scattered all over floors and tables. It was a frantic undertaking, but enjoyable.

"When the show sold a year later, Jay asked me on staff. I told him I was happy to work three days a week for him because I'm an artist, and I needed the other days to paint."

Clayberger spent most of his time at Ward's working with Bill Hurtz. He recalled, "Pete Burness was a fine animation director, and a terrific model man. He cleaned up a ton of rough drawings, while Roy Morita and Shirley Silvey were two of the best layout people around." Clayberger specialized in color and background work on the series titles and those cartoons animated at Ward's Hollywood studio, like "Fractured Fairy Tales." He left in 1964 for an art teaching position, and taught from 1965 until May 1991. Even though he was no longer on staff, Clayberger added, "I'd do freelance stuff for Jay to bail him out. I worked on the Cap'n Crunch commercials and *George of the Jungle*. Jay was his own man, and there's not too many of them left. He would always tell me he wanted color—nice, bright color! But he never forgot that he was telling a story, unlike UPA, where we also had nice color, and the graphics were exciting, but the art of telling a story wasn't developed." As for Bill Scott, "I liked Bill a lot. He was sort of crusty, and he had the sharpest tongue in town, but very funny. And a very fair guy." Clayberger was asked to go to Mexico but declined: "The animators down there were really amateurish, but unfortunately Jay couldn't get out of that."

Shirley Silvey Storyboard and layout artist Shirley Silvey was born in Los Angeles, and attended the Art Center School and Jepson Art Institute. After four years spent raising her family, she landed a job at an animation studio, where she specialized in cutout work. Following a stint at UPA ("I helped in my own little way to bungle the CBS *McBoing-Boing Show*"), Silvey worked at Churchill-Wexler doing layout and backgrounds for medical and educational films, one of which "made it to Venice for some kind of award. Then after becoming somber and morose with no work, I got a call from UPA and I became the layout designer for the Magoo *Arabian Nights* feature.

I was climbing fast. TV Spots came next, then at last the pinnacle: Ward Productions." Shirley Silvey worked at Ward's studio from December 1959 until 1973. She and Roy Morita specialized in storyboards for the "Rocky and Bullwinkle" chapters. Bill Hurtz said, "Shirley's work is great. God, she was a fantastic artist; I admired her work so much that I was a fan."

Roy Morita The importance of the late Roy C. Morita's role in the Jay Ward cartoons cannot be overstated. He was the first artist to design and work on the characters and was responsible at the beginning for more of the overall visual direction than any other artist in the Ward Productions story. Morita's wife, Alice, recalled, "He was the first artist to be contacted directly by Jay to draw a model of Bullwinkle. This was late in the 1950s. Roy worked with Jay for ten years. He went on to draw for Dr. Seuss and Walt Disney Productions." Morita and Shirley Silvey basically worked all the storyboards for "Rocky and Bullwinkle." Shirley emphatically states, "Roy was very important to the beginning of 'Rocky and Bullwinkle.' " Sam Clayberger underlined the point to this author: "In case you didn't get the feeling elsewhere, Roy Morita was very responsible for the Jay Ward look."

Designer–layout artist Roy Morita was born March 30, 1928, in San Jose, California, of Japanese parentage. He attended Chouinard Art Institute, and spent four years on design and layout at UPA. Before joining Ward, he worked at Format Films, specializing in commercials. Bill Hurtz said, "Roy died of cancer, very rapidly [November 14, 1984]. One of his last stints was at Disney. He was a kind of reserved, quiet personality, kind of a downbeat nature. Roy sure knew what he was doing, and it was always amusing when he worked for Lew Keller. If Lew asked for retakes, Roy would just totally fail to see the reason why they were necessary."

Al Wilson Like Roy Morita, Al Wilson specialized in storyboard and layout. He was born in St. Louis, Missouri, circa 1920. After completing his education he spent five years in the National Guard. Moving to Los Angeles, Wilson attended Chouinard Art Institute from 1946 to 1951. After a couple of years at Disney, he worked for various TV commercial houses before joining Jay Ward Productions in 1959.

"I was out of work so I called the cartoon union, who told me there was a place at Ward Productions. I was sort of teamed with Al Shean, and we were able to work from home and send the stuff in. I remember doing a lot of storyboards for 'Peabody,' drawing that Sherman kid. I enjoyed the four years or so, and I liked the cartoons. Shirley and Roy really gave [the TV show] the distinctive look in character design that it had."

Adrienne Diamond A character model designer, Adrienne Diamond was born in Manhattan on November 2, 1933. She grew up in Inwood, graduating from Barnard College in 1954; she majored in zoology, and was active in college in publicity and dramatics. After graduation she assisted on research at the School of Tropical Medicine and the Physicians School. While there, she helped illustrate a manual on entomology.

Diamond studied at the Art Students League as the protégée of John Bloomshield (famed society portrait painter), then won an eighteen-month scholarship to the New York Academy of Design. She entered advertising in 1955, doing sports illustration for Jim Jones Associates, a New York agency. In Los Angeles from 1957, she worked as an art director for the Malcolm Steinlauf fashion agency, then went to Animation, Inc., and UPA.

Adrienne was unique in that when she joined Jay Ward Productions, she was known to be the youngest film designer in an old-line craft industry. In fact, when only eleven years old her work had been noticed by *Superman* creator Joe Schuster, who was dating her older sister. He encouraged her to do her own comic strip, and in sixth grade at P.S. 52, New York City, she did just that: "Katy Kitten" was the result.

She also designed the models for Ward's puppet film *Watts Gnu*. Skip Craig said, "Adrienne wore short skirts way before they were the in thing, and Jay and Bill used to call her 'PK,' short for pretty knees."

Jean Washam Born in Wabash, Indiana, in 1928, Jean came to Los Angeles in 1948, and spent two years at the Holmwood Art Center School. She embarked on her animation career in the ink and paint department at Warner Brothers Cartoons, and later worked for several other toon factories (Disney, Shamus Culhane, Song Ads) as an animator. Along the way she married the late, great animation director Ben Washam, a favorite of Bill Hurtz, Jay Ward, and Chuck Jones.

Sal Faillace Born in 1930 in Larchmont, New York, Salvatore Faillace had no formal art training. He graduated from school in 1948 and worked at Famous Studios in New York. Finally tiring of Wimpy, Popeye, and Olive Oyl, Faillace ventured into television commercials. In September 1960, he journeyed across the Rio Grande after being informed that Gamma was looking for an animator. During his years in Mexico City, he ended up as an animation director on *The Bullwinkle Show*, and returned later to work on Peter Piech's *Underdog* series.

George Singer A talented and highly regarded animation veteran, George Singer spent a year directing *Rocky and His Friends* in Mexico. Born in Coney Island in 1923, Singer decided on animation at an early age. He studied at Brooklyn's Pratt Institute, and after World War II service in Europe as a combat engineer, he began his career at Famous Studios in New York. There he worked on *Popeye* cartoons. Hired by UPA–New York, he did commercials, winning several art director's awards. Singer transferred to the West Coast to work on the *Gerald McBoing-Boing Show,* then accepted an offer as a supervising director at Halas and Batchelor in London, where he directed and trained British animators for three years. After this he directed Italian commercials in Milan.

Returning to the States, Singer had an offer to work on the *Rocky* show in Mexico City. While there he supervised and trained the Mexican artists: "I enjoyed my time in the studio there under Ernie Terrazas—he taught me how to box!" It was in Mexico that he developed an ongoing interest in pre-Columbian art. After leaving the moose and squirrel, Singer notched a dizzying array of animation credits, including Ed Graham's *Linus the Lionhearted,* DePatie-Freleng's *The Inspector*, and Hanna-Barbera's *Monchichis*.

Bob Mills Bob Mills was one of the stalwarts at Television Arts with Jay Ward and Alex Anderson. A fourth-generation Californian, Mills was born in Sacramento in 1923. Following World War II he was studying at art school on the GI Bill when his sister introduced him to a friend who worked as an announcer at KSFO. This happened to be Roy Whaley, narrator of TAP's *Crusader Rabbit* pilot. Whaley suggested that Mills speak to Anderson and Ward, who were commencing production on the series. Mills mentioned this opportunity to one of his teachers, Bill Martin (who had worked at Disney on *Fantasia,* and animated Pluto). Martin gave Mills a crash course in animation; Mills then took his portfolio to TV Arts and was immediately hired: "I came in on the first story about the Texas Jackrabbits."

Mills became the show's production manager and helped set up the Los Angeles studio with Ward in 1951. "I was in charge of hiring and firing. But I was so young and stupid in those days. I remember the Disney animator Dick Huemer was out of work and he came to us looking for a job.

I actually asked him to draw Crusader for me! Here I was—this green kid—unknowingly insulting this great cartoonist.

"Jay was a happy-go-lucky-guy. He wasn't physically well, but he wouldn't show it. When *Crusader* finished in 1951, Jay kept me on the payroll for six months. Then Alex offered me a job at his ad agency. After some time there I formed my own studio, TV Cartoon Productions." Bob Mills went on to form further studios. The first was Imagination, Ink., followed by Animation House ("We did a special called *Take a Giant Step* for NBC"); in recent years he has set up Pandemonium Pictures.

THE MUSICIANS

Frank Comstock In May 1959 Frank Comstock composed the catchy theme music heard on *Rocky and His Friends*. Born in San Diego, Comstock, a trombonist, orchestrator, and arranger, worked in dance bands like Sonny Dunham's and Benny Carter's, and served a quarter century with Les Brown (Bob Hope's bandleader). He worked at Warner Brothers orchestrating many film musicals (*The Music Man, Finian's Rainbow, Hello Dolly!*) and TV shows. "I worked for Jack Webb on lots of shows like *Dragnet, The D.A.,* and six years on *Adam-12*.

"I don't remember exactly how I got to compose the Jay Ward stuff. Someone had put in a word for me because I'd done four *Magoo* theatrical cartoons at UPA. The music worked out pretty good; I did the themes for "Fractured Fairy Tales," "Peabody's Improbable History," and "Bullwinkle's Corner" as well as "Rocky." I think those cartoons are funny—they still work, the jokes are still good, and the puns are real corny. They recorded my music in Mexico." Comstock composed a few extra tracks for Ward which were used occasionally: the frantic chase music heard in the "Fairy Tale" "Riding Hoods Anonymous," for instance. Later in 1959 he wrote the music for Jay's adaptation of the Czech film *The Lost Sentry*. This music also turned up as background in a couple of the "Fairy Tales" animated in Hollywood, like "Cinderella."

Fred Steiner An artist deeply immersed in the history of music—particularly film music—Fred Steiner was born in New York on February 24, 1923. He moved to California in 1947, attending the University of Southern California, where he received a doctorate in musicology (he's often called Dr. Fred Steiner). In 1961 he wrote the music for NBC's *Bullwinkle Show*. General

Mills had requested all-new themes for the cartoons; Jay Ward wanted new music as well, so he could control future publishing rights: Comstock's deal had allowed the composer to retain rights through Criterion Music. Skip Craig said, "Coincidentally, Steiner had actually conducted the Mexican orchestra when Comstock's music was recorded back in 1959."

Steiner recalled, "I'd done some music at UPA for the CBS *Gerald McBoing-Boing Show,* and some of the people who were working for Jay, like Bill Hurtz and Bill Scott, had recommended me. My father, George Steiner, had done a lot of animation music for Fleischer and Terrytoons back east. And I always had a soft spot for animation; I really love composing for cartoons.

"I'd been living in Mexico City for a couple of years, and when we recorded the Jay Ward cartoon music, I used the Mexico City Symphony Orchestra; they were superb musicians. We did a whole tracking library, although much of it, unfortunately, was never used.

"For the 'Dudley Do-Right' opening I worked in the old tradition. When I wrote it nothing had been animated, although they gave me an idea of the timing involved. So I composed a theme that had jaunty galloping music, then I put in a suspenseful scene, then it went back to the galloping music. I was delighted to see that when Bill Littlejohn animated to it, he'd invented a cutaway scene of Nell being tied to the railway tracks to match that suspense break.

"My father and I then composed a lot of piano tracks for the 'Dudley' backgrounds. I owned a large collection of old piano music from the nineteenth century, and my father had actually played accompaniment to silent films in New York theaters. So we did all these authentic melodramatic piano tracks—arranged for four hands. I went back to Mexico City and employed two fine pianists to duet. To achieve the tinny sound we had paper clips and bits of paper attached to the piano strings. Then Jay made a very clever suggestion, and the tracks were sped up back at Glen Glenn studio; they were pitched up by about one [major] third [actually by 25 percent].

"*The Bullwinkle Show* theme was requested by Jay. He said we want a real Broadway-type opening, so we called this music 'The Show Biz Theme,' and in the closing music I wrote a sort of 'broken record' effect which was kind of just stolen from some Spike Jones thing floating around in my head.

"Bill Scott was one of the funniest people I ever met, very creative. I liked him very much. He had a project which was an animated version of *Act Without Words* by Samuel Beckett. He liked my work, so I wrote the music for this and recorded it. It was all percussion. Then the project was abandoned. Later Bill Hurtz was interested in it, so he got the [story]boards, but he got too busy with the Quaker commercials. Then Gerard Baldwin was going to have a go at it. It was never completed. [A pencil-test exists.]

"And I really liked Jay Ward. He was a completely zany guy, and I had a wonderful time working with him. The cartoons he made were great; the dialogue was so fast it used to be a source of amusement. We'd say, 'Gee, people are going to miss some of the jokes,' and Jay would laugh and say, 'That's great, that means they'll have to watch them again.'

"Jay's staff were great, too. Lew Keller was a marvelous man, and Gerry Ray was a real peach. Gerry did a lot of stuff in Mexico. Then he died of cancer, which was really unexpected, it was so sudden."

Dennis Farnon Dennis Farnon worked on more projects for Jay Ward than any other musician. His work is distinctive, often sounding like a mixture of Spike Jones, with some of the fangs removed, and Hoyt Curtin, the prolific Hanna-Barbera composer. Farnon's music employs an eclectic variety of whistles and bells, a prominent saxophone, and offbeat percussion, providing a great bouncy feel, perfect for shows like *Fractured Flickers*.

Born in Toronto on August 13, 1928, Farnon went to Chicago to study at the Midwestern School of Music at the age of nineteen. Three years later he was in California, composing and arranging for TV pilot films. In 1954 he was introduced to the animation world by scoring for *Mr. Magoo* cartoons. Farnon became the West Coast album director at RCA for several years; in 1957 he was one of the five founders of the National Academy of Recording Arts and Sciences, the organization which bestows the annual Grammy Awards.

Farnon began working for Jay Ward in 1959. He composed for the *Watts Gnu* and *Hoppity Hooper* pilots, the aborted "Winnie the Pooh" project, the *Rocky the Flying Squirrel* children's album, and the *Fractured Flickers* pilot, and he led the Bullwinkle Philharmonic Orchestra at the Bullwinkle statue unveiling in September 1961. Before 1961 was over, Farnon departed for Europe and further musical studies at Boulanger in Paris. He began composing for TV and film in England, and it was in London that he recorded his superb background music for the *Fractured Flickers* series between May and September of 1962. Of his *Flickers* music, Farnon modestly offered, "It was certainly fun to write."

For the last two decades, Dennis Farnon has created compositions for the concert hall: orchestral works, chamber music, quartets, and trios. After residing in Portugal for five years, and England for another ten, Farnon moved to Holland in 1981, where he has lived since. He recalled, "Working with Jay and Bill were some of the happiest years of my musical life; composing the *Magoo* films with Pete Burness at UPA, working with Joe Siracusa at Storyboard, and the mad hatters at Jay Ward Productions, life was a paradise of complete joy and laughter." His musical family includes older brothers Robert and Brian Farnon.

THE EDITORS

Skip Craig Born George B. Craig in Detroit Lakes, Minnesota, in November 1931, Skip graduated from Detroit Lakes High School, where he lettered in four sports. Soon after entering Hamline University, he quit to go to Hollywood, trying for any type of job with the Spike Jones Musical Depreciation Revue ("I was the world's biggest Spike Jones fanatic"). To his wide-eyed delight, he got a position as band boy and traveled with the Jones show in 1951–52, until he was drafted for the Korean conflict in 1953.

Back in Minnesota, Skip graduated from the American Institute of the Air (in 1955), and was set to be a play-by-play sportscaster when Joe Siracusa, former drummer with Spike Jones, offered him an editing job at UPA. "Joe and Roger Donley were about my two closest friends in the world. Joe gradually stacked the cutting room at UPA with his friends, all Spike Jones alumni, with Roger, Earl Bennett [better known as Sir Frederick Gas], and me."

Craig worked there from 1955 to 1959, on segments of the *Gerald McBoing-Boing Show,* numerous commercials, several *Magoo* shorts, and the feature *1001 Arabian Nights,* on which project he met Bill Scott. "This was the spring of 1958. When Roy Morita and Sam Clayberger did the *Rocky* pilot for Jay—the only pilot animated by two nonanimators!—they got me to read the track for them. Then Jay had me do the EFX [sound effects] and dub the pilot. In '59, from May till October, I read the tracks on the *Rocky* show, and then in October Roger and I went to Jay's full-time."

Recalling the sheer fun of the studio's halcyon days, Skip said, "We all worked out in the basement gym around noon. That was in the main building, and at one point Jay had a guy come down to look at expanding this area and adding a story to the building where we'd have a proper gym area, a couple of baskets and so on. One time Jay even planned to put a swimming pool in the place; he was going to put it around the statue, with a drawbridge entrance, and we could go swimming each noon! He had it all priced, and I think it only came to around $20,000 in those days, but he never followed through on these ideas. It was such a fun place, nobody wanted to leave—although financially it wasn't so great."

An amazingly meticulous and diligent fan of the industry in which he works, Skip Craig has done much invaluable research on the history of the Spike Jones band and network radio shows.

Roger Donley Music editor Roger Donley was born in 1922 in Quincy, Illinois, and grew up immersed in a world of melody: his mother was a musician and his lifelong hobby was music.

A prodigy, Donley gave a piano recital at the age of eight and an accordion recital when he was ten; by the time he reached adulthood he was a multi-instrumentalist. Attending law school at the University of Southern California, he was drafted and served in the Air Force Band in World War II. This took him to China, Burma, and India. After the war, Donley spent eight years (1947–55) playing tuba and bass with the Spike Jones band which called for expert musicianship and comedic flair.

With his broad experience in both the classical and popular music fields, and a solid background in showmanship honed in one-nighters on three continents, Donley was a natural for his recording and editing responsibilities at Ward Productions. He, like Skip Craig, had entered animation with the other Spike Jones alumni, who were all at UPA.

Roger Donley's first stint at Jay Ward's ended abruptly when postproduction transferred to Mexico after the first four *Rocky* shows. But he returned for at least three more tours of duty: *Fractured Flickers,* the Laurel and Hardy movie, and *George of the Jungle*. Donley spent a long time at Bill Melendez Productions doing the *Charlie Brown* cartoon shows, after which he retired. He died in 1995.

Joe Siracusa Joseph J. Siracusa was born in Cleveland, Ohio, in 1922, and like Donley, came from a musical family. He won a drummer's audition with Spike Jones and spent six years with the City Slickers, from 1946 to 1952. The first musician to work in UPA's cutting room, Siracusa performed occasional jobs for Ward Productions. He supervised, recorded, and cut the music on various live-action compilations for Jay Ward: *The General, Three Keaton Shorts, The Golden Age of Keaton,* and *The Vintage W. C. Fields*. He retired after working several years at DePatie-Freleng and Marvel Productions.

MISCELLANEOUS

Ted Key Ted Key, creator of the "Peabody and Sherman" segment, was born in Fresno, California, on August 25, 1912. After a stint writing radio shows for J. Walter Thompson, he became nationally famous in 1943 for his panel cartoon featuring a sassy maid named *Hazel.* This appeared in the *Saturday Evening Post* for a quarter century until 1969, and is still syndicated by King Features. A highly successful artist, Ted Key conceived about a fifth of the cover ideas for the *Post,* including many painted by Norman Rockwell. He has had thousands of other cartoons published, along with twenty-one books, and a ten-year feature for *Jack & Jill* magazine called "Diz and Liz." He has also written movies like *Million Dollar Duck, The Cat from Outer Space* (both for Disney), and *The Biggest Dog in the World.*

Ted Key had known Ward since the 1930s, when his kid brother Len went to school with Jay and Alex Anderson. Ted had attended the same school and college, graduating from the University of California, Berkeley, in 1933.

After creating "Peabody" Ted Key dropped out of the picture. But he stayed in touch with Ward, attending the Coney Island Film Festival and the Picnic at the Plaza. Key recalled, "Walter Annenberg, who owned and sold *TV Guide* and was U.S. ambassador to England, was a *Bullwinkle* fan. When Jay and Howard Brandy toured the East Coast to publicize the show, they stopped overnight at my home in Valley Forge. I called my dear friend Merrill Panitt, editorial director of *TV Guide*, and told him Jay was in town. He, too, was wild about *Bullwinkle.* So over to his house we went. There Merrill called his boss on the main line at his estate and bingo! He wanted to meet Jay! So over to his mansion we went. And that's how Bullwinkle got to appreciate, and 'meet' Renoir, Picasso, Van Gogh, and other greats, hanging on Annenberg's walls. Jay was at his best that night."

Leonard Key Associated with Jay Ward for a number of years, Len Key was involved with the sale of both *Crusader Rabbit* and *Rocky*. From 1958 to 1960 he was in charge of all sales at Ward Productions and ran the New York office. Key cofounded and set up P.A.T. in 1958.

Leonard Key was born on November 30, 1920. The younger brother of Ted Key, he attended UC Berkeley with Ward and Alex Anderson, graduating with an A.B. in 1942. In 1947 he began a career selling, merchandising, and financing film properties. Len Key was highly experienced with agency and network sales. In 1952 he won the New York Critics' Circle

Award for his Broadway coproduction of *Pal Joey,* voted Best Musical of the Year. For a time he was sales manager at Shamus Culhane Productions.

Key, by the way, is not the original family name. Leonard revealed, "Our real name is Keyser (pronounced Kaiser), but earlier this century that was not the coolest name to have."

Jerry Fairbanks Jerry Fairbanks, the supervising producer of Jay Ward's first TV venture, *Crusader Rabbit,* was born in San Francisco in 1904. After the 1906 earthquake destroyed the Fairbanks family home they moved to Arizona, then on to Mexico, where Fairbanks's father was a Pacific Railroad supervisor. As a youth Fairbanks was fascinated by photography; in high school he ran a theater and bought his first movie camera. Graduating from the University of Arizona, Fairbanks became a projectionist. In 1930 he ventured into film production, photographing the *Strange As It Seems* series for Universal. He soon became known as a specialist in the field of short subjects, with packages like *Popular Science* and *Unusual Occupations* to his credit.

Fairbanks really established his reputation with the *Speaking of Animals* shorts, which netted him Oscars in 1944 and 1946, the year he entered the infant TV industry. By the time he began producing *Crusader Rabbit* he had built a solid track record in TV with series for NBC (*Public Prosecutor* and *Musical Journeys*) as well as many commercials. Fairbanks, a professional pilot since the 1920s, died, aged ninety-one, in 1995.

Peter M. Piech Peter Piech was born in Brooklyn on June 30, 1918. Of Ukrainian extraction, Piech began in journalism, which led to a job with Luce Publications. He entered the youthful TV industry in film company First National's television division Screencraft as executive vice president of sales; Piech sold CBS its first feature film, *Knickerbocker Holiday,* and TV's first color series on two-inch videotape, *Pip the Piper.*

With P.A.T. from 1958, Piech had a reputation as a savvy salesman with a list of connections established over the years. Later he joined forces with sound man Tread Covington and Buck Biggers, from the ad agency D-F-S, to form Total Television Productions. Total produced cartoons for General Mills using the same Mexican animation facility as Jay Ward. These shows were also distributed by P.A.T., of which Piech was president; in 1960 an umbrella corporate title was formed: Leonardo TV.

Piech was in on the formation of the Mexican animation studio Gamma

Productions, in which he was a shareholder. He said, "I'm a pragmatist. Gamma did the job and did it well, and I took pride in the fact that all those Spanish artists developed their abilities. But to this day in some cartoon circles, I'm considered the Antichrist of animation."

After leaving P.A.T., Piech formed his own company, Filmtel International Corporation, which distributed the cartoons of both Ward and Total TV until 1979. He explained, "Filmtel was a successor organization responsible for packaging the various elements of the cartoon shows. And PAT Films in New York City was an offshoot which is now the distribution plant facility for all the shows." Piech spent many years in association with Jay Ward, and was heavily involved with the character licensing until Jay's death.

As Jim Critchfield observed, "Peter and Jay had many agreements, and quite a few disagreements, over the years. Peter is actually very entertaining; he's a Russian [*sic*], and a very knowledgeable and cosmopolitan person. He and Jay had good and bad times together, but it's important to acknowledge that Peter was a big player in the story, and he's still one of Jay's greatest fans. He was very proud to be associated with the cartoons." As Piech himself put it, "If I had my time over, I'd do this all again. I've had a ball."

Although he lacked the clout of the Columbia Pictures TV subsidiary Screen Gems, who funded the early Hanna-Barbera material, it should be pointed out that Piech ended up producing over four hundred original half-hour animated TV shows. In the television game that's a track record that Bullwinkle would no doubt describe as "unimpiechable!"

Alan Foshko A native of Brooklyn, Alan Foshko was born in 1934. Blessed with a gift for PR, he began his career as promotional director of Grossinger's Resort, being responsible for "productions" like fashion shows, wine tastings, and sports events. Forming his own company, Alan Foshko Productions, he handled PR for an impressive clientele of Broadway and MGM stars; he looked after talent like Barbra Streisand, Robert Redford, Anthony Perkins, and, of course, Jay Ward.

Foshko mounted several lavishly zany functions for Jay Ward. After the final Ward publicity extravaganza in 1963, Foshko joined Westinghouse as talent coordinator for *The Merv Griffin Show*. Later he traveled the world, handling promotion for movie companies. Today he runs Studio Artists in New York.

Foshko and Ward hit it off immediately: "Jay was a one-of-a-kind guy, and he was my pal. We shared the same kind of humor, completely off-the-wall.

We laughed in each other's company all the time. Jay loved to have fun, and I made him the focus of these events. All the parties we did were made with love, and a sense of enthusiasm. They were like the earliest love-ins."

Howard Brandy Howard Brandy came on board as the West Coast press agent/publicity maven for Jay Ward Productions in 1961. Born in Brooklyn on June 20, 1929, Brandy was in the music business before entering the field of public relations. Combining both, he handled PR for teen idols of the early 1960s, like Fabian and Frankie Avalon. Next he branched out, becoming a motion-picture publicist.

The long association with Jay Ward was a result of Brandy's insomnia. "I was watching television one day when on came *Rocky and His Friends*. I always had a somewhat left-of-center sense of humor, and the show immediately gained an instant fan. I tracked the people down and told them I loved their show. When I got to the apartment and met Jay and Bill they were in the middle of a bet. They were both a little overweight and Jay was betting that Bill would lose weight quicker because he had to climb two steps more than Jay every day: the table Bill did his writing at was in the kitchen, which was two steps higher up than Jay's room! Here were these two grown men talking like this, so of course I immediately fell madly in love with them.

"My first claim to fame was suggesting the Bullwinkle statue, because I'd become a statue nut while I'd been living in London. And straightaway Jay said, 'Hey, that's a great idea!' "

Howard Brandy helped concoct some truly wild ideas, like the Picnic at the Plaza Hotel and the NBC Salvation Army Parade. He was also responsible for Alan Foshko's involvement. "I was fairly shy, but Alan was great for these events; he was brilliant and he craved the limelight himself. I always felt that Alan wanted to be Mike Todd." Brandy accompanied Ward on the famous cross-country Moosylvania statehood stunt, and staged Jay and Ramona Ward's twentieth anniversary party at Frascatti's restaurant in 1963, saying, "Anyone who can stay married to Jay Ward for twenty years deserves a medal."

Brandy and Ward became close friends over the years. "Jay was one of a kind. I've never met a finer person in my life. He was generous to a fault, and he had a heart bigger than Los Angeles. He was the only employer I ever met who, if he had to fire someone, he'd take that person to a champagne luncheon first, then shower them with presents and cash. He was a genius and I always said I'd feel bad if I went for a week without a fix of Jay's company. How do you thank someone for a million laughs?"

Edward Everett Horton and Charlie Ruggles Edward Everett Horton and Charlie Ruggles need no introduction. Famous comedy actors in classic Hollywood movies since the silent days, they co-starred in several 1930s Paramount films. They were born within months of each other, and they died within months of each other. Edward Everett Horton was born on March 18, 1886, in Brooklyn; Charles Sherman Ruggles had arrived five weeks earlier in Los Angeles on February 8, 1886.

"Edward Everett" (as Ward and Scott respectfully addressed him) was six feet two inches tall and blessed with a supremely comic face. Following college, he entered showbiz in 1906, and continued performing until his death on September 29, 1970. Throughout his long film career he was a masterful scene-stealer, particularly in the famous Astaire-Rogers musicals like *Top Hat*. Horton was loved by audiences for his incredible double and triple takes, muttered asides, and fumbling. He was known for what James Robert Parish aptly described in his book *The Funsters* as "an oblique if unbelieving piercing stare."

Bill Scott often recalled his feelings of awe as he observed Horton narrating the "Fractured Fairy Tales" at such an advanced age. "One time I asked him, 'Edward Everett, to what do you attribute your energy at an age when most people are retired?' and he said, 'Well, Bill, do you know where I'm going after this recording? I'm going to my mother's birthday party!' "

June Foray recalled Horton's chauffeur picking him up and taking him to tennis matches after a session. She added that in private, Horton was something of a cheapskate: "He was really quite penurious. One evening he was wearing a really thick sweater; I mean it was so big it wouldn't quit. I remember it was winter, and I asked him where he'd bought such a magnificent garment. And he pulled that famous prissy face, and said, very proudly, 'Why, this is my high school sweater!' "

Charlie Ruggles's association with Ward was quite brief—just one year, recording the thirty-nine "Aesop and Son" episodes. Daws Butler loved working with him, and June Foray called him "a delightful old man." He was noted in films of the 1930s and 1940s for his performances as dominated husbands or timid underdogs. Gifted, like Horton, with an expressive face, Ruggles would use knowing smiles, raised eyebrows, and nervous coughs for his trademark apologetic little men. He had been a frequent radio performer—many screen actors couldn't master this totally different medium—and in the 1950s had his own show, a situation comedy called *The Ruggles,* which was also seen on TV. Charlie Ruggles died on December 23, 1970.

Chris Allen Little information was found on Chris Allen, who was also known as Melba Lee (Lee being her married name). Latterly a drama teacher at California State University, Northridge, she had been featured on radio and TV commercials, and was at one time a producer-writer in that field. A close friend of Daws Butler, she had a great time playing the title role in *Hoppity Hooper* for Jay Ward, and later executed a similar voice as Scooter in the 1966 Hanna-Barbera series *Space Kidettes.*

Not intended as a slight to the many other people who worked at or for Jay Ward's studio, certain names were simply impossible to track down. Others, sadly, had passed away, including animators like Rudy Zamora and Bob Schleh.

APPENDIX 2

REVISITING THE JAY WARD RECORDING SESSIONS

> Jay seems to have been born with an innate talent for animation sound and voice recording; in the studio he was a perfectionist.
>
> —*Leonard Key*

To many *Bullwinkle Show* fanatics, the greatest assets of Jay Ward's cartoons are their distinctive sound tracks. As George Atkins observed, "Compare the wooden and slipshod deliveries one hears today on Saturday morning animated shows to the performances heard on *Bullwinkle* and it is to compare the Old Vic to a high school rendition of *Our Town*."

The voice artists whom Ward hired were simply the best in Hollywood. Bill Scott called them "the Jay Ward Mighty Art Players" (a nod to Fred Allen's old radio show in which the comedian dubbed his stock company "the Might Allen Art Players"). Scott said, "The core of them came from radio; this is why they were so good at doubling and doing voices—it's how they earned their living in the pre-TV era. And they were all very successful radio actors. Paul Frees had two radio shows in which he was the star, June Foray was constantly sought after, being able to double on so many voices, and Daws Butler as a mimic—as the Rich Little of his time—had toured nationally, doing live material. So these were very experienced people in their field. And it should be pointed out that all three of these people were diminutive, so the chance of them making a normal go from radio into movies or live television was nil: everything would have to be scaled down for them. But as voice-overs, they hit a marvelous niche. So when we got these people in, we were getting pretty much the cream of the crop when it came to playing lots of characters."

Chief among his many production chores, the recording sessions were Jay Ward's passion. Daws Butler recalled, "We were like his toys. He loved to make us do a take over again." Ward had first taken charge of sound recording on *Crusader Rabbit* in 1948. A decade later he began working with the actors profiled here, kicking off a quarter century of the greatest character voice sessions ever held for TV cartoons.

In mid-1961, Ward and Scott discussed these performers in a newspaper article. Ward explained, "We use a narrator, so that the stories and action can jump around easily. If the narrator is 'up' in the recording session everything falls into place. If not, we have a hard night. If the actors are down, we just turn out the lights and go home."

Bill Scott added, "From 1947 to 1953 things were really tough on the radio voice people who were having trouble in their own industry and could no longer count on the movie cartoon business which started to go down the sink. It turned out that residuals on commercials for the newer medium of TV saved them, and now the voice people are in great demand and reaping the dividends. There is a magnificent golden backwash of people who can't do anything else because of their height. People like Daws Butler, Paul Frees, Mel Blanc and June Foray find gold in their mailbox most mornings."

When quizzed about their use of well-known personalities—Edward Everett Horton, Hans Conried, William Conrad (still being heard at the time on the radio version of *Gunsmoke*), and Charlie Ruggles—Scott replied, "We go for actors. It's like picking out the fish for your guppy tank. What we look for is a community fish to join our group."

Ruggles and Conried had already worked for Disney (Hans Conried's most famous role being the magnificently evil Captain Hook in *Peter Pan*), and their distinctive speech patterns worked perfectly for the subtle comedy and sly narration within Ward's scripts. Ruggles and Horton were Bill Scott's choices while "Conrad came recommended to us by Paul Frees. We were looking for a strong narrator for the 'Rocky' segments, and I'd been familiar with his radio work."

Bill Scott was no slouch either. Staff member Skip Craig would often state, "Scott is the best voice man in cartoons." Bill was more of a "natural" talent than the others, being primarily the head writer and coproducer. For a part-time actor involved in many different fields, he was a remarkably gifted player.

Two talents common to all members of Jay Ward's core team (Scott, Frees, Foray, and Butler) were a natural flair for audio comedy and an ability to create characterizations which were eccentric yet believable. Each actor was highly original—in those days there were no "old voice masters" to study. During cold rehearsal readings they immediately grasped the gist of the jokes. And all shared the radio actor's peculiar trick of occasionally misreading a line, yet delivering the joke correctly. The life of a busy voice-over artist is blessed with a degree of anonymity; Bill Scott, when asked if he enjoyed being a cartoon voice, joked, "Well, there's little glory . . . it's a golden rut."

THE RECORDING SESSIONS

In May 1959 Jay Ward began taping the first sound tracks for *Rocky and His Friends,* to provide a backlog for the new Mexican animation studio. The pilot episode of *Rocky* was slated to be the first segment for broadcast, and with several new scripts finished in April, Ward was off and running. The first regular recording session was held on Saturday, May 23, 1959, at Glen Glenn Sound on Romaine Street in Hollywood. The material that evening consisted of "Rocky" episodes 2 through 6 (episode 1, the pilot, had been recorded on February 11, 1958).

This session set the pattern for the next three and a half years: once five scripts of a particular show segment were written, they were taped in one evening. By recording at night, Ward and Scott knew there would be no conflicts with bookings. "Jay knew he could get the services of our actors more easily after 5:30 P.M.," said Scott.

Also on that first date, the two initial "Bullwinkle's Corner" segments were immortalized on tape. This became a tradition: extra fill-in bits and show bridges were done, as required, after the five main episodes were down.

For the second session, five days later, the first five "Fractured Fairy Tales" were completed. These early recordings were a little tentative (this one stretching on until three o'clock in the morning), with actors and staff getting used to the unique comedy feel of the shows, as well as forging themselves into a team familiar with one another's bag of tricks.

With the first two dates completed, production began on the marriage of sound to image. Each day Skip Craig averaged one "track reading" (in which he broke the dialogue into syllables—phonetics style—on exposure sheets, for the animators' frame-by-frame timing). For the first few months, before he was an employee, Skip worked alongside three former members of Spike Jones's band: Roger Donley, Earl Bennett, and Joe Siracusa, all of whom had experience in animation editing at UPA.

The third session date (July 14, 1959) produced five more "Rocky" episodes, followed nine days later by a test episode for "Peabody's Improbable History" with Bill Scott as Mr. Peabody and Lucille Bliss as Sherman. She was deemed unsuitable for the role and was replaced by Walter Tetley on July 29, when the first five "Peabody"s were cut.

The fourth set of "Rocky" episodes, recorded on July 30, 1959, was also the occasion when the show opening was recorded by Bill Conrad, as well as the first bridges. (Bridges are those elements in a cartoon show which serve as segues from one item to the next. The first memorable "Watch me pull a rabbit outta my hat" gag was done on this occasion.) This was the session when everything fell into place; from this point on, the countless recording dates proceeded like a well-oiled machine.

Bill Scott recalled, "When we were going hot and heavy on the *Bullwinkle* series we often recorded as much as three times a week." Skip Craig often said, "My one regret is that I never went along to one of those sessions; they must have been great."

The last "Peabody" episodes were completed on April 5, 1961. On May 26, in readiness for the switch to NBC and the revamped *Bullwinkle Show,* the first five "Dudley Do-Right" cartoons were recorded. After twenty episodes, Paul Frees, who from the start half-jokingly complained about the burden of being the narrator as well as many funny voices, was pleased to see his old crony Bill Conrad take over as narrator of the remaining "Dudley"s. Hans Conried, who had done such a splendidly oily job as the Wicked Wazir in UPA's 1959 Mr. Magoo feature, was Scott and Ward's immediate choice for Snidely Whiplash (Scott had been dialogue director on the Magoo film).

The final "Rocky and Bullwinkle" session occurred on December 11, 1962. Most of 1963 was taken up recording Cap'n Crunch's first TV spots, and doing looping and postproduction work on *Fractured Flickers*. From January 2, 1964, through December 21, 1966, the *Hoppity Hooper* series was taped in convenient four-episode blocks, the *Hoppity* format being complete stories in four segments.

From April through October of 1967, "George of the Jungle," "Super Chicken," and "Tom Slick" episodes were recorded at TV Recorders on Sunset Boulevard, where the *Rocky* pilot had been dubbed in 1958. This was the regular sound studio Ward booked from 1965 onward. *George of the Jungle,* Quaker cereal commercials, and all of Ward's unsold pilot films were recorded at TVR. Coincidentally, the studio was right next door to Jerry Fairbanks Productions, where *Crusader Rabbit* had been assembled years earlier.

The usual procedure for the voice artists was to read through the scripts once and then go straight into recording. There was no need for multiple rehearsals with such pros. Ward directed from the booth, and from the beginning Scott was the "floor" director, announcing episode titles and numbers of takes, and guiding the actors' delivery of the lines. (Ward was also talented at this and possessed an acutely sensitive ear.) Ward was in charge of script notations and ordering certain speeches redone as "pickups"—odd lines to be edited later into the okay take. A stickler for "clean" voices, Jay wanted no foggy sounds. Early on in the series he earned the monikers "Ace" and "Mr. Big," while Conrad always called him "Jay-Baby."

Ward directed the sessions wisely. He was an actor's dream: instinctively in tune, willing to stroke, and allowing creative license. The performers respected one another, and this family-team feel is obvious in the cartoons. Ward was also a great audience, and for an actor, an appreciative, laughing producer is all that's needed to elicit a sharp performance.

For ten solid years on the cartoons and another decade of commercials, the loud and supremely silly Paul Frees compulsively entertained Jay Ward. Frees craved being the center of attention, and had intuitively guessed what Lew Keller observed: "Jay loved performance, and he thought comedy was the greatest thing there is." Frees was a self-confessed show-off, and delighted in feigning irreverence for Ward and his TV shows and most especially his fellow actors. Astutely summing him up, Bill Scott said, "Frees was the most infuriating yet talented show-off son of a bitch I've ever known, but we all loved him. You just didn't dare let him know!" Frees invariably reduced William Conrad to a fit of giggles. Occasionally, like two overgrown schoolkids, one would have to leave the room while the other recorded some extra lines, in case they looked at each other and broke up.

Bill Scott recalled, "The recording sessions were the happiest time of everybody involved. Conrad, Paul, Hans Conried thought it was the greatest. Bill Conrad used to come over from shooting [on the Warner lot], in makeup and girdle, and say it was great to work with people who were professional. He would break up laughing, and although he has this deep voice, he has a high, high laugh, and when that started . . ."

However, as easy as it was to rag William Conrad, Frees found it next to impossible to repeat this with Hans Conried, who subscribed to the old school of theatrical "professionalism." Conried prided himself on not breaking up, expressing mild annoyance at too much frivolity. In truth, Conried respected Frees's talent. He understood actors well enough to realize that Frees's ego-tripping was actually a nervously compulsive trait. Besides, Paul Frees was undeniably funny, and Jay Ward loved the whole charade. To his credit, Frees was totally reliable; but in his own non-J rated words, "I just always loved to 'f—k around.' " Both he and Ward were simpatico, each retaining a measure of childlike playfulness in adult life and wearing it like a badge. Still, there was hardly a recording date in the entire twenty-five years of Jay Ward Productions when someone didn't yell, "Shut up, Paul!"

For the record, Jay Ward trivia buffs should know about two specific recording dates. On August 20, 1959, the second "Peabody" session was held, and the three female roles—Lucretia Borgia, Queen Elizabeth, and Annie Oakley—were played by Dorothy Scott, Bill's wife. Both Scotts were experienced thespians in the Church of the Ascension Players in Tujunga. Dot had done voice work at UPA with Bill, including the *Gerald McBoing-Boing Show*.

And April 19, 1960, saw the final session for the first series of "Fractured Fairy Tales." On that night June Foray had to get away early for a recording with Stan Freberg, so another actress, Julie Bennett, did three of the "Fairy Tales." Ironically, notes June, "Stan was, typically, about three hours late anyway!" (Note, too, that after this date there was a break of twelve months before the final thirty-nine "Fairy Tales" were recorded, during which time the "Aesop and Son" stories were taped over eight sessions.)

To a very large extent, the Jay Ward Mighty Art Players were responsible for the success of Ward's sound tracks. Along with the best writers in TV animation, they created the memorable audio signature of what could only be a Jay Ward Production.

REFERENCE SECTION

SYNOPSES AND VOICE CREDITS FOR THE JAY WARD CARTOONS

CRUSADER RABBIT

(Television Arts Productions, 1948–51)

NBC (Syndicated by Jerry Fairbanks Productions)

Crusader Rabbit:	Lucille Bliss
Ragland T. Tiger:	Vern Louden
Narrator:	Roy Whaley
Other Voices:	Russ Coughlin, Patti Pritchard, Tom Stanford.

(Crusader Rabbit is the only Jay Ward series for which detailed voice credits per episode do not exist.)

1–15
Crusader vs. the State of Texas (15 episodes)—The people of Texas begin deporting their jackrabbits to the North Pole. Crusader Rabbit is informed by Frank Sawbuck (famed rabbit and hare removalist) that the jackrabbits are eating all the state's carrots, thus depriving Texas's sharpshooting cowboys of their keen eyesight. Crusader changes the rabbits' diet to cream puffs.

16–35
Crusader vs. the Pirates (20 episodes)—Crusader and Rags arrive on Dunkin Island, which bobs above and below water level, and which has caused the natives to evolve into "merbunnies." Our hero foils a plot by Black Bilge and his pirate gang to steal all the silverware from New York City.

36–55
Crusader and the Rajah of Rinsewater (20 episodes)—The Rajah of Rinsewater is trapping India's tigers to steal their stripes for India ink. Crusader and Rags discover that Dudley Nightshade has replaced Prime Minister Ali Oxenfree, in order to loot the province.

56–70
Crusader and the Schmohawk Indians (15 episodes)—The diminished Schmohawk Indian tribe is helped by Crusader, who suggests they fake going on the warpath for publicity. But the timid tribe flees when General Horsewhip and the U.S. Army are called in. They land in Robber's Roost, an outlaw town run by Babyface Barracuda, who disguises his gang as Schmohawks, thus ensuring the Indians will be blamed for bank robberies.

71–90
Crusader and the Great Horse Mystery (20 episodes)—Crusader's old pal Andiron the Fire Horse needs help. The steeds of Oatville, Kentucky, are vanishing. Crusader learns that Gaston Glub (of Glub's Glue fame) is making a new superglue from horse's hooves. Unfortunately, our heroes are framed as horse thieves.

91–100
Crusader and the Circus (10 episodes)—Rags's childhood home—Colonel E. Pluribus Truepenny's traveling circus—is in trouble: the Colonel is missing, and his will states the circus will go to evil ringmaster Whetstone Whiplash and his brutish sidekick Achilles the Heel. The villains imprison Rags as "recovered circus property."

101–130
Crusader and the Tenth Century (30 episodes)—Blackheart, Brimstone, and Bigot (the nasty Blaggard brothers) terrorize Merrie Olde England. When they ask Sir Chester Chillblain for his daughter Mary

Anne's hand in marriage, the court magician casts a spell which can deliver two heroes from the future. Crusader and Rags must rescue Mary Anne from the Blaggards' castle, which is being guarded by Arson and Sterno, a two-headed fire-breathing dragon.

131–145
Crusader and the Mad Hollywood Scientist (15 episodes)—Vengeful Professor Belfry Q. Batts—a frustrated actor—invents gloom juice, to make all Hollywood actors ugly. When Crusader investigates, Rags is connected to a brain-switching machine along with Batt's assistant, Vemon the vulture. Crusader saves the day by feeding a happiness extract to the Professor.

146–170
Crusader and the Leprechauns (25 episodes)—Crusader, Rags, and Garfield Groundhog travel to Ireland with leprechaun chief Pat Finnegan to find Finn McCool XIII, a greedy giant who has driven the leprechauns from their homeland. Crusader learns that nobody has actually seen the giant, but they have seen his secretary, Dudley Nightshade.

171–195
Crusader and the Showboat (25 episodes)—Captain Huckleberry, owner of the Mississippi showboat *Levee Belle,* thinks he's being jinxed by the headless Oarsman, a river ghost. But Crusader, Rags, and Garfield discover the real villains: Whetstone Whiplash and Achilles the Heel, disguised as Sternwheel Jackson and Rhatt Butler of the *Jezebel*, a rival gambling boat.

THE ADVENTURES OF BULLWINKLE AND ROCKY

(Episodes 1–156 originally appeared on *Rocky and His Friends*)

Key to abbreviations	Regular voices
WC = William Conrad	Narrator
PF = Paul Frees	Boris
BS = Bill Scott	Bullwinkle
JF = June Foray	Rocky and Natasha

1–40
Jet Fuel Formula—Rocket J. Squirrel and Bullwinkle J. Moose accidentally discover a rocket fuel which propels them to the moon and back. Bullwinkle is put to work by the government to rediscover the formula, but our boys soon become the target of Pottsylvanian spies Boris Badenov and Natasha Fatale, and moon men Cloyd and Gidney (who don't want earth tourists on the moon). Bullwinkle must find a source for mooseberries, his secret ingredient. This leads to a great adventure which includes an ocean voyage via Captain Peachfuzz's liner the SS *Andalusia,* being marooned on Bloney Island, almost getting jailed in the sinister country of Pottsylvania, crossing the Grimalaya Mountains, and helping the moon men return home.

1. *Jet Fuel Formula—Episode One*
   WC: Narrator, General. JF: Rocky, Natasha. BS: Bullwinkle, Dr. Milton Nudnik, Subway Rider #1. PF: Boris, Sir Newton Fugg, Newsboy, Dorson Belles, George, Credney Blatt.
2. *Bullwinkle's Ride or Goodbye, Dollink*
   WC: Narrator. JF: Rocky, Natasha, 2 Grandmothers. BS: Bullwinkle, Scientist, Russian Scientist #2. PF: Boris, Lecturer, Russian #1, Council Head.
3. *Bullseye Bullwinkle or Destination Moose*
   WC: Narrator. JF: Rocky, Natasha. BS: Bullwinkle, Gidney. PF: Boris, Cloyd, General.
4. *Squeeze Play or Invitation to the Trance*
   WC: Narrator. JF: Rocky, Natasha. BS: Bullwinkle, Gidney. PF: Boris, Cloyd.

5. *The Scroodched Moose*
WC: Narrator. JF: Rocky. BS: Bullwinkle, Gidney, Moon Man. PF: Boris, Cloyd, Leader of Moon Men.

6. *Monitored Moose or The Carbon Copy-Cats*
WC: Narrator. JF: Rocky. BS: Bullwinkle, Gidney, Fearless Leader, Scientist #1. PF: Boris, Cloyd, Scientist #2.

7. *Rocky's Dilemma or A Squirrel in a Stew*
WC: Narrator. JF: Natasha, Newsboy, 2 Women. BS: Bullwinkle, Gidney, Policeman, Man #1. PF: Boris, Cloyd, Governor Abner, Man #2.

8. *The Submarine Squirrel or 20,000 Leagues Beneath the Sea*
WC: Narrator. JF: Rocky, Natasha. BS: Bullwinkle, Gidney, General Broadbeam. PF: Boris, Cloyd, Radar Man.

9. *The Bars and Stripes Forever*
WC: Narrator. JF: Rocky, Admiring Woman. BS: Bullwinkle, Gidney, Special Agent, FBI Man. PF: Cloyd, TV Announcer.

10. *Hello Out There! or There's no Place Like Space*
WC: Narrator. JF: Rocky, Natasha. BS: Bullwinkle, Gidney, Submarine Pilot. PF: Boris, Cloyd.

11. *A Creep in the Deep or Will Success Spoil Boris Badenov?*
WC: Narrator. JF: Rocky, Natasha. BS: Bullwinkle, Airline Man, Bus Man, Pilot. PF: Boris, Cloyd, Railroad Man.

12. *Ace Is Wild or The Flying Casket*
WC: Narrator. JF: Rocky, Natasha, Newsboy. BS: Bullwinkle, Fearless Leader, Gorki. PF: Boris, Gorki's Assistant.

13. *The Back-seat Divers or Mashed Landing*
WC: Narrator. JF: Rocky, Natasha. BS: Bullwinkle, Fearless Leader. PF: Boris.

14. *Bullwinkle's Water Follies or Antlers Aweigh*
WC: Narrator. JF: Rocky, Natasha. BS: Bullwinkle, Fearless Leader. PF: Boris.

15. *The Inspector-Detector or A Kick in the Plants*
WC: Narrator. JF: Rocky, Natasha. BS: Bullwinkle. PF: Boris.

16. *Canoes Who? or Look Before You Leak*
WC: Narrator. JF: Rocky, Natasha, Boy, Woman in Tunnel of Love. BS: Bullwinkle, Seaway Operator, Spectator. PF: Boris, Policeman, Tunnel of Love Operator.

17. *Two for the Ripsaw . . . or Goodbye, Mr. Chips*
WC: Narrator. JF: Rocky, Natasha. BS: Bullwinkle, Edward, Captain Plopoff. PF: Boris, Chauncey, Congressman Droopleton Bunn, Crowd Man.

18. *Farwell My Ugly or Knots to You*
WC: Narrator. JF: Rocky, Bellhop. BS: Bullwinkle, Gidney. PF: Boris, Cloyd, Theatrical Man, Code Man.

19. *Cheerful Little Pierful or Bomb Voyage*
WC: Narrator. JF: Rocky, Natasha. BS: Bullwinkle, Fearless Leader, Captain Peachfuzz, Customs Officer. PF: Boris.

20. *Summer Squash or He's Too Flat for Me*
WC: Narrator. JF: Rocky, Natasha. BS: Bullwinkle, Captain Peachfuzz, Ship's Doctor. PF: Boris.

21. *The Earl & the Squirrel or The March of Crime*
WC: Narrator. JF: Rocky, Natasha. BS: Bullwinkle. PF: Boris.

22. *Adrift in the Mist or Fog Groggy*
WC: Narrator. JF: Rocky, Natasha. BS: Bullwinkle, Captain Peachfuzz, Officer #2. PF: Boris, Officer #1, Admiral.

23. *The Deep Six or The Old Moose and the Sea*
WC: Narrator. JF: Rocky, Natasha. BS: Bullwinkle, Captain Peachfuzz, Radar Man, Baseball Announcer. PF: Boris, Sailor, Radio Man, Commander, Coast Guard Man.

24. *The Slippery Helm or Captain's Outrageous*
WC: Narrator. JF: Rocky, Natasha, Newsboy. BS: Bullwinkle, Captain Peachfuzz, Fearless Leader. PF: Boris, Newsboy.

25. *Bullwinkle Makes a Hit or I Get a Bang out of You*
WC: Narrator. JF: Rocky, Natasha. BS: Bullwinkle, Captain Peachfuzz. PF: Boris.

26. *Three on an Island or Tell It to the Maroons*
WC: Narrator. JF: Rocky. BS: Bullwinkle, Captain Peachfuzz, Fearless Leader. PF: Boris, Sam, Ship's Passenger, Native.

27. *Dancing on Air or The Pottsylvania Polka*
WC: Narrator. JF: Rocky, Natasha. BS: Bullwinkle, Fearless Leader, Feodor. PF: Boris, Crowd Member, Feodor's Pal.

28. *Axe Me Another or Heads You Lose!*
WC: Narrator. JF: Rocky, Natasha. BS: Bullwinkle, Fearless Leader, Feodor. PF: Boris, Axeman, Feodor's Pal, Jailer, Pottsylvanian.

29. *The Pen-Pals or Rock Hocky Rocky*
WC: Narrator. JF: Rocky, Lady on TV. BS: Bullwinkle, Fearless Leader, Captain Peachfuzz, Commercial Singer. PF: Boris, Jailer, Commercial Singer.

30. *The Fright-Seeing Trip or Visit to a Small Panic*
WC: Narrator. JF: Rocky. BS: Bullwinkle, Vanya, Hotel Clerk. PF: Professor, Gottwold, Doorman, Ice Cream Vendor.

31. *Boris Burgles Again or Sinner Take All*
WC: Narrator. JF: Rocky, Natasha. BS: Bullwinkle, Fearless Leader. PF: Boris.

32. *Danger Ahead or Watch Out for Falling Rockys*
WC: Narrator. JF: Rocky, Natasha. BS: Bullwinkle, Fearless Leader. PF: Boris.

33. *Avalanche Is Better Than None or Snows Your Old Man*
WC: Narrator. JF: Rocky, Natasha. BS: Bullwinkle, Echo. PF: Boris.

34. *Below Zero Heroes or I Only Have Ice for You*
WC: Narrator. JF: Rocky, Natasha. BS: Bullwinkle. PF: Boris.

35. *The Snowman Cometh or An Icicle Built for Two*
WC: Narrator. JF: Rocky, Natasha. BS: Bullwinkle, Gidney. PF: Boris.

36. *The Moonman Is Blue or The Inside Story*
WC: Narrator. JF: Rocky, Natasha. BS: Bullwinkle, Gidney, Crater Kid. PF: Boris, Cloyd.

37. *Fuels Rush In or The Star-Sprangled Boner*
WC: Narrator. JF: Rocky, Natasha. BS: Bullwinkle, Gidney, Fearless Leader. PF: Boris, Cloyd, Boat Ticket Clerk.

38. *The Pottsylvania Permanent or I've Grown Accustomed to the Place*
WC: Narrator. JF: Rocky, Natasha. BS: Bullwinkle, Gidney. PF: Boris, Cloyd, Boat Man, Vladimir.

39. *The Boundary Bounders or Some Like It Shot*
WC: Narrator. JF: Rocky. BS: Bullwinkle, Gidney, Reporter. PF: Clyod, Vladimir, Senator Fussmussen.

40. *The Washington Whirl or Rocky Off the Record*
WC: Narrator. JF: Rocky, Newsboy. BS: Bullwinkle, Gidney, Countdown Man, President. PF: Cloyd, Senator Fussmussen.

41–52

Box Top Robbery—An emergency meeting of the World Economic Council reveals that cereal box tops—the real basis of the world's monetary system—are being counterfeited. Suspicion quickly falls on Bullwinkle, who owns the world's largest collection of genuine box tops. But the culprit is really Boris Badenov, disguised as the council's security chief, Hemlock Soames; by counterfeiting box tops, he plans to clean the premiums out of store after store. Business plummets when kids can't redeem goodies with fake box tops. Rocky and Bullwinkle survive close shaves with a skyscraper's clock machinery, a runaway elevator car, and a Coast Guard depth charge, but they finally foil Boris (who is about to turn out an extra million bogus box tops) by accidentally blowing up his printing press.

41. *Box Top Robbery*
WC: Narrator, Russian Economist, JF: Rocky. BS: Bullwinkle, Economist #1, French Economist, Mr. Friendly, Policeman. PF: Fiduciary J Blurt, English Economist, Greek Economist, Arbogast, Police Chief.

42. *A Fault in the Vault or Banks a Million*
WC: Narrator. JF: Rocky, Natasha, Boy #1. BS: Bullwinkle, Grocer, Posh Economist, Meek Economist, Policeman. PF: Fiduciary, J. Blurt, Police Chief, Boy #2, Boris.

43. *Calaboose Moose or The Crime of Your Life*
WC: Narrator. JF: Rocky, Natasha, Boy, Newsboy. BS: Bullwinkle, Grocer, Panicky Man. PF: Fiduciary J. Blurt, Police Chief, Old Man, Reporter, Boris.

44. *When a Felon Needs a Friend or Pantomime Quisling*
WC: Narrator. JF: Rocky, Natasha. BS: Bullwinkle, English Economist, Announcer. PF: Boris, Fiduciary J. Blurt, French Economist, Turkish Economist.

45. *Give 'Em the Works or Rocky Around the Clock*
WC: Narrator. JF: Rocky, Mabel, Mother, Wife. BS: Bullwinkle, Boy, Woodrow. PF: Boris, Fiduciary J. Blurt, Husband, Janitor.

46. *Crime on My Hands or Hickory Dickory Drop*
WC: Narrator. JF: Rocky, Natasha. BS: Bullwinkle, Edward. PF: Boris, Fiduciary J. Blurt, Chauncey.

47. *Down to Earth or the Bullwinkle Bounce*
WC: Narrator. JF: Rocky, Natasha. BS: Bullwinkle, Economist. PF: Boris, Fiduciary J. Blurt.

48. *Fall Story or Adrift in the Lift*
WC: Narrator, 3rd Crowd Member. JF: Rocky, Natasha. BS: Bullwinkle, 2nd Crowd Member. PF: Boris, 1st and 4th Crowd Members.

49. *The Ground Floor or That's Me All Over!*
WC: Narrator. JF: Rocky, Natasha. BS: Bullwinkle, Policeman. PF: Boris, Fiduciary J. Blurt.

50. *Fools Afloat or All the Drips at Sea*
WC: Narrator. JF: Rocky, Natasha. BS: Bullwinkle, Policeman, Carruthers, First Gunman. PF: Boris, Police Captain, Commodore, Second Gunman.

51. *Water on the Brain or the Deep Six and 7/8*
WC: Narrator. JF: Rocky, Natasha. BS: Bullwinkle, Policeman, Carruthers, First Gunman. PF: Boris, Police, Police Chief, Commodore.

52. *Bullwinkle Goes to Press or All the Moose That's Fit to Print*
WC: Narrator. JF: Rocky, Natasha, Child. BS: Bullwinkle, PF: Boris, Eddie.

53–88

Upsidaisium—Bullwinkle inherits a mine from his uncle Dewlap, but it appears as though someone wants to stop our heroes from claiming this inheritance. Rocky and Bullwinkle survive a military minefield and a remote-controlled car trip before Captain Peachfuzz catches up with them in the desert. He explains that the moose's mine is on Mount Flatten, chock-full of an antigravity metal called Upsidaisium, which floats up into space. They must somehow reach the huge floating mountain, and fend off Boris and Natasha (disguised as Mojave Max and Death Valley Dottie), who want the precious metal in order to solve the chronic parking problem in Pottsylvania. Eventually our heroes steer the mountain safely to Washington and foil the evil efforts of Boris and his superior, Mr. Big.

53. *Upsidaisium*
WC: Narrator. JF: Rocky. BS: Bullwinkle. PF: Postmaster James J. Nearly, Herman the Pigeon.

54. *Big Bomb at Frostbite Falls or The Exploding Metropolis*
WC: Narrator. JF: Rocky. BS: Bullwinkle. PF: Boris.

55. *The Road to Ruin or Mine over Matter*
WC: Narrator, Indian Chief. JF: Rocky, Natasha. BS: Bullwinkle, Slim's Friend, Owl-Who-Never-Sleeps. PF: Boris, Slim, General Consternation.

56. *Two Flying Ghosts or High Spirits.*
WC: Narrator. Radio Announcer. JF: Rocky, Natasha. BS: Bullwinkle. PF: Boris, Radio Actor, Captain Peachfuzz.

57. *Crash Drive or Oedipus Wrecks*
WC: Narrator, Radio Announcer. JF: Rocky, Natasha. BS: Bullwinkle. PF: Boris, Radio Actor, Captain Peachfuzz.

58. *Fender Benders or the Asphalt Bungle*
WC: Narrator. JF: Rocky, Natasha. BS: Bullwinkle. PF: Boris, Captain Peachfuzz.

59. *Burning Sands or the Big Hot Foot*
WC: Narrator. JF: Rocky, Natasha. BS: Bullwinkle, Fearless Leader. PF: Boris, Pottsylvanian Aide.

60. *Death in the Desert or A Place in the Sun*
WC: Narrator. JF: Rocky, Natasha. BS: Bullwinkle, Chauncey. PF: Boris, Edward.

61. *The Boy Bounders or Plane Punchy*
WC: Narrator. JF: Rocky, Natasha. BS: Bullwinkle. PF: Boris, Captain Peachfuzz.

62. *A Peek at the Peak or Your Climb Is My Climb*
WC: Narrator. JF: Rocky, Natasha. BS: Bullwinkle, Bradbury, Financier #2, U.S. Maritime Commissioner. PF: Captain Peachfuzz, Bradbury's Friend, Financier #1.

63. *You've Got a Secret or Out of Sight, out of Mine*
WC: Narrator. JF: Rocky, Natasha. BS: Bullwinkle. PF: Boris, Captain Peachfuzz.

64. *Boris and the Blade or Sheik, Rattle and Roll*
WC: Narrator. JF: Rocky, Natasha. BS: Bullwinkle. PF: Boris, Captain Peachfuzz.

65. *Sourdough Squirrel or Hardrock Rocky*
WC: Narrator. JF: Rocky, Natasha. BS: Bullwinkle, Chauncey. PF: Boris, Captain Peachfuzz, Edgar.

66. *A Creep at the Switch or Sudden Pacific*
WC: Narrator. JF: Rocky, BS: Bullwinkle, Zeb, Calvin the Claims Clerk, Scurvy McMurk, Reporter. PF: Boris, Captain Peachfuzz, Zeb's Friend, Henry, Dr. Sebastian Fleegle.

67. *The Train on the Plain or The Overland Express*
WC: Narrator. JF: Rocky, Natasha. BS: Calvin, Bullwinkle, Fearless Leader, Edward. PF: Boris, Henry, Captain Peachfuzz, Chauncey.

68. *Danger in the Desert or Max Attacks*
WC: Narrator. JF: Rocky, Natasha. BS: Bullwinkle, Edgar. PF: Boris, Captain Peachfuzz, Chauncey.

69. *The Missing Mountain or Peek-a-Boo Peak*
WC: Narrator. JF: Rocky, Natasha. BS: Bullwinkle. PF: Boris.

70. *Go Down Mooses or The Fall Guy*
WC: Narrator. JF: Rocky, Natasha. BS: Bullwinkle. PF: Boris.

71. *Rocky and the Rock or Braver and Boulder*
WC: Narrator. JF: Rocky, Natasha, Newsboy #1, Board Member #3. BS: Bullwinkle, Edgar, Board Member #1. PF: Boris, Chauncey, Medicine Man, Newsboy #2, Chairman, Board Member #2.

72. *Mountain Mover or Boris Sneaks a Peak*
WC: Narrator. Agent 7. JF: Rocky, Natasha. BS: Bullwinkle, Agent 9, Agent 2. PF: Boris, Captain Peachfuzz.

73. *Bullwinkle's Rise or This Goon for Higher*
WC: Narrator. JF: Rocky, Natasha. BS: Bullwinkle, Fearless Leader. PF: Boris.

74. *Boris Bites Back or A Rebel Without a Pause*
WC: Narrator. JF: Rocky, Natasha. BS: Bullwinkle, Mr. Big. PF: Boris.

75. *Bullwinkle at the Bottom or Mish-Mash Moose!*
WC: Narrator. JF: Rocky, Natasha, Miss Glum. BS: Bullwinkle, Mr. Big. PF: Boris, Captain Peachfuzz.

76. *Double Trouble or the Moose Hangs High*
WC: Narrator. JF: Rocky, BS: Bullwinkle, Mr. Big. PF: Boris, Captain Peachfuzz.

77. *Jet Jockey Rocky or The One Point Lending*
WC: Narrator. JF: Rocky, Natasha. BS: Bullwinkle. PF: Boris, Captain Peachfuzz.

78. *Plots and Plans or Too Many Crooks*
WC: Narrator. JF: Rocky, Natasha. BS: Bullwinkle. PF: Boris, Captain Peachfuzz.

79. *The Cliff Hanger or Taken for Granite*
WC: Narrator. JF: Rocky, Natasha, Lem's Wife. BS: Bullwinkle, Mr. Big, Zeke, Radio Announcer. PF: Boris, Captain Peachfuzz, Clem, Lem, Newsboy.

80. *Supersonic Boom or The Old Mount's A-Moverin'*
WC: Narrator, Board Member #1. JF: Natasha, Pottsylvanian Wife. BS: Mr. Big, Assembly-Line Head, Car Salesman, Chairman. PF: Boris, Pottsylvanian Husband, Board Member #2, Adloff the Politician, Dr. Poppover.

81. *The Big Blast or A Many Splintered Thing*
WC: Narrator. JF: Rocky, Natasha. BS: Bullwinkle, Mr. Big, Edgar. PF: Boris, Captain Peachfuzz, Guard, Chauncey.

82. *The Steal Hour or A Snitch in Time*
WC: Narrator. JF: Rocky, Natasha. BS: Bullwinkle, Mr. Big, Guard, Chauncey. PF: Boris, Edgar, General Broadbeam.

83. *Verse and Worse or Crime Without Rhyme*
WC: Narrator. JF: Rocky, Natasha. BS: Bullwinkle, Mr. Big. PF: Boris, General Broadbeam.

84. *Truckdrivers in the Sky or Follow the Fleet*
WC: Narrator. JF: Rocky, Woman #1, Woman #2. BS: Bullwinkle, Mr. Big, Nikki, General's Aide, Man #1. PF: Boris, General Broadbeam, Chief Missile Engineer, Feodor, Radar Man, Man #2.

85. *The Squirrel Next Door or High Neighbor*
WC: Narrator. JF: Rocky. BS: Bullwinkle, Mr. Big, Soldier, Ormsby. PF: Boris, General Broadbeam.

86. *The Spell Binders or Hex Marks the Spot*
WC: Narrator. JF: Rocky, Natasha. BS: Bullwinkle, Mr. Big, Sergeant, Chauncey. PF: Boris, General Broadbeam, Edgar.

87. *Battle of the Giants or it Takes Two to Tangle*
WC: Narrator. JF: Rocky, Natasha. BS: Bullwinkle, Mr. Big, Colonel Bogus. PF: Boris, General Broadbeam.

88. *Bye-Bye, Boris or Farewell, My Ugly*
WC: Narrator. JF: Rocky, Natasha. BS: Bullwinkle, Mr. Big, Colonel Bogus, Soldier #1. PF: Boris, General Broadbeam, Soldier #2.

89–104
Metal-Munching Mice—Rocky and Bullwinkle investigate the mysterious disappearance of all the TV antennas in Frostbite Falls. The situation is causing incredible havoc: since the advent of television, the populace simply can't function without it. The trail leads to creepy old Bleakly House, where Bullwinkle discovers the lair of a horde of huge metal-munching mechanical mice led by Boris, disguised as the Big Cheese. His plan is to take over the United States by destroying all TV so that the distraught citizens will desert the country. With 100,000 moon mice ready for pillage and plunder, Bullwinkle discovers he can tame them with a ukelele and his distinctive singing voice.

89. *Metal-Munching Mice*
WC: Narrator. JF: Rocky, Citizen #2, Mother. BS: Bullwinkle, Quincy, Neighbor. PF: Sheriff Wright, Citizen #1, Carlyle.

90. *Bullwinkle Bites Back or Nothing but the Tooth*
WC: Narrator. JF: Rocky, Woman, Harry's Wife. BS: Bullwinkle, Man in Washing Machine. PF: Sheriff Wright, Harry.

91. *Knock on Wood or Bullwinkle Takes the Rap*
WC: Narrator. JF: Rocky, Myrtle. BS: Bullwinkle, Chauncey, Humphrey, Executive. PF: Sheriff Wright, Edgar, Frantic Man, Quincy Flogg, Senator Shunpike.

92. *A Knock for the Rock or the Lamp Is Low*
WC: Narrator. JF: Rocky. BS: Bullwinkle. PF: Senator Shunpike, Citizen.

93. *Window Pains or the Moosetrap*
WC: Narrator. JF: Rocky, Natasha. BS: Bullwinkle.

94. *Doorway to Danger or Doom in the Room*
WC: Narrator. JF: Rocky, Natasha. BS: Bullwinkle. PF: Boris.

95. *Boris Makes His Move or the Miceman Cometh*
WC: Narrator. JF: Rocky, Natasha. BS: Bullwinkle. PF: Boris.

96. *Big Cheese Boris or I'd Rather Be Rat*
WC: Narrator. JF: Rocky, Natasha. BS: Bullwinkle. PF: Boris.

97. *The Space Rat or Of Mice and Menace*
WC: Narrator. JF: Rocky, Natasha. BS: Bullwinkle. PF: Boris.

98. *The Shot Heard Round the World or The First National Bang*
WC: Narrator. JF: Rocky, Natasha. BS: Bullwinkle, Gidney. PF: Boris, Cloyd.

99. *The Rat Pack Attacks or Sharrup You Mouse*
WC: Narrator. JF: Rocky, Natasha, Humbert's Wife. BS: Bullwinkle, Gidney, Ring Announcer, Humbert, Orville's Dad. PF: Boris, Cloyd, Viewer, Announcer, Orville.

100. *Bucks for Boris or Rocky Pays the Piper*
WC: Narrator. JF: Rocky, Natasha. BS: Bullwinkle, Gidney, Mr. Big. PF: Boris, Cloyd, Moon Man.

101. *Fright Flight or A Rocky to the Moon*
WC: Narrator. JF: Rocky, Natasha. BS: Bullwinkle, Gidney, Mr. Big. PF: Boris, Cloyd.

102. *Bullwinkle Bellows Again or Moonin' Low*
WC: Narrator. JF: Rocky, Natasha. BS: Bullwinkle, Gidney. PF: Boris, Cloyd.

103. *Bongo Boris or The Hep Rat*
WC: Narrator. JF: Rocky, Natasha. BS: Bullwinkle, Gidney. PF: Boris, Cloyd.

104. *The Spies of Life or When a Fella Needs a Fiend*
WC: Narrator. JF: Rocky, Natasha. BS: Bullwinkle, Gidney, Mr. Big. PF: Boris, Moon Man.

105–116

Greenpernt Oogle—Bullwinkle, famous for his weather-predicting bunion, is kidnapped and taken to the island of New Greenpernt. King Bushwick the Thoity-thoid tells him that their fabled and prescient Oogle Boid is missing, and Bullwinkle must take its place as a predictions expert. After some hitches, Rocky and Captain Peachfuzz arrive and rescue the moose. They discover that Boris has birdnapped the Oogle. After our lads spirit the timid bird away from its trap, Boris ends up being caught in his own minefield.

105. *Greenpernt Oogle*
WC: Narrator. JF: Rocky, Boy, Woman on Picnic. BS: Bullwinkle, Parkinson, Lumpley, Norbert. PF: Pongo Britt, Weatherman, Hadley.

106. *The Mail Animal or Bullwinkle Stamps His Foot*
WC: Narrator. JF: Rocky. BS: Bullwinkle, Norbert, Veteran's Administration Clerk, FBI Man. PF: Sheriff Wright, Pilot, Hadley, Clerk, Health Dept. Clerk.

107. *Burgled Bullwinkle or the Moose Nappers*
WC: Narrator, Secretary, Board Member #4. JF: Rocky. BS: Bullwinkle, Norbert, Agent 8, Documentor, CIA Man, Board Member #3. PF: Captain Peachfuzz, Clerk, Agent 7, Board Members #1, #2.

108. *A Crown for Bullwinkle or Monarch Moose*
WC: Narrator, Radar Man. JF: Rocky. BS: Bullwinkle, Norbert, Major, Man at Bus Stop #2, Crook. PF: Captain Peachfuzz, Aide, Man at Bus Stop #1, Erwin (Hadley).

109. *Squirrel in the Scope or Ring Around the Rocky*
WC: Narrator. JF: Rocky, Princess Kitmala. BS: Bullwinkle, Norbert. PF: Captain Peachfuzz, Hadley, Palace Announcer.

110. *Block Party or the Happy Headsman*
WC: Narrator, Headsman. BS: Bullwinkle, Firing Commander, 2 Natives, Oogle Bird. PF: King Bushwick.

111. *The Wizard Biz or Bullwinkle Lays an Egg*
WC: Narrator, Headsman. JF: Rocky. BS: Bullwinkle, Oogle Bird. PF: Captain Peachfuzz, King Bushwick.

112. *Riptide Rocky or Drips Adrift*
WC: Narrator. JF: Rocky. BS: Bullwinkle. PF: Captain Peachfuzz, King Bushwick.

113. *Blood and Sand or Three for the Show*
WC: Narrator. JF: Rocky, Natasha. BS: Bullwinkle, Oogle Bird. PF: Boris, King Bushwick.

114. *Bullwinkle's Landing or Moosle Beach*
WC: Narrator. JF: Rocky, Natasha. BS: Bullwinkle, Oogle Bird. PF: Boris, King Bushwick.

115. *The Sand Blasters or Big Bang on the Beach*
WC: Narrator. JF: Rocky, Natasha. BS: Bullwinkle. PF: Boris, King Bushwick.

116. *The Brave and the Boulder or To Each His Stone*
WC: Narrator. JF: Rocky, Natasha. BS: Bullwinkle, Oogle Bird, Native. PF: Boris, Captain Peachfuzz, King Bushwick.

117–124
Rue Britannia—It seems that Bullwinkle (who has the inscription "Rue Britannia" imprinted on the sole of his hoof) has inherited another fortune: in England the wealthy Earl of Crankcase has left everything to the bearer of this inscription. However, there is one condition—Bullwinkle must spend a week in spooky Abominable Manor. The Earl's three greedy nephews (Filcher, Belcher, and Jay) are next in line for the booty; unsuccessful in their efforts to do in our boys, they call in a professional exterminator, who turns out to be Boris Badenov, of course.

117. *Rue Britannia*
WC: Narrator. JF: Rocky. BS: Bullwinkle, Belcher, Mr. Lamb, Physician. PF: Earl, Filcher, Jay.

118. *Earl and Water Don't Mix or Next Time, Take the Drain*
WC: Narrator. JF: Rocky. BS: Bullwinkle, Belcher, Mr. Lamb. PF: Filcher, Jay.

119. *Moose Gets the Juice or Mourning Becomes Electra-cuted*
WC: Narrator. JF: Rocky. BS: Bullwinkle, Belcher, Mr. Lamb. PF: Filcher, Jay.

120. *Episode 120 or 123*
WC: Narrator. JF: Rocky, Natasha. BS: Bullwinkle. PF: Boris, Filcher.

121. *Explosive Situation or Don't Make it Worse—It's Badenov*
WC: Narrator. JF: Rocky, Natasha. BS: Bullwinkle, Belcher, Race-Caller. PF: Boris.

122. *You've Got Me in Stitches or Suture Self*
WC: Narrator. JF: Rocky, Natasha. BS: Bullwinkle, Belcher. PF: Boris, Filcher.

123. *Fifty Cents Lost or Get That Half Back*
WC: Narrator. JF: Rocky, Natasha. BS: Bullwinkle, Belcher. PF: Boris, Filcher.

124. *The Scheme Misfires or You Can Planet Better Than That*
WC: Narrator. JF: Rocky, Natasha. BS: Bullwinkle, Mr. Lamb. PF: Boris, Filcher, Jay.

125–138
Buried Treasure—Colonel McCornpone, editor of the *Frostbite Falls Picayune Intelligence,* wants to build up the newspaper's circulation. He announces a buried treasure contest to find his Picayune Pot containing $1 million—in Confederate money. The moose and squirrel, eager to win the prize, are thwarted by Boris in the guise of Baby Face Braunschweiger; who, with his gang (the Light Fingered Five Minus Two), is after his own buried treasure: the money in the bank. Thanks to Rocky and a handy vacuum cleaner, Boris is eventually incarcerated. Bullwinkle wins the contest prize, a genuine reconditioned Stearns-Knight Runabout.

125. *Buried Treasure*
WC: Narrator. JF: Rocky, Newsboy #2. BS: Bullwinkle, Mokesby, Man Buying Paper. PF: Boris, Colonel McCornpone, Newsboy #1.

126. *A Tisket a Casket or The Bury Box*
WC: Narrator, Sheriff. JF: Rocky. BS: Bullwinkle, Spike. PF: Boris, Colonel McCornpone, 2 Men.

127. *The Bank Busters or The Great Vaults*
WC: Narrator, Three-Finger. JF: Rocky. BS: Bullwinkle, Spike, Man Under Lamp, Umpire, Angry Man. PF: Boris, Colonel McCornpone, Batter Slug.

128. *Sweet Violence or The Yegg and I*
WC: Narrator, Three-Finger. JF: Rocky. BS: Bullwinkle, Spike. PF: Boris, Slug.

129. *Many a Thousand Gone or The Haul of Fame*
WC: Narrator, Three-Finger. JF: Rocky, Little Old Lady. BS: Bullwinkle, Spike, Digging Man. PF: Boris, Colonel McCornpone, Mr. Friendly.

130. *Down to Earth or Me and My Shatter*
WC: Narrator. JF: Rocky. BS: Bullwinkle, Spike. PF: Boris, Slug. Mr. Friendly, Doctor.

131. *Hop Skip and Junk or Bullwinkle's Big Tow*
WC: Narrator, Three-Finger. JF: Rocky, Nurse. BS: Bullwinkle, Spike. PF: Boris, Slug.

132. *Bucks for Boris or The Green Paper Caper*
WC: Narrator, Three-Finger. JF: Rocky. BS: Bullwinkle, Spike, Moose Call. PF: Boris, Slug.

133. *When Moose Meets Moose or Two's a Crowd*
WC: Narrator. JF: Rocky. BS: Bullwinkle, Moose Call. PF: Boris.

134. *The Midnight Chew-Chew or Stick to Your Gums*
WC: Narrator, Three-Finger. JF: Rocky. BS: Bullwinkle, Spike, Railroad Clerk. PF: Boris, Slug.

135. *Boris Badenov and His Friends?*
WC: Narrator, Three-Finger. JF: Rocky. BS: Bullwinkle, Spike. PF: Boris, Slug, Sheriff, Mr. Friendly.

136. *Bars of Steal or The Hard Cell*
WC: Narrator, Three-Finger. JF: Rocky. BS: Bullwinkle, Spike, Policeman. PF: Boris, Slug.

137. *Subway Finish or An Underground Round*
WC: Narrator, Three-Finger. JF: Rocky. BS: Bullwinkle, Spike, Chauncey. PF: Boris, Slug, Edgar, Sheriff.

138. *The Last Edition or Five-Scar Final*
WC: Narrator. JF: Rocky. BS: Bullwinkle. PF: Boris, Sheriff, Used Car Salesman.

139–142

The Last Angry Moose—Starry-eyed Bullwinkle decides he wants to be a movie star, and heads for Hollywood with his life savings (which are stuffed in a mattress). Boris and Natasha want the moose's money and follow him to the movie capital. Bullwinkle is again duped by Boris, who excels himself in three disguises: famous Hollywood talent scout D. W. Grifter, the great dramatic coach Gregory Rat—who teaches the moose a shortcut version of the Method—and director Alfred Hitchhike. Bullwinkle, who changes his name to Crag Antler, quickly decides to give it all away when he discovers that audiences laugh at him.

139. *Last Angry Moose*
WC: Narrator. JF: Rocky, Laughing Woman. BS: Bullwinkle. PF: Railway Clerk.

140. *A Punch in the Snoot or The Nose Tattoo*
WC: Narrator. JF: Rocky, Natasha. BS: Bullwinkle. PF: Boris.

141. *Fun on the Freeway or The Quick and the Dead*
WC: Narrator. JF: Rocky, Natasha. BS: Bullwinkle. PF: Boris.

142. *Bullwinkle Makes a Movie or The Feature from Outer Space*
WC: Narrator. JF: Rocky, Natasha, Newsboy #1, Louella Parsons. BS: Bullwinkle. PF: Boris, Newsboy #2, Cowboy Star.

143–156

Wailing Whale—Whole ocean liners are being swallowed by the leviathan of the deep: the legendary wailing whale Maybe Dick. Bullwinkle and Rocky volunteer to go whale hunting. Accompanied by Captain Peachfuzz, the three are soon taken by force to the sunken city of Submerbia, where they meet Mayor Fiorello LaPompano. They discover Maybe Dick is really a mechanical monster manned by their old nemesis Boris, disguised as Captain Horatio Hornswaggle. Along with Natasha and a large gorilla named Rollo, he's been shanghaiing ocean liners, then relieving the passengers of their valuables. Rocky saves the day with the help of a squadron of British attack planes.

143. *Wailing Whale*
WC: Narrator, English Member. JF: Rocky, Newsboy. BS: Bullwinkle, Aide, Commander Binnacle, Mate, Nut-case, Meek Member. PF: Pericles Parnassus, American Commander, Survivor, Jailer.

144. *Vagabond Voyage or The Castoffs Cast Off*
WC: Narrator. JF: Rocky. BS: Bullwinkle, Benson's Aide. PF: Pericles Parnassus, Airline President, Benson, Funeral Parlor Man.

145. *Fear on the Pier or What's Up, Dock?*
WC: Narrator. JF: Rocky. BS: Bullwinkle, Meek Member, British Member, Russian Member, French Member #2. PF: Pericles Parnassus, American Member, French Member.

146. *TNT for Two or Fright Cargo*
WC: Narrator. JF: Rocky. BS: Bullwinkle. PF: Captain Peachfuzz.

147. *Underwater Eyeball or The Deep Blue See*
WC: Narrator. JF: Rocky. BS: Bullwinkle. PF: Captain Peachfuzz.

148. *Underwater Moose or The Aqua-Lunk*
WC: Narrator. JF: Rocky. BS: Bullwinkle, Sir Digby, French Cabinet Member #2, U.S. TV Viewer. PF: Captain Peachfuzz, Radio Announcer, Sir Digby's Friend, French Cabinet Member #1, TV Announcer, Railroad Man.

149. *Terror on the Seas or We've Only Begun to Fright*
WC: Narrator. JF: Rocky. BS: Bullwinkle, Edgar, French Member, English Member, Scottish Member, Messenger, Member. PF: Captain Peachfuzz, Pericles Parnassus, Chauncey, French Member.

150. *Blank Night or The Age of Nothing*
WC: Narrator. JF: Rocky. BS: Bullwinkle, Chauncey. PF: Captain Peachfuzz, Edgar, Mayor Fiorello LaPompano.

151. *Defective Story or A Muffled Report*
WC: Narrator. JF: Rocky. BS: Bullwinkle. PF: Captain Peachfuzz, Mayor Fiorello LaPompano.

152. *Leaky Lyrics or Bullwinkle Plugs a Song*
WC: Narrator. JF: Rocky. BS: Bullwinkle. PF: Captain Peachfuzz.

153. *Follow the Swallow or The Inside Story*
WC: Narrator. JF: Rocky. BS: Bullwinkle. PF: Boris, Captain Peachfuzz.

154. *Playtime for Rollo or Rest in Pieces*
WC: Narrator. JF: Rocky, Natasha. BS: Bullwinkle. PF: Boris, Captain Peachfuzz.

155. *A Whale of a Tale or Thar She Blows Up*
WC: Narrator. JF: Rocky, Natasha. BS: Bullwinkle, Featherby. PF: Boris, Captain Peachfuzz, Commodore.

156. *Fast and Moose or Charley's Antler*
WC: Narrator. JF: Rocky, Natasha. BS: Bullwinkle, Featherby. PF: Boris, Commodore.

(Episodes 157-366 originally appeared on *The Bullwinkle Show*)

157–164
The Three Moosketeers—In the province of Applesauce Lorraine, good king Wuncelaus is deposed by nasty Francois Villain. Athos, one of the original Three Musketeers, enlists the aid of our heroes, mistaking Rocky and Bullwinkle for the other two Musketeers (Porthos and Aramoose). Bullwinkle

narrowly escapes a guillotine blade and imprisonment in the dungeon, but he disguises himself as a carpet cleaner and routs the evil Villain, thereby restoring the king to his rightful place.

157. *Three Moosketeers*
WC: Narrator. JF: Rocky. BS: Bullwinkle, King Wuncelaus, Philippe Mignon, Aide, Clerk. PF: Francois Villain, Athos.

158. *Foiled Again or Don't Fence Me In*
WC: Narrator. JF: Rocky. BS: Bullwinkle, Philippe Mignon, Citizen. PF: Francois Villain, Athos.

159. *Squeeze Play or Glad We Could Get Together*
WC: Narrator. JF: Rocky. BS: Bullwinkle, Philippe Mignon. PF: Francois Villain, Athos, Chess Player.

160. *Just Desserts or Operator, We've Been Cut Off*
WC: Narrator. JF: Rocky. BS: Bullwinkle. PF: Francois Villain, Athos.

161. *Severed Relations or How to Get a Head*
WC: Narrator. JF: Rocky. BS: Bullwinkle. PF: Francois Villain, Athos.

162. *That's the Way the Cookie Crumbles or Me and My Chateau*
WC: Narrator. JF: Rocky. BS: Bullwinkle, King Wuncelaus, Spectator #1. PF: Francois Villain, Athos, Spectator #2.

163. *A Raw Deal or Two Aces and a Pair of Kings*
WC: Narrator. JF: Rocky. BS: Bullwinkle, Pretender #1, Chef, Coronation Man. PF: Athos, King Wuncelaus, Pretender #2, Guard.

164. *Rocky Draws the Line or Who's Got My Ruler?*
WC: Narrator. JF: Rocky. BS: Bullwinkle, Coronation Man. PF: Francois Villian, Athos, Politician.

165–182
Lazy Jay Ranch—Rocky and Bullwinkle buy the Lazy Jay Ranch in Squaw's Ankle, Wyoming. They meet Lazy Jay, the world's most slothful man, who discloses the shocking news that they now own a worm ranch. Meanwhile Boris (disguised as Scots cowboy Black Angus) is after some valuable rocks on the property. The moose and squirrel decide to drive their underground herd to the nearby fishing resort of Angel's Cramp, which boasts thousands of fish but no bait. They survive an underwater truck journey and some depth charges, while Boris attempts to rob the Hogbreeder's National Bank. Squaw's Ankle finally becomes a tourist attraction.

165. *Lazy Jay Ranch*
WC: Narrator. JF: Rocky. BS: Bullwinkle, Black Eagle, Technician (Jim), Trampas, Two Gun Twombly #2. PF: Cowboy Actor, Technician #2, Two Gun Twombly #1.

166. *Fast and Moose or The Quick and the Dead*
WC: Narrator. JF: Rocky. BS: Bullwinkle. PF: Mayor, Dudley Digg.

167. *Buzzard Bait or The Carrion Call*
WC: Narrator. JF: Rocky. BS: Bullwinkle. PF: Mayor, Lazy Jay.

168. *Rocky Rides Again or Small in the Saddle*
WC: Narrator. JF: Rocky. BS: Bullwinkle. PF: Boris, Lazy Jay.

169. *The Last Angry Angus or Hot Scotch*
WC: Narrator. JF: Rocky. Natasha. BS: Bullwinkle. PF: Boris, Lazy Jay.

170. *Our Town or Home of the Grave*
WC: Narrator, Basil. JF: Rocky, Natasha. BS: Bullwinkle, Calvin. PF: Boris, Lazy Jay, Durward.

171. *The Big Countdown or Tally in Our Alley*
WC: Narrator. JF: Rocky, Natasha. BS: Bullwinkle. PF: Boris.

172. *Aches and Planes or The Old Chisel 'Em Trail*
WC: Narrator. JF: Rocky, Natasha. BS: Bullwinkle. PF: Boris.

173. *Bucket-Headed Bullwinkle or Pail-Face Moose*
WC: Narrator. JF: Rocky, Natasha. BS: Bullwinkle, Finlayson. PF: Boris, Penworthy.

174. *Make-Believe Monster or Once Upon a Crime*
WC: Narrator. JF: Rocky, Natasha. BS: Bullwinkle, Whatsat. PF: Boris.

175. *Chew Chew Baby or Stick to Your Gums*
WC: Narrator. JF: Rocky, Natasha. BS: Bullwinkle, Prospector. PF: Boris, Mervin, Manager.

176. *Rain of Terror or The Desperate Showers*
WC: Narrator. JF: Rocky, Natasha. BS: Bullwinkle, Finlayson. PF: Boris, Man.

177. *The Lightning Bugs or Nuts and Volts*
WC: Narrator. JF: Rocky, Natasha. BS: Bullwinkle. PF: Boris, Citizen.

178. *The Bush Pusher or Beri Beri Who's Got the Berry?*
WC: Narrator, Singer. JF: Rocky, Natasha. BS: Bullwinkle, Singer. PF: Boris, Mayor, Fisherman, Singer.

179. *Underwater Trap or No Air in the Snare*
WC: Narrator. JF: Rocky, Natasha. BS: Bullwinkle. PF: Boris.

180. *Boris Bounces Back or The Rubber Heel*
WC: Narrator. JF: Rocky, Natasha. BS: Bullwinkle. PF: Boris, Mr. Wangle.

181. *Boris Takes a Town or The Night Mayor*
WC: Narrator. JF: Rocky, Natasha. BS: Bullwinkle. PF: Boris, Mr. Wangle.

182. *Just Boris and Me or The Yegg and I*
WC: Narrator. JF: Rocky, Natasha. BS: Bullwinkle. PF: Boris, Mr. Wangle, Mayor.

183–208

Missouri Mish Mash—Bullwinkle sets off to Missouri to attend the annual moose convention. He and Rocky avoid assassination attempts by Boris and Fearless Leader, then board the SS *Huck Finn* and arrive in Peaceful Valley. Unfortunately they land right in the middle of a 150-year-old feud between the Hatfuls and the Floys. Boris disguises himself as two clansmen—Devil Dan Hatful and Felonious Floy—in an effort to stop our lads from finding a fabulous bowler hat called the Kirward Derby, which turns anyone who wears it into the smartest person in the world. The Derby is somewhere in Missouri, so Boris hypnotizes Bullwinkle into finding it; sure enough, it's been sitting in a hat shop. It certainly works well: when Bullwinkle puts the hat on he can speak fluent French and discuss Einstein's theory. Next the moon men, Cloyd and Gidney, turn up claiming ownership of the hat. Rocky decides to take the Derby to Washington, with Boris and Fearless Leader desperate to stop him.

183. *Missouri Mish Mash*
WC: Narrator. JF: Rocky. BS: Bullwinkle, Fearless Leader, Calvin, Clarence, Tiddler #2. PF: Calvin's Friend, Checker Player, Mort, Tiddler #1, Charlie Parlorcar, Railway Clerk, Georgiy.

184. *Landslide on the Rails or Bullwinkle Covers His Tracks*
WC: Narrator. JF: Rocky, Natasha. BS: Bullwinkle, Fearless Leader. PF: Boris, Georgiy.

185. *Rocky and the Rock or Taken for Granite*
WC: Narrator. JF: Rocky, Natasha. BS: Bullwinkle. PF: Boris.

186. *Trouble Upstairs or Bats in the Boris*
WC: Narrator. JF: Rocky, Natasha. BS: Bullwinkle, Fearless Leader. PF: Boris, Dmitriy.

187. *Boris on a Broomstick or The Flying Sorcerer*
WC: Narrator. JF: Rocky, Natasha. BS: Bullwinkle, Fearless Leader. PF: Boris, Dmitriy.

188. *Boris Lends a Hand or Count Your Fingers*
WC: Narrator. JF: Rocky, Natasha. BS: Bullwinkle. PF: Boris.

189. *Mud-Munching Moose or Bullwinkle Bites the Dust*
WC: Narrator, Clive. JF: Rocky. BS: Bullwinkle, Caleb, Ephraim Floy. PF: Boris, Hatful, Floy.

190. *Devil Dan Thinks It Over or Feud for Thought*
WC: Narrator. JF: Rocky. BS: Bullwinkle, Fearless Leader, Countdown. PF: Boris, Hatful, Professor.

191. *Calling Fearless Leader or Whistle for the Missile*
WC: Narrator. JF: Rocky, Natasha. BS: Bullwinkle, Fearless Leader, Executioner, Clem. PF: Boris, Professor, Harlow.

192. *Rocky Takes the High Road or Missile in the Thistle*
WC: Narrator. JF: Rocky, Natasha. BS: Bullwinkle, Fearless Leader. PF: Boris.

193. *Dollars and Scents or Putting on the Dog*
WC: Narrator, Witness. JF: Wife. BS: Bullwinkle, Fearless Leader, Newt. PF: Boris, Hadley.

194. *One of Our Meese Is Missing or Heads You Lose*
WC: Narrator, Witness. JF: Wife. BS: Fearless Leader, Caveman. PF: Boris, Aristotle, Einstein, Hillbilly.

195. *Bullwinkle Makes His Bid or Going! Going! Gun!*
WC: Narrator. JF: Rocky. BS: Bullwinkle, Fearless Leader, Zeke. PF: Boris, Hillbilly, Isaac Newton, Galileo.

196. *The Vanishing American or No Moose Is Good Moose*
WC: Narrator. JF: Rocky. BS: Bullwinkle, Fearless Leader, Zeke. PF: Boris, Hatful, Alfred.

197. *Hello, Ma Booby or Pleased to Beat Ya*
WC: Narrator. JF: Rocky. BS: Bullwinkle, Fearless Leader. PF: Boris, Dmitrij, Martha Washington.

198. *Under Bullwinkle's Bowler or The Wide, Open Spaces*
WC: Narrator. JF: Rocky. BS: Bullwinkle, Fearless Leader. PF: Boris, Hat-Seller.

199. *Million Dollar Carton or Jack in the Box*
WC: Narrator. JF: Rocky. BS: Bullwinkle, Fearless Leader. PF: Boris, Hat-Seller.

200. *Two at One Blow or The Devil Beheader*
WC: Narrator. JF: Rocky, Natasha. BS: Bullwinkle, Fearless Leader. PF: Boris.

201. *Flower in the Hat or The Rose Bowler*
WC: Narrator. JF: Rocky. BS: Bullwinkle, Fearless Leader. PF: Boris.

202. *A Snitch in Time or The Finking Man's Thilter*
WC: Narrator. JF: Rocky, Natasha. BS: Bullwinkle, Fearless Leader. PF: Boris.

203. *Boomerang Bowler or Boris Makes a Comeback*
WC: Narrator. JF: Rocky, Natasha. BS: Bullwinkle, Fearless Leader. PF: Boris, G-Man.

204. *All in Fever Say Aye or The Emotion Is Carried*
WC: Narrator, Genie. JF: Rocky, Teacher. BS: Bullwinkle, Gidney, Headmaster, Ugbert the Ugly, Guards 1 and 3. PF: Boris, Cloyd, Agent, Nozmo, Lyndon, Kirwood, Guard 2.

205. *Too Much Too Moon or What Makes Lunar Tick?*
WC: Narrator. JF: Rocky. BS: Bullwinkle, Gidney, Fearless Leader, Ugbert the Ugly. PF: Boris, Cloyd, Nozmo, Lyndon, Kirwood.

206. *Flying Bullets or A Cartridge in a Pear Tree*
WC: Narrator. JF: Rocky, Natasha. BS: Bullwinkle, Gidney, Fearless Leader, Moon Man. PF: Boris, Cloyd, Nozmo.

207. *The Crepe Hangers or Brighten the Coroner Where You Are*
WC: Narrator. JF: Rocky, Natasha. BS: Bullwinkle, Gidney, Edgar. PF: Boris, Cloyd, Chauncey, Man.

208. *Double Trouble or Two's a Crowd*
WC: Narrator. JF: Rocky. BS: Bullwinkle, Gidney, Fearless Leader, Hatful. PF: Boris, Cloyd, Floy, Man, Politician.

209–222.

Topsy Turvy World—Captain Peachfuzz enlists the aid of Rocky and Bullwinkle to help find out what's causing a change in the world's weather patterns. Of course Boris Badenov is behind the scheme—he and Natasha are disguised as Santa and Alf Elf, in a mad plan to tip the world upside down so that Santa can go up people's chimneys (thus carrying Christmas presents up, for himself). Bullwinkle and Rocky land on the island of Riki Tiki, where they survive a crocodile-infested swamp, a cannibal stew pot, and being skinned by the now freezing Riki Tikians. Peachfuzz saves them by bartering with the natives for a box of trinkets.

209. *Topsy Turvy World*
WC: Narrator. JF: Rocky, Receptionist. BS: Bullwinkle, Mr. Crotchet, Old Man. PF: Mr. Flappenstrap, Citizen, Mayor.

210. *Funny Business in the Books or The Library Card*
WC: Narrator. JF: Rocky. BS: Bullwinkle, Chauncey, Agent. PF: Captain Peachfuzz, Edgar, Cletus Bookbinder, X-9.

211. *Topsy Turvy Time or Emit Yvrut Yspot*
WC: Narrator. JF: Rocky. BS: Bullwinkle. PF: Captain Peachfuzz, Professor Werner Von Beige, Citizen.

212. *Bullwinkle Takes the Wheel or The Bum Steer*
WC: Narrator. JF: Rocky. BS: Bullwinkle, Chauncey. PF: Captain Peachfuzz, Edgar.

213. *The Ocean Waves or Hi, Divers*
WC: Narrator. JF: Rocky. BS: Bullwinkle. PF: Captain Peachfuzz, Professor Von Beige.

214. *(Untitled Episode)*
WC: Narrator. JF: Rocky, Natasha. BS: Bullwinkle. PF: Boris, Captain Peachfuzz, Professor Von Beige.

215. *Six O'Clock Low or Bullwinkle Gets the Point*
WC: Narrator, Native #1. JF: Rocky, Natasha, Newsboy, Wife, Eskimo. BS: Bullwinkle, Scientist, British Scientist, Salesman, Native #2. PF: Boris, Professor Von Beige, Sir Basil, Husband.

216. *Boris Goes for Broke or A Friend in Need Is a Fiend . . . Indeed*
WC: Narrator, Native. JF: Rocky, Natasha. BS: Bullwinkle. PF: Boris, Captain Peachfuzz, Professor Von Beige.

217. *The Fright Before Christmas or A Visit from Saint Nicholouse*
WC: Narrator, Elf. JF: Rocky, Natasha. BS: Bullwinkle, Sales Clerk, Elf, Native. PF: Boris.

218. *Soups On or Rocky Goes to Pot*
WC: Narrator. JF: Rocky. BS: Bullwinkle, Sam. PF: Boris, Mbutu.

219. *Snowbank Squirrel or Bullwinkle Gets the Drift*
WC: Narrator. JF: Rocky, Natasha. BS: Bullwinkle. PF: Boris, Captain Peachfuzz, Professor Von Beige.

220. *Claus and Effect or Yule . . . Be Sorry*
WC: Narrator, Sam. JF: Rocky, Natasha. BS: Bullwinkle, British Man, Russian, Harold, Native. PF: Boris, Professor Von Beige, Bobby, Commissar, Clint, Chief.

221. *Boom at the Top or The Angry Young Moose*
WC: Narrator. JF: Rocky, Natasha. BS: Bullwinkle. PF: Boris, Captain Peachfuzz, Professor Von Beige, Native Chief.

222. *Fur, Fur Away or Hair Today, Gone Tomorrow*
WC: Narrator. JF: Rocky, Natasha. BS: Bullwinkle, Elf #1. PF: Boris, Captain Peachfuzz, Professor Von Beige, Santa (Arthur Godfrey), Elf #2.

223–228.

Painting Theft—Boris steals ten old masters from the Paris Art Museum, mails them to Bullwinkle's address, and escapes to America. Meanwhile the moose thinks the paintings are wallpaper and decides to brighten up his chicken coop with them. Next he whitewashes the whole coop, covering up the valuable masterpieces. Horrified, Boris now has to buy them back, but which ones are they? Bullwinkle has gone art crazy, producing whitewash after whitewash and setting the art world afire (the moose is commissioned to do a Christmas cover for the *Saturday Evening Post*). Fortunately the missing masterpieces do finally make it back to the museum.

223. *Painting Theft*
WC: Narrator. JF: Rocky, Natasha. BS: Bullwinkle, Museum Director, Gendarme #3 (Henri). PF: Boris, Gendarmes #1 and 2, Mailman.

224. *Transatlantic Chicken or Hens Across the Sea*
WC: Narrator. JF: Rocky, Natasha. BS: Bullwinkle, Museum Director, Henri. PF: Boris, Security Guard, Security Chief, Aristide.

225. *Portrait of a Moose or Bullwinkle Gets the Brush*
WC: Narrator, Reporter. JF: Rocky, Natasha. BS: Bullwinkle, Movie Critic, Artist #1, Politician #2, Museum Man. PF: Boris, Jack Benny, Artist #2, Politician #1, Senator.

226. *Bullwinkle Busts a Brush or The Cleft Palette*
WC: Narrator. JF: Rocky, Natasha, Newsboy. BS: Bullwinkle, Price McVincent, Ernest. PF: Boris, Ernest's Friend.

227. *Boris Badenov Presents or The 20-inch Scream*
WC: Narrator. JF: Rocky, Natasha. BS: Bullwinkle. PF: Boris.

228. *Dollars to Doughnuts or The Wonderful World of Cruller*
WC: Narrator. JF: Rocky, Natasha. BS: Bullwinkle, Fearless Leader, Price McVincent, Frenchmen #2 and 4. PF: Boris, Frenchmen #1 and 3, Paint Salesman.

229–232

The Guns of Abalone—Rocky and Bullwinkle must silence the Guns of Abalone when Boris threatens to blow up the world. In this short but frantic adventure, our heroes' plane is shot down over the Rock of Gibraltar, they are imprisoned, find a secret passage, escape a firing squad, and are put on a ship which sinks in a storm. Their longboat lands on the island of Abalone, where they confront Boris and Natasha. Boris finally bungles his plan by aiming all five cannons at one another.

229. *Guns of Abalone*
WC: Narrator. JF: Rocky, Natasha, Newsboy. BS: Bullwinkle, General Crenshaw. PF: Boris, Captain Schnader, Inquisitive Man.

230. *Falling Stars or Only a Plumber Should Plummet*
WC: Narrator. JF: Rocky. BS: Bullwinkle, Man #1, Carruthers's Friend. PF: Boris, General Carruthers, Firing Squad Major.

231. *I'm Out of Bullets or Pour Me Another Shot*
WC: Narrator. JF: Rocky, Natasha. BS: Bullwinkle, Sailor. PF: Boris, Captain Peachfuzz, Firing Squad Major.

232. *Seasick Bullwinkle or How Green Was My Moose*
WC: Narrator. JF: Rocky, Natasha. BS: Bullwinkle. PF: Boris, Captain Peachfuzz.

233–240

Treasure of Monte Zoom—Boris and Natasha are in Frostbite Falls planning to find the hidden treasure of Monte Zoom, which lies at the bottom of Lake Salle De Bain. Rocky and Bullwinkle get lost in the town's waterworks system. Boris eventually finds the treasure chest, but Bullwinkle has the key to open it. The prize is an old car (an Apperson Jackrabbit) made out of 14-karat gold. Boris disguises himself as a used-car dealer and trades a cardboard cutout for the Jackrabbit.

233. *Treasure of Monte Zoom*
WC: Narrator. JF: Rocky, Natasha. BS: Bullwinkle. PF: Boris, Crow.

234. *Flood Waters or Drown in the Valley*
WC: Narrator. JF: Rocky, Natasha. BS: Bullwinkle. PF: Boris.

235. *A Leak in the Lake or The Drain Maker*
WC: Narrator. JF: Rocky, Natasha. BS: Bullwinkle, Tenant #2. PF: Boris, Singing Tenant.

236. *Bullwinkle Cleans Up or The Desperate Showers*
WC: Narrator. JF: Rocky, Natasha. BS: Bullwinkle, Superintendent. PF: Boris, Tenant.

237. *Boris Bashes a Box or The Flat Chest*
WC: Narrator. JF: Rocky, Natasha. BS: Bullwinkle. PF: Boris.

238. *One, Two, Three, Gone! or I've Got Plenty of Nothing*
WC: Narrator. JF: Rocky, Natasha. BS: Bullwinkle. PF: Boris.

239. *All That Glitters or Baby, It's Gold Outside*
WC: Narrator. JF: Rocky, Natasha. BS: Bullwinkle. PF: Boris.

240. *Boris Wheels and Deals or A Profit Without Honor*
WC: Narrator. JF: Rocky, Natasha. BS: Bullwinkle, Andy Grift. PF: Boris.

241–248

Goof Gas Attack—The government is in a panic trying to discover the reason behind the sudden moronic behavior of the nation's top scientific minds. Rocky and Bullwinkle, traveling by train, meet up with Captain Peachfuzz at McKeesport, Pennsylvania. He tells our boys that Pottsylvania has developed Goof Gas, which Boris has been spraying at America's leading smart-alecks and whiz kids. The nasty spy smuggles some gas into a missile base and sets off a multiple launch, but Rocky is able to redirect all the missiles out over the ocean and toward Pottsylvania.

241. *Goof Gas Attack*
WC: Narrator. JF: Rocky. BS: Bullwinkle, 2 Professors, Doctor's Aide. PF: Janitor, Armbruster, Hotchkiss, Doctor, Detective.

242. *The Brain Drainers or Malice in Wonderland*
WC: Narrator. JF: Rocky, Natasha. BS: Bullwinkle. PF: Boris.

243. *The Dunderheads or Feeling Zero*
WC: Narrator. JF: Rocky, Natasha. BS: Bullwinkle, Fearless Leader, Reporter, Dr. Fleegle. PF: Boris, Captain Peachfuzz, Professor, Fleegle's Assistant.

244. *Three to Go or Crash on Delivery*
WC: Narrator. JF: Rocky, Teacher. BS: Bullwinkle, Launch Man, Suzie, Dr. Smallhausen, Chancellor. PF: Captain Peachfuzz, Countdown Man, Johnny, Chancellor's Aide.

245. *McKeesport on the Prod or The Pennsylvania Poker*
WC: Narrator, Scientist. JF: Rocky, Natasha. BS: Bullwinkle, Fearless Leader, Board Member, Goof Gas Inventor. PF: Boris, Captain Peachfuzz, Gerhardt, Board Member.

246. *Hare-Brained Boris or The Dumb Bunny*
WC: Narrator. JF: Rocky, Natasha. BS: Bullwinkle, Professor, Senators #2 and 3. PF: Boris, Opera Singer, Senator #1.

247. (*Untitled Episode*)
WC: Narrator. JF: Rocky, Teacher. BS: Bullwinkle, Guard. PF: Boris, Captain Peachfuzz, Doctor, Senator.

248. *5-4-3-2-1 or The Quick Launch Counter*
WC: Narrator. JF: Rocky, Natasha. BS: Bullwinkle, Fearless Leader, Guard, Scientist #2. PF: Boris, Captain Peachfuzz, Scientist #1, Werner.

249–260

Banana Formula—Boris steals a formula for a silent explosive called Hush-a-Boom. He writes it on the inside of a banana, which is then eaten by Bullwinkle, who can apparently remember every meal he ever ate. Boris invites Rocky and Bullwinkle to a free weekend at Lake Kitchie Itchie mountain lodge, where the boys survive various assassination attempts before escaping on a river steamer. There they are bound and gagged by two security agents working for Captain Peachfuzz. When Boris tries to poison Bullwinkle with a drink containing Hush-a-Boom, an explosion foils his plans, and he's arrested for being a litterbug.

249. *Banana Formula*
WC: Narrator. JF: Rocky, Natasha, Newsboy. BS: Bullwinkle, Dr. Bermuda Schwartz. PF: Boris. Hypotenuse, General.

250. *Boom Town or Destination Schwartz*
WC: Narrator. JF: Rocky, Natasha. BS: Bullwinkle, Dr. Bermuda Schwartz, Fruit Cart Proprietor. PF: Boris.

251. *The Flat of the Land or A Rolling Stone Gathers No Moose*
WC: Narrator. JF: Rocky, Natasha. BS: Bullwinkle. PF: Boris.

252. *Mack the Knife or Operation: Moose*
WC: Narrator. JF: Rocky, Natasha. BS: Bullwinkle, Fearless Leader, Policeman, Juvenile Court Judge. PF: Boris.

253. *Two Days to Doom or The Last Weekend*
WC: Narrator. JF: Rocky, Natasha. BS: Bullwinkle. PF: Boris.

254. *Two Moose Is Loose or Which One Has the Phoney?*
WC: Narrator. JF: Rocky, Natasha, Jayne Moosefield. BS: Bullwinkle, Fearless Leader. PF: Boris, Dmitrij.

255. *The Moose and The Monster or Nothing but the Pest*
WC: Narrator. JF: Rocky, Natasha. BS: Bullwinkle, Fearless Leader. PF: Boris, Dmitrij.

256. *Testing 1, 2, 3, or Tape a Number*
WC: Narrator. JF: Rocky, Natasha. BS: Bullwinkle, Fearless Leader, Ben. PF: Boris, Joe.

257. *The Villain's Victory Dance or The Jig Is Up*
WC: Narrator. JF: Rocky, Natasha. BS: Bullwinkle, Fearless Leader, Ben. PF: Boris, Captain Peachfuzz, Joe.

258. *The Missing Moustache or Hair Today, Gone Tomorrow*
WC: Narrator. JF: Rocky, Natasha. BS: Bullwinkle, Joe. PF: Boris, Captain Peachfuzz, Ben.

259. *Boom at the Top or Bullwinkle Loses His Head*
WC: Narrator. JF: Rocky, Natasha. BS: Bullwinkle, Safecracker. PF: Boris, Captain Peachfuzz.

260. *Boris Talks to Himself or Mockingbird Heel*
WC: Narrator. JF: Rocky, Natasha. BS: Bullwinkle, Fearless Leader, Sheriff. PF: Boris, Captain Peachfuzz, Telegram Boy.

(For the final season, the numbering system was changed to continue from episode 301)

301–310

Bumbling Brothers Circus—Twin cirus owners Hugo and Igo Bumbling bring their show to Frostbite Falls. Boris, disguised as lion tamer Claude Badley, is employed by the circus. He lets a lion loose, but the musically inclined Bullwinkle tames the savage beast with a "hum-a-comb." The moose becomes the new lion tamer. After using an elephant's trunk to douse a fire lit by vengeful Boris, Rocky becomes the circus elephant trainer. Surviving an encounter with hostile Indians, Rocky is fired when Boris feeds the elephants peanuts loaded with reducing pills. But Boris's plan backfires when he and Natasha get stuck inside an artificial lion disguise.

301. *Bumbling Brothers Circus*
WC: Narrator. JF: Rocky. BS: Bullwinkle, Igo Bumbling, Citizens #1 and 4, Charlie Parlorcar. PF: Boris, Hugo Bumbling, Citizens #2, #3, #5, Zeb.

302. *Lion in the Bedroom or The Cat's Pajamas*
WC: Narrator. JF: Rocky, Natasha. BS: Bullwinkle, Igo, Timekeeper. PF: Boris, Hugo.

303. *A Red Letter Day or Drop Us a Lion*
WC: Narrator. JF: Rocky, Natasha. BS: Bullwinkle, Igo. PF: Boris, Hugo.

304. *The Fire-Eaters or Hot Lips*
WC: Narrator. JF: Rocky, Natasha. BS: Bullwinkle, Igo. PF: Boris, Hugo.

305. *The Show Must Go On or Give 'Em the Acts*
WC: Narrator. JF: Rocky, Natasha. BS: Bullwinkle, Igo. PF: Boris, Hugo, Arizona Man.

306. *Looney Lightning or Nuts and Volts*
WC: Narrator. JF: Rocky. BS: Bullwinkle, Igo, Chauncey, Indian. PF: Boris, Hugo, Edgar.

307. *The Fire Chaser or Bullwinkle Goes to Blazes*
WC: Narrator. JF: Rocky, Natasha. BS: Bullwinkle, Big Indian, Indian Brave. PF: Boris.

308. *Flaming Arrows or Bullwinkle Meets His Match*
WC: Narrator, Humorous Indian #3. JF: Rocky. BS: Bullwinkle, Igo, Chauncey, Indian #1, Humorous Indian #2. PF: Boris, Hugo, Edgar, Humorous Indian #1.

309. *It's in the Bag or Rocky Gets the Sack*
WC: Narrator. JF: Rocky. BS: Bullwinkle, Igo. PF: Boris, Hugo.

310. *A Short Weight for All Seats or One of Our Trunks Is Missing*
WC: Narrator. JF: Rocky, Natasha. BS: Bullwinkle. PF: Boris.

311–316

Mucho Loma—In the Mexican village of Mucho Loma (English translation: Much Mud), Rocky and Bullwinkle must capture Guadalupe, a masked noisemaker who calls himself Zero. Zero's valiant steed Esmerelda deposits the boys in a well; then Bullwinkle disguises himself as the bandit. When the moose is tossed in jail, Rocky has to spring him with a cigar containing TNT. They finally capture Zero, who is exonerated—as Rocky sympathetically explains, the misguided bandit didn't realize he was breaking any laws.

311. *Mucho Loma*
WC: Narrator. JF: Rocky. BS: Bullwinkle, Jose, Sheriff, Citizen #1, Town Councilman. PF: Zero, Mexican, Citizen #2, Council Member.

312. *The Boys Bounce Back or Springtime in the Rocky*
WC: Narrator. JF: Rocky. BS: Bullwinkle, Town Councilman, Sheriff. PF: Zero, Mexican, Judge.

313. *Rock Meets Rock or Thud and Blunder*
WC: Narrator. JF: Rocky. BS: Bullwinkle, Mexican, Sheriff. PF: Zero, Judge.

314. *A Watery Grave or Drown Among the Sheltering Palms*
WC: Narrator. JF: Rocky. BS: Bullwinkle. PF: Zero, Old Berry.

315. *The Unsatisfied Customer or Why Not Try Brand-X*
WC: Narrator, Mexican #3. JF: Rocky. BS: Bullwinkle, Mexican #2. PF: Zero, Posse Man, Mexican #1, Judge.

316. *The Inferior Decorators or The Walleyed Moose*
WC: Narrator. JF: Rocky. BS: Bullwinkle, Sheriff. PF: Zero, Judge.

317–322
Pottsylvania Creeper—Rocky and Bullwinkle don't have a plant to enter in the annual Frostbite Falls Flower Fair and Plant Pageant, until Boris and Natasha sell them a bean supposedly descended from Jack's original beanstalk. In reality the seed is a man-eating monster called the Pottsylvania Creeper which quickly grows to a fearsome size, covering the village like a blight. It starts dropping seeds which begin to engulf the entire country. In desperation the people decide to be nice to the vicious plant, and it begins to wilt. One remaining seed lands on a submarine returning Boris, Natasha, and Fearless Leader to Pottsylvania.

317. *Pottsylvania Creeper*
WC: Narrator. JF: Rocky, Natasha. BS: Bullwinkle, Caleb. PF: Boris, Caleb's Friend.

318. *Four for the Show or Two Pairs of Plants*
WC: Narrator. JF: Rocky, Natasha. BS: Bullwinkle, Player #1. PF: Boris, Mayor, Player #2, Policeman.

319. *Beaned by a Blossom or The Petal Pushers*
WC: Narrator. JF: Rocky, Natasha. BS: Bullwinkle, Fearless Leader. PF: Boris, J. Edgar Bloomer, Citizen.

320. *Vacation Daze or Visit to a Small Panic*
WC: Narrator. JF: Rocky, Natasha. BS: Bullwinkle, Fearless Leader, Eph, Old Citizen. PF: Boris, Eph's Friend, Mayor.

321. *The Worryin' of the Green or The Look of the Irish*
WC: Narrator. JF: Rocky, Natasha, Newsboy #1. BS: Bullwinkle, Fearless Leader, Chauncey, Secretary of Agriculture, Secretary of Commerce, Plant Trainer, George Washington. PF: Boris, Newsboy #2, Secretary of State, Secretary of Interior, Secretary of Defense, Edgar, Washington's Father.

322. *It's Only a Flesh Wound or Better Lead Than Dead*
WC: Narrator. JF: Rocky, Mrs. Johnson. BS: Bullwinkle, Fearless Leader, Man Phoning White House, Effeminate Man, President, Doctor, Dmitri's Friend. PF: Boris, Man Phoning Air Force, Psychiatrist (M. T. Skull).

323–326
Moosylvania—Boris wants a lifetime supply of fiendish tricks, so he holds an evil contest, which Bullwinkle somehow wins. The prize is a complete set of the *Encyclopedia Badenov,* containing sticks of TNT attached to the page describing Bullwinkle's birthplace, Moosylvania. The moose decides to claim statehood for Moosylvania by flying to Washington, D.C.; Boris disguises Butte, Montana, as the capital.

323. *Moosylvania*
WC: Narrator. JF: Rocky, Natasha, Fred's Wife. BS: Bullwinkle, Gurney's Friend, Jewelry Seller. PF: Boris, Robber, Mailman.

324. *Blast Off Speedia with Encyclopedia or Off to Heaven with Volume Seven*
WC: Narrator. JF: Rocky, Natasha, Betsy Ross. BS: Bullwinkle, Merle, Politician. PF: Boris, Otis.

325. *Resign Your Fate to a 52nd State or Moosylvania Mania!*
WC: Narrator. JF: Rocky, Natasha, Mother. BS: Bullwinkle, Merle. PF: Boris, Selwyn, Dad.

326. *Bad Day at Flat Rocky or A Record in Bullwinkle's Blot*
WC: Narrator. JF: Rocky, Natasha. BS: Bullwinkle, Voter. PF: Boris, Senator.

327–332

Ruby Yacht—In Veronica Lake, Bullwinkle discovers a ruby-encrusted yacht. He enters the special boat in the annual Frostbite Falls Flotilla Festival. Coincidentally, a Pasha in Lower North Pakistan wants this "ruby yacht of Omar Khayam" and sends his vizier to haggle with the moose. Rocky and Bullwinkle are put aboard the SS *Plankton* and taken to the Pasha's palace, where they are charged with theft. Bullwinkle is about to be thrown into a cobra pit, but Rocky demands a trial. While Bullwinkle fakes having a fit (not much of a stretch), Rocky constructs a red dummy yacht, and they're allowed to return home.

327. *Ruby Yacht*
WC: Narrator. JF: Rocky, Librarian. BS: Bullwinkle. PF: Digger Deeper, Senior Citizen, Jeweler.

328. *Let's Drink to the Ruby or Stoned Again*
WC: Narrator. JF: Rocky, Newsboy. BS: Bullwinkle, Pasha. PF: Vizier, Jeweler, Newsreader.

329. *Rimski and Korsakoff Go to Palm Springs or Song of Indio*
WC: Narrator. JF: Rocky, Miss Plumfort. BS: Bullwinkle, Pasha, Featherby, Miles Standoffish, Board Members #1 and 2, Fred. PF: Vizier, Featherby's Friend, Mayor, Crook, Barney.

330. *The Malady Lingers On or I Bought You Violence for Your Furs*
WC: Narrator. JF: Rocky. BS: Bullwinkle, Police Sergeant, FBI Agent, Captain. PF: Vizier, Mayor, Chief, Mate.

331. *The Deep Six or It's Tough to Fathom*
WC: Narrator. JF: Rocky. BS: Bullwinkle, Pasha, Captain. PF: Vizier.

332. *The New Delhi-catessen or Judgment at Bloombergs*
WC: Narrator. JF: Rocky. BS: Bullwinkle, Pasha. PF: Vizier.

333–338

Bullwinkle's Testimonial Dinner—The citizens of Frostbite Falls decide to give Bullwinkle a testimonial but Bullwinkle's only shirt boasts a Tabasco sauce stain. The nearest available laundry is Ed Foo Yung's in Shanghai, China. Bullwinkle is mistakenly given a package meant for Boris and Natasha; the package contains an atom-bomb wristwatch. The two spies, along with agent One Ton Lee, discover Rocky and Bullwinkle on a nearby junk. Bullwinkle gives the package back to Boris, who only gets as far as the city dump.

333. *Bullwinkle's Testimonial Dinner*
WC: Narrator. JF: Rocky, Granny Goodfoot. BS: Bullwinkle, Man. PF: Generous Man, Mayor.

334. *Hello, Orient or That's Some Dandy-Looking China You Have There*
WC: Narrator. JF: Rocky, Natasha, Miss Bracegirdle. BS: Bullwinkle, Mr. Frapp. PF: Boris, Ed Foo Yung, Mayor.

335. *Let's Blow Up New York or We Bombed 'Em at the Palace*
WC: Narrator. JF: Rocky, Natasha. BS: Bullwinkle, Mr. Frapp. PF: Boris, Ed Foo Yung.

336. *Exploding Population or Pull Yourself Together*
WC: Narrator. JF: Rocky, Natasha. BS: Bullwinkle, One Ton Lee. PF: Boris, Ed Foo Yung.

337. *Up The River or Yangtze with the Laughing Face*
WC: Narrator. JF: Rocky, Natasha. BS: Bullwinkle, One Ton Lee. PF: Boris, Ed Foo Yung.

338. *The Bomb in the Cellar or Bullwinkle Lowers the Boom*
WC: Narrator. JF: Rocky, Natasha. BS: Bullwinkle, One Ton Lee. PF: Boris, Chinese Authority, Shirt-seller.

339–344

The Weather Lady—The citizens of Frostbite Falls buy a fortune-telling machine in the shape of a lady; they name it "Ruth Booth." Apart from predicting the weather, she plays cards, never dealing less than four of a kind. Boris and Natasha spirit her away to Watchowee Falls, where a gambling boat is moored. Rocky and Bullwinkle fail to retrieve the weather lady and must raise enough money to bet on her. When Bullwinkle arrives with a second prediction machine, the greedy spies steal both units, escaping into a lifeboat, which promptly sinks.

339. *Weather Lady*
WC: Narrator. JF: Rocky, Natasha, Aggie. BS: Bullwinkle, Bill, Man. PF: Boris, Mayor, Newsreader.

340. *The Rolling Stone or Look Maw, No Moss*
WC: Narrator. JF: Rocky, Natasha. BS: Bullwinkle, Hiram Trump, Citizen. PF: Boris, Mayor.

341. *A Southern-Style Breakfast or How Many Grits Can You Eat?*
WC: Narrator. JF: Rocky, Natasha. BS: Bullwinkle, Gambler #1, Lucky Louie Ledbetter. PF: Boris, TV Announcer, Gambler #2.

342. *Bartender, Turn Those Lights Off or A Shot in the Dark*
WC: Narrator. JF: Rocky, Natasha. BS: Bullwinkle, Man. PF: Boris, Man.

343. *Duel Controls or Put It in Second*
WC: Narrator. JF: Rocky, Natasha. BS: Bullwinkle, Boris's Second, Boarder. PF: Boris, Man, Duel Judge.

344. *They Didn't Pick Up Our Option or Show Down*
WC: Narrator. JF: Rocky, Natasha. BS: Bullwinkle, Onlooker #2, Man #2. PF: Boris, Onlooker #1, Man #1.

345–350

Louse on 92nd Street—Bullwinkle J. Moose is the only one brave enough to testify against feared and vicious gangster Fingers Scarnose, who happens to be Boris Badenov's idol. When Bullwinkle accidentally takes the Scarnose gang's getaway car, they follow him. Now our endangered moose must hide out until the trial day. Boris offers his services to Scarnose. Rocky and Bullwinkle escape to a mink farm, but they are traced; Bullwinkle is sold to Boris as the biggest mink. Finally, after Rocky saves his pal from a sawmill, the court trial proceeds and Scarnose is sent to jail.

345. *Louse on 92nd Street*
WC: Narrator. JF: Rocky, Natasha, Mrs. Scarnose, Claire Loose Booth. BS: Bullwinkle, Captain Harvey "Blood and Viscera" Linkenfurter, Fact-Finder #2. PF: Boris, Mr. Scarnose, Fact Finder #1, DA.

346. *Bullwinkle Sneaks a Peek or There's Room in the River*
WC: Narrator. JF: Rocky. BS: Bullwinkle, Policeman, APB Man. PF: Boris, Police Chief.

347. *The Half Shot Moose or Testify My Eye*
WC: Narrator. JF: Rocky, Newsboy. BS: Bullwinkle, APB Man, Man #2. PF: Boris, Fingers Scarnose, Man #1.

348. *Whatever Happened to Joel Kupperman? or Get That Quiz Kid*
WC: Narrator, Lawyer. JF: Rocky, Natasha. BS: Bullwinkle, DA. PF: Boris, Fingers Scarnose, Reporter, Assistant DA.

349. *Doing the Big Apple or May I Have the Next Dunce?*
WC: Narrator. JF: Rocky, Natasha. BS: Bullwinkle. PF: Boris, Mink Farmer.

350. *The Act Is Over or The Big Mink Is the Fink*
WC: Narrator. JF: Rocky, Natasha, Newsboy. BS: Bullwinkle, Judge. PF: Boris, Mink Farmer, Prosecutor.

351–362

Wossamotta U—Wossamotta University desperately needs a successful football team. Two football scouts observe Bullwinkle propelling Rocky skyward, and sign the moose up as a passer. Bullwinkle's actual sports prowess is minimal, but with Rocky's help, they win the first game, 66–60. Boris and Natasha turn up and decide to fix a game; Natasha convinces Bullwinkle that her little brother will be thrown off the opposing team if Wossamotta wins. After our boys see through the scam, Wossamotta becomes the country's top team. Fearless Leader enters the stakes; he and Boris coach a vicious new team called the Mud City Manglers. To make the odds even higher, Boris dresses his team as girls. The Manglers cheat, intimidate the referee, and dig trenches with gun emplacements. Rocky and Bullwinkle employ Civil War plans rather than conventional football plays. In the final quarter, Boris decides to mine the whole end zone, but lucky Bullwinkle scores the winning touchdown, miraculously missing every land mine.

351. *Wossamotta U*
WC: Narrator, Professor #4. JF: Rocky. BS: Bullwinkle, Edgar, Deaf Man, Angry Professor #1, Professor #2, Professor #5. PF: Rocky Knute, Chauncey, Chancellor, Professor #3, Scout.

352. *A College for Two or Rock Enrolls*
WC: Narrator. JF: Rocky. BS: Bullwinkle, Edgar, Professor. PF: Rocky Knute, Chauncey, Chancellor, Counselor.

353. *The Hidden Ball Play or Goal Is Where You Find It*
WC: Narrator. JF: Rocky, Natasha. BS: Bullwinkle, Herdlicker. PF: Boris, Rocky Knute, Chancellor, Pass Receiver.

354. *Wager at Dawn or Early to Bet*
WC: Narrator. JF: Rocky, Natasha. BS: Bullwinkle. PF: Boris, Student.

355. *Standing Room Only or Bullwinkle Sells Out*
WC: Narrator. JF: Rocky, Natasha. BS: Bullwinkle, Manny, Team Member. PF: Boris, Whizzer.

356. *Bullwinkle Scores Again or Fool's Goal*
WC: Narrator. JF: Rocky, Natasha. BS: Bullwinkle, Fearless Leader, Dr. Isosceles Digit, Hockaby, Team Member. PF: Boris, Chancellor, Professor.

357. *Rogues' Gallery or Hold That Line-Up*
WC: Narrator, Strangler. JF: Rocky, Natasha, Newsboy #1. BS: Bullwinkle, Fearless Leader, Thug #1. PF: Boris, Rocky Knute, Chancellor, Thug #2, Back Stabber, Newsboy #2.

358. *Male Bags or Homely Are the Brave*
WC: Narrator. JF: Rocky, Natasha. BS: Bullwinkle, Fearless Leader, Manny, Bob Waterbucket. PF: Boris, Rocky Knute.

359. *Mine Eyes Have Seen the Gory or Moose's In the Col' Col' Ground*
WC: Narrator. JF: Rocky. BS: Bullwinkle, Fearless Leader, Mangler #1, Referee, "Gertrude." PF: Boris, Colonel Jefferson Beauregard Lee, Mangler #2, "Sybil."

360. *Bullwinkle's Battle Plan or Civil Defense*
WC: Narrator. JF: Rocky, Natasha. BS: Bullwinkle, Manny, Referee, Rufe. PF: Boris, Colonel Beauregard, Lefty, Man.

361. *Bullwinkle Buys a Fence or Pickets Charge*
WC: Narrator. JF: Rocky, Natasha. BS: Bullwinkle, Fearless Leader, Manny, Referee. PF: Boris, Colonel Beauregard, Lefty, Mangler.

362. *A Rock for Rock or To Each His Stone*
WC: Narrator, Bookie #2. JF: Rocky. BS: Bullwinkle, Fearless Leader, Referee, Nicky, Charley. PF: Boris, Bookie #1, Mangler, Charley's Friend.

363–366

Moosylvania Saved—Pottsylvania's treasurer has stolen the treasury, leaving the evil little nation flat broke. Fearless Leader employs the aid of a machine called Advise-a-Vac, which tells him that money can be found in Moosylvania, where Rocky and Bullwinkle happen to be vacationing. Boris announces that the moose and squirrel are marooned, thus turning Moosylvania into a disaster area. Emergency rations arrive and the island begins to sink under the weight. Rocky floats the island to safety with some surplus bubble gum. Boris and Natasha steal all the goodies and head across the river, but their raft sinks.

363. *Moosylvania Saved*
WC: Narrator. JF: Rocky. BS: Bullwinkle, Fearless Leader. PF: Boris, Anatol.

364. *(Untitled Episode)*
WC: Narrator. JF: Rocky, Natasha. BS: Bullwinkle, Fearless Leader. PF: Boris.

365. *(Untitled Episode)*
WC: Narrator. JF: Rocky, Natasha. BS: Bullwinkle, Fearless Leader. PF: Boris.

366. *Moosylvania Mish Mash or A State of Confusion*
WC: Narrator. JF: Rocky, Natasha. BS: Bullwinkle, Fearless Leader. PF: Boris.

FRACTURED FAIRY TALES

Narrator: Edward Everett Horton

Key to abbreviations

DB:	Daws Butler	JB:	Julie Bennett (episodes 49, 50, 52 only)
JF:	June Foray	JW:	Animated by Jay Ward Productions
BS:	Bill Scott	TVS:	Animated by TV Spots.
PF:	Paul Frees (episodes 31–35 only)		

1. *Goldilocks*—Goldilocks learns a valuable lesson about misusing people's property. JF: Tusineida Woofenpickle (aka Goldilocks), Mama Bear. DB: Bruce Bear, Oswald.

2. *Jack & the Beanstalk* (Title onscreen: *Fee Fi Fo Fum*)—A slow-witted giant can't remember how to say "Fee Fi Fo Fum," thus allowing Jack to escape. JF: Jack's Mother, Giant's Wife, Singing Harp. DB: Jack, The Giant. BS: Fairy Godmouse, Magic Hen.

3. *Rapunzel*—Rapunzel and a charming prince foil a wicked witch. DB: Husband, Prince. JF: Wife, Witch, Rapunzel. (JW)

4. *Puss in Boots*—A clever cat accomplishes the impossible: his master, the Marquis, finally takes a bath. DB: Ogre, Puss. BS: Jack the Miller's Son, King.

5. *The Enchanted Fish*—A poor fisherman meets a mermaid who grants wishes, but his greedy wife makes trouble. BS: Fisherman. JF: Wife, Mermaid. DB: Jeeves.

6. *The Little Tailor*—The king offers his daughter's hand in marriage to a tailor, who must first kill a unicorn in the woods. DB: Tailor, King. BS: Ralph Giant. JF: Princess, Small Woman.

7. *Rumpelstiltskin*—PR man Rumpelstiltskin becomes Gladys's agent, in exchange for her first child. JF: Gladys. DB: Rumpelstiltskin. BS: King, Town Crier. (JW)

8. *The Princess and the Pea*—A greedy court jester disguises his friend Clyde as a missing princess. BS: King, Clyde Clod. DB: Million-Laughs Charlie. JF: Princess.

9. *Beauty and the Beast*—A hideous beast must get kissed by a beauty if he is to become handsome. DB: Beast. JF: Old Woman, Amazonian Woman, Juliet, Beauty. (JW)

10. *Sweet Little Beet*—The invisible Prince Fascinato wants a bride; Beet and her two ugly sisters audition. JF: Prunelda, Grinessa, Sweet Little Beet. DB: Prince Fascinato. BS: Winnie.

11. *Dick Whittington*—in London, a sharp-talking cat becomes ambitious Dick Whittington's manager. BS: Dick Whittington, Citizen of Poppin' Full of Squares. DB: Puss, Mr. Fitzwarren, King. JF: Miss Alice, Queen.

12. *Tom Thumb*—Minuscule Tom forms a juvenile delinquent gang, and is subsequently psychoanalyzed. DB: Father, Tom Thumb, Cop, Parliamentarian, Citizen #3, King. BS: Admiring Person, Merlin, Gang Member, Inspector Snoot, Citizen #2. JF: Farmer's Wife, Newsboy, Citizen #1. Edward Everett Horton: Citizen #4.

13. *The Elves and the Shoemaker*—A depressed artist wants to be a shoemaker like his idol Hermann Capuccino, but first he must "suffer." DB: Easel Painter, Elf #2. BS: Elf #1, Hobo, Direction Giver. JF: Easel Painter's Wife.

14. *Cinderella*—Bankrupt Prince Fascinato needs to marry an heiress but instead meets Cinderella, who is selling pots and pans on commission to the Good Fairy. JF: Cinderella. DB: Prince Fascinato. BS: Fairy Godmother, Frobisher. (JW)

15. *Snow White*—A sarcastic Magic Mirror tells the Wicked Queen about Snow White; but first the Queen must join the Seven Dwarves' Health Club. JF: Wicked Queen, Snow White. BS: Magic Mirror, Dwarf with gland trouble, Dwarf #2, Max. DB: Head Dwarf, Dwarf #3. (JW)

16. *Sir Galahad*—Young Sir wants to be a knight over the objections of his father, who wants the boy to follow him into the clown biz. BS: Harry Galahad, Lackey, King. DB: Town Clerk, Sir Galahad. JF: Bessie Galahad, Damsel.

17. *King Midas*—Greedy Midas craves the love of his subjects, so he can tax them even more. DB: Midas, Town Crier, Citizen. BS: Benson, Bead, Bangle, Bauble, Soldier. JF: Cat Owner.

18. *Pinocchio*—Pinocchio wants to be brave so he can become a real boy, but "kindly" old Geppetto gets him a TV show, begging him to "stay wood." BS: Geppetto, TV Director, Cameraman. DB: Pinocchio, J. Quincey Flogg. JF: Good Fairy. (TVS)

19. *Little Red Riding Hood*—Red, who sells riding hoods in Hollywood, needs a wolf skin and snares naive Walter Wolf, who must dispose of his Grandma. JF: Red, Wealthy Customer, Mama Wolf. DB: Walter Wolf. BS: Zookeeper.

20. *Sleeping Beauty*—A prince realizes he can make money out of Sleeping Beauty; instead of awakening her, he markets her comatose form by building a theme park called Sleeping Beautyland. DB: Prince. JF: Yolanda, Sleeping Beauty. (JW)

21. *Hansel and Gretel*—Hansel and Gretel find the Witch's gingerbread house, but the Witch turns the boy into an aardvark. JF: Wife, Gretel. DB: Woodchopper, Hansel. BS: Witch, Talking Duck. (TVS)

22. *Cinderella Returns*—After embarrassing herself by trying to snag Prince Edgar the Mild, Cinderella discovers he's already married, to her Fairy Godmother! BS: Fairy Godmother, Bertie. JF: Cinderella. DB: Prince Edgar the Mild. (JW)

23. *Snow White, Incorporated*—A tale of corporate climbers: the Wicked Queen is head of Witchpak; Snow runs Consolidated Dwarfs, an agency for showbiz midgets. JF: Queen, Snow White. BS: Mirror. DB: Dwarfs, Prince. (TVS)

24. *Jack and the Beanstalk*—When Jack joins baseball club the Boston Beavers they win all their games. BS: Big Lip Leo, Giant. DB: Player, Jack Umpire, Opposing Coach. (TVS)

25. *The Pied Piper*—A musician who rids the kingdom of mice is asked by the King to exterminate his mother-in-law, but piper and victim fall in love. DB: Flatt Player, Mouse #1, Theater Patron. JF: Mouse #2, Queen, Ticket Lady. BS: King.

26. *Puss in Boots #2*—A cunning cat grants three wishes to a gullible young man. DB: Puss. BS: The Hero, Ogre. JF: Wife. (TVS)

27. *Leaping Beauty*—A witch turns the popular Leaping Beauty into a crashing bore, and she is banished to the forest. JF: Leaping Beauty. BS: Witch, Ponsonby. DB: King, Prince Charming. (TVS)

28. *Tom Thumb #2*—(also called *Tiny Tom*)—A woodchopper tries in vain to get his microscopic son to grow. The lad finally leaves to seek a bride. JF: Ma, Wife. BS: Pa. DB: Tom. (TVS)

29. *Slipping Beauty*—A witch forgets her appointment to cast a sleeping spell on a girl who is meant to be awakened by a prince. JF: Frances Beauty. BS: Witch. DB: Prince, Wolf. (TVS)

30. *Aladdin's Lamp*—Aladdin's lamp shop is a front for a gambling joint, but the King demands a lamp. DB: Aladdin, Grand Vizier. BS: King. JF: Jeannie, Sally.

31. *Rumpelstiltskin Returns*—A contest-crazy girl is helped by Rumpelstiltskin, who wants her child—until he realizes the boy is a lummox. DB: Rumpelstiltskin. JF: Girl. PF: Duke of Dunder. (TVS)

32. *The Enchanted Fish* (title on-screen: *The Magic Fish*)—A poor chimney sweep buys a supposedly magic fish, then suffers nothing but bad luck. DB: Chimney Sweep, Pirate. PF: Fishmonger, King, King's Brother. JF: Messenger. (TVS)

33. *The Frog Prince*—An oversupply of witches results in a fight over a frog; the frog has so many spells cast on him he angrily confronts the witches' union. DB: King, Head Witch. PF: Witch #2, Frog. JF: Witch #1, Witch #3, Princess, Witch #4.

34. *The Pied Piper #2*—A mute man blows pies from his pipe, until his tempting tobacco-leaf pie causes all who eat it to disappear. DB: Merchant. PF: Customer #1, Customer #2, King. JF: Queen. (TVS)

35. *Prince Darling*—A good fairy turns a wicked boy into a "horrid kind of thing," until he learns to be kind. DB: Prince Darling, Kind King, Langston. PF: Insulting Cat, George, Hunter. JF: Good Fairy, Baby, Celia the Shepherdess. (JW)

36. *The Ugly Duckling*—A talented but ugly duck wants to be a movie star, and undergoes plastic surgery. DB: Ugly Duckling, Talent Scout #2, Doorman, Plastic Surgeon. BS: Talent Scout #1, Reflection, J. B. Hogfat, Director, Producer, Insulting Janitor. JF: Fainting Woman, Little Boy. (JW)

37. *Son of Rumpelstiltskin*—To get her child back a princess must guess a funny little man's name, but he's even forgotten it himself. DB: Rumpelstiltskin, King. BS: Father, Miller, Streetworker, Wise Man. JF: Daughter. (TVS)

38. *Beauty and Her Beast*—An ugly girl becomes beautiful every time she sits on her mule. BS: Old Woodchopper. JF: His Plain Daughter. DB: Handsome Young Prince.

39. *The Golden Goose*—A dullard is rewarded with a golden goose; but everyone in the kingdom becomes stuck to the bird. BS: Father, Poetic Son, Musical Son, Wealthy Merchant, Robber, King. DB: Dumb Son, Little Man, Castle Wise Man. JF: Laughing Princess. (TVS)

40. *The Enchanted Frog*—Philbert Frog grows to human size and thinks he's an enchanted prince. BS: Singing Suitor, Frank, Townsman, Angry Suitor, Firing Squad Captain. DB: Philbert, King. JF: Mama Frog, Princess. (JW)

41. *The Goose and the Golden Egg*—A goose pretends to lay a golden egg in order to avoid being cooked, but when war breaks out she discovers she really can lay golden ones. DB: King Newton

of Fig, Duke's Aide, Soldier #2. BS: Castle Cook, Duke Parkington of Hog, Soldier #1. JF: Goose, Newsboy. (TVS)

42. *Riding Hoods Anonymous*—A wolf is trying to "kick the riding hood" habit, but Red and her equally violent Grandma don't believe him. JF: Red Riding Hood, Grandma. BS: Wolf. (JW)

43. *The Shoemaker and the Elves #2*—A shoemaker is ordered by the king to stop making shoes, but two overzealous elves try to help him. DB: Shoemaker. BS: King, Elf #2. JF: Elf #1. (TVS)

44. *Speeding Beauty*—A beauty is changed into a horse and a prince decides to race her. But she constantly falls asleep short of the finish line. BS: Witch, Clyde. JF: Princess. DB: Prince, Merlin Le Roy. (TVS)

45. *The Three Little Piggs*—Henry Q. Wolf tries courting the three wealthy Pigg sisters, but his greed goes unrewarded. JF: Portland Pigg, Penelope Pigg, Alice Pigg, Cassandra. BS: Telegram Boy. DB: Henry Q. Wolf. (TVS)

46. *Goldilocks and the Three Bears*—Goldie opens her winter resort in summer, and the Three Bears take over in her absence. JF: Goldilocks, Mama Bear. DB: Papa Bear, Clyde Bear. BS: Baby Bear. (TVS)

47. *Son of Beauty and the Beast*—Prince Fletcher, son of the famous Beast, can't follow in his father's footsteps; he decides to get a book written about his life. DB: Fletcher, Guard. BS: Soldier, Cook, Court Counselor, Sordid J. Scrivener, Cop. JF: Girl, Winona Witch, Woman.

48. *Androcles and the Lion*—Androcles pulls a thorn from the foot of a Bert Lahr–type lion; years later they meet again. BS: Wise Man, Master, Lion, Prisoner. DB: Androcles, Scorekeeper.

49. *The Fisherman and His Wife*—A struggling fisherman is granted three wishes by a talking fish, but the man and his wife soon lose everything. DB: Fisherman. JB: Wife. BS: Talking Fish, Puss in Boots. (TVS)

50. *The Goblins*—The Goblins move into a mountain and terrorize the populace, then abduct Irene, the King's daughter. BS: Treasurer, Aide, Announcer, Goblin #2, Prince Goblin. DB: King, Goblin #1, Sam, Curdy, Direction Finder, Goblin Priest. JB: Poetic Girl, Irene. (JW)

51. *Snow White Meets Rapunzel*—A witch cuts off Rapunzel's hair so that she can't let it down; the prince must learn how to fly in order to reach her. BS: Dwarf, King. JF: Snow White, Witch, Rapunzel. DB: Prince. (TVS)

52. *The Little Princess*—When a little princess grows to giant size, the heavily taxed citizens advertise for a suitor in order to marry her off. JB: Little Princess, Citizen #4. DB: King, Citizens #2 and #5, Treasurer, Tax Collector, Writer, Strange Little Man, Citizen #7. BS: Citizen #1, Pipe Smoker, Citizen #3, Lawyer, Efficiency Expert, Desperate Man, Citizen #6. (TVS)

53. *Thom Tum*—Thom Tum is a tiny lad until a Good Fairy turns him into a giant with a ravenous appetite. BS: Wallace, Aide, Duck. JF: Wallace's Wife, Good Fairy. DB: Thom Tum, King, Town Crier.

54. *Slow White and Nose Red*—A miller has two daughters whose love for the forest animals is almost their father's undoing. DB: Miller, Bachelor #1, Slowpoke. JF: Slow White, Nose Red. BS: Bachelor #2, Marriage Counselor, Sean.

55. *Prince Hyacinth and the Dear Little Princess*—Fairy 53 helps poor King Dom, whose son has a nose like a casaba melon. DB: King Dom, Red Fox Leader, Prince Hyacinth. JF: Queen, Dear Little Princess. BS: Fairy, Warlock, Citizen.

56. *The Giant and the Beanstalk*—A sequel to "Jack and the Beanstalk"—twenty years later Jack is wealthy from his Golden Harp business. JF: Giant's Wife, Jack's Secretary. BS: Giant's Son, Magic Goose, Sorcerer. DB: Bean Seller, Jack Junior.

57. *The Enchanted Fly*—An enchanted fly grants the King's every wish; finally the King becomes a fly (until he meets a certain tailor). DB: King, Fink-sayer, Tailor. BS: Fly, Royal Minister, Friend, Other King. JF: Betty.

58. *Felicia and the Pot of Pinks*—A woodcutter leaves a chicken to his son Bruno, and a pot of pinks to his daughter Felicia. BS: Woodchopper, Chicken, Talking Cabbage. DB: Bruno, Prince Pinky. JF: Felicia, Magic Tree.

59. *Hans Klinker*—Hans is a born musician; this story involves a pair of silver skates and the Zuyder Zee race. JF: Brunhilde, Mama. BS: Papa. DB: Hans, Waterfront Boss.

60. *The Witch's Broom*—Grizelda—Witch of the Year—falls hopelessly in love with a handsome prince. JF: Grizelda, "Princess." BS: Witch's Boss, Psychiatrist, Mirror, King. DB: Handsome Prince, Minister.

61. *Son of King Midas*—Midas's son finds it impossible to follow in his father's footsteps. BS: Midas, Dentist Major, Dean, Patient, Angry Patient, Helpful Patient. DB: Proxy, Midas Junior. JF: Old Witch.

62. *The Magic Chicken*—The path to the hand of a merchant's daughter includes a magic chicken, golden axes, and an ogre. DB: Aladdin. BS: Father, Guard, Man #1, Ogre. JF: Hilda, Chicken.

63. *Aladdin and His Lump*—Aladdin must look for a new lamp when his old one is stolen by an evil sorcerer. DB: Aladdin. BS: Genie, Uncle, Sorcerer.

64. *The Enchanted Gnat*—A tinker has three sons, each of whom is granted a magic wish; the son named Nathaniel is a real menace. BS: Tinker, Brother #3. DB: Nat, Brother, Sprite, Brother #2. JF: Witch.

65. *Milo and the Thirteen Helmets*—At Dragon U, poor Milo the Dragon has been a senior for forty years and still hasn't graduated. BS: King Arthur, Citizen, Milo. DB: Sir Cumference, Dean. JF: Wife.

66. *The Prince and the Popper*—In the town of Tootsie Lavendeur, a popper overthrows an evil prince, saving the kingdom's champagne. DB: Champagne Man, Popper, Good Prince. BS: Scientist, Man, Evil Prince. JF: Wife.

67. *Booty and the Beast*—Handsome Alden Farquhar, sick of being pursued by all the beautiful maidens, wants to be turned into a beast. DB: Alden Farquhar. JF: Witch, Maidens #1, 2, 4. BS: Scared Man, Real Estate Man, Maiden #3.

68. *Little Fred Riding Hood*—Little Fred Riding Hood is granted a wish after helping two strange little people. DB: Fred, Little Man #2. BS: Little Man #1, Woman #2. JF: Mother, Women #1, 3, 4.

69. *Goldilocks and the Three Bears*—Goldilocks, a home economist, helps the Three Bears move to an apartment. DB: Bear. JF: Mother, Ethel, Home Economist. BS: Junior, Preacher.

70. *The Ugly Almond Duckling*—An ugly duck from the Yangtze River in China takes up music and tours as a bandleader. BS: Emperor, Ugly Duck. DB: Cook, Duck #1, Duck #2. JF: Teacher, Frog.

71. *John's Ogre Wife*—Prince John and Princess Tinsel are deliriously happy until mean witch Grumpira turns Tinsel into an ogre. JF: Tinsel. DB: John. BS: Grumpira.

72. *The Absent-minded King*—A forgetful king wants to find a bride, but to do so he must remember a magic word; he must also face a giant, some vicious thorns, and a witch. DB: King. BS: Aide, Prime Minister. JF: Magic Blue Fairy, Princess, Witch, Forgetful Girl.

73. *The Mysterious Castle*—In the kingdom of Easy Pickins, man of the year Schuyler Sugg must determine who dwells in a spooky black castle. DB: Scalawag, Schuyler Sugg, Citizen #2, Scared Man. BS: Victim, Citizen #1, Mayor, Farmer. JF: Woman.

74. *The Little Tinker*—A tinker confronts a giant troll who wants his "People Pot" repaired. JF: Tinker's Wife, Townswoman, Princess. BS: Tinker, Townsman, Troll, Woodsman. DB: Tinker's Son, King.

75. *Tale of a Frog*—Julius Frog is unhappy, believing "people have more fun than frogs." But after his Fairy Frogmother turns him into a "people" he's not so sure. JF: Mother Frog, Fairy Frogmother, Princess. DB: Julius Frog, Sergeant. BS: Bully, Recruiting Officer, Medical Officer.

76. *The Teeth of Baghdad*—A set of false teeth provides the clue to the identity of the rightful ruler of Baghdad. DB: Fakir, Sultan, License Officer, Passerby #2, Dentist. BS: Soldier, Passerby #1, Grand Vizier, Vizier's Aide.

77. *The Little Man in the Tub*—A poor boy with the unfortunate name Delicia finally scrapes up some money, but ends up with mother-in-law problems. DB: Delicia. BS: Wishing Well Voice, Sword Owner, Man in Tub, Ogre. JF: Maiden, Mother-in-law.

78. *Red White*—A duke and a fair maiden are both endowed with hair that's "redder than red." DB: Duke. BS: Magic Mirror, Fairy Godmother. JF: Red White.

79. *Cutie and the Beast*—Cutie tries to turn a beast into a prince, but the tables are eventually turned. BS: Clock Maker, Wise Man. JF: Cutie. DB: Beast.

80. *The Flying Carpet*—A rug seller tells the king that a carpet with a hole in it is really a magic carpet which can fly. BS: Rug Seller. DB: Sultan, Carpet Man, Fortuneteller. JF: Princess.

81. *The Count and the Bird*—A gullible Count is a dupe for the local charlatans; he finds a bird that lays eggs containing gold coins, but loses his fortune on a wager. BS: Charlatan, Gambler, Tailor. DB: Count Basil. JF: Newsboy, Wife.

82. *The Tale of a King*—Nothing-Ham is a kingdom where nothing ever happens, so the king decides to make up a "keen story" about his daughter. JF: Queen, Princess, Witch. DB: King, Messenger. BS: Storyteller, Tailor, Lad, Troll.

83. *Sweeping Beauty*—A frumpish castle maid discovers that a series of catnaps will make her beautiful. JF: Esmerelda Fump. DB: Prince Robin of Redbreast, King's Friend. BS: King, Freddy the Court Magician.

84. *The Wishing Hat*—A boy named Booby helps a Brownie and is rewarded with a red wishing hat; he finally turns into an owl. BS: Booby, Captain of the Royal Guard. DB: Father, Brownie, Rich Guest. JF: Guest's Wife.

85. *Son of Snow White*—Joe White, handsome son of Snow White, faces his opponent—a handsome prince. DB: Prince Charming, Wicked Prince Virgil, Sleazy. JF: Snow White, Wicked Queen, Flo White. BS: Joe White, Magic Mirror, Dirty.

86. *Jack B. Nimble*—A sly caretaker is banished; he enters into a prosperous magic-fountain business. DB: Jack B. Nimble. BS: Judge, Gnome. JF: Gloomy Woman, Gloria.

87. *Potter's Luck*—A potter's boiling temper does him in when he is used as a guinea pig by a group of witches. DB: Potter. JF: Potter's Wife, Witch, Witch #2, Good Fairy. BS: Witch #3.

88. *The Magic Lychee Nut*—A young man asks his honorable father's permission to marry; an old man gives him some magic lychee nuts. BS: Sneezing Man, Charlie, Aa-Choo's Son. DB: Sneezing Man's Friend, Aa-Choo, Old Man, Robber. JF: Wife.

89. *The King and the Witch*—A king is tricked into marrying an ugly witch but is saved by a magic wishbone. DB: King, Citizen #2. BS: Citizen #1, Butcher, Citizen #4, Adviser, Troll, Aide. JF: Citizen #3, Witch.

90. *The Seven Chickens*—A prince meets the king's six beautiful daughters, who have all been changed into chickens—the seventh chicken is the witch. BS: King, Handsome Knight. DB: Prince. JF: Witch. (Animated in Hollywood)

91. *A Youth Who Set Out to Learn What Fear Was*—A young boy named Swinburne knows no fear, but he must learn how to shudder. DB: Swinburne, Elf, King, Ogre. BS: Maynard, Father. JF: Queen.

BULLWINKLE'S CORNER

Key to abbreviations

BS: Bill Scott = Bullwinkle
JF: June Foray = Rocky
PF: Paul Frees = Boris

1. *The Swing*—Bullwinkle demonstrates a swing with the help of a bull. JF: Rocky. BS: Bullwinkle.
2. *Little Miss Muffet*—Rocky wants to know what a "tuffet" is. JF: Rocky. BS: Bullwinkle.
3. *The Horn*—Rocky portrays an accomplished musician named Little Boy Blue. JF: Rocky. BS: Bullwinkle.
4. *Where Go the Boats*—Bullwinkle goes boating down a stream. JF: Rocky. BS: Bullwinkle.
5. *My Shadow*—The moose and his shadow end up in fisticuffs. JF: Rocky. BS: Bullwinkle.
6. *I Love Little Pussy*—A Mother Moose classic (featuring a tiger). JF: Rocky. BS: Bullwinkle.
7. *Taffy*—The tale of a Welshman and his friend. BS: Bullwinkle. PF: Boris (Taffy).
8. *Wee Willie Winkie*—Bullwinkle runs upstairs and downstairs in his nightgown, until the police investigate. JF: Rocky, Frantic Woman. BS: Bullwinkle, Cop #1. PF: Cop #2.
9. *Little Jack Horner*—Bullwinkle has trouble baking a pie. JF: Rocky. BS: Bullwinkle.
10. *The Queen of Hearts*—The knave is Boris, who steals the tarts. JF: Rocky. BS: Bullwinkle. PF: Boris.
11. *Tom, Tom, the Piper's Son*—*Dragnet*-style cops question Bullwinkle about a stolen pig. BS: Bullwinkle, Cop #2. PF: Cop #1.
12. *Barbara Frietchie*—The Civil War is reenacted. BS: Bullwinkle. PF: Stonewall Boris.
13. *Rocky Bye Baby*—Network censors force the removal of a baby from the treetop. BS: Bullwinkle. PF: G. J.
14. *The Village Blacksmith*—Bullwinkle is the smithy, in a salute to Longfellow. JF: Rocky. BS: Bullwinkle.
15. *The Children's Hour*—Dedicated to baby-sitters everywhere. JF: Rocky. BS: Bullwinkle.
16. *The Barefoot Boy*—The barefoot boy is Rocky, who meets a bear. JF: Rocky. BS: Bullwinkle.
17. *The Raven*—Edgar Allan Poe à la Bullwinkle, in a moody reading. JF: Rocky. BS: Bullwinkle.
18. *Woodman, Spare That Tree*—Ranger Bullwinkle prevents Boris from cutting down a tree. BS: Bullwinkle. PF: Boris (Woodman).
19. *Excelsior*—Bullwinkle dramatizes Longfellow once again. JF: Rocky. BS: Bullwinkle, Villager.
20. *Simple Simon*—Simon is Bullwinkle; he wants to taste pie man Boris's wares. JF: Rocky. BS: Bullwinkle. PF: Boris (Pie-man).

21. *Hickory Dickory Dock*—Bullwinkle is no match for a little mouse. JF: Mouse. BS: Bullwinkle. PF: Doctor.

22. *Little Bo Peep*—Bullwinkle foils sheep rustler Boris. BS: Bullwinkle. PF: Boris (Sheriff).

23. *The Daffodils*—Bullwinkle is thrown in jail for picking flowers. BS: Bullwinkle. PF: Boris (Park Ranger—Judge—Prison Guard).

24. *The Bee*—Bullwinkle's taste for honey proves his undoing. BS: Bullwinkle, The Bee.

25. *Peter Piper*—Bullwinkle meets Peter Piper, who tells the moose of his sister Suzie. BS: Bullwinkle. PF: Peter Piper.

26. *Pat-a-Cake*—Bullwinkle shows off his culinary skills. JF: Rocky. BS: Bullwinkle.

27. *Thanksgiving Day*—The saga of a sleigh ride. JF: Rocky. BS: Bullwinkle. PF: Wolf.

28. *Sing a Song of Sixpence*—Boris almost beheads Bullwinkle the baker. JF: Rocky BS: Bullwinkle, Bird. PF: Boris (King).

29. *How to Be Happy (Though Miserable)*—Boris takes over the poetry corner. BS: Bullwinkle. PF: Boris.

30. *The Wind*—Bullwinkle recites in galelike conditions. BS: Bullwinkle. PF: Boris.

31. *How to Train Your Doggy—For Fun and Profit*—Bullwinkle displays mastery over his dog (the first "Mr. Know-It-All" segment). JF: Rocky. BS: Bullwinkle.

32. *The Arrow and the Song*—Bullwinkle the archer runs into a policeman. BS: Bullwinkle. PF: Irish Cop.

33. *Jack Be Nimble*—Bullwinkle gets into trouble with the Hop, Skip, and Jumpers' Union. BS: Bullwinkle. PF: Boris (Jack B. Nimble).

34. *Morey Had a Little Lamb*—Rocky must take drastic measures to save Bullwinkle. JF: Rocky. BS: Bullwinkle.

35. *See a Pin*—Boris Badenov doesn't believe in good luck. BS: Bullwinkle. PF: Repairman, Boris.

36. *How to Tame Lions—and Get a Little Scratch—on the Side—of Your Head*—Mr. Know-It-All proves to be a great lion tamer. JF: Rocky. BS: Bullwinkle.

37. *How to Cook a Turkey's Goose*—One must first have a turkey to cook. JF: Rocky. BS: Bullwinkle, Turkey.

38. *Swimming Can Be Fun—and Wet*—An "antlered-fire-winged-goofus" finds it difficult to swim. JF: Rocky, BS: Bullwinkle. PF: Boris.

39. *How to Sell Vacuum Cleaners—and Clean Up*—The customee (or salesman) has three major rules for getting to the customer. JF: Rocky. BS: Bullwinkle. PF: Boris, Dog.

40. *How to Cure the Hiccups*—Don't let Boris join in. JF: Rocky. BS: Bullwinkle. PF: Boris.

41. *Old Mother Hubbard*—Bullwinkle meets a starving dog. BS: Bullwinkle. PF: Dog.

42. *The Cherry Tree*—Squire Hatchett objects to Bullwinkle climbing his cherry tree. BS: Bullwinkle, Friend. PF: Hatchet.

43. *Tommy Tucker*—The heartwarming story of a singing waiter. BS: Bullwinkle. PF: Customer, Manager.

44. *Grandfather's Clock*—We meet Bullwinkle's Grampa Moose. JF: Rocky. BS: Bullwinkle, Grampa.

45. *A Wet Sheet and a Flowing Sea*—A salty yarn by that old mariner Bullwinkle. JF: Rocky. BS: Bullwinkle. (Last of the poetry format)

46. *How to Open a Jar of Pickles*—Some jars are difficult—but it won't stop our moose. JF: Rocky. BS: Bullwinkle.

47. *How to Get into the Movies Without Buying a Ticket*—Boris is the theater manager. JF: Rocky. BS: Bullwinkle. PF: Boris.

48. *How to Catch a Bee and Make Your Honey Happy*—Catching a bee in Death Valley. JF: Rocky. BS: Bullwinkle.

49. *How to Be a Cow Puncher—Without Getting Hit Back*—Boris is foreman of the cattle drive. JF: Rocky. BS: Bullwinkle. PF: Boris, Rodeo Announcer.

50. *How to Escape from Devil's Island—and Get Away from It All*—Ten years served of a thirty-day sentence! JF: Rocky. BS: Bullwinkle. PF: Boris (Warden).

51. *How to Shoot Par*—Bullwinkle is hampered by an unusual iron, and a sand trap. JF: Rocky. BS: Bullwinkle.

52. *Magic Made Easy (the Hard Way)*—Trouble with a "living pincushion." JF: Rocky. BS: Bullwinkle.

53. *How to Turn a Beastly Failure into a Monstrous Success*—Meet Llewellyn, a nice monster. JF: Rocky. BS: Bullwinkle.

54. *How to Remove a Moustache—Without Getting Any Lip*—A bank robber joins this lecture. JF: Rocky. BS: Bullwinkle. PF: Bankers #1 and #2, Barber, Robber, Judge.

55. *Falling Asleep on the Job Can Lead to a Rude Awakening*—Mr. Know-It-All shows how easy it is to stay awake. JF: Rocky. BS: Bullwinkle.

56. *How to Remove an Unwanted Guest from Your House—and Make More Living Room*—A guest overstays his welcome, infuriating the host. JF: Rocky. BS: Bullwinkle.

57. *How to Be a Star Reporter*—Bullwinkle's city editor turns out to be Boris. JF: Rocky. BS: Bullwinkle. PF: Boris (Editor).

58. *How to Do Stunts in the Movies—Without Having the Usher Throw You Out*—Famous Hollywood director C. B. puts his stuntman through a harrowing experience. JF: Rocky. BS: Bullwinkle. PF: Boris.

59. *How to Run the Four Minute Mile—in Ten Seconds*—Speed, endurance, and antlers. JF: Rocky. BS: Bullwinkle.

60. *Wouldn't a Trophy Look Good over Your Fireplace—or How to Get a Head*—Boris is the faithful Indian guide. JF: Rocky. BS: Bullwinkle. PF: Boris. (Faithful Indian Guide).

61. *How to Be a Barber—or Ten Ways to Clip Your Fellow Man*—Bullwinkle can't get customers for his barbershop. JF: Rocky. BS: Bullwinkle. PF: Boris, Captain Peachfuzz.

62. *How to Water-Ski—or Five Steps to Easy Drowning*—Rocky shows us how an expert handles water skiing. JF: Rocky. BS: Bullwinkle. PF: Boris.

63. *How to Be an Indian in One Easy Lesson—or You Can Be a Tonto, Pronto*—Bullwinkle models what the well-dressed Indian will wear this coming season. JF: Rocky. BS: Bullwinkle.

64. *How to Own a Hi-Fi on a Low Income—and I.Q.*—Bullwinkle speaks for music lovers everywhere. JF: Rocky. BS: Bullwinkle. PF: Boris, Voice of Sir Harry Lauder.

65. *How to Be a Human Fly*—Boris lends a hand as Bullwinkle climbs a tall building. JF: Rocky. BS: Bullwinkle.

66. *The Most Economical Form of Transportation—Hitchhiking*—Bullwinkle's in trouble when Boris is the hitchhikee. JF: Rocky. BS: Bullwinkle. PF: Boris (Driver).

67. *How to Be a Hobo—or Ten Easy Steps to a Bum Career*—The hardships of a hobo's life. JF: Rocky. BS: Bullwinkle.

68. *How to Disarm a Live 5000 Megaton TNT Bomb in Your Own Workshop in Your Spare Time to Amuse Your Friends—or Just Yourself Even*—Bullwinkle tries for 100 percent safety—well, 99 percent anyway! JF: Rocky. BS: Bullwinkle.

69. *How to Be a Beatnik*—Bullwinkle reads cool poetry in a coffeehouse. JF: Rocky, Natasha. BS: Bullwinkle. PF: Boris.

70. *How to Conquer your Acrophobia*—Mr. Know-It-All takes us to a skyscraper for a parachute jump. JF: Rocky. BS: Bullwinkle.

71. *How to Fix a Flat, and Retire—Your Car*—Bullwinkle demonstrates how to handle a flat tire. JF: Rocky. BS: Bullwinkle.

72. *How to Avoid Tipping the Waiter*—Trying to avoid tipping Boris will be difficult. JF: Rocky. BS: Bullwinkle. PF: Boris.

73. *Fan Club (A)*—Boris gives the secret code and Bullwinkle does his good deed for the day. JF: Rocky, Old Lady. BS: Bullwinkle. PF: Boris, Captain Peachfuzz.

74. *Buying a Used Car*—Find an honest salesman—not Boris! JF: Rocky. BS: Bullwinkle. PF: Salesman.

75. *How to Be a Archeologist—and Dig Ancient History*—Mr. Know-It-All takes us to Egypt and the Pyramids. JF: Rocky. BS: Bullwinkle. PF: Abdul Ben Boris.

76. *How to Take Your Covered Wagon Through the West—While Being Attacked by Over 2000 Savages*—Bullwinkle tries to outwit Indians. JF: Rocky. BS: Bullwinkle.

77. *Fan Club (B)*—How to enlarge the membership. JF: Rocky, Natasha. BS: Bullwinkle. PF: Boris, Captain Peachfuzz.

78. *How to Sell the Encyclopedia, Door-to-Door*—A good door-to-door salesman must outwit the customer. JF: Rocky. BS: Bullwinkle.

79. *Fan Club (C)*—Bullwinkle gives a demonstration on selling Fan Club cookies. JF: Rocky, Natasha, Housewife. BS: Bullwinkle. PF: Boris, Captain Peachfuzz.

80. *How to Wash Windows—and Be a Smash Success*—First make sure there's a window to wash. JF: Rocky. BS: Bullwinkle.

81. *Fan Club (D)*—Bullwinkle's lecture: how to get elected. JF: Rocky. BS: Bullwinkle. PF: Boris, Captain Peachfuzz.

82. *Fan Club (E)*—Boris disguises himself as publicity genius Jim Moranski to help Bullwinkle's drive for club membership. JF: Rocky, Newsboy. BS: Bullwinkle, Applicant. PF: Boris (Publicity Man).

83. *Fan Club (F)*—The big Fan Club telethon; Boris does impersonations. JF: Rocky, Natasha. BS: Bullwinkle. PF: Boris, Captain Peachfuzz.

84. *Boris' Fan Club*—Tired of the high standards of the Bullwinkle and Rocky Fan Club, Boris starts his own, using TV commercials to attract members. JF: Natasha. BS: Bullwinkle, Announcer, Boris's Twin. PF: Boris.

85. *Fan Club (G)*—At the annual Fan Club picnic, Natasha wins the "Queen" contest. JF: Rocky, Natasha. BS: Bullwinkle. PF: Boris, Captain Peachfuzz.

86. *How to Win Friends—and Be Influential with People*—Mr. Know-It-All quotes from his best-seller. JF: Rocky. BS: Bullwinkle.

87. *How to Be a Successful Baseball Umpire*—In trying to show the importance of impartiality, Bullwinkle encounters a lot of opposition. JF: Rocky. BS: Bullwinkle. PF: Boris.

88. *How to Interview a Scientist That Is Working on a Top Secret Project*—The scientist is more interested in finding a subject for his own experiment. JF: Rocky. BS: Bullwinkle, Chicken. PF: Boris.

89. *Fan Club (H)*—Ingmar Badenov directs "She Can't Pay the Rent"; Bullwinkle can't remember his lines. JF: Rocky, Natasha. BS: Bullwinkle, Dudley Do-Right. PF: Boris.

90. *Fan Club (I)*—To publicize their club, Bullwinkle starts a club newspaper. JF: Rocky. BS: Bullwinkle. PF: Boris, Captain Peachfuzz.

91. *How to Become a Successful Member of the U.S. Peace Corps*—Bullwinkle demonstrates diplomacy gone awry. JF: Rocky. BS: Bullwinkle, Computer.

92. *How to Get Your Money Back, If Not Completely Satisfied*—Bullwinkle discovers one hitch in the store's promise—it doesn't specify who must be completely satisfied. JF: Rocky. BS: Bullwinkle. PF: Boris.

93. *How to Direct Temperamental Movie Stars*—Bullwinkle shows masterful psychology with child star Little Muriel Merkle (Boris). JF: Rocky. BS: Bullwinkle. PF: Boris (as Muriel Merkle, Hoot Mix, Zip Farnsworth).

94. *How to Have a Hit Record*—Bullwinkle tries to promote his new record. JF: Rocky. BS: Bullwinkle. PF: Boris (as Disc Dawson).

95. *Making Your Neighbor Quiet Without Making Him Angry*—In trying to keep the noise down Bullwinkle winds up in jail. JF: Rocky. BS: Bullwinkle. PF: Angry Man.

96. *How to Play Winning Tennis*—Bullwinkle as a tennis star. JF: Rocky. BS: Bullwinkle. PF: Boris.

97. *Selling These Here Soap Flakes*—Bullwinkle, disguised as a washer repairman, gets caught in the washing machine. JF: Rocky. BS: Bullwinkle. PF: Boris.

98. *How to Be a Top Flight Stock Salesman*—Bullwinkle sells Boris stock, which proves worthless. JF: Rocky. BS: Bullwinkle. PF: Boris.

99. *How to Teach a Mean Bully a Lesson at the Beach*—From Bullwinkle's new book. He defends Natasha's honor when a bully kicks sand. JF: Rocky. BS: Bullwinkle.

PEABODY'S IMPROBABLE HISTORY

Key to abbreviations

BS:	Bill Scott	= Peabody (heard in every episode)
WT:	Walter Tetley	= Sherman (heard in every episode)
PF:	Paul Frees	
JF:	June Foray	
DS:	Dorothy Scott	

1. *Ben Franklin*—We meet Peabody, Sherman, and the WABAC machine (and, briefly, Ben Franklin). PF: Orphanage Man, Judge, Publius Maximus, Benjamin Franklin. WT: Newsboy.

2. *Napoleon*—Napoleon's suspenders are missing. Thus, he can't draw his sword to order his troops forward. PF: Napoleon, Pierre LeKomo, Pirate, Townsmen #1, #3. BS: Pirate Chief, Townsman #2. WT: Girl.

3. *Lord Nelson*—Nelson can't go into battle against the Spanish fleet because his boat is tied to the dock. PF: Nelson, Spanish Captain, Admiral, Hawser Guard. BS: Spanish Mate.

4. *Wyatt Earp*—The indisposed Earp can't face notorious Aces Wilde, and Peabody takes his place. PF: Wyatt Earp, Aces Wilde, BS: Informer, Bartender, Aide.

5. *King Arthur*—The King is having bad luck—it's Black Tuesday. PF: King Arthur, Merlin, Sir Round. BS: Frantic Man.

6. *Franz Schubert*—Schubert's symphony is unfinished when his piano is stolen by a music hater. PF: Franz Schubert, Vienna Police Chief. BS: Neighbor.

7. *Lucrezia Borgia*—Lucrezia meets her match when Peabody concocts a devilish mix of the world's poisons. PF: Lord of Pisaro. DS: Lucrezia Borgia.

8. *Sir Walter Raleigh*—Raleigh delivers a waterlogged cargo to a furious Queen Elizabeth. PF: Walter Raleigh. DS: Queen Elizabeth.

9. *Robert Fulton*—Fulton, the inventor of the steamboat, is pitted against the clipper ship in a race. BS: Robert Fulton, Fortescue. PF: Robert E. Leech.

10. *Annie Oakley*—Buffalo Bill arranges a shooting match between Annie and Forrest Primeval. DS: Annie Oakley. PF: Buffalo Bill, Forrest Primeval.

11. *The Wright Brothers*—Wilbur and Orville are sabotaged by a giant bird named—what else?—Kitty Hawk. PF: Wilbur. BS: Orville.

12. *George Armstrong Custer*—Custer leads his men right into an Indian camp; Peabody must cook wild-berry pies so they can escape. PF: Custer, Indian Chief. BS: Two soldiers.

13. *Alfred Nobel*—Nobel is due to meet a delegation to demonstrate his invention, TNT. PF: Nobel, Delegate.

14. *Marco Polo*—Marco is rescued from prison by Peabody and Sherman, who trick Kublai Khan. PF: Marco Polo, Kublai Khan.

15. *Richard the Lionhearted*—King Richard's cowardice ensures he'll lose the war against the Saracens. PF: Soldier, King Richard, Chief of Staff. BS: Messenger.

16. *Don Juan*—Don Juan, the great Spanish lover, has onion breath. PF: Don Juan. JF: Senorita.

17. *William Tecumseh Sherman*—General Sherman can't reach Atlanta due to an overpriced toll bridge. PF: General W. T. Sherman, Toll Keeper.

18. *The First Kentucky Derby*—Colonel Beauregard's horse, Alert, certainly doesn't live up to his name. PF: Colonel Beauregard. BS: Shorty, Horse Doctor.

19. *P. T. Barnum*—Shady trapeze artists Hyde and Sick are half owners in Barnum's circus. PF: Barnum, Sick. BS: Freddy the Highdiver, Hyde.

20. *Stanley and Livingstone*—Stanley and Livingstone are captured by cannibals, until Peabody rescues the chief's father from the river. PF: Dr. Livingstone, Cannibal Chief. BS: Mr. Stanley.

21. *Louis Pasteur*—Pasteur's cow, Fifi, thinks she's a chicken and won't give milk needed to help in the research on pasteurization. PF: Louis Pasteur, Gaston. BS: Scientist.

22. *Robin Hood*—Robin has lost his memory and Prince John is threatening to cut off England's kipper supply. PF: Little John, Robin Hood, Sheriff of Nottingham, Announcer. BS: Friar Tuck, Prince John, JF: Maid Marian.

23. *Robinson Crusoe*—Condominium resorts are being built on Crusoe's island. Crusoe hates crowds. PF: Estate Agent, Robinson Crusoe.

24. *Ponce de León*—Ponce's men have regressed to infancy after drinking from the Fountain of Youth. PF: Ponce de León, Indian #1, Seminole Chief. BS: Indian #2.

25. *Leonardo da Vinci*—Mona Lisa can't smile for da Vinci—she has a bad toothache. PF: Da Vinci, Dentist.

26. *Captain Matthew Clift*—Clift is taught how to swim by Peabody in time for the English Channel swim. PF: Matthew Clift.

27. *Paul Revere*—Revere can't get to Lexington—he has no horse to ride on, only a pig. PF: Mrs. Revere, Paul Revere, General. BS: Mayor of Lexington.

28. *Confucius*—Confucius has been kidnapped and is being held prisoner on a Chinese junk. PF: Confucius, Police Officer. BS: Kidnapper (Genghis Ex-Khan).

29. *The Battle of Bunker Hill*—The Americans are ordered not to fire until they see "the whites of their eyes"—but the British are wearing sunglasses. PF: Lieutenant, English Officer, General Burgoyne, Cockney Soldier. BS: English Officer #2, Major, English Soldier.

30. *Vasco Núñez de Balboa*—Balboa is having eye trouble; he can't see the Pacific Ocean in order to discover it. PF: Balboa, Eye Doctor, Governor of Panama, Sir Augustus Coney. BS: Soldier.

31. *John L. Sullivan*—Sullivan's mustache is so heavy he can't fight Jake Kilrain for the championship. PF: O'Hara, Kilrain's Manager. BS: Barber, Ring Announcer, Jake Kilrain, Referee.

32. *Stephen Decatur*—Decatur, lieutenant of the *Enterprise*, plots to set fire to the Philadelphia, but can't find a match. PF: Stephen Decatur, Chief of Police, Sergeant #1. BS: Soldier, Sergeant #2.

33. *Race of the* Tom Thumb—Peter Cooper races his locomotive (the *Tom Thumb*) against a horse and carriage. PF: Peter Cooper, Judge, Opponent.

34. *Alexander Graham Bell*—Bell is having trouble inventing the telephone; he gets involved in a football match. PF: Alexander Graham Bell, Rimsky. BS: Korsakoff.

35. *The Pony Express*—Wells Fargo want to put the Pony Express out of business, so they send a message on a huge boulder. BS: Wells, Charlie. PF: Pony Express Manager, Indian Chief.

36. *Christopher Columbus*—Gaspar Viego attempts to sabotage Columbus's expedition by setting course for Africa. PF: Columbus, Queen Isabella, Gaspar Viego. BS: Ferdinand, Aide.

37. *Nero*—-Nero hates fire—it's his violin teacher, Oddpuss Rex, who is the arsonist. PF: Nero, Oddpuss Rex, Angry Man. BS: Henchman.

38. *Pancho Villa*—Villa and his gang threaten to raid the town of El Famino. PF: Gonzalez, Pancho Villa, Mayor, Old Man Mose. BS: Henchman, Bank Teller.

39. *Lord Francis Douglas*—Peabody helps Douglas and his party to conquer the Matterhorn. PF: Francis Douglas, Italian. BS: Guide, Climber, Luigi.

40. *Sitting Bull*—Sitting Bull takes over a hotel lobby. PF: Sitting Bull, Hotel Manager. BS: Finster.

41. *Commander Peary*—Peary is captured by Eskimos. PF: Peary, Eskimos Chief.

42. *The French Foreign Legion*—The Sheik gives the Foreign Legion's sergeant a going-away present—a watch with a time bomb attached. PF: Sheik Finook, French Sergeant, Arab Soldier. BS: Sergeant Pierre.

43. *Guglielmo Marconi*—Marconi can't invent radio because his wiring goes through a canal. PF: Gugllelmo Marconi, Giuseppe Pasto, Guard.

44. *Scotland Yard*—The Crown jewels are stolen and Peabody suspects international smugglers. PF: Chief inspector.

45. *John Holland*—Holland's submarine won't submerge. PF: John Holland, Admiral.

46. *Louis the Sixteenth*—Peabody finds the missing King Louis XVI, who is imprisoned in the Bastille. PF: Captain of Guards, Marie Antoinette, Warden, Louis XVI. BS: Balloon Salesman.

47. *Francisco Pizarro*—Pizarro is placed before a squad of spear throwers by the chief of the Incas. PF: Chief, Francisco Pizarro. BS: Wife, Lieutenant, Indian.

48. *Daniel Boone*—To free Daniel Boone, Peabody challenges a top Indian warrior. PF: Daniel Boone. BS: Indian Chief.

49. *Jesse James*—Peabody disguises himself as Santa Claus in this encounter with Frank and Jesse James. BS: Frank James. PF: Jesse James, Engineer, Bank Manager, Townsman, Robber.

50. *William Shakespeare*—Shakespeare's new play is *Romeo and Zelda*, but Francis Bacon is sabotaging it. PF: Francis Bacon, William Shakespeare. BS: Umpire.

51. *Zebulon Pike*—A baseball game helps in the climbing of Pike's Peak. PF: Zebulon Pike, Climber #2. BS: Climber #1

52. *The First Golf Match*—Peabody, involved in the first golf match, plays against a Scots farmer. PF: McSnide. BS: Angus, McPherson.

53. *William Tell*—Peabody outwits Austrian governor Gessler, saving the day for William Tell and his son Joey. WT: Joey Tell. PF: William Tell. BS: Governor Gessler, Announcer.

54. *James McNeill Whistler*—Whistler can't paint his mother—she's a hyperactive fan of the Old West and won't sit still in her chair. PF: James Whistler, Whistler's Mother.

55. *Ferdinand Magellan*—Magellan becomes a matador and must face a huge bull. PF: Ferdinand Magellan. BS: King Charles V, Butcher.

56. *Sir Isaac Newton*—Sir Isaac proves his theory of gravity with an apple and a polo match. PF: Isaac Newton. BS: Fruit Peddler.

57. *Kit Carson*—Carson suffers from a very bad memory. PF: Kit Carson. BS: Indian.

58. *The First Caveman*—The first cavemen are terrified of a sabre-toothed tiger. PF: Caveman. BS: Caveman #2.

59. *Johannes Gutenberg*—Gutenberg's printing press will be a flop unless he can find paper. PF: Gutenberg.

60. *Buffalo Bill*—Buffalo Bill's railroad workers have no food. Peabody, and some red underwear, end the famine. PF: Cook, Buffalo Bill.

61. *Hans Christian Oersted*—Oersted, helped by Peabody, invents the first compass. PF: Oersted.

62. *Leif Eriksson*—Eriksson's beard is so heavy he can't board his Viking ship. PF: Leif Eriksson, Barber. BS: King of Norway.

63. *John Sutter*—Sutter suffers from an addiction to Chinese fortune cookies, but finally discovers gold. PF: Hop Toy, John Sutter.

64. *Ludwig van Beethoven*—Beethoven doesn't want to compose "The Moonlight Sonata"—he wants to be a cook. PF: Beethoven.

65. *Calamity Jane*—Calamity Jane takes a liking to driving a stagecoach loaded with dynamite. PF: Citizen of Deadwood, Townsman. JF: Calamity Jane. WT: Crowd noise.

66. *Cornwallis's Surrender*—Cornwallis finally surrenders to Washington, after a fast trip to England. PF: Washington, Charles Cornwallis. BS: Guard, Cornwallis's mother.

67. *The First Indian-Head Nickel*—Talbot Heffelfinger's attempt to paint an Indian's portrait is thwarted by a bear. PF: Talbot Heffelfinger, General, Indian.

68. *Jules Verne*—In going around the world in eighty days, Verne is helped by some Yale collegians. PF: Jules Verne, Foreign Legion Officer, Italian, Yale Student.

69. *Casanova*—Italy's lover is imprisoned. The guards are female, and he refuses to leave the jail and write his memoirs. PF: Casanova. BS: Warden, Maximilian. JF: Female Guards.

70. *Lawrence of Arabia*—Lawrence dons an Arab disguise and defeats the Turkish army. PF: Colonel, T. E. Lawrence. BS: Sultan.

71. *Bonnie Prince Charlie*—Charlie is a basketball star who outdribbles the British soldiers. BS: Soldier, Sentry, Guard. PF: Scotsman, Grenadier.

72. *Paul Julius Reuter*—Reuter beats his rival Fritz Grimmelschausen to set up the first news agency. PF: Reuter.

73. *Geronimo*—Geronimo trades an autographed picture of Tonto for a horse. BS: General Crook. PF: Geronimo.

74. *The Great Wall of China*—Chop Suey Louie finances the building of the Great Wall of China. PF: Fungus Khan, Chop Suey Louie. BS: Rock Shop Man, Cement Seller.

75. *The Marquis of Queensberry*—Peabody, with very little help from the Marquis, sets up the rules of boxing. PF: Marquis, Cockney, Waiter. BS: Race Caller, Club Member.

76. *Jim Bowie*—Bowie's famed knife is auctioned off. PF: Bowie, General, Mr. Penn, Mr. Butterfield. BS: Jack.

77. *Edgar Allan Poe*—Poe can't write horror stories—he needs inspiration but seems to be totally fearless. PF: Poe.

78. *The Charge of the Light Brigade*—Tennyson, assisted by Peabody, rounds up his Light Brigade. PF: Lord Cardigan, Higginbotham, Scorekeeper, Doctor. BS: Chesney, Colonel Fotheringay.

79. *The Royal Mounted Police*—The Mounties always get their man, but notorious criminal Ottawa O'Toole is a woman. PF: Constable Archibald Woolley. BS: Pettigrew.

80. *The First Bullfight*—Porfirio Garbonza can't find a bull for the first bullfight. PF: Arena Manager, Profirio Garbonza, Croupier.

81. *The Building of the Great Pyramid*—Young prince Ahmed Fez is a menace to King Cheops. PF: King Cheops.

82. *John James Audubon*—A Zebrides chicken keeps disappearing, and Peabody helps Audubon locate her. PF: Audubon, The Suspect, Alastair the Cook.

83. *Mata Hari*—Mata Hari is sought by a Scotland Yard inspector. The trail leads to the Argonne Forest. PF: Admiral, Scotland Yard Inspector.

84. *Galileo*—In this episode Sherman subs for the ailing hound, and finds that Galileo can't get into the tower of Pisa. PF: Galileo, Frenchman. BS: Locksmith, Policeman.

85. *Wellington at Waterloo*—Wellington fails to show up for the Battle of Waterloo. PF: Sergeant, Duke of Wellington, French Driver, French Guard. BS: French Sentry.

86. *Florence Nightingale*—Florence Nightingale can't find oil for her famous lamps. JF: Florence Nightingale. PF: General, Russian Soldier.

87. *Henry the Eighth*—Henry VIII wants jelly with his breakfast toast. PF: Henry VIII, Cook. BS: Contest Man, Sailor.

88. *The First Indianapolis Auto Race*—Barnaby Victor and Carman Dioxide are pitted in the first Indianapolis Auto Race. PF: Barnaby Victor, Carman Dioxide.

89. *Captain Kidd*—Peabody learns that a slot machine is the key to his problem with the bloodthirsty pirate. PF: British Captain, Captain Kidd.

90. *The Texas Rangers*—Peabody outshoots the Dallas Kid; Sherman recruits some Texas Rangers. BS: Governor, Laredo Citizen, Bullwinkle. PF: Captain R. J. Hotchkiss, Cowboy, Dallas Kid.

91. *Cleopatra*—Prince Ptolemy is defeated by Julius Caesar, who has sent Cleo down the Nile. PF: Prince Ptolemy, Julius Caesar, Carnival Barker. JF: Cleopatra. BS: Soldier.

AESOP AND SON

Narrator: Charlie Ruggles as Aesop

Key to abbreviations

DB: Daws Butler = Aesop Junior
JF: June Foray
BS: Bill Scott

1. *The Lion and the Mouse (Pilot Episode)*—A sassy mouse asks a lion to prove who is really king of the beasts, via a display of bravery, kindness and generosity. DB: Junior, Mouse, Deaf Gorilla, Freddy. BS: Lion, Barney, Mouse's Wife. (Animated in Hollywood by Jay Ward Productions)
2. *The Mice in Council*—A group of mice must decide who is to bell a nasty cat. DB: Junior, Mouse, Murphy. BS: Old Mouse, Cat, Ice-Cream Vendor.
3. *The Fox and the Stork*—A social-climbing fox is disillusioned by the snobbish Mr. Stork. DB: Junior, Fox. BS: Stork, Chicken.
4. *The Wolf in Sheep's Clothing*—Al Wolf's wife is expecting, and she craves roast lamb—but the sheepdog is a problem. DB: Junior, Al Wolf. JF: Myrna Wolf. BS: Butcher, Sheepdog, Sheep Shearer.
5. *The Hare and the Tortoise*—A hare with an unnatural appetite is driven to distraction by a tortoise who must be the world's slowest delivery boy. DB: Junior, Delivery Tortoise, Grocer. BS: The Hare.
6. *The Hare and the Hound*—An opportunistic hound takes advantage of a hare until a skunk comes to the rescue. DB: Junior, Hound, Cop. BS: Hare, Skunk.
7. *The Hares and the Frog*—A sharp-talking frog becomes a hare's manager and comes up with the gimmick of promoting his client as "Top Critter." DB: Junior, Second Hare, Frog, Bear, Wolf. BS: Hare, Aggressive Critter.
8. *The Frogs and the Beaver*—Two covetous frogs, Romeo and Julius, wreck a beaver's resort home and his rustic cabin. DB: Junior, Romeo Frog. BS: Julius Frog, The Beaver.
9. *The Lion and the Aardvark*—A tyrannical lion advertises for a moth killer; three applicants (a fox, a bear, and a hoot-owl) audition. There is no aardvark in the story. DB: Junior, The Weasel, The Fox, The Hoot-Owl. BS: The King, The Bear.
10. *The Jackrabbits and the Mule*—Two prospecting jackrabbits continually harass an industrious mule. DB: Junior, Flem. BS: Charlie, The Mule.
11. *The Dog and the Shadow*—A dog's shadow begins acting independently. DB: Junior, The Dog, Shady Character, Dog Catcher. BS: The Tout, Charlie. (Animated in Hollywood)
12. *The Cat and Fifteen Mice*—After rejecting Disneyland, some mice decide to move to a lighthouse, but a tough tomcat follows them. DB: Junior, Moe, Cat. BS: Manny.
13. *The Goldfish and the Bear*—A fox and a crow suggest that a lazy bear try harder to contribute to the community stew pot. DB: Junior, The Crow, "Jack" Bear. BS: Fox, Pelican, Eagle.
14. *The Vain Crow*—A narcissistic crow pretends to be a peacock. DB: Junior, Dumb Crow, Peacock, Policeman. BS: Vain Crow, Henchman to Peacock. JF: Peahen, Crow.
15. *The Canary and Musical Hares*—Rabbits Johann and Ludwig are itinerant musicians; they are joined by a persistent canary. DB: Junior, Ludwig, Canary. BS: Johann.
16. *The Fox and Three Minks*—Three minks must unite against a fox who wants their fur. DB: Junior, Mink #1, Mink #3. BS: Mush-head Mink, Shakespearian Fox.

17. *The Owl and the Wolf*—A wolf with a clock fetish disguises himself as the Masked Clock and robs stage passengers of their watches. DB: Junior, Wolf, Inspector Owl. BS: Bear, Turtle.

18. *The Centipede and the Snail*—The hopeless centipede and hapless snail try to train for the annual forest race. DB: Junior, Centipede. BS: Snail.

19. *The Fox and the Owl*—A shiftless fox breaks the law so he can be put in the pillory; people throw food at him and he's very happy—until they begin to throw rocks. DB: Junior, The Fox, The Judge. BS: The Shop owner, The Old Owl, The organ-grinder.

20. *The Hound and the Wolf*—A wolf is continually outwitted by Mauler, a highly competent sheep-dog. DB: Junior, The Wolf, Mauler. BS: Gus, The Crafty Wolf, Santa Claus.

21. *The Fox and the Winking Horse*—A crafty fox teams up with Dobbin, a horse, whose magic wink causes people to bounce on their heads and thus empty their pockets. DB: Junior, The Fox, The Posse Leader. BS: The Sheriff, Bank President, Engineer. (Animated in Hollywood)

22. *The Sick Lion*—Leo D. Lion suffers from a psychosomatic sneeze caused by his father, who years ago tried to suppress his son's singing ambitions. DB: Junior, Animal, Leo's Friend, Concert Host, Opera Singer, Father Lion. BS: Leo D. Lion. (Animated in Hollywood)

23. *The Porcupine and the Tigers*—Mr. and Mrs. Tiger are slobs who throw all their dinner scraps out the window; they're kept awake at night by a rare bone-eating porcupine. DB: Junior, "Tiger-Baby." JF: "Kitten."

24. *Son of The Masked Clock*—A sequel to episode 17: Guy Wolf, son of the Masked Clock, blows his inheritance. DB: Junior, Guy, The Cop. BS: The Attorney, The Guard, Tommy Gunn, Police Chief, Bakersfield Man.

25. *The Hen and the Cat*—Florence Chicken falls in love with Tom Cat but is allergic to him. DB: Junior, Tom Cat. JF: Florence Chicken, Tom's Wife. BS: The Other Hen, The Wizard Owl.

26. *The Chicken and the Ducks*—A freezing chicken joins the ducks and flies south for the winter, overcoming the ducks' objections to his presence. DB: Junior, The Chicken, Feeney. BS: The Hen, Murdock.

27. *The Coyote and the Jackrabbits*—Hasty J. Rabbit, recently retired, is annoyed by his bullying neighbor, an obnoxious coyote. DB: Junior, Hasty J. Rabbit, The Coyote. BS: Wallace, The Doctor.

28. *The Rooster and Five Hens*—A handsome rooster is pursued by the five Leghorn sisters. DB: Junior, Holdup Villain, Old Owl. BS: Rooster, Bully. JF: Matronly Hen, Cooking Hen, Muscular Hen, Egg-laying Hen, Zelda Hen.

29. *The Three Bears*—Charlie and Edna Bear are visited by their rich uncle Fabian, who won't include them in his will unless they can make him happy. DB: Junior, Uncle Fabian, Golf Pro, Owl in Cave. BS: Charlie Bear. JF: Edna Bear.

30. *The Robin, the Pelican and the Angleworm*—An angleworm holds King Leo for ransom; a robin and a pelican must rescue the king. DB: Junior, The King's Aide, Private-Eye Fox, The Robin. BS: The King Leo I, The Pelican, The Worm.

31. *The Eagle and the Beetle*—A nearsighted eagle swoops down on the wrong prey, so a beetle offers to navigate. DB: Junior, The Eagle, The Mouse. BS: Animal, The Rabbit, The Beetle.

32. *The Fox and the Hound*—MCA Fox, an incompetent Hollywood agent, is saved by Freddie Feeney, a dog who can levitate. DB: Junior, The Dog, C.B. BS: MCA (Murgatroyd Cornelius Applefinger).

33. *The Bears and the Dragon*—Two itinerant bears vie with each other to be knighted by Leo XXXII. DB: Junior, Leo XXXII, Maxie Bear. BS: Town Crier, Card Player, Bear #2, The Fox. JF: Maiden.

34. *The Fox and the Woodsman*—Aesop thinks this will be the Great American Fable: Reynard, a good fox with a sneaky face, is betrayed by a nasty man with an honest face. DB: Junior, The Fox, Townsman. BS: Townsman #2, Huntsman, Honest Faced Man, The Rat.

35. *The Country Frog and the City Frog*—A naive frog falls for a big-city showgirl frog, but she keeps him broke. DB: Junior, The Buyer, The Circus Owner, The Golfer. BS: Country Frog, Buyer #2. JF: Ann Phibian.

36. *The Fox and the Rabbit*—Foxini the Great employs a pickpocket rabbit as his magician's assistant. DB: Junior, Foxini the Great. BS: Boss, Rabbit, Officer.

37. *The Hare and the Tortoise*—The old hare's grandbunny inspires a rechallenge to race the famous tortoise. DB: Junior, Race Caller, The Tortoise, The Grandbunny. BS: Hare, Rabbit.

38. *The French Poodle and the Alley Cat*—An artistic poodle must compete with an alley cat in the fashion-wear industry. DB: Junior, The French Poodle. BS: The Alley Cat. JF: Two Female Voices.

39. *The Fox and Three Weasels*—Three crooked weasels are employed by soup king Tycoon J. Fox; he wants them to steal some new ingredients. DB: Junior, Tom, Larry, Buyer #1, Buyer #3, Broomington, The Judge. BS: Dick, Tycoon J. Fox, Buyer #2.

DUDLEY DO-RIGHT OF THE MOUNTIES

	Key to abbreviations	
BS:	Bill Scott	= Dudley
PF:	Paul Frees	= Narrator and Inspector Fenwick
JF:	June Foray	= Nell
HC:	Hans Conried	= Snidely
WC:	William Conrad	= Narrator 2

1. *The Disloyal Canadians*—Snidely Whiplash smuggles furs across the Canadian border with his band of "musicians." PF: Narrator, Inspector Fenwick, Mayor. HC: Snidely Whiplash. BS: Dudley, Frantic Man. JF: Nell.

2. *Finding Gold*—Dudley looks for gold to win the heart of fickle Nell Fenwick. PF: Narrator, Inspector Fenwick. JF: Nell. BS: Dudley. HC: Snidely.

3. *Stokey the Bear*—Stokey the Bear is hypnotized by Snidely into becoming an arsonist. PF: Narrator, Inspector Fenwick. HC: Red Wood, Snidely. BS: Lumberjack, The Fire Chief, Dudley.

4. *Mortgagin' the Mountie Post*—Snidely forecloses the mortgage on the RCMP camp. PF: Narrator, Inspector Fenwick. BS: Dudley, Circus Owner. HC: Snidely. JF: Nell.

5. *Trap Bait*—Snidely baits a trap for Dudley, using Horse, Nell, and Inspector Fenwick. PF: Narrator, Inspector Fenwick. HC: Snidely. BS: Dudley. JF: Messenger Boy, Nell.

6. *The Masked Ginny Lynne*—Nell decides to go into show business as masked singer Ginny Lynne. PF: Narrator, Inspector Fenwick. JF: Nell. BS: Dudley, Barney, A Man. HC: Snidely.

7. *The Centaur*—The morale at the Mountie post crumbles when Dudley captures a "centaur." PF: Narrator, Inspector Fenwick. HC: Snidely. BS: Dudley, Bruno.

8. *Railroad Tracks*—Dudley disguises himself as Nell in an attempt to capture Snidely, who has been tying defenseless people to railroad tracks. PF: Narrator, Inspector Fenwick. HC: Snidely. BS: Dudley, Train Driver. JF: Nell.

9. *Foreclosing Mortgages*—Cruel Snidely goes on a mortgage-foreclosing rampage in the middle of winter. PF: Narrator, Inspector Fenwick. HC: Snidely. BS: Dudley. JF: Mortgaged Lady, Nell.

10. *Snidely Mounted Police*—Snidely decides to compete with the RCMP, forming his own band of villainous Mounties. PF: Narrator, Snidely Mountie #1, Inspector Fenwick. HC: Snidely. BS: Dudley, Homer, Horse, Good Mountie, Snidely Mountie #2, Bank Teller. JF: Nell, Two Women.

11. *Mother Love*—Snidely spreads the rumor that he is Dudley's younger brother, but Dudley begins mollycoddling him. PF: Narrator, Inspector Fenwick. HC: Snidely. BS: Homer, Dudley. JF: Nell.

12. *Mountie Bear*—Dudley arrests a bear, who joins the Mounties. PF: Narrator, Inspector Fenwick. HC: Snidely. BS: Dudley, Homer, JF: Woman, Nell.

13. *Inspector Dudley Do-Right*—Inspector Fenwick is impersonated by Snidely. PF: Narrator, Inspector Fenwick. HC: Snidely. BS: Homer, Dudley. JF: Nell.

14. *Recruiting Campaign*—Dudley recruits new Mounties, then battles Finster, Snidely's new monster. WC: Narrator. PF: Inspector Fenwick, Tor. HC: Snidely. BS: Dudley. JF: Nell.

15. *Out of Uniform*—Dudley's clothes are stolen; he will be in trouble if he's found "out of uniform." PF: Narrator, Inspector Fenwick. HC: Snidely. BS: Homer, Dudley. JF: Nell.

16. *Lure of the Footlights*—Whiplash and Do-Right form a vaudeville act. PF: Narrator, Showbiz Agent, Inspector Fenwick. HC: Snidely. BS: Homer, Dudley. JF: Nell.

17. *Bullet-Proof Suit*—A bored Nell takes up knitting, but is tricked into creating a bulletproof Snidely suit. PF: Narrator, Inspector Fenwick. HC: Snidely. BS: Homer, Dudley. JF: Nell, Mortgage Victim.

18. *Miracle Drug*—A pox epidemic breaks out, and Dudley must bring back a miracle drug from Quebec. PF: Narrator, Inspector Fenwick, Earnshaw. HC: Snidely, Renfrew. BS: Dudley.

19. *Elevenworth Prison*—Snidely breaks out of Elevenworth Prison in a submarine. WC: Narrator. PF: Warden, Rollo, Inspector Fenwick. HC: Snidely. BS: Guard, Dudley, Admiral Dewey Dare.

20. *Saw Mill*—Nell rejects Snidely, so he ties her to the sawmill's conveyor belt. PF: Narrator, Inspector Fenwick. BS: Dudley, Preacher, Mailman. JF: Nell. HC: Snidely.

21. *Mountie Without a Horse*—Snidely, disguised as a visiting colonel, orders the Mounties to ride rocking horses. WC: Narrator. PF: Inspector Fenwick, Train Conductor, Robber #1. BS: Dudley, Colonel Ogden Krimcrammer, Robber #2. HC: Snidely.

22. *Mother Whiplash's Log Jam*—Snidely is marketing Mother Whiplash's Log Jam. (This story reveals Dudley's background.) WC: Narrator. BS: Dudley. JF: Dudley's Mother, Eloise, PF: Inspector Fenwick. HC: Snidely.

23. *Stolen Art Masterpiece*—Canada's most priceless art masterpiece is stolen by Snidely. WC: Narrator, BS: Museum Guard, Museum Owner, Dudley. PF: Inspector Fenwick, Captain. HC: Snidely.

24. *Mechanical Dudley*—Snidely invents a mechanical Dudley Do-Right. PF: Narrator, Inspector Fenwick, Citizen. HC: Snidely. BS: Homer, Dudley. JF: Nell.

25. *Flicker Rock*—Flicker Rock hits Dudley on the noggin, and he begins seeing things. PF: Narrator, Inspector Fenwick BS: Homer, Dudley. HC: Snidely. JF: Nell.

26. *Faithful Dog*—Dudley, wanting to emulate Renthrew, his Mountie hero, obtains a "faithful dog"—actually a wolf. WC: Narrator, PF: Inspector Fenwick, Renthrew. BS: Dudley. HC: Snidely. JF: Nell.

27. *Coming-Out Party*—Snidely gate-crashes Nell's coming-out party. WC: Narrator. PF: Inspector Fenwick. BS: Dudley, Homer. HC: Snidely. JF: Nell, Hat-Check Girl, Woman.

28. *Robbing Banks*—Snidely disguises himself as a Mountie and robs banks. WC: Narrator. PF: O. D. Pringle, Inspector Fenwick. BS: Oberlin, Gate Man, Dudley. HC: Snidely. JF: Nell.

29. *Skagway Dog Sled–Pulling Contest*—Dudley challenges Snidely in the annual Skagway dogsled–pulling contest. WC: Narrator, Corporal Muggerdugger. PF: Mayor, Inspector Fenwick. BS: Dudley, Mountie. HC: Snidely. JF: Nell.

30. *Canadian Railway's Bridge*—Snidely is continually destroying the Canadian Railway's bridge. WC: Narrator. PF: Foreman, Rollo, Toll Collector, Inspector Fenwick. BS: Engineer Potter, Janitor, Dudley, Tippecanoe N. Tyler. HC: Snidely.

31. *Niagara Falls*—Snidely constructs a dam to stop Niagara Falls from falling. WC: Narrator. HC: Snidely. PF: Inspector Fenwick, Captain. BS: Dudley. JF: Nell.

32. *Vic Whiplash's Gym*—Snidely decides to run a fitness center: Vic Whiplash's Gym. WC: Narrator. BS: Dudley, Employer #2. JF: Nell, Woman. PF: Inspector Fenwick, Employers #1, 3, and 4, Lumber Captain, Citizen. HC: Snidely.

33. *Marigolds*—Snidely, aware that Dudley is allergic, wears a suit made of marigolds. WC: Narrator. HC: Snidely. BS: Dudley, Homer. JF: Nell. PF: Inspector Fenwick.

34. *Trading Places*—Nell trades places with Dudley and brings in Snidely and his gang. WC: Narrator. HC: Snidely. BS: Dudley, Homer. JF: Nell. PF: Inspector Fenwick.

35. *Top Secret*—Dudley must try to keep Whiplash away from a top secret project. WC: Narrator. HC: Snidely. BS: Dudley. JF: Nell. PF: Inspector Fenwick, Barber, Walter.

36. *The Locket*—Nell gives incentive lockets to both Dudley and Snidely. WC: Narrator. HC: Snidely. BS: Dudley, Homer. JF: Nell. PF: Inspector Fenwick.

37. *The Inspector's Nephew*—Whiplash is mothered by Dudley, who has mistaken him for the Inspector's nephew, Melvin. WC: Narrator. HC: Snidely. BS: Dudley, Homer. JF: Melvin Fenwick. PF: Inspector Fenwick, Nasty Noogle.

38. *Matinee Idol*—Snidely is signed by a movie producer and becomes a matinee idol, but talkies ruin his career. WC: Narrator, HC: Snidely. BS: Dudley. JF: Movie Actress. PF: Talent Scout, Inspector Fenwick.

39. *Snidely Arrested*—Nell decides to read books on law, and gets Snidely off the hook in a courtroom trial. WC: Narrator, Bailiff. HC: Snidely. BS: Dudley, Judge. JF: Nell. PF: Inspector Fenwick.

HOPPITY HOOPER

Key to abbreviations

CA:	Chris Allen	= Hoppity
BS:	Bill Scott	= Fillmore
PF:	Paul Frees	= Narrator
HC:	Hans Conried	= Waldo
AR:	Alan Reed (episodes 1 and 2 only)	= Fillmore
WC:	William Conrad (episodes 101–104)	= Narrator

(Four chapters to each story, except "Golf" and "Hopeless Diamond," which run two chapters each)

1–4

Ring-a-Ding Spring—This story introduces us to Hoppity, Waldo, and Fillmore. The boys discover that water from Ring-a-Ding Spring causes hair to grow, and opportunistic Waldo names the hair-restorer Q Bald. Millionaire miser Cyrus Flugelhorn, who is rich from marketing wigs, toupees, and scalp wax, sends hit man One-Way Windrip to do our friends in.

1. *Ring-a-Ding Spring* PF: Narrator, Sheriff. CA: Hoppity. AR: Fillmore. HC: Waldo Wigglesworth.

2. *The Thing in the Spring (Pilot Episode)* PF: Narrator, Announcer #2, One-Way Windrip. CA: Hoppity, Girl in Commercial. BS: Newsboy, Announcer #1, Man in Commercial, Man. AR: Fillmore, Cyrus Flugelhorn. HC: Waldo.

3. *Dressed to Kill or Three's a Shroud* PF: Narrator, Man #2, Hairdresser, Crudley, One-Way Windrip. BS: Man #4, Reporter, Cyrus Flugelhorn, Fillmore. CA: Movie Star, Hoppity. HC: Waldo, Man #1 and Man #3.

4. *How to Straighten a Hairpin* PF: Narrator, One-Way Windrip. BS: Cyrus Flugelhorn, Old Man, Fillmore. CA: Hoppity, Society Woman. HC: Waldo.

5–8
Rock 'n' Roll Star—Waldo, looking for another scheme, decides to turn Hoppity into a new rock and roll sensation named Baby Hooper. The frog becomes a hit with The Croak, until Susan Swivelhips, Waldo's jilted ex-girlfriend, gets even by introducing another hit called The Boing. Ever resourceful, Waldo combines the two fads into the Croak & Boingenanny.

5. *Rock 'n' Roll Star* PF: Narrator, B. J. BS: J. B., Customer, Fillmore. CA: Hoppity. HC: Waldo.

6. *Whatever Happened to Baby Hooper?* PF: Narrator, Simithers, Man. BS: Leon, Bum, Fillmore. CA: Hoppity, Teacher. HC: Waldo, Rich Man.

7. *Pardon Me, But Your Image's Showing, or Turn in Your Wig, Waldo—I'd Know You Anywhere* PF: Narrator. BS: Man #1 and #2, Woman, Fillmore. CA: Hoppity, Susan Swivelhips. HC: Waldo.

8. *Laugh and the World Laughs with You, Croak and You Croak Alone, or A Boing in the Hand Is Worth Two in the Bush* PF: Narrator. BS: Fillmore. CA: Hoppity, Susan Swivelhips. HC: Waldo.

9–12
Diamond Mine—Waldo turns a vacant lot into a do-It-yourself diamond mine, but the digging disturbs an underground race called the Mole People, and their leader, King Glubby the Third, captures the lads.

9. *Diamond Mine* PF: Narrator, Man #1. BS: Man #2, Fillmore. CA: Hoppity. HC: Waldo.

10. *Sandy Claws Strikes Again or Howzat Grab Yer?* PF: Narrator, Gobbo, King Glubby. BS: Fillmore. CA: Hoppity. HC: Waldo, Announcer.

11. *Six Feet Under or The Mole Folks at Home* PF: Narrator, King Glubby. BS: Fillmore. CA: Hoppity, Lady Mole. HC: Waldo.

12. *The Real Low-Down or Hoppity Gets to the Bottom of Things* PF: Narrator, King Glubby, Gobbo. BS: Fillmore. CA: Hoppity. HC: Waldo.

13–16
Costra Nostra—The notorious crooks Costra and Nostra attempt to kidnap the Faubus Flytrap baby (heir to the Flytrap insecticide fortune) by using Fillmore in a Central Park concert, but they mistake Hoppity for the baby. With the help of Susan Swivelhips our heroes capture the bad guys.

13. *Costra Nostra* PF: Narrator, Clyde, Nostra. BS: Clem, Costra, Fillmore. CA: Hoppity. HC: Waldo.

14. *The Ice Box Caper or Fillmore Blows It Cool* PF: Narrator, Nostra. BS: Costra, Fillmore. CA: Hoppity, Susan Swivelhips. HC: Waldo.

15. *A Lark in the Park or Will the Real Faubus Flytrap Please Stand Up!* PF: Narrator, Nostra. BS: Fillmore, Faubus Flytrap, Costra. CA: Hoppity, Susan Swivelhips. HC: Waldo.

16. *Hoppity Hooper's Blooper or Costra Nostra Does the Bossa Nova* PF: Narrator, Nostra, Cop. BS: Costra, Fillmore. CA: Hoppity, Susan Swivelhips. HC: Waldo.

17–20

The Giant of Hoot'n'Holler—After fleeing town (where Waldo tried his beauty cream on the Sheriff's wife) the boys run into Tiny, the huge but harmless Giant of Hoot'n'Holler. Waldo puts him on a basketball team called the Dribblers Five Minus Two. They begin beating all comers, until Tiny decides to quit the team.

17. *The Giant of Hoot'n'Holler* PF: Narrator, Sheriff. BS: Fillmore. CA: Hoppity, Sheriff's Wife. HC: Waldo.
18. *Tree-top Tall or Things Are Looking Up* PF: Narrator, Giant. BS: Fillmore. CA: Hoppity. HC: Waldo.
19. *The Game's the Same or Hi'ya, Sport* PF: Narrator, Shoe Man, Giant. BS: Fillmore. CA: Hoppity. HC: Waldo.
20. *Waldo the Weeper or The Bawl's in the Other Court* PF: Narrator, Giant, All-Star Coach. BS: Fillmore. CA: Hoppity, Bean Seller. HC: Waldo.

21–24

Detective Agency—Waldo tires of being in trouble with the law and forms the I-Spy Detective Agency. Their first case involves searching for the Lost Duchess of Dashit Hall, but the notorious *Lime Juice Louis* and his gang have exactly the same goal in mind.

21. *Detective Agency* PF: Narrator, Sheriff, Client, Badley-Bent. BS: Fillmore, Informer. CA: Hoppity. HC: Waldo.
22. *The Lowdown on the Blow-Up or Hallelujah, I'm a Bomb* PF: Narrator, Badley-Bent, Mugsy. BS: Fillmore, Lime Juice Louis, Woman #2. CA: Hoppity, Woman #1. HC: Waldo.
23. *Portrait of a Thief or Lime Juice Louis Gets Framed* PF: Narrator, Mugsy, Badley-Bent, Chauncey. BS: Fillmore, Edgar, Lime Juice Louis, Dudley Do-Right. CA: Hoppity. HC: Waldo.
24. *What's Cooking or Hoppity's Plots and Plans* PF: Narrator, Badley-Bent, Mugsy, The Earl of Cloves. BS: Fillmore, Lime Juice Louis. CA: Hoppity. HC: Waldo.

25–28

Olympic Star—As Waldo begins training Fillmore to be an Olympic track star, a giant bird swoops down and carries Hoppity off to Boise, Idaho. Waldo thinks Hoppity jumped all the way. Next the bird swoops down and grabs Waldo, who finally cures the big bird of this obsession; the bird releases Waldo, who plummets to earth. The Olympic officials think Waldo is the greatest pole-vaulter of all time.

25. *Olympic Star* PF: Narrator. BS: Fillmore. CA: Hoppity. HC: Waldo.
26. *Look Before you Leap or It Don't Mean a Thing If You Ain't Got That Spring* PF: Narrator, Announcer. BS: Fillmore. CA: Hoppity. HC: Waldo.
27. *Waldo, Waldo, Wherefore Art Thou, Waldo or Wigglesworth Visits Birdland* PF: Narrator, Big Bird. BS: Fillmore, Man. CA: Hoppity. HC: Waldo.
28. *Big Bird Is Watching You or Howzat Grab Yer?* PF: Narrator, Big Bird, Man, Announcer. BS: Fillmore, Olympics Man. CA: Hoppity. HC: Waldo.

29–32

Ghost—Waldo sets up a fortune-telling business and orders Fillmore to impersonate a ghost, but Wilbur—a real ghost who is lonely—shows up. Waldo then enters the haunting business.

29. *Ghost* PF: Narrator, Onlooker #1. BS: Fillmore, Onlooker #3. CA: Hoppity, Onlookers #2 and #4. HC: Waldo.

30. *Spook Watchers or Let's Join the Ghost Guard* PF: Narrator, Ghost. BS: Fillmore. CA: Hoppity, Onlooker. HC: Waldo.

31. *A-Haunting We Will Go or The Ghost Is Clear* PF: Narrator, Wilbur, Employee, Bully. BS: Fillmore, Mr. Pearson. CA: Hoppity, Mrs. Pearson, Claire, Susan Swivelhips. HC: Waldo.

32. *Who's Haunting Who? or Which Witch Is Which?* PF: Narrator, Wilbur. BS: Fillmore. CA: Hoppity, Claire, Susan Swivelhips. HC: Waldo.

33–36

The Masked Martin—Foggy Bog is being plundered by the notorious burglar the Masked Martin, who steals Waldo's clothes and liverwurst sandwich. Waldo is later mistaken for the Masked Martin; the real villain is arrested after he steals Fillmore's bugle.

33. *The Masked Martin* PF: Narrator, Alfred. BS: Fillmore, Tycoon. CA: Hoppity. HC: Waldo.

34. *Elementary, My Dear Fillmore or Show Me a Liverwurst and I'll Show You a Thief* PF: Narrator, Masked Martin. BS: Fillmore, Husband. CA: Hoppity, Wife. HC: Waldo.

35. *Waldo's Alley or Catch As Catch Can* PF: Narrator, Accuser #1, Cop. BS: Fillmore, Scared Man, Accuser #2. CA: Hoppity. HC: Waldo.

36. *Waldo Keeps a Straight Face or The Man in the Ironed Mask* PF: Narrator, Cop #1, Masked Martin, Cop #3. BS: Fillmore, Cop #2, Chief. CA: Hoppity. HC: Waldo, Irish Cop.

37–40

Jumping Frog Contest—Our friends head to California to enter Hoppity in the big Jumping Frog Contest. Some thugs, led by Buckshot Brown, are entering Hennery the Kangaroo as a fake frog. They kidnap our little amphibian and replace him with a fake Hoppity Hooper.

37. *Jumping Frog Contest* PF: Narrator, Customers #1 and #4, Buckshot Brown. BS: Fillmore, Customer #2, Shorty. CA: Hoppity, Customer #3. HC: Waldo.

38. *Hoppity's Dead End or Canyon Fodder* PF: Narrator, Buckshot Brown. BS: Fillmore, Shorty. CA: Hoppity. HC: Waldo.

39. *Two for the Money or Hoppity's Double Trouble* PF: Narrator, Buckshot Brown, Kangaroo, Entrant #2. BS: Fillmore, Shorty, Judge, Entrants #1 and #3. HC: Waldo.

40. *The Joint Is Jumping or Springtime for Hennery* PF: Narrator, Hennery the Kangaroo, Buckshot Brown. BS: Shorty, Judge, Fillmore. CA: Hoppity. HC: Waldo.

41–44

The Traffic Zone—in this takeoff on *The Twilight Zone,* Fillmore gets stuck in a strange dimension where everyone turns into talking vegetables. The bear is now a giant turnip and the boys discover they must somehow reenter the Traffic Zone to become their old selves again. Finally they are granted an audience with the Grand Asparagus.

41. *The Traffic Zone*
PF: Narrator. BS: Fillmore. CA: Hoppity. HC: Waldo.

42. *(untitled Episode)* PF: Narrator, Citizen #2, #5, #9, Fred. BS: Fillmore, Mayor, Citizens #1, #4, #8. CA: Hoppity, Citizens #3, #7. HC: Waldo, Citizen #6.

43. *The Vegetarians on Plant Me Now, I'll Dig You Later* PF: Narrator, Citizen, BS: Fillmore, Husband, Mayor. CA: Hoppity, Wife. HC: Waldo.

44. A *Fine Kettle of Succotash or Who Put the Wigglesworth in Mrs. Murphy's Chowder?* PF: Narrator, Spanish Onion. BS: Fillmore, Grand Asparagus. CA: Hoppity, Avocado, Woman. HC: Waldo.

45–48

Wottabango Corn Elixir—chased by sundry creditors, our boys safely cross the state line, then make up some of Waldo's Indian Guide Elixir. Discovering it packs an explosive wallop, Waldo decides to sell the stuff as fuel for the sport of auto racing.

45. *Wottabango Corn Elixir* PF: Narrator, Chief. BS: Fillmore, Botany Teacher, Werner Von Braunbear. CA: Hoppity. HC: Waldo, Indian.

46. *A Kernel of Artillery or That's My Pop!* PF: Narrator, Man #2, Grandpa, Sheriff. BS: Fillmore, Indian, Man #1, Wilbur. CA: Hoppity, Grandma, Nurse, Wife. HC: Waldo.

47. *Dangerous Crossing or Waldo Meets the 5:15* PF: Narrator, Leadfoot Lew Keller, Drag Racer #1. BS: Fillmore, Drag Racer #2. CA: Hoppity. HC: Waldo.

48. *Speed to Burn or What Kind of Fuel Am I?* PF: Narrator, Drag Racer #3. BS: Fillmore, Drag Racers #1 and #2. CA: Hoppity, Fan. HC: Waldo.

49–52

Frog Prince—Hoppity, learning the story of the Frog Prince of Monomania, decides to go there and rescue him. But the guards mistake Hoppity for the real Prince Teddy, just as the prince's wicked uncle plans to marry his nephew off to the Princess of Pugnacia.

49. *Frog Prince of Monomania* PF: Narrator, Lupo, Sentry. BS: Fillmore, Frog Prince, Magician. CA: Hoppity. HC: Waldo.

50. *Let Sleeping Pills Lie or Take a Powder* PF: Narrator, Lupo, Sentry, Edgar, Guard #1. BS: Chauncey, Guard #2, Prince Teddy, Magician, Fillmore. CA: Hoppity. HC: Waldo.

51. *Father of the Frog or Wedding Bills Are Breaking up that Old Dad of Mine* PF: Narrator, Uncle Lupo, Ticket Seller. BS: Prince Teddy, Magician, Fillmore. CA: Hoppity, Princess. HC: Waldo.

52. *Hoppity's Bride and Joy or I'd Rather Be Dead Then Wed* PF: Narrator, Lupo. BS: Magician, Prince Teddy, Bishop, Guard, Fillmore. CA: Princess, Hoppity. HC: Waldo.

53–56

Colonel Clabber Limburger Cheese Statue—The town statue of Colonel Oswald Clabber is stolen. Our heroes soon discover that monuments from all over the world (like the Leaning Tower of Pisa and Big Ben) are disappearing. It transpires that millionaire miser Cyrus Flugelhorn, from the first Hoppity story, is behind the scheme: he's rich enough to see the world, but can't be bothered traveling. Boris Badenov makes a cameo appearance in episode #55.

53. *Colonel Clabber Limburger Cheese Statue* PF: Narrator, Employment Man, Crook #2. BS: Crook #1, Fillmore. CA: Hoppity. HC: Waldo.

54. *Out on a Limb-Burger or Cheese It, the Cops* PF: Narrator, Crook #1, Sheriff, Carruthers. BS: Crook #2, Tour Guide, Prime Minister, Fillmore. CA: Tourist, Hoppity. HC: Waldo.

55. *A Corner in Steal or The Big Robber Band* PF: Narrator, Carruthers, Chauncey, Man, Egyptian, Boris Badenov. BS: Prime Minister, Edgar, Italian, French Man, News Man, Announcer. CA: Hoppity. HC: Waldo.

56. *A Place in the Sun or That's Clabber All Over* PF: Narrator, Cyrus Flugelhorn, Henchman #1. BS: Henchman #2, Fillmore. CA: Hoppity. HC: Waldo.

57–60

The Giant Cork—Fillmore constructs an atomic-powered corkscrew but it goes haywire and bores into the earth. A giant jet of water precedes the creation of a new volcano, and Hoppity volunteers to plug it up with a giant cork.

57. *The Giant Cork* PF: Narrator, Old Man. BS: Announcer, Fillmore. CA: Hoppity. HC: Waldo.

58. *The Hole Truth or I'll Dig You Later* PF: Narrator, Doctor J. Roscoe Hoppenclimber, Farmer. BS: Meter Reader, Fillmore. CA: Hoppity. HC: Waldo.

59. *How to Stop a Volcano or Lava, Come Back to Me* PF: Narrator, Home Owner, Sheriff, Doctor Hoppenclimber, Curtis Wrong, Edgar. BS: Chauncey, Property Owner, Fillmore. CA: Hoppity. HC: Waldo.

60. *The Maw the Merrier or Hoppity Drops In* PF: Narrator, Curtis Wrong, Doctor Hoppenclimber. BS: Fillmore. CA: Hoppity. HC: Waldo.

61–64
Ferkle to Hawaii—Ferkle's friend Bilgebottom makes a wager that Ferkle's car can't go anywhere in the USA in three days. Our boys offer to drive Mr. Ferkle's car, the Ferkle 500. But Bilgebottom cheats by hiring the crooks from RAT to sabotage our heroes. After battling a giant squid, Hoppity, Waldo, and Fillmore make it to Hawaii.

61. *Ferkle to Hawaii* PF: Narrator, Ferkle, Man from RAT. BS: Billsbottom, RAT Chief, Fillmore. CA: Hoppity. HC: Waldo.

62. *My Old Flame or Your Gas Is As Good As Mine* PF: Narrator, Man from RAT. BS: RAT Chief, Man form RAT #2, Fillmore. CA: Hoppity. HC: Man from RAT #3, Waldo.

63. *The American Way to Go or Hooray for the Red, White and Blooie* PF: Narrator, Captain Meano. BS: Man from RAT #1, Chief RAT, Mate. CA: Hoppity. HC: Man from RAT #2, Waldo.

64. *Submarine Sandwich* PF: Narrator, Ferkle. BS: Billsbottom, Fillmore. CA: Hoppity. HC: Waldo.

65–68
Halloween—Hoppity, Waldo, and Fillmore drive into the haunted village of Ware, and are invited to a Halloween ball. They discover a group called the Horrible Order who plan to silence all the roosters so that they won't crow at dawn.

65. *Halloween* PF: Narrator, Boris Karloff. BS: Ware Villager, Fillmore. CA: Hoppity. HC: Waldo.

66. *The Witch of Ware or The Flying Sorceress* PF: Narrator, Bela Lugosi. BS: Fillmore. CA: Hoppity. HC: Waldo.

67. *Some Enchanted Evening or Voo-Doo Something to Me* PF: Narrator, Bela Lugosi. BS: Werewolf Guard, Roosters, Vaughn Monroe, Fillmore. CA: Witch, Hoppity. HC: Waldo, Specter.

68. *Down in the Mouth or Fangs a Million* PF: Narrator, Bela Lugosi. BS: Guard, Rooster, Fillmore, Child. CA: Hoppity. HC: Waldo.

69–72
Christmas—Santa Claus hires some temporary elves to speed up production, not realizing they are the villainous gang led by Little Poison. The gang plan to take presents, not give them. Our three heroes help Saint Nick.

69. *Christmas* PF: Narrator, Santa Claus, Little Poison. BS: Foreman Alf, Fillmore. CA: Hoppity. HC: Waldo.

70. *Tough Sledding or I Only Have Ice for You* PF: Narrator, Santa Claus, Little Poison. BS: Reindeer Salesman, Criminals #2 and #3, Fillmore. CA: Hoppity. HC: Criminal #1, Waldo.

71. *Making a Hit with Santa or I'm Dreaming of a Wide Christmas* PF: Narrator, Santa Claus, Little Poison, Chauncey. BS: Criminal #1, Rent-a-Car Man, Edgar, Fillmore. CA: Hoppity. HC: Criminal #2, Waldo.

72. *Oh, You Skid or An Icicle Built for Two* PF: Narrator, Santa Claus, Little Poison. BS: Criminal #2, Big Charlie, Cop, Fillmore. CA: Kid #1, Hoppity. HC: Criminal #1, Waldo.

73–76

Horse Race Follies—The boys are sold a worthless racehorse called Big Dud, who runs backward and falls asleep. Then they discover that if Fillmore blows his bugle, Big Dud turns into a speedster. Naturally some crooks steal the bugle.

73. *Horse Race Follies* PF: Narrator, Race Caller, Horse Owner #2, Organ Grinder. BS: Horse Owner #1, Fillmore. CA: Woman, Hoppity. HC: Waldo.

74. *You'd Better Believe It or Don't Nag Me* PF: Narrator, Horse Owner #2. BS: Stable Boss, Horse Owner #1, Big Dud, Fillmore. CA: Hoppity. HC: Waldo.

75. *The Bronco Bill or Pay-Up Charlie Horse* PF: Narrator, Horse Owner #1, Race Caller. BS: Stable Boss, Horse Owner #2, Fillmore. CA: Hoppity. HC: Waldo.

76. *Waldo with Mustard or Hold the Onions* PF: Narrator, Race Caller, Horse Owner #1. BS: Horse Owner #2, Fillmore. CA: Hoppity. HC: Waldo.

77–80

Jack and the Beanstalk—Our boys are in Kansas, where they meet the mother of Jack, a boy who disappeared forty years ago. They climb a beanstalk and discover that Jack married a female giant. After reuniting Jack and his mother, the girl giant discovers she has in-law trouble.

77. *Jack and the Beanstalk* PF: Narrator, Jack. BS: Fillmore. CA: Jack's Mother, Hoppity. HC: Waldo.

78. *A Hassle in the Castle or The Fee Fi Fo Fumble* PF: Narrator, Flight Announcer, Jack. BS: Copilot, Fillmore. CA: Giant, Hoppity. HC: Waldo, Ed the Pilot.

79. *The King Size Surprise or Jolly Green Trouble* PF: Narrator, Jack, BS: Fillmore. CA: Giant, Hoppity. HC: Waldo.

80. *Spot on the Wall or The Flat of the Land* PF: Narrator, Jack, Ev. BS: Charlie, Fillmore. CA: Giant, Jack's Mother, Hoppity. HC: Senator, Waldo.

81–84

Granny's Gang—Grandma Jessica James forms a gang of old ladies who rob banks. When our boys help the police, the Granny Gang pretend to knit sweaters for them, but the sweaters are actually straitjackets. After being rescued by ham actor Clyde Wrinklebetter (who sounds like Dudley Do-Right, and who calls everyone Nell), the lads hire a group of old men to woo the Granny Gang.

81. *Granny's Gang* PF: Narrator, Cop. BS: Old Lady #2, Newsboy, Fillmore. CA: Jessica James, Hoppity. HC: Old Lady #1, Newsboy #2, Waldo.

82. *Boom in the Room or Bomby Weather* PF: Narrator, Mr. Gloomeyer, Cop #1. BS: Charlie, Cop #2, Ella-Mae, Fillmore. CA: Jessica James, Hoppity. HC: Waldo.

83. *The Big Splash or Bridge over the River Cry* PF: Narrator. BS: Cora, Fillmore. CA: Jessica James, Hoppity. HC: Waldo.

84. *On the Wrong Track or The Big Wheel* PF: Narrator, Phillip, Old Man #3 (Homer), Sheriff. BS: Clyde Wrinklebetter, Old Man #1 and Old Man #4, Fillmore, Old Lady. CA: Old Lady #2, Jessica James, Hoppity. HC: Old Man #2, Bertha, Waldo.

85–86

Golf—The boys are digging ditches. Fillmore strikes a rock with such force that Waldo enters him in the Foggy Bog Golf Open. If Fillmore wins, Waldo can pay off his disgruntled creditors.

85. *Golf Toumament* PF: Narrator. BS: Fillmore, Major Grigsby. CA: Hoppity. HC: Waldo.

86. *Divot Diggers or The Wearing of the Green* PF: Narrator, Creditor #1 & 4, Golfer #2. BS: Scorekeeper, Golfer #3, Creditor #2 & 3, Fillmore, Announcer. CA: Hoppity. HC: Waldo.

87–88

Hopeless Diamond—Fillmore reads the others a story he has written, and the events all come true: the lads are offered the Hopeless Diamond, which brings bad luck. Two river pirates want to steal it from them.

87. *The Hopeless Diamond* PF: Narrator, Falling Man. BS: Lumberjack, Fillmore. CA: Hoppity. HC: Waldo.

88. *Darn the Luck or Summer, Spring and Fall!* PF: Narrator, Pierre. BS: Mate, Fillmore. CA: Hoppity. HC: Waldo.

89–92

Dragon of Eubetchia—King Pippin the Green of Eubetchia declares war on the USA. Waldo receives a letter telling him he's inherited Dankmoor Castle. The boys will be beheaded if Waldo can't defeat a huge talking Dragon; actually the beast is simply hungry and he gets to eat one of Hoppity's chocolate pecan upside-down cakes. Waldo becomes the Dragon's showbiz manager.

89. *The Dragon of Eubetchia* PF: Narrator, Treasurer, Aide, Court Member #2, Royal Courier. BS: King Pippin the Green, Trembly, Court Member #3, Police Officer, Fillmore. CA: Hoppity. HC: Court Member #1, Waldo.

90. *The Part-Time Peer or Knight for a Day* PF: Narrator, Royal Courier, Treasurer, Aide, Headsman. BS: King Pippin the Green, Polite Man, Fillmore. CA: Hoppity. HC: Captain of Guards, Waldo.

91. *Where's Waldo? or A Knight to Remember* PF: Narrator, Dragon. BS: Onlooker #1, Fillmore. CA: Hoppity. HC: Onlooker #2, Waldo.

92. *The Inside Story or Alimentary, My Dear Hoppity* PF: Narrator, Dragon. BS: King Pippin, Fillmore. CA: Hoppity. HC: Waldo.

93–96

Rare Butterfly Hunt—Lepidopterist Dr. Dingbat asks the boys to help him find the rare Horribilis butterfly in a South American jungle. They are captured by the Quivery Indians. Fillmore disguises himself as a six-foot butterfly until they finally snare the real one.

93. *Rare Butterfly Hunt* PF: Narrator, Chauncey. BS: Edgar, Front-Page Frisby, Dr. Donald Dingbat, Fillmore. CA: Hoppity. HC: Waldo.

94. *The Butterfly Collectors or I Wanted Wings* PF: Narrator, Native #2, Native Cheftin. BS: Dr. Dingbat, Native #3, Fillmore. CA: Hoppity. HC: Native #1, Waldo.

95. *The Statue Speaks or Idol Chatter* PF: Narrator, Native Chieftain. BS: Dr. Dingbat, Bullwinkle, Dudley Do-Right, Fillmore, Butterfly. CA: Hoppity. HC: Waldo.

96. *Fillmore in a Flap or Coming In on a Wing and a Bear* PF: Narrator, Native Chieftain, Native #2. BS: Dr. Dingbat, Native #3, Fillmore, Butterfly. CA: Hoppity. HC: Native #1, Waldo.

97–100

Oil's Well at Oasis Gardens—Guest star Boris Badenov sells Waldo a worthless piece of desert. When Fillmore strikes oil, Waldo names the land Boondockia, but a syndicate of oil magnates, led by the evil Sahara Vaughn, try to do away with our heroes.

97. *Oil's Well at Oasis Gardens* PF: Narrator, Boris Badenov, Politician #2, Federal Man, Sahara Vaughn. BS: High Singer, Indian, Politician #1, Ali, Fillmore. CA: Hoppity. HC: Waldo.
98. *The Night Crawlers or Oily to Bed, Oily to Rise* PF: Narrator, Government Agent #2, Senator, Oil Man #2, Sahara Vaughn. BS: Government Agent #1, Oil Man #1, Ali, Fillmore. CA: Hoppity. HC: Waldo.
99. *A Negative Approach or More Film for Fillmore* PF: Narrator, Sahara Vaughn. BS: Ali, Fillmore. CA: Hoppity. HC: Waldo.
100. *The Rains Came or The Froggy, Froggy Dew!* PF: Narrator, Boris Badenov, Sahara Vaughn, Happy Folks #1, #3, and #5. BS: All, Repossessor, Happy Folks #2 and #6, Fillmore. CA: Happy Folk #7, Hoppity. HC: Happy Folk #4, Waldo.

101–104

Wonder Water—Waldo invents Wonder Water, which gives Fillmore a terrific "Sunday Punch"—he accidentally knocks out boxing champ Dirty Poole. A championship bout is arranged, but the crooks steal the Wonder Water.

101. *Wonder Water* WC: Narrator, Sparring Partner, Spectator #1. BS: Manager, Spectator #3, Fillmore. CA: Hoppity. HC: Spectator #2, Waldo.
102. *The Champ and the Chump or That Little Old Haymaker... Him!* WC: Narrator, Dirty Poole, Spectator #1. BS: Manager, Announcer, Newsboy, Reporter, Spectator #3, Fillmore. CA: Hoppity. HC: Spectator #2, Waldo.
103. *The Holy Mackerel or Half-Shot in the Dark* WC: Narrator, Dirty Poole. BS: Manager, Fillmore. CA: Hoppity. HC: Waldo.
104. *There's a Bear in There or Tree's a Crowd* WC: Narrator, Dirty Poole. BS: Manager, Ring Announcer, Fillmore, Fight Commentator. CA: Hoppity. HC: Waldo.

GEORGE OF THE JUNGLE

Key to abbreviations

DB:	Daws Butler	
JF:	June Foray	= Ursula
BS:	Bill Scott	= George
PF:	Paul Frees	= Narrator, Ape, District Commissioner

(Director's name follows episode title)

1. *The Sultan's Pearl* (Gerard Baldwin)—300 Pound Pearl, the sultan's favorite back scratcher, is stolen by arch fiends Titheridge and Plumtree PF: Narrator, Border Guard #2, Ape, Plumtree. DB: Sheik Ali Bay-Window, Titheridge, Border Guard #1. BS: Security Guard, George. JF: Ursula, 300 Pound Pearl.
2. *Oo-Oo Birds of a Feather* (Frank Braxton)—The oo-oo birds are being poached for their aphrodisiac tail-feathers. PF: Narrator, Admiring Man #3, Weevil. DB: Fritz, Admiring Man #1, Dog, Oo-Oo Bird, Tiger. BS: Admiring Man #2, George. JF: Fritz's Wife, Dowager, Princess Elsa, Ursula.

3. *The Malady Lingers On* (Pete Burness)—George's pet elephant Shep is ailing, so Dr. Kilimandaro is called to help. PF: Narrator, Ape. JF: Nurse, Ursula, Gaw-Gaw Bird, BS: George, Doctor.

4. *Ungawa the Gorilla God* (Bill Hurtz)—The District Commissioner and Shep are going to be sacrificed by the Boondocki tribe. PF: Narrator, Commissioner, Commentator. JF: Woman, Ursula. BS: George, Tooki Tooki Bird. DB: Witch Doctor.

5. *Little Scissor* (Fred Calvert)—Little Scissor is responsible for a pygmy uprising. PF: Narrator, Commissioner, Ape. DB: Pygmy, Guard. BS: George, Little Scissor, Pygmy Bandit.

6. *Monkey Business* (Jim Hiltz)—Ape is captured by animal tamer Claude Badley when a trained ape is needed for a TV show. PF: Narrator, Ape. BS: Claude Badley, George, Tooki Tooki Bird. JF: Ursula. DB: Ernest Confab.

7. *Next Time, Take the Train* (Gerard Baldwin)—Dr. Chicago sabotages the Nairobi and Grand Trunk Railway by stealing the tracks. PF: Narrator, Commissioner. BS: Carruthers, George. JF: Aunt Mae, Aunt Jemima. DB: Carruthers's Friend, Dr. Chicago.

8. *The Desperate Showers* (Pete Burness)—Ursula is to be sacrificed to the Great Juju so that it will finally rain. PF: Narrator, Ape. BS: Native Witch Doctor, George, Tooki Tooki Bird. JF: Ursula. DB: Chief.

9. *The Treasure of Sarah Madre* (Pantomime Pictures—subcontracted)—George and the Commissioner are after Sarah Madre's treasure, but so are the villains Tiger and Weevil. PF: Narrator, Ape, Commissioner, Weevil. BS: George, The Horse, Hungry Customer. JF: Ursula, Sarah Madre. DB: Tiger.

10. *The Trouble I've Seed* (Bill Hurtz)—Dr. Chicago is responsible for plants that steal. PF: Narrator, Commissioner, Ape, Laughing Plant. BS: George, Man with Refrigerator, Curious Man, Angry Householder. JF: Ursula. DB: Dr. Chicago, Policeman.

11. *Dr. Schpritzer, I Presume?* (Gerard Baldwin)—George must search for famous missing gallstone specialist, Dr. Alfred Schpritzer. PF: Narrator, Commissioner, Ape. BS: King, George. DB: Dr. Alfred Shpritzer.

12. *Rescue Is My Business* (Fred Calvert)—The shady Bumbashooti witch doctor becomes George's manager but demands payment from any people who are rescued by his client. PF: Narrator, Ape, Sinking Man. BS: Assistant Witch Doctor, George, Hunter, Tooki Tooki Bird. JF: Ursula. DB: Evil Witch Doctor.

13. *Big Flop at the Big Top* (Bill Hurtz)—The Ring-a-Ding Brothers employ Tiger and Weevil to snare George for their circus. PF: Narrator, Ring-a-Ding #2, Weevil, Ape. BS: Fettucini, George. JF: Lady in Distress, Ursula. DB: Ring-a-Ding #1, Tiger.

14. *The Chi Chi Dog* (Steve Clark)—Fabulously wealthy Sir Alfred Canine desperately wants a rare Chi Chi dog. PF: Narrator, Ape, Commissioner. BS: George, Doc. JF: The Lady Claudia, Ursula. DB: Sir Alfred Canine, Merv.

15. *A Man for All Hunting Seasons* (Pete Burness)—Big-game hunter the Duke of Ellington has trophy heads of every creature—except an Ape Man. PF: Narrator, Ape. BS: George. JF: Ursula, Cynthia. DB: Duke of Ellington.

16. *The Forest's Prime Evil* (John Walker)—Avaricious property developer Jerry Mander is going to bulldoze the Mbwebwe Valley in order to build Tsetse City. PF: Narrator, Ape, Mannie. BS: George. JF: Ursula. DB: Jerry Mander.

17. *Kings Back to Back* (Bill Hurtz)—Arrogant old millionaire Seymour Nudnik competes with George for the King of the Jungle title; he buys his votes. PF: Narrator, Ape, Commissioner. BS: George, The Hippie. JF: Ursula. DB: Seymour Nudnik.

SUPER CHICKEN

Key to abbreviations

DB: Daws Butler
JF: June Foray
BS: Bill Scott = Super Chicken
PF: Paul Frees = Narrator, Fred

(Director's name follows episode title)

1. *One of Our States Is Missing* (Jim Hiltz)—Henry Cabot Henhaus is pitted against old schoolchum Appian Way, who has "kidnapped" Rhode Island. PF: Narrator, Edgar, Fred. BS: Chauncey, Super Chicken, Frantic Farmer. DB: Passenger, Urgent Man, TV Announcer, Appian Way.
2. *The Zipper* (Gerard Baldwin)—Arch villain the Zipper invents a bomb to blow up the world. PF: Narrator, News-spreader #3, Fred. DB: The Zipper, News-spreader #2, Onlooker #1, Citizen #1, Little Boy. BS: News-spreader #1 and #4, Onlooker #2, Citizen #2, Super Chicken.
3. *Rotten Hood* (Fred Calvert)—Rotten Hood and his band of merry man, Fried Tucker, rob from the rich, but don't give any to the poor. PF: Narrator, Fried Tucker, Citizen #2, Fred. DB: Rotten Hood, Citizen #1. BS: Super Chicken, Citizen #3.
4. *The Oyster* (John Walker)—Master criminal the Oyster steals the world's largest pearl. PF: Narrator, Hornbeck, Fred. DB: The Oyster. BS: Super Chicken, Melville.
5. *The Elephant Spreader* (Bill Hurtz)—The evil Prince Blackhole of Calcutta removes elephants from India in a mad scheme to tip the world on its side. PF: Narrator, Fred. JF: Mrs. Fingerknot, Alvin's Wife, Charlie's Wife. DB: Hubert Fingerknot, Charlie, Secretary of the Exterior, Prince Blackhole of Calcutta. BS: Super Chicken, Alvin, Woman #2, The Cab Driver, Pinjab.
6. *Merlin Brando* (Pantomime Pictures—subcontracted)—Wizard Merlin Brando, told by his Magic Mirror that Super Chicken is his superior, lures our hero into a trap. PF: Narrator, Magic Mirror, Fred. DB: Merlin Brando. BS: Super Chicken. JF: Voice Recording.
7. *Wild Ralph Hiccup* (Jim Hiltz)—Wild Ralph Hiccup, a cowboy bandit, robs people on airplanes, then parachutes to a getaway. PF: Narrator, Fred. DB: Wild Ralph Hiccup. JF: Arthur's Wife. BS: Super Chicken, Arthur, Henchman.
8. *The Geezer* (Jim Hiltz)—Crabby old codger the Geezer steals a geyser in order to open a car wash. PF: Narrator, Fred. DB: Park Ranger, the Geezer. BS: Super Chicken.
9. *Salvador Rag Dolly* (Bill Hiltz)—Mad inventor Rag Dolly makes toys that hold up people attending birthday parties. PF: Narrator, Fred. DB: Little Boy, Citizen, Salvador Rag Dolly. BS: The Father, the Policeman, Super Chicken. JF: Little Girl, The Mother, Talkie-Tilly Doll.
10. *The Easter Bunny* (Gerard Baldwin)—It appears as though the Easter Bunny has turned bank robber, but it's really Louie the Lapin in disguise. PF: Narrator, The Easter Bunny, Fred. JF: Newsboy, Little Old Lady. DB: Bank President, Bank Teller #1, Man #2, informative Citizen, Police Chief. BS: Policeman, Man #1 Super Chicken, Bank Teller #2.
11. *The Noodle* (Jim Hiltz)—Notorious and brainy bank robber the Noodle drops a watermelon on Super Chicken, and our hero suffers amnesia. PF: Narrator, Onlooker #3, Fred. DB: Noodle, Onlooker #2. BS: Beastly, Onlookers #1 and #4, Super Chicken.
12. *The Fat Man* (Fred Calvert)—A parody of *The Maltese Falcon:* the Fat Man and his butler Shingles steal the Maltese Duck. PF: Narrator, The Fat Man, Fred. DB: Indignant Man, Shingles. BS: Super Chicken, Black Magic Man.
13. *Briggs Bad-Wolf* (Jim Hiltz)—Stressed-out actor Briggs Bad-Wolf believes he really is the villain he's been portraying. PF: Narrator, Brick Mason, Fred. DB: Briggs Bad-Wolf, Theater Patron. BS: Super Chicken. JF: Red Riding Hood.

14. *The Laundry Man* (Bill Hurtz)—Laundry man Shrimp Chop Fooey and his Number One Son are true money launderers—they wash fingerprints off stolen greenbacks. PF: Narrator, Big Buck Balucci, Fred, Number One Son. DB: Laundry Man. BS: Super Chicken.
15. *The Muscle* (Steve Clark)—Bad guy the Muscle steals a 7,000-pound diamond-studded dumbbell from a gymnasium. PF: Narrator, Fred. DB: McTasty, The Muscle. BS: Super Chicken, Henchman.
16. *Dr. Gizmo* (Gerard Baldwin)—Mad Gizmo escapes from police custody and goes on a crime rampage. PF: Narrator, Fred. DB: Doctor Gizmo. BS: Super Chicken, Cop, Holdup Victim.
17. *The Wild Hair* (Bill Hurtz)—A living troupee runs loose from a laboratory and starts a spree of destruction. PF: Narrator, Igor, Houston Mayor, Fred. DB: Doctor Could-Be, Terrified Man. BS: Super Chicken.

TOM SLICK, RACER

	Key to abbreviations		
DB:	Daws Butler		
JF:	June Foray	=	Marigold
BS:	Bill Scott	=	Tom, Gertie
PF:	Paul Frees	=	Race Caller

(Director's name follows episode title)

1. *The Bigg Race* (Bill Hurtz)—Tom competes in a race sponsored by millionaire Tiny Bigg. Baron Otto Matic drives the Blacktop Ramshocker. PF: Race Caller, Baron Otto Matic, Sir Philip Prince. BS: Gertie Growler, Tom Slick. JF: Marigold. DB: Clutcher.
2. *Tom Slick and the Monster Rally* (Lew Keller)—In Transylvania, Tom competes with Count Lew Gosi, who drives the Red Corpuscle Bloodmobile. PF: Race Caller, Monte Carloff. JF: Marigold, Sepulchra. BS: Tom Slick, Gertie Growler, Lobo Fanguzzi, Peasant. DB: Spooky Man, Count Lew Gosi.
3. *The Cupp Cup Race* (Jim Hiltz)—Tom competes in a speedboat race against Anson Snobsworthy V, who operates the Twin Prowed Surf Slurper. PF: Race Caller, Sir Thomas Cupp, U-boat Commander. BS: Tom Slick, Gertie Growler. JF: Marigold, Wilma Willow. DB: Anson Snobsworthy V, Henchman, Bilgerat, Ringo Starfish.
4. *Dranko the Dragster* (Fred Calvert)—Tom competes in a drag race against alien Dranko, and tough guy Harley Angel, who drives the Switchblade Chop Popper. PF: Race Caller, Steve McQueasy, Harley Angel. BS: Arnold Forthcoming, Tom Slick, Gertie Growler. JF: Marigold. DB: Dranko.
5. *Send in a Sub* (Gerard Baldwin)—Tom competes in a submarine race against nasty cheat Anthony J. "Lucky" Pool. PF: Race Caller. DB: Anthony J. Pool, Floyd Britches. BS: Tom Slick, Gertie Growler. JF: Marigold, Brenda, Sonia Nar.
6. *The Mach Buster Trophy* (Pantomime Pictures—subcontracted)—Tom competes in an airplane race against Baron Otto Matic, who is flying the Snuff Wing Cowl Howler. PF: Race Caller, Baron Otto Matic, Inquisitive Man #3. BS: Buster Mach, Lenny Johns Inquisitive Man #2, Tom Slick, Gertie Growler. JF: Marigold, France LaBelle. DB: Ivan Awfulitch, Clutcher, Inquisitive Man #1, Loan Company Man.
7. *Snow What?* (Bill Hurtz)—Tom competes in a snowmobile race against Baron Otto Matic, who drives the Frostoblast Igloo. PF: Race Caller, Baron Otto Matic, Vittorio Vermicelli. BS: Vittorio Vermicelli (also), Tom Slick, Gertie Growler. JF: Marigold. DB: Clutcher, Roy Almonte.
8. *The Great Balloon Race* (Gerard Baldwin)—Tom competes in a balloon race against Baron Otto Matic. PF: Race Caller, Baron Otto Matic. BS: Tom Slick, Gertie Growler, Ponsfoot, Fellini Scallopini. DB: Clutcher, Sir Stanley Steamer, French Official. JF: Marigold.

9. *I've Been Railroaded* (John Walker)—Tom competes in a locomotive race against Lionel Switchback IV, who drives the Ram Steam Boil Bomber. PF: Race Caller. BS: Tom Slick, Gertie Growler, Krudney, Carruthers Toe-Tippy, Railway Announcer. JF: Marigold. DB: Lionel Switchback IV.

10. *Overstocked* (Jim Hiltz)—Tom competes in a stock car race against Sweet Willie Rollbar, who drives the Chrome Fang Panther-Prong. PF: Race Caller. BS: Tom Slick, Gertie Growler, Luther Gene Sodbuster, Smiling Sid Schlock. JF: Marigold. DB: Sweet Willie Rollbar, Morse O. Leum.

11. *The Sneaky Sheik* (Bill Hurtz)—Tom competes in a dune buggy race against Howya Ben Boobie, who drives the Squat Wheel Camel Choker. PF: Race Caller, Gas Station Man. BS: Tom Slick, Gertie Growler. JF: Marigold. DB: Sneaky Sheik (Howya Ben Boobie), Sanford Nitty.

12. *The Cheap Skateboard Derby* (Fred Calvert)—Tom competes in a motorized skateboard race against nasty Rocco Roller. PF: Race Caller. BS: Tom Slick, Gertie Growler, Channing Jawbeaver. JF: Marigold. DB: Rocco Roller, Birdwell S. Cheap.

13. *The Double Cross Country Race* (Gerard Baldwin)—Tom competes against Baron Otto Matic, who gets stuck on a cloverleaf highway-intersection. PF: Race Caller, Baron Otto Matic. BS: Tom Slick, Gertie Growler. JF: Marigold. DB: Clutcher.

14. *The Apple-Less Indian 500* (John Walker)—Tom competes in a Big Wheel race against Baron Otto Matic, who drives the Black Log Cross Wheeler. PF: Race Caller, Baron Otto Matic. BS: Tom Slick, Gertie Growler. JF: Marigold. DB: Clutcher, Indian.

15. *The Irish Cheapstakes* (Gerard Baldwin)—In Ireland, the Baron becomes "Art O'Matic" in a race against Tom, who is helped by Gertie's awful singing voice. PF: Race Caller, Baron Otto Matic. BS: Tom Slick, Gertie Growler, Sean O'Malley. DB: Clutcher. JF: Marigold.

16. *The Badyear Blimp* (Bill Hurtz)—Tom competes in a blimp race against Baron Otto Matic's Chain Drive Sky Hooker. PF: Race Caller, Baron Otto Matic. DB: Stretch Snapback, Clutcher, Fledge Sparrow. BS: Tom Slick, Gertie Growler, Danny Druff, Man with No Guests, Man. JF: Marigold.

17. *The Swamp Buggy Race* (Fred Calvert)—Tom competes in a swamp buggy race against Baron Otto Matic, who dresses up in drag as Wilma Mae Boondocker. PF: Race Caller, Baron Otto Matic. DB: Clutcher. BS: Tom Slick, Gertie Growler, Billy Joe Halfacre, Wally George Boughmoss. JF: Marigold.

FRACTURED FLICKERS EPISODES AND VOICE CREDITS

Key to abbreviations

HC: Hans Conried (Series Host)
BS: Bill Scott
PF: Paul Frees
JF: June Foray

Episode 1

Bullfight—PF: Charlie. BS: Rudy.
Model Interview—JF: Model. PF: Model Agent.
The 39 Stoops—BS: Film Director.
Guest Interview (Rose Marie)
Tarfoot of the Apes—HC: Narrator. BS: Professor, Scientist #3, Maid. JF: Jane. PF: Tarfoot, Scientist #2, Reginald Snively Wappington-Jones, Native Chief.
Route 56—JF: Announcer, Fuzz. BS: Clod.

Episode 2

The Fly by Night Airlines Deluxe Movie Flight (Down to Earth)—BS: Captain, Movie Voice, Spectator #3. PF: Copilot, Movie Narrator, Spectator #1. JF: Stewardess (Miss Finster), Spectator #2.
Cornell Goes Wilde—HC: Narrator, Football Player #2. PF: Jack Headstrong, Footballer. BS: Coach, Heckler, Footballer #1. JF: Rosa Picardy, Miss Placement.
Guest Interview—Fabian.
Egg Institute—HC: Announcer. JF: Woman in Bath.
Do Me a Flavor—HC: Narrator. BS: Albert K. Seltzer, Phosphate's Friend. PF: George, German, Conrad Phosphate, Emaline's friend. JF: Old Lady, Madeleine La Farge, Flavor Tester, Imogene Cola, Emaline Gargly.
Shady Grove Hotel—BS: Announcer.

Episode 3

The Death of a Travelling Salesman—HC: Narrator, Man, Cop #1. JF: Mildred, Selma, Lolita O'Brien. BS: Willie Roman, Lucellus Blanc, Cop #2. PF: Client, Manny, Ernest Hemenhaw.
A Salute to Industry—PF: Announcer.
Guest Interview—Gypsy Rose Lee.
San Francisco—PF: Narrator. BS: Cigar Smoker, Man in Fog. JF: Woman.
The Clover Boys at Camp—PF: Narrator, Tom Clover, Harry Clover. JF: Tom's ex-wife. BS: Dick Clover, Roger, Grandad.

Episode 4

The Frink Story—PF: Narrator, Butler. BS: Thomas Alva Frink, Eli Pitney. JF: Girl.
Shoe Store—BS: Announcer.
Apache Shane's High Noon Stagecoach to Virginia City, via Alamo, Oklahoma—HC: Narrator. PF: The Giddyap Kid, Bartender. BS: Stage Passenger, Sham O'Tanta, Dance Caller. JF: Dolly Finster.
Guest Interview—Allan Sherman.
From Rags to Twitches (A Hollywood Story)—HC: Narrator. JF: Edna Mae Furd. PF: Creditor, Director, Home Roller Announcer, Floor Wax Director. BS: Janitor, Client, George, Soap Announcer, Eye Training Announcer, Actor. Hair-Piece—PF: Narrator.

Episode 5

The Cut-Away—PF: Announcer. BS: Frederick Figg.
Hands Across the Fee—BS: Doctor. PF: Otto Umlaut. JF: Gretchen Schimmelfarb.
Guest Interview—Annette Funicello.
Dinky Dunstan—Boy Cheerleader—PF: Narrator, Effeminate Student, Chancellor, Dean Stucker. BS: Student, Dinky Dunstan, Student #2 (Feeney). JF: Mary Lou Beazley.
The Adventures of Harry & Ozziet—PF: Narrator. JF: Ozziet. BS: Harry, Mr. Bratley.

Episode 6

A Moving Story—PF: Narrator. BS: Moving Man.
Pasadena, California—PF: Narrator.
Guest Interview—Edward Everett Horton.
The Prince and the Poppa—HC: Narrator. BS: King Fritzchel, Soldier #2, Puppet, Dueling Instructor, Butler, Boopy's Friend, Old Woman, Man with Crown, General Hockfleisch. PF: Treasurer, Soldier, Charlie, Prince Boopy, Heckler, Driver, Farmer. JF: Damsel, Tish, Heppelfinger.
Fearless Follicle's Hair Remover—HC: Announcer.

Episode 7

The Man of the Hour—PF: Announcer. BS: Narrator, Claude Vanderwilt, other voices.
What Is Jay Ward Really Like?—HC: Narrator. PF: Jay Ward, Man #2, Reginald Nose. JF: Gladys. BS: Rob Sterling, Irving, Man #1, Man #3.
(A Special Announcement) National Restaurant Week—PF: Announcer.
Guest Interview—Paula Prentiss.
The Barber of Stanwick—PF: Narrator, Customer, Hairdresser, Client's friend, Man #2, Man #5, Man

#7, Tony's friend, Old Customer. JF: Natalie, Mother, Woman, Miss Pomfritt. BS: Zeke's Manager, Client, Zeke, Man #1, Man #3, and Man #6, Barber, Tony, Effeminate Man.
Mother's Day—BS: Eddie Lawrence Voice.

Episode 8
Lovely Las Pulgas—HC: Narrator. PF: Native Guides. BS: Crying Man, Caller. JF: Dying Woman.
Guest Interview—Sebastian Cabot.
The Quitter—HC: Narrator. BS: Smoker #1, Marvin Detweller, Announcer #2, Shorty, Bearded Man, Ad Man #2, Ad Executive, J. B. PF: Smokers #2 and #4, Ad Man Executive #2, Waiter, Announcer.
The Nineteenth Century—BS: Bunker Waltite, Insurance Agent. PF: Brudenko Man, Grover S. Tweet, Mr. Clump. JF: Driver.

Episode 9
Saturday Night at the Auto Races—PF: Announcer, Chicken Singer. JF: Chicken Surprise Voice. BS: Chicken Singer.
Jungle Bums—BS: Dalt Wisley, Buffalo, Rhino, Giraffe, Monkey #2. PF: Lion, Hippo, Monkey, Gorilla, Hunter, Baboon. JF: Mother Giraffe.
Guest Interview—Roddy McDowall.
Behind the Scenes—"Half Baked Alaska"—BS: Director.
Elephants Are Funny—PF: Italian, Householder. BS: Gumbadi, Teacher, Groom, Man, Cop, Elephant. JF: Woman, Bride, Mae West, Woman with Veil, Banished Woman.
Safety Message—PF: Announcer.

Episode 10
Previews of Next Week's Shows—PF: Announcer.
The Fatal Question—PF: Narrator, Walter, Man #2, Doctor #3, Officer. BS: Man with Hiccups, Man #1, Man #3, and Man #4, Doctor #2. JF: Woman, Woman #2.
A Letter from Camp—BS: Elroy. JF: Mabel. PF: Dickie.
Guest Interview—Vivien Della Chiesa.
Mr. G. Whizz—HC: Narrator. PF: Mr. G. Whizz. BS: Chess Player.
The Blackboard Bungle—PF: Narrator, Mr. Spinoza, Cyril, Henchman. BS: Principal, Mr. O'Brien, Freddie Finkeldoofer, PTA Man, Drama Teacher. JF: Marjean Freeble.
Bride and Gloom—Eddie Lawrence Voice.

Episode 11
Saturday Night at the Horse Races—PF: Announcer (Del Mar), Singer. BS: Upsides Gum Announcer, Singer, Crying Man.
Hollywood Magazine of the Air—JF: Lolly Popsons. BS: Actor, Boyfriend, Tab Hunter.
Guest Interview—Connie Stevens.
The Auditor's Report—JF: Secretary, Miss Peckthorpe. PF: J. B. Bostwick, Cop, Guard, Police Chief, Crossword Man, Chief's Assistant. BS: Mr. Bentwhistle, Mr. Osgood.
Burpaseltzer—PF: Announcer.
Coming Distractions (The Grim, Grim World of the Wonderful Brothers Sisters)—PF: Announcer. BS: Man at End.

Episode 12
Who Is This Man?—PF: Announcer.
Friendly Land Grab Real Estate Company—PF: Announcer.
The Annual Flemmy Awards—PF: Announcer, Dr. Zebra, Walter, Winchell, Peter Lorre, Theater Man. BS: Ruby Wheeler, Doctor, Dr. K-C, Frank Nutty, Heckler, Matt Dodge, Professor Wizzard, Friendly, Sports Commentator, Agent. JF: Miss Rebstock, Katy, Schoolteacher, Rocky, Tour Guide, Theater Girl.
Guest Interview—Rod Serling.
Fungo Foster—PF: Narrator, Howie Dingle, Hometown Manager, Hecklers #1 and #3. BS: Fungo Foster, Man in Street, Foster's Brother, Sports Voice, Heckler #2, Umpire. JF: Willa Mae Conky, Mrs Foster.
Owed to an Indian—BS: Narrator.

Episode 13

Hey, Boating Fans—PF: Announcer. BS: Man.
The Dalt Wisley Program—PF: Announcer, Coupon Man, Strong Man, Accountant #4. BS: Dalt Wisley, Employee, Screaming Man, Accountant #3, Singing Man. JF: Child, Mother, Accountant.
Guest Interview—Connie Hines.
How the West Was Lost—PF: Narrator, Direction Giver, Fighting Man, Foreman, Jesse. BS: Pecos Pruitt, Chicken Flicker Man, Old Man, Cowboy, Jesse's Friend. JF: Mavis, Mrs. Puyster De Witt.
Minute Mystery No. 592733—PF: Narrator. BS: Elephant, Pop Henry, Sherman Oaks. JF: Mata Hari.

Episode 14

This Here's My Life—BS: Narrator.
A Salute to Chicago—PF: Announcer. BS: Itchy Man, Giggler.
Guest Interview—Cesar Romero.
Hymie and Me—BS: Erich Von Stucker, Soldier #2, Waiter, Husband. PF: Soldiers #1 and #3, Irving Dandy, Shorty Woods, Man at Table. JF: Undine Flugelmeyer, Girl at Table, Girl in Audience, Wife, TV Actress.
Scrutiny (U.S. In the Twenties)—PF: Narrator. BS: Man, Adolf Hitler, Enrico Caruso.

Episode 15

The Big Contest—PF: Announcer. BS: Husband.
Fun Things to Do In Backward Countries—BS: Announcer, Laugher.
Guest Interview—Diana Dors.
Minute Mystery No. 896014—PF: Narrator. BS: Joseph Rebstock, Falling Man, Man in Parachute, Sherman Oaks.
Teen-age Tips—PF: Arthur Godfrey, Merle Squint, Joking Man, Jingle Singer, Charlie Dugan. BS: Ricky Teenage, Jingle Singer. JF: Wanda Jean Obese.
Foam King of the Mad Dogs—PF: Announcer, Narrator. BS: German, Foam.

Episode 16

Saturday Night at the Bike Races—PF: Announcer. BS: Commercial Voice.
Deadsel—America's Luxury Car—PF: Announcer.
Spike that Rumor!—PF: Narrator, Clyde. BS: Merle, Barber, Soldier, Zelda Ben Gurion, Gay Man.
Tan Vicky's Gyms—PF: Announcer. BS: Man, Tan Vicky.
Guest Interview—Bullwinkle J. Moose.
The Yetta Hari Master Spy Kit—HC: Announcer.
Minute Mystery No. 402564—PF: Narrator. BS: Wolf Howl.
Ode to an Engineer—BS: Poet.

Episode 17

Who Is This Man? No. 2—PF: Narrator.
A Salute to New York—PF: Narrator. BS: Commercial Announcer, Blind Man, Man Watching Fight.
Destructo—Full Scale Tank—BS: Announcer.
Guest Interview—Deborah Walley.
The Tilton Hotel—PF: Narrator, Merle. BS: Ned.
Uncle Sam Wants You Guys!—BS: Recruiting Man. PF: Announcer.
Minute Mystery No. 5—PF: Narrator. BS: Howl.

Episode 18

The Adventures of Yangtze Derringer—BS: Yangtze, Toulouse. PF: Narrator.
Acid Indigestion—PF: Announcer. JF: Woman.
Charlatan Hotels—PF: Announcer. JF: Wife. BS: Man.
Saturday Night at the Movies—BS: Hero, Knothead, Pool Announcer, Blade Announcer. PF: Announcer. JF: Heroine.
Guest Interview—Paul Lynde.
The Fractured Flickers Annual Company Picnic—PF: Narrator. BS: Employee.
Doctor Overbite's Betterbreath—PF: Announcer. BS: George.

Return Marvin D. Snark to Washington—BS: Announcer, Indian, Supporter, Marvin Snark. PF: Narrator. JF: Housewife, Movie Star.
Believe It . . . or Don't—PF: Narrator.

Episode 19
The Big Contest—PF: Announcer.
National Safety Month—PF: Announcer. BS: Announcer #2.
Maidenform Gunbelts—BS: Announcer, Lox. PF: Announcer #2.
Jay Ward Prevues—PF: Announcer, Mr. Fred. BS: Mr. Nojak, Uncle Martini, Jay Ward. JF: Gladys, Princess.
Fairyton Cigarettes—PF: Fairyton Announcer. BS: Man.
Guest Interview—Anna Maria Alberghetti.
Astrology—PF: Announcer. JF: Heavenly Day.
Pick Your College—PF: Announcer. BS: Orton, Tailor. JF: Orton's mother.
Hey, Culture Fans!—BS: Announcer.
Odd Occupations—PF: Announcer. JF: Woman on Beach. BS: Schoolkid, Teddy.

Episode 20
Saturday Night at the Channel Swim—PF: Announcer. BS: Commercial Announcer.
Bunkwood Country Club—PF: Spokesman. JF: Woman.
Guest Interview—Ruta Lee.
National Healthy Week—PF: Announcer. BS: Man.
The Charge of the Light Brigade—HC: Narrator. BS: Irving Fink.
A Salute to the American Worker—PF: Announcer, BS: Messenger, Sneezing Man.
B.P. & E.—BS: Announcer, Mad Man. PF: Announcer #2, Peter Lorre.
Who Is This Man? No. 3—PF: TV Presenter.
Hysteria Airlines—PF: Announcer.

Episode 21
Believe it . . . or Don't (No. 2)—PF: Narrator.
Dangerous Ben Magrew—PF: Narrator. BS: Ben Magrew, Bert.
Guest Interview—Barbara Eden.
I Remember Maybelle—BS: Horace Silverspoon, Nicky Ivanitch. JF: Maybelle, Mrs. Ivanitch. PF: Dr. Ivanitch.
Carper's Little Liquor Pills—JF: Old Lady. PF: Announcer.
Who Are the Dark Horse Candidates?—PF: Announcer.
How to Be a Finders Keepers—BS: Announcer.

Episode 22
Scrutiny (Great Men Through The Ages—Hippocrates to Einstein)—PF: Announcer. BS: Whispering Man, A. G. Bell, Dr. Guppy.
F-Bar-F Dude Ranch—BS: Announcer, Singer. PF: Singer.
Where Has Hollywood Glamor Gone?—PF: Fag Announcer.
Guest Interview—Bob Denver.
Beaver Brothers—PF: Announcer. BS: The Phantom of the Opera.
The El Rancho Gordo Story—JF: Narrator. BS: Countess Finkelstein, Mr. Dicky.
Minute Mystery No. 6—PF: Narrator.
Fractured Flickers Lost and Found Department—PF: Announcer.

Episode 23
The Big Contest No. 3—PF: Announcer. BS: Sneezer.
Your City Needs You!—Be a Lady Cop—BS: Announcer, Crowd Voice.
Hollywood Low-Down—BS: Announcer, Movie Crew Man, Kentucky Feldman, Dickie Bird, Tijuana Cop, Drunk, Guard. PF: Narrator, John Dallas. JF: Cleo Niles.
Bee Tissues—PF: Announcer.
Guest Interview—Pat Carroll.
A Salute to the Fractured Flickers Scouts of America—PF: Announcer. BS: Vocal FX.

Saturday Night at the Sundae—PF: Announcer (Rocky Rhodes), Commercial Announcer #2. BS: Commercial Announcer, Sneezer, Singing Woman.

Episode 24
David Whelper Presents (The Raw Ring Twenties—The Hoodlum Era Part 1)—PF: Waldo Winkle. BS: Buze Cola Announcer.
Olympic Training Film—PF: Announcer, Al Dunn. BS: Commentator.
Fractured Flickers Auction—PF: Fag Announcer.
Guest Interview—Bob Newhart.
What Is a Fractured Flickers Fan Really Like?—PF: Announcer. BS: Neighbor. JF: Commercial Announcer.
Believe It . . . or Don't No. 3—PF: Announcer.

Episode 25
To Yell the Truth—JF: Anna Marie Lesser, Imposter. PF: Announcer.
Fractured Flickers Consumers Bureau Report—PF: Announcer. BS: Seal.
(A Public Service) Fractured Flickers Guide to Income Tax Fun—PF: Announcer. BS: Giggling Man.
Guest Interview—Ursula Andress.
A Day of Destiny—BS: Pomfritt. PF: T. J. Lovelace, Bellhop, Columnist, Policeman, Desk Sergeant, J. B. Prindle. JF: Marsha Mallow, Newsboy.
Tower of London—PF: Narrator, Mitty. BS: Reginald Tower.
Fractured Flickers—All Pro Team—PF: Commentator, Sneezer. BS: Sneezer, Reginald Tower.

Episode 26
Saturday Night at the Jail Break—PF: Announcer (Al Catraz), Woman. BS: Announcer #2.
A Salute to Los Angeles—PF: Announcer, Singer, Heckler #2. BS: Scared Man, Singer, Hecklers #1 and #3, Kidnapped Man, Hanged Man.
Who Asked for It?—PF: Effeminate Announcer.
Guest Interview—Zsa Zsa Gabor.
Cow-Tux—Western Formal Wear—BS: Announcer.
Fractured Flickers Dream Analysis Plan—BS: German Man. PF: Lawrence of Arabia, Man.
The Big Contest Report—BS: Announcer, Man. PF: Fred Lamarr.

ON-SCREEN CREDITS

ROCKY AND HIS FRIENDS

ABC network

First Season 1959–60

Producers	Jay Ward, Bill Scott
Executive Producer	Ponsonby Britt, O.B.E.
Directors	Bill Hurtz, Ted Parmelee, Gerry Ray, Gerard Baldwin, Jim Hiltz
Animation	Val-Mar Studios
Writers	Chris Hayward, Chris Jenkyns, George Atkins
Voices	E. E. Horton, June Foray, Paul Frees, Bill Conrad, Walter Tetley, Daws Butler

And a host of others, including Skip Craig, Al Shean, Roy Morita, William Schleh, Harvey Siegal, and Sam Clayberger
Theme Music composed by Frank Comstock
Recorded by Glen Glenn Sound
Producers Associates of Television, Inc.

Second Season 1960–61

A Producers Associates of Television, Inc., Production
Copyright 1960 Ward-P.A.T. Productions, Inc.

Producers	Jay Ward, Bill Scott
Directors	Gerard Baldwin, Pete Burness, Bill Hurtz, Gerry Ray, Bob Schleh, George Singer, Ernie Terrazas
Writers	George Atkins, Chris Hayward, Chris Jenkyns, Lloyd Turner
Animation	Gamma Productions
Associate Producer	Edwin A. Gourley
Voices	Edward Everett Horton, June Foray, Paul Frees, Bill Conrad, Walter Tetley
Design and Layout	Sam Clayberger, Dave Fern, Frank Hursh, Dan Jurovich, Joe Montell, Roy Morita, Al Shean, Shirley Silvey, Sam Weiss, Al Wilson
Supervised by	Harvey Siegel
And a Host of Others	Barbara Baldwin, Skip Craig, Adrienne Diamond, Art Diamond, Roger Donley, Sal Faillace, Carlos Manriquez, Jesus Martinez, Bob Maxfield, Dun Roman, Jean Washam

THE BULLWINKLE SHOW

NBC network

Third, Fourth, and Fifth Seasons, 1961–64

Produced by Jay Ward, Bill Scott
A Producers Associates of Television Production
Peter Piech, Producer
Animation by Gamma Productions
Bud Gourley, Producer

Directors	Bill Hurtz, Pete Burness, Ted Parmelee, Lew Keller, Sal Faillace, Gerard Baldwin, George Singer
Writers	Chris Hayward, Lloyd Turner, Chris Jenkyns, George Atkins, Al Burns
Actors	June Foray, Paul Frees, Edward Everett Horton, Hans Conried, Bill Conrad, Walter Tetley
Artists	Sam Clayberger, Adrienne Diamond, Art Diamond, Roy Morita, Al Shean, Shirley Silvey, Al Wilson, Barbara Baldwin
Editor	Skip Craig
Theme Music	Fred Steiner
Additional Music	Dennis Farnon, George Steiner
Executive Producer	Ponsonby Britt

FRACTURED FLICKERS

(1963–64, syndicated)

Producers	Jay Ward, Bill Scott
Your Host	Hans Conried
Actors	June Foray, Paul Frees
Writers	Bill Scott, Chris Hayward, Lloyd Turner, Jim Critchfield, George Atkins, Al Burns
Music	Dennis Farnon, Fred Steiner

Edited by	Skip Craig
Sound Editor	Roger Donley
Title Animation	Bill Hurtz, Jim Hiltz
Executive Producer	Ponsonby Britt, O.B.E
A Jay Ward Production	
(1963) JW Productions, Inc.	

HOPPITY HOOPER

ABC network

1964–67

Producers	Jay Ward, Bill Scott
Directors	Pete Burness, Bill Hurtz, Lew Keller
Writers	Chris Jenkyns, Bill Scott
Film Editor	Skip Craig
Designers	Sam Clayberger, Roy Morita, Shirley Silvey
Voices	Chris Allen, Hans Conried, Paul Frees
Animation by	Gamma Productions S.A. de G.V.
Production Director	Harvey Siegel
Associate Director	Jamie Torres V.
Animation Supervisor	Sam S. Kai
Layout Supervisor	Joe Montell
Executive Producer	Ponsonby Britt
A Jay Ward Production	
In association with Producers	Associates of Television, Inc.
Executive Producer	Peter Piech

GEORGE OF THE JUNGLE

ABC network

1967–68

Executive Producers	Ponsonby Britt, O. B. E., Jay Ward, Bill Scott
Scripts	Chris Jenkyns, Jim MacGeorge, John Marshall, Jack Mendelsohn, Lloyd Turner
Directors	Gerard Baldwin, Frank Braxton, Pete Burness, Paul Harvey, Jim Hiltz, Bill Hurtz, John Walker
Music	Stan Worth, Sheldon Allman
Supervisor Production	Helen Hanson
Production	Betty Brenon, Jan Gusdavison, Doris Nelson
Editing	Skip Craig, Roger Donley
Animators	Bob Bachman, Howard Baldwin, Herman Cohen, Phil Duncan, Bob Goe, Fred Madison, Bob Maxfield, Gary Mooney, Barrie Nelson, Jack Schnerk, Rod Scribner, Rudy Zamora, Alan Zaslove
Design	Sam Cornell, Don Ferguson, Don Jurwich, Bob Kurtz, Roy Morita, Rosemary O'Connor, Shirley Silvey
Background	Sam Clayberger, Bob McIntosh, Gloria Wood
Jay Ward Productions, Inc.	

MISCELLANEOUS MATERIAL AND EXTRA SHOW ANIMATION

ROCKY AND HIS FRIENDS and THE BULLWINKLE SHOW

ROCKY SHOW OPENING 1 Parade and fireworks (Two versions—General Mills and Tootsie Roll billboards)

ROCKY SHOW OPENING 2 "A Thunder of Jets" and Bullwinkle in balloon

ROCKY SHOW CLOSING 1 Credits in gift box (Two versions—General Mills and Tootsie Roll billboards)

ROCKY SHOW CLOSING 2 Bullwinkle has wristwatch-hourglass

SYNDICATED ROCKY SHOW OPENING AND CLOSING—Circus wagon

OLD COMMERCIAL INTROS

A.		Bullwinkle is a projectionist.
B.		Bullwinkle is a painter.

OLD SPECIAL FEATURE INTROS

A.		Bullwinkle does a soft-shoe routine.
B.		Bullwinkle pulls a bear from his hat.

(following descriptions from Bill Scott's official NBC master list)

COMMERCIAL INTRODUCTIONS

A.	CI-Private	Rocky and Bullwinkle are soldiers.
B.	CI-Teacher	"Bullwinkle is a Dope."
C.	CI-Fortune	Bullwinkle is disguised as a fortune-teller.
D.	CI-Fish	Rocky and Bullwinkle find a message in a bottle.

SPECIAL FEATURE INTRODUCTIONS

A.	SF-Lion	Bullwinkle pulls a lion from his hat.
B.	SF-Tiger	Bullwinkle pulls a tiger from his hat.
C.	SF-Rhino	Bullwinkle pulls a rhinoceros from his hat.
D.	SF-Rocky	Bullwinkle pulls Rocky from his hat.
E.	SF-Singer	Bullwinkle misses a high note and gets hit in the face by his formal shirt.
F.	SF-Juggler	Bullwinkle juggles three balls and misses.

ROCKY EPISODE INTROS

A.	REI-1	Bullwinkle falls on clothesline.
B.	REI-2	Bullwinkle falls on an awning.
C.	REI-3	Rocky does a high dive.
D.	REI-4	Rocky and Bullwinkle are mountain climbers.

ROCKY EPISODE CLOSING

A.	Daisy	Rocky and Bullwinkle pop out from sunflowers.

FAIRY TALE INTROS

A.	FTI-1	Giant and dwarf carrying a sign.
B.	FTI-2	Bullwinkle is dressed as a ballerina.
C.	FTI-3	A witch uses her magic wand.

FAIRY TALE CLOSINGS

A.	FTC-1	A dwarf is hit on the head by a sign that says "The End."
B.	FTC-2	A piece of chalk writes "The End" (2 versions—blue or gray background).

PEABODY INTROS

A.	PI-1	March with Cleopatra.
B.	PI-2	Peabody and Sherman use various stages of transportation to enter history.
C.	PI-3	Peabody and Sherman use paintings to enter history.

PEABODY CLOSE
Little street sweeper.

DUDLEY OPENING TITLES
Nell is tied on railroad tracks by Snidely, and Dudley rides by on his horse.

AESOP OPENING TITLES
Aesop chisels his name in granite while the son uses a high-speed drill.

AESOP CLOSE
Same as FTC-2.

BULLWINKLE SHOW OPENING TITLES—PART 1
Neon sign treatment of titles.

BULLWINKLE SHOW OPENING TITLES—Part 2
Shooting the lights on the Bullwinkle neon.

BULLWINKLE EPISODE OPENING TITLES
A. Orchestra leader (Bullwinkle leads a jukebox)
B. Spelling (group of letters finally forms "Bullwinkle")

BULLWINKLE SHOW CLOSING TITLES—Part 1
Neon credits for Peter Piech, Jay Ward, Bill Scott.

BULLWINKLE SHOW CLOSING TITLES—Part 2
Remainder of credits.

MISCELLANEOUS

ROCKY AND BULLWINKLE SAVINGS STAMPS CLUB (Animated promotional film)
VIC DAMONE SPECIAL (Animated—Bullwinkle Bossanova)
BULLWINKLE PUPPET (Live intros [76 filmed items])
BULLWINKLE PUPPET (Station promos [85 filmed items])

FRACTURED FLICKERS—Opening and closing animation.

THE NUT HOUSE—Opening animation, running animated gags featuring Nut House Squirrel, Jet Plane, Chain.

HOPPITY HOOPER—Opening, episode opening, commercial intro (Fillmore hits the TV set), commercial intro (Hoppity asks Fillmore the time), lead-in (Hoppity previews next show), lead-in (Four Hoppity Hoopers appear), show close (Hoppity says it's time to go), closing credits.

GEORGE OF THE JUNGLE—Show opening (George song—long version), George episode opening (George song—short version), Super Chicken episode opening (Super Chicken song), Tom Slick episode opening (Tom Slick song), commercial bridge (Message from Tooki Tooki Bird), commercial bridge (George says "George of Bungle"), commercial bridge (George is wrestling Leon the Lion), lead-in (Ape previews next show).

The Garry Moore Show (CBS, 1966)

Flicker Songs
1. "These Boots are Made for Walkin' "
2. "Strangers in the Night"
3. "The Maine Stein Song"
4. "I See Your Face Before Me"
5. "California, Here I Come"

6. "You Go to My Head"
7. "Hello, Dolly"
8. "Downtown"
9. "Summer Wind"
10. "Wives and Lovers"

Special Animation blackouts
1. Out of Gas
2. Canary
3. Plug
4. Conversation
5. Do You Remember?

Compilation Feature Films

1. *The Crazy World of Laurel and Hardy*
2. *The Vintage W. C. Fields*
3. *Those Marvelous Benchley Shorts*
4. *Buster!* (original title: *The Golden Age of Buster Keaton*)
5. *Three Comedies* (aka *Three Shorts*)
6. *The General*
7. *That's Comedy* (not completed)

Animation for Feature Compilations
1. *The Vintage W. C. Fields*
2. *Those Marvelous Benchley Shorts*

PILOT FILMS

SUPER CHICKEN (1965)
William Conrad: Narrator.
Paul Frees: Eggs Benedict, Fred, Cop.
Bill Scott: Super Chicken (Hunt Strongbird, Jr), Bank Teller.

GEORGE OF THE JUNGLE (1965)—"E FLAT ELEPHANTS"
Hans Conried: Narrator.
Bill Scott: George, Tooki Tooki Bird.
June Foray: Jane, Rosie.
Paul Frees: Charlie, Ape.

HAWKEAR: FRONTIER SCOUT (1969)
Paul Frees: Narrator, Commander, Indian Chief.
June Foray: Mrs. Kincaid.
Bill Scott: Guard, Pierced Arrow.
Daws Butler: Hawkear.

FANG, THE WONDER (?) DOG (1971)
Paul Frees: Narrator, Pa Appleknocker, Policeman #2.
Bill Scott: Grampa Appleknocker, Dog Catcher, Policeman #1, Fireman #1.
Daws Butler: Freddie Appleknocker, Husband, Fireman #2.
June Foray: Wife, Furrier, Customer, Panicking Woman.

RAH! RAH! WOOZY (1980)
(Working title: Woozy State)
Paul Frees: Narrator, Football Announcer, Footballer.

Bill Scott: Morey Mouse, Coach Weepy Mudbank, Crazy Ribs.
Daws Butler: Hamilton Hamster.
June Foray: Cheerleader.

LIVE ACTION PILOTS

THE WATTS GNU SHOW (1959)
Opening—Bill Scott: Announcer #1. Paul Frees: Announcer #2.
Intro—Bill Scott: Watts Gnu.
Reporter—Bill Scott: Byron Line. Paul Frees: Samuel Hopkins.
Take Us Back to the Good Old Days—Bill Scott: Peter Lorre. Paul Frees: Boris Karloff.
Mike Mallat, Public Private Eye—Bill Scott: Mike Mallat. June Foray: Blondie.
The Race—Bill Scott: Clem McClam.
Africa—Paul Frees: Sir Gradely Pentwhistle.
Fashion—Dorothy Scott: Miss Terry Cloth.
What's My Line-Up?—Bill Scott: Watts Gnu. June Foray: Miss Arleen Freen. Joy Terry: Prudence Prunepucker. Paul Frees: Random Punsmith, Rex Carnivore, Stagehand.
Half Shot at Sunrise—Paul Frees: Narrator, Harry, The Brazos Kid. Bill Scott: Singer, Ram. June Foray: Molly.
The No Account Mountie—Dave Fulmer: Nelson. Fran Osborn: Jeanette.
Closing.

Credits—Producers: Jay Ward, Bill Scott. Whips provided by: Simon Legree, Inc. Birdcalls by: Waldo Lydecker. Toupees: The American Doily Corporation. Writers: George Atkins, Chris Hayward. Songs by: Forman Brown, Leon Pober. Musical Director: Bob Thompson. Midnight Oil: American Petroleum Institute. Puppets by: Harry Burnett, Naomi Littell, Malcolm Wilkes. Administrative Assistants: Bill Oberlin, Sam Clayberger. Editors: Jess Papal, Edna Bullock. Miss Gabor's gown: Jenkel of California. Director: Alan Lee, for Consul Films. Orgy Scenes staged by: Flabbey Rents. Executive Producer: Ponsonby Britt, O.B.E. Mr. Britt's Money provided by: the Widows and Orphans Benevolent Fund.

THE NUT HOUSE (1963)
Sketches—Opening, Drop a Bag of Water on a Friend, Viewer's Potpourri Digest, Falcon Monologue, Potpourri, Skydiving, The Nut House Choir, Hollywood Marriages, Nut House Commercials, Mona Lisa, Potpourri, Barge on the Nile, Hello Mom! This Is Your Son Alvin, Closing

Credits—Producer/Director: Charles S. Dubin. Guests flown In by Pep Pills. Writers: Bob Arbogast, George Atkins, Allan Burns, Chris Hayward, Art Keane, Jack Margolis, Hal Parets, Lloyd Turner. Ballets devised and choreographed by Herb Ross. Piano bench courtesy of Ponsonby Britt. Musical director: Jerry Fielding. Choral director: Johnny Mann. Special material: Marty Charnin & Mary Rogers and Jim Rusk. Title music: Fred Steiner. Animation director: Pete Burness. Audience courtesy of: The Old Folks Home. Executive producers: Jay Ward, Bill Scott.

Cast—Andrew Duncan, Don Francks, Fay De Witt, Jane Connell, Len Maxwell, Alan Sues, Adam Keefe, Muriel Landers, Ceil Cabot, Tony Holland, Marilyn Lovell, Mara Lynn, Jack Sheldon, Kathy Kersh.

MISCELLANEOUS TV COMMERCIALS

General Mills

(All feature Rocky and Bullwinkle unless otherwise noted)

Trix	Troubadour, Breakfast Table, Nestlé Quik Offer
Cocoa Puffs	Singer, TV Announcer
Jets	Bicycle Race, Boxer

Wheathearts	Wiggle Picture, Ghost, Balloon Offer (Peabody and Sherman)
Cheerios	Aesop and Son (Two spots), Coloring Book Kit, Bullwinkle's Corner (Three spots—Thanksgiving, Old Mother Hubbard, It's Not That I Don't Trust You William Tell), Casey at the Bat, Pogo Stick, Ballet, Canoe, Pole Vault, Trapeze, Surfboard, Racing Cheerios, Bowling, Judo, Rowing, Wall-Spring, Springboard Diver, Tennis, Bicycle, Barrel Jump, Football, Ice-Skating, Badminton (last 19 feature Bullwinkle only), Silent Movies
Lucky Charms	Thief, Dig (Boris and Natasha)
Frosty O's	Cold Breakfast (Dudley and Nell)
Generic	General Mills billboards (two), Thanksgiving Day Parade promos, ABC-TV *Rocky* show promos (two), NBC-TV *Bullwinkle Show* promos (four)

Miscellaneous Advertisers

Sweets Company	Tootsie Roll billboards (two)
American Chicle	Dentyne billboard
Peter-Paul	Peter-Paul candy billboard
Ideal Toy	Garden of Toys (Rocky and Bullwinkle)
Kenner	Presto Sparkle paint set (Bullwinkle)
Colgate-Palmolive	Soaky bath products (Three with Rocky and Bullwinkle)
Fire Prevention Council	Smokey the Bear (Four with Rocky and Bullwinkle)
Southern California Gas Companies	Your gas range (six spots)
Nielson's All Guernsey Milk	
First Federal Savings	
Generic Used Car Promo	
Associated Grocer Foodmarkets	
The *Fresno Bee* newspaper	
United Bank Check Card	Two spots with Dudley and Nell
Shakey's Pizza	Various TV and radio spots
Bubble-Up	(Live action, not completed)
Burger King	B.K. the Great
Auto Club (two spots-Bullwinkle Puppet)	
Bullwinkle Quiz *Game* (Puppet)	

NBC Promos

Meet the Mess
Statistics Can Be Fun
Moose Reel
Moosylvania Promos
Rocky and His "Fiends"
Who Needs It
He/She
Clyde
Bird
Announcer
Rocky and Bullwinkle Olympic Fund

COMMERCIALS FOR THE QUAKER OATS COMPANY

Note: This list, while comprehensive, is incomplete. The dates listed are production dates only; a commercial listed from late 1968 may not have been seen on TV until early 1970. Some of these commercials were reused with giveaway premium tags added, and a few were unfinished projects. Not noted are revised versions, Canadian versions, or repeats. The list includes Quaker cereal commercials, as well as spots for Quaker's Burry cookie division. Also noted are Ward's Aunt Jemima waffles commercials.

1963 **Cap'n Crunch**—Breakfast on the *Guppy*, Wild Man of Borneo, Sweet, Clock, Little Old Grocer, Cap'n Crunch Sails Again (Industrial film), Singalong with Cap'n Crunch, Foe Below, Crunch's Crunch

1964 **Cap'n Crunch**—Cap'n Crunch's Treasure Chest, Cap'n Crunch at the World's Fair, Cap'n Crunch Sweet Tooth, Mopey Dick, Buried Treasure, The Eskimo, Cap'n Crunch Meets Robinson Crusoe

1965 **Cap'n Crunch**—Great Grain Robbery, Cap'n Crunch and Ponce De León, The Parrot, Jean La Foote, Cap'n Crunch and the Mermaid, Astronaut, Redskin Rumble
Quisp & Quake—Joint Intro, Upside Down Bandits, Giant Saw, Dam Has Busted, Hard Sell, Question, Best, No Time, Roaring Flames, Rock Croc, Switch, Meteor Mites.

1966 **Cap'n Crunch**—Bosun's Whistle, Secret of the Crunch, Baggies, Where's Cap'n Crunch? Sea Dog Takes the Cake, King Neptune, Maneater, Mutiny, My Friend Sea Dog, Ship's Model
Quisp & Quake—Planet Q, Ravening Wolves, Half Bake, Ring Promo, Giant Cave Cat. Excuse Me Fellas (Two versions), Face to Face (Two versions)
Monster Munch—Gorilla

1967 **Cap'n Crunch**—La Foote's Footsies, The Leash, Imprint Set, Munch Box, Cap'n Kid, Airline Sticker, Colonel Krispo, Fort La Foote, Foreign Coins, Iron-On Decals, Colonel Krispo Again, Crunchberry Island, Crunchberry Beast Intro
Quisp & Quake—Roaring Cataract, Dr. Uh-Uh, Dart Target, Quisp to the Rescue, The Shopper, Quake Lends a Hand, Keep the Peace, Double Challenge, Hat Promo, Matchbox Cars (with Cap'n Crunch), Elephant Pass

1968 **Cap'n Crunch**—Shipshake Intro, Mutiny on the Bouncy, Birthday Sweepstakes, The Magic Word, Shipshake Maker, The Duel, Giant Clam, Crunchberry Picker, The Cage, What Is a Crunchberry?, Giant Sea Horse, Firing Squad, Big Tiny, The Shake-In, Shaking Contest, Hungry Lion, Some Like It Hot, Welcome Woody, Seadog Sweepstakes, Travel Stickers, Here Comes Tugboat Granny, Telescope Promo, Tortoise Race
Quisp & Quake—Nutrition Story, Time Bomb, Big Ben, Abdominal Snowman, Subsonic Atomic Car, Opera Star, Mad Ball of Yarn, Lost Dutchman, Daylight Robbery, Space-Quaft & Glowies, New Improved Quake Intro, Adventure Book & Mini-Movie Promo
Aunt Jemima—Waffle Whiffer Intro, How to Catch a Waffle Whiffer, Diving Bell, Sky Diver
Captain Vitamin—Mudderov Pearl, Bill Poster
Frosted Oat Flakes—Desert Bandit, Stampeding Elephant, Fire-Breathing Dragon, Stage Holdup
Scooter Pie Cookies—Jack and the Giant, To a Kid, Glad To (last two are 10-second spots)
Mr. Chips Cookies—Intro
Fudge Town Cookies—The Critters, Won the West, Full of Fudge (last two are 10-second spots)

1969 **Cap'n Crunch**—Pipetruck, The Counterfeiter, Explosive Crunchberry, Peanut Butter Crunch Intro, Shake-a-Baker, Giant Moa, Smedley Makes Tracks, The Big Skate, Frying Dutchman, Lost in the Fog, In the Trunk, Alaskan Wolves, Rustlers, Clear the Decks, The Lagoon Monsoon, There's Cookie Island, Map Painter, Match Box Car Offer, Sumter Fires Again, Barbary Pirates
Scooter Pies—Jack and the Giant, The Wishing Well, Free Wheeling (all with Cap'n Crunch)
Quisp & Quake—The Mine Rescue, Whynchataka Peak, Runaway Missile, The Magnetic Storm, Nosagref (One Word), Cosmic Clouder & Mini-Movie Offer, Matchbox Two, Explorer Kit & Quispmobile (last two with Cap'n Crunch)
Mister E—Light Finger, Caught in the Switch (with Quisp)
Captain Vitaman—Vitaman Intro, Meet the Baron, Meet Milton Burgle
Vitaman the Great—Disappearing Elephant, Big Top
Gauchos Cookies—The Derby, Gauchos P-J, Question (last two are 10-second spots)
Cinnamon Flakes—Booster and Brewster Intro
Crackles—The Merry-Go-Round
Mr. Chips Cookies—More Chocolate, Doctor
Pronto—The Tightrope
Frosted Oat Flakes—Polly, Zoomerang Givewawy
Cinnamon Bear Cereal—Intro, The Climbers

1970 **Cap'n Crunch**—The Berry Pickers, Snap'n Catch, Fingers Finnegan, Super Cars, Forget-Me-Quick, Charging Rhino, Where's Smedley, Poppin' Ships, Balloon Buster, Super Rings
Quisp & Quake—The Quakemobile, The Visitor, Dusted Moon Buster, Timer, Meet Max
King Vitaman—King Vitaman Intro, Intro Teaser, Not So Bright Knight, Castle Surrounded, The Tower, Magni-Viewer, Battering Ram, William the Conker, The Blue Baron, The Wager
Aunt Jemima—Bell Tower

1971 **Cap'n Crunch**—Candy Factory Promo (Two versions), Telephone Booth, Weirdo Sisters, Talking Boxes, Double Crunch, Two into One, The Foggy Don't, Kid's Favorites, Ding Buster, Everybody Smile, No Room, Snagtooth Snelliguster
Quisp & Quake—Vote, Vote No, They Like Me, Save Quake, Quangaroo Intro, Surprise, Simon in the Store, Rain Dance
Aunt Jemima—Haunted House, Abandoned Mine, Rowboat, Hammock
King Vitaman—Wrong Way Sidney, Dragon, The Moat, Sidney Carries the Mall, Candy Factory Promo

1972 **Cap'n Crunch**—Crunching Contest, The Glacier, The Quiz, Even in Fog, Fake Whale, Thirty Seconds Flat, Storm at Sea, Cinnamon Crunch Intro, Look What I Get, Just Zis Once, He Found Out, New Labels, Mohawk, Crunch Muncher
Quisp & Quake—Sudden Hospitality, The Land of One, Great Race, Great Race Directions, Orangeania, Shopping List
Aunt Jemima—French Toast Waffle Whiffer, Wallace Makes Up His Mind, Sure Fooled You

1973 **Cap'n Crunch**—Pirate Kit, Parachute Smedley, Anvil, Smedley Captured, Fire Down Below, The Black Knight, Lightning Bolt, We Got a Problem, Give Me Ze Names, Earphones, Get out of the Galley, I Gotcha Bird
Quisp & Quake—Great Race Final, The Quakealyzer, Leaning Giant, Gronk
Aunt Jemima—Football Team, Balanced Breakfast, Blueberry Waffles, The Side Car, Which One's Wallace?, Jumbo Intro, You Bet Your Beany

1974 **Cap'n Crunch**—Smedley's Broad Jump, C.B.'s Concerto, All Us Sharks, Smedley and the Safe, The Cap'n's Tip, Smedley Skips Rope, Smedley's Record, Sic 'Em C.B., Lucky You, It's a Tie

1975 **Cap'n Crunch**—Punch Crunch Intro, Two Treed, Two Left Feet, Light on His Feet, Two to Tango, The Contest, Breakfast in the Hold, The Chicken, One Nice Thing, On the Table, Sure to Make a Hit, Cereal Flag, New Song

1976 **Cap'n Crunch**—Little Old Lady, Lifeboat, Water Spout, Now Hear This, One Thing in Common, Spanish Galleon, Let My C.B. Go, C.B. on the CB, C.B. the Scientist, C.B. the Engineer, C.B.'s Alarm, Echo Canyon, Thief in the Night, Aha Eee Hee Oho, Midnight Snack, Pirates' Parrot, Haunted Castle, Burger King Promo

1977 **Cap'n Crunch**—The Cliff, Mesa Land, Crunchberry Plucker, The Rajah, Elephant Trappers, On the Dunes, The Circus, The Cage, The Octopus, Rope Trick, Invisible Goo Goo, In Ze Dark, Carlysle Is Missing

1978 **Cap'n Crunch**—You Found Me, Give It Back, Something Better, Melvin, Smedley Comes A-Runnin', I Heard You, Smedley Misses, Fancy Table, Where's the Bear?, Little Kid, Gesundheit, Dancing Package, Lotta Crunch, The Seagull

1979 **Cap'n Crunch**—A Big Kid, Drop In, Blind Man's Buff, What a Plan, Smedley's Pole Vault, Smedley and the Raging River, Funhouse Freddy
Half-sies—Half Moat, Half Tunnel, Rope Trick

1980 **Cap'n Crunch**—C.B. and the Fireflies, If You Are, I Say to Myself, Fun and Games Book Offer, LaFoote Sweepstakes, How You Like Zat, Now You Do, He Show Me, A Good Thing Too, Picture and Paint Set
Half-sies—The Best Half, Field Day, Half Door Half Stairs
Hi-Lo's—Playground; Circus and Ship Shape (Projects, uncompleted)

1981 **Cap'n Crunch**—LaFoote Junior, I Got It, Cap'n Crunch Sweepstakes, C.B. Lights Up, His Favorite Food, Is C.B. Smart?, Brighten Up a Morning. They're Playing My Song, Laughing Pirate, Smedley's Math, C.B. Adrift, Just Asking, LaFoote on the Air, C.B. Photo

1982 **Cap'n Crunch**—How Do Elephants Kiss?, Koko Crunch Intro, How to Find an Elephant, You Believe That?, Smedley and the Cave, Classroom, The Mystery of Crunch Island, Mr. Chockle, Garfingle, Crunch Money Promo
Half-sies—Pole Vault, Umbrella

1983 **Cap'n Crunch**—Wish, Little Pirate, C.B. Has To, Hat Trick, Safe At Last, C.B.'s Shopping Spree, Adventure Sweepstakes, Crunch Island Secret, Two Seconds, Phone Monster, Those Two, Telescope

1984 **Cap'n Crunch**—Mount Crunchmore, Clock-a-Dial, Treasure of Crunch Island, Tickleberry, Weird Wolf, C.B. Movie, Alien, Smedley in the Maze, Crabgrass, C.B. Speaks, Chockle Crunch-Mother, Chockle Crunch-King

GLOSSARY OF ANIMATION TERMS

Animation. General term for the branch of filmmaking which creates the illusion of movement. For the scope of this book, it refers to the traditional studio animation process, chiefly based on character drawings, and involving a number of different people in various creative departments. Much to Jay Ward's chagrin, any actual "animation" on his early shows was strictly in the eye of the beholder.

Animator. The artist responsible for drawings; key animators do the most important (or "extreme") drawings, while the in-between drawings—containing action falling between extreme points of movement—are handled by assistant animators, commonly called "in-betweeners."

Background. The flat painted artwork serving as the setting of a scene (such as a forest) over which the character action drawings, on cels, are individually photographed.

Cel. Abbreviation for celluloid, a thin transparent sheet on which animation drawings are traced in ink (or more recently by a Xerox photocopying process).

Checker. The person responsible for the production stage in which all scene elements are double-checked against exposure sheets for mistakes, before photography commences. The Mexican checkers on Jay Ward's early shows should have been taken out and offered a cigarette and a last wish.

Dailies. Also called "rushes," these are prints of the previous day's shooting which will reveal potential mistakes.

Designer. The studio artist responsible for a cartoon's overall visual look; the designer and director work closely together.

Dialogue. The spoken part of a cartoon sound track, sometimes generically called the narration. The most highly regarded element in Jay Ward's cartoons.

Director. The top creative person working on a cartoon. The director is in charge of the team of artists, to whom he or she conveys how the script will be handled.

Editor. The person who assembles the various scenes and shots, plus sound track elements, into a finished cartoon. Sometimes the sound track will be handled by an assistant "sound editor."

Exposure sheets. Also called "X" sheets: a printed form sheet containing frame-by-frame instructions for the camera department when the completed artwork is ready for photographing. (A frame is a single photo on a strip of film. When projected, there are twenty-four frames of film per second.)

Ink and paint. The department of artists who transfer animation drawings to cels; first the inkers trace the drawings on the front of cels; then the painters apply the colors on the reverse side. More recently superseded by a Xerographic process.

Layout. The essential blueprint for the cartoon. The layout artist, or scene planner, details the background, actions, and camera movements for each scene.

Limited animation. A process which reduces full animation (that is, the lush, flowing, highly detailed motion seen in, for example, Disney cartoons) to the movement of mere key poses and selected parts of a character. A cheaper and much faster form of animation, employed superbly in the 1950s at UPA; until the late 1980s, a sadly wasted art form.

Looping. Replacing a portion of sound track, for reasons of revision, clarity, or foreign language.

Mixing. Combining various sound track, elements (voices, music, sound effects) into a single track, or two tracks. The process, when matching final mix to image, is called "dubbing."

Model sheet. A series of reference drawings for the animators, which show a cartoon character in various angles and positions. Helps ensure consistency from artist to artist.

Moviola. A machine used in production, which contains a small screen and a speaker. It can play back various sound tracks, and is also used by the editor for synchronizing picture and sound in the editing process. Newer flatbed viewers (like the Steenbeck) have superseded older Moviolas.

Pencil test. A film of the animation drawings used to check the flow and timing of a sequence before the ink and paint process begins.

Poses. The extreme drawings of a character's movements (pose-to-pose), later filled in with in-between drawings.

Postproduction. That work which is done following photography, such as editing, laboratory developing and printing, and final dubbing.

Predirection. Predirection of Jay Ward cartoons was performed in Hollywood for the benefit of the Mexican animation team. It involved all steps (storyboard, track reading, design, and layout) prior to the so-called below-the-line work in Mexico City—animation, ink and paint, camera, dubbing, lab.

Producer. The head person, like Jay Ward, responsible for both show and studio administration (budget, overheads, staff, contracts, scheduling). The executive producer credit was often taken by the financing company, as P.A.T. did on the 'Rocky' series.

Production supervisor. Person assisting the producer, in charge of the minutiae of administrative duties. For example, Helen Hanson's role on *George of the Jungle*.

Roughs. The original sketchy animation drawings, later smoothed over by a "cleanup" artist.

Script. The text of a cartoon containing dialogue and visual instructions. Jay Ward's scripts actually looked like mini radio plays.

Sponsor. The advertiser who buys a TV show, paying most of the production costs and network airtime charges, thus exercising some control over the show. In the 1950s it was common for the sponsor to own TV shows, developing them through their advertising agencies (as General Mills did with *Rocky and His Friends* through Dancer-Fitzgerald-Sample). Rising costs led to alternating or cosponsor arrangements, with two advertisers sharing costs. This was often done on a major-minor basis: a half-hour show like *Rocky* contained three commercial minutes; General Mills as the major paid for two minutes and Sweets Company (the minor) paid the remaining one minute. Sponsorship died out in the mid-sixties, being replaced by the more efficient purchasing of minutes and half minutes by participating or individual advertisers.

Storyboard. Before layout, the storyboard is the actual shot-by-shot plan of a film. A storyboard consists of a series of drawings containing captions of the action and sound, arranged in comic-strip fashion.

Track reader. A technician who listens to the dialogue track and measures each vowel and consonant onto exposure sheets (containing frame-by-frame gradations) so that action and sound will be synchronized. Skip Craig performed this task for Jay Ward. After thirty-nine years he's still at it, working on Disney's animated TV shows ("I must have read hundreds of miles of track by now").

Workprint. A print of the film used by the director and editor as a rehearsal for eventual release prints.

BIBLIOGRAPHY

Books

Brasch, Walter M. *Cartoon Monikers: An Insight into the Animation Industry*. Ohio: Bowling Green University Popular Press, 1983.

Bruce, Scott, and Bill Crawford. *Cerealizing America*. Boston: Faber and Faber, 1996.

Cawley, John, and Jim Korkis. *How to Create Animation* Las Vegas: Pioneer Books, 1990.

———. *The Encyclopedia of Cartoon Superstars*. Las Vegas: Pioneer Books, 1990.

———. *Cartoon Confidential*. California: Malibu Graphics, 1991.

Chunovic, Louis. *The Rocky and Bullwinkle Book*. New York: Bantam Books, 1996.

Culhane, Shamus. *Talking Animals and Other People*. New York: St. Martin's Press, 1986.

Dunning, John. *Tune In Yesterday: The Ultimate Encyclopedia of Old-Time Radio*. New Jersey: Prentice-Hall, 1976.

Edwards, R. Scott, and Bob Stobenor. *Cel Magic: Collecting Animated Art*. California: Laughs Unlimited, 1991.

Erickson, Hal. *Television Cartoon Shows: An Illustrated Encyclopedia. 1949–1993*. North Carolina: McFarland & Company, 1995.

Freberg, Stan. *It Only Hurts When I Laugh*. New York: Times Books, 1989.

Grossman, Gary H. *Saturday Morning TV*. New York: Dell Publishing, 1981.

Javna, John. *Cult TV*. New York: St. Martin's Press, 1985.

Lenburg, Jeff. *The Encyclopedia of Animated Cartoons*. New York: Facts on File, 1991.

Maltin, Leonard. *Of Mice and Magic*. New York: McGraw-Hill, 1980; revised 1987 by Plume-N.A.L.

Peary, Gerald and Danny Peary (Editors). *The American Animated Cartoon*. New York: Dutton, 1980.

Rovin, Jeff. *The Illustrated Encyclopedia of Cartoon Animals*. New York: Prentice-Hall Press, 1991.

Solomon, Charles. *Enchanted Drawings: The History of Animation*. New York: Alfred A. Knopf, 1989.

Woolery, George. *Children's Television: The First 35 Years. 1946–1981*. Metuchen, N.J.: Scarecrow Press, 1983.

Magazine Articles

Adler, Dick. "Fat Is Beautiful!" *TV Guide*, November 6, 1971.

Amory, Cleveland. "And Now, a Brief Message." *TV Guide*, August 18, 1971.

Bayles, Soni. "First Person—Bill Scott." *California Living*, December 2, 1984.

Beck, Roger. "Bullwinkle: The Moose with the Most." *TV-Radio Mirror*, January 1962.

Butler, Daws. "Creating Radio Drama for Today's Listeners." *The Commercial Actor*, Vol. 2, #33 March 1977.

———. "How to Be an Impersonator." *Radio Life*, February 9, 1951.

Carlson, Bruce. "Bullwinkle: the Minnesota Connection." *Minne Hal Hal*, Volume 4, #1, 1991.

Cawley, Jr., John. "A Hound Called Huckleberry." *Starlog* (undated)

Cohen, Karl. "Animation Made for Kid's TV before Crusader Rabbit." *Animatrix#5* 1989.

———. "The Origins of TV Animation: Crusader Rabbit and Rocky and Bullwinkle." *Animatrix #4* 1987–88.

———. "The Influence of Crusader Rabbit on Ruff and Reddy." *Animatrix#5*, 1989.

———. "The Jay Ward Studio: An Appreciation." *Animation*, Fall 1989.

Cox, Raymond H. "Out of Sight, but Not Out of Mind." *TV Collector Vol. 2, #37* July–August 1988.

Davis, Erik. "Rock and Bull." *Village Voice*, August 7, 1990.

Dorf, Shel. June Foray Interview. *Comics #54*, 1988.

Etcheverry, Paul. Bill Scott interview. *Animania*, 1982

Evanier, Mark. "Daws Butler Dies at 71." *Comics Buyers Guide #760*, June 10, 1988.

Farber, Jim. "Rock Lives." *Entertainment Weekly*, February 8, 1991.

Fuerst, Jeffrey. "The New Cult Status of Rocky and Bullwinkle." *Animation*, Spring 1988.

Fury, David. "The Fat Man Is Back." *Movie Collectors' World #325*, September 15, 1989.

Gray, Milt. Daws Butler Interview. *Funnyworld #18*, 1978.
Gray, Milton. June Foray interview. *Funnyworld #18*, 1978.
Hurtz, Bill. "Bill Scott." *Cartoonist Profiles*, 1978.
Kaiser, Robert Blair. "Who Said Talk's Cheap?" *TV Guide*, May 13, 1972.
Kaplan, David A. "A Moose for All Seasons." *Newsweek*, March 18, 1991.
Korkis, Jim. Bill Scott interview. *AniMato*, 1990.
———. Bill Scott interview. *Filmfax*, 1995.
Lowry, Brian. "Daws Butler: The Master's Voice." *Starlog*, March 1987.
Mallory, Michael. "The Woman Behind the Squirrel." *Comics Scene #13*: (undated).
Maltin, Leonard. "TV Animation: The Decline and Pratfall of a Popular Art." *Film Comment*, January-February 1975.
———. Hans Conried interview. *Film Fan Monthly*, 1970.
McCrohan, Donna. "Rocky and Bullwinkle." *TV Gold*, 1986.
Patten, Fred. "Two and a Half Carrots Tall." *Comics Scene*, 1981.
Scott, Bill. "The Case for Animated TV Spots." *Broadcasting*, August 15, 1960.
Stumpf, Charles K. "The Great Gildersleeve and Walter Tetley." *The World of Yesterday, #13*, October 1977.
Thingvall, Joel. "Jay Ward and Friends." *Mediascene #21*, September-October 1976.
Tomashoff, Craig. "The Moose Is on the Loose." *Tower Video Collector*, February/March 1991.
Williams, Martin. "A Purple Dog, a Flying Squirrel, and the Art of Television." *Evergreen Review*, 1961.
Wilmot, Judy. "The Voice of Bullwinkle." *Stop #3*, 1982.
(Unsigned). "Bill Scott at UCLA." *Animatrix #3*: Fall 1986.
(Unsigned). Paul Frees interview. *The Commercial Actor*, 1978.
(Unsigned). "Of Moose and Men." *Newsweek*, December 4, 1961.
(Unsigned). "Jay Ward: Vidiot's Delight." *Playboy*, August 1963.
(Unsigned). Article on June Foray. *Radio Life*, July 1, 1945.
(Unsigned). Article on June Foray. *Radio Life*, March 17, 1946.
(Unsigned). Article on June Foray. *Radio Life*, June 15, 1947.
(Unsigned). Article on June Foray. *Radio Life*, February 29, 1948.
(Unsigned). Article on June Foray. *Radio Life*, April 13, 1951.
(Unsigned). Article on Paul Frees. *Radio Life*, October 31, 1948.
(Unsigned). Article on Paul Frees. *Radio Life*, December 1, 1950.
(Unsigned). Article on William Conrad. *Radio Life*, October 26, 1947.
(Unsigned). Article on William Conrad. *Radio Life*, June 27, 1948.
(Unsigned). "A Bullwinkle Bonanza." *TV Guide*, March 16, 1991.
(Unsigned). "Bullwinkle vs. NBC." *TV Guide*, August 11, 1962.
(Unsigned). "Cannon Keeps on the Run." *TV Week* (Australia), August 9, 1975.
(Unsigned). "He Plays Conried to the Hilt." *TV Guide*, August 31, 1963.
(Unsigned). "The Horns of Bullwinkle's Dilemma." *TV Guide*, January 20, 1962.
(Unsigned). "The Accent's on Versatility." *TV Guide*, April 23, 1960.
(Unsigned). April Fool's Day Supplement, *TV Guide*, April 1, 1963.
(Unsigned). Daws Butler article. *TV Guide* (undated, circa 1962).

Newspaper Articles

Austin, John. "You Never See Her." *National Enquirer*, January 28, 1968.
Bazemore, Robert. "Paul 'The Voice' Is Seen Back Home." *Lerner Newspapers*, November 6, 1962.
Beck, Andee. "Of Moose and Men." *The News Tribune*, February 18, 1991.
Bender, Harold. "Building a Better Moosetrap." *Pictorial TView*, February 25, 1962.
Cames, Del. "Bullwinkle Creator Welcomes Lawsuits." *Denver Post*, February 7, 1964.
Carroll, Jerry. "A Voice That's Money in the Bank." *San Francisco Chronicle*, February 5, 1980.
Champlin, Charles. "His Yogi Bear Voice Leaves Lasting Imprint." *Los Angeles Times*, May 20, 1988.
Christon, Lawrence. "Days of Wine and Bullwinkle." *Los Angeles Times*, November 13, 1988.

Conrad, William. "Confessions of a Plump Private Eye." *Los Angeles Times*, 1972.
Downing, Jim. "All Those Mayors Were So Courteous." *Tulsa Tribune*, November 22, 1962.
Elliot, Jack. "Jay Ward Reveals . . . The Perils of Producing." *Sunday Star-Ledger*, November 25, 1962.
Fanucchi, Kenneth. "Can't Place the Face, but the Voice Is Sure Familiar." *Los Angeles Times*, October 10, 1976.
———. Folkart, Burt A. "Paul Frees, Man of Many Voices, Dies."*Los Angeles Times*, November 6, 1986.
Daws Butler obituary. *Los Angeles Times*, May 20, 1988.
Hellman, Jack. "Light and Airy." *Daily Variety*, August 12, 1965.
Houser, John G. "What's the Score."*Daily Variety*, May 3, 1961.
Kaplan, David A. "Rocky and Bullwinkle Brave the Comeback Trail." *New York Times*, May 7, 1989.
Kleiner, Dick. "You Hear Voice, Seldom See Face." *The (Gainesville) Times*, August 13, 1964.
Knapp, Dan. "Frees and His Poster People." *Los Angeles Times*, November 28, 1970.
Krier, Beth Ann. "Wackiest Trading Post on the Strip." *Los Angeles Times*, February 17, 1972.
McDonnell, John. "A 30-Year Career as the Audio Portion of Show Business." *Los Angeles Herald Examiner*, April 27, 1975.
Mount, Jenny. "Rocky Redux: Bullwinkle and Friends Ride Again." *The Blade*, March 10, 1991.
Paynter, Susan. "Iss Moose and Squirrel." *Seattle Post-Intelligencer*, March 4, 1991.
Phillips, Pat. "Heard, Not Seen, Is Key to June's Record Success." *The Citizen-News*, March 18, 1961.
Purcelli, Mario. "A Voice Yes—An Ego, No." *Times-Chicago*, November 1962.
Reining, Paul. "Man Who Can't Draw Straight Line." *The National Tattler*, October 22, 1972.
Reynolds, Janet. "Of Moose and Men." *The Hartford Advocate*, March 7, 1991.
Rosenthal, Phil. "PBS Pulls Gem Out of Hat with 'Of Moose and Men.' " *(Los Angeles) Daily News*, March 11, 1991.
Scott, Jim. "Rocky's Best Friend—Jay Ward." *(Berkeley) Daily Gazette*, October 17, 1960.
Simons, Jeannie. "Careers Are a Lot of Talk." *The Plain Dealer*, February 27, 1968.
Smith, Cecil. "Conrad Finds His Niche in Cannon." *Los Angeles Times*, 1971.
Solomon, Charles. "Bullwinkle: Still Amoosing at 25." *Los Angeles Times*, November 8, 1984.
———. "A Gleeful Tribute to Rocky and Bullwinkle." *Los Angeles Times*, March 12, 1991.
———. "The Animator's Animator." *Los Angeles Times*, December 8, 1985.
Stern, Fredric. "Bill Scott of Tujunga: Life Isn't Rocky for Bullwinkle Anymore." *Los Angeles Times* (undated).
Sullivan, Elizabeth. "Moose on the Loose." *Boston Globe*, September 24, 1961.
Tepper, Ron. "Moose with the Moosetest." *Free Press, Detroit*. October 8, 1961.
Wloszczyna, Susan. "Rocky Moose-tique." *USA Today*, February 8, 1991.
(Unsigned). "An Invisible Star." *The American*, April 30, 1961.
(Unsigned). "Paul Frees: TV's Insurance Policy." *Los Angeles Herald Examiner*, March 3, 1963.
(Unsigned). "Man of Many Voices." *Pittsburgh Press*, November 1962.
(Unsigned). "J. Ward Can't Do Wrong." *Southern California Teamster Journal*, January 19, 1972.

Special Sources

Files, tapes and business correspondence donated by Bill Scott.
Correspondence donated by Leonard Key, George Atkins and others.
Original scripts by Daws Butler for his workshop; "What is a Daws Butler?"—his potted autobiography; workshop notes to students.
ABC Publicity Features, "Invisible TV Star of *Rocky and His Friends* makes money talking to Herself," September 21, 1960.
L. A. County Museum of Art program notes for "remembering Bill Scott," May 31, 1986.
Bill Scott studio autobiography, written in 1960.
"The Giant with the Beer Can" (magazine article draft by Bill Scott) 1960.
Ludwig Von Drake—New Disney star (Walt Disney Publicity).

Paul Frees memorial service, by June Foray, November 7, 1986.
Bill Scott memorial service, tape December 1985.
Jay Ward memorial service, tape October 1989.
Articles and tapes donated by Daws Butler, Corey Burton, Charles Ulrich, Mark Kausler, Ray Cox and David Mruz.
Artwork donated by Bill Hurtz, Bill Scott, Bob Mills, Alex Anderson and others.

Index

ABC, 52, 70, 85, 88, 92, 141, 148, 160, 164, 167–68, 234, 242, 261–62, 302, 304
  censorship by, 154, 155
Action for Children's Television (ACT), 253, 297
"Aesop and Son," 121, 139, 143, 146, 147, 149, 150, 151–57, 161, 168, 176, 191, 236, 242, 394–96
Allen, Chris, xix, 235, 345
Allman, Sheldon, 266, 268
Anderson, Alex, 5, 10–32, 46, 61, 65, 73, 76, 168, 241, 285, 291, 292–93, 302, 304, 308, 313
  background of, 7–10
  Crusader Rabbit and, 14–24, 26–29, 115, 278, 283
Atkins, George, 3, 72, 99, 108, 117, 121, 122, 166–67, 214, 217, 260, 287, 297, 324–25
  Fractured Flickers and, 224, 225, 230, 231, 232
  on Ward, 281, 282, 290
Aubrey, James T., 259
Avery, Tex, 13, 38–39, 51, 96, 117

Bagnall, George, 29, 58n
Baker, Bruce, 244, 246
Baldwin, Gerald, 84, 86, 87, 88, 236, 260, 281, 328–29
Barbera, Joe, 29
Bastian, Bob, 15
"B Boys, The," 61, 63
Beck, Roger, 190–91
Bemiller, Bob, 15, 29–30
Benchley, Robert, 299, 300–301
Bender, Harold, 191
Berkeley Gazette, 6n, 149–50
Blanc, Mel, 45, 51–52, 134
Bliss, Lucille, 11–12, 15–16, 26
Bonsall, Shull, 25, 30, 58n, 59, 136, 283, 288
  Crusader Rabbit and, 27–28, 29
Boris and Natasha, xvi, 51, 106–107, 109–11, 114–15, 123–24, 144, 145–46, 154–55, 191, 194, 205, 238, 239–40, 241, 260, 314

Boris and Natasha, 312n
Bowen, Jerry, 15
"Box Tops Robbery" caper, 135–36, 137, 147, 156–57
Brandy, Howard, 53, 166, 175, 176–77, 192, 194–200, 204, 219, 223, 227, 229, 282, 283, 286, 344–45
Brown, Forman, 99
Bubble-Up, 299
Buffalo Billy, 40
Bugs Bunny Show, The, 135, 159, 234
Bullwinkle Coloring Book, 211
Bullwinkle comic strip, 193–94, 260
Bullwinkle J. Moose, xv, 30, 31, 106, 109, 123, 124, 214, 223, 238, 260, 269, 273, 302
  origins of, 21, 32
  statue of, 176–77, 178, 288–89
  voice of, 47, 48, 144, 309
"Bullwinkle's Corner," 72, 73, 84n, 88, 122–25, 141, 148, 158, 161, 204, 385–89
  "Mr. Know-It-All," 123, 124, 148, 164–65, 193
  poetry, 122–24
  "The Rocky and Bullwinkle Fan Club," 123, 124, 204n
Bullwinkle's Family Food 'n' Fun Restaurants, 308–309
Bullwinkle Show, The, xxi, 3, 31, 123, 124, 142, 159–61, 164, 166–89, 238–42, 246, 278, 302, 310, 416
  audience for, 4, 165
  Bullwinkle puppet, 41, 185–87, 189, 206–208
  critical reaction to, 184–85, 187–88
  "Dudley Do-Right of the Mounties," *see* "Dudley Do-Right of the Mounties"
  lawsuits, 181–82, 188
  premiere of, 175–76, 185
  promotion of, 166–67, 175–80, 187, 192–204, 208–209, 212–14
  reruns of, 234, 242, 302
Burness, Pete, 87, 95–96, 137, 149, 217, 235, 236, 247, 248, 326–27
Burns, Allan, 2, 166–67, 198, 216–17, 226, 273, 293, 294, 310, 316–17
  George of the Jungle and, 259–60
  Quaker Oats commercials and, 244, 245–46, 248
  on Ward, 280, 283, 289, 290
Burton, Corey, xix, xx, xxi, 308, 309
Butler, Daws, xviii–xx, 40, 41, 50–53, 118, 134, 153–58, 247, 248, 254, 264, 271, 295, 307
  profile of, 119–21

Canada Dry, 58, 59, 60, 62
Cannon, Bobe, 43, 159
Capitol Records, 51–52, 57, 113, 118
Cap'n Crunch, 120, 121, 190, 204, 243, 244, 245–48, 250–54, 295, 301
"Captain Cutlass," 297
Captain Peter "Wrongway" Peachfuzz, 107, 112, 114, 145, 183, 205–206
Carlin, Roger, 47, 62, 64, 66, 69, 71, 100–101
"Carrots and King," 58–59, 70
Carrots and the King, 97
CBS, 43, 52, 208, 214–18, 259, 272, 273
Censorship and interference by sponsor, ad agency, and network, 129, 132, 135–36, 137, 146–48, 153, 154–57, 173–74, 183–84, 187, 188, 189, 191, 206–10
Charrow, Fred, 58
Chauncey and Edgar, 107, 112, 238
Cheerios commercials, 124, 157, 187, 211, 244, 260
Chicago Sun-Times, 266–67
Christon, Lawrence, 279
Clampett, Bob, 39, 40, 268, 288
Clayberger, Sam, 58, 93, 94, 298, 331–32
"Clobbered Classics," 133
Cocoa Marsh, 59–60, 62
Cohen, Karl, 11, 12, 125, 304
Columbia University, 213–14

Colvig, Pinto, 52
Comic Strips of Television, The, 10–14
Compton Advertising Agency, 244, 245–46, 247
Comstock, Frank, 74, 133, 336
Conrad, Bill, xx, 50, 54–57, 176, 247, 248, 258
background of, 54–56
"doubling" by, 56, 145, 183
narration of, 49, 54, 56–57, 108, 169, 181, 258, 314
Conried, Hans, 45, 176, 204, 233n, 291, 311
Fractured Flickers and, 158, 171, 172, 222n, 225–26, 229, 232, 233
profile of, 171–72
voices of, 56, 158, 168, 170–72, 235, 237
Cornell, Sam, 309
"Cosgrove the Magician," 133
Coughlan, Russ, 12
Craig, Skip, xx, 58, 60, 61, 72n, 80, 91, 96, 98, 121, 133, 173, 174, 220, 223, 235, 248, 254–55, 273, 274, 294, 297–301, 339–40
The Bullwinkle Show and, 177, 178, 182, 194–96
Fractured Flickers and, 225–33
George of the Jungle and, 259–60, 266, 270, 271–72
The Nut House and, 215, 216
on Ward, 282–90, 307–309, 312
Crazy World of Laurel and Hardy, The, 274–75
Critchfield, Jimmy, 232, 233, 235, 260, 273, 292, 295, 298, 299, 309, 323–24
on Ward, 284–85, 286–87, 291
Crusader Rabbit, 6, 14–30, 41, 62, 115, 283, 288, 301, 355–56
creation of, 9, 10–11
revival of, 26–30, 47, 58n, 59, 119
Culhane, Shamus, 44, 45, 63
Culhane Productions, Shamus, 43, 44–45, 47, 58
Curtin, Joe, 19

Daily Variety, 16, 147
Dancer-Fitzgerald-Sample (D-F-S), 161, 284
Hoppity Hooper and, 234
Rocky and His Friends and *The Bullwinkle Show* and, 63, 65, 71, 76, 82, 85–89, 91, 92, 94, 96, 98, 129, 130, 135–39, 143, 146–48, 155–57, 164–65, 167–68, 172, 174, 182, 189, 201, 209, 242
Davis, Arthur, 37–38
Daws Butler: Voice Magician, 53
Desilu Productions, 218, 228
Diamond, Adrienne, 334
Disney, 8, 15, 34, 36, 50, 51, 55, 137, 162, 245, 262, 272, 308, 311–12, 314
Dobkin, Larry, 45
Donley, Roger, 226, 272, 340
Douglas, Jack, 203
Dranko, Bob, 94
Driscoll, Don, 27
Dubin, Charles S., 216
Dudley Do-Right and His Friends, 242
"Dudley Do-Right of the Mounties," 10, 12–13, 23, 117, 133–34, 153, 168–75, 188, 191, 204, 225, 233, 236, 304, 314, 396–98
Dudley Do-Right of the Mounties (film), 312n, 314
Dudley Do-Right's Emporium, xx, 72n, 295, 298, 305–306, 307
Duncan, Phil, 67, 250, 299

Eastman, Phil, 41, 42, 73
"Elementary, My Dear Rocky," 302
Etcheverry, Paul, 34, 37

Faillace, Sal, 140, 150, 161, 168, 204, 334–35
Fairbanks, Jerry, 14–15, 16, 17, 20, 24–25, 27, 38, 44, 342
Fang, The Wonder (?) Dog, 296–97, 420
Farnon, Dennis, 158, 160, 177, 225, 232–33, 236, 338–39

Fern, Dave, 131, 140
Fielding, Jerry, 216, 274
Fields, W. C., 275, 289, 299, 300, 306, 308
Fields, W. C., Jr., 274
Fleischer, Max, 34, 73
"Flicker Songs," 273, 301
Flinstones, The, 135, 159, 160, 163, 164, 235
Flynn, Joe, 252
Foray, June, xviii–xxi, 2, 39, 50, 134, 176, 186, 192–93, 222, 255, 308, 311
  background of, 51–52
  voices of, 2, 49, 52–53, 118–21, 145–46, 157, 170, 225, 246, 247–48, 252, 309
Foshko, Alan, 175, 196, 202–203, 212, 213, 218–23, 343–44
Four Star, 43, 47
"Fractured Fairy Tales," 3, 53, 72, 73, 74, 85, 88, 90, 92, 117–22, 126, 135–36, 139, 143, 146, 147, 148, 149, 151, 154, 155, 156, 158, 164, 168, 189, 191, 204, 236, 242, 301, 304, 306, 314, 379–85
Fractured Flickers, 135, 161, 163, 167, 172, 190, 211, 224–33, 246, 257, 262, 285, 294, 410–15, 416–17
  publicity for, 218–23
Freberg, Stan, 20, 39, 40n, 41, 45, 51, 52, 112, 113, 118, 243
Freeman, Donald, 138, 185
Frees, Paul, xviii–xx, 45, 56, 134, 186, 254, 307, 308
  background of, 49–50
  death of, 311
  voices of, 49, 50–51, 53, 54, 99, 110, 128–29, 132, 144–45, 146, 158, 169, 170, 225, 232, 235, 237, 240, 247, 258, 262–65, 268, 272, 288
Freleng, Friz, 307
Frostbite Falls Far-Flung Flier, The, 311, 312n
Frostbite Falls Review, The, 21–22, 45–46
Fuerst, Jeffrey, 311
Fuson, Chuck, 15, 23

Gamma Productions, 141, 146, 149, 150, 151, 157, 160, 161, 166, 168, 174, 176, 204, 211, 235, 236, 256–58
Ganon, Bob, 20, 28, 29, 136, 148
Gardiner, Reginald, 137
Garry Moore Show, The, 233, 273
General Mills, 244, 260, 284, 421–22
  Hoppity Hooper and, 234, 235, 236, 256
  Rocky and His Friends and *The Bullwinkle Show* and, 63, 65–71, 75–78, 85, 91, 92, 96, 97, 104, 120, 130–31, 132, 134, 137, 139, 141, 143, 146, 147–48, 150–54, 156, 159, 160, 166, 174–75, 178–80, 182, 188, 189, 191, 192, 201, 209, 242
  Watts Gnu pilot and, 211
George of the Jungle, 67, 171–72, 238, 257, 259–72, 278, 294, 295, 312, 417, 420
"George of the Jungle," 259–60, 261–66, 269, 271–72, 304–306, 406–407
George of the Jungle (film), 272, 314
Gerald McBoing-Boing, 41, 43, 55, 118, 127, 171
Gleason, Jimmy, 35
Glossary of animation terms, 426–27
Gloyd and Gidney, 107
Goodman, Hal, 18
Gourley, Bud, 69, 80, 90
Grade, Lew, 227
Graves, Peter, 252
Gray, Milton, 52
Green Chritma, 113
Grossman, Gary, 17, 253
Gruver, Bernie, 72–73, 80, 93

"Hamhock Jones," 11, 12
Hanan, David, 72

Hanna, William, xix, 26–27, 29
Hanna-Barbera Productions, xix, xx, 17, 43, 60, 84–85, 90, 95, 97, 100, 119, 120, 158, 163, 164, 235, 245, 271
founding of, 29
Happy Hooper, 59
Harrison, Rich, 272, 300
Harvard Graduate School of Business, 6, 85, 213, 279
Harvey, Paul, 266
Hawkear, Frontier Scout, 295–96, 420
Hayward, Chris, 41, 50, 133, 134, 170, 178, 197–98, 220, 235, 239, 243, 267, 273, 288, 289, 292, 294, 317–19
Crusader Rabbit and, 29
Fractured Flickers and, 224–29, 232
The Nut House and, 214
Rocky and His Friends and *The Bullwinkle Show* and, 73, 111, 124, 126, 127–28, 145, 151, 153, 168–69, 172, 173, 174, 190, 205
on Ward, 280, 290–91, 291
Watts Gnu and, 99
Hayward, Linda (née Simmons), 54, 194, 224, 227, 232, 235, 243, 245, 266, 282–83, 287–88, 289, 292
Heffernan, Harold, 230–31
Henning, Barbara, 218
Henry, Bob, 61
Hilberman, Dave, 59n
Hiltz, Jim, 84, 86, 87, 95–96, 225, 272, 301, 329–30
Hollywood Reporter, The, 56, 167
Hoppity Hooper, 135, 149, 150, 161, 167, 171, 234–38, 256, 417
"Hoppity Hooper," 133–34, 142, 398–406
Horton, Edward Everett, 118, 126, 164, 229, 344
Hotchkiss, Charles, 63, 66, 81, 90, 94, 167–68
Houser, Dwight, 182
Hubley, John, 36, 41, 243
Humphrey, Pat, 199
Hursh, Frank, 87, 89, 140
Hurtz, Bill, 7, 23, 35–41, 45, 55, 67, 73–74, 79, 104, 122, 130, 146, 159, 200–202, 202, 235–36, 242, 245, 248, 250, 252, 254, 258, 260, 271, 300, 301, 309, 310, 311, 325–26
Fractured Flickers and, 225
George of the Jungle and, 262, 266, 271
Mexican operations and, 81–84, 86–87, 88–89, 91, 92–93, 94, 131
on Ward, 281, 282, 283, 284, 285, 287, 292, 295, 297–98
Hurwood, Bernhardt, 133
Hyams, Joe, 161

Independent Television Corporation, 227–28
Ising, Rudy, 34–35, 37
Jamieson, Doug, 246
Jam Session, 60–61, 64
Jay Ward Productions, *see* Ward Productions, Jay
"Jay Ward Productions Workshop," 158–59
Jay Ward's Intergalactic Film Festival, 274, 301–302
Jenkyns, Chris, 59, 72, 121, 153, 170, 227, 235, 298, 311, 322–23
Johnson, Gordon, 71, 76, 77, 85, 86, 87–88, 89, 90, 91, 94, 96, 100, 104, 123, 130, 131, 137, 138, 141, 143, 147, 148, 164, 174, 178, 189, 201–202
Johnson, Harry, 246
Johnson, Russ, 14, 25
Jones, Chuck, xx, 37, 250
Jones, Franky, 284
Julian, Paul, 93
Jurovich, Dan, 131

Kai, Sam, 257
Kanter, Albert, 64
Kay, Monte, 60
Keaton, Buster, 226–27, 299–300, 306

Keene, Art, 231
Keller, Lew, 5, 173, 238, 248, 285, 286, 287, 288, 295, 304, 309, 310, 327
Kennedy, John F., 199, 216, 223, 230
Key, Leonard, 14, 20, 26, 27, 28, 29, 31, 77–78, 100, 130, 282, 299, 341–42
  Rocky and His Friends and, 47–48, 58, 59, 60, 61, 62–63, 65–66, 69, 71, 75–76, 77
  sales for Ward Productions, 97, 98, 133, 141
Key, Ted, 61, 70, 100, 125, 126, 192, 341
Kilgore, Al, 195, 211
Kimball, Charlie, 91, 174
King Leonardo and His Short Subjects, 160–61, 256–57
King Vitamin, 252
Kinney, Jack, 48
Kirby, Durward, 181–82, 188
"Kirward Derby," 112, 181–82, 188, 201
Knotts, Don, 134, 268, 269
Knox-Reeves agency, 146
Korkis, Jim, 36, 39, 42, 67, 71, 235, 307
Kurtz, Bob, 312

Lah, Mike, 27, 252
Lantz, Walter, 51
Laugh-In, 215, 216, 217
Lee, Alan, 99
Leeds, Peter, 45
Levy, Al, 76–77
"Lighter Side of American History, The," 301
Lilly, Lou, 39
Limited animation, 8–9, 16, 17–18, 262
Littlejohn, Bill, 23, 67, 250
Livingstone, Alan, 51–52
"Lone Masked Man, The," 297
Los Angeles Times, 7, 248, 279, 290, 310
Louden, Vern, 12

McDonald, Tom, 73, 81
McElmurray, Chuck, 93
MacGeorge, Jim, 268, 273
McKenna, Bernadine, 155
McLaren, Norman, 62n
McNamara, Don, 27
Magic of Christmas, The, 142
Maltin, Leonard, 4, 128, 249, 250
Manriquez, Carlos, 74, 80, 88–89
Marshall, John, 272
Martine, Ted, 15
Martinez, Jesus, 79, 88
Mason, James, 42, 227
Mason, Ken, 244n, 246, 248, 254, 285
Mazursky, Paul, 214
MCA, 163, 191, 313
Melendez, Bill, 73
Merchandising, 72, 123, 148, 167, 187, 201, 204n, 211, 244, 246, 261, 295, 305–306, 307, 313, 314
MGM, 34, 50, 51, 96
Miles, Sylvia, 203, 223
Miller, Marvin, 134
Mills, Bob, 15, 23, 62, 335–36
Mishkin, Lee, 15
Mr. Big, 112, 144
Mr. Magoo, 41, 63
Mr. Magoo, 135
Mitchell, Whitney, 294
Monroe, Phil, 35, 36, 37, 41, 81
Montell, Joe, 96, 204, 257
Moore, Gary, 272–73, 275
Moose-a-Rama, 242
Morita, Roy, 58, 333
Mother's Records and Snarf Company, 275
Mruz, David, 21

Nagurski, Bronko, 21, 241
Natasha, *see* Boris and Natasha
Natwick, Grim, 15
NBC, 78, 130, 153
  Bullwinkle Show on, 130, 142, 159, 160, 161, 167–89, 206–10, 238, 242
  Crusader Rabbit and, 14, 16, 17, 21, 24–25

Neufeld, Rosen, Bash & Associates, 142, 160
New Bullwinkle Show, The, 304–307
Newton, Dwight, 147, 154, 176
Nichols, Luther, 5–6, 281, 285
Nickelodeon's "Nick at Nite," 242, 312
Nuthouse, The (film), 301
Nut House, The (pilot), 214–18, 233, 257, 259, 272, 273, 301, 421
Nye, Louis, 134

Oberlin, Bill, 177, 178, 288–89
"Officer, You Dropped Your Purse," 272
Of Moose and Men, 283
O'Hara, Betty, 143
Oleson, Robert, 15
Ossininkle, John, 193
Owens, Gary, 53, 266

Paramount, 38–39, 51, 97
Parmelee, Ted, 42, 73, 80, 92, 94, 327–28
Parnes, Paul, 158
Patten, Fred, 14, 18, 23, 27, 136
"Peabody's Improbable History," xvi, 70, 72, 84n, 88, 92, 94, 125–29, 140, 141, 146, 149, 151, 153, 154, 155–56, 158, 161, 389–93
  attempted censorship of, 129, 132, 137
Phineas T. Phox, Adventurer, 44–45, 63
Piech, Peter, 65, 66, 70, 101, 111, 114, 130, 141, 160, 182, 192, 193, 201, 204, 211, 233, 242, 256, 258, 308, 342–43
  financing of *Rocky* series, 62, 63–64, 72, 76, 77
"Piper's Show, The," 132–33
Plattes, Cy W., 65, 123, 166, 174–75, 178, 192, 193
Playhouse Pictures, 43, 47
Pober, Leon, 99
"Prince Fred," 272
Probert, George, 298
Producer's Associates of Television (P.A.T.), 47, 62, 64, 65, 69–77, 84, 91, 100, 122, 146, 148, 182, 193, 204, 238, 260, 284, 311
Publicity, 161–64, 175–80, 187, 190–204, 208–209, 212–14, 282–83
  "Coney Island Film Festival," 218–23, 228, 279
  "Moose's Day Parade," 202–204
  "Moosylvania" statehood, 196–202, 246
  "Operation Loudmouth," 166–67

Quaker Oats commercials, 67, 121, 195, 237, 243–55, 257, 261, 272, 284, 294, 295, 298, 307, 423–25
  Cap'n Crunch, *see* Cap'n Crunch
Quartet Films, 43, 63
Quisp & Quake commercials, 172, 248–50, 251

Radio-TV Daily, 200
"Ragnar the Chicken," 297
Rah Rah Woozy, 304, 420–21
Ray, Gerry, 11, 12, 13, 15, 18, 19, 23, 25, 80, 81, 95–96, 136–37, 328
RCA, 29, 58n
Reed, Alan, 235
Rivera, Tony, 94
Roach, Hal, 273, 275
"Rocky and Bullwinkle," 3, 4, 41, 56–57, 72, 78–81, 84n, 88, 92, 94, 103, 105–16, 135–36, 141, 144–46, 149, 151, 152, 154–55, 201–202, 204, 205, 211, 239–42, 246, 258, 303, 304, 305, 311, 356–79
Rocky and Bullwinkle & Friends, 314
Rocky and Bullwinkle Movie, The, 314
Rocky and His Friends, 15, 17, 31, 65–158, 182, 191, 278, 284, 297, 415–16
  "Aesop and Son," *see* "Aesop and Son"

Rocky and His Friends (*continued*)
audience for, 3, 4, 132, 138, 143, 147, 161–63
Boris and Natasha, *see* Boris and Natasha
budget for, 65–66, 70, 73, 84–85, 85, 89, 90, 96, 131, 141, 148, 284
"Bullwinkle's Corner," *see* "Bullwinkle's Corner"
censorship of, *see* Censorship and interference by sponsor, ad agency, and network
"Fractured Fairy Tales," *see* "Fractured Fairy Tales"
Mexico studio, *see* Val-Mar Productions
naming of, 71
"Peabody's Improbable History," *see* "Peabody's Improbable History"
pilot for, 46, 47, 48–49, 57–65, 150
premiere of, xv, 1–2, 91, 96, 101–102
puns and wordplay, xvii, 109, 113–14, 126, 151, 164
reruns, 164, 167–68, 211
reviews of, 103–104
"Rocky and Bullwinkle," *see* "Rocky and Bullwinkle"
satire and parody in, 3, 106, 107–108
sound quality, 96, 101, 132, 138, 140
subject matter of, xvi–xvii, 3, 105, 106, 112–13, 144, 145
Rocky and His Friends (record), 158, 161
"Rocky-Bullwinkle Savings Stamps Club and Peace Patrol, The," 161, 187
Rocky the Flying Squirrel, xv, 30, 31, 106, 108, 137 origins of, 21
Rocky the Flying Squirrel, see Rocky and His Friends, pilot for
Rohauer, Raymon, 226–27, 274, 300
Roman, Dunbar "Dun," 245, 329
Mexican operations and, 87, 88, 90, 92–93, 94, 131, 132
Ruff and Ready, 17, 29, 43, 100
Ruggles, Charlie, 151, 153, 157–58, 344–45
Runaway animation, 48, 66, 71, 257–58
Rush, Chris, 309

Sahl, Mort, 20, 60–61
Saltzman, Harry, 64
San Diego Union, 137–38, 185
Schaefer, Meyer, 111
Schlatter, George, 215
Schleh, Bob, 69, 80, 89, 137, 140, 141, 148, 149, 150, 160
Scholl, Russ, 15
Schwartz, Norman, 225
Schwartz, Zachary, 59n
Scott, Bill, xix–xxi, 3, 4, 8, 20, 50, 61, 135, 159, 193, 222, 235, 274, 282, 286, 287, 295–96, 298, 301, 302, 304, 307, 308, 309–11, 314
background of, 32–33, 268, 310–11
Bullwinkle puppet and, 41, 186–87
death of, 309–10
early career of, 37–43
Fractured Flickers and, 158, 224, 227–33
George of the Jungle and, 260–64
interviews, 138, 161, 162, 163
The Nut House and, 214–16
Quaker Oats commercials and, 243, 244, 246–48, 251, 252, 254–55
retrospectives on comedians, 299–301
Rocky and His Friends and *Bullwinkle Show,* 21, 31, 46–189, 201, 206, 209, 240, 241
testimonial to Jay Ward, 277–79
voices of, xix, 31, 34, 35, 46–47, 48, 53, 54, 55, 99, 118, 121, 132, 134, 144, 157, 158, 160, 170, 225, 235, 237, 258, 262, 264, 269, 271, 309
Watts Gnu Show and, 98
during World War II, 33–37
Scott, Dorothy, 39, 55, 72, 94, 310
Scott, Jim, 149–50
Scott, Keith, 272, 314

Screen Gems, 29, 60
Second City Troupe, 215
Selzer, Eddie, 38
Shakey's Pizza, 298–99
Shean, Al, 45, 58, 59, 73–74, 88, 90, 94–95, 125, 140, 282, 330–31
Shield Productions, 27, 28, 29
Shimkin, Arthur, 158
Shows, Charlie, 39–40, 43, 44, 45
Sidney, George, 29
Siegel, Harvey, 69, 80, 89, 140, 204, 257
Silverman, Fred, 260
Silvey, Shirley, 332–33
"Simpson and Delaney," 149, 160, 161
Singer, George, 80, 131, 132, 140, 168, 335
Siracusa, Joe, 300, 340
"Sir Melvin," 259
Skelton, Red, 182, 188, 190
Slezak, Walter, 133
Smith, Frank, 250
Snidely Whiplash, 169, 170, 173, 188, 225
Solomon, Charles, 302, 304
Sparey, John, 18, 23, 29–30
Speaking of Animals, 38–39, 44
Stahmer, Waynem, 11
Stanford, Tom, 11, 15, 274, 301
Stan Freberg Show, The, 52
Stanley, Jim, 215–16
Stanley, John, 30
Steiner, Fred, 48, 172, 186, 218, 233, 336–38
Steiner, George, 172, 233
Stewart, James G., 140
"Stokey and Bear," 173–74, 188
Stone Associates, 72
Storyboard Co., 43, 47
Stringer, Dave, 164
Stupor Bowl, The, 302–304
Styles, Hal, 288
Sullivan, Elizabeth, 176
"Super Chicken," 262, 266, 267–69, 272, 304, 408–10
Super Chicken (1965 pilot), 258–59, 260, 261, 268, 420
"Super Chicken Show, The" (1960 concept), 134, 138, 142, 150, 161, 267–68
Sutherland Productions, 42–43, 55, 112–13

Ted Turner Cartoon Network, 242, 312
Television Arts Productions, Inc., 10–29
Terrazas, Ernest, 73, 74, 79–80, 89, 94, 150
Terry, Paul, 8, 9
Terrytoons, 8, 9, 73
Tetley, Walter, 127–28
"That's Comedy," 301
"That Was the Town," 256
Thomas, Frank, 36, 144
Thornton, Teri, 275
Time for Beany, 19–20, 39–41, 44, 99, 118, 177, 288
Tojo Studios, 48, 62
"Tom Slick," 232, 262, 269–72
Tonight Show with Johnny Carson, The, 220, 228, 279
Torres Vasquez, Jaime, 168, 257
Total Television, 160, 242, 256–57, 258, 308
Travis, Robert, 76, 77
Turnbull, Bill, 33, 37, 38
  The Nut House and, 214, 215
Turner, Lyoyd, 4, 18, 38, 41, 73, 111, 121, 122, 124, 128, 134, 145, 151, 174, 235, 237–38, 251, 258, 267, 268, 270, 273, 294, 295, 296–97, 297, 299, 310, 319–22
  Bullwinkle Show and, 168, 172, 174, 190, 205, 206
  Fractured Flickers and, 225, 231–32
  on Ward, 280–81, 287, 190, 291–92
TV Guide, 166, 178, 183–84, 207–208, 209, 214
TV-Radio Mirror, 190–91

TV Recorders, 58
TV Spots, 20, 28, 29, 30, 117, 136, 148, 160–61

Ulrich, Charles, 86–87, 130, 242, 266, 311
"Uncle Lefty" 272
Uncle Waldo's Cartoon Show, 238
United Productions of America (UPA), 41–42, 43, 51, 55
Universal Recorders, 57
Universal Studios, 51, 313, 314
University of California at Berkeley, 5, 8, 26, 278–79

Valdez, Gustavo, 66, 79, 84, 89
Val-Mar Productions, 48, 66–69, 71, 72, 73, 81–96, 101, 129, 135, 138–40, 284
  early staff of, 79–80
  improvement in output of, 131, 137, 140–41, 149
  renamed Gamma Productions, 141
Vane, Ed, 261
Variety, 103–104, 161, 176, 218, 229–29
Village Voice, The, 164

Walt Disney, *see* Disney
Ward, Billie, 291, 292
Ward, Jay, xix–xx
  animation business, start in, 7, 9–10
  background of, 4–7
  death of, xxi, 312–13
  described, 2, 3, 277–93, 295
  education of, 5, 6, 10, 85, 213, 278–79
  health problems, 6–7, 9, 20, 61, 62, 63, 64, 65, 67, 76, 161, 223, 281–82, 283, 284, 312
  interviews, 138, 149–50, 161–63, 190–91
  production companies, *see individual praoduction companies, e.g.* Ward Productions, Jay; Television Arts Productions, Inc.
  real estate business, 6–7, 24, 26, 30, 150, 278
  see also individual projects
Ward, Ramona, xx, 6–7, 10, 23, 25, 61, 203–204, 248, 280, 282, 284, 292
Ward, Ron, 294–95, 298, 301, 305
Ward, Tiffany, 312–13
Ward Films, Jay, 97–98, 141
Ward Productions, Jay, xvii, xx, 1, 74, 80–81, 130–31, 141–42, 150, 176
  closing of, 309
  creation of, 30, 57
  early staff of, 80–81
  payroll, 289–91
  recording sessions, 347–52
  who's who of, 315–46
  see also specific projects
Warner Brothers Cartoons, 37–38, 42, 51, 262
Washam, Ben, 67, 81, 250, 299
Washam, Jean, 334
Watts Gnu Show, The, 97, 98–99, 141, 142, 150, 163, 167, 211, 224, 301, 421
Weaver, Pat, 273
Weiss, Sam, 94
Whaley, Roy, 12
White, Spaulding, 15
White, Volney, 15
Wight, Read, 59
Williams, Jack, 15
Williams, Martin, 163–64
Wilson, Al, 333–34
Witbeck, Charles, 163
Woolery, George, 266
Worth, Stan, 266, 268

Zamora, Rudy, 73, 87, 90, 93, 94, 131, 132, 137, 140
Zimbert, Richard, 261